Resisting Reality

Resisting Reality

Social Construction and Social Critique

SALLY HASLANGER

OXFORD
UNIVERSITY PRESS

OXFORD
UNIVERSITY PRESS

Oxford University Press is a department of the University of Oxford.
It furthers the University's objective of excellence in research,
scholarship, and education by publishing worldwide.

Oxford   New York
Auckland   Cape Town   Dar es Salaam   Hong Kong   Karachi
Kuala Lumpur   Madrid   Melbourne   Mexico City   Nairobi
New Delhi   Shanghai   Taipei   Toronto

With offices in
Argentina   Austria   Brazil   Chile   Czech Republic   France   Greece
Guatemala   Hungary   Italy   Japan   Poland   Portugal   Singapore
South Korea   Switzerland   Thailand   Turkey   Ukraine   Vietnam

Oxford is a registered trade mark of Oxford University Press in the UK and certain other countries.

Published in the United States of America by Oxford University Press
198 Madison Avenue, New York, NY 10016

© Oxford University Press 2012

Library of Congress Cataloging-in-Publication Data
Haslanger, Sally Anne.
Resisting reality: social construction and social critique /Sally Haslanger.
p. cm.
ISBN 978-0-19-989262-4 (pbk.: alk. paper)—ISBN 978-0-19-989263-1 (hardcover: alk. paper)
1. Social constructionism. 2. Critical theory. 3. Feminism. 4. Social sciences—Philosophy. I. Title.
HM1093.H38   2012
300.1—dc23   2011044301

1 3 5 7 9 8 6 4 2

Printed in the United States of America
on acid-free paper

CONTENTS

PART THREE   LANGUAGE AND KNOWLEDGE

ACKNOWLEDGMENTS

Although writing philosophy is usually a solitary business, doing philosophy is a collaborative process, whether we acknowledge it or not. The collaboration can happen in face-to-face conversations, or through reading or listening to others. I began writing the essays in this book twenty years ago. The ideas and arguments that appear here depend on input from many others, including students, colleagues, friends, conference participants, interlocutors at colloquia, well-known and little known authors, and random acquaintances whom, at this point, I cannot even name. So first, and importantly, I want to express my gratitude for my communities—both academic and non-academic—that enable rich and challenging conversation, and the willingness of so many to share their thoughts with me. I regret that I cannot give each of you the individual credit that you deserve.

Most of the chapters in this volume were published separately and have their own acknowledgments, so rather than trying to list everyone who has helped me with this project, I want to use this opportunity to express special thanks to a few, with the understanding that whatever I say here barely scratches the surface.

I have known Charlotte Witt since I was in graduate school at Berkeley, and for thirty years she has been a wonderful friend, colleague, and collaborator. She has pushed me when I needed pushing, supported me when I needed support, and been an invaluable interlocutor on personal, professional, and philosophical issues. Her input has not only made my feminist work better, but has made it possible.

Rae Langton, my close friend and colleague at MIT, has also been an important part of my life since the late 1980s. Her ideas have inspired me, her writing has moved me, and her friendship has sustained me. She shows by example all that feminist philosophy can be and *do*. I feel privileged to know her and am forever grateful for her friendship.

Years ago at I supervised Elizabeth Hackett's dissertation on Catharine MacKinnon's epistemology. Not only was it a joy to work with Beth, but the hard work we did together enabled me to appreciate much more deeply than I had before the philosophical richness of MacKinnon's work. Beth became a good friend and colleague, and years later we collaborated on a textbook *Theorizing Feminisms* (Oxford 2005). Beth's insights into feminist method and the goals of feminist theorizing have influenced me deeply, and her commitment to philosophical feminism, and making space for it within academia, has helped me keep hope alive during hard times.

Louise Antony is another close friend who has been a companion from the start in doing analytic feminism: my first feminist publication was a response to Louise and Charlotte's invitation to contribute to *A Mind of One's Own*. Her high standards, incisive intelligence, and political intensity challenge me in the best way and keep me up at night searching for answers. She has been invaluable in working on this book, and in so much else.

When I was at the University of Michigan, Abigail Stewart was the Director of Women's Studies. Abby was my first feminist mentor. The most precious gift— of many—that Abby gave me was the awareness that feminist theory is its own interdisciplinary intellectual project and that even I, a philosopher, was qualified to do it. Such work is answerable to rigorous intellectual standards, but different standards than those represented in philosophy. Abby unyoked my thinking from the burdensome cart of academic philosophy and gave me a voice. She has also been an inspiration and role model in working on gender equity issues in the academy. I admire her beyond words, and I would not be where I am today without her guidance, vision, and support.

Elizabeth Anderson and I were colleagues at the University of Michigan, and it was the first time I had a colleague in my own department doing feminist work. Liz's work has had a huge influence on me, and her straightforwardness, confidence, and integrity gave me strength in times of doubt. While Abby freed me from the artificial constraints of academic philosophy, Liz took for granted that philosophical feminism *is* philosophy. The combination allowed me to form a new, less fragmented, intellectual identity and the courage to own it.

Since moving to Cambridge, I have had the good fortune to have Lawrence Blum as a friend. Larry's commitment to doing and teaching philosophy in ways that matter nourishes me and keeps me grounded in my own values. His unqualified willingness to take up hard issues, his attention to detail, his thoughtful self-reflectiveness and his appreciation of the importance of philosophical community have made a huge difference to how and why I still identify as a philosopher.

For the many ways they have helped me over the years and inspired me, I'd like to thank: Linda Martín Alcoff, Anita L. Allen, Nancy Bauer, Robert Gooding-Williams, Kimberly Leighton, Elisabeth Lloyd, Charles Mills, Jennifer Saul, Jacqueline Stevens, and Ronald Sundstrom. Thanks especially to Mary Kate McGowan who, in addition to her insight and friendship over the years, read through and gave me excellent comments on an early version of the manuscript when I was still trying to turn it into a monograph.

Special thanks to Ásta Sveinsdóttir and Ishani Maitra who were my grad students at MIT and helped me found the Workshop on Gender and Philosophy in 2000. Ishani and Ásta created a warm and welcoming feminist space for me at MIT and have been fabulous feminist interlocutors. And they have given me the greatest gift by going on to do *such* great work. More recently, Kate Manne and Kenneth Walden have given me valuable feedback on the material in this collection and have been a great pleasure to work with.

To all those who have participated in the Workshop on Gender and Philosophy, I am very grateful. WOGAP has sustained me and given me so much to think about over the years. Special thanks to the regulars, including Candice Delmas, Heidi Lockwood, Alice MacLachlin, Alison McIntyre, Charles More, Serena Parekh, Ronni Sadovsky, Suzanne Sreedhar, Jacqueline Taylor, Catherine Wearing; and to my assistants over the years (who have also contributed to my thinking in many ways), including Dylan Bianchi, Rachael Briggs, Jennifer Carr, Helena deBres, Tom Dougherty, Romelia Drager, Roxanne Fay, Lyndal Grant, Elizabeth Harman, Jerome Hodges, Ginger Hoffman, Adam Hosein, Kate Manne, Sarah McGrath, Melissa Schumacher; and to other regular participants already mentioned. The Philosophy Section in the Department of Linguistic and Philosophy at MIT is a great place to do philosophy and I feel privileged to have been part of the community since 1998. Thanks to all the faculty and graduate students who have overlapped with me there.

For the wonderful conversations and comments over the years that have influenced my thinking, thanks to: Alia Al-Saji, Luvell Anderson, Anat Biletzky, Susan Brison, Sylvain Bromberger, Joshua Cohen, Ann Cudd, Tracy Edwards, Catherine Elgin, Janet Farrell-Smith, Heath Fogg-Davis, Jorge Garcia, Joshua Glasgow, Heidy González, Elizabeth Harman, Diana Henderson, Emily Hipchen, Jules Holroyd, Richard Holton, Adam Hosein, Alison Jaggar, Karen Jones, Evelyn Fox Keller, Christine Koggel, Roxanne Kurtz, Mika Lavaque-Manty, Christopher Lebron, Kimberly Leighton, Sarah-Jane Leslie, Annabelle Lever, Koffi Maglo, Ron Mallon, Kate Manne, Lionel McPherson, Ifaenyi Menkiti, Maria Morales, Stephen Nathanson, Ruth Perry, Anne Phillips, Ryan Preston, Margaret Rhodes, Mark Richard, Sarah Richardson, Lisa Rivera, Gideon Rosen, Ronald Sandler, Naomi Scheman, Laura Schroeter, Tommie Shelby, Susan Silbey, Sarah Song, Quayshawn Spencer, Robert Stalnaker, Natalie Stoljar, Ronald Sandler, Judith Thomson, Manuel Vargas, David Velleman, Kenneth Walden, Ralph Wedgwood, Andrea Westlund, Ajume Wingo, David Wong, and Christopher Zurn. Randal Parker and Kayley Vernallis were among my earliest conversation partners on feminist issues and I am deeply grateful for their enduring friendship and inspiration.

Over the years I have received two fellowships that have given me valuable time to work. In 1995–1996 I was a fellow at the National Humanities Center;

and I received an American Council of Learned Societies Fellowship that gave me leave in the spring of 2002. I am very grateful for this financial support.

The complexities of my life outside academia would never have permitted me to devote the necessary time and energy to this book without the help of Ingleed August, Stasia Barrett, Adam Corbiel, Joe Forth, Crystal Kanode, Melissa Kavanagh, Philip Laidlaw, and Angela Tiexiera. For their love, support, and wisdom, I am forever grateful to my sister supervisors of the Angels Without Wings Choir at St. Paul A.M.E. Church, Marilyn Bradshaw, Tanya English, Velma Jeffers, Ronda Martinez, and Helen Mitala. My dear friends M. J. Jensen, Deb Levy, Ricardo Maldonado, Mariko Sakurai, Lynn Shirey, Patricia Weinmann, Elizabeth Wood—and my wonderful dog Sparky—have sustained me through it all.

Isaac and Zina, my children, are woven into the texture of my days and the shape of my consciousness. So much of what I have learned in writing this book, I have learned from and through them. They provide the opportunity for experience and the occasion for thought. I am so blessed to have them in my life. And Stephen, my amazingly brilliant, funny, and humble companion: thanks for doing the dishes *every night* and for all you are, have been, and will be.

I thank the editors and publishers who have granted permission to reprint the essays appearing in this volume. Original publication information follows:

Chapter 1: "On Being Objective and Being Objectified." In *A Mind of One's Own: Feminist Essays on Reason and Objectivity*, eds. Louise M. Antony and Charlotte E. Witt. (Boulder, CO: Westview Press, 1993), pp. 85–125.

Chapter 2: "Ontology and Social Construction." *Philosophical Topics* 23:2 (Fall 1995): 95–125.

Chapter 3: "Social Construction: The 'Debunking' Project." In *Socializing Metaphysics*, ed. Frederick Schmitt. (Lanham, MD: Rowman and Littlefield, 2003), pp. 301–325.

Chapter 4: "Feminism in Metaphysics: Negotiating the Natural." In the *Cambridge Companion to Feminism in Philosophy*, eds. M. Fricker and J. Hornsby. (Cambridge: Cambridge University Press, 2000), pp. 107–126.

Chapter 5: "Family, Ancestry and Self: What Is the Moral Significance of Biological Ties?" In *Adoption and Culture* 2 (2009): 91–122.

Chapter 7: "Gender and Race: (What) Are They? (What) Do We Want Them to Be?" *Noûs* 34:1 (March 2000): 31–55.

Chapter 8: "Future Genders? Future Races?" In *Philosophic Exchange* 34 (2003–4): 4–27. Edited version reprinted in *Moral Issues in Global Perspective* (2nd ed.), ed. Christine Koggel (Peterborough, ON: Broadview Press, 2005): 102–115.

Chapter 9: "You Mixed? Racial Identity Without Racial Biology." In *Adoption Matters: Philosophical and Feminist Essays*, eds. Charlotte Witt and Sally Haslanger (Ithaca: Cornell University Press, 2005), pp. 265–289.

Chapter 10: "A Social Constructionist Analysis of Race," in B. Koenig, S. Lee, and S. Richardson, eds., *Revisiting Race in the Genomic Age* (New Brunswick, NJ: Rutgers University Press, 2008, pp. 56–69).

Chapter 11: "Oppressions: Racial and Other." In *Racism, Philosophy and Mind: Philosophical Explanations of Racism and Its Implications*, eds. Michael Levine and Tamas Pataki. (Ithaca: Cornell University Press, 2004), pp. 97–123.

Chapter 12: "What Knowledge Is and What It Ought To Be: Feminist Values and Normative Epistemology." *Philosophical Perspectives* 13 (1999): 459–480.

Chapter 13: "What Are We Talking About? The Semantics and Politics of Social Kinds." *Hypatia* 20:4 (Fall 2005):10–26.

Chapter 14: "What Good Are Our Intuitions? Philosophical Analysis and Social Kinds." *Proceedings of the Aristotelian Society Supplementary Volume*, vol. 80, no. 1 (2006): 89–118.

Chapter 15: "'But Mom, Crop-Tops *Are* Cute!' Social Knowledge, Social Structure and Ideology Critique," *Philosophical Issues*, 17, The Metaphysics of Epistemology, 2007, pp. 70–91.

Chapter 16: "Language, Politics and 'The Folk': Looking for 'The Meaning' of 'Race.'" *The Monist* 93:2 (April 2010): 169–187.

Chapter 17: "Ideology, Generics, and Common Ground," in Charlotte Witt, ed., *Feminist Metaphysics: Explorations in the Ontology of Sex, Gender and the Self* (Dordrecht and London: Springer 2011), pp. 179–207.

Resisting Reality

Introduction[1]

In the summer of 1963, my family moved from Westport, Connecticut, to Shreveport, Louisiana. I was eight years old. My mother was from Massachusetts, my father from Wisconsin. My family had moved often, even living a stretch of time in south Texas, and all four of the kids (I'm the youngest) had been born in different states. Nevertheless, we were considered "Yankees," and we came to town ignorant of the local social codes and racial norms.

Shreveport was in the midst of the upheaval of the civil rights movement when we arrived. A short article from the *New York Times* that July captures the moment:

> 10 Arrested in Shreveport
>
> SHREVEPORT, LA, July 19 (AP)—Negroes stage sit-ins at the lunch counters of two downtown stores today. The police broke up the demonstrations quickly, arresting 10.
>
> An order to pick up Charles Evers of Jackson, Miss., was also issued. Mr. Evers is the Mississippi field secretary for the National Association for the Advancement of Colored People and the brother of Medgar Evers, the slain Negro civil rights leader. (*New York Times* 1963)

Medgar Evers had been assassinated just a month before.

I was mostly oblivious to the civil rights protests in Shreveport. My world had just been turned upside down by this sudden move, and I was preoccupied with adjusting to a new home and neighborhood, a new school, a new climate, and the loss of all that had been left behind. What I do remember, though, is the constant correction and physical interventions that were attempts to retrain me to conform to the local norms of gender and race. These didn't come from my parents or siblings—they knew as little as I did about how to behave—but from teachers, neighbors, and strangers. The corrections did not come with explanations, either. Instead, I might be yanked away from a car door (I had been planning to sit in the front seat next to the Negro driver rather than in the back seat), or grabbed by the arm and scolded

---

[1] Thanks to Kate Manne, Charlotte Witt and Stephen Yablo for excellent comments on earlier drafts.

for my loud (and probably "know it all") tone of voice. I had learned how to be a privileged white girl in Connecticut, but this did not do in Shreveport, where Jim Crow and Southern gentility still had a hold. I had to relearn how to enact privilege, whiteness, and femininity. At the same time, I also had a sense, both from what I had known in my previous world and from things I overheard at home, that this new way of being wasn't quite right.[2] I was so confused.

I believe that early confusions can sometimes motivate philosophical reflection. In my case everyday routines and assumptions were dramatically disrupted at an age when I knew enough to ask why, but not enough to figure out the answers. Although this was a source of considerable unhappiness at the time, I believe it also taught me valuable lessons about the contingency of "common sense," the embodiment of social structures, and implicit training in political values. These early lessons have prompted me to both action and inquiry. I am a feminist. I am antiracist and committed to social justice more broadly. I am an adoptive mother of two African-American children in open adoptions. I am also a philosopher who believes in the power of ideas. Social justice will never be achieved by just working to change beliefs, for the habits of body, mind, and heart are usually more powerful than argument. However, knowledge of the workings of social structures and their appropriation of bodies is crucial. The essays in this collection are some of the fruits of my inquiry, arising out of and directed towards action. I will begin by summarizing some of the broad themes. The following three sections of this introduction correspond roughly to the divisions of chapters that follow; the final section considers themes that are more integrated throughout the essays.

Social Construction

The idea of social construction is an important tool in contemporary social theory. Social constructionist accounts of what it is to have a gender, race, ethnicity, sexuality, and the like systematically challenge everyday assumptions about what is "natural." However, in spite of consensus that we need to be attentive to social construction, there is striking diversity in how the term 'social construction' is used and what it is taken to imply. The multiplicity of uses across contexts and disciplines has, over time, reduced the value of the term in discussion. But the points that social constructionists have been trying to make remain important. This book explores the claim that something is socially constructed. The essays included are written over a span of almost twenty years and are

---

[2] In case it isn't obvious, I should note that my parents were not liberal or even especially politically minded. Their goal seemed to be simply to adapt and get along, though they had some qualms about the forms of racial segregation they had not encountered so directly before.

informed by work in contemporary feminist and race theory; they also draw on recent work in analytic metaphysics, epistemology, and philosophy of language. The overarching goal is to clarify and defend the more specific proposals that race and gender are socially constructed, and to situate these proposals within a broader philosophical and political picture.

The contemporary literature on race and gender is not only concerned with social and political questions; central to it are questions concerning reality, knowledge, and nature. For example, the claim that something is a "social construct" (or "*merely* a social construct") sometimes suggests that it is illusory, or at least less than fully real. And yet can we accept that race and gender are unreal? For those in subordinated positions, it sometimes seems that race, gender, age, disability, and such are all *too* real. So we need to ask: What is the illusion (if any), and what is the reality (if any) in social constructions?

Moreover, traditional efforts to justify racist and sexist institutions have often relied on viewing women and people of color as inferior *by nature*. There is an unmistakable pattern of projecting onto subordinated groups, as their "nature" or as "natural," features that are instead (if manifested at all) the result of social forces. If one function of references to "nature" is to limit what is socially possible, thereby "justifying" pernicious institutions, we must be wary of any claim that a category is "natural." Yet it would be ridiculous to maintain that there are *no* limits on what social arrangements are possible for human beings. So, what is the relationship between social constructions and natural facts? Is there any meaningful distinction between the natural and the social? Do race and gender differ with respect to their "naturalness"?

And further, in claiming that race and gender are socially constructed, we seem to be treating each as a unified category—as if we can isolate what it means to be a woman, or to be Black, by giving an analysis that applies in each and every case. But we are complex social beings with not *only* a gender or *only* a race, but with a gender, a race, a class, a nationality, a sexuality, an age, a collection of abilities and disabilities, and more. Many feminists have argued that the social forces that form us, and their effects, cannot be decomposed into discrete elements (Lugones and Spelman 1983; Spelman 1988; Crenshaw 1989; Harris 1990). Is it possible to give a unified account of gender or race, while still affirming the interdependence and experiential blending of an individual's lived social positions? Can we assume that terms such as 'woman' or 'race' have determinate meanings? If not, how should we proceed—politically and theoretically? What is the best methodology for theorizing about social categories? What determines the meaning(s) of contested terms?

Even these quick examples demonstrate that topics in metaphysics, epistemology and philosophy of language are not far below the surface of debates over social construction: What is real and what isn't? How do we know what's real? Is there reality beyond what's natural? Is the natural "fixed," setting immutable constraints on us? How does our language hide or reveal aspects of reality? What illusions does it promote? These are all questions that demand consideration as part of social theory.

My overall strategy is to distinguish several different ways in which things are "socially constructed." For example, consider a simplified account of the construction of race or gender: to be a member of the subordinate group in question is to be viewed and treated in a certain way by the dominant group (and usually others). Members of the subordinate groups typically internalize and eventually come to resemble and even reinforce the dominant's image because of the coercive power behind it. Thus the dominants' view appears to be confirmed, when in fact they simply have the power to enforce it.

There are several different elements of this picture that could qualify as social constructions, for example, the dominant group's (mistaken) view of the subordinate; each group's self-understandings; the lived (economic, political) divisions between the groups; the group classification system; and even members of the groups themselves. In understanding these different phenomena, we are sometimes concerned with unmasking illusions that are projected onto groups: attention to the illusions is one source of the suspicion that social constructions aren't "real." In other cases we are concerned to emphasize that the causes of apparent group differences are at least mediated by social forces: attention to the profound effects of the social is one source of suspicion of the "natural." And accounts of this sort supplement individualistic explanations of behavior with explanations that emphasize the impact of social structures. Although post-structuralism and postmodernism have taught us to be wary of "totalizing" structural explanations, we cannot avoid talking about practices and institutions and local structures if we are to understand group oppression.

In this book, I aim to provide accounts of race and gender that clarify the sites and forms of construction involved, and that can also be fruitfully employed in the quest for social justice. In particular, I am interested in certain forms of oppression that are read into, marked upon, and lived through the body. The process of marking groups and naturalizing their subordination is an element in virtually all oppression, yet the form and degree of bodily involvement varies. The markers of race and gender, like the markers of disability and age, are not accessories that might be added or dropped, habits to be taught or broken; they are parts of our bodies and "as-if" indelible. Although other forms of oppression may be equally lasting, and may be more severe, it is both analytically and politically valuable to have a framework within which we can explore contemporary forms of embodied oppression (see also Alcoff 2006). In this project I focus on only two dimensions of embodiment: race and gender; this is not to suggest that they are the most important or that a full account can be achieved without looking at other dimensions as well. Rather, this is just where I begin. My hope is that the tools I provide in exploring these dimensions will be helpful in studying others.

Race and Gender

Given the complexity of the phenomena, I argue for a focal analysis that defines race and gender, in the primary sense, as social classes (see Ch. 7). A focal analysis explains a variety of phenomena in terms of their relations to one that is theorized, *for the purposes at hand*, as the focus or core phenomenon.[3] For my purposes, the core phenomenon is the pattern of social relations that constitute men as dominant and women as subordinate, of Whites as dominant and people of color as subordinate. An account of how norms, symbols, identities, and such are gendered or raced is then given by reference to the "core" sense.

My accounts focus on the social relations constituting gender and race, because these relations are an important site of injustice. As a result, on my account, neither gender nor race is an intrinsic feature of bodies, even though the markers of gender and race typically are. To have a race is not to have a certain appearance or ancestry, and to have a gender is not to have a certain reproductive anatomy. I embrace the feminist slogan that *gender is the social meaning of sex* and extend this by arguing that *race is the social meaning of "color."* To avoid confusion, I use the terms 'woman' and 'man' to refer to genders and 'male' and 'female' to sexes, 'Black' and 'White' (upper case) to refer to races and 'black' and 'white' (lower case) to refer to "colors."[4] Sex and "color" have social meaning to the extent that the interpretation of someone as male or female, white or asian, has implications for their social position: the roles they are expected to play in the social context, the norms in terms of which they will be evaluated, the identities they are expected to have, and the like. Such implications are easily demonstrated, hence, on my view, gender and race are real. However, their reality in the contemporary context is the product of unjust social structures, and so should be resisted.

I have found it useful to present the idea of a focal analysis by using a pair of overlapping diagrams:

On the view I favor, the social relations defining gender and race consist in a set of attitudes and patterns of treatment towards bodies as they are perceived (or imagined) through frameworks of salience implicit in the attitudes. These pat-

---

[3] Focal analyses have played an important role in philosophy since Aristotle. I believe G. E. L. Owen coined the term 'focal meaning' (G. E. L. Owen 1986). As Owen describes it (1986, 184): "A world such as 'medical,' [Aristotle] says, is not univocal—it has various definitions answering to its various senses, but one of these senses is primary, in that its definition reappears as a component in each of the other definitions. If to be a medical man is to be XY, to be a medical knife is to be of the sort used by a man who is XY (1236a15–22)." I differ from many using the concept by emphasizing that the core or focal meaning may differ depending on one's theoretical purposes.

[4] I discuss the distinctions between sex and gender, "color" and race extensively in Chapter 6. Note that "color" (with scare quotes) on my view is not just skin color, but any socially meaningful features taken in a context as (alleged) indicators of ancestral links to a particular geographical region.

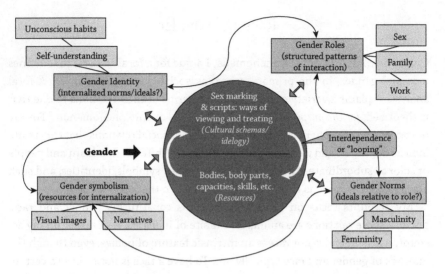

Figure 0.1 "Focal" Analysis of Gender

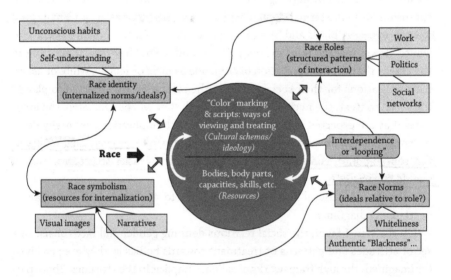

Figure 0.2 "Focal" Analysis of Race

terns of thought and action take different forms depending on time, place, context, culture, and they generate divisions of labor, roles, norms, identities, and so on that are specific to the location. Gender varies tremendously cross-culturally and transhistorically, but there are, I argue, important structural similarities across these variations. Roughly, women are those subordinated in a society due to their perceived or imagined female reproductive capacities. It follows that in those societies where being (or presumed to be) female does not result in subordination along any dimension, there are no women. Moreover, justice requires that where there is such subordination, we should change social relations so there will be no more women (or men). (This will not require mass femicide! Males and females may remain even where there are no men or women.) However, although men and women are the only genders we currently acknowledge, if we understand gender as the social meaning of anatomical sex, then there is room in my account for the development of alternative non-hierarchical genders based on reinterpretations of sexual differences. Such genders may be radically different from ones we can now imagine.

I argue that in some ways race is parallel to gender: races are (roughly) those groups that are situated hierarchically due to the interpretation of their physical features as evidence of their ancestral links to a particular geographical region. As with gender, the social relations that constitute race vary cross-culturally and transhistorically, but there are structural parallels across these different contexts. Although I am in favor of cultural diversity, we should aim to eliminate these "color" hierarchies; on my view, to eliminate "color" hierarchy is to eliminate race. (Similarly, this is not to recommend genocide! Cultural and non-hierarchical ethnic groups may remain even where there are no races.)

To capture the specificity of the social position of an individual, it would be a mistake, of course, to consider just gender or just race. I suggest that we can gain insight into the phenomenon of intersectionality by (roughly) superimposing the diagrams offered in figures 0.1 and 0.2. Imagine race, gender, and other social positions to be like gels on a stage light: the light shines blue and a red gel is added, and the light shines purple; if a yellow gel is added instead of the red, the light shines green. Similarly, gender is lived differently depending on the racial (and other) positions in which one is situated. Just as a light may appear different colors depending on which combination of gels it is filtered through, the gender norms for Black women, Latinas, and White women differ tremendously, and even among women of the same race, they differ depending on class, nationality, sexuality, religion, historical period, and so on. However, just as we can gain understanding of the green light on the stage by learning it is created by a combination of blue and yellow gels, and can adjust the light by manipulating the gels, the hope is that we can gain understanding of the lived experience of those who are gendered and raced by having the analytical tools to distinguish them.

As I've mentioned, the "focus" of my analyses are the relations that constitute some embodied groups as dominant and others subordinate. However, as indicated in figures 0.1 and 0.2, these relations are part of broader structures that are both pervasive and entrenched. Gender and race are systematically maintained in a culture because they are performed and internalized. The interdependence of the different elements of the structure is illustrated in figures 0.1 and 0.2 by the boxes surrounding the core relations that give bodies racial and gendered meaning.

Begin with the upper right box in the diagrams: The interpretation of human bodies as "fit" for some activities (and not others) motivates and "justifies" divisions of labor and the separation of domains and forms of activity, that is, social roles. For these roles, then, there are norms (lower right): what it takes to do that labor or activity *well*. For example, those interpreted as having a female body are regarded as fit or suited for mothering, which is taken to entail a different relation to small children than fathering. Correspondingly, there are different norms for mothering and fathering: even if the norms for mothering and fathering differ across time and culture, what makes a good mother is not thought to be the same as what makes a good father. But if females are expected to perform the role of mothering and to perform it well, then rather than coerce them to fulfill this role, it is much better for females to be motivated to perform it. So the norms must be internalized, that is, they must be understood as part of one's identity and defining what would count as one's success as an individual (upper left box in the diagram). Ideally, one will develop unconscious patterns of behavior that reinforce the role in oneself and others and enable one to judge others by its associated norms. And in order for large groups of people to internalize similar or complementary norms, there must be a cultural vocabulary—concepts, narratives, images, scripts, cautionary tales—that provide the framework for action (lower left box). The cultural vocabulary, of course, will be very complex, for the scripts and images for an White able-bodied 20-something rural Southern (U.S.) Christian woman will have elements that pertain to the multiple social roles and norms she is expected to satisfy. Not all complex positions will have defined roles or norms, and not all defined roles will be consistent.

Although I have described the broader structure illustrated in figures 0.1 and 0.2 in a sequence that suggests linear causation from gender relations, to gender roles, norms, identities, and then symbolism, this is misleading, for there is a thoroughgoing causal interdependence. My claim is not that gender relations are the focal category because they *cause* these other social phenomena; rather I am making an analytical point in keeping with the concept of focal meaning. Consider the question: What makes being weak and helpless a gender norm for women in some contexts and yet not others? In other words, by virtue of what is weakness feminine in certain contexts? If we just consider weakness itself, or even the representations of weakness in that context (are they typically images of females?), we won't have an explanation. Rather, what's required is an examination of the roles that women are expected to occupy in that context. These, of course, will be varied. What we will often find, however, is that weakness is a norm for women in certain classes/races/periods and not others, corresponding to the sort of role that women of that sort are assigned, or corresponding to the reference domain (weakness is not a norm for women in childbirth). By considering how weakness functions in context to make one "well-suited" for some roles and not others, we can disentangle the social factors that situate weakness as feminine. For example, it might have been a norm for "Southern belles" to be weak, but not for their maids, because it is a crucial indicator of race and class privilege that females are relieved of the burdens of physical work and are to be cared for by males and non-privileged females. The link between gender norms and gender roles invites an interrogation of the complex interaction between different dimensions of privilege and subordination. In the example just considered, the norm of weakness is a social mechanism for coercing White women into their proper place within a race and gender hierarchy that brings with it both privilege and disadvantage. Moreover, the dominant norms dictating that women should be weak but Blacks should be strong puts Black women in an impossible bind; they cannot possibly excel in the terms set by the dominant culture. So this form of analysis also calls attention to the fact that what's construed as "feminine" in a culture may be the norm for only a privileged group, making women in subordinated groups either invisible or apparently inferior qua women.

Several broad themes emerge in my discussion of race and gender. First, individuals stand in complicated relationships to the collectively formed and managed structures that shape their lives. Structures take on specific historical forms because of the individuals within them; individual action is conditioned in multiple and varying ways by social context. Theory, then, must be sensitive to this complexity: focusing simply on agents or simply on structures will not be adequate in an analysis of how societies work and don't work, or in a normative evaluation of them (Sewell 1992). We must be attentive simultaneously to both agents and structures.

Second, although in understanding agents we must do justice to experience, we must also be aware that we are bodies, and in the practices of day-to-day life, the movement, location, and meaning of our bodies often has little to do with the agent's consciousness or intentions. As a result, it must be a nontrivial part of feminist and antiracist efforts, not just to change minds, but also to retrain bodies, and not just to retrain bodies, but to change the material conditions that our bodies encounter on a daily basis.

And third, in understanding structures we must be sensitive to the interplay between material and cultural dimensions of social life (Young 1980). In interdisciplinary feminist studies, scholars have learned to play close attention to the complex relationship between representations and the material reality of the social world. Both ordinary narratives and "scientific" theories sustain structures of power; unjust allocations of resources appear to provide evidence for certain cultural myths. Dialogue across disciplines has urged humanists to consider the material circumstances that condition representation, and has led social scientists to recognize the complex ways that institutions are interpreted, reinterpreted, and resisted by the agents within them. Social theory, as I aspire to do it, must be always alert to the interdependence of material and cultural realities.

Although in a single project I cannot do full justice to the relationships between agents, human bodies, cultural meanings, social structures, and the

material conditions for social life, I hope to reveal some crucial sites where interaction between these elements makes a difference.

Language, Knowledge, Method

It is important to note that I am not offering a phenomenology of gender or
race. A phenomenological approach to social categories studies the first-person
lived experience of those positioned in that category (Smith 2009). Feminist
phenomenology is a valuable part of the study of women's oppression (e.g.,
Young 1990; Bartky 1990; Al-Saji 2010), as are studies in the phenomenology of
race (e.g., Fanon 1967; Gordon 2007; Yancy 2008). However, interdisciplinary
social theory, more broadly, draws on a range of methods from the social sciences and philosophy to understand, explain, and critique society. Although
first-person experience is an important source of evidence for any social theory,
the primary subject matter of the sort of social theory I'm undertaking is not
experience, but social structures and the social relations that constitute them.

However, one might reasonably complain that it is not necessary to be a phe-
nomenologist to find the analyses of gender and race that I offer to be counterintuitive. Who on earth would ever find intuitively plausible an analysis of
woman according to which women are, by definition, subordinate? Given that
the analyses are at odds with any ordinary understanding of the terms, on what
basis can I meaningfully claim that I have captured what gender and race *are*, or
what terms such as 'woman,' 'man,' 'White,' 'race,' mean? The analyses I offer are
not only at odds with the phenomenology of being gendered or raced, but with
common sense.

One response to this complaint is that social theory is not in the business of
trying to capture common sense and, as already mentioned, need not be true to
the phenomenology of first-person experience. Do we expect economics to provide a theory of the market that accords with our common-sense ideas or that is
phenomenologically realistic? Surely not. The market works, in part, because of
its ability to mystify those engaged in its transactions. An adequate economic
theory attempts to see through such mystification to explain and predict changes
and trends. To do so, it will need to have definitions of key terms, for example,
labor, unemployment, profit, that differ from our common sense understanding.

In keeping with this thought, one might want to distinguish *theoretical* and
non-theoretical uses of terms. Lots of terms have a life both within a theoretical
project and also in everyday usage, for example, 'energy,' 'force,' 'solid,' and we
do not require scientific theories (whether in natural or social science) to change
in order to accommodate ordinary intuitions. It would not be unreasonable to
claim that the accounts of *race* and *gender* that I offer are theoretical and should
be evaluated by theoretical standards. But what is the relationship between

theoretical and non-theoretical meanings of a term? Is a term such as 'energy,' or 'woman,' ambiguous, that is, does it have multiple meanings, theoretical and non-theoretical? Is the common sense term 'woman' a different term from the various theoretical terms 'woman'? And how might a theoretical account of gender or race play a role in social critique?

Many of the essays in this collection consider these issues of meaning indirectly, and a few more directly. On my view, there is not a sharp line between ordinary language and theory, and it would be a mistake to treat the terms in question as ambiguous. My approach to meaning is influenced by three broad movements in contemporary analytic philosophy: naturalism, scientific essentialism, and semantic externalism. Books have been written on each, and anything I say here, or in the chapters that follow, will barely scratch the surface. However, I will say a bit about each to give some background context relevant to my project and then explain why I believe that these movements are more friendly to the project of critical social theory than is sometimes supposed.

Although it took me years to recognize its influence, V. W. O. Quine's essay, "Two Dogmas of Empiricism" (1951) was at the core of my philosophical training, and my impulses in metaphysics, epistemology, philosophy of language and even normative theory are tutored by Quine's legacy. Much of modern philosophy has relied on a sharp divide between propositions allegedly necessary, true by virtue of meaning, and known a priori, and propositions that are contingent, true by virtue of the world, and known a posteriori. "Two Dogmas," along with Quine's other work, challenged this divide. On Quine's view, all inquiry is of a piece and results are justified by satisfying a variety of criteria, both logical and empirical. There is no sharp line between those parts of inquiry that tell us what the world is like and those parts that create the tools—including definitions of new terms or redefinitions of old ones—for understanding it.

> The lore of our fathers is a fabric of sentences. In our hands it develops and changes, through more or less arbitrary and deliberate revisions and additions of our own, more or less directly occasioned by the continuing stimulation of our sense organs. It is a pale gray lore, black with fact and white with convention. But I have found no substantial reasons for concluding that there are any quite black threads in it, or any white ones. (Quine 1976, 132)

Nor is there a sharp line between science, philosophy, and ordinary efforts to make sense of the world:

> . . . my position is a naturalistic one: I see philosophy not as an *a priori* propaedeutic or groundwork for science, but as continuous with science. I see philosophy and science as in the same boat—a boat which, to

revert to Neurath's figure as I so often do, we can rebuild only at sea
while staying afloat in it. There is no external vantage point, no first
philosophy. All scientific findings, all scientific conjectures that are at
present plausible, are therefore in my view as welcome for use in philosophy as elsewhere. (Quine 1969, 126–7)

Although Quine himself was skeptical of "meanings," semantic externalists
such as Putnam, Kripke (1980), and Burge (1979) embraced his naturalizing
impulse and proposed that the meaning of a term is its referent, and determining what the meaning is requires empirical inquiry. Although the ordinary
person may use words meaningfully to refer to things having in mind only a
vague, non-individuating, or even mistaken description of them, the meaning is
not, correspondingly, vague or incomplete. This is because, as Putnam put it,
"'meanings' just ain't in the head!" (Putnam 1973, 704). Rather, our ordinary
referential efforts succeed directly, without mediation by a Fregean sense or implicit description, and knowledge of meaning is an achievement that requires
expertise, not something we gain simply by linguistic competence.

Semantic externalism, in the work of Putnam and Kripke, came hand in
hand with scientific essentialism. The scientific essentialist holds that it is possible to discover a posteriori the essence of a kind such as water or gold. For
example, according to the scientific essentialist, we know (a priori) that if what
it is to be water *just is* to be H_2O, that is, if water = H_2O, then water is essentially H_2O. So if we learn through scientific inquiry that water *just is* H_2O, then
we can infer that water is essentially H_2O. Because one of the premises of this
argument relies on empirical investigation, the conclusion is a posteriori.
However, it is important to note that the conclusion that water is essentially
H_2O is fallible. Our best chemical theory says that water *just is* H_2O, but we
know that no scientific theory is infallible. Scientific results are overturned,
rejected, eclipsed, regularly. So if we come to have reason to reject the claim
that water *just is* H_2O, likewise we will have to revise our understanding of the
essence of water.

If we combine naturalism, semantic externalism, and scientific essentialism,
then we get a view according to which we regularly communicate about the world
with only a partial grasp of what we are talking about: the boundaries of our
references are not clear, nor is it clear what features are crucial for distinguishing
the individuals or kinds we speak of. This can only be determined holistically in
light of broader considerations about our purposes, the inquiry we are engaged
in, the community we are part of, and expert information from those with
greater empirical knowledge of the domain. Recently semantic externalists have
further explored the dynamic aspect of meaning that allows ongoing reinterpretation of meaning in light of past practice and present concerns (Bigelow and
Schroeter 2009; but see also Quine 1972).

For most conversations the incomplete hold we have on meanings doesn't matter, for we are good at figuring out enough to communicate and get by. But the indeterminacy of our grasp of meanings also allows for confusion and mystification; one goal of social theory, as I see it, is to clarify meanings with social justice in mind. Although Putnam, Kripke, et al. were keen on the holistic nature of our inquiry, they also tended to be biased in favor of the natural sciences in seeking the a posteriori conditions for membership in a kind. But an externalist bias towards the natural sciences is not warranted, for social kinds are no less real for being social. I argue that in the social domain we should rely on social theorists, including feminist and antiracist theorists, to help explicate the meanings of our terms. Much can be gained, I believe, by including *both social science and moral theory*—broadly construed—in the web of belief that has a bearing on our inquiry.

I discuss explicitly some ways in which this approach to language, knowledge, and metaphysics can be useful to social theorists in Chapters 1, 14, and 16. Let me suggest, very briefly, how these ideas apply to the social domain. It is my view that although we have terms to describe the practices in which we engage and the institutions of which we are a part, we usually have only the vaguest idea of what we are actually doing. Most of our knowledge of practice is know-how; it is implicit, embodied. However well this serves us in some situations (we should be grateful that so much of it is implicit, for we could not manage without habits of mind and body), there are times when we need a fuller understanding of what is going on. Charles Taylor suggests:

> In a sense, we could say that social theory arises when we try to formulate explicitly what we are doing, describe the activity which is central to a practice, and articulate the norms which are essential to it. . . . But in fact the framing of theory rarely consists simply of making some continuing practice explicit. The stronger motive for making and adopting theories is the sense that our implicit understanding is in some way crucially inadequate or even wrong. Theories do not just make our constitutive self-understandings explicit, but extend, or criticize, or even challenge them. (Taylor 1985, 93–4)

The theorist who studies a social practice (or whatever) is not talking about something wholly new. It is the same practice that we've been talking about and engaging in all along, but without a clear understanding. The social theorist undertakes to place the practice within a larger social matrix. Taylor suggests that in some cases the theorist

> . . . alters or even overturns our ordinary everyday understanding, on the grounds that our action takes place in an unperceived causal context,

and that this gives it a quite different nature. But there are also theories which challenge ordinary self-understanding and claim that our actions have a significance we do not recognize. But this is not in virtue of an unperceived causal context, but because of what one could call a moral context to which we are allegedly blind. (Taylor 1985, 95)

The failure of understanding that the social theorist aims to correct is not a lack that only some of us have; it comes with being an ordinary agent living in a culture whose practices we engage in, often "unthinkingly," just as we speak our native language. Broader causal and moral reflection on the practice, however, may reveal it to be quite different from what we might have imagined, or even what we thought pre-theoretically. This is potentially a crucial moment of demystification, and, as I see it, calls for an approach to language that allows radical revisions to our ordinary understandings of what we are talking about, based on a broad-based inquiry. In short, social theory needs, at least, semantic externalism and a holistic Quinean naturalism. At this point it will be helpful, I believe, to say more about my general approach to social theory and social critique.

Social Theory and Social Critique

Social critique is an interdisciplinary enterprise that comes in many forms. One central form takes aim at existing social institutions, laws, and practices, for example, health care policies, the gendered distribution of family work, racial profiling, and argues that they are bad or unjust. Let's call this *institutional critique* (allowing the notion of 'institution' to be very broad). It is tempting to see such critique as involving two steps. One step involves describing the social practice in question in a way that highlights those features that are relevant to normative evaluation. Another step invokes explicitly normative concepts to evaluate the practice as just, reasonable, useful, good, or not.

In my experience, philosophers tend to neglect the first step. In some cases they miss the social level of analysis completely (focusing instead on the individual or the state); in other cases they note it, but are insensitive to the challenges of describing it well or aptly. (This latter weakness may be exacerbated by the assumption that fact and value should be kept separate, so description must be value-neutral and normative concepts only become relevant once description is done and evaluation begins.) Non-philosophers, in contrast, tend to neglect the second step. Although they are committed to social justice and skilled at describing the social world in ways that reveal its tensions and constraints, they are uncomfortable in the face of moral disagreement or disagreement about values, and are unfamiliar with the resources of moral and political theory, both normative and meta-normative.[5] As a result, they are often wary of outright normative vocabulary and prefer more implicit evaluative judgments that avoid theoretical scrutiny.[6]

As I see it, the two steps are deeply interdependent: in order to describe the world in a way that is apt for moral evaluation, one must have an appreciation of the multiple dimensions of moral value and adequate language to describe features that moral theory is, or should be, attentive to. Moreover, moral theory should provide grounds for evaluation and remediation that are informed by rich descriptions and our best theories of the social world. Attention to this interdependence of description and evaluation encourages critical reflection on the resources available for these tasks: Do our descriptions—ordinary or theoretical—capture what's morally significant? Do our evaluations address the complexity of social life? Should we revise concepts or introduce alternative narrative tropes to expand our expressive repertoire?

Ideology Critique

Reflection on the terms used for description and evaluation will sometimes reveal that institutional critique needs to be supplemented by *ideology critique*. Ideology critique focuses on the conceptual and narrative frameworks that we employ in understanding and navigating the world, especially the social world. Elizabeth Anderson describes the critique of a concept this way:

> A critique of a concept is not a rejection of that concept, but an exploration of its various meanings and limitations. One way to expose the limitations of a concept is by introducing new concepts that have different meanings but can plausibly contend for some of the same uses to which the criticized concept is typically put. The introduction of such new concepts gives us choices about how to think that we did not clearly envision before. Before envisioning these alternatives, our use of the concept under question is *dogmatic*. We deploy it automatically, unquestioningly, because it seems as if it is the inevitable conceptual framework within which inquiry must proceed. But envisioning alternatives, we convert dogmas into *tools*; ideas that we can *choose* to use or not, depending on how well the use of these ideas suits our investigative purposes. (Anderson 2001, 22)

[5] Although I use 'they' to refer to both groups, I find myself situated, sometimes in one, other times in the other, with all their strengths and weaknesses.

[6] The histories of the disciplines make sense of these tendencies: social scientists are "scientists" so their research should be "objective" in the sense of value neutral; philosophers are not "scientists" and their realm of expertise is normative inquiry, so they should leave the description to the scientists (or common sense).

I would add that in order to create the critical distance that gives us "choice," critique need not introduce a wholly new concept, but can just suggest a revision to a concept or a new understanding of a concept. Ideology critique disrupts conceptual dogmatism and extends this method further to other representational tools, capacities, and culturally mediated patterns of response; it raises questions about their aptness, what they capture and, importantly, what they leave out, distort, or obscure.[7]

The term 'ideology' has a long and complicated history and in recent years some have rejected the concept of ideology in favor of the notion of 'discourse' (Hoy 2004). However, I have chosen to stick with a rather broad notion of ideology that plausibly captures the less controversial core of both notions. Alan Hunt and Trevor Purvis argue, for example:

> . . . ideology and discourse refer to pretty much the same aspect of social life—the idea that human individuals participate in forms of understanding, comprehension or consciousness of the relations and activities in which they are involved. . . . This consciousness is borne through language and other systems of signs, it is transmitted between people and institutions and, perhaps most important of all, it *makes a difference*; that is, the way in which people comprehend and make sense of the social world has consequences for the direction and character of their action and inaction. Both 'discourse' and 'ideology' refer to these aspects of social life. (Purvis and Hunt 1993, 474; see also McCarthy 1990, 440)

Although from this quote it might appear that ideology is always conscious and intentional, on my view, ideology includes habits of thought, unconscious patterns of response, and inarticulate background assumptions (see also Taylor 1985, chap. 1, esp. pp. 36, 46, 54; Althusser 1970/2001). In this regard my own use of the term is probably closer to Bourdieu's (1977) notion of *habitus* than either a Marxian concept of 'ideology' or a Foucauldian notion of 'discourse' (Foucault 1982). Let me emphasize, though, that 'ideology,' in the intended sense, is not a pejorative term. It is an essential part of any form of social life because it functions as the background that we assimilate and enact in order to navigate our social world.

Although societies tend to have dominant ideologies, ideologies differ across social groups, and alternatives to dominant ideologies are ubiquitous at every level. Individuals who navigate different social spaces become expert at a kind of

---

[7] Miranda Fricker (2007) introduces the term 'hermeneutic disablement' and discusses the kinds of epistemic and political injustice that arise when our concepts fail us. Such circumstances call for ideology critique.

social code-switching; not only forms of speech, but manner of self-presentation, degrees of self-revelation, style of reasoning, and such change from context to context, to accommodate the ideology of the milieu. These ideologies, and the practices they partly constitute, *make a difference,* as Purvis and Hunt say. In particular, they enable both the reproduction and disruption of social inequality by guiding our perceptions and responses to existing social conditions.

One crucial task of ideology critique is to reveal ideology as such. In some cases this will involve calling attention to aspects of the discursive frameworks that we consciously employ, their history, and their relation to the practices and institutions they underwrite. This is sometimes called *genealogy*.[8] In other cases, however, ideology is invisible to us, that is, it is *hegemonic*, and it is necessary to articulate it and make it accessible for critical reflection. Questions of aptness or justice don't arise for what is taken for granted. However, once articulated, ideology can (in principle) be debated and reformed. So one goal of ideology critique is to elucidate the conceptual and narrative frameworks that undergird our social interaction, thus making them available for critical examination.

In some cases, ideology critique can succeed in its critical task simply through redescription; once the social phenomenon in question is seen anew, it is clear that it is problematic, even immoral. The problem might have been simply that the previous description of the phenomenon did not adequately capture the morally relevant features, or that the descriptive tools we employed were not well-suited to the evaluative tools we were attempting to apply. In these cases, the burden of argument lies in the reinterpretation of the phenomenon, not in moral theory per se. For example, once we recognize that non-consensual sex in marriage is rape, or that domestic violence is assault, we don't need an elaborate moral theory to tell us that we should change our evaluation of it from permissible to impermissible. At some point we may legitimately want to know what is the best moral theory to explain what's wrong with rape or assault, but such explanation is not necessary to critique the practice of marital rape and domestic violence within a context in which there is consensus that rape and assault are wrong.

Correlatively, it might be that a genealogy (or other reconsideration) of our evaluative concepts demonstrates their weaknesses and, once they are revised, it becomes clear that social phenomena we thought benign are not, or vice versa. For example, reflection on the concept of patriotism may reveal that although it is often assumed that patriotism requires an unconditional support for one's nation, especially in times of war, a better understanding of patriotism involves a commitment to values somehow fundamental to the nation, for example, enshrined in founding documents. Patriotism, then, may be exhibited in criticism of national policy, war resistance, and civil disobedience

---

[8] I discuss one approach to genealogy in this volume, Chapter 13.

when the nation's actions violate its central values. Ideology critique, as I understand it, occurs against a backdrop in which some values are assumed; it is not part of its task to provide a foundation for normative evaluation or answers to metaethical questions.

There are several specific issues concerning social phenomena that make the tasks of description and evaluation especially challenging. Social structures, as such, are not part of our ordinary experience and so can be hard to notice and describe; moreover, our most familiar terms of moral evaluation apply first and foremost to individuals, though we are also comfortable bringing states and the explicit actions of states (laws, policies, and such) under moral scrutiny. What is less clear is how to describe the target and choose the right terms of evaluation when we are considering the huge array of social practices, traditions, and norms. Should fashion be subject to moral evaluation? What about etiquette or cuisine? Or religious practices? Or art? What is relevant when we evaluate the social organization of families, child rearing, and education, work? How is an evaluation of a social practice related to the evaluation of individuals who engage in it?

In saying that social structures are hard to notice, I'm not suggesting that people are unaware of the social practices in which they engage. Food, family, and work are a huge part of everyday life (though notably not a huge part of philosophical inquiry), and people are well aware of that. What is hard to notice—and sometimes even grasp—are the structural features of everyday practices and the interconnections between them. For example, food choices are related not only to health, cultural tradition, money, and lifestyle, but also the growth of agribusiness, global food security, animal well-being, environmental degradation, and economic exploitation (Roberts 2008). At this point in time, the moral questions we need to ask about food concern its place in a broad social structure with complex causes and effects. This echoes Taylor's point in the quote above: the social theorist's task is to situate a practice within a broader causal and moral context that those engaged in the practice ordinarily aren't aware of.

But what is a social structure? I discuss this question at length in some of the chapters that follow, but very briefly, on my view, a social structure is a set of interdependent practices. Practices, in turn, are shared dispositions (schemas) to respond to certain parts of the world (resources); some of these dispositions are encoded as beliefs and other attitudes, but some are merely habitual responses (Sewell 1992). Social practices are more or less coordinated. Coordination can be facilitated by adjusting salient parts of the world to trigger the right dispositions, for example, signs, to exit. Social structures are not unique to humans. Non-human animals engage in interdependent forms of coordinated behavior as well. Humans, however, have distinctive capacities to critique and change the practices, and to design them for conscious ends. However, because social structures often involve coordinated responses—both habitual and intentional—by many individuals, they can be very hard to change.[9]

Gaining insight into what a social structure is doesn't immediately solve the problem of how to evaluate it, however. For example,

(i)   As indicated before, it can be difficult to locate the object of moral evaluation. For example, what precisely is "the heteronormative family"? It is not a particular family, of course; it isn't the set of families with homophobic beliefs or attitudes; it isn't the set of traditional two-parent families. It is a complex set of interdependent practices, cultural resources, laws, policies, and such, that privilege heterosexual couples and their biological offspring living together. But how, exactly, do we adequately describe, much less evaluate *that*?

(ii) Social structures constitute our social world and serve as frames of meaning within which we act as social beings. Our desires and intentions, our sources of pleasure and pain, are partly a function of the schemas we have internalized and which also partly constitute the structure. If moral evaluation relies on what satisfies preferences or desires, what causes pleasure and pain, how can we both rely on these states of mind to guide our evaluation and also critique these states of mind as conditioned by problematic structures? What is the ground of critique?

(iii) Individual practices that make up an unjust structure may be harmless in themselves and so not a proper target of critique; it may be only the systematic interdependence of multiple practices that creates the injustice. But social structures are often sufficiently complex that it is difficult to identify not only their causes, but also their effects. Given that we are rarely in a position to experiment with whole societies, how do we isolate the particular source of the problem? And unless we know the source, how can we proceed with moral evaluation—which practice or practices are the problem?

(iv) Social structures are created and sustained by us, collectively, but are not within any individual's control; they are often not even within any group's

---

[9] A careful reader will note that I never define the term 'social,' here or in the essays that follow. This is not an accident. I believe that it is not possible to define 'social' in non-circular terms, so an analysis, strictly speaking, is not possible. This does not rule out giving an account of the social, but the contours of this, like those of any account, will depend on the particular project, the purposes for which one needs a notion of the social, and so on My approach to this, as in other cases, is to employ a focal analysis. For my purposes, coordinated activity is the focal notion. Social relations are those that constitute and support the coordination, and social groups consist of those standing in these relations. This approach allows for forms of sociality that are quite demanding (Margaret Gilbert's excellent work (e.g., Gilbert 1989) on activities such as taking a walk together would be included), social-structural groups that are social groups in a more attenuated sense (Young 2000), and even the sociality of bees and flocks of geese.

control. However, it is often assumed that we are only morally responsible for what we can control. Should we conclude that social structures are not within the scope of moral evaluation?

How should we proceed? It will be useful to say a bit about my identification with critical theory and what I think a critical theory can and cannot do. This will help us think a bit further about the possibility of social critique.

Critical Theory

Ideology critique is often associated with critical theory. Critical theory is situated theory. It is situated in two ways: epistemically and politically. Critical social theory begins with a commitment to a political movement and its questions; its concepts and theories are adequate only if they contribute to that movement. A feminist or antiracist critical theory does not attempt to be "neutral" on questions of race or gender, but begins with the assumption that current conditions are unacceptably unjust and a commitment to understand and remedy that injustice. Consider Nancy Fraser's characterization:

> To my mind, no one has yet improved on Marx's 1843 definition of critical theory as "the self-clarification of the struggles and wishes of the age." What is so appealing about this definition is its straightforwardly political character. It makes no claim to any special epistemological status but, rather, supposes that with respect to justification there is no philosophically interesting difference between a critical theory of society and an uncritical one. However, there is, according to this definition, an important political difference. A critical social theory frames its research program and conceptual framework with an eye to the aims and activities of those oppositional social movements with which it has a partisan, though not uncritical identification. . . . Thus, for example, if struggles contesting the subordination of women figured among the most significant of a given age, then a critical social theory for that time would aim, among other things, to shed light on the character and basis of such subordination. It would employ categories and explanatory models that revealed rather than occluded relations of male dominance and female subordination. And it would demystify as ideological any rival approaches that obfuscated or rationalized those relations. (Fraser 1989, 113)

Critical theories arise out of social activism. The questions they ask are those that are important for bringing about social justice in a particular time and place. They do not begin by asking what justice is, in the abstract, and, unless it is important for the purposes of the movement, attempt to provide a universal account of justice. Often a universal account of justice isn't necessary to improve the situation, for the activism is a response to a situation that is straightforwardly unjust. Alternatively, the situation may not appear obviously unjust, but the challenge is then to reframe it so the injustice becomes salient. In such cases, the theoretical task is to demystify the situation to reveal what is easily acknowledged to be unjust. The task is to turn a complaint into a critique.

In keeping with the embeddedness of critical theory, feminist social critique need not attempt to argue that a social practice is sexist or racist from a starting point that all rational inquirers must endorse. It is assumed that not all rational inquirers have the understanding or the values that constitute a feminist outlook, though perhaps they could and should. The first goal is to find or construct the conceptual and evaluative frameworks that do justice to the phenomena that are the source of complaint, the phenomena that give rise to the movement. Of course there will be political and practical questions about how to use critical frameworks to promote social justice; appropriating the rhetoric of the dominant discourse may sometimes be politically necessary. But the demystification that comes from ideology critique reveals the need for, and often promising directions for, social change.

Critical theory, like all good theories, aims to be empirically adequate. However, as just indicated, it also has a practical aim: it should be helpful to those committed to furthering the aims of social justice through the movement in question, for example, the feminist and/or antiracist movement. This is not as radical as it might sound. Theories offer a response to the needs present in a social context; among other things, they offer a framework of concepts for understanding a domain. Consider, for example, medicine, engineering, economics. In addition to allowing us to make true, or empirically adequate, statements, the point of the theory is to provide resources that can inform us as we navigate the world. The framework of concepts serves as a tool. This means that justified truth is not enough; practical significance is an additional condition of success. So a critical theory, like other theories, should be judged according to several criteria: (1) Does it meet ordinary epistemic standards of empirical adequacy, consistency, and the like? (2) Are its concepts apt? Do they reveal the phenomenon in a way that helps us provide an answer to our guiding questions? (3) Does it function as part of a larger picture that enables us to address our practical concerns? (see also (Anderson 1995a)). The point of theory in such cases is not to convince someone that there is a problem, or to prove to an unbeliever that a particular belief is the only rational option, but to answer a question, to address a concern.

To say that critical theory is epistemically (as well as politically) situated, is not to reject the goal of objective inquiry (Anderson 1995a; Anderson 1995b; Anderson 2011). Once we acknowledge that the questions we ask arise out of a particular social-historical context and that we draw on familiar assumptions and metaphors as sources of intelligibility, then it is only reasonable to be alert to the potential distortions as well as the glimpses of truth our epistemic position affords. In fact, one might argue that any plausible empiricism has to take into account the situatedness of knowing in order to address the potential for bias: the idea that multiple observers of a phenomenon are desirable in order to increase objectivity is itself an acknowledgement of the situatedness of perception and cognition. The task is not, I believe, to aim for objectivity by repositioning oneself as an abstract subject, suspending all "subjective" beliefs and values. We need not view the philosopher as a "neutral" observer of a realm of concepts. Instead, we can embrace the limitations and opportunities of our position and to undertake self-consciously situated inquiry, that is, inquiry that arises from and speaks to social conditions at a particular historical moment.

'Situated knowledge' is a term that one often finds associated with *standpoint epistemology* (Hartsock 1983). Standpoint epistemology is a cluster of views according to which a socially situated perspective is granted epistemic privilege or authority with respect to a particular domain; *feminist* standpoint theories, in particular, typically grant such privilege to members of subordinated groups. Usually the privilege in question is granted over the domain of social relations that oppress them. A commitment to *situated knowers* is, however, a weaker commitment than a commitment to standpoint epistemology. To claim that knowers are situated is to claim that what we believe or understand about something is affected by how we are related to it. This is consistent with themes already discussed: if being a member of a certain social category brings with it pressure to learn the practices and internalize the norms and expectations of that category, it is not surprising that this process would reveal some phenomena and obscure others, depending on the social position one occupies. A commitment to situated inquiry does not commit one to *privileging* any particular perspective or to the idea that one is unable to "step outside" one's particular perspective.

But, one might ask, how does it help to say that feminist social critique or antiracist social critique begins with the commitments and projects of feminism and must be evaluated relative to that domain? It would seem that either there is a single "approved" feminist viewpoint that offers social criticism but few will endorse it (since so few occupy the "approved" feminist viewpoint); or there are multiple feminist viewpoints and there are multiple critiques, but no coherence and so little power in the account.

These are real concerns, but they are concerns for virtually any disciplined inquiry in which there is disagreement about the subject matter, the methods, or the precise standards for acceptability. There is always a trade-off between the breadth of the target audience for an argument and the strength of its conclusions. Moreover, the fact of disagreement does not undermine a theoretical endeavor, but potentially strengthens it. However, the multiplicity of feminist perspectives raises two deep issues: first, if feminist critical theorists are doing both institutional and ideology critique in very different contexts, facing different political and cultural pressures, should we expect feminism to offer a single coherent "theory," "framework," or utopian vision? If not, then what does it offer? And is it meaningful to use the term 'feminist *theory*'? Second, if feminist critical theory is situated, as suggested, and looks to those in subordinate positions for insight into the practices and structures they enact, how can the theory challenge or demystify the dominant understanding of the practices? The majority will plausibly reflect back to the theorist the dominant understandings and reject critical reframings. Must it rely on "experts" or "theorists" as authorities to validate its claims? Is ideology critique, then, inevitably epistemically (and politically) elitist?

Let me say something brief about each of these issues in turn. As I see it, feminist critical theory does not offer a broad overarching "theory" or utopian vision that can be applied across the board. As I mentioned before, critical theory is not primarily in the business of constructing normative theories from scratch, but of exploring the opportunities within and limits of existing normative and descriptive frameworks. Even if there were rational consensus on a single universal theory of justice, the job for critical theorists would be to engage in critique of its conceptual and narrative presuppositions. As Anderson described above, the result of critique would not necessarily be a rejection of the theory's principles and frameworks; critique might yield reflectively endorsement of them as tools in the work for justice. What feminist critical theory does offer is a range of strategies, priorities, and tools for doing both institutional and ideology critique. Some of these may be very abstract and useful in many contexts; others may be only locally useful. But it is not necessary to develop a single coherent position in order to promote social justice. There are many very different ways for women and members of other subordinated groups to flourish. And the goal of feminist critical theory is to open up those possibilities, not to define a single approved form of life.

This still leaves the question of epistemic and political authority: Whose values and whose insights count in doing critique? It is important first to set aside the suggestion that critique is only successful if those in subordinate positions, that is, those in whose name the movement in question seeks justice (immediately?) endorse it. The idea of situated knowers allows that those situated in a particular social position may have special access to certain phenomena, but also that they may be especially vulnerable to mystification. All of us are dogmatic about aspects of the conceptual and narrative frameworks we employ—agency would not be possible without an assumed cultural frame, a language, a set of basic social dispositions. It is hardly surprising that efforts to disrupt this frame in order to reflect on it meet with suspicion and a rejection of alternatives. Nevertheless, critical theorists are committed to the possibility that anyone can engage in critique—not just intellectuals, not just the elite. (Historically one feminist version of this is consciousness raising; in the 21st century it is more often called "raising awareness.") Critical theory is anti-elitist not because it takes every idea or every reaction equally seriously, but because its methods are based on a capacity to critically reflect that we all share. Consider Anderson again:

> Reason is the power to change our attitudes, intentions, and practices in response to reflection on the merits of having them or engaging in them. . . . reflective endorsement is the only test for whether a consideration counts as a reason for having any attitude or engaging in any practice of inquiry: we ask: on reflecting on the ways the consideration could or does influence our attitudes and practices and the implications of its influencing us, whether we can endorse its influencing us in those ways. If we can reflectively endorse its influence, we count the consideration as a reason for our attitudes or practices. (Anderson 1995b, 53)

Ideology critique invites us to withhold reflective endorsement from our ordinary ways of thinking and speaking to consider whether and how they guide our participation in unjust structures; critique gives us alternatives to explore. It does not follow from our shared capacities for reasoned reflection that feminists will all agree, or that any critical theorist will find universal (or even broad) endorsement of the revisionary frameworks she proposes. Consensus is a standard no theorist can be expected to meet, even those committed to anti-elitist and situated epistemologies.

But even if critical theorists cannot gain the endorsement of everyone subordinated by the institutions and practices they critique, a crucial feature of critical theory is that it supposed to make a difference. In its early forms, the idea was that critical theories are "inherently emancipatory" (Geuss 1981, 2). I've articulated a much weaker form of this criterion, suggesting that a critical theory must be judged, in part, by its practical pay-off. It must be useful to the movement. Is this a reasonable basis for evaluation?

One way of developing this idea would be to claim that a critique is acceptable only when it can gain a foothold among those adversely affected by the practice or structure being criticized; in other words, it is a necessary condition on acceptable critique that the subordinated and their allies find it illuminating or useful, that it contributes to their quest for social justice.[10] This condition would

---

[10] Taylor suggests something along the lines I'm suggesting: "Put tersely, our social theories can be validated, because they can be tested in practice. If theory can transform practice, then it can be tested in the quality of the practice it informs. What makes a theory right is that it brings practice out in the clear; that its adoption makes possible what is in some sense a more effective practice" (Taylor 1985, 104).

be both a strength and a weakness: on one hand, it is easy to imagine that there are unjust social structures that are so ingrained that few directly affected can recognize their harm. Shouldn't we count a critique that demonstrates the injustice of those structures as acceptable, nevertheless? On the other hand, if the success of a social critique depends on the reflective responses and choices of those affected, we build respect for their autonomy into the practice of critique. Acceptable feminist social critique, on this view, must be meaningful to the women in whose name it speaks. This is not to say that it must be compatible with everything women say or desire, but that social critique is an adequate tool in a context only if it can reach those whose complaint it allegedly articulates.

What should we say, then, about unjust structures that one cannot convince the affected are problematic or unjust? Are they not unjust? On the view I am exploring, there may be compelling theoretical grounds for claiming that a particular structure is unjust, but a critique based on that theory may nevertheless be less than fully acceptable.[11] Theoretical soundness is not all that critical theory aims for. A broad failure by those affected to sign-on to social critique—at least under conditions where they are willing and able to understand it and evaluate it fairly—is defeasible evidence that there is something left out, for example, that some part of the critique needs to be revised. Dissent does not determine that the critique or the values on which it relies are illegitimate, but it does show that it is not functioning as the tool it is designed to be; this may require us to not accept it until after further inquiry to determine what is going wrong.

Although there are appealing features of this approach to acceptability, there is something untoward in saying that a theory is acceptable only if it is (broadly?) accepted. (Are those who initially accept it accepting an unacceptable theory that becomes acceptable only once others have accepted it?) Moreover, whether a theory is broadly accepted may depend on highly contingent issues such as publicity. However, given that there are several criteria on which critique should be judged, and effectiveness or usefulness is only one, it is reasonable to have a variety of evaluative terms that reflect this. As Anderson emphasizes: ". . . there are many goals of scientific inquiry. Multiple goals support multiple grounds for criticizing, justifying, and choosing theories besides truth" (Anderson 1995a, 53). She continues by providing some examples:

- "The theory, although it asserts nothing but truths, may be trivial, insignificant or beside the point: it doesn't address the contextual interests motivating the question."

---

[11] Another, perhaps better, option would be to claim that a critique is satisfactory if it could be effective, should more accept it (assuming also that its claims are well-justified and its concepts apt), but unless it is useful to those needing it, it is not fully successful (because it doesn't have the practical import that successful critique must have).

- The theory "may be biased: it offers an incomplete account, one that pays disproportionate attention to those pieces of significant evidence that incline towards one answer, ignoring significant facts that support rival answers."
- "The theory may be objectionable for trying to answer a question that has illegitimate normative presuppositions."
- The theory may "misconceive the relevant legitimate interests [motivating the inquiry], and thereby classify together phenomena that should be separated or exclude phenomena that should be included in a class."
- The theory may employ a classification "based on illegitimate contextual values and for that reason should be rejected altogether."
- The theory may rely on "methods that foreclose the possibility of discovering that we have certain valuable potentialities or that certain important differences or similarities exist among the subjects being studied" (Anderson 1995a, 53–4).

We might add that even a theory that employs open-ended methods to organize significant truths and apt classifications to answer a legitimate question may still fail to make a substantial difference. It may not achieve broad reflective endorsement. It may not help the cause of social justice. Perhaps what we need is a distinction between an acceptable theory and a (wholly) successful one. A critical theorist not only aims for an acceptable theory that satisfies the various epistemic criteria Anderson outlines (and potentially others as well), but also a successful theory that makes a difference, one that has meaning within a social movement.

There are at least two ways that a critical theory might be acceptable in Anderson's sense and still, in some sense, fail. On one hand, the failure might be purely political: the theory gains reflective endorsement by a significant number of those who have the opportunity to consider it fairly, but it doesn't help the cause for any number of practical reasons; an extreme version could be that the leaders of the movement are killed or imprisoned. On the other hand, the failure might be more epistemic: the theory does not receive reflective endorsement even after opportunities for reflection have been offered. Those who ask the question motivating the inquiry just don't find it illuminating. This suggests that the theory is missing a bridge that allows a shift from seeing the world in one way, to seeing it in another. This "bridge," however, may not be simply a matter of ideas. Charles Taylor suggests:

> . . . we have great difficulty grasping definitions whose terms structure the world in ways which are utterly different from or incompatible with our own. Hence the gap in intuitions doesn't just divide different theoretical positions, it also tends to divide different fundamental options in life. The practical and the theoretical are inextricably joined here. It may not just be that to understand a certain explanation one has to

sharpen one's intuitions, it may be that one has to change one's orientation—if not in adopting another orientation, at least in living one's own in a way which allows for greater comprehension of others. Thus . . . there can be a valid response to 'I don't understand' which takes the form, not only 'develop your intuitions,' but more radically 'change yourself.' (Taylor 1985, 54)

This suggests that critique may fail to garner broad endorsement not because the theory itself is unacceptable or because the inquirers are epistemically at fault, but because the social context does not provide for ways of being that are necessary in order to find value in the critique. Social critique is a process of re-thinking the practices that we constitute partly through our thinking, of trying out new responses to the world in place of the old responses that have come to seem problematic. The task is to situate ourselves differently in the world, not just to describe it more accurately. Although we can go some way in this direction by thinking and acting in new ways, social conditions may make it rational for one to resist such change (Cudd 2006).

Nevertheless, critique is sometimes fully successful. Clear examples include critical reframings of marital rape, domestic violence, hate speech, and sexual harassment. These are cases in which feminist critique has been incorporated into law. But social critique is not always a legal matter (though relevant legal permissibility or impermissibility must be ensured). There are valuable critiques of just about any contemporary practice, for example, the care economy (Folbre 2002; Kittay 1998), mass incarceration (Alexander 2010; McLennan 2008), re-productive freedom (Roberts 1997), aesthetic/cosmetic surgery (Heyes 2007), pornography (MacKinnon 1987; Langton 2009), disability (Wendell 1996), the American diet (Roberts 2009; Pollan 2008), consumerism (Schor 1999), milita-rism (Enloe 2007), orientalism (Said 1978), the social contract (Mills 1997; Mills and Pateman 2007), race (Appiah 1996), gender (Butler 1990), gender/race (Alcoff 2006), and sex (MacKinnon 1989; Fausto-Sterling 2000), to mention just a tiny sample. This just is so much of what feminist and antiracist intellectuals do. And success should not only be gauged by political progress towards justice. Even if social justice is a only a distant hope, not to be achieved in our lifetime, and social change only minimal, we can gain much through clarity about our current circumstances: we become more aware of the injustices in which we par-ticipate; we can identify and perform acts of resistance; and our attitudes, for example, of sadness, regret, celebration, remorse, and frustration, are better attuned to the reality that warrants them.[12]

The title of the book, *Resisting Reality,* is intentionally ambiguous. On one hand, it reflects a common resistance to recognizing the reality of the social

---

[12] Thanks to Kate Manne for pointing out how having our attitudes attuned to the injustice around us is valuable even if there is little hope for change.

world and the tendency of theorists, in particular, to opt for an anti-realist approach to social categories such as race. I reject this approach and argue throughout for the reality of social structures and the political importance of recognizing this reality. On the other hand, given that much of the (very real) social world consists of unjust social structures, I think this reality must be resisted. Another theme in the book is that one of the main goals of social constructionism is to lay bare the mechanisms by which social structures are formed and sustained so that we are better positioned to locate the levers for social change. We should not resist seeing the reality that we should, in fact, resist; in fact, disclosing that reality is a crucial precondition for successful resistance.

Originally I intended this book to be a monograph developing an overarching argument. It now seems best to publish it as a collection of essays with closely interconnected themes. Part of what made a monograph difficult was the issue of audience. I have had in mind multiple audiences to whom different parts of the book speak more or less directly: students interested in social theory, feminists and anti-racists in a broad range of disciplines, analytic philosophers, legal theorists and policy makers, adoption advocates, perhaps a few non-academic activists who can tolerate my academic prose. Given the range of audiences, there will certainly be parts where each of you feels left out of the discussion. And there will be parts where you can't believe I have ignored a literature you are familiar with and, perhaps, even contributed to. I apologize. I wish I could have researched more, said more, understood more. I hope if you keep reading there will be a thread drawing you back in and insight to make it worthwhile.

It is a rare book that has "timeless" value. But especially because of the nature of the project, my hope is that this book will be, at best, useful for a while, and will then become obsolete as our social conditions and narrative resources evolve. What you'll find is my effort to sustain a delicate balancing act— balancing race and gender; agents and structures; bodies and subjectivities; material realities and cultural interpretations. In the end, there may be a great crash as the edifice topples of its own weight, but there is something valuable to be learned from giving attention to these various elements. It is my hope that although methodologically I'm deeply entrenched in philosophy, my arguments will speak across disciplines, and will provide resources for us to work together, at least in the short run, towards greater justice.

Works Cited

Alcoff, Linda Martín. 2006. *Visible Identities: Race, Gender, and the Self*. New York: Oxford University Press.

Alexander, Michelle. 2009. *The New Jim Crow: Mass Incarceration in the Age of Colorblindness*. New York: The New Press.

Al-Saji, Alia. 2010. Bodies and sensings: On the uses of Husserlian phenomenology for feminist theory. *Continental Philosophy Review* 43(1):13–37.

Althusser, Louis. 1970. Ideology and ideological state apparatuses. In *Lenin and Philosophy and Other Essays*. Trans. Ben Brewster New York: Monthly Review Press, 2001. http://www. marxists.org/reference/archive/althusser/1970/ideology.htm.

Anderson, Elizabeth S. 1995a. Knowledge, human interests, and objectivity in feminist epistemology. *Philosophical Topics* 23(2): 27–58.

——. 1995b. Feminist epistemology: An interpretation and a defense. *Hypatia* 10(3): 50–84.

——. 2001. Unstrapping the straitjacket of 'preference': A comment on Amartya Sen's contributions to philosophy and economics. *Economics and Philosophy* 17(1): 21–38.

——. 2011. Feminist epistemology and philosophy of science. *The Stanford Encyclopedia of Philosophy* (Spring 2011 Edition), Edward N. Zalta (ed.), http://plato.stanford.edu/archives/spr2011/entries/feminism-epistemology/.

Appiah, Kwame Anthony. 1996. Race, culture, identity: Misunderstood connections. In *Color Conscious: The Political Morality of Race*. Ed. K Anthony Appiah and Amy Gutmann. Princeton: Princeton University Press.

Bartky, Sandra. 1990. *Femininity and Domination*. New York: Routledge.

Bigelow, John, and Laura Schroeter. 2009. Jackson's classical model of meaning. In *Minds, Ethics and Conditionals: Themes From the Philosophy of Frank Jackson*. Ed. Ian Ravenscroft. Oxford: Oxford University Press.

Bourdieu, Pierre. 1977. *Outline of a Theory of Practice*. Trans. Richard Nice. Cambridge: Cambridge University Press.

Burge, Tyler. 1979. Individualism and the mental. *Midwest Studies in Philosophy* 4: 73–121.

Butler, Judith. 1990. *Gender Trouble*. New York: Routledge.

Crenshaw, Kimberlé W. 1993. Demarginalizing the intersection of race and sex: A black feminist critique of antidiscrimination doctrine, feminist theory, and antiracist politics. In *Feminist Legal Theory: Foundations*, ed. D. Kelley Weisberg. Philadelphia: Temple University Press.

Cudd, A. E. 2006. *Analyzing Oppression*. New York: Oxford University Press, USA.

Enloe, Cynthia. 2007. *Globalization and Militarism: Feminists Make the Link*. Lanham, MD: Rowman and Littlefield Publishers.

Fausto-Sterling, Anne. 2000. *Sexing the Body: Gender Politics and the Construction of Sexuality*. New York: Basic Books.

Folbre, Nancy. 2002. *The Invisible Heart: Economics and Family Values*. New York: The New Press.

Foucault, Michel. 1982. *The Archaeology of Knowledge and the Discourse on Language*. Trans. A. M. Sheridan Smith. New York: Pantheon Books.

Fraser, Nancy. 1989. What is critical about critical theory: Habermas and gender. In *Unruly Practices: Power Discourse and Gender in Contemporary Social Theory*. Cambridge: Polity Press.

Fricker, M. 2007. *Epistemic Injustice: Power and the Ethics of Knowing*. New York: Oxford University Press.

Gilbert, Margaret. 1989. *On Social Facts*. Princeton: Princeton University Press.

Gordon, Lewis R. 1999. *Bad Faith and Antiblack Racism*. Amherst, NY: Humanity/Prometheus Books.

Geuss, Raymond. 1981. *The Idea of a Critical Theory: Habermas and the Frankfurt School*. Cambridge: Cambridge University Press.

Harris, Angela P. 1990. Race and essentialism in feminist legal theory. *Stanford Law Review* 43(3): 581–616.

Hartsock, Nancy. 1983. The feminist standpoint: Developing the ground for a specifically feminist historical materialism. In *Discovering Reality*. Ed. Sandra Harding and Merrill Hintikka. Dordrecht: Klewer.

Heyes, Cressida. 2007. *Self Transformations: Foucault, Ethics, and Normalized Bodies*. New York: Oxford University Press, USA.

Hoy, David Couzens. 2004. *Critical Resistance: From Poststructuralism to Post-Critique*. Cambridge, MA: MIT Press.

Kittay, Eva F. 1998. *Love's Labor: Essays on Women, Equality, and Dependency*. New York: Routledge.

Kripke, Saul. 1980. *Naming and Necessity*. Cambridge, MA: Harvard University Press.

Langton, Rae. 2009. *Sexual Solipsism: Philosophical Essays on Pornography and Objectification*. Oxford: Oxford University Press.

Lugones, Maria C., and Elizabeth V. Spelman. 1983. Have we got a theory for you! Feminist theory, cultural imperialism and the demand for the woman's voice'. In *Women's Studies International Forum* 6(6): 573–81.

MacKinnon, Catharine. 1987. *Feminism Unmodified*. Cambridge, MA: Harvard University Press.

———. 1989. *Towards a Feminist Theory of the State*. Cambridge, MA: Harvard University Press.

McCarthy, Thomas. 1990. The critique of impure reason: Foucault and the Frankfurt School. *Political Theory* 18(3): 437–69.

McLennan, Rebecca M. 2008. *The Crisis of Imprisonment: Protest, Politics, and the Making of the American Penal State, 1776–1941*. Cambridge: Cambridge University Press.

Mills, Charles. 1997. *The Racial Contract*. Ithaca: Cornell University Press.

New York Times (1923–Current file); July 20, 1963; ProQuest Historical Newspapers The New York Times (1851–2007), p. 9.

Owen, G. E. L. 1986. "Logic and metaphysics in some earlier works of Aristotle." In *Logic, Science, and Dialectic: Collected Papers in Greek Philosophy*. Ithaca: Cornell University Press.

Pateman, Carole, and Charles Mills. 2007. *Contract and Domination*. Cambridge: Polity Press.

Pollan, Michael. 2008. *In Defense of Food: An Eater's Manifesto*. New York: Penguin Press.

Purvis, Trevor, and Alan Hunt. 1993. Discourse, ideology, discourse, ideology, discourse, ideology. . . . *The British Journal of Sociology* 44(3): 473–99.

Putnam, Hilary. 1973. Meaning and reference. *The Journal of Philosophy* 70(19): 699–711.

Quine, W. V. 1961. Two dogmas of empiricism. In *From a Logical Point of View*. Cambridge, MA: Harvard University Press.

———. 1969. Natural kinds. In *Essays in Honor of Carl G. Hempel*. Ed. Nicholas Rescher. Synthese Library 24. Dordrecht: Klewer.

———. 1972. Review of *Identity and Individuation*. By Milton K. Munitz. *The Journal of Philosophy* 69(16): 488–97.

———. 1976. Carnap and logical truth. In *The Ways of Paradox, and Other Essays*. Cambridge, MA: Harvard University Press.

Roberts, Dorothy. 1997. *Killing the Black Body: Race, Reproduction, and the Meaning of Liberty*. New York: Pantheon Books.

Roberts, Paul. 2008. *The End of Food*. Boston: Haughton-Mifflin.

Said, Edward. 1978. *Orientalism*. New York: Pantheon.

Schor, Juliet B. 1999. *The Overspent American: Why We Want What We Don't Need*. New York: Harper Paperbacks.

Sewell, William. 1992. A theory of structure: Duality, agency, and transformation. *American Journal of Sociology* 98(1): 1–29.

Smith, David Woodruff. 2009. Phenomenology. *The Stanford Encyclopedia of Philosophy* (Summer 2009 Edition), Edward N. Zalta (ed.), http://plato.stanford.edu/archives/sum2009/entries/phenomenology/.

Spelman, Elizabeth. 1988. *The Inessential Woman*. Boston: Beacon Press.

Taylor, Charles. 1985. *Philosophy and the Human Sciences*. Cambridge, UK: Cambridge University Press.

Wendell, Susan. 1996. *The Rejected Body: Feminist Philosophical Reflections on Disability*. New York: Routledge.

Yancy, George. 2008. *Black Bodies, White Gazes: The Continuing Significance of Race*. Lanham, MD: Rowman & Littlefield Publishers, Inc.

Young, Iris Marion. 1980. Socialist feminism and the limits of dual systems theory. *Socialist Review* 10 (2/3): 169–88.

———. 1990. *Throwing Like a Girl and Other Essays in Feminist Philosophy and Social Theory*. Bloomington: Indiana University Press.

———. 2000. *Inclusion and Democracy*. Oxford: Oxford University Press.

PART ONE

SOCIAL CONSTRUCTION

On Being Objective and Being Objectified

1. Introduction

One of the common themes in feminist research over the past decade has been the claim that reason is "gendered" or, more specifically, that reason is "male" or "masculine." Although feminists have differed in their interpretations of this claim and the grounds they offer for it, the general conclusion has been that feminist theory should steer clear of investments in reason and rationality, at least as traditionally conceived. For example, we should avoid an epistemology that privileges reason or the standpoint of reason; we should avoid theories of the self that take rationality to be a defining trait; and we should avoid endorsing moral and political ideals that glorify reason and the reasonable "person" (read: man).

The feminist resistance to ideals of reason has at least two different strands. On one strand, giving reason prominence is problematic by virtue of what it leaves out; our views (and our lives) are distorted by a failure to recognize and properly value what has traditionally counted as "feminine." It is not that reason is inherently objectionable, but allowing ourselves to be preoccupied with the significance of reason reflects a bias toward men, or the "masculine," which feminism ought to challenge.[1] Thus we might aim in our theorizing to integrate "feminine" perspectives and attributes that have been contrasted with reason,

---

[1] There is an enormous amount of feminist research offering critiques of male bias in traditional disciplines. Important anthologies focusing on critiques of traditional philosophical projects include Sandra Harding and Merrill B. Hintikka, eds., *Discovering Reality: Feminist Perspectives on Epistemology, Metaphysics; Methodology, and Philosophy of Science* (Dordrechr: D. Reidel, 1983): Carol Gould, ed., *Beyond Domination: New Perspectives on Women and Philosophy* (Totowa, N.J.: Rowman and Littlefield, 1984); Carole Pateman and Elizabeth Gross, eds., *Feminist Challenges: Social and Political Theory* (Boston: Allen and Unwin, 1986); Eva Kittay and Diana Meyers, eds., *Women and Moral Theory* (Totowa, N.J.: Rowman and Littlefield, 1987); Ann Garry and Marilyn Pearsall, eds., *Women, Knowledge, and Reality* (Boston: Unwin Hyman, 1989); Alison Jaggar and Susan Bordo, eds., *Gender/Body/Knowledge: Feminist Reconstructions of Being and Knowing* (New Brunswick, N.J.: Rutgers University Press, 1989).

or we might recognize an alternative "feminine" reason in addition to the more traditional "masculine" reason.[2]

On the other strand, reason itself is more deeply implicated in our oppression; the problem is not one that can be solved by a shift in emphasis—in short, by a new appreciation of the feminine. Offering a positive characterization of this second strand is tricky, for there are markedly different views about how reason is implicated and what we should do about it. But the core idea is that a rational stance is itself a stance of oppression or domination, and accepted ideals of reason both reflect and reinforce power relations that advantage white privileged men.[3] On this view, the point is not to balance the value of reason with feminine values, but to challenge our commitments to rational ideals.

On the face of it, it may seem misguided for feminists to pursue these challenges. It has long been a feminist project to resist the association between women and the "feminine," and even to question the very categories of "masculine" and "feminine." If feminists now take up the project of revaluing the feminine, aren't we reinforcing rather than combating traditional stereotypes? Should we not be wary of ideals of femininity that have been defined in the context of male dominance?[4]

---

[2] A paradigm example of this latter project is Carol McMillan's *Women, Reason, and Nature* (Princeton, N.J.: Princeton University Press, 1982). See also Sara Ruddick, "Maternal Thinking," *Feminist Studies* 6 (Summer 1980): 342–67. This general strategy has been widely pursued in the context of theories of moral reasoning, often inspired by Carol Gilligan's *In a Different Voice: Psychological Theory and Women's Development* (Cambridge, Mass.: Harvard University Press, 1982).

[3] This line of thought is relatively common among French feminists and feminist postmodernists. See, e.g., Elaine Marks and Isabel de Coutivron, eds., *New French Feminisms: An Anthology* (Amherst, Mass.: University of Massachusetts Press, 1980); Luce Irigaray, *Speculum of the Other Woman*, tr. Gillian C. Gill (Ithaca, N.Y.: Cornell University Press, 1985); Susan Bordo, "The Cartesian Masculinization of Thought," *Signs* 11 (1986): 439–56; Jessica Benjamin, "Master and Slave: The Fantasy of Erotic Domination," in *Powers of Desire*, ed. A Snitow, C. Stansell, and S. Thompson (New York: Monthly Review Press, 1983): 280–99; Evelyn Fox Keller, *Reflections on Gender and Science* (New Haven, Conn.: Yale University Press, 1985). Helpful commentaries explicating important themes in this line of thought include Toril Moi, *Sexual/Textual Politics* (New York: Methuen, 1985); and Chris Weedon, *Feminist Practice and Poststructuralist Theory* (Oxford: Basil Blackwell, 1987). For a different approach to the same issue, see also Susan Griffin, *Woman and Nature: The Roaring Inside Her* (New York: Harper and Row, 1978); and Mary Daly, *Gyn/ecology: The Metaethics of Radical Feminism* (Boston: Beacon Press, 1978).

[4] Many feminists have cautioned against theorizing an alternative "feminine" kind of reason. These include Genevieve Lloyd, *The Man of Reason: "Male" and "Female" in Western Philosophy* (Minneapolis: University of Minnesota Press, 1984), esp. 105; Robert Pargetter and Elizabeth Prior, "Against the Sexuality of Reason," *Australasian Journal of Philosophy*, supplement to vol. 64 (June 1986): 107–19; Jane Flax, "Postmodernism and Gender Relations in Feminist Theory," in *Feminism/Postmodernism*, ed. Linda Nicholson (New York: Routledge, 1990), 39–62; Christine DiStefano, "Dilemmas of Difference," in Nicholson, ed., *Feminism/Postmodernism*, 63–82. One alternative to the idea of "feminine reason" has been to locate instead a "feminist standpoint" that offers an alternative to the ideal of "masculine reason" as well as a critique of femininity. See, e.g., Nancy Hartsock, *Money, Sex, and Power* (Boston: Northeastern University Press, 1984); and Alison Jaggar, *Feminist Politics and Human Nature* (Totowa, N.J.: Rowman and Allenheld, 1983). This strategy too has received sustained criticism. See Sandra Harding, *The Science Question in Feminism* (Ithaca, N.Y.: Cornell University Press, 1986).

Moreover, although it is clear that the rhetoric of reason is often used to marginalize and silence women, an appeal to the value of reasoned debate is also a way of opening up a discussion to criticism of standard assumptions. Because an important element in the traditional conception of reason is the value it accords to honest public debate and self-criticism, women's insistence on standards of reason should be one way to combat the dogmatism that fuels patriarchy. If we reject the value of rational reflection and reasoned discussion, then what acceptable methods are left to criticize entrenched positions and to mediate between conflicting points of view? How are we to construct and evaluate our own feminist positions? Even if there are flaws in traditional accounts of reason, must we conclude that they are hopelessly flawed?[5]

This brief glance at some of the issues that arise in considering the claim that reason is gendered shows that we face two huge stumbling blocks: the first is the concept of reason, the second is the concept of gender. Both are highly contested concepts: attempts at their analysis spark profound disagreement. Often it is unclear in the context of debate what account of reason or gender is under discussion, making it unclear who is speaking to whom, where there is disagreement and where there is not. Given the vast amount of interdisciplinary literature on the issue, literature drawing from different traditions and speaking to different audiences, the task of sorting through the discussion seems intractable.

In what follows I will pursue the following strategy. In the first part of the chapter, I consider what it is for a concept or a point of view to be "gendered." Drawing on the idea that gender should be defined in terms of social relations, I begin with the idea that concepts or attributes are gendered insofar as they function as appropriate norms or ideals for those who stand in these social relations. After modifying and elaborating this idea, I turn to ask whether and to what

---

[5] Important work in evaluating feminist critiques of rationality and in reconstructing conceptions of reason include Helen Longino, "Feminist Critiques of Rationality: Critiques of Science or Philosophy of Science," *Women's Studies International Forum* 12 (1989): 261–69, and *Science as Social Knowledge* (Princeton, N.J.: Princeton University Press, 1990); Mary Hawkesworth, "Feminist Epistemology: A Survey of the Field," *Women and Politics* 7 (Fall 1987): 115–27, and "Knowers, Knowing, Known: Feminist Theory and Claims of Truth," *Signs* 14 (1989): 533–57; Sandra Harding, "The Instability of Analytical Categories in Feminist Theory," *Signs* 11 (1986): 645–64, and *The Science Question in Feminism* (Ithaca, N.Y.: Cornell University Press, 1986); Susan Hekman, "The Feminization of Epistemology: Gender and the Social Sciences," *Women and Politics* 7 (Fall 1987): 65–83; Judith Grant, "I Feel, Therefore I Am: A Critique of Female Experience as a Basis for Feminist Epistemology," *Women and Politics* 7 (Fall 1987): 99–114; Donna Haraway, "Situated Knowledges: The Science Question in Feminism and the Privilege of Partial Perspective," *Feminist Studies* 14 (Fall 1988): 575–99; Seyla Benhabib, "Epistemologies of Postmodernism: A Rejoinder to Jean-François Lyotard," *New German Critique* 33 (1984): 104–26; Iris Young, "The Ideal Community and the Politics of Difference," *Social Theory and Practice* 12 (Spring 1986): 1–26.

extent the norms of rationality are specifically appropriate to the role defining the social category of men. To make progress in answering this question, we need at least a working definition of gender.

In the second part of the chapter, I begin by considering Catharine MacKinnon's proposal for defining the social relations that constitute gender. On her view, gender is defined in terms of sexual objectification: roughly, women as a class are those individuals who are viewed and treated as objects for the satisfaction of men's desire. In short, women are the sexually objectified, men the objectifiers. She argues, moreover, that rationality, construed as a stance of objectivity, is an ideal that sustains the inequality of power on which sexual objectification depends. MacKinnon's account of gender has often been criticized for focusing too narrowly on a specific form of gender oppression. But even allowing that there are a plurality of different relations which constitute gender, MacKinnon's work still provides a compelling analysis of one of them. Moreover, working with MacKinnon's concrete analysis of gender enables us to explore in some detail the connections between objectification and objectivity.

Drawing on MacKinnon's critique of objectivity, I undertake to explicate a set of epistemic and practical norms that would, under conditions of social hierarchy, legitimize and sustain objectification. I argue that there is an ideal recommending "neutrality" and "aperspectivity" whose satisfaction both contributes to success in the role of objectifier and is sufficient for functioning as a collaborator in objectification. However, I argue against MacKinnon's stronger claim that satisfaction of this ideal is sufficient for functioning in the social role of a man. I conclude that the ideal is contextually "gendered" and so a proper target for feminist concern, though it is not in the strong sense "masculine."

Before continuing, let me emphasize that for the bulk of the chapter I will try to remain as neutral as possible on the issue of what counts as reason or rationality. My strategy here is to approach the question of whether reason is gendered by way of a better understanding of gender. If there are some epistemic or practical ideals that are gendered, we should determine what they are; whether these ideals are "really" what has traditionally been meant by 'rationality,' or whether they are currently what we mean by 'rationality,' is an important question but not my immediate concern.

I should also note that to my mind, there is something peculiar about engaging in discussion and reasoned debate over the value, or legitimacy, or reality, of reason and rationality. If there is something wrong with our commitments to reason, I doubt we'll find it this way (and I don't know what we could do about it if we did). But this is just to say that in this chapter, I will be assuming that at least some minimal conception of reasoning and some minimal norms of rationality are not at stake in the discussion.

2. Gender and Social Construction

In order to understand the charge that reason is "masculine" or "gendered," it is important to sketch some of the background work that has been done on gender.[6] It is no easy task, since there are deep disagreements among theorists about what specific account we should give of gender or whether we should seek to give an account at all. Some of the concerns have even prompted the suggestion that the concept of gender is no longer a useful theoretical tool, and this in turn has raised the specter of "post-feminism."[7] The project of this chapter is (thankfully) a few steps back from that cutting edge, for the charge that reason is "gendered" or "masculine" arises from feminist views which allow that the notion of gender is at least dialectically appropriate. So I will begin by working briefly through some of the distinctions and themes that the critique of reason draws upon in order to situate the more detailed discussion that will follow.

Sex and Gender

For the time being, let us restrict ourselves to speaking of human beings. Let us use the terms 'male' and 'female' to indicate a classification of individual human beings on the basis of anatomical difference. For our purposes it is not important to specify exactly what anatomical differences count, though primary sex characteristics are a place to start. Let us allow that the distinction between males and females is neither exhaustive nor exclusive and that the terms may be vague—that is, given that human beings display a range of anatomical diversity, we can allow that there are individuals who do not fall neatly within either class and that there are others who fall within both. Further, let us leave it open whether such an anatomical classification is "natural" or "social," "real" or "nominal." And let us say that two individuals are of different *sex* just in case each falls

---

[6] Useful papers include Joan Scott, "Gender: A Useful Category of Historical Analysis," *American Historical Review* 91 (December 1986): 1053–75; Jane Flax, "Gender as a Social Problem: In and For Feminist Theory," *Amerikastudien/America Studies* 31 (1986): 193–213, and "Postmodernism and Gender Relations"; Donna Haraway, "'Gender' for a Marxist Dictionary," in her *Simians, Cyborgs, and Women: The Reinvention of Nature* (New York: Routledge, Chapman, and Hall, 1991), 127–48. For important early attempts at defining gender in terms of social relations, see also Gayle Rubin, "The Traffic in Women: Notes on the Political Economy of Sex," in *Toward an Anthropology of Women*, ed. Rayna Rapp Reiter (New York: Monthly Review Press, 1975), 157–210; and Sherry Ortner, "Is Female to Male as Nature to Culture?" in *Women, Culture, and Society*, ed. Michelle Rosaldo and Louise Lamphere (Palo Alto, Calif.: Stanford University Press, 1974), 67–87.

[7] See, e.g., Susan Bordo, "Feminism, Postmodernism, and Gender Scepticism," in Nicholson, ed., *Feminism/Postmodernism*, 133–56; and DiStefano, "Dilemmas of Difference," esp. 73–78.

within one and only one of the two classes, and they don't fall within the same class.[8]

It is commonplace in feminist research that we must distinguish sex from gender.[9] In keeping with this research, let us use the terms 'man' and 'woman' to indicate gender difference (allowing that boys may fall within the gender *man* and girls within the gender *woman*). Although it *might* be that the distinctions of sex and gender are extensionally equivalent—that is, that all and only females are women and all and only males are men—the basis for the gender classification is not anatomical; rather, its basis lies in social relations.

To see the general point, it is useful to consider other straightforward examples of distinctions based in social relations. Consider a scapegoat. An individual is a scapegoat not by virtue of their intrinsic features but by virtue of their relations to others: anyone, regardless of their bodily features, character, and so on can function as a scapegoat in the right circumstances. What makes you a scapegoat is the role you play in a social group. Consider a landlord. One is a landlord by virtue of one's role in a broad system of social and economic relations which includes tenants, property, and the like. Even if it turned out as a matter of fact that all and only landlords had a closed loop in the center of their right thumbprint, the basis for being counted a landlord is different from the basis for being counted as having such a thumbprint. Likewise for gender, one is a woman, not by virtue of one's intrinsic features (for example, body type), but by virtue of one's part in a system of social relations which includes, among other things, men.[10]

---

[8] The suggestion that sex may not be a binary classification and that it may be socially constructed appears, of course, in Michel Foucault; see, e.g., *The History of Sexuality, Vol. 1: An Introduction*, tr. Robert Hurley (New York: Vintage/Random House, 1980). This suggestion has also been endorsed by many feminist theorists. For useful discussions, see Monique Wittig, "One Is Not Born a Woman," *Feminist Issues* 1 (Winter 1981): 47–54, "The Category of Sex," *Feminist Issues* 2 (Fall 1982): 63–68; Judith Butler, "Variations on Sex and Gender: Beauvoir, Wittig, and Foucault," in *Feminism as Critique*, ed. S. Benhabib and D. Cornell (Minneapolis: University of Minnesota Press, 1987), 128–42; and Donna Haraway, "A Manifesto for Cyborgs: Science, Technology, and Socialist Feminisms in the 1980's" in her *Simians, Cyborgs, and Women*, 149–81.

[9] This "commonplace," however, is not as straightforward as it may seem, and it is not accepted across the board. The distinction between sex and gender has been challenged as presupposing and reinforcing a problematic contrast between "nature" and "culture." See, e.g., Moira Gatens, "A Critique of the Sex/Gender Distinction," in *Beyond Marxism? Interventions after Marx*, ed. J. Allen and P. Patton (Sydney: Intervention Publications, 1983), 143–63; Haraway, "'Gender' for a Marxist Dictionary." esp. 133–34; and Butler, "Variations on Sex and Gender." However, it is by no means obvious that in drawing the distinction between sex and gender, one is thereby committed to saying that sex is a natural category; my concern here is to emphasize the social character of gender, allowing that sexual difference must also be given a social analysis, one plausibly interdependent with the analysis of gender.

[10] Roughly, an intrinsic property of x is one that x has simply in virtue of itself, regardless of the properties of other things—e.g., x could have that property even if it were the only thing existing. Intrinsic properties need not be essential and may be temporary. An extrinsic property of x is one that x has not simply in virtue of itself; x's having the property depends on the properties of other things as well.

Gender is a relational or extrinsic property of individuals, and the relations in question are social.[11] If gender rests in this way upon the organization of social life, we should at least entertain the possibility that just as a change in social relations could have the result that there are no landlords and tenants, a change in social relations could have the result that there are no men and women, even if there continue to be males and females.

It is natural to ask next: What are the social relations that constitute gender? Here things become theoretically difficult, for although it seems plausible that gender difference appears cross-culturally and trans-historically, we must at the very least allow that the specific social relations constituting gender differ from culture to culture. But the recognition of broad social differences raises the question whether gender can be understood as a unitary phenomenon at all.[12] Moreover, there is a theme among feminists that the social relations that give rise to gender distinctions are relations of domination; in particular, they are oppressive to women.[13] However, gender oppression does not typically occur in isolation

[11] At this point, in saying that the relations are "social" I mean simply to indicate that they concern certain relations that hold between individuals by virtue of their place in a social system. My point is completely neutral on the issue of whether or not we should be realists about properties or think that all properties and relations are "merely conventional." Any plausible nominalism or conventionalism will have the resources to distinguish social properties and relations from others in the sense intended. See Ian Hacking, "World—Making by Kind-Making: Child Abuse as an Example," in *How Classification Works*, ed. Mary Douglas (Edinburgh: University of Edinburgh Press, 1992), especially sec. 1–2.

[12] Important works discussing the ethnocentric and imperialistic tendencies in feminist accounts of gender include Cherrie Moraga and Gloria Anzaldúa, eds., *This Bridge Called My Back: Writings by Radical Women of Color* (Watertown, Mass.: Persephone, 1981); bell hooks, *Ain't I a Woman: Black Women and Feminism* (Boston: South End Press, 1981); Audre Lorde, *Sister/Outsider* (Trumansburg, N.Y.: Crossing Press 1984); Maria Lugones and Elizabeth Spelman, "Have We Got a Theory for You: Feminist Theory, Cultural Imperialism, and the Demand for 'The Woman's Voice,'" *Women's Studies International Forum* 6 (1983): 573–81; Elizabeth Spelman, *The Inessential Woman: Problems of Exclusion in Feminist Thought* (Boston: Beacon Press, 1988); Elizabeth Weed, ed., *Coming to Terms: Feminism, Theory, Politics* (New York: Routledge, Chapman, and Hall, 1989); Gayatri Spivak, "Explanation and Culture: Marginalia," in *In Other Worlds: Essays in Cultural Politics*, ed. Gayatri Spivak (New York: Routledge, Chapman, and Hall, 1988), 103–17, and her "Feminism and Critical Theory," in Spivak, ed., *In Other Worlds*, 77–92. For a useful discussion of ethnocentric bias in the feminist critique of rationality, see, e.g., Uma Narayan, "The Project of Feminist Epistemology: Perspectives from a Nonwestern Feminist," in Jaggar and Bordo, *Gender/Body/Knowledge*, 256–69.

[13] For an important discussion of this claim, see Catharine MacKinnon, *Feminism Unmodified: Discourses on Life and Law* (Cambridge, Mass.: Harvard University Press, 1987), ch. 2. See also Flax, "Postmodernism and Gender Relations," esp. 45, 49; Monique Wittig, "The Straight Mind," *Feminist Issues* 1 (Summer 1980): 103–11, "Category of Sex," and "One Is Not Born a Woman." It is important to note that not all social relations are hierarchical (e.g., being a friend is not), and not all hierarchical relations are relations of domination (e.g., although plausibly the relations of doctor-patient, mother-daughter, and so on are hierarchical, they are not themselves relations of domination). Unfortunately, the distinctions between social, hierarchical, and dominance relations are sometimes conflated.

from other forms of oppression; the social relations that constitute gender will be part of a system of social relations, and such systems also serve to ground other distinctions such as race and class. What distinguishes those social relations that constitute *gender*? On what basis (if any) can we meaningfully isolate gender from other hierarchical social distinctions, and gender oppression from other forms of oppression? Are anatomical facts concerning sex and reproduction important for distinguishing gender from other social categories, and gender oppression from other oppressions?[14]

Gender-Norms

There are several strategies for addressing the questions just raised which have been proposed and criticized in the feminist literature. Before I return to the issue of specifying what relations constitute gender, we need to consider a related distinction between "gender-norms": *masculinity* and *femininity*. Gender-norms are clusters of characteristics and abilities that function as a standard by which individuals are judged to be "good" instances of their gender; they are the "virtues" appropriate to the gender.

Because the notion of a "norm" is used in different ways, an example will help illustrate the notion I am relying on. Consider a paring knife. Something counts as a paring knife only if it has features that enable it to perform a certain function: it must be easily usable by humans to cut and peel fruits and vegetables. We can distinguish, however, between something's marginally performing that function and something's performing the function excellently. A good paring knife has a sharp hard blade with a comfortable handle; a poor paring knife might be one that is so blunt that it crushes rather than cuts a piece of fruit, it might be too large to handle easily, and so on. Those features that enable a paring knife to be *excellent* at its job, are the "virtues" of a paring knife. (Something that functions as a good paring knife may function as a poor screwdriver and, when nothing else is available, a good screwdriver may function as a poor paring knife. Although having a sharp pointed blade is a virtue in a paring knife, having such a blade is not a virtue in a screwdriver.) In general, our evaluation of the goodness or badness of a tool will be relative to a function, end, or purpose, and the norm will serve as an ideal embodying excellence in the performance of that function.

Likewise, masculinity and femininity are norms or standards by which individuals are judged to be exemplars of their gender and which enable us to function excellently in our allotted role in the system of social relations that

---

[14] For a discussion of the political interplay between categories of sex and gender, see references in notes 8 and 9 above. See also Evelyn Fox Keller, "The Gender/Science System; or, Is Sex to Gender as Nature Is to Science?" *Hypatia* 2 (Fall 1987): 37–49.

constitute gender. Although I won't be able to make these ideas perfectly precise, the leading idea is that at least some roles have a point or a purpose; to name a few fairly clear examples, consider the roles of teacher, cook, doctor, firefighter, rabbi, pilot, waitress, plumber. For each role there are performances that would count as successes and others that would count as failures; in general, one can do a better or worse job at them. The suggestion is that gender roles are of this kind; gender-norms capture how one should behave and what attributes are suitable if one is to excel in the socially sanctioned gender roles.

In the traditional privileged white Western scenario, to be good at being a man (that is, to be masculine), one should be strong, active, independent, rational, handsome, and so on; to be good at being a woman, one should be nurturing, emotional, cooperative, pretty, and so on. For example, I am a woman because I stand in various gender-constitutive relations to others (often whether I choose to or not); however, I am not in the traditional sense a "good woman" because I don't live up to this ideal of femininity. Judged against the standard of such traditional gender-norms—that is, judged in terms of how I function in the traditional role of woman—I do not excel. Although I don't aspire to satisfying this ideal, this doesn't prevent others from judging me in its terms.

I noted above that there are difficulties in specifying the social relations that constitute gender, especially if we seek to understand it as a cross-cultural phenomenon; these difficulties are echoed and amplified in the project of specifying the content of gender-norms. We should be wary of postulating a single gender-norm for women across cultures or even within a cultural group:

> A glance at women's magazines, for example, reveals a range of often competing subject positions offered to women readers, from career woman to romantic heroine, from successful wife and mother to irresistible sexual object. These different positions which magazines construct in their various features, advertising, and fiction are part of the battle to determine the day to day practices of family life, education, work, and leisure.[15]

Moreover, gender-norms vary markedly with race, class, and ethnicity. To use a particularly apt example in the context of this chapter, there are studies that suggest that although developed capacities for abstract thought and intellectual activity are part of a masculine gender-norm for some privileged groups of men in Western communities, these elements of the masculine norm do not persist across class.[16]

---

[15] Weedon, *Feminist Practice and Poststructuralist Theory*, 26.

[16] See, e.g., Jean Grimshaw, *Philosophy and Feminist Thinking* (Minneapolis: University of Minnesota Press, 1986), 62.

Because our values and the structure of our lives have an impact on each other, the norms and the roles tend to adjust to each other. The acceptance of new roles for women can result in the recognition of new "women's virtues," and the appeal of new norms can result in changes in social roles.[17] But we should keep in mind that norms and roles can also fall desperately out of sync when the norms remain rigid while social roles change; gender-norms "often take on complex lives and histories of their own, which often bear little resemblance to their functional roots."[18] In the course of these complex histories, norms can become internally contradictory, making it impossible to live up to them or to structure a coherent life around them.[19] Such incoherence in the norms may indicate that they no longer reflect the allotted social roles, or it may reflect an incoherence in the roles themselves.

In contexts where gender roles are well entrenched, the corresponding norms function *prescriptively*: not only do they serve as the basis for judgments about how people ought to be (act, and so on), but also we decide how to act, what to strive for, what to resist, in light of such norms.[20] This prescriptive force is backed by social sanctions. In aspiring to a gender-norm, you aim to conform your behavior to those ideals that make you especially suited to your allotted role; if you don't aspire to the norm or if you don't manage to conform, you can

[17] For example, in some affluent Western communities the ideal of the "supermom" has replaced the ideal of the "homemaker" as a gender-norm for women (is this a new "femininity"?). We should also note that gender-norms may function differently if women take control of defining the social relations that constitute gender—i.e., being a "good woman" within a women's community may require satisfying very different norms than those traditionally counted as feminine. Note that feminist resistance to the claim that gender categories are constituted by relations of domination is sometimes supported by the thought that the category of women should be defined *by* and *for* women in terms of a more empowering self-conception; such a definition would plausibly not employ relations of domination. This constructive project is highly contested, for there is a clear danger of replacing one set of oppressive gender roles (and gender-norms) with another. One alternative is to resist the construction of gender categories altogether, likewise resisting the consolidation of (at least binary) gender-norms. We might instead recommend a "subversive recombination of gender meanings" (see Judith Butler, "Gender Trouble, Feminist Theory, and Psychoanalytic Discourse," in Nicholson, ed., *Feminism/Postmodernism*, 333). See also Theresa de Lauretis, "*Feminist Studies/Critical Studies*: Issues, Terms, and Contexts," in her *Feminist Studies/Critical Studies* (Bloomington: Indiana University Press, 1986), 1–19.

[18] DiStefano. "Dilemmas of Difference," 70.

[19] E.g., the idea that a "good" woman is asexual, combined with the idea that a "good" woman is responsive to men's sexual desire, offers women little room to negotiate a coherent relation to sexuality. For a discussion of such contradictions in the context of moral evaluation, see Kathryn Morgan, "Women and Moral Madness," *Canadian Journal of Philosophy*, supplementary vol. 13 (Fall 1987): 201–25.

[20] However, we should note that norms may entail features that are not in any obvious way under our control; hence, our strivings to satisfy the accepted norm may be pointless and even tragic. Self-mutilation and self-starvation are not uncommon consequences of the felt need to satisfy accepted gender-norms.

expect censure, sometimes mild, sometimes severe. Moreover, those social relations that constitute gender (including, for example, the organization of parenting) provide a context in which children tend to internalize the locally endorsed gender-norms.[21] Thus conformity to our proper gender role comes to seem right and good, and perhaps most significantly, internally motivated rather than socially enforced. As a result, we should expect that socially endorsed gender-norms will *reflect and reinforce* the local pattern of gender relations.

However, we should also note that the properties constituting the norms can also function *descriptively*: some individuals have the properties in question and others do not. In a society where gender-norms are generally agreed upon and well entrenched, and where individuals are fairly successful in living up to them, corresponding generalizations about the differences between men and women, even about males and females, may be descriptively adequate.[22] Noting such generalizations, there is an unmistakable tendency to conclude that a woman is "by nature" or "essentially" feminine (and a man masculine). In short, the prescriptive role of the norms is not acknowledged, and gender differences are taken to be natural or inevitable.[23] But this inference is mistaken: Even if the generalizations are accurate, their accuracy may simply reflect the impact of the

---

[21] A broad range of feminists have been keen to incorporate the suggestion that our conceptions of self and world bear the marks of gender, largely due to the influence of early childhood experience. In internalizing the relevant gender-norms, we develop "gender identities"; these gender identities represent reality—self and world—in a form that motivates our participation in the assigned gender role. The literature on this is enormous. Important examples include Nancy Chodorow, *The Reproduction of Mothering: Psychoanalysis and the Sociology of Gender* (Berkeley: University of California Press, 1978); Dorothy Dinnerstein, *The Mermaid and the Minotaur: Sexual Arrangements and Human Malaise* (New York: Harper and How, 1976); Jane Flax, "Political Philosophy and the Patriarchal Unconscious: A Psychoanalytic Perspective on Epistemology and Metaphysics," in Harding and Hintikka, eds., *Discovering Reality*, 245–81; Keller, *Reflections on Gender and Science;* Naomi Scheman, "Individualism and the Objects of Psychology," in Harding and Hintikka, eds., *Discovering Reality*, 225–44. For an important critical discussion of this work, see Butler, "Gender Trouble."

[22] It is important to note, however, that when gender-norms are well-entrenched, individuals are often interpreted as living up to them even when they don't: a woman may be assumed to be nurturing, weak, or dependent even when she isn't. (Others may make these assumptions about her, and she may also make these assumptions about herself.)

[23] Another temptation prompted by generalizations that women are feminine and men are masculine is to define the social categories of gender in terms of conformity to idealized gender-norms—i.e., to take the social class of women to consist of those who are feminine. This, too, is a mistake, but for different reasons. On this view, it is rightly acknowledged that gender differences are the result of social forces; but in taking femininity to be the mark by which one qualifies as a woman, the analysis loses much of its power as a critique of patriarchy's assumptions about women. Delimiting the class of women in terms of the standards of femininity treats unfeminine women as not "really" women at all and ignores the possibility of women's resistance to the norm; worse still, because socially endorsed conceptions of "femininity" will reflect race, class, heterosexual, religious, and ethnic bias, by defining women as those who are feminine we are in danger of repeating the exclusion and marginalization that feminism is committed to redressing.

norms and the pattern of social relations that underwrites the acceptance of those norms.[24]

In contrast, the theoretical framework I have sketched emphasizes the prescriptive role of gender-norms and highlights the fact that gender is grounded in broad social arrangements. Particular traits, norms, and identities, considered in abstraction from social context, have no claim to be classified as masculine or feminine. The classification of features as masculine or feminine is *derivative*, and in particular, depends on prior *social* classifications. For example, consider the claim that sensitivity to interpersonal relationships is a feminine trait. In considering this claim we must not suppose that such sensitivity is inherently feminine or that its status as feminine is determined biologically, or psychologically, or by virtue of its inclusion in an extrasocial (be it "natural" or "metaphysical") archetype of Woman. Not only does such reification fail to accommodate the broad cultural differences in the content of gendered ideals; worse still, the reliance on such archetypes masks the fact that the status of ideals as masculine or feminine rests upon an organization of social life in terms of "proper" roles and functions.[25] The ideals are gendered because the roles for which they count as ideals constitute gender.

I stress this dependence of gendered ideals on social arrangements because it highlights one issue in the problematic of justifying social arrangements. Ideals present themselves as standards or excellences to be valued; if we assume that the "right" ideals are given by authority (for example, by nature or God), then it is tempting to justify a distribution of social roles by virtue of the opportunities they provide to achieve the given ideals. If nurturing is an inherently feminine excellence and bravery is an inherently masculine excellence, then it might seem justified to distribute social roles in a way that facilitates women's opportunities to nurture and men's opportunities to be brave. But if we allow that ideals are functionally rooted in roles and activities, this strategy loses its force. An excellent slave is one who is obedient; an excellent master is one who exercises control. But such ideals of slavishness and mastery do not justify the institution of slavery because the ideals gain their prescriptive force only in a context where we assume the appropriateness (or inevitability) of the social roles of master and slave. In short, an ideal is appropriate only insofar as we are justified in endorsing the social role for which it functions as the ideal; the ideal does not, in turn, justify the role.

[24] This point has been made repeatedly over the centuries. See, e.g., John Stuart Mill, *The Subjection of Women*, in *Essays on Sex Equality*, ed. Alice Rossi (Chicago: University of Chicago Press, 1970). We will discuss later some of the mechanisms that all too often obscure this point.

[25] For a convincing and engaging discussion of this point, see Christine Delphy, "Protofeminism and Antifeminism," in *French Feminist Theory*, ed. Toril Moi (Oxford: Basil Blackwell, 1987), 80–109. See also Iris Young, "Is Male Gender Identity the Cause of Male Domination," in *Throwing Like a Girl and Other Essays in Feminist Philosophy and Social Theory* (Bloomington/Indianapolis: Indiana University Press, 1990), 36–61.

This argument is aimed primarily at those who would claim that naturally or transcendentally "given" ideals of masculinity and femininity warrant a gendered division of social life. But it is also intended to motivate the concern that the value we accord to masculinity or femininity cannot be easily separated from the value we accord the corresponding gender roles. If the gender roles are oppressive and constitute a system of male domination, then we should be cautious in theoretically appropriating either masculine or feminine virtues, even if our intention is to construct a revised ideal of human virtue.

3. Masculine Rationality

Within the Western philosophical tradition, the capacity to reason has been crucial to accounts of the self, and ideals of rationality have been construed as important elements in normative accounts of knowledge and morality. It is also clear that these ideals of rationality and rational selves have typically been defined in contrast to what are assumed to be characteristic features and capacities of women: Women are guided by emotion or feeling rather than reason; women are not capable of impartiality or abstract thought; women are more intuitive and closer to nature than men, and so on.[26] Moreover, anyone who displays a tendency to diverge from rational ideals (or virtually anything that does so) counts as feminine.[27] It is striking that even very different accounts of rationality agree on the contrast with assumed "feminine" attributes. The significance of this contrast supports the hypothesis that in spite of efforts to cast rationality as a "human" ideal, it is in fact a masculine one. That rationality is masculine is explicitly stated by some philosophers, and this assumption also forms a backdrop to common Western conceptions of gender difference that have a deep influence on everyday life.

Insofar as allegedly gender-free accounts of knowledge, morality, and personhood offer ideals defined by their contrast with femininity, patriarchy turns one of its neatest tricks. The reification of masculine ideals as human ideals ensures that one's efforts to be feminine will consistently undermine one's efforts to realize the ideal for persons (and similarly the ideals for morality and knowledge). Women face an impossible choice that carries censure either way: be a good person but fail as a woman, or be a good woman and fail as a person. This is no small consequence. As Judith Butler notes,

---

[26] See Lloyd, *Man of Reason*.

[27] Just about anything can be (and has been) interpreted as exemplifying the norms of femininity and masculinity. Useful examples of the projection of gender-norms onto individuals of other kinds is available in feminist work in science (especially biology). See, e.g., Helen Longino and Ruth Doell, "Body, Bias, and Behavior: A Comparative Analysis in Two Areas of Biological Science," *Signs* 9 (1983): 206–27; and Haraway, *Simians, Cyborgs, and Women*, esp. pts. I–II.

The social constraints upon gender compliance and deviation are so great that most people feel deeply wounded if they are told that they exercise their manhood or womanhood improperly. In so far as social existence requires an unambiguous gender affinity, it is not possible to exist in a socially meaningful sense outside of established gender norms. . . . If human existence is always gendered existence, then to stray outside of established gender is in some sense to put one's very existence into question.[28]

Initially it is tempting to think that the mistakes of this tradition can be easily remedied by excising the problematic claims about women and femininity. One might propose, for example, that conceptions of rational selves and the ideals of rationality need not be defined in contrast to femininity; they can stand on their own as ideals for both men and women. This proposal acknowledges that rational ideals have been associated with men and are assumed to be masculine; but it goes on to claim that we should simply reject these associations and assumptions. The traditional conceptions of femininity were misguided: To be a good woman (or a good man) just is to be a good person (in one or another of the traditional senses). In short, the sexism of the tradition is not inherent in its accounts of the self or the role of reason; rather, its sexism lies in a failure to see that, as a matter of fact, the accounts apply equally well to all of us.

But feminist work on gender raises doubts about this apologetic strategy. If rational ideals have been defined in contrast to feminine ideals, then there is reason to think that underlying these ideals we will find a division of gender roles. As I've already argued, norms are not gendered simply by being associated with men or women; they are gendered by providing ideals that are appropriate to the roles constituting gender.[29] Masculine norms are excellences appropriate to men's social role, and masculine identities are conceptions of self and world that justify one's place and activities in this role by presenting the activities as appropriate, good, natural, or inevitable. If we simply extend masculine norms to everyone and take the masculine conception of self and world to apply generally, we would seem to be committed to the view that everyone should occupy the social role (and so take up the perspective on social life) that was once

---

[28] Butler, "Variations on Sex and Gender," 132.

[29] Unfortunately, many feminist theorists speak as if a concept is masculine simply by virtue of being "associated" with men: "The basic thesis of the feminist critique of knowledge can be stated very simply: the privileging of the rational mode of thought is inherently sexist because, at least since the time of Plato, the rational has been associated with the male, the irrational with the female" (Hekman, "Feminization of Epistemology," 70). As should be clear from my discussion thus far, I find this "simple statement" of the thesis too weak to do justice to the depth of the feminist critique; at the very least, more needs to be said about the nature of the association, showing it to be more than "mere" association, in order to sustain the feminist challenge.

granted only to men. In effect, this move assumes that what was a model for life within one social category among others can (and should) become a model for all of us.

The initial worry is that if reason itself is masculine, then simply granting that rational ideals properly apply to everyone, regardless of gender, reflects a bias toward men. We might ask, If the ideals of rationality are ideals appropriate to men's social role, by what right do we extend these ideals to "human" ideals? What are we to make of the ideals appropriate to women's social role, particularly those that are defined in contrast to rationality? Likewise, if philosophical accounts of self and world only reflect how things seem from the social position of boys and men, and *not* how things seem from the social position of girls and women, then by what right do we expect everyone to endorse these conceptions? The concern is that masculine ideals appear to offer, at best, only a partial model of human life. One pressing question is how, or whether, we might remedy such a partial model. Should we aim to integrate the different perspectives?

We can extend and deepen these questions by noting that it is by no means obvious whether it is warranted to extend men's social role, and its corresponding rational ideals and excellences, to everyone. Whether such an extension is even possible will depend, of course, on how one conceives of gender and, in particular, how the ideals of rationality are grounded in gender. But the worry gains focus if we attend to the hypothesis mentioned above that gender roles are defined relationally and hierarchically—for example, just as someone is a landlord by virtue of standing in a certain (hierarchical) relation to another who is a tenant, someone is a man by virtue of standing in a certain (hierarchical) relation to another who is a woman. Because gender roles are situated within complex social arrangements, we cannot simply assume that it is possible or warranted to generalize masculine roles or to integrate masculine and feminine ideals.

For example, we cannot coherently extend some social roles to everyone: it is not possible for everyone to take up the role of being a free slave-owner. For different (very material) reasons, it is not possible for everyone to live the life of pure contemplation, "unsullied" by menial labor and uninterrupted by the needs of the young, the sick, and the elderly.[30] Although some other roles can be generalized, we should hesitate to do so: Even though it is possible for everyone to function as a scapegoat with respect to some group of others, proposing that everyone should function in the role of scapegoat and endorse its corresponding ideals would be misguided. So we should ask, What are the roles for which rationality is an appropriate ideal? What roles are motivated and authorized by a

---

[30] For a wonderful discussion of whether and to what extent philosophical conceptions and ideals of self can be extended to include women, see Susan Okin, *Women in Western Political Thought* (Princeton, N.J.: Princeton University Press, 1979).

conception of rational selves? In particular, if rationality is an ideal for men's social role, and if gender is defined relationally, then can we coherently endorse rationality without also endorsing those social relations that constitute gender and without also endorsing a contrasting ideal for women?

It is important to note that these questions have correlates concerning feminine norms and ideals. For example, if feminine norms such as "intuitiveness," "partiality," and "situatedness" offer ideals particularly suited to the gender roles of women, we should question whether these feminine norms can be "de-gendered" to free them from their links to social arrangements of gender oppression. This shift of focus from masculine ideals to feminine ideals raises doubts about the strategies of "gynocentric" feminists who seek to remedy the Western tradition's emphasis on reason by revaluing what are traditionally conceived as feminine virtues.[31] Understanding that gender and gender-norms are grounded in social relations, we may have reason to challenge not only masculine norms and identities but also feminine ones. If masculine and feminine ideals can be realized only in social contexts organized by gender relations, or if their realization functions to sustain existing gender relations, then if gender relations are relations of domination, those who seek to end gender oppression should reject both masculine and feminine ideals.

At this stage of the discussion, I have not yet offered an argument which shows that reason is gendered. The point noted early in this section—that traditional accounts of rational ideals characterize them in contrast to femininity—lends plausibility to the claim that such ideals are gendered. But it remains to be shown in what sense, and to what extent, an endorsement of reason functions to sustain oppressive gender roles. In order to provide such an argument, we will need to look at a more detailed account of gender and reason. We will turn to this task shortly. Before doing so, however, we must consider in more detail the relationship between norms and roles.

The questions raised above suggest two underlying suspicions. The first is that those situated in certain oppressive or problematic roles succeed (for example, their activities are furthered and sustained) by satisfying the ideals of reason. The second is that those who satisfy the ideals of reason thereby function in a problematic or oppressive social role; that is, simply satisfying the ideals of reason is enough to situate you in the role of oppressor. Plausibly, in both cases we would have grounds to question the value of reason if we are concerned to promote social change. Moreover, these suspicions become specifically feminist if the oppressive social roles in question are gender roles. But these two suspicions need further clarification before we can make a compelling case against the ideals of reason.

---

[31] For a valuable discussion and defense of "gynocentric" feminism that is sensitive to these concerns, see Iris Young, "Humanism, Gynocentrism, and Feminist Politics," in her *Throwing Like a Girl*, 73–91.

So far I have repeatedly suggested that norms or ideals are "suitable" or "appropriate" to specific social roles. Admittedly, these notions remain obscure; as a start toward clarification, it will help to introduce a couple of distinctions that will play a role in the arguments that follow. As indicated above, I am assuming that some roles have a point or a purpose and that certain performances in these roles count as successes and others as failures. Further, I will assume that excellence in an ongoing role will require a reliable disposition to perform successfully. Drawing on these ideas we can say that a norm is *appropriate* to a social role just in case those functioning in the role will have a greater chance of success (in that role) if they satisfy the norm; in other words, satisfying the norm would make for, or significantly contribute to, (reliable) success in the role. So, an "appropriate" norm for a role is one whose satisfaction will, other things being equal, take you from merely meeting the minimal conditions for the role to doing a better, or even excellent, job at it.

Promoting excellence in oppressive social roles is something we should aim to avoid; we should not assume, however, that the value of a norm can be judged simply in light of its contribution to excellence in a given social role. Consider, for example, the roles of master and slave. Plausibly, "good" masters are those who (among other things) are kind and compassionate toward their slaves. Such kindness on the part of good masters may help sustain the social institution of slavery by encouraging slaves' loyalty and hard work. But the fact that kindness contributes to success in the role of master should not lead us to reject the value of kindness in general; nor should we even conclude that it is wrong for those who are masters to be kind and compassionate toward their slaves, suggesting, perhaps, that they should be cruel and heartless instead. We can continue to value kindness, even the kindness of masters, while acknowledging that it is a norm appropriate to an oppressive social role. Nevertheless, we must acknowledge that a master's kindness is worrisome insofar as it functions to perpetuate the institution of slavery. And there is something clearly wrong in encouraging individuals to be good masters: In order to be a good master, one must also be a master, and this role we have reason to reject.

As a step toward sorting through these complications, we can note that some norms are separable from the social role for which they are appropriate and some aren't. One may have features that would contribute to success in a particular role without functioning in that role and without that role even being socially available. For example, suppose we were to characterize a good tenant as one who pays the rent on time and is considerate of others (does not disturb their neighbors, does not destroy others' property, and so on). These features are appropriate to the role of tenant: They contribute to success in being a good tenant, and they serve as standards by which tenants are evaluated.

However, one of the elements in this specified tenant ideal, namely, being considerate of others, is separable from the relations constituting the social category of tenant. Satisfying this norm does not entail one's participation in the role of tenant because one can be considerate of others without being a tenant. In contrast, the condition that one pay one's rent on time is not separable in this way. One can satisfy the condition of paying one's rent on time only if one is a tenant; in satisfying this norm, one thereby satisfies the conditions for being a tenant. If one is not a tenant, then not only is the ideal inappropriate, but there is no way to satisfy it short of becoming a tenant. Similarly, a good teacher reliably informs and guides others in learning, listens carefully, and encourages enthusiasm for the subject. Listening carefully is separable from the role of teacher, but reliably informing and guiding others in learning is not. Satisfying the latter plausibly entails that one functions as a teacher (assuming, of course, that one need not be a teacher by profession to be a teacher).

These examples illustrate two points. First, some norms are such that satisfying them entails one's participation in a particular social role; these norms are *constitutively grounded* in a social role; but in the case of conjunctive norms or ideals, even if as a whole they are constitutively grounded in a social role, they may have elements that are separable from the role.[32] Second, if a norm is constitutively grounded in a social role that is defined relationally—for example, as the role of tenant is defined in relation to landlords—then satisfying the norm will require that social arrangements provide for such relations. Because of the relational character of the role of tenant, satisfying the tenant ideal requires that someone is a landlord. If the tenant ideal is appropriate to some, then there is a landlord ideal appropriate to others. Thus commitment to a norm that is constitutively grounded in a relational social role presupposes the appropriateness of a contrasting and correlative ideal.

We should note, however, that there is a middle ground between norms that are constitutively grounded in a particular social role and ones that are wholly separable from the given role. As I characterized the conditions for the constitutive grounding of a norm in a role, it is (conceptually) necessary that anyone who satisfies the norm functions in that role—necessarily, anyone who pays their

---

[32] Note that in defining constitutive grounding in terms of entailment, I am not distinguishing between cases in which the entailed conditions are presupposed by the entailing conditions (as might be claimed of the tenant example) and those in which they are not presupposed but in which they count as more straightforward sufficient conditions (as in the teacher example). For classic attempts at characterizing the difference between presupposition and entailment, see, P. F. Strawson, *Introduction to Logical Theory* (London:Methuen, 1952), and "Reply to Mr. Sellars," *Philosophical Review* 63 (1954): 216–31.

rent on time is a tenant. However, we should note that whether and how one is situated in a role will often depend on contextual factors; therefore, satisfying a norm may be sufficient for functioning in a role in some contexts but not in others.[33]

Consider first a relatively straightforward example: the ideal life of pure contemplation mentioned above. There is nothing about satisfying this ideal, in and of itself, that makes one dependent on the work of others for one's sustenance and survival. The life of pure contemplation is not constitutively grounded in the role of dependent by virtue of the concepts employed in the ideal: angels could satisfy it without functioning in a dependent role. And yet as a matter of fact, given the material conditions of human life, any adult who comes even close to satisfying this ideal will, in doing so, function in a dependent role. That is to say, given certain background conditions, satisfying the ideal is sufficient for functioning in the social role of a dependent.

In the case of pure contemplation, the background conditions that we just assumed—for example, the human need for food and shelter—are general and, at least to some extent, apply to all of us; but other background conditions will be socially specific. Consider the ideal for an investigative journalist. Plausibly, in order to be an excellent investigative journalist, one should "relentlessly" pursue and publicize information of concern to the general public. Note, however, that the social roles of those who satisfy this norm will vary greatly depending on their social context. Someone who satisfies this norm under a dictatorship where such journalistic efforts are prohibited by law will thereby function in the role of a criminal and will be subject to prosecution. (More important, perhaps, those who satisfy the norm in such contexts take up a role of resistance.) However, satisfying this journalistic norm will not be sufficient for being a criminal, or for resistance, under a democracy where journalistic freedom is legally protected. Thus one could realize the same ideal, even in substantively the same way, in two different social contexts and yet in doing so function in very different social roles.[34]

Let us say (roughly) that a norm or an ideal is *contextually grounded* in a social role just in case, given specified background conditions, satisfying that norm is

---

[33] We should note that in determining whether a norm is *appropriate to a role*, parallel issues arise: Is satisfying the norm required in any context in order to excel at the role? Or does satisfying the norm contribute, in a given context, to excellence in the role? Because it is relatively common to acknowledge the contextual factors in determining a norm's appropriateness to a role, my discussion here will focus on the constitutive/contextual distinction with respect to grounding.

[34] Clearly the journalistic ideal mentioned may be satisfied in a variety of different ways and by a variety of different actions. Two journalists may end up in different social roles because they realize the norm through different courses of action. My point here, however, is that even if a journalist were to pursue the same course of action as in fact she does, but under different background conditions, she could be cast in a different social role.

or would be sufficient for functioning in that role.[35] No doubt determining whether an ideal is contextually grounded in a particular social role will be a difficult project that will rely on controversial assumptions about the context in question. These contextual complications are not typically a focus of attention in evaluating norms or ideals; instead we describe the ideals in ways which are largely indeterminate with respect to who or what satisfies them, and with respect to how and when they are satisfied (though, as feminist work has shown, often sexist background assumptions play a crucial role in our evaluations). We may grant that in evaluating a norm it is important to determine the variety of possible ways that it can, in principle, be realized and the conceptual limits on its realization. But it is only by considering how norms and ideals are realized in *context* that we can effectively determine their consequences, and their value, for our thoroughly situated lives.[36]

As I mentioned above, our evaluation of norms goes hand-in-hand with an evaluation of the roles in which they are grounded. On the face of it, we might think that if a norm is grounded in a socially problematic role, then we should reject the norm; in rejecting the norm, we often hope to discourage others from assuming the role. However, if a norm is contextually grounded in a problematic social role, the appropriate move may not be to give up the norm; rather, it may be warranted instead to change the background conditions connecting the norm with the role. For example, plausibly in those contexts in which realizing the ideal of investigative journalist renders one a criminal, we should continue to endorse the role of investigative journalist and its norms but work to change the social conditions that are responsible for a journalist's criminal status.

---

[35] In offering this condition it is important to note that there has been significant philosophical attention devoted to the problem of articulating and evaluating conditionals that depend upon the specification of relevant background conditions. A classic statement of the problem appears in Nelson Goodman, "The Problem of Counterfactual Conditionals," *Journal of Philosophy* 44 (February 1947): 113–28; also his *Fact, Fiction, and Forecast*, 2d ed. (Indianapolis: Bobbs-Merrill, 1965). See also Roderick Chisholm, "Law Statements and Counterfactual Inference, *Analysis* 15 (April 1955): 97–105; J. L. Mackie, "Counterfactuals and Causal Laws," in *Analytical Philosophy*, ed. R. J. Butler (New York: Barnes and Noble, 1962), 66–80. It remains a standing problem how to set limits on the assumed background conditions so that the conditional yields a substantive requirement; in this case, the problem is how to set constraints on the background conditions to avoid the result that any norm whatsoever is grounded in a given social role, yet without describing the constraints so that the conditional in question trivially holds. I will not undertake to solve this problem here. I trust that the argument I will discuss below does not depend for its plausibility on working through the details of this issue.

[36] It is important to keep in mind that the contextual grounding of a norm in a role need not contribute to success in that role and that the norm need not count as part of an ideal "for" that role, in the ordinary sense. For example, what makes you an excellent journalist may, under certain conditions, result in your being a criminal without making you a good criminal. Nevertheless, noting that norms are not only constitutively but also contextually grounded in roles highlights the fact that our "virtues" may unexpectedly cast us in roles for which they were never intended.

Having noted these differences in the way in which norms and ideals might be "appropriate to" or "grounded in" social roles, we can now gain clearer focus on the task of showing that reason is masculine, or gendered. In section 2, I suggested that traits are "gendered" insofar as they make for excellence in socially endorsed gender roles. Although this captures part of the idea, the discussion in this section expands and develops the initial suggestion. I have proposed that a norm is *appropriate* to a social role just in case satisfying that norm would make for or significantly contribute to successful functioning in that role. Further, broadly speaking, a norm is *grounded in* a social role just in case (allowing restricted background conditions) satisfying the norm is sufficient for functioning in the role, perhaps successfully, perhaps not. Let us say that a norm is *weakly gendered* just in case it is appropriate to a gender role, and that it is *strongly gendered* just in case it is grounded—either constitutively or contextually—in a gender role.

We can now reconsider the two "underlying suspicions" that prompted this discussion. The first suspicion was that those situated in oppressive social roles succeed—and, further, their roles are perpetuated—because they satisfy the ideals of reason. The second was that satisfying the ideals of reason was itself enough to situate you in an oppressive social role. If we assume that men's role is problematic—that it is oppressive to women—then these two suspicions correspond respectively to the charges that the ideals of reason are weakly gendered and that they are strongly gendered.[37] But the arguments I've offered show that we must be careful in drawing broad conclusions about the value of reason, or lack of it, based on the claims that it is gendered.

If we find that the norms of rationality are weakly gendered (that their satisfaction contributes to success in men's social role), this does not establish that we should reject them wholesale; it may be, for example, that satisfying the norms of rationality is separable from gender roles and has independent value. Nevertheless, there is significant political import in showing that the norms of rationality are weakly gendered. Consider again the example of a kind master. However laudable individual acts of kindness on the part of masters may be, insofar as these acts contribute to the perpetuation of slavery as an institution, the political consequences of these acts are abhorrent. It is a sad fact about social

---

[37] There is, however, one qualification we must add. It is a complicated matter to determine whether the features that promote success in a social role are responsible for perpetuating the role. Consider doctors: A successful doctor is one who heals her patients. It is tempting to say that healing patients, although required for a doctor's success, is not responsible for perpetuating the role of doctor; it's the fact that people get sick, in spite of good doctors' efforts, that perpetuates this role. But we should also note that people getting sick can't be all that is responsible for sustaining the social role of doctor, since it is easy to imagine how in contexts where all doctors are bad at their job, the role might lose credibility and eventually disappear. Thus I suggest that the features that contribute to success in a role will, at least indirectly, perpetuate the role.

life that the good we manage to accomplish may, in a broader context, sustain much more severe harm; and this harm is all too often masked by the good deeds that sustain it. If satisfying the norms of rationality enables men to excel in their social role, and does so specifically in a way that perpetuates male dominance, then knowing this is an important factor in unmasking the forces that prevent social change.

Moreover, if we find that rationality is weakly gendered, it does not follow that those who are rational stand in oppressive gender relations; nor does it follow that promoting ideals of rationality also promotes oppressive gender roles.[38] (One can promote kindness without promoting slavery.) However, if the norms of rationality are strongly gendered, say, if they are grounded in men's social role, then one who satisfies these norms thereby functions socially as a man. If the grounding is contextual, we should look hard at both the norms and the particular background conditions that link the norms with the role. But if men's social role is a role of domination, then on finding that rationality is grounded in this role, we can then insist that under the specified background conditions, satisfying the norms of rationality is offensive.

I'll now turn to consider a series of arguments designed to show that there is an ideal of objectivity that is both weakly and strongly gendered—in particular, masculine. The arguments I consider are based largely on an interpretation of Catharine MacKinnon's work, though there are points at which I employ a rather free hand in reconstructing the main line of thought. My goal is not to do justice to the full complexity of MacKinnon's views, but to draw on her insights in developing a critique of one conception of objectivity. I begin by explicating MacKinnon's account of the relation that constitutes categories of men and women. I then turn to consider what norms are appropriate to the role defined for men. Following MacKinnon's lead, I argue that there is a cluster of epistemic and practical norms, an ideal I label "assumed objectivity," that contributes to success in men's role and helps sustain a gendered division of social life. This shows that the ideal is weakly masculine. I then consider her further claim that this ideal of assumed objectivity is contextually grounded in men's social role; in particular, I ask whether satisfying this ideal is sufficient, under conditions of male dominance, for functioning as a man. I argue that it is not. Though I do not believe that MacKinnon's arguments accomplish the goal of showing that assumed objectivity is strongly masculine, I suggest that this ideal is contextually grounded in a different, but still problematic, social role.

---

[38] This theoretical possibility is important, for it allows us to claim that there may be ideals appropriate to women's social role that are, nevertheless, separable from this role. Just as satisfying some traditionally masculine ideals may not be sufficient to cast one in a man's role, satisfying some traditionally feminine ideals may not be sufficient to cast one in a woman's role. We may hope that this will allow us to endorse some of the traditional feminine ideals without supporting social arrangements of gender oppression.

4. Gender Relations: MacKinnon on Gender

In sketching some of the distinctions that play a role in recent feminist theory, I intentionally skirted controversial issues which now need attention. In particular, if we are to give substantive content to the claim that reason is gendered, we need an account of the social relations that constitute gender. Allowing that the category of gender is contested within feminist theory, is it possible to chart a path through some of the controversies?

There is a growing trend in current feminist research which recommends that although we should employ the concept of gender in our theorizing, we should not treat gender as a unified category.[39] On this "pluralistic" approach to gender, we acknowledge that gender is constituted through a variety of social relations, without aiming to specify what these relations have in common (perhaps opting for Wittgensteinian "family resemblances"?). In effect, we take gender relations to comprise an irreducibly disjunctive class.[40] Whether or not we accept this as our final conclusion, it is reasonable to grant that, at least at this stage, our theoretical efforts are best spent in exploring the range of relatively determinate relations that constitute gender; further, we may grant that it is not a criterion of success in our inquiry that gender can be given a unified analysis.

In keeping with this strategy, our emphasis should be on the task of proposing and employing admittedly partial, temporary, and context-sensitive gender distinctions. As a result, the charge that reason is gendered will not have a unique substantive content; its interpretation will depend on what gender relations are at issue. In the discussion that follows I will evaluate one instance of this charge, employing MacKinnon's account of gender as constituted by sexual objectification. To simplify my discussion I will often gloss over these limitations, speaking as if the account offers a definition of the relation that constitutes the social categories of men and women as such. I trust that given the allowances just sketched, we can proceed with an acknowledgment of the relevant qualifications.

Catharine MacKinnon's work on gender and objectivity is part of a large systematic project with broad repercussions for ongoing political and legal debates.[41]

---

[39] See, e.g., Haraway, "Manifesto for Cyborgs" and "Situated Knowledges"; Butler, "Variations on Sex and Gender" and "Gender Trouble"; and de Lauretis, "Feminist Studies/Critical Studies."

[40] For example, consider the relation "is a mother of." Employing a pluralistic approach to mothering relations, we might claim that one can be a mother of someone either by contributing the ovum from which they developed, by giving birth to them, by adopting them, or by playing a certain role in their parenting; in effect, we would claim that the conditions for being a mother are irreducibly disjunctive and heterogeneous.

[41] MacKinnon develops her position on gender and objectivity in "Feminism, Marxism, Method, and the State: An Agenda for Theory," in *Feminist Theory: A Critique of Ideology*, ed. Nannerl O. Keohane, Michelle Z. Rosaldo, and Barbara C. Gelpi (Chicago: University of Chicago Press, 1982), 1–30 (hereafter FMMS-I) (originally published in *Signs* 7 [1982]: 515–44); "Feminism, Marxism, Method, and the State: Toward Feminist Jurisprudence," Signs 8 (1983): 635–58 (hereafter FMMS-II); *Feminism Unmodified;* and *Towards a Feminist Theory of the State* (Cambridge, Mass.: Harvard University Press, 1989).

Her work is deeply grounded in a commitment never to lose sight of the terrible concrete reality of sexual violence against women. MacKinnon's account of gender falls largely within the specific theoretical framework I sketched above: Gender categories are defined relationally—one is a woman (or a man) by virtue of one's position in a system of social relations.[42] So one's gender is an extrinsic property, and assuming that we can survive even dramatic changes in our social relations, it is not necessary that we each have the gender we now have, or that we have any gender at all. MacKinnon's account adds to this background three main claims: (1) The relations constituting gender are, by definition, hierarchical. That men dominate women is not a contingent truth; relations of domination *constitute* the categories of man and woman. (2) Gender relations are defined by and in the interests of men. (3) Gender is "sexualized."[43] To quote MacKinnon:

> Male and female are created through the eroticization of dominance and submission. The man/woman difference and the dominance/submission dynamic define each other. This is the social meaning of sex and the distinctively feminist account of gender inequality.[44]
>
> Gender emerges as the congealed form of the sexualization of inequality between men and women.[45]
>
> A theory of sexuality becomes feminist methodologically, to the extent that it treats sexuality as a social construct of male power: defined by men, forced on women, and constitutive of the meaning of gender.[46]

[42] I say that MacKinnon's account falls "largely" within the framework, because she is more critical of the distinction between sex and gender than I have been here. Claiming that sex and gender are interdependent, she chooses to use the terms 'male' and 'man' and the terms 'female' and 'woman' interchangeably. See her *Feminism Unmodified*, 263(n5), and FMMS-II, 635(nl). Although I will continue to use the man/woman terminology when speaking of gender, in quotations I will leave her terminology as is.

[43] See, e.g., MacKinnon, *Feminist Theory of the State*, 113. Note that this third element in the analysis of gender—i.e., that gender is "sexualized"—is what distinguishes MacKinnon's analysis from a broad range of others. Many of the accounts are inspired by the thought that the category of women is defined as "other" to men; as I interpret these analyses, they share with MacKinnon both the idea that gender is irreducibly hierarchical and that our "otherness" is projected onto women by and in the interests of men. As has been frequently noted in the literature, however, there are "other others" besides women. MacKinnon's emphasis on sexuality seems to offer a way of distinguishing the hierarchical categories of gender from other hierarchical categories, such as race, class, and so on. But this way of distinguishing gender (and gender oppression) won't work if, as MacKinnon sometimes suggests, all hierarchy is "sexualized."

[44] Ibid., 113–14. See also *Feminism Unmodified*, 50.

[45] MacKinnon, *Feminism Unmodified*, 6.

[46] MacKinnon, *Feminist Theory of the State*, 128.

To put the point bluntly: One is a man by virtue of standing in a position of eroticized dominance over others; one is a woman by virtue of standing in a position of eroticized submission to others.[47] The modes and forms of dominance, submission, and eroticization may vary from culture to culture, context to context[48]; moreover, it is not necessary that one be anatomically female to be a woman or anatomically male to be a man, though, of course, this is the norm.[49]

But this blunt statement of the point is incomplete, for we need some better understanding of "eroticized dominance/submission" in order to connect it to the idea of objectification, and men's power to define the terms. As I interpret MacKinnon's position, if dominance/submission is eroticized, then the submissive participant must be viewed, at least by the dominant participant (though often by both participants), as being an object for the satisfaction of the dominant's desire. This desire presents her submissiveness to him, and his domination of her, as erotic. (We should keep in mind that on MacKinnon's view it is not because of some "purely natural" male urge toward domination or female impulse toward submission that subordination in its various forms is found erotic or stimulating. Desire is socially conditioned; locally, the most extreme and effective vehicle of this conditioning is pornography.[50])

So how is eroticized dominance/submission connected to objectification? For our purposes there are two points to highlight: First, if dominance/submission is eroticized, then the submissive participant is both *viewed as* and *treated as* an

[47] It is important to note that on MacKinnon's analysis, eroticized domination/submission is the definition of sex, or at least "sex in the male system"—i. e., under male supremacy. (See ibid., 140.) So sex is the relation in terms of which MacKinnon defines the social categories of man and woman. However, it is also important to recognize that on her view not all loving physical intimacy is sex (ibid., 139) and that many other interactions, "from intimate to institutional, from a look to a rape," can qualify as sex on her terms (ibid., 137). Although I recognize the importance of MacKinnon's strategy to define sex in terms of domination, here I am downplaying her account of sexuality and pornography in order to highlight other aspects of her account. I regret that in doing so, my exposition fails to reflect many of the important connections she draws.

[48] MacKinnon herself does not endorse the pluralist approach just sketched; rather, she takes her account of gender to capture the basic structure of all gender relations. She does allow, however, that there are cultural variations in the way this structure is instantiated. See MacKinnon, *Feminist Theory of the State*, 130–32, 151; *Feminism Unmodified*, 53; and FMMS-I, 24(n55).

[49] MacKinnon quotes C. Shafer and M. Frye, "Rape and Respect," in *Feminism and Philosophy*, ed. Mary Vetterling-Braggin et al. (Totowa, N. J.: Littlefield, Adams, 1982), 334: "Rape is a man's act, whether it is a male or female man, and whether it is a man relatively permanently or relatively temporarily; and being raped is a woman's experience, whether it is a female or male woman and whether it is a woman relatively permanently or relatively temporarily." MacKinnon comments: "To be rapable, a position that is social, not biological, defines what a woman is" (*Feminist Theory of the State*, 178, 179). See also *Feminism Unmodified*, 52, 56.

[50] For further discussion of these issues in connection with MacKinnon's analysis, see Andrea Dworkin, *Pornography: Men Possessing Women* (New York: Perigee, 1981), and *Intercourse* (New York: Free Press, 1987).

object of the dominant's desire.[51] Second, the submissive participant is viewed in functional terms: She is *for* the satisfaction of his desire. Let us concentrate here on the first point. (I will return to the second point in the next section.) On MacKinnon's view, the relation of objectification that constitutes gender requires both attitude and act. Gender is a distinction of power that is *read into* and *imposed upon* women: "Men treat women as who they see women as being."[52] The category of women is, in a sense, that group of individuals onto which men project and act out their desire.

However, we must take special note of the act, for the dominance inherent in gender is not just in the content of the desire—for example, a wish for dominance. Nor is the dominance merely a matter of projection: of viewing certain individuals through the lens of one's desire to dominate them. For this projection "is not just an illusion or a fantasy or a mistake. It becomes *embodied* because it is enforced."[53] On MacKinnon's view, one who objectifies another has the power to enforce compliance with his view of them.[54] The power and the force are socially real: In the United States during 1989, according to Federal Bureau of Investigation (FBI) reports, a woman was raped on average every six minutes, and nine out of ten women murdered were murdered by men;[55] and according to the National Coalition Against Domestic Violence, a woman was beaten on average every fifteen seconds.[56]

---

[51] On the issue of the intentionality in sexual abuse, see Hacking, "World-Making by Kind-Making." Hacking's essay is very useful in understanding that social categories are those which depend, at least in part, on being viewed as categories. He argues convincingly that it is problematic to extend social categories to other times and contexts if there is reason to doubt whether the relevant concepts were available for conceptualizing the categories in question. So, one might argue, in contexts where concepts such as desire, submission, and the like are not available, there is no gender. MacKinnon seems to be sensitive to this issue in claiming (contra the Freudians) that infants "cannot be said to possess sexuality" in her sense (*Feminist Theory of the State*, 151).

[52] MacKinnon, *Feminism Unmodified*, 172.

[53] Ibid., 119.

[54] For an especially clear statement of this claim, see ibid., 233–34(n26). MacKinnon contrasts objectification, which requires actual power to dominate, with stereotyping, which need not: "Objectification is the dynamic of the subordination of women. Objectification is different from stereotyping, which acts as if it is all in the head" (ibid., 118, 119). See also ibid., ch. 2. I take it that individual women can stereotype men, but women do not objectify men (at least not normally or as easily) because we don't have the social power. Although an analysis of social power is important to flesh out MacKinnon's account of gender, I will not offer one here.

[55] Federal Bureau of Investigation, *Uniform Crime Reports for the United States*, 1989 (Washington, D.C.: GPO, 1990), 6, 15. According to this report, there were 94,504 forcible rapes (p. 10), with forcible rape defined as "the carnal knowledge of a female forcibly and against her will. Assaults or attempts to commit rape by force or threat of force are included, however statutory rape (without force) and other sex offenses are excluded" (p. 14). Needless to say, rape often goes unreported. Credible estimates of rapes far surpass the FBI statistics; some suggest we should multiply the FBI numbers by as much as ten.

[56] National Coalition Against Domestic Violence, Fact Sheet, in "Report on Proposed Legislation S2754," 27. On file with the Senate Judiciary Committee.

In individual cases, the dominant party who sexually objectifies another need not exercise this power directly; the force behind the submissive participant's compliance may have been exercised in other contexts and in indirect ways. Moreover, the dominant party may have, and may maintain, the power to enforce compliance even if in some cases he attempts force and fails; power doesn't guarantee success. But the fact of the dominant participant's real power is a necessary condition for objectification. Because this inequality of power is a condition of objectification, and because gender is defined in terms of objectification, gender is, by definition, hierarchical: Those who function socially as men have power over those who function socially as women.

Although gender is defined relationally in terms of social roles which in principle could be taken up by different individuals at different times (and no doubt in individual cases are), socially these roles have "congealed": it is a particular group of individuals who are assigned the status "man" and another group the status "woman." Broadly speaking, men are male, women are female, and males have the power to dominate females.[57] However, it is important to note that objectification is not "the cause" of male dominance. That males objectify females presupposes that males have power over females; this follows from the conditions on objectification. Moreover, objectifying *attitudes*—for example, attitudes representing females as "sex objects"—may function socially to sustain inequality of power, but having such attitudes does not, by itself, give one power. MacKinnon's analysis of gender is not intended to provide a causal account of the origins of male dominance. Rather, it is an account which locates gender within a system of hierarchical social relations; as we shall see, one point of highlighting objectification is to explain how, in certain contexts, male dominance is self-sustaining.

So, in MacKinnon's terms, the social category of women is that group of individuals who are viewed functionally as objects for the satisfaction of men's desire, where this desire is conditioned to find subordination stimulating, and where men have the power to enforce the conformity of those they so perceive to their view of them.[58] Male supremacy grants a particular group of individuals

---

[57] On MacKinnon's view, pornography is at least locally responsible for conditioning the particular sexual dynamic within which the domination of *females* is erotic. Yet she says surprisingly little about why it is that females, on the whole, have been marked as women. Her idea seems to be that because dominance is rationalized by biological difference, women's bodies come to be the "location" for gender to play itself out (see, e.g., *Feminist Theory of the State*, 54–59); however, because there is a general tendency to rationalize domination biologically, other embodied differences (race, age, weight, and so on) can and do provide alternative locations (*Feminist Theory of the State*, 179).

[58] Using the relation of sexual objectification, the structure of this definition of gender seems to be (roughly) as follows: x *is a woman* iff there is a y such that y sexually objectifies x; x *is a man* iff there is a y such that x sexually objectifies y. It is more tricky to define male supremacy. We might begin by considering this: A social system S *is a system of male supremacy* iff for all female x and male y in S, x's being female licenses (via S's norms, institutions, divisions of labor, and so on) any y's sexual objectification of x, and it is not the case that y's being male licenses any x's sexual objectification of y.

this power over others. It is important to note that on this account women are *not* defined as those who are submissive, or as those who *actually* satisfy men's conception of what is desirable; nor are women defined as those who have a feminine identity or who satisfy the norms of femininity (though this account will enable us to explain why many women will). In effect, what we share, as women, is that we are perceived and treated as sexually subordinate. Our commonality is in the eye, and the hand, and the power, of the beholder.

This last point becomes evident through an analogy between the concept of gender and the concept of meat. What counts as meat varies from culture to culture; the distinction between meat and not-meat is not marked simply by what animal flesh humans can digest (though in some cases the distinction may be coextensive with this). The class of things that count as meat for a given group of people is determined by their attitudes, desires, and appetites. What do the deer, the tuna, and the lamb have in common that the horse, the dolphin, and the kitten lack? The former are (at least locally) objects of socially trained human appetite; they are viewed and treated as objects for human consumption, and their lives are endangered as a result. The category of meat is not a "natural" category; like gender it is social, relational, and hierarchical. Like gender, the category of meat is a "fiction" which humans have the power to enforce and so to make all too real through practices of domestication, hunting, and fishing. As (many) vegetarians aim for a day when nothing will fall within the category of meat, (many) feminists aim for a day when no one will fall within the category of women.[59]

MacKinnon's account of gender, like others that define gender hierarchically, has the consequence that feminism aims to undermine the very distinction it depends upon. If feminism is successful, there will no longer be a gender distinction as such—or, allowing that there are a plurality of relations that serve to constitute gender and a plurality of feminist projects, we can say that one goal of feminism is to fight against the sexual subordination that constitutes these categories of men and women. "The refusal to become or to remain a 'gendered'

[59] This is not intended as an argument that a consistent feminist should also be a vegetarian (though I do believe that eating animals is, in most circumstances, wrong). Nor am I suggesting that the analogy is perfect; there are admittedly important differences between women and meat. Nor am I arguing that one should never view and treat things as objects for the satisfaction of one's desires; it will surely depend upon what sorts of things and what sorts of circumstances are in question. The analogy, however, does raise the possibility that, as explicated, MacKinnon's account fails to provide a sufficient condition for being a member of the category of women: If one finds cooking erotic, then it may be that one sexually objectifies food. But if we define women as the sexually objectified, this, I take it, would be an undesirable consequence. MacKinnon mentions that sex is like cuisine, though she doesn't suggest that a meal can function socially as a woman (*Feminist Theory of the State*, 132). One strategy to begin solving this problem would be to add conditions to the analysis of sexual objectification that require intentionality (i. e., the having of attitudes) of the subjugated participant.

man or woman . . . is an immanently political insistence on emerging from the nightmare of the all-too-real, imaginary narrative of sex and race."[60] "To refuse to be a woman, however, does not mean that one has to become a man."[61]

5. Objectivity and Objectification

Working with MacKinnon's account of gender and her conception of the social relations that constitute men and women, can we construct an argument for the claim that reason is gendered or, more specifically, masculine? As I sketched above, I will divide this question in two[62]: First, is rationality weakly masculine? That is, considering those who function as men, does it make for or specifically contribute to their success as men? If so, how does it do so? Second, is rationality strongly masculine? That is, does one who satisfies the norms of rationality thereby function socially as a man?

MacKinnon does not often use the term 'rationality', though when she does, it appears that she takes it to be equivalent to 'objectivity'. And most often she applies the terms to stances or points of view: One's point of view is rational, iff it is objective, iff it is "neutral," "distanced," or "non-situated."[63] In a compressed, though typical, statement of her position, MacKinnon claims:

> The content of the feminist theory of knowledge begins with its criticism of the male point of view by criticizing the posture that has been taken as the stance of "the knower" in Western political thought. . . . [That stance is] the neutral posture, which I will be calling objectivity—that is, the non-situated, distanced standpoint. I'm claiming that this is the male standpoint socially, and I'm going to try to say why. I will argue that the relationship between objectivity as the stance from which the world is known and the world that is apprehended in this way is the relationship of objectification. Objectivity is the epistemological stance of which objectification is the social process, of which male dominance is the politics,

[60] Haraway, "'Gender' for a Marxist Dictionary," 148.

[61] Wittig, "One Is Not Born a Woman," 49.

[62] It is important to keep these steps distinguished. Even if we are able to establish the strong claim that if one is a man, then one is a "good" or "successful" man *just in case* one is rational, we still cannot conclude that if one is rational, then one functions as a man—namely, that rationality is grounded in men's social role. The latter claim requires a separate argument.

[63] For MacKinnon's uses of the term 'rationality,' see, e.g., *Feminist Theory of the State*, 96–97, 114, 162, 229, 232; FMMS-II, 636(n3), 645. For the connections between objectivity, neutrality, and aperspectivity see, e.g., *Feminism Unmodified*, 50; *Feminist Theory of the State*, 83, 97, 99, 114, 162–64, 211, 213, 232, 248. 1 will assume that one is objective iff one's stance is objective if one satisfies the norms of objectivity.

the acted-out social practice. That is, to look at the world objectively is to objectify it. The act of control, of which what I have described is the epistemological level, is itself eroticized under male supremacy.[64]

Here MacKinnon claims that the stance of objectivity is the stance of those who function socially as men.[65] This would seem to commit her to the claim that one functions socially as a man if and only if one satisfies the norms of objectivity. Given my readings of her arguments, I think we can charitably recast her point in terms of the conditions for weak and strong gendering: Objectivity is strongly masculine because satisfying the norms of objectivity is sufficient, at least under conditions of male dominance, for being a sexual objectifier. And objectivity is weakly masculine given that those who function as men are successful in this role, at least in part, because they are objective.

In the next several sections I will concentrate on the charge that objectivity is weakly masculine; I will then turn to the question whether objectivity is strongly masculine. So the question now before us is this: Given someone who is a sexual objectifier, what would make for their (reliable) success in that role?[66] (In answering this question, my emphasis will be on what makes for an ideal objectifier, bracketing the fact that men are not just objectifiers but are *sexual* objectifiers. When we turn to the charge that objectivity is strongly masculine, I will then consider how sexuality figures in the picture.)

The Epistemology of Objectification

As outlined above, if one objectifies something (or someone), one views it and treats it as an object for the satisfaction of one's desire; but this is not all, for objectification is assumed to be a relation of domination where one also has the

---

[64] MacKinnon, *Feminism Unmodified*, 50.

[65] See also MacKinnon, *Feminist Theory of the State*, 114, 121–24, 199, 213, 248–49; *Feminism Unmodified*, 50–52, 54–55, 150–51, 155; FMMS-I, 23–25, 27; FMMS-II, 636, 640, 644–45, 658.

[66] There are several points we should be attentive to in considering the ideal objectifier. First, given that objectification requires both thinking and acting, excellence at objectification will require that one meet standards governing both thought and deed. Thus we should expect that the norm of objectivity in question will contain both epistemic and pragmatic elements. Second, one most fully realizes the ideal for those roles that are defined in terms of a *power* to act when one is *exercising* that power—e.g., a doctor is one who is able to heal others, but a doctor is most fully a doctor when she is actually healing someone. Moreover, one who excels at such a role should reliably have the power to act and should be able to sustain her power—e.g., a good doctor reliably heals her patients and sustains this power to heal. Third, one is more likely to succeed in roles that require sustaining a course of action (and a set of attitudes) if one's actions (and attitudes) are guided by norms or principles that legitimate them—e.g., even though a good doctor may sometimes rely on hunches or guesses, this works only against the backdrop of her reliance on medical knowledge and practice. This last point is important, for we evaluate actions and attitudes themselves as "good" or "warranted" in light of their relation to principles that are used to justify them.

power to enforce one's view. Objectification is not just "in the head"; it is actualized, embodied, imposed upon the objects of one's desire. So if one objectifies something, one not only views it as something which would satisfy one's desire, but one also has the power to make it have the properties one desires it to have. A good objectifier will, when the need arises—that is, when the object lacks the desired properties—exercise his power to make the object have the properties he desires. So if one does a "good" job in objectifying something, then one attributes to it properties which it in fact has. Thinking alone doesn't make it so, but thinking plus power makes it so. "Speaking socially, the beliefs of the powerful become proof [proven?], in part because the world actually arranges itself to affirm what the powerful want to see. If you perceive this as a process, you might call it force."[67] Or, as Monique Wittig puts it: "They are *seen* black, therefore they *are* black; they are *seen* as women, therefore they *are* women. But before being *seen* that way, they first had to be *made* that way."[68]

This suggests that an ideal objectifier is in the epistemic position of (at least) having some true or accurate beliefs about what he has objectified.[69] Such beliefs attribute to the object properties that it has, and these (post hoc) attributions would seem to be as empirical and as publicly accessible as you like.[70] We must note that the possibility of accurate description is not what distinguishes the objectifier's position, or the objective stance, from others: "Because male power has created in reality the world to which feminist insights, when they are accurate, refer, many of our statements will capture that reality, simply exposing it as specifically male for the first time."[71] So we may allow that there is *something* accurate about an (ideal) objectifier's view of things; moreover, one need not be an objectifier in order to acknowledge such claims as accurate or, more generally, to make accurate claims oneself.

As I read MacKinnon's view of objectification, however, there is an aspect of illusion in objectification that we have not yet captured. The illusion on the part

---

[67] MacKinnon, *Feminism Unmodified*, 164.

[68] Wittig, "One Is Not Born a Woman," 48–19.

[69] It is interesting to consider whether being a successful or ideal objectifier places one in a privileged epistemic position with respect to the consequences of one's objectification. Consider an argument that such an objectifier is incorrigible: S is incorrigible with respect to p iff (necessarily) if S believes p, then p is true. Suppose S is a successful objectifier, and S, in objectifying x, views x as F. Because S, by hypothesis, is ideally successful, if x is not F, then he exercises his power to make it the case that x is F; so S's belief that x is F is (or will soon be) true. So it would seem that (necessarily) if S is an ideal objectifier with respect to x, and S believes x is F, then x is F. In short, if S believes that x is F, and x is not (at least eventually) F, then S must not be an ideal objectifier. Admittedly, there are temporal qualifications that disrupt the argument and divert us from the standard notions of incorrigibility, but the suggestion provides food for thought.

[70] See MacKinnon, *Feminist Theory of the State*, 100: "Of course, objective data do document the difficulties and inequalities of woman's situation."

[71] MacKinnon, *Feminism Unmodified*, 59; *Feminist Theory of the State*, 125.

of the objectifier (an illusion often shared by the objects of his objectification) is that these post hoc attributions are true by virtue of the object's *nature* and not by virtue of having been enforced. The important distinction here is between properties that are part of (or follow from) an object's "nature," and those that are mere accidents. This distinction has a long and complex history in Western philosophy, but there are three themes relevant to our purposes here:[72] (1) All objects have a nature or essence; to be an object is (in some significant sense) to have a nature; it is by virtue of their nature that objects are members of kinds or species. This allows that there are also other legitimate classifications of objects in terms of accidental similarity or shared properties, but we should distinguish these classifications from those that group things in accordance with their natures. (2) Natures determine what is normal or appropriate—what is natural—for members of the kind. Natures serve to explain the behavior of the object under normal circumstances. (3) An object's nature is essential to it—that is, the object cannot exist without having those properties which constitute its nature.

Returning to objectification, if one objectifies something, one views it as an object for the satisfaction of one's desire. The suggestion I am pursuing is that in objectifying something one views it as *having a nature* which makes it desirable in the ways one desires it, and which enables it to satisfy that desire.[73] For example, if men desire submission, then in objectifying women men view women as having a nature which makes them (or, under normal circumstances, should make them) submissive, at the same time as they force women into submission. The illusion in successful objectification is not in the reports of its consequences— the women who have been forced to submit do submit; the illusion is in, so to speak, the modality of such claims—women submit *by nature*.[74]

---

[72] An important source for this conception of natures is Aristotle. See, e.g., *Physics* I–II and *Metaphysics* VII–IX. A wonderful commentary on Aristotle's conception of natures is Sarah Waterlow, *Nature, Change, and Agency in Aristotle's Physics* (Oxford: Oxford University Press, 1982).

[73] Although MacKinnon rarely puts the point in this way, I think making explicit the objectifiers commitment to natures helps in understanding her position. For example, she describes pornography (and some of its horrors) in these terms: "Women's bodies trussed and maimed and raped and made into things to be hurt and obtained and accessed, *and this presented as the nature of women*" (my emphasis) (MacKinnon, *Feminism Unmodified*, 147). See also MacKinnon, *Feminist Theory of the State*, 138.

[74] This modality is ambiguously expressed (or obscured) in the verb 'to be.' The verb 'to be' is notoriously ambiguous; there are two uses at issue here. Consider the claim: women are submissive. It could be used to express an empirical generalization: As a matter of fact, all (or most) women are submissive. It could express a fact about women's nature: All individual women are, by their nature, submissive. MacKinnon's arguments highlight problems that arise when this ambiguity is not acknowledged (see, e.g., MacKinnon, *Feminism Unmodified*, 55, 59, 154, 166, 174; and *Feminist Theory of the State*, 99, 122, 125, 204). MacKinnon also suggests a potential ambiguity in the claim: Women are equal to men. Again the modality of the verb 'to be' is an issue: To claim that women *are* equal obscures the fact that women are not actually equal; nevertheless we may allow that women *should be* equal (see, e.g., MacKinnon, *Feminism Unmodified*, 39–40, 59, 171, 178–79; and *Feminist Theory of the State*, 163, 231, 240, 242).

Hence, the point that men view women *as objects* is not simply the point that men view women as something to use for their pleasure, as means and not ends. To view women as objects is to view women as a (substantial) kind; it is to view individual women as having a Woman's Nature. As the objectifier sees it, it is distinctive of this (alleged) kind that those features he finds desirable or arousing in women are a consequence of their nature, and so under normal circumstances women will exhibit these features. As we will consider further below, it follows from this view that women who fail to have those features men find desirable should be considered as deviant or abnormal. And if women are to develop in accordance with their nature, we should provide circumstances in which they will have those features. From the point of view of the objectifier, his view of women captures their individual nature; MacKinnon aims to unmask this illusion: "See: what a woman 'is' is what you have *made* women be."[75]

So what is the epistemic position of one who successfully objectifies something? A successful objectifier attributes to something features that have been forced upon it, and he believes the object has these features "by nature."[76] In the relevant cases, this latter belief concerning the nature of the object—let us call this his "projective belief"—is false. But then what role does that belief play? Answering this takes us to the issue of neutrality.

Neutrality and Aperspectivity

As I've indicated, MacKinnon claims that "neutrality" and "distance" or "nonsituatedness" characterize the stance of objectivity, and that this stance functions as the norm for those who objectify others. This gives us little to go on. Neutrality between what? Distance from what? Drawing on several themes in MacKinnon's work, I will aim in this section to motivate an ideal of objectivity,

---

[75] MacKinnon, *Feminism Unmodified*, 59. It is important to keep distinct the objectifier's view of women from MacKinnon's own account of gender. Consider a particular woman, Rachel. On the objectifier's view, Rachel is a woman by nature; this is her essence which explains why, under normal circumstances, she is feminine. If she is not feminine (submissive, sexually desirable), it is because circumstances are frustrating and inhibiting her true nature. On MacKinnon's view, Rachel is a woman because she is viewed by an objectifier as having a nature that is responsible for those features he finds desirable and is treated accordingly. MacKinnon's move is subtle—it uses the intended or perceived definition of a kind to function in the definition of an accident: Men take women to be submissive by nature; those whom men take to be submissive by nature (and whom they force into submission) constitute the category of women; but no woman is a member of that category by nature.

[76] Of course, the objectifier need not formulate explicitly the commitment to "natures," in particular, to a "Woman's Nature." In the next section I will indicate the epistemic role of an objectifier's projective beliefs; I hope this will be sufficient to illustrate what sort of beliefs might qualify.

consisting of a cluster of epistemic and practical norms, which is appropriate for the role of successful objectifier.[77]

What we are seeking is that set of norms that would effectively and reliably guide a successful objectifier's beliefs and actions, and whose general endorsement would sustain his position of power. We may assume that one in this role is situated in a position of power; success in this role requires maintaining the power to objectify others in an ongoing way.

Consider the objectifier's projective belief that the object of his domination has the properties "by nature" which, in fact, he has enforced. Two questions will guide the discussion: First, what role does this belief play in sustaining the objectifier's position of power? Second, what kind of justification could an ideal objectifier offer for this belief? Clearly these questions are closely connected, for if an ideal objectifier guides his beliefs and actions in accordance with a set of principles that legitimate them, then one would expect that in a social context where the principles are generally endorsed, his behavior would seem appropriate and his social position would be (relatively) safe. This allows that in contexts where the principles are not generally endorsed, a good objectifier might still guide his actions by these principles, but his position of power would be more tenuous insofar as others would challenge the principles guiding his behavior.

In following the thread of MacKinnon's discussion, I will pursue the following suggestion: (1) If the accepted norm for practical decision making is to adapt one's actions to accommodate natures, and (2) if the accepted epistemic norm for determining a thing's nature is to read it off of observed regularities, and (3) if in seeking regularities we are enjoined to deny or ignore our own contribution to the circumstances we observe, then the objectifier's beliefs and actions will appear "legitimate" and the unequal distribution of power that sustains objectification will be preserved.

As mentioned above, the belief that objects have natures plays a significant explanatory role: an object behaves as it does, under normal circumstances, because of its nature. So, regular patterns in the behavior of objects can and should be explained, at least in part, by reference to qualities of the objects themselves. Moreover, it is not possible to change something's nature. An object's nature is essential to it; a change with respect to an object's nature destroys the object. This suggests that in practical decision making we ought to be attentive to things' natures. It won't do to try to fry an egg on a paper plate; there's no point in trying to teach a rock how to read. Because the world is not

---

[77] My reconstruction of MacKinnon's argument draws primarily from the following chapters in *Feminism Unmodified*: "Desire and Power" 46–62; "Not a Moral Issue," 146–62; and "Frances Biddle's Sister," 163–97; and from *Feminist Theory of the State*: "Consciousness Raising," 83–105: "Method and Politics," 106–25; "The Liberal State," 157–70; and "Toward Feminist Jurisprudence," 237–49. Some of the arguments in these chapters originally appeared in MacKinnon, FMMS-II.

infinitely malleable to our wants or needs, reasonable decision making will accommodate "how things are," where this is understood as accommodating the natures of things, the background conditions constraining our action.[78]

But of course it is a difficult matter to figure out what the natures of things are. If natures are responsible for regular behavior under normal circumstances, it is a plausible strategy to begin by inferring or postulating natures on the basis of observed regularities. Given the assumption that practical decision making should accommodate "the nature of things," this epistemic strategy has practical repercussions; it also leaves some important issues unaddressed. First, it will matter whose observations count (for example, only "normal" observers?), how we adjudicate disagreement, and what terms are classed as "observational." Second, if the point is to find natures, the strategy of inferring or postulating natures on the basis of actual observed regularities assumes that ordinary (observed) circumstances are "normal." Allowing for the possibility that current circumstances are not, broadly speaking, normal—that things are not expressing their natures in their regular behavior—accommodating regular behavior may *not* be justified by the need to cope with the real constraints the world presents.

The procedure of drawing on observed regularities to set constraints on practical decision making would appear to be a paradigm of "neutral," "objective," or "reasonable" procedure. And yet the ideal objectifier exploits this combined epistemic and practical norm—and its gaps—to his advantage. I'll offer here only a sketch of how this is done. We are asked to begin by assuming that actual circumstances are "normal." Looking around us, we discover rough generalizations capturing differences between men and women; more women than men satisfy the (contextually specific) norms of femininity and have a feminine gender identity internalizing those norms. Considering those gender categories of men and women constituted by sexual objectification, there are notable differences between men and women in line with the corresponding norms of dominance and submission.

However, if we take such existing gender differences as evidence for the different "natures" of men and women, and so structure social arrangements to accommodate these natures, then we simply reinforce the existing gendered social roles—that is, we sustain those social arrangements in which men dominate and women submit. "Once power constructs social reality . . . the subordination in gender inequality is made invisible; dissent from it becomes inaudible as well as rare. What a woman is, is defined in pornographic terms; this is what pornography does. If [we] look neutrally on the reality of gender so produced, the harm that has been done will not be perceptible as harm. It becomes just the

---

[78] On the idea that reasonable decision making should accommodate "how things are" and that we should "conform normative standards to existing reality," see, e.g., MacKinnon, *Feminism Unmodified*, 34, 164–66, 176, 178; and *Feminist Theory of the State*, 162–64, 218–20, 227, 231–32.

way things are."[79] Once we have cast women as submissive and deferential "by nature," then efforts to change this role appear unmotivated, even pointless. Women who refuse this role are anomalies; they are not "normal" observers, and so their resistance, recalcitrant observations, and even their very efforts to speak may be ignored. Strangely, against this backdrop it is of no help to insist that women are rational agents capable of freely deciding how to act, for then it simply appears that women, by nature, rationally choose their subordinate role.[80] As a result, there is even less motivation for social change.

These reflections suggest that what appeared to be a "neutral" or "objective" ideal—namely, the procedure of drawing on observed regularities to set constraints on practical decision making—is one which will, under conditions of gender hierarchy, reinforce the social arrangements on which such hierarchy depends. But the argument for this conclusion is still incomplete, for one could object by claiming that observed regularities do not support the claim that women are, by nature, submissive. Straightforward empirical research would appear to show that many of the features the objectifier attributes to women "by nature" are a product of contingent social forces.

This is where the objectifier must resort to a norm of "distance," to a claim of aperspectivity. Initially it is plausible to offer this as a meta-norm that dictates what claims you, as an effective objectifier, should make about your results: (1) claim that your observations are not conditioned by your social position (though the claims of the subordinate are); and (2) claim that you have had no impact on the circumstances you are observing—you see what is happening without being part of it. If you can get others who already accept the proposed norms of neutrality to accept these claims about your standpoint, then your position of power is (relatively) safe.

In effect, if you are going to be successful in objectifying others, the best way to do it is to present the results of your objectification as "how things are," not to be evaluated and changed, but to be accepted as part of the circumstances we all must accommodate in steering a course through life. The norm of aperspectivity, at least in this context, functions to mask the power of the objectifier, thereby reinforcing the claim that the observed differences between men and women are a reflection of their natures. By this move the objectifier casts gender differences as asocial and amoral: We aren't responsible for things' natures, so morality has no foothold.[81]

---

[79] MacKinnon, *Feminism Unmodified*, 59. See also ibid., 52–53, 59, 155, 166; and *Feminist Theory of the State*, 94, 99–100, 104, 117–18, 124–25, 128, 163–64, 198, 204, 218–20.

[80] See, e.g., MacKinnon, *Feminism Unmodified*, 172; and *Feminist Theory of the State*, 153–54, 174–75, 209.

[81] Although strictly speaking we aren't responsible for things' natures, within the broadly Aristotelian tradition we are thought to be responsible for seeing that things exemplify their natures as fully as possible. For example, if it is part of a woman's nature that she beat children, then she *ought* to, and we should "facilitate" her doing so. Thanks to Charlotte Witt for this point.

And because we cannot change something's nature, there is nothing to be done about it anyway.

So what epistemic and practical role does the objectifier's projective belief play in the process of objectification; or, in other words, what is the role of those beliefs that attribute to the object her enforced properties "by nature"? In general, such beliefs concerning the nature of things function as a linchpin to convert observation to practical justification; under conditions of gender hierarchy they enable the objectifier to use the observable consequences of his domination to justify his continued domination. But the objectifier's projective claims can function to reinforce his position of power over others only because he works in a context where norms of epistemic and practical neutrality are generally endorsed, and where he has convinced others of his aperspectivity (at least with respect to the object of his domination).

Assumed Objectivity

Should we conclude from this argument that theoretical positions committed to "natures" are politically suspect? Should we conclude that those who accommodate empirical regularities in deciding how to act objectify others? I don't think so; but to see why not we need to make the argument a bit more precise. In stating the norms of neutrality and aperspectivity at issue, it would be desirable to offer more substantive detail than I will here; such detail can make a difference to the arguments. But in the context of this chapter my concern is to state the basic ideas that form the basis for a more precise formulation, not to provide that formulation.

What exactly is the ideal of objectivity at issue, and how is it connected to objectification? Let us take *absolute objectivity* to consist (roughly) of three norms:

- *Epistemic neutrality*: take a "genuine" regularity in the behavior of something to be a consequence of its nature.
- *Practical neutrality*: constrain your decision making (and so your action) to accommodate things' natures.
- *Absolute aperspectivity*: count observed regularities as "genuine" regularities just in case: (1) the observations occur under normal circumstances (for example, by normal observers), (2) the observations are not conditioned by the observer's social position, and (3) the observer has not influenced the behavior of the items under observation.

The point of absolute aperspectivity is to limit application of the norm of epistemic neutrality—only those observations that satisfy the aperspectivity conditions (1) through (3) are a legitimate basis for drawing conclusions about the nature of things. We should note, however, that because the objectifier's projective beliefs are not based on observations satisfying the constraints of absolute aperspectivity, they are not justified by the principles of absolute objectivity. At the very least the objectifier fails to satisfy conditions (2) and (3). But the ideal objectifier gets around this by relying on a supplemental principle of aperspectivity:

• *Assumed aperspectivity*: if a regularity is observed, then assume that (1) the circumstances are normal, (2) the observations are not conditioned by the observers' social position, and (3) the observer has not influenced the behavior of the items under observation.[82]

Assumed aperspectivity entitles us to claim that any regularity we observe is a "genuine" regularity and so reveals the nature of the things under observation. In effect, we may apply the principle of epistemic neutrality to any regularity we find, because assumed aperspectivity bridges the gap between observed regularities and genuine regularities. It is this norm of assumed aperspectivity which enables the objectifier to conclude that his observations (which themselves may be accurate) are a guide to things' natures; in effect, the norm provides a basis for his projective beliefs. Let us call the ideal of objectivity which consists of absolute objectivity supplemented by the norm of assumed aperspectivity the ideal of *assumed objectivity*.

The broad question before us is whether and to what extent this ideal of assumed objectivity is gendered—more specifically, is it either weakly or strongly gendered. Let us ask first: Is this ideal *appropriate* to the role of men—that is, to what extent does it contribute to excellence in men's social role; and second, is the ideal *grounded* in men's social role—that is, is this an ideal whose satisfaction is sufficient for functioning as a man?

As I read MacKinnon's argument, we should conclude that the ideal of assumed objectivity is weakly masculine. It is appropriate to the role of objectifier in two ways: First, an objectifier who satisfies this ideal will reliably form the projective beliefs required for objectification and will act accordingly; moreover, a commitment to the ideal would provide him with principles to guide and

---

[82] Although there is considerable vagueness and obscurity in the principles I have suggested, there is one qualification that deserves special note. In my statement of the principles of absolute aperspectivity and assumed aperspectivity, I have relied on the notion of an "observed regularity." In the philosophical literature a "regularity" is typically taken to be a true universal generalization, and an "observed regularity" to be such a generalization for which we have observational evidence. However, as I am using the term I mean to allow that there are regularities that fall short of being universal generalizations, either because they don't strictly hold of all members of the class or because they only hold for cases that have actually been observed up to a point in time. Those who prefer to reserve the term 'regularity' for the stricter usage might instead think in terms of "observed patterns."

legitimate his objectifying behavior. Second, if the ideal is broadly endorsed, then it is at least likely that the objectifier's position of power, necessary for his continuing objectification, will be preserved. (We may assume that if the ideal is appropriate to the role of objectifier, it is appropriate to the role of sexual objectifier.)

To see these points, remember that we are considering how one who meets the minimal conditions as an objectifier might sustain a practice of successful objectification and so become an "excellent" objectifier. It is perhaps easiest to judge individuals' excellence in this role, as in many others, by whether they conform to principles that consistently recommend and justify their objectifying behavior. Objectifiers who conform to the norms of assumed objectivity will qualify, in this sense, as excellent. A man, for example, who objectifies women will view them and treat them as having a nature which makes them what he desires them to be; but he must also have the power to enforce this view. As discussed above, objectification occurs under conditions of inequality where some individuals have power over others. It is plausible that under such conditions there will be consequences of inequality evident in observable and regular differences between the unequal parties. But then, assuming that men will be witness to these regularities, those men who satisfy the norm of assumed objectivity will have reason to view women and treat women as they appear under the conditions of inequality—that is, as subordinate. The norms tell us to observe the differences and behave accordingly: see, women are subordinate (submissive, deferential, . . .), so treat them as subordinate (submissive, deferential, . . .). By the standards set by assumed objectivity, such objectifying beliefs and actions are justified. Those objectifiers who conform to these standards will reliably and consistently fulfill their role, given the social power to do so.[83]

Moreover, assumed objectivity contributes to sustaining that social power, at least in contexts where its norms are broadly endorsed. It is plausible that insofar as you are in a position to justify your behavior in light of broadly shared epistemic and practical norms, your social position is relatively secure. The relevant regularities that provide the basis for the objectifier's projective beliefs are generally accessible and, we may assume, accurate. So if the ideal of assumed

---

[83] Because here we are concentrating on what is required for being a "successful" or "excellent" objectifier, we must allow that there are objectifiers who meet the minimal conditions for objectification but who aren't guided by and don't satisfy the ideal of assumed objectivity. They do it, but they don't do it "well." Objectifying well requires mastering the "art" of objectifying in a sustained and reliable way. If the argument I've sketched is convincing, one won't be an ideal objectifier unless one's projective beliefs are based on observable regularities. "Poor" objectifiers may be highly imaginative, or they may work under conditions in which there isn't an established social hierarchy, so the relevant differences between dominant and subordinate are missing. But without (publicly accessible) justification, it will be more difficult to sustain a practice of objectification, and one's power will be more easily challenged. In short, good objectification may depend on a developed practice of objectification that has established the regularities needed to be effective.

objectivity is generally endorsed, then the inference to the projective belief and the consequent practical decisions will be broadly recognized as legitimate. Thus a general endorsement of the ideal of assumed objectivity reinforces the objectifier's position of power and contributes to his ongoing success.

The considerations just offered suggest that the ideal of assumed objectivity is weakly masculine, because satisfying the ideal contributes to success in the role of objectifier and, therefore, to success in the role of sexual objectifier. Should we also conclude that the ideal is strongly masculine? Let me begin by asking whether it is grounded more broadly in the role of objectifier: Is satisfying the ideal sufficient for objectifying others? MacKinnon suggests that it is: "to look at the world objectively is to objectify it."[84] Let us recall that an ideal might be grounded in a social role either constitutively (if it is not possible to satisfy the ideal without functioning in that social role) or contextually (if given specified background conditions satisfying the ideal are sufficient for functioning in the role). I think we may grant that satisfying the ideal of assumed objectivity is not constitutively grounded in the role of objectifier; our focus should be on contextual grounding.

In considering the ways in which the ideal of assumed objectivity contributes to the success of an objectifier, we saw that under conditions of gender inequality, one who observes regular differences between men and women and who satisfies the ideal will view women as subordinate, treat women as subordinate, and be justified, by those standards, in doing so. But this is not sufficient, in general, to be an objectifier or, more specifically, to sexually objectify women. I propose that the ideal of assumed objectivity is contextually grounded, not directly in the role of objectifier, but in the role of collaborator in objectification.

To explain, remember that one objectifies something just in case one views it and treats it as an object that has by nature properties which one *desires* in it and, further, one *has the power* to make it have those properties. (Sexual objectification adds to each of these two further conditions: The desire in question is an erotic desire, and the desire is for dominance/submission.) Let us say that one *collaborates in objectifying* something just in case one views it and treats it as an object that has by nature properties which are a consequence of objectification, that is, properties which are a consequence of the forces sustaining social hierarchy. Collaboration differs from objectification insofar as one may collaborate in objectifying something without viewing it in terms of one's projected desire: One may not find the properties attributed to the object desirable—they may be viewed as undesirable, perhaps simply "natural" or "inevitable." Collaboration also differs from objectification insofar as one who collaborates need not have the power to force her view of things upon them. Nevertheless, collaboration is not simply a passive process of allowing others to carry on with their objectification;

---

[84] MacKinnon, *Feminism Unmodified*, 50 (quoted above).

a collaborator shares with both sorts of objectifiers a pattern of thought and action. A woman who views women as weak and inferior by nature, and acts accordingly, collaborates in objectification, though in doing so she need not objectify women.

So if we consider a context of gender inequality—let's say a context where male dominance is widespread—we may assume that there will be generally observable differences between men and women that are a consequence of men's forcing their view of women on women. Individuals in this context who are aware of these differences and who satisfy the norm of assumed objectivity (at least with respect to these observed regularities) will view the differences as "natural" and will act to accommodate gender difference. This, I take it, is sufficient to function in the role of a collaborator in objectification. In short, the ideal of assumed objectivity is contextually grounded in the role of collaborator; the relevant background conditions for this grounding are that the one who satisfies the ideal (a) does so in a context of social hierarchy, (b) is aware of the observable consequences of this hierarchy, and (c) applies the norm to these observations.

I state these background conditions in terms of social hierarchy rather than gender hierarchy, because we may allow that there are other forms of objectification besides sexual objectification (for example, racial objectification); correspondingly, there are other forms of collaboration. The argument just offered suggests that the ideal of assumed objectivity is sufficient for functioning in a specific collaborative role relative to the social context and one's application of the norms. For example, in a context where both racial and sexual domination are in place, one who observes both racial and sexual differences, and who satisfies the norms of assumed objectivity with respect to both, will collaborate in both racial and sexual objectification; if one satisfies the norms only selectively, one may, for example, collaborate in racial but not sexual objectification or in sexual but not racial objectification.

We should not conclude, however, that any and every case in which one satisfies the ideal of assumed objectivity, even under conditions of social hierarchy, is sufficient for functioning as a collaborator. This is to say that all three of the above stated background conditions (a)–(c), not just the first, must be met before drawing the connection between assumed objectivity and collaboration. This is because there are contexts, even under conditions of soscial hierarchy, in which one observes regularity in something's behavior, assumes that it is a consequence of its nature, and acts to accommodate this nature, without thereby collaborating in objectification.

For example, I observe that watering begonias with ammonia kills them; I assume that this is a consequence of their nature, and I adjust my actions so that I water begonias with ammonia only if I want to kill them. I don't try to change the fact that begonias die when watered with ammonia. In this case, the relevant property of begonias is not a consequence of objectification; that they have this property is not due to social coercion. I satisfy the ideal of assumed objectivity with respect to my observations of begonias, but I don't collaborate in objectifying them. It is central to objectification that social facts are treated as natural facts and so are cast as immutable; assumed objectivity legitimates this error. But where the observable regularities used as a basis for drawing conclusions about natures are not the result of social coercion or force, there is no objectification and so no collaboration in objectification.

Similarly, if I observe that people regularly die when deprived of food and shelter for an extended period, and I take this to be a result of their nature, and also accommodate this fact in deciding how to act, I don't collaborate in objectification. Again, that there are conditions under which we cannot survive is not a consequence of objectification. The important point to note here is that one objectifies someone (or something) only if the properties one takes to be part of her nature are properties she has as a consequence of social forces. The fact that a human organism will stop functioning under conditions of physical deprivation is not plausibly a result of social forces. Again, the element of illusion—the masking of social/moral facts as natural facts—is missing; this illusion is a crucial element of both objectification and collaboration.

Objectivity and Sexual Objectification

The argument I have just offered for the conclusion that assumed objectivity is contextually grounded in the role of collaborator, falls considerably short of the thesis that satisfying this ideal of objectivity is sufficient for being a sexual objectifier. It falls short in two important ways. First, I have argued that in a limited variety of cases, satisfying the norm of assumed objectivity is sufficient for functioning as a collaborator, not as an objectifier. Second, I have left sexuality virtually out of the picture. To be fair, I should acknowledge that MacKinnon does sketch an argument for the claim that in being objective one functions as a sexual objectifier.

Let us grant that we are considering whether assumed objectivity is contextually grounded in the role of men under conditions of male dominance. Further, let us say that one takes up an *objectivist stance* toward something, just in case on the basis of assumed objectivity, one views it as an object having certain properties "by nature," and takes this as a constraint in deciding how to act. The hypothesis under consideration is that if you are an objectivist in this sense, then your relationship to the object is one of sexual objectification. What must be shown is that if one takes up such an objectivist stance toward something, then (1) one views it and treats it as having by nature properties one desires, (2) one has the power to force it to have these properties (and sometimes exercises this power), and (3) one desires subordination and finds force erotic.

MacKinnon's argument for this claim relies on three controversial premises (my numbering indicates a link with each of the required points above):

1+. In general, to view something as an object is to view it as having, by nature, certain properties that one finds useful or desirable: "The object world is constructed according to how it looks with respect to its possible uses."[85]

2+. One's stance toward an object is objective only if one has made (or makes) it have the properties one attributes to it: "What is objectively known corresponds to the world and can be verified by being pointed to (as science does) because the world itself is controlled from the same point of view."[86]

3+. All domination or control is eroticized: "The act of control . . . is itself eroticized under male supremacy."[87]

So the picture is this: In taking up the objectivist stance toward something, you project your needs/desires onto it (taking the desired properties to be part of its nature, even if it doesn't currently exhibit them); you make it have the properties you project; and you find this control erotic. One thereby sexually objectifies the "object" of this stance. If the social role of men is the role of sexual objectifier, then taking up the objectivist stance is sufficient for being a man.

Although I have only indicated the barest outline of MacKinnon's argument, I will not undertake to explicate it further here. I offered some examples in the previous section which suggest that at least premises (1+) and (2+) are seriously overstated. Even more effective counterexamples to these claims could be easily constructed. Further, if we accept MacKinnon's premises, then we lose the distinction between objectification and collaboration; as sketched above, a collaborator is an objectivist who conforms her beliefs and actions to the objectifier's projected reality. But she need not find this reality desirable and she need not have the social power to enforce it. If MacKinnon's premises are accurate, this is not an available position: On her view an objectivist not only desires objects to have the properties she takes to be part of their nature, but is in a position to make them conform to her view. Yet it is mysterious, for example, why taking up an objectivist stance should be thought sufficient for having such power.

More important, however, I think the basic strategy of MacKinnon's argument—a strategy all too common among feminist theorists—is deeply flawed. The strategy is to take a powerful analysis of how the social world has been shaped

---

[85] Ibid., 173; see also 307(nl7).

[86] MacKinnon, *Feminist Theory of the State*, 122.

[87] MacKinnon, *Feminism Unmodified*, 50 (also quoted above). See also her *Feminist Theory of the State*, 137–38, 147.

by male power and desire, and to extend this analysis to the world as a whole. For example, take a powerful account of pornography as a mechanism by which the social category of women is constructed, and suggest that there are analogous accounts for all categories. But such generalization, rather than strengthening MacKinnon's position, weakens it.

MacKinnon's analysis of gender and sexual objectification is important and effective because it vividly captures the very real power that men have over women, power backed by violence and hatred and law. In spite of the horror of it, it is empowering to recognize that the threat of male violence has significantly formed the social world as women know it and live it. What has been done can maybe be undone. If we claim, however, that the power that has determined gender categories is the *same power* that has determined all categories, then we deflate the social analysis of this power with the simple thought that much of what the world is like is not within the control of people, societies, cultures, languages, and so on. In short, in the effort to generalize our insights we lose the contrast between what we do have significant control over and what we don't. Fortunately we are not omnipotent; we don't have the power "to force the world to be anyway [our] minds can invent."[88] Men don't have this power; neither do women; neither do "cultures," and so on. The fantasy of such power may be useful in casting our current categories as open to critique, but believing in the fantasy, I submit, is as dangerous as supposing that our current categories capture Nature's "givens."

The analysis of gender categories as socially constructed succeeds as a critique of traditional ideas about men and women in part because it targets the specific mechanisms of social control that are responsible for the observable differences between men and women. It is the contrast between these mechanisms of control and naturalistic or deterministic causal mechanisms—for example, mechanisms that are responsible for the observable differences between, say, water and ammonia—that lends support to the hope that social change is possible. There may be a complex social analysis of why we are interested in the difference between ammonia and water and why we are keen to distinguish them, but it is implausible to suggest that specific mechanisms of social control are responsible for their difference. If we insist that the mechanisms responsible for any apparent natural differences are the same mechanisms that are at work in constructing gender difference, we lose our focus on what social power consists in.

If we suppose, for example, that the explanation of gender difference should apply in explaining all differences, then it is plausible to seek a common denominator in the variety of explanations offered. But seeking such a common explanatory strategy distracts the effort for social change; there are two temptations that lead us astray. On the one hand, if we note the significance of causal explanation in understanding regular patterns in things' behavior, it is

---

[88] MacKinnon, *Feminist Theory of the State*, 122.

tempting to resort to a social or psychological determinism in explaining gender; thus it becomes obscure, once again, how the power that constructs gender is both optional and, more important, subject to moral appraisal. On the other hand, it is tempting to relocate the source of gender oppression in a "pattern of thought" common to all efforts at differentiation—for example, a pattern that attributes natures to things. This shifts our attention from a concern with the concrete mechanisms of social control and relocates the problem "in our heads"—as if domination and abuse would end if we just stopped the bad habit of thinking that things have natures (or if we stopped distinguishing things or postulating unified categories). Worse still, taking our thoughts to be the problem can lead to an intellectual nihilism that deprives us of the resources for constructing viable alternatives to existing social arrangements.

Analyses of categories that purport to be natural in terms of hierarchical social relations (for example, analyses of gender, race, sex) have highlighted the political import of the distinction between the social and the natural; and plausibly such analyses should prompt us to reevaluate all our judgments about what is natural and what is social. But even if systematic doubt and extra caution are warranted *for every case*, this does not support a wholesale denial of the distinction between natural categories and social categories. Nor does it give us grounds for thinking that a commitment to things having "natures" is antifeminist; in particular, recognizing that I am not by nature a woman leaves untouched the broader question of whether I have a nature and, strange as it may sound, whether my nature is natural or not.[89] Generalizing the strategy behind a social analysis of gender across the board may seem a promising way to combat a dogmatic insistence on the immutability of life as we know it. But concrete analyses of socially constructed categories do not warrant sweeping conclusions about "all language" and "all categories," and the hasty generalization of our analyses both theoretically and politically weakens the force of our position.

6. Conclusion

Thus far I have argued that there is a complex epistemic and practical norm—what I have called the ideal of "assumed objectivity," which is appropriate to the role of objectifier: realizing this ideal enables objectifiers to be better objectifiers,

---

[89] It is important to note that one may be committed to natures without being a "naturalist." Although the term 'naturalist' covers many different views, typically naturalists are committed to thinking that natural science has a privileged status in finding natures; moreover, naturalists privilege physical properties over others. But the idea of a "natural" property is ambiguous between a physical property that natural science studies and a property that is part of, or follows from, something's nature. Plausibly, Catholicism is committed to natures, but it is not committed to naturalism.

and its endorsement perpetuates objectification. If there is a social category of men defined by the relation of sexual objectification, then (assuming that someone can be a good sexual objectifier only if they are a good objectifier) the ideal is appropriate to at least one significant gender role for men. From this we should conclude that the ideal of assumed objectivity is weakly masculine.

I have also argued that the ideal of assumed objectivity is contextually grounded in the role of collaborator in objectification. Under conditions of social hierarchy, those who observe the consequences of inequality and apply the norms in assumed objectivity to their observations will function socially as collaborators. I also argued, however, that one can satisfy the ideal of assumed objectivity under these specific background conditions and not function as an objectifier or as a sexual objectifier. Thus we should conclude that the ideal, at least with respect to these conditions, is not grounded in men's social role and so is not strongly masculine. Of course, this leaves open the question whether there are other gender roles, and other background conditions, with respect to which the ideal is strongly masculine.

What should we make of these conclusions? To what extent do they offer reason to reject the ideal of assumed objectivity? We should begin by noting that the ideal of assumed objectivity is a cluster of principles; it consists of assumed aperspectivity, along with the principles in absolute objectivity (epistemic neutrality, practical neutrality, and absolute aperspectivity). The arguments I have considered, even if they pose a challenge to the value of the ideal as a whole, do not offer grounds for rejecting *all* of the constituent principles in the ideal; nor do they offer grounds for deciding which constituent principle, or principles, to reject. What problems the ideal may cause are a consequence of the principles being employed in conjunction.[90] This is important, for it shows that one cannot plausibly use the argument I have outlined against those who endorse something less than the full conjunction of principles. The argument is ineffective, for example, against those who accept that things have natures which we must accommodate in our decision making, but who deny that we can read off natures from just any apparent regularity; it is also ineffective against those who make quick inferences to natures but who think there's no general imperative to accommodate or respect them.

In introducing the charge that rationality is gendered, I suggested that its being so would constitute a challenge to the Western philosophical tradition's emphasis on ideals of reason and rational selves. Given the arguments just offered, have we a basis for claiming that the traditional commitments of epistemology and metaphysics are male biased or that they sustain male domination? Certainly we cannot answer this question without a detailed examination of the

---

[90] Admittedly, one might argue that each of the principles are weakly masculine because in contexts where the other principles are realized, they contribute to success in the role of men. This illustrates both the difficulty and the importance of having clear criteria for what can count as "background conditions." See note 35 above.

philosophical positions that have been offered. I would suggest, however, that it is difficult to situate the charge that assumed objectivity is gendered as a critique of traditional epistemology and metaphysics.

Undoubtedly philosophers have relied on the ideal of assumed objectivity in constructing accounts of human nature and in offering moral, political, and epistemological theories; moreover, they have relied on it in ways that are politically problematic. But we must also acknowledge that the norm of assumed objectivity does not capture a broad range of philosophical ideals of rationality; and it does not do justice to the sensitivity philosophers have shown concerning the problem of postulating natures. Those working within a (broadly) empiricist tradition are happy to rely on observed regularities in forming their theories, but they are notoriously opposed to attributing natures to things; those working within (broadly) Aristotelian and rationalist traditions are happy to attribute natures to things, but they do not do so on the basis of observed regularities alone. Thus it would seem that important figures in the traditional philosophical canon not only explicitly reject the ideal of assumed objectivity, but also offer resources for demonstrating its weaknesses and for constructing alternatives.

However, even if the conclusion that assumed objectivity is gendered does not provide a direct indictment of those pursuing traditional projects in epistemology and metaphysics, neither can we rest content, thinking that these projects have been vindicated. For example, we should ask: In what cases does the explicit rejection of assumed objectivity belie a deeper reliance upon it? What are the alternatives to assumed objectivity? Are there other conceptions of objectivity—conceptions offering weakly or strongly gendered ideals—playing a role in philosophical theorizing? And are there additional ways that norms and ideals can be gendered beyond those we have discussed?

Having noted some limitations of the arguments considered, we still face the more difficult question of how these arguments bear on our evaluation of assumed objectivity. Given that the ideal of assumed objectivity is weakly masculine and contextually grounded in the role of collaborator in objectification, should we reject the ideal? Let us return to the examples (discussed above) of the kind masters, and the journalists whose excellence renders them criminals. In these cases, it seemed plausible that we should continue to value kindness and the virtues of journalists, but work to change the circumstances that made for their offensive consequences. Is assumed objectivity an ideal like these? Should we broadly endorse, even abide by, its norms, but work to undermine the social hierarchy that makes for its offensive consequences?

I submit that we should reject the ideal of assumed objectivity—at least in the unqualified form we've considered it—for the suggestion that we might endorse it while working to undermine the existing social hierarchy leaves us in an unmanageable position. There are two issues to address: First, should we accept the ideal of assumed objectivity as binding on us—should we accept its norms to guide our attitudes and actions? Second, should we support and value the activities of others who live by those norms, even if we don't? In answering these questions, it matters who is included in the "us," who counts as "we." The "we" I am speaking of, and to, is culturally and historically situated. We live under conditions of social hierarchy, a hierarchy in which one has power by virtue of being, for example, male, white, straight. More important, I am assuming that we are committed to changing this.

If we accept the norms of assumed objectivity as binding on us, then our efforts at social change would be, by its lights, not only unmotivated but unjustified. Because we live under circumstances of social hierarchy and are aware of the consequences of this hierarchy, the ideal of assumed objectivity would instruct us to collaborate in the existing patterns of objectification: we should view and treat the subordinate as subordinate. In short, our circumstances satisfy the background conditions under which assumed objectivity renders one a collaborator. But in committing ourselves to social change we reject these attitudes and these actions, viewing them as wrong and unjustified. Such a conflict is unmanageable. Faced with such a conflict, assumed objectivity is clearly the commitment to revise. Moreover, if we allow that others, also situated under conditions of social hierarchy, legitimately guide their attitudes and actions by the ideal of assumed objectivity, then this legitimacy will extend to their collaborative activities. But then it becomes obscure on what basis we demand that they change.

In these respects the ideal of assumed objectivity is unlike kindness and unlike journalistic excellence; in those cases there is no conflict between valuing the ideals and being committed to social change. Admittedly, there are actual cases in which satisfying the ideal of assumed objectivity is not offensive, even when its constituent norms are employed in conjunction. And there are times and places in which the background conditions are not those of social hierarchy, so satisfying the ideal will not render one a collaborator. But unfortunately, we are not in such a time or place, and endorsing unrestricted application of the ideal will only keep us from getting there.

Acknowledgments

I would like to thank Elizabeth Anderson, Louise Antony, Susan Brison, Susan Donaldson, Cynthia Freeland, Beth Hackett, Elisabeth Lloyd, Will Kymlicka, Maria Morales, Laura Murphy, Jay Wallace, Alison Wylie, and Stephen Yablo for their encouragement, comments, and helpful discussion on the topics of this essay; for this, as well as valuable editorial assistance, special thanks to Charlotte Witt. Thanks also to Wayne Sumner and the Philosophy Department at the University of Toronto for their generosity in making available to me the resources of the university while I was on leave from the University of Pennsylvania.

2

Ontology and Social Construction[1]

1. Introduction

One of the most important projects of feminist theory has been to question traditional assumptions about what is "natural"; in particular, theorists have worked to disclose the variety of cultural mechanisms by which we "become" the gendered, raced, and sexual beings that we are. In a context where what is "natural" has been assumed to be fixed by nature, and so inevitable, appropriate, or even good, demonstrating the deep contingency of such categories of identity and their associated patterns of behavior has significant political force. Moreover, this research questioning our assumptions about what is natural shows that in a significant range of cases—at least in the case of race, gender, and sexuality—our efforts to classify things as "natural" or "objective" have failed, and this has prompted a general critique of the methods we have used to justify our classifications, as well as the political institutions built to accommodate them.

There is a broad consensus in this research that the reason why the previous models of justice, knowledge, and reality have gone so wrong is that they ignore the force of *social construction*; and yet there is striking diversity in how the term 'social construction' (and its cognates) is used and, consequently, in what revisions to the old models are proposed. In addition to the claims that race, gender, and sexuality are socially constructed, it is also claimed, for example, that "the subject," "identity," "knowledge," "truth," "nature," and "reality" are each socially

[1] Many thanks to Elizabeth Anderson, Louise Antony, Stephen Danvall, Ann Gamy, Beth Hackett, Lloyd Humberstone, Joe Levine, Rae Langton, Naomi Scheman, Elliott Sober, Candace Vogler, and Stephen Yablo for helpful discussions and/or comments on earlier drafts of this paper. This chapter is an extended version of my "Objective Reality, Male Reality, and Social Construction," in Ann Gamy and Marilyn Pearsall, eds., *Women, Knowledge, and Reality*, 2d ed. (New York: Routledge, 1996). Earlier versions were presented at the conference "New Directions in Epistemology," at Monash University, August 1993, and at the Central Division Meeting of the American Philosophical Association, Chicago, Ill., April 1995. At the latter, Candace Vogler was the commentator.

constructed.[2] On occasion it is possible to find the claim that "everything" is socially constructed or that it is socially constructed "all the way down."[3] But once we come to the claim that *everything* is socially constructed, it appears a short step to the conclusion that there is no reality independent of our practices or of our language and that "truth" and "reality" are only fictions employed by the dominant to mask their power.[4]

Dramatic claims rejecting the legitimacy of such notions as "truth" and "reality" do appear in the work of feminist theorists, yet one also finds there a deep resistance to slipping into any form of idealism or relativism.[5] For example, to quote Catharine MacKinnon's typically vivid words:

> Epistemologically speaking, women know the male world is out there because it hits them in the face. No matter how they think about it, try to think it out of existence or into a different shape, it remains independently real, keeps forcing them into certain molds. No matter what they think or do, they cannot get out of it. It has all the indeterminacy of a bridge abutment hit at sixty miles per hour.[6]

Bridge abutments and fists in the face are "independently real" at least in the sense that no individual or community of individuals can simply think them out

---

[2] For a diverse selection of texts that take up these claims, see, e.g., Peter Berger and Thornas Luckmann, *The Social Construction of Reality* (New York: Doubleday, 1966): Teresa de Lauretis, "Feminist Studies/Critical Studies: Issues, Terms, and Contexts," in Teresa de Lauretis, ed., *Feminist Studies/ Critical Studies* (Bloomington: Indiana University Press, 1986), 1–19; Evelyn Fox Keller, "Making Gender Visible in the Pursuit of Nature's Secrets.' in *Feminist Studies/Critical Studies*, 67; bell hooks, *Talking Back* (Boston: South End Press. 1989); Judith Butler, *Gender Trouble* (New York: Routledge, 1990). esp. ch. 1.; Naomi Scheman, "From Hamlet to Maggie Verver: The History and Politics of the Knowing Subject," in her *Engenderings: Constructions of Knowledge, Authority and Privilege* (New York: Routledge. 1993), 106–25; Chris Weedon, *Feminist Practice and Poststructuralist theory* (Oxford: Basil Blackwell. 1987).

[3] See, e.g., Nancy Fraser on Foucault in her *Unruly Practices* (Minneapolis: University of Minnesota Press, 1989), 3, 59–60.

[4] This seems to be the conclusion drawn by radical social constructionists. See, for example, Bruno Latour and Steve Woolgar, *Laboratory Life: The Social Construction of Scientific Facts* (London: Sage, 1979).

[5] Even Jane Flax, who embraces the postmodern critique of "the seductive tyranny of metaphysics, truth, the real," claims later in the same essay that she is unwilling to "deny the existence of subjectivity or an 'outer' reality constituted in part by nontextual relations of domination" (Jane Flax, *Thinking Fragments* [Berkeley: University of California Press, 1990], 189, 219). Donna Haraway is another who is clear that we must find a way to embrace the social construction of knowledge together with "a no-nonsense commitment to faithful accounts of a 'real' world"; see Donna Haraway, "Situated Knowledge: The Science Question in Feminism and the Privilege of Partial Perspective." in her *Simians, Cyborgs, and Women* (New York: Routledge, 1991), esp. 187.

[6] Catharine MacKinnon, *Toward a Feminist Theory the State* (Cambridge, Mass.: Harvard University Press, 1989). 123. See also her *Feminist Unmodified* (Cambridge, Mass.: Harvard University Press, 1987), 57.

of existence; fortunately, less-threatening parts of the physical world are similarly real—a change in my thinking, by *itself*, cannot make my body, my friends, or my neighborhood go out of existence, nor thankfully can a change in anyone else's. To bring about a change in the world, you have to do more than just think about it. However, if we want to maintain a notion of independent reality, we should consider to what extent the research on social construction challenges the idea. If a strong case can be made for the claim that *reality* is socially constructed and, further, that what's socially constructed is *not* independently real, then we may have to consider a more radically revisionary view about the world.

My project in this paper is to explore the claim that *reality* is socially constructed; more broadly, I hope to show how debates over such philosophical notions as "truth," "knowledge," and "reality" can be relevant to feminist and antiracist politics. In the following section I will consider what it means to say that something is socially constructed and will distinguish several senses of the term (allowing that there are also many others); I've chosen to set out this rather complex set of distinctions because their differences become significant in the arguments that follow. I'll then turn to consider how far the claim that reality is socially constructed commits us to denying that the world is, at least in part, independent of us. I will examine a strategy of argument claiming that because *knowledge* is socially constructed, there is no objective (and so no independent) reality. I argue, however, that even if this strategy provides good reason for rejecting one conception of "objective reality," this does not force us into either skepticism or idealism, for there are other ways of conceiving what it means to be real and other ways of conceiving an "independent" reality. My intention here is not to offer an argument *for* realism, or *for* an independent reality; rather, it is (more modestly) to understand and evaluate some of the arguments that may seem to challenge such commitments.

2. Social Construction

As mentioned above, the notion of "social construction" is applied to a wide variety of items and seemingly with rather different senses.[7] At least initially it is useful to think of social constructions on the model of artifacts.[8] In addition to straightforward artifacts like washing machines and power drills, there is a clear sense in

[7] A good place to begin in considering recent uses of the phrase 'social construction' is Berger and Luckmann, op. cit.; for a recent survey of uses of the term, especially in the sociology of knowledge, see Sergio Sismondo, "Some Social Constructions," *Social Studies Science* 23 (1993): 515–53.

[8] Whether, ultimately, social construction should be understood in terms of artifacts is controversial; in particular, the suggestions that artifacts require agents to produce them and that artifacts invite a matter-form analysis have been targeted as problematic. See, e.g., Judith Butler, *Bodies That Matter* (New York: Routledge, 1993), ch. 1.

which, for example, the Supreme Court of the United States and chess games are artifacts, as are languages, literature, and scientific inquiry. Because each of these depends for its existence on a complex social context, each is in the broad sense in question a social construction. So, let's say:

> *Generic social construction*: Something is a social construction in the generic sense just in case it is an intended or unintended product of a social practice.

Although it is fair to say that, generally speaking, social constructions are artifacts, this leaves much open, since there are many different kinds of artifacts and ways of being an artifact. In perhaps the paradigm case of artifacts, human beings play a causal role in bringing an object into existence in accordance with a design plan or to fulfill a specific function. However, the idea of artifact, and with it the idea of social construction, extends well beyond this paradigm case: Human intention or design is not always required (natural languages and cities are certainly artifacts, but they are not the work of an intentional agent or artisan); in other cases the issue does not concern origins but whether the conditions for being the kind of object in question make reference to social practices. For example, categories of individuals such as professors or wives and other *social* kinds count as social constructions because the conditions for being a member of the kind or category include *social* (properties and) relations: The category of wives counts because you can't be a wife unless you are part of a social network that provides for an institution of marriage.

These examples suggest a distinction between *causal* and *constitutive* senses of construction that is important, for it makes a big difference to how we should evaluate the claim that something is socially constructed. For example, in some contexts, to say that "gender" is socially constructed is to make a claim about the causes of gender-coded traits in individuals; that is, it is to claim that insofar as women are feminine and men are masculine, this is due (at least in part) to social causes and is not biologically determined.[9] Presumably, in order to evaluate this claim, we would have reason to consider data from the social sciences, including psychology, sociology, anthropology, and history.

However, in other contexts the claim that "gender" is socially constructed is not a causal claim; rather, the point is constitutive: Gender should be understood as a social category whose definition makes reference to a broad network of

---

[9] In the context of psychology, the claim is often more specific, viz., that our own self-attributed gender, or gendered sense of self, is a result of social forces and is not biologically determined. In the feminist literature, one finds the term 'gender identity' being used in different ways, e.g., sometimes for the psychological phenomenon of self-ascribed gender, sometimes for one's gendered characteristics more broadly, and sometimes for the social category one has been ascribed to.

social relations, and it is not simply a matter of anatomical differences.[10] In this case, gender is introduced as an analytical tool to explain a range of social phenomena, and we evaluate the claim by considering the theoretical usefulness of such a category.[11] There is room for much debate here, not only over the question whether we should employ such a category, but if we do, how we should define it, that is, what social relations (or clusters of social relations) constitute the groups *men* and *women*. (The debates here parallel others in social theory: One might debate whether the category "middle class" is useful to explain a range of social phenomena and, if so, how we should define it.)

To help keep distinct these different ways in which the social can function in construction, let's distinguish:

> *Causal construction*: Something is causally constructed iff social factors play a causal role in bringing it into existence or, to some substantial extent, in its being the way it is.

> *Constitutive construction*: Something is constitutively constructed iff in defining it we must make reference to social factors.[12]

We need to consider causal construction further, for things get quite complicated when we consider how social factors can have an effect on the world (we'll also return to constitutive construction below). At least in the case of human beings, the mere fact of how we are (even potentially) described or classified can have a direct impact on our self-understandings and our actions, because typically these descriptions and classifications bring with them normative expectations

[10] A significant amount of feminist work over the past two decades has been concerned with gender as a social category. For important examples, see Joan Scott, "Gender: A Useful Category of Historical Analysis," *American Historical Review* 91 (1986): 1053–75; Donna Haraway, "'Gender' for a Marxist Dictionary," in her *Simians, Cyborgs, and Women*. See also, Sally Haslanger, "On Being Objective and Being Objectified," chapter 1 of this volume, esp. secs. 2 and 4; and Linda Alcoff, "Cultural Feminism versus Post-Structuralism," *Signs* 13 (1988): 405–36. esp. 433–36.

[11] A "social constructivist" approach to a given domain is typically set in opposition to an "essentialist" approach. Because there are different senses in which things are socially constructed, it is not surprising that the term 'essentialism' also has a variety of uses. For example, those who are concerned to assert social construction as a causal thesis about the social origins of certain traits or capacities tend to interpret the opposing essentialism as a commitment to biological determinism; however, in contexts where constructionists are postulating a social category, essentialism is usually taken to be the view that all members of the category share some (intrinsic?) feature(s). Both of these "essentialisms" are different from the kind of modal (or Aristotelian) essentialism discussed in contemporary analytic metaphysics.

[12] I intend this definition of constitutive construction to be applicable to objects, kinds of objects. properties, or concepts. Some may find it puzzling that I speak of defining objects and features of objects, since contemporary philosophers have often insisted that terms or concepts are the (only) proper subjects of definition. I take it, however, that the seeming unanimity on this point is breaking down, and I want to allow broad flexibility in the notion of constitutive construction. See Kit Fine, "Essence and Modality," *Philosophical Perspectives* 8 (1994): 1–16.

and evaluations. This works in several ways. Forms of description or classification provide for kinds of intention; for example, given the classification "cool," I can set out to become cool, or avoid being cool, and so on. But also, such classifications can function in justifying behavior—for example, "we didn't invite him, because he's not cool"—and such justifications, in turn, can reinforce the distinction between those who are cool and those who are uncool.[13]

The main point to note here is that our classificatory schemes, at least in social contexts, may do more than just map preexisting groups of individuals; rather our attributions have the power to both establish and reinforce groupings which may eventually come to "fit" the classifications. In such cases, classificatory schemes function more like a script than a map. This gives us a narrower conception of social construction falling under the more general rubric of causal construction. On this conception something is socially constructed if what or how it is depends on a kind of feedback loop involving activities such as naming or classifying.[14] Sometimes this form of construction is called "linguistic" or "discursive" construction,[15] so I'll keep with this terminology:

> *Discursive construction*: Something is discursively constructed just in case it is the way it is, to some substantial extent, because of what is attributed (and/or self-attributed) to it.

I'd say that there is no doubt that in this sense you and I are socially constructed: We are the individuals we are today at least partly as a result of what has been attributed (and self-attributed) to us. In other words, there is a sense in which adult human beings are a special kind of artifact.[16]

---

[13] No doubt with time the term 'cool' will come to seem awkward and dated as an honorific; such changes in the terminology used to establish social groups are inevitable. If the reader finds "being cool" no longer socially desirable, substitute in the examples whatever term currently functions in its place.

[14] Ian Hacking explicitly mentions such a "feedback loop" in "The Sociology of Knowledge about Child Abuse," *Nous* 22 (1988): 55. See also Ian Hacking, "The Making and Molding of Child Abuse," *Critical Inquiry* 17 (1990/91): 253–88.

[15] Note that a discourse, and so discursive construction, will involve more than spoken language. See Nancy Fraser, "The Uses and Abuses of French Discourse Theories for Feminist Politics," in Nancy Fraser and Sandra L. Bartky, eds., *Revaluing French Feminism* (Bloomington: Indiana University Press, 1992). 177–94. For a clear explanation of one feminist appropriation of Foucault's notion of "discourse," see, also, Joan Scott, "Deconstructing Equality-verses-Difference: or, The Uses of Poststructuralist Theory for Feminism," *Feminist Studies* 14 (1988): 33–50.

[16] The claim that adult human beings are artifacts allows that we are constructed from "natural" materials—e.g., flesh and blood—though this would seem to presuppose a clear distinction between the natural and the social. For helpful discussions questioning feminist uses of this distinction, see Marilyn Frye, *The Politics of Reality* (Freedom, Calif.: The Crossing Press, 1983). 34–37; Moira Gatens, "A Critique of the Sex-Gender Distinction," in J. Allen and P. Patton, eds., *Beyond Marxism? Interventions after Marx* (Sydney: Interventions Publications, 1983); and Judith Butler, *Bodies That Matter*, esp. ch. 1.

Things get even more complicated, though, because there's still another wrinkle to consider. The idea of discursive construction depends on there being descriptions, distinctions, and classifications at hand whose attribution to things makes a difference—I am the way I am today because people have had the linguistic and conceptual resources to describe me as, for example, "smart" or "stupid," "attractive" or "ugly." There is yet another sense of social construction in which it makes sense to say that *these classificatory schemes themselves*—our distinctions such as smart or stupid, attractive or ugly, rather than the things that respond to them—are socially constructed. Very roughly, to say that such a scheme is socially constructed is to say that its use is determined, not by the "intrinsic" or "objective" features of the objects to which it is applied, but by social factors.[17]

This characterization is purposely vague; so to help us explore some of the issues involved in it let's go back to the example of "being cool": In considering our use of the distinction between those who are cool and those who are uncool, it is plausible to conclude that the distinction is not capturing intrinsic differences between people; rather it is a distinction marking certain social relations—that is, it distinguishes status in the in-group—and the fact that it is employed in any given context is a reflection of the importance of in-group and out-group relations. For example, suppose I need a way to establish a cohort; I do so by calling those I like "cool" and those I don't "uncool." The distinction does not capture a difference in the individuals so-called except insofar as they are related to me (based on my likes and dislikes), and its use in the context is determined not by the intrinsic or objective coolness of the individuals but by the social task of establishing a cohort.[18]

---

[17] Note that I do not mean to equate "intrinsic" with "objective" features. Intrinsic features are, roughly, those that an object has "by virtue of itself alone": i.e., they are nonrelational properties. In this context we can take objective features to be (very roughly) those that an object has independently of its representation by an inquiring subject. At the very least. not all objective features are intrinsic; e.g., *orbiting the sun* is an extrinsic or relational property of the earth that is plausibly objective. The earth orbits the sun or doesn't, independently of what we think about it. Note that, in the examples below, I assume that in attributing "coolness" to someone we are suggesting that they have an *intrinsic* quality of coolness. I'm now not convinced that this is right, because the attribution of coolness seems to allow that there are some relational features relevant to someone's being cool, e.g., owning an electric guitar; instead it may be that what's at issue is the "objectivity" of coolness— we suggest that coolness has nothing to do with our representations, when in fact it does. For ease of presentation, I've focused on intrinsicness in the examples, though a more complete discussion would have to show greater sensitivity to the particular nuances of "cool."

[18] Though if I am successful and there is solidarity in the cohort, we may come to act alike, dress alike, value similar things, etc., and this can provide substantive content to the notion of "coolness": eventually there may be a genuine (intrinsic) difference between the cool and uncool. For an up-to-date sample of who's and what's *really* cool, you can contact the "Who's Cool in America Project" though the World Wide Web at: http://www.attisv.com/-getconl/index.shtml. You can even submit an application stating why you think you are cool, and a "CoolBoard" determines whether you are.

Noting the influence of social forces upon the distinctions we draw, let us define this third form of social construction, as follows:

> *Pragmatic construction*: A classificatory apparatus (be it a full-blown classification scheme or just a conceptual distinction or descriptive term) is socially constructed just in case its use is determined, at least in part, by social factors.

Construed in its weakest form, the point in claiming that a given distinction is pragmatically constructed is simply to say that our use of that distinction is as much due to contingent historical and cultural influences as to anything else; we inherit vocabularies and classificatory projects and decide between alternatives based on utility, simplicity, and such. This point is easy to grant; it would be hard to deny that the discursive resources we employ are socially conditioned in these ways and more. In a stronger form, however, the point is that social factors *alone* determine our use of the distinction in question; in short it is to emphasize that there's no "fact of the matter" that the distinction captures. So let's distinguish two kinds of pragmatic construction:

> A distinction is *weakly pragmatically constructed* if social factors only partly determine our use of it.

> A distinction is *strongly pragmatically constructed* if social factors wholly determine our use of it, and it fails to represent accurately any "fact of the matter."[19]

We'll come back to the weak form of pragmatic construction shortly; let me first unpack this strong form further, because there is an ambiguity in the suggestion that there's no fact of the matter that such a pragmatically constructed distinction captures. In the example of "cool," I use the term to establish my cohort, and in doing so my ascriptions are guided by my likes and dislikes; so there may be a real social distinction (admittedly parochial) that corresponds to my use—I call Mary

---

[19] As will become clear in what follows, this characterization of strong pragmatic construction is oversimplified, even misleading, in its suggestion that in the relevant cases social concerns *wholly* determine our use of the distinction. In the case of "cool," because our use tracks *some* real distinction (status with respect to the in-group), facts about individuals we label "cool dudes" matter to whether we apply the term (e.g., whether they dress a certain way, behave a certain way, etc.). What I'm trying to capture, however, is the fact that our usage is not being guided by some actual property of individuals that corresponds to the intended content (intrinsic coolness) and that what property (or properties) substitutes for it is determined by social concerns. In terms I introduce below, we could say that what operative concept substitutes for the manifest concept is determined wholly by social factors. Let me also emphasize that by labeling the different forms of pragmatic construction "weak" and "strong" I do not intend to imply that the more socially motivated a distinction, the less real; we have very strong social reasons for marking certain real distinctions.

and George "cool," Susan and John "uncool," and the application of the terms corresponds to who I like and who I don't. But note also that in attributing "coolness" to someone, I'm doing so with the background assumption in play that the "coolness" is an intrinsic feature of the individual and is not merely a matter of whom I like. In calling Mary and George "cool," I'm suggesting that there is something cool *about them* that has nothing to do with me—supposedly, it's *their coolness* that warrants my use of the term. It is here that the question of fact arises: Insofar as I am attributing intrinsic coolness to someone, my attribution misfires since no one is, so to speak, cool *in themselves*. In such cases I want to say that my attributions of coolness are false—there is no fact about their coolness that I am accurately representing, even if my use of the terms corresponds to some other features of the individuals, for example, whether or not I like them.[20] So, *strong pragmatic constructions are, in an important sense, illusions projected onto the world; their use might nevertheless track—without accurately representing—a genuine distinction.* The main point is that in cases of strong pragmatic construction there are no available facts corresponding to the intended content—in the case at hand, about intrinsic coolness or uncoolness—that my attributions could be tracking, so instead, we might conclude, they must be functioning *wholly* as a means to a social goal.

On the face of it, there is a significant difference between weak and strong pragmatic construction. In cases of weak pragmatic construction our choices of descriptive terms, classificatory schemes, and so on, are conditioned by social factors (values, interests, history, etc.), but of course this is compatible with those terms' and classifications' capturing real facts and distinctions. The world provides us with more facts and distinctions than we could ever know what to do with; acknowledging that what ones we bother to notice or name is largely determined by our background and interests does not impugn in any general way the accuracy of our attributions.[21] In cases of strong pragmatic construction, however, the attributions are, by hypothesis, not accurately capturing facts, though there is an illusion that they are.

It is important to note that because in the case of pragmatic construction, what's constructed is (at least primarily) a distinction or classificatory scheme, the thought that our classifications are socially constructed leads naturally to the idea that *knowledge* is socially constructed. Given the preceding discussion, we must allow that there are different ways to cash out the claim that knowledge

---

[20] Others will likely question whether I've made a genuine assertion at all, and still others may suggest that I've said something true but misleading. The issues that arise here parallel debates over antirealism and realism in other domains; in effect I am proposing here an "error theory" about coolness, where others might endorse a realism or noncognitivism (though shortly I will modify this view somewhat). But this is a debate we need not settle here. For a general discussion of the alternatives, see Geoffrey Sayre-McCord, "Introduction: The Many Moral Realisms," in his *Essays on Moral Realism* (Ithaca, N.Y.: Cornell University Press, 1988); and Paul Boghossian, "The Status of Content," *Philosophical Review* 99 (1990): 157–84.

[21] See John Dupré, *The Disorder of Things* (Cambridge, Mass.: Harvard University Press, 1993), ch. 1.

is socially constructed, but we can cast two of them in terms of weak and strong pragmatic construction. Roughly:

> Our *knowledge* is weakly/strongly socially constructed (in the relevant senses) iff the distinctions and classifications we employ in making knowledge claims are weakly/strongly pragmatically constructed.

We now have three basic senses of construction to work with: causal, constitutive, and pragmatic. To see how these can become intertwined let's consider the project of debunking strong pragmatic constructions. Return once again to the case of "cool": Attributions of "coolness" have an effect on how individuals interact. "Cool dudes" are *discursively constructed*. But on the analysis I've been proposing, this happens as a result of a false and importantly misleading representation of the facts. I am suggesting that in contexts where "coolness" functions as a serious form of evaluation, there is general complicity in the belief that cool behavior is a result of a character trait (the person's *being* cool) that is the real basis for the evaluation. Cool dudes want their coolness, so to speak, to "shine through" in their behavior, dress, and so on, so that they will win approval by the in-group; and the in-group acknowledges a distinction between *being* cool and just acting cool. Cool things (objects, dress, actions) are the things cool people approve of (or would approve of). To debunk the belief that there is a special quality of coolness that warrants the designation "cool," we show that there is no such property of "coolness" (so understood) and, in fact, that the application of the term "cool" is determined wholly by the interests and concerns of the in-group. In other words, "coolness," when debunked, is revealed as a *constitutive construction*; that is, the concept doing the work of determining when the term should be applied makes essential reference to social factors (that is, in-group status).

But we must be careful here: What counts as the concept "cool"? Once we have disrupted the coolness illusion, there seem to be two different concepts playing a role in our use of the term. On the one hand, there is the concept that actually determines how we apply the term to cases, that is, (roughly) being such as to conform to the standards of the in-group. Let's call this the *operative* concept. On the other hand, there is the concept that users of the term typically take (or took) themselves to be applying, that is, being intrinsically or objectively cool, where this is supposed to be the objective basis for the in-group standards. Let's call this the *manifest* concept. In attributing "coolness" (or "uncoolness") to someone, we are using the apparent objectivity of the manifest concept of "coolness" as a mask for the explicitly social content of the operative concept. But which of these two concepts is the concept "cool"? Both seem to be reasonable candidates. When we sincerely say that someone is "cool," or when we begin the debunking project by insisting that we are mistaken in our attributions of coolness—no one is *really* cool—what's at issue is the manifest concept; but once the debunking project has taken hold, it is tempting to break the illusion by saying that we were wrong about what "coolness" involved and that coolness itself is a constitutive construction. In this we shift from thinking of "cool" in terms of the manifest concept to the operative concept.

So in saying that "coolness" is a social construction, one could have in mind either (or both) (i) that "cool" individuals are discursively constructed (the pattern of behavior found in "cool" individuals is caused by a complex system of attribution and response) or (ii) that the operative concept expressed when we use the term "cool" is constitutively constructed (our use of the term "cool" is actually governed by conditions that concern in-group status, and the content normally associated with the term is a mask for these social conditions). These two ideas are intertwined because the discursive construction of "cool" individuals partly depends upon the (masked) attribution of the constitutively constructed concept "cool."

To see more clearly how these different kinds of social construction function, let's shift from the somewhat artificial example of "cool" I've been using to something more substantive and, for some, more familiar. I'll run briefly through the different kinds by using an example of the social construction of gender. As usual, allow at least a provisional distinction between sex and gender. Gender is defined relationally: Men and women are two groups defined by their social relations to each other. I've argued elsewhere,[22] drawing on the work of Catharine MacKinnon, that we can usefully model one process by which gender is constructed roughly as follows: The ideal of Woman is an externalization of men's desire (so-called Woman's Nature is what men find desirable); this ideal is projected onto individual females and is regarded as intrinsic and essential to them. Accepting these attributions of Womanhood, individual women then internalize the norms appropriate to the ideal and aim to conform their behavior to them; and, in general, behavior towards women is "justified" by reference to this ideal. This, in turn, is responsible for significant empirical differences between men and women.

In this example, individual women are *discursively constructed*; that is, we are the individuals we are because of the attribution (and self-attribution) of Womanhood to us or, more simply, because we've been viewed (and so treated) as having a Woman's Nature. Because discursive construction is a kind of causal construction, it is also correct to say that individual women are *causally constructed*. The ideal of Woman's Nature, however, is *strongly pragmatically constructed*; it is an illusion projected onto women whose basis lies in complex social-sexual relations, not in the intrinsic or essential features of women. As in the case of "cool," we debunk the idea of Woman's Nature and find two concepts at work: The manifest concept of Woman's Nature—understood as defining *what women are by nature* in traditional terms—is an illusion; the operative concept being masked by it is constitutively constructed in terms of men's (socially conditioned) sexual

---

[22] Haslanger, "On Being Objective and Being Objectified." Chapter 1 of this volume.

responses. Further, the distinctions between both man and woman, and male and female (taken as groups of individuals) are *weakly pragmatically constructed*; the fact that we draw these distinctions as we do is to be at least partly explained by social factors, though there are also very real differences between both men and women, male and female.

To summarize, the following would be plausible examples of each kind of construction:

> *Discursively (and so causally) constructed*: individual women; cool dudes.
> *Strongly pragmatically constructed*: Woman's Nature; intrinsic coolness.
> *Constitutively constructed*: the operative concept of "coolness"; the operative concept of "Woman's Nature."
> *Weakly pragmatically constructed*: The distinction between men and women, between male and female; the distinction between those who wear black t-shirts more than once a week and those who don't.

3. The Social Construction of Reality

Given the different kinds of social construction just sketched, there are a variety of different senses we might give to the claim that *reality* is socially constructed. For example, the claim might be that human beings are in some significant way involved in bringing about or constituting everything there is or, more specifically, that our linguistic and conceptual activities are responsible for how things are. Alternatively, the claim might be that how we conceive of reality is determined wholly or partly by social factors. Are any of these claims plausible? And if so, should we be led to give up the idea that there is a world (in some sense) "independent" of us?

The Causal Construction of Reality

Consider, for the moment, causal construction. Is it plausible that the entire world—not just Earth, but everything there is—is a human artifact, even allowing that the mechanisms of construction might be highly complex and mediated? Is the world, for example, a product of our efforts at classification? I don't think so. Clearly human beings have had an enormous effect on things: Mountains are damaged by acid rain, the polar icecaps are melting. And it is equally clear that our actions and classificatory efforts can make a big difference to the nonhuman world: Microbes adapt to our classifications of them by becoming immune to our antibacterial agents.[23] But not everything is so responsive to our

---

[23] See Ian Hacking, "Making Up People," in Thomas Heller, Morton Sosna, and David Wellberg, eds., *Reconstructing Individualism* (Stanford, Calif.: Stanford University Press, 1986), 222–36.

activities, much less simply to our activities of naming; our causal powers, however grand, are limited; and it would be a conceptual stretch to suggest that something should count as an artifact by virtue of even the most remote human influence. (Even if we have had some causal impact on Alpha Centauri, does this make it a human artifact?)

But more important for our questions about independence, the model of causal construction seems to presuppose (at least in some cases) that the mind and world are distinct things that causally interact in complex ways. It is part of this presumption, I believe, that the world we affect exists independently of us, for the model is typically used to point out the extent to which human practices have had an impact on the world.[24] For example, opinions about what is appropriate for humans to eat and so about what counts as "food" have had a huge causal impact on the size, distribution, and behavior of animal populations. We may even want to say that in the causal sense, domesticated cows and chickens are socially constructed. But the deer in the woods and the chickens in the barnyard (or more commonly, on the factory farm) are, nonetheless, independently real. Whatever might be at stake in claiming that there is an "independent reality," the concern is not to insist upon a reality untouched by the actions of human beings. So at the very least, granting that the mind and the world each significantly affects the other does not itself require us to compromise the idea of independence at stake in maintaining that some things are independently real. And even if the case could be made that reality (as a whole) were causally constructed, this reality might nonetheless be independent of us, for in general, claiming that something is causally constructed does not challenge its independent reality.[25]

---

[24] See Sismondo, op. cit., 524. Note that for this reason more radical social constructivists, especially those in science studies concerned with the construction of scientific objects, may be wary of seeing causal construction as a genuine type of social construction.

[25] One might argue that even here I am working with too narrow an understanding of causal construction. Harking back to the concerns of nineteenth-century philosophy, the claim that the world is a social artifact can seem to have a transcendental ring. In particular it suggests that there is a transcendental agent (whether it be a "transcendental ego" or some transcendental notion of "society" or "language") that is not a part of nature but nevertheless is causing, producing, or otherwise constituting the natural world in a rather special way. But this transcendental conception of an "artifact" is no longer believable; whatever worries one might have about the idea of "nature," it is clear that there are no such transcendental agents "outside of" or "prior to" nature. Surely groups of embodied human animals are not such agents, nor are the spoken languages of such animals: We finite beings are not doing the work of constituting the entire inanimate world. And if we aren't doing it, no one else is. Here I am intending to situate myself within a tradition of mild naturalism: We are embodied beings functioning as an integral part of the world, as are our minds, and our languages, and our social systems. This mild naturalism is not only a familiar background assumption in contemporary philosophy but also functions as the background for many of the feminist critiques of earlier philosophical projects. Although there are vestiges of transcendental epistemology in some postmodern and feminist epistemologies, I take it that these are problematic aspects of those projects and should be avoided.

Pragmatic Construction of Our Concept of Reality

Let us turn, then, to pragmatic construction. There can hardly be a doubt that the distinction we draw between what's real and what's unreal is pragmatically constructed at least in the weak sense; that is, social factors play a role in determining our applications of the distinction. There are at least two different ways that social factors play an inevitable role in our application of *any* distinction. First, the fact that we have the linguistic and conceptual resources to draw the distinction in question (and that we have any interest in doing so) will always depend upon contingent historical and cultural factors; so the fact that the distinction is available in our conceptual repertoire at all is largely a social matter.

Second, any particular effort (at a particular time) to apply a distinction to something is influenced by social factors. For example, my ability to distinguish effectively *As* from *Bs* may depend on my confidence, ignorance, intelligence, bias, the incentives and costs, and such. So social factors play a role both in determining the content of the distinctions we make and in our efforts to apply them. The real-unreal distinction appears no different from any other in these respects, and I take these points to be completely uncontroversial. So there's at least one sense in which reality is socially constructed: The distinction between real and unreal—in fact, all of the substantive distinctions we employ—is weakly pragmatically constructed. But as suggested before, it is perfectly compatible with this that our distinctions are accurately capturing genuine—and independent—facts.

A full discussion of this last point could go on at some length, but it will be useful to respond briefly to a couple of concerns here. One might object to the claim that our socially situated inquiries capture independent facts as follows: Insofar as our inquiries are interest-laden, they cannot yield knowledge; so even if there is an independent world, we could never know that there is. Note first that the only way for this argument to get off the ground is for it to presuppose a distinction between cognitive and noncognitive interests, for any knowledge-producing inquiry must rely upon some cognitive values, for example, truth, evidence, consistency. To abjure all interest-laden inquiry would require giving up on knowledge altogether. But even if we restrict the scope of the argument to noncognitive interests, the premise that knowledge requires interest-free inquiry is problematic, for substantive interests and values need not distort; instead, they may enhance our ability to gain knowledge.[26] I believe that noncognitive values have a crucial role in the production of knowledge and cannot be eliminated, so I reject the premise that knowledge requires interest-free inquiry.

But more to the point, there are two separate issues here. To claim that socially situated inquiry can *capture* independent facts is not to claim that such

---

[26] See, e.g., Elizabeth Anderson. "Knowledge, Human Interests, and Objectivity in Feminist Epistemology," *Philosophical Topics* 23, no. 2 (1995): 27–58; and Alison Wylie, "Doing Philosophy as a Feminist: Longino on the Search for a Feminist Epistemology," *Philosophical Topics* 23, no. 2 (1995): 345–58.

inquiry gives us *knowledge* of the facts. It is possible to have true belief that is not knowledge. As I have just indicated, I believe that our inquiries often do provide knowledge of real distinctions and independent facts; but all I am claiming here is that the historical and social contingencies that affect our inquiries need not prevent us from forming true beliefs. No doubt some will see this as a leap from the frying pan into the fire, for in the context of these debates, any reference to "truth" is taken as problematic. In supposing that we can make sense of the notion of "truth" am I not supposing that there is a "ready-made world"? And doesn't this beg the question?

Two points may be helpful here. First, in some contexts, it seems, to say that a statement is true is to claim for it the status of Absolute Truth or to commit oneself to the project of finding One Truth; or it is a claim to have found what is natural, or inevitable, or necessary. But in other contexts saying that a statement is true does not entail any such grandiose claims. It's true that I just finished my mug of tea; it's true that the tea bag is sitting wet and soggy at the bottom of the mug; it's true that I'd love a refill. There is nothing absolute, inevitable, necessary, or epistemically privileged about these very mundane claims; they are, nonetheless, true. And it is this fairly ordinary notion of truth that I have in mind in considering whether the inevitable social conditions for inquiry prevent us from forming true beliefs.

Second, I do, in some sense of the term, believe in a "ready-made world." As should be clear from the discussion above, however, this is not to say that the world hasn't been profoundly affected by human activity; rather, it is to say that there are things in the world that satisfy our descriptions of them, without our having to "constitute" them in any sense through our cognitive efforts. (That is, our descriptions may have an impact on things, but they do so via the kinds of causal processes we've already considered in connection with discursive construction.) Does this commitment to such a world "beg the question"? Not in this context. My goal in working through the various forms of social construction is to determine if there is an argument for the claim that reality is socially constructed that requires us to revise the idea that there is such a "ready-made" world; thus, I unabashedly begin with the belief and evaluate the challenges to it. Because the project is to determine how effective arguments are against the belief, it need not be (in fact, should not be) suspended for the discussion. Admittedly, such burden-of-proof arguments are frustrating; but I hope it can be acknowledged that they have their place.

Strong Pragmatic Construction

So it appears that without compromising the idea that there is an independent world, we can grant that reality is socially constructed in this sense: The distinction we draw between what's real and what's not is weakly constructed, that is, social factors partly influence our efforts to describe the world. Is there any further reason this should lead us to be skeptical about there being a world independent of us? It might seem so if we could extend the case for pragmatic construction to show that the real-unreal distinction is *strongly pragmatically constructed*. Remember that a distinction is strongly pragmatically constructed if it is one whose purported applications are wholly determined by social factors and it fails to accurately represent "the facts." If there are arguments to show that the real-unreal distinction is constructed in this strong sense, then it would follow that our use of it is misguided and doesn't "capture" anything; what we take to be reality is simply a fiction. On this view, reality is socially constructed in the sense of being, like intrinsic coolness and "Woman's Nature," merely an illusion.

The question before us now is whether there are further considerations that should lead us from acknowledging the influence of social factors on knowledge to the more controversial suggestion that we should regard the notion of an "independent reality" as a fiction. For the purposes of this chapter, I want to focus on a cluster of arguments aiming to show that the idea of a "reality" independent of us, sometimes called "objective" reality, is a kind of social projection. We are urged to conclude from these arguments that any meaningful sense of reality must be "perspectival," or "epistemically conditioned," and so we are not entitled to take a realist approach (however limited or modest) towards our classificatory schemes.[27]

The broad strategy of the arguments in question is to suggest that because our efforts at describing, classifying, and understanding are inevitably influenced by social factors, we are misguided to think that we are in a position to accurately represent an "independent reality"; instead, the "reality" that presents itself as the (external) *object* of our epistemic efforts is actually better understood as a *product* of our efforts. (Think back to the example of "cool": Our apparent attributions of intrinsic or objective coolness turned out to be misguided; instead, we found that these attributions were better understood as concerned with the responses of a particular social group and that the object described was better understood as an artifact of our descriptive efforts.) Drawing on the distinctions

---

[27] I put the epistemic qualifications on reality in scare-quotes to indicate that they are intentionally left vague at this point—what exactly they mean is controversial and often obscure. I will elaborate on at least one interpretation in discussing MacKinnon's view below. In this chapter I'll use the term 'realist' roughly as follows: A 'minimal realist' with respect to a domain of discourse is one who takes some of the statements in that domain to express truths; an 'ontological realist' (usually referred to simply as a 'realist') believes that some truths obtain independently of our conceptual or representational activities. Needless to say, these characterizations are vague, and the notion of "independence" I am relying upon needs further explanation, but this is not work I can do here. Note, however, that it is not my view that only things that are "independently" real are real; I only claim that some things that are real are "independently" real.

we discussed earlier, the arguments invite us to reflect on the pragmatic construction of knowledge in order to recognize our role in the discursive and constitutive construction of reality.

I speak of a "cluster" of arguments, however, because the strategy involves two interdependent levels of argument. On the one hand, to show that "reality" is pragmatically constructed, we are asked to consider a broad range of cases in which we attempt to describe the world. The goal is to demonstrate why in each case it is mistaken to understand our classificatory efforts on the model of sorting independently existing things, and to show how "reality" is being constructed rather than "mirrored" in our inquiry. Because a clear pattern develops in these examples, the question arises whether *all* of our seemingly "objective" classifications can be analyzed in the same way. If we could develop a critical method that would show the force of construction in all of our ordinary classifications and descriptions, this would lend credibility to the general metaphysical concerns about the notion of "reality" as such.

But this first level of argument can only be effective in challenging the general notion of reality if the chosen examples are paradigmatic, that is, if our analysis of them could be plausibly extended to all of our efforts to describe the world. The second level of argument, however, targets the notion of reality more directly by asking us to consider the specific distinction between what counts as "real" and "unreal," and what we might mean by speaking of an "independent reality." The goal is to argue that when we call something 'real' we are not accurately describing, or even tracking, a world independent of us; instead, the designation 'real' functions like 'cool' simply to mark a socially meaningful fiction; and thus "reality" as we conceive it is an illusion. As we will see, this second level of argument focuses on a specific philosophical vision of what's real and what's not.

In the sections that follow, I begin by considering the substantive and controversial example of rape to determine the extent to which it might function as a model for unmasking the (strong) pragmatic construction of a wide range of substantive distinctions. I then turn to consider to what extent the distinction between real and unreal is pragmatically constructed. I'll argue that the general strategy of challenging the notion of an independent reality by working from pragmatic construction fails at both levels, even though the example of rape is in significant respects compelling.

4. "Male" Reality

As suggested above, the first level of argument for the conclusion that reality is a strong pragmatic construction involves analyzing how social factors influence our descriptions of a wide range of phenomena. It is promising to begin by analyzing our use of concepts involving race, gender, class, or sexuality, but the goal is to develop a model that can apply across the board. So our task is to look at familiar and concrete cases: What is the actual basis for the divisions and distinctions we employ every day? Are any of these distinctions accurately mapping the world? Or are they systematically serving some other function?

It is a fairly common feminist claim that what is put forward as "objective" reality is rather "male" reality. One interpretation of this claim is that things are not actually designated 'real' by virtue of some objective or intrinsic fact about them but, rather, by virtue of their relation to "us," where the "us" in question is a rather narrow class of white privileged males. (Think of the example of "cool" mentioned before—what's cool is what "we" like, though masked as an intrinsic quality of the objects or individuals in question.) In defending this claim, the goal at this stage is to show how the various different classifications and categories we employ implicate men in some way. Although it is plausible that different cases will require different kinds of analysis, even with one case we can begin to evaluate whether the steps of the particular analysis are compelling and to what extent they can be generalized.

One of the most commonly discussed examples of the "male" construction of reality is rape, and one of the most compelling discussions is MacKinnon's. Rape laws vary from jurisdiction to jurisdiction (and there have been some important changes in rape law over the past two decades): nevertheless, there have been three relatively common aspects relevant to defining rape. First, the definition of rape centers around penetration; for example, in traditional common law, "intercourse" or "carnal knowledge" was required, and contemporary law typically requires that there is "some penetration, however slight."[28] Second, typically rape requires that the sexual act in question involve more than "the normal level of force." And third, the woman must not have consented. But, as MacKinnon argues, each of these conditions are (at least as they are interpreted in practice) peculiarly male oriented. She points out:

> The law to protect women's sexuality from forcible violation and expropriation defines that protection in male genital terms. Women do resent forced penetration. But penile invasion of the vagina may be

---

[28] MacKinnon, *Toward a Feminist Theory of the State*, 295 n. 2. Some states have revised the definition of "intercourse" or "sexual conduct" used in rape law to include oral and anal penetration; Michigan law includes "any other intrusion, however slight, of any part of a person's body or of any object into the genital or anal openings of another person's body" (quoted in Susan Estrich, *Real Rape* [Cambridge, Mass.: Harvard University Press, 1987], 83). Note, however, that penetration or "intrusion" is still required; so the question remains: Why is sexual assault that involves penetration or "intrusion" considered worthy of special treatment? Are there not acts that from a woman's point of view would be experienced as more sexually violating than some penetrations?

less pivotal to women's sexuality, pleasure, or violation, than it is to male sexuality. This definitive element of rape centers . . . upon one way men define loss of exclusive access. In this light, rape, as legally defined, appears more a crime against female monogamy (exclusive access by one man) than against women's sexual dignity or intimate integrity.[29]

Further, to define the "normal level of force" beyond which something counts as rape, it is taken for granted that "normal" male sexuality involves some amount of force. So what counts to distinguish rape from "normal" sex is not the *victim's* "point of violation" but rather what is socially accepted male sexual behavior. Finally, the standards for women's presumed consent depend in important ways on their relationship to men; daughters, and, by extension. young girls and virginal women, are presumed not to consent, wives and prostitutes are presumed to consent (and in many cases there is no action that counts as registering their nonconsent).[30] The complexities of consent deepen when we note further that what matters in establishing a rape charge is whether the perpetrator had reason to think that the woman was consenting, not whether she actually consented. So in considering whether an alleged rape was real, what seems to matter is what the event in question means to men and whether it is in their interest to view it as real. The example of rape seems to be a paradigm case in which the (legal?) distinction between what's real and what's not is being drawn from the point of view of a particular group.[31]

To further illustrate how men's point of view functions to define the terms we use, MacKinnon frequently mentions Justice Stewart's comment when asked to define obscenity. He said, "I know it when I see it."[32] On her view, he's right in a way that he didn't realize, for something is obscene, not in itself, but by virtue of provoking certain responses in men; because Stewart experiences it as obscene, it is obscene, and he's in a position to know it. So on MacKinnon's analysis of masculinist practice, a rape counts as real, an obscene photograph counts as real, not "in itself' and not because some "reasonable person" would decide so given the facts, but due to how men respond to such events and such objects.

---

[29] MacKinnon, *Toward a Feminist Theory of the State*, 172.

[30] Ibid., 175.

[31] It is important to note that on MacKinnon's view, one's "point of view" is not the same as one's experience or perception. For example, rape law may be framed from the "male point of view" even if there are many men who do not experience the desire for sexual ownership. What matters is whether the law is framed to accommodate the needs and interests of those who excel in the social position defined for men; those who do excel in this social position will typically have internalized the norms, and so will have the associated experience, e.g., the desires, anxieties, etc.

[32] MacKinnon, *Feminism Unmodified*, 90, 147; *Toward a Feminist Theory of the State*, 196–7.

Reflecting on the rape example, it appears that the issue focuses on how we should define rape. Let's suppose the masculinist defines rape in terms of the three conditions mentioned (penetration, force, nonconsent) and maintains that whether or not a rape occurred must be determined by what a reasonable person would decide given all the facts. MacKinnon's discussion raises two objections. First, the accepted definition of rape is partial, because its implicit definition of sexual integrity is partial: It privileges men's responses to sexual situations and accommodates their needs, anxieties, and interests. And second, (she claims) there is no neutral or "objective" fact about what rape "really" is; and likewise, there is no neutral or objective point of view from which we can define rape. (Though on her view, there may be a non-neutral point of view—viz., a woman's point of view, or a feminist point of view, that we are entitled to draw upon in framing rape law.)

How do we employ the model of strong pragmatic construction in these sorts of cases; that is, what is the illusion being projected onto the world? Here's a suggestion: Considering the legal conditions sketched above, one might try to define rape in two steps. The first step tries to capture a rather vague "common-sense" view of rape:

> (R) X rapes y iff x and y have sex that violates y's sexual integrity; the second step tries to spell this out:
> (SI) X and y have sex that violates y's sexual integrity iff x and y have nonconsensual sex that involves the forced penetration of y's vagina by x's penis.

This two-step definition is clearly unacceptable, for by assuming that when sexual integrity is violated there is a penis and vagina involved, it is deeply heterosexist; and in assuming that the violation is always of the one with the vagina, it is deeply sexist. But on MacKinnon's account there is an even deeper problem, for as suggested above, the definition undertakes to define sexual integrity in terms that merely reflect heterosexual men's desire for exclusive access to women's bodies. According to the proposed definition (and contrary to some appearances), a violation of women's sexuality is not defined in terms of women's desires or needs; instead it is defined by projecting onto women what violates heterosexual men's desire for sexual ownership.

The key here is to see that the legal understanding of "rape" is premised on an understanding of women's sexual integrity that is an illusion. Strictly speaking (SI) defines what *violates* women's sexual integrity, but clearly this account depends on assumptions about what *constitutes* women's sexual integrity; for example, because the act of nonconsensual forced penetration is taken to be not only sufficient but also necessary for sexual violation, any sexual act other than this one is presumed compatible with women's sexual integrity. But this image of "Women's Sexual Integrity" is an illusion; in other words, the so-called "sexual integrity" implied by (SI) doesn't exist. Why not? Because at the very least if you listen to women talk about their experiences of sexuality, you'll find that they have a very different idea (and among them very different ideas) about what violates their sexual integrity—nonconsensual forced penetration might be part of it, but it surely isn't all. So if rape is defined by (R) and (SI) together, then rape too is a kind of illusion—one cannot violate something ("Women's Sexual Integrity" so-defined) that doesn't exist.

But of course we want to say that rape does exist, that rape *isn't* an illusion. How can we make this claim in the context of this analysis? In keeping with the analogy with "cool," MacKinnon's strategy does not allow us to claim that there is a "Real" essence of rape or obscenity that the common use of such terms [as in (R) and (SI)] misses. In other words, we're not to think that there is an "objective" fact—one that is independent of us and our self-interpretations—about what is rape and what isn't (just as we're not to think that there is an "objective" fact about coolness, independent of us and our self-interpretations). According to MacKinnon, rape isn't an *objective* fact, but neither is it an illusion; it is a fact of women's experience that must be understood from women's—or more accurately, a feminist—point of view. On this view, rape—and in turn, sexual integrity—can only be defined from a point of view; the question is, whose point of view counts? To use a slogan, rape is what rape means, sexuality is what sexuality means: the question is, to whom? And more generally, reality is what reality means; and again the question is, to whom?

Although these last questions are pressing and need well-thought-out answers, they are not directly on our topic; so I'm not going to offer even a tentative answer. Rather, the point of the example of rape is to explain what it might mean to describe reality as "male" and, more generally, to illustrate how our classificatory practices and decisions about what to count as "real" can depend in crucial ways on a particular group's responses and point of view (without it being obvious that they do). The example also shows how claims to map "objective" reality in setting up classification schemes can have disturbing political consequences, for the rhetoric of objectivity can serve to mask the privileging of the dominant group's interests. In many contexts, the struggle to determine what's real is in part a political fight about what relations to "us" count and about who is included in the "us."

But it is unclear from this example what general conclusions we are entitled to draw concerning our classificatory efforts. Remember that the point of considering this example was to lend plausibility to the broader claim that reality *as a whole* is socially constructed in the strong sense of being, like "coolness," a socially useful fiction. Can we extend the analysis of coolness, and now the masculinist understanding of rape, to other things? To everything?

5. Constructed Reality?

MacKinnon is emphatic that there is no objective reality and that reality is socially constructed in a strong sense. And yet, we have no clear indication of how to generalize her analysis of rape to other concepts. On the face of it, this would seem a difficult task; for example, are our concepts like 'water', 'dog', 'tree' to be understood in terms of the responses of particular groups or, more specifically, as defined from men's point of view? Moreover, as the quote at the beginning of this paper about the bridge abutment demonstrates, Mac-Kinnon is not ready to give up the notion of reality—even an independent reality—altogether. How should we interpret this? What is her notion of so-cially constructed reality?

Her view emerges from an analysis of practice. When the masculinist employs terms such as 'rape' or 'obscene' or, importantly for our purposes, 'real', he does so based on his own responses to things. But this is not a peculiarity of the mas-culinist. In general, whenever any of us speak of an object, we use criteria in-volving some relation that the object bears to us; when we call something F, we do so because of its place in our picture of things or its meaning from our point of view. However, if this is all we're ever doing in calling things F, you might go further to claim that to *be* F must be just to have such a place in our picture. The guiding thought here is that because what we think or know about things is always conditioned by our particular social position, all we can ever meaning-fully say about them is how they are related to that position. So although we sometimes appear to be talking about how things are "in themselves," we're ac-tually only speaking of how things seem to us, that is, of social facts.[33] From this, MacKinnon concludes that we must give up the idea that our thought cap-tures a "reality" with a "nonsocially perspectival" "content;[34] more specifically she claims that "there is no ungendered reality or ungendered perspective."[35] For, she asks, "What is a purely ontological category, a category of 'being' free of social perception?"[36]

On this interpretation, MacKinnon is using the insight that social criteria govern our use of a given term F to debunk our "common-sense" idea of what it

---

[33] It may seem odd to think of the fact in question as a "social fact," for after all, when I describe or classify something, I do so on the basis of how the thing in question relates to *me*, and whatever the relation between myself and the object may be, it isn't obviously a *social* relation. (Though what counts as a "social relation" is far from clear.) However, the criteria I employ are social in the sense that the application-conditions for any term are socially, not privately, specified; so in claiming that I can only speak of how things seem *from here*, what counts as "here" is not the individual conscious-ness but, rather, the social context that determines meanings.

[34] MacKinnon, *Toward a Feminist Theory of the State*, 83.

[35] Ibid., 114.

[36] Ibid., 119.

is to be *F*. Nothing is *F* "in itself"; rather to be *F* is to stand in some relation to us (a relation that may vary from case to case).[37] In terms we discussed above, all concepts (more specifically, all of our operative concepts) are constitutively constructed. She then uses this idea to challenge one understanding of an "independent" reality and to form an alternative conception of what it is to be real. If we mean by "independent reality," the way things are "in themselves," then, she argues, there is no way to speak of (or to think of, or to experience) a world that is "independent" of us, because the only world we can speak of is the one that is constituted through our perspective. However, in contrast, the real world, in any meaningful sense, is the world we speak of (think of, and experience); so, she concludes, we must learn to embrace in a general way the implication of perspective in what it is to be real.[38] In keeping with this, it is important to note that even though MacKinnon's strategy works to unmask patriarchal concepts as reifying men's interests and men's point of view, her next step is *not* to aspire to concepts that are purged of all perspective. Instead, she urges us to endorse a feminist perspective, and with it, to constitute the world anew.

---

[37] Looking closely, we can see that MacKinnon's position develops in two steps: First, allow that any meaningful *criteria* for employing a term will always implicate us; e.g., the criteria will involve reference to conditions under which the thing in question normally appears *to us* or is meaningful *to us*. Then, second, treat the criteria for employing a term as its *meaning* or *intension*; i.e., equate the epistemic basis for our attributions with the property we are attributing. As stated, both steps apply to all terms, but they have the particular result that the property we are attributing to something in saying that it is real is a kind of social property: To be real is always to be real to someone, to some group, or from some point of view. Although in this analysis the reference to some "us" or other is ineliminable, in saying what is real we nevertheless capture genuine social facts concerning "us."

I'm relying here on some distinctions that have functioned implicitly in the discussion so far. In applying any term, there are several things at issue: First, there is the class of things to which the term applies, i.e., the *extension* of the term. (Here we might note a further difference between the class of things to which the term truly or accurately applies and the class to which it purportedly applies in a given pattern of use; so we might distinguish the extension from the *purported extension*.) Second, there are the properties attributed to the things in so distinguishing them, i.e., the *intension* of the term. (With the distinction between manifest and operative concepts in mind, we might also want to distinguish the intension from the *purported intension*.) And third, there is the *criterion* by which we judge whether something falls into the class or not. A criterion for use is an epistemic notion concerning those conditions under which we do (or should) apply the term. (Note that the notion of a criterion has both a descriptive and normative use.)

[38] MacKinnon is concerned that her view not be dismissed as relativism. She does not allow that each group's determination of what is real is equally good or that it doesn't matter which "reality" we adopt. It is a political matter what "reality" we adopt and so take as a basis for our actions; in effect, different points of view generate competing realities, and to decide between them is to take a moral stand. MacKinnon's own moral stand is unequivocal; she proposes that we stop acting on the basis of what is real *to men* and instead begin to take seriously what is real *to women*. More specifically, we should adopt the point of view of feminism ("unmodified") and accept (and work to create) the reality it endorses. This is not "women's reality" in the sense of what females think; one might say that it is a feminist standpoint which does not claim greater objectivity than other standpoints but which claims our allegiance on the basis of its contribution to gender equality. (See also note 31.)

So on MacKinnon's view, the masculinist and feminist worlds we constitute are in an important sense not independent of us, because we cannot eliminate and should not ignore the fact that they are constituted from and through perspectives; nonetheless, in perhaps another (and weaker) sense they are independent, for we are not demigods, and we do not create and control them—they may not be wholly independent of us, but we should not conclude that they are wholly dependent upon us either. As MacKinnon illustrated before, simply describing or naming something as, say, a bridge abutment cannot make it so. She resists realism, but she is also firmly opposed to any form of idealism; we cannot build a feminist world with thought alone, we need action as well.

There is much that is compelling about MacKinnon's overall position—in particular, MacKinnon's concern with the social and political factors in all knowledge is important; and she is right to claim that the meanings of some terms are irreducibly social. But the question is how far to extend these insights. Unfortunately, her argument for perspectival realities rests crucially on the dubious claim that because we only have a basis for classifying or describing something if it bears some relation to us, the content of our classifications inevitably captures those relations.[39] The problem is that even if we grant that the epistemic criteria for applying any term will implicate us in some way, we need not equate such social *criteria* with the *content* of our attribution.[40] For example, the criterion we employ (and plausibly should employ) for judging whether something is water is how it looks and tastes; but to say that something is water is to classify it as a kind of liquid (i.e., as H_2O), where this classification concerns the composition of the liquid and not how it appears to us.[41] In this case and in most others there is a clear contrast between the criteria for applying a concept and its content, and thus far we've been given no reason for thinking that a conflation of the two is necessary. In other words, social factors may play an unavoidable

---

[39] There are reasons for questioning my interpretation of MacKinnon's argument, specifically its attribution to her the belief that we must understand the content of a term in terms of the criteria for its use. There is some evidence in her work that, for reasons similar to Rorty's, she rejects a representationlist epistemology; if so, I'm not sure how, if at all, the content of a term would be determined. For an excellent discussion of MacKinnon's epistemology, see Elizabeth Hackett, "Catharine MacKinnon's 'Feminist Epistemology,'" (Ph.D. diss., University of Pennsylvania, 1996). Drawing on parallels with Rorty and Kuhn, Hackett's interpretation offers MacKinnon a much more sophisticated position than I can do justice to here.

[40] Admittedly, it is not uncommon to find authors conflating the criterion for the application of a term and the meaning of a term. (This is not surprising since much of what we say on these matters is ambiguous: In considering what is the *basis for* the application of a term, it is often unclear whether we are inquiring into the truth conditions or the evidential basis.) But for the most part, the conflation of criteria and truth conditions is a mistake.

[41] Ironically, there are echoes of verificationism in MacKinnon's epistemology, for at least in the argument just considered, she needs to equate the meaning of a term with our methods for determining when it applies.

role in determining the ways we employ the concepts we do, but this is no reason for thinking that our concepts can't capture facts about the world as it is "in itself." On occasion we do get things right, sometimes due to luck, or other times hard work, or even insight.

In summary, MacKinnon's analysis of rape shows in detail how strong pragmatic constructions typically work: A particular group's interests and desires come to be projected onto the world in the service of some (often pernicious) social goal, where the supposed fact being represented is missing. For example, the masculinist projects his need for sexual ownership onto women and reads it as "Women's Sexual Integrity" (and not only expects women to live up to it but legally enforces it as well); but actual women's sexuality does not support his view of things.[42] In such cases of projection, the social factors determining how we use our terms are masked, with the result that the projections are made to seem "objective," "natural," or "inevitable," when, of course, they aren't. But we must be careful before generalizing this model to all cases; sometimes social forces do affect how and why we view the world in a certain way, without preventing us from forming accurate beliefs about the world that exists beyond our perspective. Social forces (together with my own desires and interests) are responsible for my belief that right now the street outside my window is wet (it has been raining); but its wetness consists in properties of the pavement that have nothing to do with me or my conceptual repertoire. So MacKinnon's example and the argument developed from it do not offer us reason for thinking that reality as a whole is a strong pragmatic construction or that we should modify our understanding of an "independent" reality to grant that all reality is socially conditioned. What we *believe* to be real may be deeply conditioned by our point of view; but what is real is another matter.

6. "Objective" Reality

Even if MacKinnon's argument is not compelling, however, her discussion does leave some uncertainty about what to make of the idea of an *independent* reality. What does the idea amount to, and what work does it do for us? In pressing

---

[42] My use of the masculine pronoun here should not mislead, for it is important to allow that women can take up a masculinist perspective and so come to think about their own sexual integrity and other women's in masculinist terms. The contradictions between what women learn to think about themselves and what they actually experience are often a source of confusion, pain, and struggle. Whether or not there is a way to define "women's sexual integrity" or "women's experience" that includes all women is a highly contested issue; MacKinnon is often labeled (and dismissed) as "essentialist" for seeming to suggest that there is. But note that MacKinnon's project is primarily negative—living in a masculinist world, she is undertaking to show that whatever we might come to see as women's experience(s) or women's point(s) of view, *it isn't this*.

these questions, we move to the second level of argument I mentioned earlier: Rather than using the first strategy of working to develop an analysis that debunks all of our efforts to describe the world, we instead focus attention directly on the distinction between real and unreal and on the concept of an independent reality. The worry is that if the real-unreal distinction *in particular* is constructed in the sense of being nothing more than a social projection, then we would have to conclude that there are no facts about what's real and what's not, and the idea of an independent reality would be a kind of fiction.

Let us begin again with the acknowledgment that all of our distinctions are weakly pragmatic—what ones we choose to employ and how we do so are at least partly determined by social factors; it follows that our use of the real-unreal distinction is weakly pragmatic. So the question before us now is whether there are further considerations which should lead us from acknowledging the influence of social factors on knowledge to the more controversial suggestion that we should regard the notion of an "independent reality" as a fiction. The following argument is one that can be found explicitly in some writers and is implicit in many others.[43] The general strategy was initially motivated as a critique of what is alleged to be a modernist picture of knowledge and reality, though the picture takes on a positive momentum of its own. (Whether it was actually endorsed by any modernist philosophers is a difficult historical issue I'm not going to get into.)

On the picture under attack, knowledge and reality are intimately connected: What is real is what can be objectively known.[44] Objectivity, on this view, is in its primary sense an epistemological notion. Roughly:

(ObInq) An inquiry is *objective* in the relevant sense just in case the way the world is and the rationality of the inquirers are the only factors that determine its outcome.

So, an objective view of some subject matter is one that a purely rational inquiry into the subject would eventually yield.[45] This epistemic notion of "objectivity" is then applied derivatively to ontology—as in "objective reality"—by virtue of the following equivalence:

---

[43] My characterization of the argument is much simplified, but I have in mind works such as Richard Rorty, *Philosophy and the Mirror of Nature* (Princeton, N.J.: Princeton University Press, 1979); Hilary Putnam, *Reason, Truth, and History* (Cambridge: Cambridge University Press, 1981); Catharine MacKinnon, *Toward a Feminist Theory of the State*, esp. ch. 6; Sandra Harding, *Whose Science? Whose Knowledge?* (Ithaca, N.Y.: Cornell University Press, 199 I), esp. ch. 6; and others.

[44] For one typical characterization of the objectivist target, see MacKinnon, *Toward a Feminist Theory of the State*, 97.

[45] See Gideon Rosen, "Objectivity and Modern Idealism," in M. Michael and J. O'Leary-Hawthorne, eds., *Philosophy in Mind* (Dordrecht: Kluwer, 1994), 277–319. Rosen's paper offers an excellent discussion of the problems that arise in even framing a notion of objective reality.

(ObRel) An object or a fact is objectively real just in case it is (or can be) objectively known.

Moreover, on this view there is no notion of reality other than objective reality. (Note that this is only one of many accounts of objectivity; nevertheless, in the remainder of this section I will be using the term 'objective' as indicated here.)

At least in this crude formulation, such a conception of "objective" inquiry is not plausible, and it is now a commonplace to deny that such pure inquiry is possible. For (at least) the reasons sketched above, we must acknowledge that the results of all human inquiry are conditioned by social factors.[46] But if we continue to think that reality must be equated with what is objectively knowable, then since nothing is objectively knowable (in the relevant sense), it appears that we should conclude that there is no such thing as "reality," that is, that nothing is objectively real. In short, "Reality" or "objective reality" is as much an illusion as "pure inquirers" and "objective knowledge."

Having rejected the idea that there is an "objective reality," however, it then seems plausible to offer an analysis of our purported references to what's real in line with our previous example of "cool." When we attribute "reality" to something, our attribution does not capture a fact about the object itself (since, by hypothesis, the fact we purport to be attributing is not available); rather such attributions correspond to a distinction in how things are related to us; in other words, things are graced with the term 'real' not by virtue of some intrinsic fact about them but by virtue of some relevant social fact, for example, our finding them useful or, perhaps, politically expedient.[47] Yet, as in the case of "cool," there is an illusion implicit in our attributions, since the background assumption is that what's real is not a matter of how things are related to us but rather a matter of an intrinsic feature of things. This illusion is, of course, politically significant, for the distinction between what's real and what's not has important social consequences. As we've noted before, by masking our own contribution to what counts as real we mask the problematic political motivations for such discriminations and often cast them as natural or inevitable. So on this view we are to conclude that "objective reality" is an illusion masking the social factors that are actually responsible for the distinctions we draw between what's real and what's not.

---

[46] Of course there may be subtleties to add to the formulation that the kinds of social factors mentioned don't prevent an inquiry from being objective; and it may be that such a crude view was never actually held by anyone. But historical accuracy is not my concern here, since the point is to capture what's motivating the broad-scale anti-objectivist.

[47] See, e.g., MacKinnon, *Feminism Unmodified*, 173: "The object world is constructed according to how it looks with respect to its possible uses."

7. Being Real

That's the sketch of the argument; let's now go through it a bit more carefully. We should note first that the argument is concerned with a particular practice of employing the terms 'real', 'reality', and their cognates; so far I've spoken vaguely about "our use" of the terms, but this is potentially misleading since it is unclear who the "we" are whose use is in question.[48] For the moment, let's just call it the "objectivist use" of the terms, keeping in mind that we are analyzing a particular practice.

The objectivist use of the terms 'real' and 'unreal' involves both a discrimination between two classes of things (the class of things designated 'real' and those designated 'unreal') and an interpretation of the basis for that discrimination. In particular, the anti-objectivist argument is directed against those who apply the term 'real' rather narrowly, alleging to employ as their criterion whether it is possible to have objective knowledge of the thing or not. Against this use of the term, the critical argument aims to show, first, that nothing satisfies the alleged criterion and, second, that there is really another criterion being employed in making the relevant discriminations, one that is grounded in certain responses to the things in question.

At this stage, I think we should grant that there's something wrong with an objectivist criterion for applying the term 'real' (viz., one requiring "objective knowledge"), so it is implausible that the classes of things the objectivist designates as 'real' and 'unreal' are being judged accurately by that standard, in spite of his belief that they are. The question is whether there is another criterion, or range of criteria, implicit in the objectivist's discriminations, and what they might be. Here the anti-objectivist will claim that there is always another criterion doing the work, and more specifically, it is one that draws on social facts or implicates "us" in some way (relating the object in question to our needs, interests, desires, social roles, etc.).

Of course, this statement of the point is rather vague, but exactly what social facts are relevant and how "we" are implicated varies depending on which anti-objectivist account you are considering—in MacKinnon's account we just discussed, male needs and interests are at the heart of the story. Moreover, what social factors determine how the terms are used may vary from context to context. But in spite of this vagueness, I think there is reason to be concerned about the whole strategy of argument.

Suppose we do grant that there are objectivist uses of the terms 'real' and 'reality' or, more generally, that there are ways of determining what is real and

---

[48] E.g., it is unclear whether it is supposed to be philosophers (modernist or otherwise), judges, or the person on the street who supposedly uses the terms precisely as sketched. It might also be that the use in question is one that few people are entirely consistent about and that, instead, it tends to accompany certain roles.

what isn't that purport to be epistemically objective but in fact are based on so-cially loaded criteria. This raises a challenge to the notion of an independent re-ality only if we accept the thesis that such a reality is *by definition* that which can be objectively known, that is, only if we accept (ObRel) as characterizing what it is to be objectively (or independently) real. This is an easy thesis to reject, espe-cially for one with realist inclinations; for the whole point of speaking of an inde-pendent reality is to emphasize that there is no necessary connection between what's real and what human beings know or can (in practice) know. Strangely, it appears that the argument as sketched would only be convincing to someone who was already committed to an epistemically constrained conception of re-ality and should not be convincing to those realists it purportedly sets out to target.

So there are several plausible responses to the argument that "objective re-ality" is an illusion. We could start by rejecting the most questionable premises: We could reject the proposed link between (objective) knowledge and (objective) reality, as stated in (ObRel). Or we could reject the proposed definition of objec-tive knowledge in (ObInq). I find both of these options appealing. But suppose for the sake of argument that the only way to conceive of an "objective" reality is in terms of what is objectively known; that is, suppose we decide to accept both of these premises. Then we probably should conclude that the correlative idea of reality is equally nonsensical.[49] However, even if we grant that there is no *objec-tive* reality, it still doesn't follow that there is no *independent* reality or that there are no genuine facts of the matter that it would be good to know. To give up the idea of "objective reality," as we've been considering it, is simply to give up the idea that there are things which determine, in and of themselves, without any social factors playing a role, how they are known. It seems clear that because language and knowledge are socially conditioned, there are no things like this.

What's at least partly at stake here is how *we* want to employ the notion of "the real" or "reality." Assuming that the idea of an independent reality can only be defined in terms of objective knowledge grants too much to the objectivist. For as suggested above, at least one plausible idea of an "independent" reality is one that places no epistemic conditions on what it is to be real. At least initially, we might take the property of being real at face value: To be real is to exist. Or perhaps: For an object to be real is for it to exist; for an event to be real is for it to occur; for a fact to be real is for it to obtain. These explications are unillumi-nating to be sure and may well need further analysis; my point is not to endorse an intentionally naive view but rather to suggest the first steps of an account that views what's real in nonepistemological and nonsocial terms. We will, of

---

[49] This, I take it, is sometimes Rorty's view. See, e.g., Richard Rorty, "The Contingency of Language," in his *Contingency, Irony, and Solidarity* (Cambridge: Cambridge University Press, 1989), 3–22.

course, need an epistemology (and I think a feminist epistemology) to help us decide what to believe exists, what definitions to accept, and so on. But I see no good reason in the arguments we've considered so far to collapse the epistemology-ontology distinction. When I say that something is real, my assertion is true just in case the thing in question exists; this is so even if the criteria I employ in making the judgment are socially loaded and even if my utterance also expresses the value it has in my conception of things.

8. Conclusion

Are there any general conclusions we can draw from this discussion? How profoundly does the idea of social construction affect our projects in metaphysics and epistemology? There is no doubt that the idea of discursive construction should play a significant role in our ontological theorizing. Because reality does have a way of conforming itself to our conception of it, the line between artifacts and natural objects must continually be challenged and contested. We must be aware that the classifications we employ in our theorizing may not be capturing differences already there, but may be responsible for creating them. But we have no reason yet to conclude that there are only artifacts or that our classificatory endeavors are so powerful as to leave nothing untouched.

Moreover, epistemologically, we must acknowledge the force of pragmatic construction. Our classificatory schemes, our distinctions, and our judgments are inevitably influenced by many different social factors; and some of our judgments are not tracking any facts but are instead only perpetuating socially meaningful illusions. Moreover, we must be attentive to the possibility that the terms we use are defined by and in the interest of dominant social groups. But from this it does not follow that the only function of judgment is the social one of perpetuating useful stories or that our judgment can only represent a social world. It may well be that our point of view on the world is always socially conditioned; but there is no reason to conclude that the world we have a point of view on is likewise socially conditioned. We must distance ourselves from the objectivist tendencies to limit our vision of what's real, but we must be careful at the same time not simply to accept perspectivist limitations in their place. I would propose that the task before us is to construct alternative, modestly realist, ontologies that enable us to come to more adequate and just visions of what is, what might be, and what should be.

3

Social Construction

The "Debunking" Project

Introduction

The term 'social construction' has become a commonplace in the humanities. Its shock value having waned and its uses multiplied, the metaphor of construction has, as Ian Hacking puts it, "become tired" (Hacking 1999, p. 35). Moreover, the variety of different uses of the term has made it increasingly difficult to determine what claim authors are using it to assert or deny and whether the parties to the debates really disagree.

In his book *The Social Construction of What?*, Hacking offers a schema for understanding different social constructionist claims along with a framework for distinguishing kinds or degrees of constructionist projects. Hacking's efforts are useful, but his account leaves many of the philosophical aspects of social construction projects obscure, as are the connections, if any, with more mainstream analytic philosophy projects. My goal in this chapter is to argue that although Hacking's approach to social construction is apt for some of those working on such projects, it does not adequately capture what's at issue for an important range of social constructionists, particularly many of us working on gender and race. Moreover, a different way of understanding social construction reveals interesting connections and conflicts with mainstream analytic projects.

I agree with Hacking that it isn't useful to try to determine what social construction "really is" because it is many different things, and the discourse of social construction functions differently in different contexts. So instead I focus on a particular kind of social constructionist project, one I call a "debunking project," to consider how exactly it is supposed to work, how it differs from other constructionist projects, and what, if any, metaphysical implications it has.

Given the multiple uses of the term 'social construction,' one might wonder why it matters whether this or that project is properly characterized as a form of social constructionism. And of course, in the abstract it matters very little. But

nt academic context, the classification of some view as social
t can mean that it is not worth taking seriously or, alternatively,
~ of the views to be taken seriously. Insofar as the label carries such
~ut, it is useful to differentiate some of the various constructionist projects
so that their intellectual affiliations and incompatibilities can be clarified.

Hacking on Social Construction

Hacking suggests that in order to understand social construction, we should ask
first: What is the point of claiming that something is socially constructed? He
offers this schema for understanding the basic project:

> Social construction work is critical of the status quo. Social construc-
> tionists about X tend to hold that:
>
> 1. X need not have *existed*, or need not be at all as it is. X, or X as it is at
>   present, is not determined by the nature of things; it is not inevitable.
>
> They often go further, and urge that:
>
> 2. X is quite bad as it is.
> 3. We would be much better off if X were done away with, or at least
>   radically transformed. (Hacking 1999, p. 6)

In order for a claim of social construction to have a point, however, there is a
precondition to be satisfied: "(0) In the present state of affairs, X is taken for
granted, X appears to be inevitable" (Hacking 1999, p. 12).

In this schema, X can range over very disparate kinds of things, including ideas,
concepts, classifications, events, objects, persons. Allegedly socially constructed
things include: child abusers, the self, quarks, the concept of the economy, the
classification "woman refugee." Especially important to Hacking is the distinction
between constructing *ideas* (which includes concepts, categories, classifications, etc.)
and constructing *objects* (e.g., Hacking 1999, pp. 10–11, 14, 21–22, 28–30, 102, etc.).
(Note that Hacking's understanding of "objects" is broad and includes: people, states,
conditions, practices, actions, behavior, classes, experiences, relations, material
objects, substances [i.e., stuffs], unobservables, and fundamental particles (Hacking
1999, p. 22).) Although X in the schema above ranges over both ideas and objects, he
urges us to be clear which we are talking about in order to avoid confusion.

Condition (0), on Hacking's account, is a necessary condition for a work to be
considered "social constructionist" at all. Cases that don't appear to satisfy (0),
for example, the "invention" of Japan (Hacking 1999, pp. 12–13) and the construction of "obvious" social kinds, don't qualify as genuine social constructionist

projects. Hacking offers a framework for classifying the variety of constructionist views (given (0)), with respect to their acceptance of claims (1)–(3):

> *Historical constructionist:* Contrary to what is usually believed, X is the contingent result of historical events and forces, therefore (1): X need not have existed, is not determined by the nature of things, etc.
>
> *Ironic constructionist:* Historical constructionism PLUS: at this stage we cannot help but treat X as "part of the universe," but our way of thinking may evolve so that X is no longer viewed in this way.
>
> *Reformist constructionist:* Historical constructionism PLUS (2): X is quite bad as it is. Although we cannot at this stage see how to avoid X, we should try to improve it.
>
> *Unmasking constructionist:* Historical constructionism PLUS if we understand the function of X socially, we will see that it should have no appeal for or authority over us.
>
> *Rebellious constructionist:* Historical constructionism *PLUS* (2): X is quite bad as it is. And (3), we would be much better off if X were done away with or radically transformed.
>
> *Revolutionary constructionist:* Historical constructionism *PLUS* (2): X is quite bad as it is. And (3), we would be much better off if X were done away with or radically transformed. In addition, the revolutionary constructionist acts to do away with X. (Hacking. 1999, pp. 19–20)

It is important to note that it is common to all of Hacking's constructionists that they use a claim about the contingent causes or historical source of the phenomenon X to support the idea that X need not have existed or need not have been "at all as it is." He says explicitly, for example, that "construction stories are histories" (Hacking 1999, p. 37; also p. 48); and the point, as he sees it, is to argue for the contingency or alterability of the phenomenon by noting its social or historical origins. So, if one were to argue, on Hacking's account, that the idea of refugee were socially constructed, then the point would be that the idea of refugee is the result of historical events, that we might have lacked that idea and have had other ideas instead.

Idea-Construction

In keeping with Hacking's account, let's distinguish the "idea-constructionist" project and the "object-constructionist" project, and focus for the time being on idea-constructionist projects. Given the account so far, it isn't clear how any idea-constructionist project should be able to get off the ground, for it seems implausible that they satisfy condition (0). *Of course* what concepts and so what ideas we have is the result of social-historical events; who is in the business of denying that? (Hacking seems to agree—1999, p. 69.) It would seem to be a matter of common sense that concepts are taught to us by our parents through our language; different cultures have different concepts (that go along with their different languages); and concepts evolve over time as a result of historical changes, science, technological advances, and so on.[1] Let's (albeit contentiously) call this the "ordinary view" of concepts and ideas.[2] Moving to more theoretical domains, even the most arch realist who believes that our concepts map "nature's joints" allows that groups come to have the concepts they do through social-historical processes. So what could possibly be the excitement in claiming that any particular concept emerges as a result of historical events and forces? If Hacking feels free to deny that a book such as *Inventing Japan* is a social constructionist project because it is too obvious that Japan is a social entity and so condition (0) is not satisfied (Hacking 1999, p. 13), why should we not similarly rule out all attempts to reveal the historical origins of a particular idea or concept, that is, all purportedly idea-constructionist projects?

To answer this we need to elaborate Hacking's account further. Let's begin by considering what, on Hacking's view, is supposed to be controversial or interesting in the claim that some idea or other is constructed. Hacking identifies three "sticking points"—presumably implicit in (1) or in the inference to (1)—that arise in debates between constructionists and nonconstructionist. (Although his discussion of these sticking points focuses on constructionist debates concerning natural science, it appears at various points he intends them to be characteristic of constructionist debates more generally, so I'll articulate them in more general terms.)

On his account, constructionists with respect to a domain D, for example, the natural world, mental illness, rocks, are sympathetic to (a) the contingency of our understanding of D; (b) nominalism about kinds in D, or more precisely, a denial that the domain D has an inherent structure; and (c) an explanation of the stability of our understanding of D in external rather than internal terms. Letting the domain be the natural world, the constructionist claims (or tends to claim) that a scientific theory different from current scientific theory might

---

[1] Ideas are similar, but perhaps less conditioned by language and more specific to the individual.

[2] Hacking more often speaks of the social construction of "ideas" and sometimes of the social construction of "the idea of X (in its matrix)" where the matrix is the social setting "within which an idea, a concept or kind, is formed" (Hacking 1999, pp, 10–11). The emphasis on ideas and matrices rather than concepts doesn't change the ordinary view, for if on the ordinary view concepts are influenced by society and concepts are generally thought to play a role in any idea, then ideas will be too. Given that the matrix is the social context for the idea, including, for example, in the case of woman refugee: "a complex of institutions, advocates, newspaper articles, lawyers, court decisions, immigration proceedings" (Hacking 1999, p.10), the ordinary view would certainly hold that the idea in its matrix is conditioned by social forces.

nonetheless have emerged and been as successful in its own terms as ours is in our terms (Hacking 1999, pp. 68–80); that the natural world does not have an "inherent structure" (Hacking 1999, pp. 80–4); and that the best explanation of the stable elements of current scientific theory relies on factors external to science, for example, the educational system that instills in aspiring scientists the practices and the background assumptions that give rise to the dominant theory (Hacking 1999, pp. 84–95). So on Hacking's view the idea-constructionist thesis is not simply that our ideas have a history, or that what concepts we have is influenced by social forces. Rather, the idea-constructionist holds a cluster of theses opposing what is taken to be a standard explanation of the origins of our ideas or theories and why we retain them. (Henceforward I'll use the term 'idea-constructionism' for this cluster of theses, not just the simpler claim that our ideas are the contingent result of social/historical events and forces.)

Let's take a moment to spell out the idea-constructionists' adversary a bit further. The question on which the debate hinges seems to be: Are the origin and stability of our ideas/classifications determined by "how the world is," more specifically, by the domain they purport to describe? As Hacking sees it, the constructionist says "no," and the adversary says "yes." But the suggestion that the domain of inquiry "determines" our classifications of it is a bit puzzling. Hacking clearly states that the kind of determination at issue is causal determination: the nonconstructionist maintains that the domain *D* has an inherent structure, that our understanding of *D* is in some sense inevitable because the inherent structure of *D* causally determines how to understand it, and that our understanding of *D* is stable because the stable structure of the world sustains it. Hacking's idea-constructionist claims, in contrast, that the results of our inquiry into *D* "are not predetermined," in particular that they are "not determined by how the world is" (Hacking 1999, p. 73), and that we remain stably committed to the results, not because the content of our theories supports them, but due to social and psychological forces at work. Hacking explicitly claims that the constructionist's point is "not a logical one" (Hacking 1999, p. 73) and emphasizes later that the real issue for constructionists is not semantics, but the dynamics of classification (Hacking 1999, p. 123). Although there is a metaphysical issue lurking behind the debate, namely, whether the world has an inherent structure, this is at issue only because the nonconstructionist invokes such a structure in explaining the origins and stability of our beliefs.

Let's call the constructionist's adversary Hacking has described a "world-idea determinist" to contrast it with Hacking's idea-constructionist who is trying to show that the results of our inquiry into *D* are not only not determined by the inherent structure of the world, but in fact "are not determined by anything" (Hacking 1999, p. 73). Within a debate between these opposing sides, it might seem interesting to claim that some idea of ours has social-historical origins, for the alternative seems to be that the world's inherent structure, by itself, determines what ideas we use to describe it. There may well be, as Hacking strives to show, some scientists who maintain something as extreme as world-idea determinism, so the point is worth making. But casting social construction-ism in general in these terms has several serious drawbacks:

First, the target world-idea determinism is not plausible on its face, and one does not need anything as strong as idea-constructionism to defeat it. To claim that our ideas and the classifications we use to frame them (pick any domain you want) are not in any way influenced by social conditions but are inevitable and stable because they map the relevant domain's inherent structure rules out even a minimal fallibilism.[3] Surely even good scientific method requires one to allow that new data may defeat one's best theory, and conceptual innovation will be called for; certainly ordinary nonscientists, philosophers and the like don't take themselves to be infallible about any domain except perhaps the contents of their own consciousness and simple arithmetic.

Second, although the claim that our ideas are conditioned by social and his-torical events is plausible, Hacking has expanded idea-constructionism into something quite implausible. In the end, idea-constructionism rejects norma-tive epistemology altogether and opts instead for sociology: reasons for belief are replaced by causes, justifications with explanations, semantics with dy-namics (Hacking 1999, pp. 90–2, 121–24). It's one thing to acknowledge that the causal routes responsible for our way of thinking travel through and are influ-enced by the contours of our contingent social structures; it's another thing to entirely replace questions of justification with questions of causation. Although some social constructionists take this line, it is a quite radical position that hardly seems supported by the core idea-constructionist observation that our ideas are the product of social and historical forces.[4]

Third, the world-idea determinist position Hacking describes as the target of social constructionists is not a common view in philosophy and is not the sort of thing that is likely to be accepted by anyone who accepts what I've claimed is an ordinary view about ideas and concepts, namely that what ones we have are con-ditioned by our culture. If world-idea determinism is the social constructionists' target, it isn't surprising that philosophers in general and metaphysicians in

---

[3] Different sorts of fallibilism may be relevant here because Hacking uses the term 'idea' to cover both concepts/classifications and theses or propositions. My point is that it is rare to find someone who holds that *either* their concepts/classifications are inevitable, given how the world is, deter-mined by the inherent structure of the world, and so on, or that their beliefs/theoretical commit-ments are.

[4] It should be noted that Hacking allows idea-constructionism to come in degrees, so plausibly world-idea determinism does too. So the adversary for a moderate constructionist may be someone who allows that reasons and justification, not just causes and explanation, are appropriate consid-erations in discussing a theory. But as I suggest below, the interesting moderate cases deserve more attention than Hacking accords them.

particular have paid little attention to the social constructionist literature. But more important, Hacking's constructionist doesn't have much to say to the non-specialist or nonacademic, for it rejects the "ordinary view" of concepts. This is a problem, for as Hacking himself claims, "most people who use the social construction ideas enthusiastically want to criticize, change, or destroy some *X* that they dislike in the established order of things" (Hacking 1999, p. 7). We constructionists are, on the whole, a politically motivated bunch. But what a waste of breath and ink it would be if our target is a view that most people would find quite bizarre.

Determinism?

If world-idea determinism is not a worthy target of the social constructionist, then is there something nearby that we should be considering? There are three separate issues concerning the relationship between our classifications and the world that lie in the background of Hacking's discussion: (1) what *causes* us to use certain classifications/concepts, (2) by virtue of what is a concept or classification *apt*, and (3) what, if anything, *justifies* our use of one classification scheme as opposed to another? If one is primarily interested in the origins of our ideas, then the debate between Hacking's idea-constructionist and the world-idea determinist seems to represent two ends of a spectrum of possible views. Plausibly our ideas and classifications are the product of some combination of worldly input from perception and experience and social input from language, practices, and the like. The debate as presented by Hacking is not very interesting because neither extreme view is plausible and very little is offered to cover the more interesting middle-ground.

However, if, for example, one is interested in what makes a particular scheme apt, then the issues look quite different. In a telling passage, Hacking describes the constructionist's nominalism as follows:

> If contingency is the first sticking point [between the constructionist and the non-constructionist], the second one is more metaphysical. Constructionists tend to maintain that classifications are not determined by how the world is, but are convenient ways in which to represent it. They maintain that the world does not come quietly wrapped up in facts. Facts are the consequences of the ways in which we represent the world. The constructionist vision here is splendidly old-fashioned. It is a species of nominalism. It is countered by a strong sense that the world has an inherent structure that we discover. (Hacking 1999, p. 33)

Here, as mentioned before, the broad background question seems to be: are our classifications determined by how the world is or not? If the question is, what causes us to have the classifications we do, then we have simply returned to the old world-idea determinist question: are we caused to have the classification scheme we have by the structure of the world itself? And we can agree that social-historical factors play a role. But nominalism and its adversaries aren't about what causes our classifications but what determines their correctness or aptness. The question is: is the aptness (correctness, fittingness) of our classifications determined by the structure of the world, or is their aptness determined by our choice? In other words, which way does the direction of fit run: are our classifications apt because they fit the world, or are they apt because the world fits them? In either case, aptness is not a matter of causal determination. The "inherent structurist" (Hacking's substitute term for 'realist' in the debate with the "nominalist") doesn't think that the world *causes* our classifications to be apt, neither does the nominalist think that our acts of classifying *cause* the world to have a structure. If the idea-constructionist and the inherent structurist are going to have a debate about nominalism, questions about the causal origins of our beliefs aren't really relevant.

If any part of the idea-constructionist project were to have metaphysical implications, one would expect them to show up in the constructionist's commitment to nominalism. But on Hacking's account there is no basis in the constructionist arguments for denying that the domain of our inquiry, whatever it may be, has an inherent structure. The main constructionist premise is that our concepts and ideas are the product of historical forces and could have been different. As suggested above, this is entirely consistent with the most arch realism, or "inherent structurism" about kinds (as Hacking would seem to agree—1999, p. 80). We're left, then, with nothing of metaphysical interest in the idea-constructionist project (assuming that a bald denial of a metaphysical thesis is not metaphysically interesting).

A third question in this general area (in addition to what causes us to use certain classifications and what makes them apt) is what justifies our use of the classifications we've chosen. This issue seems to lie in the background behind Hacking's "third sticking point" between the idea-constructionist and the world-idea determinist. This sticking point, as characterized by Hacking, concerns the causes of the stability of our ideas, or the results of our inquiry. Why, for example, do Maxwell's Equations or the Second Law of Thermodynamics remain stably entrenched in our physics (Hacking 1999, p. 86)? Why do we continue to use the periodic table of the elements in our chemistry? The idea-constructionist maintains that this stability is due entirely to "external factors." Hacking is frustratingly unclear where he intends to draw the line between "internal" and "external" factors, but the discussion as a whole suggests that the world-idea determinist is supposed to think that the inherent structure of our domain of inquiry is somehow causally responsible, ruling out the influence of ordinary human interests, contingent facts about the point of our inquiry, or what technology we have available to test our hypotheses.[5]

But the problem is that again the issue has been framed in causal terms for the benefit of Hacking's constructionist. It should be obvious that the results of any inquiry are at least partly conditioned by the circumstances of inquiry, the kind of technology that is available to the inquirer, the attitudes and biases of the inquirers, and the like, and should the circumstances, technology, resources, and so on change, this is likely to influence what conclusions we draw. Again, one need not be a social constructionist to grant this. It may be that there are scientists who believe that natural laws are "facts we run up against" (Hacking 1999, p. 86) as if their effect is then to write themselves in our notebooks. But again, if this is the constructionist target, it is hard to understand why it should be interesting to philosophers or the general public.

A nearby question that the constructionist rhetoric often seems to be addressing is: what justifies us in our ongoing commitment to a theory, classification scheme, and so on. This isn't, or isn't obviously, a causal question. Many different factors contribute to the justification of a theory, including coherence, supporting evidence, simplicity, fruitfulness, and so on. These are sometimes called "constitutive values" of inquiry. Feminists have also argued that contextual values are relevant to justification, for example, whether the question motivating the theory is legitimate, whether the methods allow for certain evidence to emerge, whether the community of researchers exhibits a certain diversity (Longino 1980; Anderson 1995). With the distinction between "constitutive" and "contextual" values in mind, it is possible to identify several views that seem to be floating around in the discussion. One extreme view is that nothing *justifies* our use of a particular classification scheme; the best we can do is *explain* why we use this or that classification scheme by doing sociology, or Foucauldian genealogy, perhaps. An opposing extreme view is that the world itself—its inherent structure—justifies us: because our ideas are caused by the inherent structure of the world, they're justified. But the more philosophically interesting options concern what norms—contextual, constitutive, or some combination of both—are the basis for justification. But this last set of options aren't seriously considered in the discussion.

Unfortunately, the debate Hacking has described between the social constructionist and the world-idea determinist seems to frame it either as entirely

---

[5] Sometimes Hacking represents the issue of stability as a question of whether, given the methods we've embraced, the technology available to us, and so on, we could have come up with different results. Of course if we allow that we could have used the methods or the technology better or worse than we actually did, we could have reached different results. The more serious question is whether using the technology to its limits and following the methods perfectly could yield different and incompatible results. It's hard to see how one could give a general answer to this question, for it would depend crucially on what methods and what technology one had in mind.

concerned with the causes of the stability of our ideas, or as a debate between the two most radical and implausible of the views regarding justification. So again his idea-constructionist seems to be of little interest to the philosopher or anyone but a few radicals in the science wars.

Constructed Objects

Having devoted considerable attention to Hacking's account of the idea-constructionist project, we should now turn to consider object-construction. Hacking's work on the social dynamics that produce certain kinds of people is important; his historically nuanced discussion of social categorization in, for example, the "helping professions," provides rich resources for thinking about how the social world comes to be as it is (Hacking 1986, 1991, 1992, 1995b, 1999). This work finds a place in his discussion of social construction under the rubric of "object construction." Moreover, object constructionism has, I believe, more to offer the metaphysician than we found in the idea-constructionist project.

According to Hacking's account of object-construction, some objects, in particular some objects that we might not expect to be, are the product of social-historical forces. What are some examples? Possibly the self (Hacking 1999, pp. 14–16); more plausibly, on Hacking's view, people of *certain kinds*. What kinds? Women refugees, child viewers of television, child abusers, schizophrenics. The key to understanding this claim is what Hacking calls *interactive kinds* (Hacking 1999, pp. 32, 102–105).

> The "woman refugee" [as a kind of classification] can be called an "inter-active kind" because it interacts with things of that kind, namely people, including individual women refugees, who can become aware of how they are classified and modify their behavior accordingly. (Hacking 1999, p. 32)

The classification "quark," in contrast, is an *indifferent kind*: "Quarks are not aware that they are quarks and are not altered simply by being classified as quarks" (Hacking 1999, p. 32). As Hacking elaborates the idea of an interactive kind it becomes clear that the interaction he has in mind happens through the awareness of the thing classified, though is typically mediated by the "larger matrix of institutions and practices surrounding this classification" (Hacking 1999, p. 103; also pp. 31–2, 103–106).

So, for example, the idea or classification "woman refugee" is a socially constructed idea (along the lines we considered in the previous sections); but this classification occurs within a matrix of social institutions that has a significant effect on individuals. Thus, Hacking argues, the individuals so-affected are themselves socially constructed "as a certain kind of person" (Hacking 1999, p. 11). For example, if a particular woman is not classified as a woman refugee,

> she may be deported, or go into hiding, or marry to gain citizenship. . . . She needs to become a woman refugee in order to stay in Canada; she learns what characteristics to establish, knows how to live her life. By living that life, she evolves, becomes a certain kind of person [a woman refugee]. And so it may make sense to say that the very individuals and their experiences are constructed within the matrix surrounding the classification "women refugees." (Hacking 1999, p. 11)

To understand Hacking's view of "object construction," the first point to note is that our classificatory schemes, at least in social contexts, may do more than just map preexisting groups of individuals; rather our attributions have the power to both establish and reinforce groupings that may eventually come to "fit" the classifications. In an earlier essay, drawing on Hacking's work, I referred to this as "discursive" construction.[6]

> *discursive construction:* something is discursively constructed just in case it is (to a significant extent) the way it is because of what is attributed to it or how it is classified. (Haslanger 2012 [1995], p. 99)

Admittedly, the idea here is quite vague (e.g., how much is "a significant extent"?). However, social construction in this sense is ubiquitous. Each of us is socially constructed in this sense because we are (to a significant extent) the individuals we are today as a result of what has been attributed (and self-attributed) to us. For example, being classified as an able-bodied female from birth has profoundly affected the paths available to me in life and the sort of person I have become.

Note, however, that to say that an entity is "discursively constructed" is not to say that language or discourse brings a material object into existence de novo. Rather something in existence comes to have—partly as a result of having been categorized in a certain way—a set of features that qualify it as a member of a certain kind or sort. My having been categorized as a female at birth (and consistently since then) has been a factor in how I've been viewed and treated; these views and treatments have, in turn, played an important causal role in my

---

[6] Note that a discourse, and so discursive construction, will involve more than spoken language. See Fraser (1992). For a clear explanation of one feminist appropriation of Foucault's notion of "discourse," see also Scott (1988).

becoming gendered a woman. Having been categorized as a "widow," Christiana was forced to endure harsh rituals that disrupted her family (her children were hired out as servants) and caused her to become seriously ill.[7] Widows in many parts of the developing world are denied basic human rights, for example, they are often stripped of property, subjected to violence, and face systematic discrimination in custom and law. In a context where widowhood is associated with certain material and social conditions that are imposed after the death of one's husband, it is plausible to say that widows constitute a social group or kind, and that one's being a widow, that is, being a member of that social kind or sort, is a result of social forces: Christiana's being a widow (in a sense that entails suffering the social and material deprivations), is a result of her having been categorized as a widow in a matrix where that categorization carries substantial weight.

One might resist this description of things on several counts. To begin, one might object that Christiana's fate was caused not by being *categorized* as a widow but by her husband's death. Admittedly, it is misleading to say that it was the *categorization* alone that made her a widow; but likewise it is misleading to suggest that it was the death alone. (Note that if the husband didn't actually die, but is thought to have died, the effects of being categorized as a widow might be the same as if he actually died.) The cause of her misfortune was his death in a social matrix where the death, or presumed death, of one's husband signals, at least ordinarily, a debilitating change in social status. Can we be clearer on both the source and the product of the construction?

Hacking is especially interested in a certain kind of object construction, namely, construction works by the social context providing *concepts* that frame the *self-understanding* and *intentions* of the constructed agent. In cases like this, agents incorporate (often consciously) socially available classifications into their intentional agency and sense of self; but as their self-understanding evolves, the meaning of those classifications evolves with them. This forms a "feedback loop" (hence the term: 'interactive kinds') between what we might think of as objective and subjective stances with respect to the classification. Hacking's paradigm

---

[7] Christiana's story was reported on http://www.womenforwomen.org/ in 2002. The story has now been replaced by other more recent examples.

For more information on Widowhood Practices, see also EWD (Empowering Widows in Development): http://www.widowsrights.org/index.htm. According to the EWD literature, "In widowhood, a woman joins a category of women among the most marginalized, and invisible. There is little research to inform public opinion or goad governments and the international community to action Widows hardly figure in the literature on poverty or development.

See also the Widows' Development Organization (WiDO), Nigeria: http://www.widoafrica. org/. However, harsh treatment of and ritualized oppression of widows is not specific to Africa, see: http://www.womenaction.org/ungass/caucus/widows.html.

examples concern the labeling of various mental illnesses: multiple personality disorder, autism, and posttraumatic stress disorder. Individuals are diagnosed with such illnesses; treatment plans are developed; their self-understanding is modified. In some cases groups of those diagnosed develop support groups, communities, and political movements. As their self-understanding and behavior changes, however, the diagnosis and patient profile must evolve to take this into account.

To emphasize the importance of the agent's active awareness in this process, we might call this "discursive *identity* construction." This is a construction of *kinds* of people because (at least according to Hacking) people fall into certain kinds depending on their identities, where "identity" is understood as a psychological notion intended to capture one's self-understanding and the intentional framework employed in action. Through being categorized as a widow, Christiana comes to think of herself as a widow, to act as a widow, to live as a widow, that is, she becomes a certain kind of person. Hacking would have us say that she has been constructed "as a widow." We might unpack this as: her self-understanding as a widow (and pattern of her actions conforming to this understanding) is the result of having been classified as a widow. No doubt this is an important claim: that certain identities and ways of life come into existence and evolve in response to social and theoretical categorization (especially categorization that emerges in psychology and social work) has important social and political implications (Hacking 1995, esp. chs. 14–15). But at the same time it isn't entirely surprising that how people think about themselves is influenced by what vocabularies they are given. Is there something more behind the idea of object construction?

Reflecting on Christiana's widowhood reveals that Hacking's emphasis on the construction of "identities" is overly narrow in several respects. Note first that the notion of *kind* in philosophy has several different uses. On one use it is meant to capture a classification of things by essence: things fall into kinds based on their essence, and each thing falls only into one kind. On this view, horses constitute a kind because they share an equine essence, but red things don't constitute a kind because apples, t-shirts, and sunsets don't share an essence. However, on a more common use, the term 'kind' is used as equivalent to "type" or "sort" or "grouping." So far I've been using the term 'kind' in the latter sense and will continue to do so. Of course, there are many ways to sort people into groups. One way is in terms of their (psychological) "identity." Other ways include: by appearance, ancestry, religion, neighborhood, income, nationality, parental status, even by insurance carrier or long distance phone service. If we are exploring the ways in which categorization can have an impact on what sort of person we are, then its impact on our "identities" is one thing to look at. But if we are concerned with the ways in which categorization can cause or perpetuate

injustice, then it will be useful to look at effects that aren't necessarily internalized in the way that Hacking suggests, that is, effects of classifications that
aren't used to frame our intentions and don't come to be part of our self-
understandings. In moving away from an emphasis on the psychological we are
also in a position to rethink the sources of construction and to expand them
beyond a narrow range of "discourse" that focuses on concepts and language to
other aspects of the social matrix.

Christiana's husband dies. The death, at some level, is a biological event. That
it was Christiana's *husband* who died, is, of course, a social matter, for marriage
is a social institution. What about Christiana's becoming a widow? This is more
complicated still, for the meaning of "widowhood" varies across social groups.
Social constructionists interested in the impact of categorization on individuals
are usually interested not only in the nominal classification "widow" or "wife"
(etc.), but also in the system or matrix of practices and institutions that create
"thick" or "robust" social positions, that is, social positions that entail a broad
range of norms, expectations, obligations, entitlements, and so on. It is one
thing to have one's husband die; it is another thing to be socially positioned as a
"widow" in a community where widowhood is a subordinated status.

The distinction between "thick" and "thin" social positions I'm relying on
deserves more attention than I can devote to it here. However, the basic idea is
that some social positions carry with them more demanding norms, expectations, and obligations than others; some carry more privileging entitlements
and opportunities than others. "Thin" social positions carry very little social
weight. "Thick" social positions can empower or disempower the groups
standing in those positions. Being a widow in the contemporary United States
is a much thinner social position than being a widow in, say, the region where
Christiana lives.

Given the norms and expectations that constitute the position of widow in
some contexts, women who lose their husbands are disempowered. Typically in
contexts where a group is systematically mistreated, there are explanations and
rationalizations of the mistreatment. For example, in some traditions, because a
widow has special connection to the deceased she is considered unclean and
must go into ritual seclusion. She may not touch herself, even to bathe or feed
herself. She relies on older widows to care for her. Initially she may be given no
clothes or only "rags"; eventually she must wear special clothes of mourning. If
she refuses (as some Christians do) to participate in the rituals, she is, in effect,
"excommunicated" from the village: the villagers are prohibited from communicating with her or engaging in any commerce with her (Korieh 1996, chs. 2, 3).

Needless to say, someone whose belongings are taken from her, is dressed in
rags, and is denied the opportunity to bathe and feed herself will likely appear
"unclean." In this case, the widow's supposed metaphysical uncleanliness is the
justification for the rituals that result in her physical uncleanliness and social

alienation (she may not touch herself, even to bathe, *because* she is unclean). Although her eventual condition may itself seem evidence for the rightness of the treatment, of course it is simply evidence for its effectiveness.

In such contexts the social constructionist is concerned to argue that the thick social position of "widow" is not naturally or metaphysically justified, that her appearance is not evidence of the rightness of the rituals, that the practices structured apparently as a response to the condition of "widowhood" actually create the condition. (On this sort of self-fulfilling ideology more generally, see Geuss 1981, pp. 14–15.) Although there may be independent social reasons, to maintain rituals in spite of false natural or metaphysical assumptions underlying them, usually the social constructionist's point is to argue that the rituals or practices in question are unjust and should not be maintained in their current form and that the supposed metaphysical or natural justification for them is misguided.

This example of widowhood is intended to show that there is something wrong with seeing object construction as a process that primarily works with and on ideas. On Hacking's account, object construction starts with a socially available concept or classification that is incorporated into an individual's self-understanding. The concept is then modified as her self-understanding evolves and ultimately the changes force a reconceptualization of the classification by others. This is an important and interesting phenomenon. But focusing on this process makes it seem that the impact of social forces on us and the locus of social change is primarily cognitive: social categories are offered to us that we internalize and modify, offering back a revised classification that others then adjust to (or not). Disrupt the classifications and you disrupt the social structure.

Hacking of course allows that ideas occur in matrices, so there are structural and material elements playing a role in making the classification concrete. But a matrix is a complex, usually unwieldy, and somewhat haphazard collection of institutions and practices together with their material manifestations. Narratives and scripts accompany the practices; rules are part of the institutions. But one may be profoundly affected by the matrix without accepting the narrative, following the script, or even knowing the rules. A Christian widow in a non-Christian context may refuse to "identify" as a widow or to participate in the local widowhood practices. Nevertheless, the status of widow is, without her acquiescence, imposed upon her. I would propose that she is, as much as the more compliant woman, socially positioned as a widow, that is, a member of the social kind *widow*.

Moreover, the matrix may shape one's life without one's falling into any of its articulated classifications. Consider Christiana's children who were sent to live with others as servants after she was widowed. There may be no named category or social classification: "child of a widow," but there is nonetheless a social position created by widowhood practices for the fatherless children. And it might be an important political move to make this category explicit, to name it, to argue that the severe economic consequences of a father's death are not "necessary" or "natural," to empower the children within it, and lobby for a reconceptualization of their entitlements.

So although language and explicit classification can play an important role in identifying groups and organizing social practices around groups, and although group membership can become an important part of one's self-understanding, it is also important to note how social matrices have an impact on groups of individuals without the group being an explicit or articulated category and without the members of the group internalizing the narrative and the norms associated with it. In other words, we need a way of thinking about "object construction" or better, the formation of social kinds, that acknowledges the causal impact of classification, but also gives due weight to the unintended and unconceptualized impact of practices.

In summary, in thinking about the ways that classification can make a difference (pun intended) it is important not to focus so narrowly on "identities" that we lose sight of the ways that classification can affect us without influencing our self-understanding or without our even being aware of it. We need also to account for the ways that social practices can constitute "thick" social positions without explicit categorization being, at least in the first instance, a primary factor in creating or maintaining the position. This suggests at least a two-dimensional model is required to understand this form of social construction: one dimension represents the degree to which explicit classification is a causal factor in bringing about the features that make for membership in the kind (as opposed to the features being an unintended byproduct of social practices); the other dimension represents the degree to which the kind in question is defined by "identification" with the social position.[8] For example, widowhood in some parts of the world is an explicit category that has an impact on creating and maintaining a "thick" social position; yet one need not identify with that position in order to be positioned as a widow (one might be positioned as a widow while rebelling against it). Child of a widow is an implicit category, though again one need not identify with that position in order to occupy it. Other positions,

---

[8] Thus far I've been assuming that the kinds we're concerned with correspond with "thick" social positions, that is, positions defined within a network of social relations and typically entail a range of norms, expectations, obligations, entitlements, and so on. But one might argue that not all social kinds are like this and, more significantly, our classifications and practices can have a significant impact on the world that extends well beyond this. Hacking himself has used the example of classifying some microbes as pathogenic; this classification can have a profound effect on the kinds of microbes so classified. One might argue, then, that certain bacteria are socially, even discursively, constructed insofar as they are the result of mutations in previous bacteria that we classified as pathogenic and treated with antibiotics. Those interested in the subtle (and not so subtle!) effects of humans on ecosystems might have use for speaking of social construction in this broad sense.

however, involve greater agency in conformity to the practices defining them; for example, the category of student, refugee, or voter. Even here, though, we should distinguish conformity to the practices, and acceptance of the assumptions behind them. For example, a refugee may conform to the rules defining refugee status, without coming to think of herself *as a refugee,* or intentionally acting *as a refugee.*

In the previous section we saw how the social world had a causal impact on our ideas; in this section we've considered how the social world (including our ideas and classifications) has an impact on things to form them into kinds. The—perhaps by now obvious—point is that ideas and objects interact in complex ways and transform each other over time. Broadly speaking, social construction is about this complex interaction. Thus far it may appear that social construction is all about causation (this, after all, seems to be Hacking's view); but there remain questions about kinds and classification that have not yet been addressed.

Social Kinds

One of the important messages of Hacking's work on social construction is that we must distinguish *what* is allegedly being constructed, namely ideas or objects, in order to avoid confusion. In other words, he has focused on distinguishing different *products* of construction, but in every case construction is a causal *process.* But we should also be careful to distinguish different ways in which things are constructed, in particular, different ways things might "depend for their existence" on a social context.

Hacking believes that gender is a perfect example of a case in which the idea and the object are both socially constructed:

> There are many examples of this multi-leveled reference of the X in "the social construction of X." It is plain in the case of gender. What is constructed? The idea of gendered human beings (an idea), and gendered human beings themselves (people); language; institutions; bodies. Above all, "the experiences of being female." One great interest of gender studies is less how any one of these types of entity was constructed than how the constructions intertwine and interact. (Hacking 1999, p. 28)

Here Hacking suggests that "gender" (in different senses) is both an idea-construction and an object-construction. Gender is an idea-construction because the *classification* men/women is the contingent result of historical events and forces and does not correspond to and is not stable due to the world's inherent structure. And yet the classifications "woman" and "man" are interactive kinds: gender classifications occur within a complex matrix of institutions and practices, and being classified as a woman (or not) or a man (or not) has a profound effect on an individual, both in terms of the social consequences for her and in terms of her experience and self-understanding. That is, women and men are constructed *as gendered kinds of people.*

Although on Hacking's view the claim that gender is constructed has more than one sense, on both senses it is a causal claim: the point is either a causal claim about the source of our "ideas" of man or woman or a claim about the causes of gendered traits. However, there are contexts in which the claim that gender is socially constructed is not a causal claim; rather the point is constitutive. The point being made is that gender is not a classification scheme based simply on anatomical or biological differences, but should be understood as a system of social categories that can only be defined by reference to a network of social relations. In this case, the concept of gender is introduced as an analytical tool to explain a range of social phenomena, and we evaluate the claim by considering the theoretical usefulness of such a category (Scott 1986).[9] There is room for much debate, not only over the question whether we should employ such a category, but if we do, how we should define it, that is, what social relations (or clusters of social relations) constitute the groups *men* and *women.* The debates here parallel others in social theory: One might debate whether the category "underclass" is useful to explain a wide range of social and cultural phenomena and, if so, how we should define it.

Although Hacking is generous in suggesting that feminist theorists, following Beauvoir, have been important in developing the notion of construction, he suggests that the claim that gender is socially constructed is redundant, and not, at least at this point in time, particularly useful (Hacking 1999, p. 39). Gender is, on any definition, a social phenomenon: "no matter what definition is preferred, the word ['gender'] is used for distinctions among people that are grounded in cultural practices, not biology" (Hacking 1999, p. 39). The point seems to be that if one means by the claim that gender is socially constructed the constitutive claim that gender is a social category, then one's point is no better than a tautology. That the social classifications *men* and *women* are social classifications is redundant. "If gender is, by definition, something essentially social, and if it is constructed, how could its construction be other than social?" (Hacking 1999, p. 39).

---

[9] There are moments when Hacking seems to acknowledge that some forms of construction are not causal but constitutive. I discuss one such passage below (Hacking 1999, p. 39), but his discussion does not reveal an understanding of the distinction. For example, constitutive constructions are treated as "add-on" entities, "the contingent product of the social world" (Hacking 1999, p. 7). This misses the point that a social construction claim may function to challenge the presumed content of our conceptual repertoire and not simply its origins. More on this later.

It is odd that Hacking should frame his rhetorical question this way, for as we've seen, on his view, to say that something is socially constructed is to say that it is, in some way, socially caused. But we should avoid conflating social kinds with things that have social causes. Sociobiologists claim that some social phenomena have biological causes; some feminists claim that some anatomical phenomena have social causes, for example, that height and strength differences between the sexes are caused by a long history of gender norms concerning food and exercise.[10] It is an error to treat the conditions by virtue of which a social entity exists as causing the entity. Consider, for example, what must be the case in order for someone to be a husband in the contemporary United States: A husband is a legally married man. Being a legally married man does not *cause* one to be a husband; it is just what being a husband consists in.

It is also significant that not all social kinds are obviously social. Sometimes it is assumed that the conditions for membership in a kind concern only or primarily biological or physical facts. Pointing out that this is wrong can have important consequences. For example, the idea that whether or not a person is White is not simply a matter of their physical features, but concerns their position in a social matrix, has been politically significant, and to many surprising.

To help keep distinct these different ways in which the social can function in construction, let's distinguish:

> *X is socially constructed causally as an F* iff social factors (i.e., *X's* participation in a social matrix) play a significant role in causing *X* to have those features by virtue of which it counts as an *F*.

> *X is socially constructed constitutively as an F* iff *X* is of a kind or sort *F* such that in defining what it is to be *F*, we must make reference to social factors (or: such that in order for *X* to be *F*, *X* must exist within a social matrix that constitutes *F's*).

In summary, social constructionists are often not just interested in the causes of our ideas and the social forces at work on objects, but are interested in how best to understand a given kind, and in particular whether it is a natural or social kind. Because on Hacking's view social constructionisms are concerned with causal claims, it doesn't capture what's interesting in claiming that something is, perhaps surprisingly, a social kind.

---

[10] For example, recent race theorists such as Lucius Outlaw suggest that race is a social category but caused by natural forces (Outlaw 1996). Hacking himself also mentions Hirschfeld, but really muddles the debates over race and essentialism (Hacking 1999, pp. 16–18).

Natural Structures and Social Structures

How should we construe the constructionist project of arguing that a particular kind is a social kind? What could be interesting or radical about such a project? Is Hacking right that it is not useful to point out that a social kind is a social kind?

I am a White woman What does this mean? What makes this claim apt? Suppose we pose these questions to someone who is not a philosopher, someone not familiar with the academic social constructionist literature. A likely response will involve mention of my physical features: reproductive organs, skin color, and so on. The gender and race constructionists will reject this response and will argue that what makes the claim apt concerns the social relations in which I stand. In effect, the constructionist proposes a different and (at least in some contexts) surprising set of truth conditions for the claim, truth conditions that crucially involve social factors. On this construal, the important social constructionist import in Beauvoir's claim that "one is not born but rather becomes a woman," is not *pace* Hacking (Hacking 1999, p 7) that one is caused to be feminine by social forces; rather, the important insight was that being a woman is not an anatomical matter but a social matter; for Beauvoir in particular "Here is to be found the basic trait of woman: she is the Other in a totality of which the two components are necessary to one another" (Beauvoir 1989, p. xxii; also 1989, pp. xv–xxxiv).

This project of challenging the purported truth conditions for the application of a concept I call a "debunking" project. A debunking project typically attempts to show that a category or classification scheme that appears to track a group of individuals defined by a set of physical or metaphysical conditions is better understood as capturing a group that occupies a certain (usually "thick") social position. Hacking is right that the goal is often to challenge the appearance of inevitability of the category, to suggest that if social conditions changed, it would be possible to do away with the category. But an important first step is to make the category visible *as a social category*. This sometimes requires a rather radical change in our thinking. For example, elsewhere, following in Beauvoir's now long tradition, I have argued for the following definitions of man and woman:

S is a woman iff

(i) *S* is regularly and for the most part observed or imagined to have certain bodily features presumed to be evidence of a female's biological role in reproduction;

(ii) that *S* has these features marks *S* within the dominant ideology of *S*'s society as someone who ought to occupy certain kinds of social position that are in fact subordinate (and so motivates and justifies *S*'s occupying such a position); and

(iii) the fact that *S* satisfies (i) and (ii) plays a role in *S*'s systematic subordination, that is, *along some dimension, S*'s social position is oppressive, and *S*'s satisfying (i) and (ii) plays a role in that dimension of subordination.

S is a man iff

(i) *S* is regularly and for the most part observed or imagined to have certain bodily features presumed to be evidence of a male's biological role in reproduction;

(ii) that *S* has these features marks *S* within the dominant ideology of *S*'s society as someone who ought to occupy certain kinds of social position that are in fact privileged (and so motivates and justifies *S*'s occupying such a position); and

(iii) the fact that *S* satisfies (i) and (ii) plays a role in *S*'s systematic privilege, that is, *along some dimension, S*'s social position is privileged, and *S*'s satisfying (i) and (ii) plays a role in that dimension of privilege.

(Haslanger 2012 [2000])

These definitions are proposed, not as reconstructions of our commonsense understanding of the terms *man* and *woman* but as providing a better explanation of how gender works.

What does this mean? There are two clusters of questions that should be distinguished. The first is whether employing a classification *C* (e.g., a distinction between the two groups as defined above) is theoretically or politically useful. The second is whether the theoretical understanding of *C* captures an ordinary social category, and so whether it is legitimate or warranted to claim that the proposed definitions reveal the commitments of our ordinary discourse. Those who hold the view that we have privileged access to the meanings of our terms will be suspicious of any attempt to provide radical analyses of our discourse. However, such semantic confidence is not warranted. It is broadly recognized that we often don't know exactly what we are talking about—at least not in all senses of "what we're talking about"—and that reference can be successful even under circumstances of semantic ignorance. I, like Putnam, cannot distinguish between beeches and elms. But that does not prevent my words "beech" and "elm" from referring to the correct species of tree (Putnam 1975b, 1973). If, however, there is no avoiding some form of semantic externalism, then it is perfectly reasonable to suppose that familiar terms that we ordinarily think capture physical kinds in fact capture social kinds.

To see how this might work, consider an early (simplified) version of scientific essentialism (Putnam 1975b, 1973; Kripke 1980). The term 'water' may refer to the natural kind *water* even in contexts where no one is in a position to say what all and only instances of water have in common, for reference can be fixed by ostending certain paradigm instances with the intention to refer to the kind shared by the paradigms. The ordinary speaker might not be in a position to say what the kind in question is, or even identify the paradigms (I cannot point out a beech tree). Rather, we rely on a "semantic division of labor": I intend to mean by "beech" what others who are familiar with the paradigms mean, and it is up to the "experts" to determine what kind the paradigms share. Putnam and others assumed that the relevant "experts" would be *natural scientists* (the issue was framed as a question about the use of natural kind terms), and that the kind sought by the experts would be the *essence* of the paradigms.[11] However, we need not accept these naturalistic and essentialist assumptions. In my mouth, the term 'underclass' refers to a social kind even though I am not in a position to define the kind. I defer to certain social scientists to refine the relevant range of paradigms and to provide a social theory that gives explanatory weight to this category and determines its extent. If I come to learn the currently accepted definition of 'underclass' and believe that it has problematic implications or presuppositions, then I may need to stop using the term. Note, however, that although in the examples thus far I have supposed that the speaker intends to participate in the semantic division of labor, semantic externalism does not depend on my intention to defer. Even if I think I know perfectly well what arthritis is, when I believe that I have arthritis in my thigh, the content of my belief is determined by experts on joint disorders (Burge 1979).

---

[11] Note that Hacking himself relies on a version of scientific essentialism in clarifying the sense in which, for example, "autism" is a social construct. He argues:

> Now for the bottom line. Someone writes a paper titled "The Social Construction of Childhood Autism." The author could perfectly well maintain that (a) there is probably a definite unknown neuropathology P that is the cause of prototypical and most other examples of what we now call childhood autism; (b) the idea of childhood autism is a social construct that interacts not only with therapists and psychiatrists in their treatments, but also interacts with autistic children themselves, who find the current mode of being autistic a way for themselves to be.
>
> In this case we have several values for the X in the social construction of X = childhood autism; (a) the idea of childhood autism, and what that involves; (b) autistic children, actual human beings, whose way of being is in part constructed. But not (c) the neuropathology P, which ex hypothesi, we are treating as an indifferent kind. A follower of Kripke might call P the essence of autism. For us, the interest would not be in the semantics but the dynamics. How would the discovery of P affect how autistic children and their families conceive of themselves; how would it affect their behavior? (Hacking 1999, p. 121)

Hacking, however, inherits the naturalistic bias of the early scientific essentialists in allowing that there may be an underlying kind that the natural scientist discovers, but in ignoring the possibility that in other cases there are social kinds underlying our discourse that the social scientist discovers.

Debunking constructionists can be understood as relying on a kind of semantic externalism. We use the terms 'Black,' 'White,' 'Hispanic,' and 'Asian.' But can an ordinary speaker say what it is that all and only White people have in common? We can identify a range of quite different cases. Contemporary race theorists have argued that the cases don't fall within a meaningful biological kind. One conclusion, then, is to maintain that the term 'White race' is vacuous, that the predicate "is a White person" has no extension (Appiah 1996). The social constructionist about race will claim, however, that the cases share membership in a social kind. This is not to claim that they all share an essence, so are all essentially White, but that our best social theory finds the category useful and provides an account of what the cases have in common (Haslanger 2012 [2000]). The goal is not *just* to find something that all and only the cases have in common. Rather, it is to find a theoretically valuable kind that captures more or less the usual range of samples or paradigms. Both scientific and social theory can tell us that what we thought was a paradigm case of something doesn't fall within the kind it proposes as the best extension of our term. Whether we go with the theory or our pretheoretic beliefs about the extension is a judgment call of the sort made in the process of finding reflective equilibrium.

Of course, social constructionists often make great efforts to distance themselves from the kind of realism that is commonly associated with scientific essentialism. Scientific essentialism is associated with many views in metaphysics, epistemology, and philosophy of language that are not part of the debunking constructionist's agenda. For example, it is open to the constructionist to maintain that theoretical commitment to certain kinds or categories is at least partly a political choice, especially in the context of social theory. This brings us back to some of the issues raised in the discussion of object construction.

Recall the widow Christiana and her children. As noted above, there may not be an explicit or named social category *child of widow,* yet in developing a social theory for the society in question, it may be important to introduce such a category in order to understand the social and economic forces that result in the outcomes one is concerned to explain. What outcomes one is interested in explaining, what social forces one postulates, what form of explanation one seeks, are matters that are influenced by constitutive and contextual values (Anderson 1995). Moreover, the theoretical decisions may have political repercussions. One may, for example, introduce a category for *child of widow* in order to point out injustice and argue for changes to existing practices and institutions.

More complicated are decisions about how to theorize social categories for which there are explicit terms, for example, widow, Hispanic, woman, middle-class. There will be many cases in which what is common to the range of paradigms could be captured by several different theoretical models or several different classifications within a model. For example, consider 'widow.' In considering widows where widowhood is a "thick" social position and involves practices of subordination, one might choose to define the term 'widow' (or the corresponding term in the native language) thinly to mean simply "woman whose husband has died," and to argue that widows need not and should not be treated as they are. Alternatively, one might choose to define the term 'widow' to capture the thick social position—with its associated rituals and deprivations—and to argue that there should be no more widows. A third option would be to seek a middle-ground: to define 'widow' so it is not so tightly bound to the practices of a particular society that we cannot consider the fate of widows across cultures but theorize the category (roughly) as a site of subordination grounded in the loss of standing provided by one's husband, due to his death. Each of these options (and others) will not only have theoretical advantages and disadvantages, but will also have political advantages and disadvantages both locally and more globally.

There are two points to be drawn from this example. First, although typically debunking constructionists will want to "debunk" the assumption that a social category is grounded in or justified by nonsocial (natural or metaphysical) facts, there may also be cases in which the project is to "debunk" the assumption that a thick social category is grounded in and justified by thinly social facts (possibly in conjunction with natural or metaphysical facts). So, one might argue that ("thick") widowhood is a social construct, where the point is that it is wrong to see widows as the social kind consisting of women whose husbands have died, and who for some reason or other come to be poor, childless, and filthy. Rather, the claim would be that the ("thick") condition of widows as poor, childless, and so on, is something that "we"—our institutions and practices—have created. The purpose here would not be to suggest that the ordinary notion of "widow" is wrongly thought to be a natural category, but that the social position of widow is more robustly social than ordinarily thought.

Second, the debunking constructionist may need to respond to the two questions raised above in different ways depending on context: (1) is the classification C useful politically and/or theoretically useful, and (2) should we take the theoretical classification C to capture the commitments of ordinary discourse? How one answers these questions will depend on many factors, including of course theoretical and empirical concerns. But it will also depend on one's broader purposes in theorizing, the political context of one's theorizing, and one's particular position within that context.

Conclusion

Although Hacking's discussion of social construction is valuable and provides insight into the ways in which the notion of construction is often used and misused, there are important constructionist projects he neglects. In particular, he tends to ignore or dismiss the kind of project I've been calling the "debunking" project in which constructionists argue that there is a theoretically important social kind or category that has not been adequately acknowledged, or not been adequately acknowledged to be social. Debunking constructionists may seem to be offering radical and implausible "analyses" of our ordinary concepts, in fact they can be better understood as working within a semantic externalist model that looks to social theory to provide us with an account of our social terms, just as scientific essentialism looks to the physical sciences to provide an account of our naturalistic terms. Debunkers sometimes surprise us, however, in suggesting that what we thought were natural terms are in fact social terms.

There are of course many philosophical issues the debunking constructionist needs to address; the project raises interesting philosophical questions about the relationship between, for example, our everyday understandings of social phenomena and social theory, our everyday understandings of what we mean and what might make our terms apt, the epistemic demands/constraints on theorizing and the political demands/constraints on theorizing. But in raising these questions, debunking constructionism, in contrast, say, to Hacking's "idea-constructionism," is much more philosophically palatable and meaningfully engaged with ongoing work in philosophy in general and metaphysics in particular.

Acknowledgments

Thanks to Roxanne Fay, Rae Langton, Ishani Maitra, Agustin Rayo, Ásta Sveinsdóttir, Kayley Vernallis, and Stephen Yablo for discussion of earlier versions of this chapter. Thanks also to Frederick Schmitt for comments on an earlier draft.

Works cited

Anderson, Elizabeth S. 1995. "Knowledge, Human Interests and Objectivity in Feminist Epistemology." *Philosophical Topics* 23(2): 27–58.
Appiah, K. Anthony. 1996. "Race, Culture, Identity: Misunderstood Connections." In *Color Conscious: The Political Morality of Race*, eds. K. Anthony Appiah and Amy Guttman. Princeton: Princeton University Press, pp. 30–105.
Beauvoir, Simone de. 1989. *The Second Sex*. Translated by H. M. Parshley. New York: Vintage.
Burge, Tyler. 1979. "Individualism and the Mental." In *Midwest Studies in Philosophy* 4: *Studies in Metaphysics*, eds. P. A. French, T. E. Uehling, and H. Wettstein. Minneapolis: University of Minnesota Press, pp. 73–121.
Fraser, Nancy. 1992. "The Uses and Abuses of French Discourse Theories for Feminist Politics." In *Revaluing French Feminism*, eds. Nancy Fraser and Sandra Bartky. Bloomington: Indiana University Press, pp. 177–194.
Geuss, Raymond. 1981. *The Idea of a Critical Theory*. Cambridge: Cambridge University Press.
Hacking, Ian. 1986. "Making Up People." In *Reconstructing Individualism: Autonomy, Individuality and the Self in Western Thought*, edited by T. C. Heller, M. Sosna, and D. E. Wellbery. Stanford, CA: Stanford University Press, pp. 222-236.

————. 1991. "The Making and Moulding of Child Abuse." *Critical Inquiry* 17: 253–88.

————. 1992. "World Making by Kind-Making: Child Abuse for Example." In *How Classification Works: Nelson Goodman among the Social Sciences*, eds. M. Douglas and D. Hull. Edinburgh: Edinburgh University Press, pp. 180–238.

————. 1995. *Rewriting the Soul: Multiple Personality and the Sciences of Memory*. Princeton: Princeton University Press.

————. 1999. *The Social Construction of What?* Cambridge, MA: Harvard University Press.

Haslanger, Sally. 2012 [1995]. "Social Construction: The "Debunking" Project." Chapter 3 of this volume.

————. 2012 [2000]. "Gender and Race: (What) Are They? (What) Do We Want Them To Be?" Chapter 7 of this volume.

Korieh, Chima Jacob. 1996. "Widowhood among the Igbo of Eastern Nigeria." www.uib.no/hi/korieh/chima.html (accessed September 2002).

Kripke, Saul. 1980. *Naming and Necessity*. Cambridge, MA: Harvard University Press.

Longino, Helen. 1980. *Science as Social Knowledge*. Princeton: Princeton University Press.

Outlaw, Lucius. 1996. *On Race and Philosophy*. New York: Routledge.

Putnam, Hilary. 1973. "Meaning and Reference." *The Journal of Philosophy* 70: 699–711.

————. 1975. "The Meaning of 'Meaning'." In *Mind, Language and Reality*. Cambridge: Cambridge University Press, pp. 215–71.

Scott, Joan. 1986. "Gender: A Useful Category of Historical Analysis." *American Historical Review* 91: 1053–75.

————. 1988. "Deconstructing Equality-versus-Difference: Or, The Uses of Poststructuralist Theory for Feminism." *Feminist Studies* 14: 33–50.

4

Feminism in Metaphysics

Negotiating the Natural

Introduction[1]

Metaphysics has never been without critics. Plato's efforts have repeatedly been a target of attack; Hume ranted against the metaphysicians of his day; and one of the founding missions of logical positivism was to show that metaphysical claims are meaningless. More recently, feminist theorists have joined the chorus. To reveal among academic feminists that one's specialization in philosophy is metaphysics is to invite responses of shock, confusion and sometimes dismissal. Once after I gave a presentation at an American Philosophical Association meeting on social construction, a noted senior feminist philosopher approached me and said, "you are clearly very smart, and very feminist, so why are you wasting your time on this stuff?" Academic feminists, for the most part, view metaphysics as a dubious intellectual project, certainly irrelevant and probably worse; and often the further charge is leveled that it has pernicious political implications as well.[2]

Academic feminism has never been without critics either. If academic theorizing is an effort to achieve objective accounts of the world and its parts, and if feminism is a political movement guided by substantive moral and political values, then, some have suggested, the idea of academic feminism is oxymoronic.[3] Philosophers have been especially keen to discount the relevance of

[1] For valuable discussion on related topics, many thanks to Elizabeth Anderson, Richard Holton, Rae Langton, Mary Kate McGowan, and Sam Ruhmkorff. For that and comments on an earlier draft, thanks to Miranda Fricker, Jennifer Hornsby and Stephen Yablo. Special thanks to Miranda and Jen for their patience and excellent editorial advice.

[2] E.g., N. Fraser and L. Nicholson, "Social Criticism without Philosophy: An Encounter Between Feminism and Post-modernism," in L. Nicholson, ed., *Feminism/Postmodernism* (New York: Routledge, 1990), pp. 19–38; J. Butler, "Contingent Foundations," in J. Butler and J. Scott, eds., *Feminists Theorize the Political* (London and New York: Routledge, 1992), pp. 3–21.

[3] E.g., S. Haack, "Epistemological Reflections of an Old Feminist," *Reason Papers* 18 (Fall 1993), 31–43.

feminist thinking to research outside of normative moral and political theory, and the idea that feminism might have something to contribute to metaphysics is often regarded as ridiculous.[4] Reality is what it is, and the metaphysician's goal should be to discover what it is apart from the social and political values we bring to it.

These representations of metaphysics and of academic feminism are distorted and presuppose cartoon versions of contemporary research in the two areas. Yet even if we allow that there are more subtle understandings of metaphysics and feminist inquiry, the questions remain: is there a place within feminist inquiry for metaphysics? Does feminist theory have anything to offer metaphysicians? My goal in this chapter is to begin to answer these questions, with full awareness that both subject areas are too large, too multifaceted, and too contested to capture comprehensively. The best I can hope to do is make clear what facet of each I'm considering as we proceed. At the start I should also make clear that my discussion will focus exclusively on Anglo-American metaphysics and Anglo-American feminism.

With this limitation in mind, we need to ask: what is metaphysics, anyway? Oversimplifying considerably, it can be organized into three main parts: (i) A study of what there is, or what is real. (This area is also known as *ontology*.) For example, Are minds distinct from bodies? In addition to physical objects, does the world include properties, natural kinds, universals, essences? (ii) A study of the basic concepts employed in understanding ourselves and the world, for example existence, predication, identity, causation, necessity, (iii) A study of the presuppositions of inquiry, or first principles.

There has been significant feminist work addressing many substantive ontological issues: personal identity, mind/body, free will.[5] The question I will focus on here is how feminism might contribute to the more abstract issues in metaphysics. What would it mean to have a feminist theory of causation or modality? Can feminist inquiry help us discover the basic categories of being?

Feminists themselves disagree about whether and how feminist inquiry might engage with metaphysics. It is important to distinguish at least two different reasons behind their attitude of suspicion. Some have argued that the questions and claims of certain dominant metaphysical theories are male-biased, and recommend less male-biased replacements; whereas others have argued that feminists have good reason to reject the project of metaphysics altogether. Feminist critique of the second sort resists the temptation to engage in

---

[4] E.g., J. Searle, "Rationality and Realism: What is at Stake?," *Daedalus* 122 (1993), 55–83

[5] See, e.g., Susan James, "Feminism in Philosophy of Mind: The Question of Personal Identity," and Naomi Scheman, "Feminism in Philosophy of Mind: Against Physicalism," both in Miranda Fricker & Jennifer Hornsby (eds.), *The Cambridge Companion to Feminism in Philosophy*. (Cambridge: Cambridge University Press, 2000), pp 29–48 and pp. 49–67.

any metaphysical theorizing; though, as we shall see, metaphysical issues are not completely ignored.

I shall elaborate these critiques a bit further in the following sections, offering some examples. Both forms of critique, I believe, raise important questions, but are also flawed. After considering these flaws I will suggest some ways to build on their strengths to develop yet another approach to feminist metaphysics.

Androcentric versus Gynocentric Metaphysics

In the 1980s there was a surge of feminist work that looked behind the debates over concrete political issues such as sexual violence, reproductive rights, and equal pay, to consider how sexist beliefs are embedded in our theorizing.[6] Some of this work was motivated by the awareness that (supposed) reasoned debate was not always an effective tool for combating sexism because its epistemological and metaphysical assumptions were preventing certain points of view from being heard or taken seriously. It became clear that science and philosophy are at least as prone to sexism as any other social institution; what's worse, they often provide the tools to buttress the institutions that are the more immediate problem.

Blatantly sexist theories—ones that assert women's inferiority to men, claim that women's subordination is good or appropriate, or recommend gender-stereotyped behavior—are not absent from philosophy. But feminist theorizing in this period also raised questions about the less obvious ways that philosophical theorizing contributes to women's subordination. One important form of such critique is directed at *androcentrism*. Very briefly, a theory is androcentric if it takes males or masculinity to be the norm against which females and femininity are considered deviant,[7] or if it considers its subject matter from the point of view of men and simply ignores women or women's perspective.[8] Let me mention just two sample arguments that raised the question of androcentric bias in metaphysics.[9]

In their paper, "How Can Language be Sexist?," Merrill and Jaakko Hintikka argue that an ontology of discrete particulars is biased towards males.

[6] E.g., S. Harding and M. Hintikka, eds., *Discovering Reality* (Dordrecht: D, Reidel, 1983).

[7] As is common, I use the terms 'male' and 'female' to refer to the two standard anatomical sexes, 'man' and 'woman' to refer to the two standard genders (understood as social positions), and 'masculine' and 'feminine' for the norms associated with the genders.

[8] See E. Anderson, "Feminist Epistemology: An Interpretation and Defense," *Hypatia* 10 (Summer 1995), 58–59.

[9] Psychoanalytic feminism offers another sort of androcentric critique not discussed here. See, e.g., J. Flax, "Political Philosophy and the Patriarchal Unconscious," in Harding and Hintikka, eds., *Discovering Reality*.

[W]omen are generally more sensitive to, and likely to assign more importance to, relational characteristics (e.g. interdependencies) than males, and less likely to think in terms of independent discrete units. Conversely, males generally prefer what is separable and manipulatable. If we put a premium on the former features, we are likely to end up with one kind of cross-identification and one kind of ontology, if we follow the guidance of the latter considerations, we end up with a different one.[10]

Hintikka and Hintikka go on to point out that "Western philosophical thought" has emphasized art ontology of discrete objects "individuated by their intrinsic or essential (non-relational) properties," and has been "unfavorably disposed towards cross-identification by means of functional or other relational characteristics." They ask, "Is it to go too far to suspect a bias here? It seems to us that a bias is unmistakable in recent philosophical semantics and ontology."[11] In response they recommend Jaakko Hintikka's contextually based methods for cross-identification.

Iris Young argues in her paper "Pregnant Embodiment: Subjectivity and Alienation" that attention to the phenomenology of pregnancy "jeopardizes dualistic metaphysics altogether. There remains no basis for preserving the mutual exclusivity of the categories of subject and object, inner and outer, I and world."[12] For example, "Pregnancy challenges the integration of my bodily experience by rendering fluid the boundary between what is within, myself, and what is outside, separate. I experience my insides as the space of another, yet my own body."[13] Pregnancy does not only make vivid the "externality of the inside,"[14] however, but also challenges a disembodied conception of agency based in the "dichotomy of subject and object." In the experience of pregnancy, Young argues, awareness of the body need not be in tension with the accomplishment of one's aims. "The pregnant woman experiences herself as a source and participant in a creative process. Though she does not plan and direct it, neither does it merely wash over her; rather she *is* this process, this change."[15]

These critiques have in common the idea that metaphysical theorizing as we've known it tends to draw uncritically on experiences and patterns of thought

[10] M. Hintikka and J. Hintikka, "How Can Language Be Sexist?" in Harding and Hintikka, eds., *Discovering Reality*, p. 146.

[11] Ibid., p. 146.

[12] I. Young, "Pregnant Embodiment," in her *Throwing Like a Girl and Other Essays* (Indianapolis: Indiana University Press, 1990), p. 161; see also I. Young, "Breasted Experience," in *Throwing Like a Girl*, pp. 189–209.

[13] "Pregnant Embodiment," p. 163.

[14] Ibid., p. 163.

[15] Ibid., p. 167.

that are characteristically male or masculine, and ignores or devalues those that are characteristically female or feminine, in a context where there is no reason to think that the male or masculine perspective deserves to be privileged. This charge of androcentrism is not simply a political charge, but concerns the epistemic credentials of a theory. If men and women do differ systematically in their perspectives on the basic features of reality (let's call these proposed perspectives 'androcentric' and 'gynocentric' perspectives), and if a particular metaphysical theory has reflected only the androcentric perspective, then it is right to charge it with male-bias. Likewise, theorizing entirely from a gynocentric perspective would not be warranted unless there were grounds for privileging a gynocentric perspective on the issue. Perhaps for this reason, this genre of feminist critique has been more effective in revealing the limitations of mainstream views than in defending gynocentric ontologies.

Note, however, that many feminists reject this form of critique. In the first place, it is very difficult to establish convincingly systematic differences between the perspectives of men and women on the kinds of phenomena in question. As feminist philosophers of science have often pointed out, research "documenting" the differences between men and women along stereotypical lines has often been credited with accomplishing much more than the evidence warrants because it tells us what we've been taught to expect.[16] Because the stereotypes also serve socially to keep women in their place (marking those who fail to fit the stereotype as deviant), this research requires heightened scrutiny.[17]

One major difficulty in establishing that there are systematic differences between men's and women's perspectives is that men and women are so tremendously varied as individuals, and across race, class, culture and historical period. As a result it becomes very difficult to describe the experiences of women "as a group." Consider Young's reports of the phenomenology of pregnancy. The problematic of embodied agency that her experience eloquently refutes is actually culturally specific. It is not hard to imagine a different scenario in which the extent of agency involved in being pregnant is simply not an issue, or in which the mother does not experience herself as an agent in the process. This might occur either because the cultural meanings of pregnancy do not engage the issue of agency, or because of the individual history of the woman or the pregnancy in question. A single experience of the breakdown of subject/object or inner/outer

---

[16] See C. Tavris, *The Mismeasure of Woman* (New York: Simon and Schuster, 1992).

[17] Note, e.g., that Hintikka and Hintikka cite as the basis for their claim about cognitive differences between the sexes a study on children in second to fourth grades that was already twenty years old when they published their paper. When they generalize the result to "women," they cite a paper that still only surveys research on children, and moreover, questions their empirical premise: E. E. Maccoby, "Sex Differences in Intellectual Functioning," in E. E. Maccoby, ed., *The Development of Sex Differences* (Stanford: Stanford University Press, 1966), esp. pp. 27, 41–42.

in pregnancy (such as Young's) can be enough to challenge the reigning metaphysical dichotomies. But in such a case it is difficult to charge the dominant view with *androcentrism* if the claim is only that it is insensitive to the experiences of some pregnant women. In short, we need to ask: what exactly is a "gynocentric" perspective? Must a "gynocentric" perspective capture the experiences of all or most women? And if not all women have access to a "gynocentric" perspective, do efforts to describe such a perspective rely on problematic normative stereotypes about how women *should* be?

It is plausible that gender is a factor affecting one's perspective on the world. But if gender itself is a culturally variable phenomenon, then it may not be possible to capture the mediating force of gender in terms of a shared content to be found in women's thought. This being said, however, it would be wrong to neglect the failings of a theory that systematically ignored or devalued a female or feminine perspective, as it appears in context. Consider for example a context where women are socialized to be sensitive readers of emotions and men are socialized to be emotionally insensitive. A theory constructed in that context (by those who are socialized in this way) that denied the reality of emotion would be at least *contextually androcentric*. In making the charge of "contextual" androcentrism, however, care must always be taken to look carefully at the potentially complex meanings of gender in the context, as well as variations across contexts.

To sustain a distinctively gynocentric metaphysics, one would have to argue that either having a female body, or being socialized as a female, provides one with better access to reality.[18] However, those who are committed to the idea that there are distinctive (and competing?) androcentric and gynocentric perspectives, and yet are wary of privileging any perspective, may opt instead for the idea that neither men nor women know what is real because it is impossible to overcome the distorting effects of gender (and other social factors) on our thinking. This is the direction Jane Flax takes:

> To the degree that thought depends upon and is articulated (to ourselves and others) in language, thought and the "mind" itself will be socially and historically constituted. No ahistorical or transcendental standpoint exists from and by which the Real can be directly and without construction/distortion apprehended and reported in or by thought.[19]

[18] See, e.g. N. Hartsock, "The Feminist Standpoint: Developing the Ground for a Specifically Feminist Historical Materialism," in Harding and Hintikka, eds., *Discovering Reality*, pp. 283–310; and S. B. Hardy, "Empathy, Polyandry, and the Myth of the Coy Female," in Ruth Bleier, ed., *Feminist Approaches to Science* (New York: Pergamon, 1986), pp. 119–46.

[19] J. Flax, "The End of Innocence," in Butler and Scott, eds., *Feminists Theorize the Political*, p. 453.

The idea seems to be that once gender (and other social factors) mediates our access to reality, it does not make sense to claim privilege for a gynocentric perspective; no perspective can tell us what's "Real."

Many metaphysicians are likely to hear this as a bold metaphysical view (how can you tell what would distort reality without some access to undistorted reality as a basis for comparison?). Setting such concerns aside, however, the thought is clear enough: because our thinking is culturally conditioned, we are not able to discover what is really "Real." So any scheme of metaphysics that attempted such a project of discovery would be profoundly misguided. If one adopted this view, one might then go on to argue that a gynocentric perspective is preferable, not because women have privileged access to reality, but on the basis of other virtues, perhaps epistemic, perhaps political. This challenge goes well beyond a critique of particular metaphysical claims. So let us now turn to the broader critiques of metaphysics as a whole.

Feminist Anti-foundationalism

In describing the subject area of metaphysics (in my introduction), I set out what I take to be the central questions without saying much about the method for addressing them, or more generally, the epistemology of metaphysical inquiry. What methods should we employ to analyze our basic concepts or to discover the categories of being? Suppose it is true that we don't have "direct" access to reality. Does it follow that the project of metaphysics is impossible or indefensible?

It is difficult to emphasize too strongly that method has always been a matter of controversy within metaphysics. Unsurprisingly, method in metaphysics has reflected the influence of broader trends in epistemology. In periods where foundationalist epistemology was dominant, foundationalism tended to be dominant in metaphysics. (By *foundationalism* I mean here the philosophical view that a belief is justified only if it is itself certain, or is derivable from premises that are certain.) But in periods where foundationalism has been questioned, metaphysicians have worked with other epistemic frameworks. In mid-century, ordinary language philosophers were keen both to address questions about what there is and to provide conceptual analyses of basic metaphysical concepts through subtle reflection on ordinary language; and linguistic/semantic analysis is to this day an important and much-used tool in addressing metaphysical questions. Language is assumed to be a medium through which we have access to what there is; and there is no assumption that the truths being analyzed are known with certainty. In the context of post-Quinean metaphysical debate, the thought that we might have *or need* certainty, or direct access to reality, in order to make legitimate ontological claims, has been rejected.

Despite this, it is not uncommon to find feminist theorists criticizing metaphysics because of its "foundationalism." There are two strands to this critique (though some theorists focus on one strand, others on the other). The first concerns the nature of our access to reality. Do we have direct access to reality, for example unmediated by gender socialization or other cultural norms, and does the project of metaphysics assume that we do? The second concerns the "foundational" role of metaphysical claims in non-metaphysical theorizing. Does metaphysics function to constrain our theorizing within patriarchal limits by setting unquestioned and unquestionable starting points? The two issues can be linked; for if metaphysicians wrongly assume that we have unmediated access to reality when in fact our access is culturally conditioned by background sexist and racist beliefs, and if metaphysics also functions to constrain our theorizing within the limits it sets, then this poses a very serious problem for any effort to overcome oppressive attitudes and practices.

I'll return in the next section to consider the first strand of this critique in more detail. A more pressing issue is that the critique has as its target a very substantive conception of metaphysics that is, as far as I can tell, completely outdated. Let me sketch what I take to be a very widely endorsed approach to metaphysics in the contemporary Anglo-American tradition, which I'll call the *aporematic* approach. Here one begins inquiry by asking a question and looking for answers. Theorizing starts when one finds a particular puzzle, tension, or contradiction in the answers, either in one's beliefs on the question or, more generally, in the claims made on a certain topic. The goal is to resolve these puzzles in order to achieve a broadly consistent set of beliefs, allowing beliefs to be weighted according to plausibility. Other theoretical virtues may also play a role, though the question of which virtues and what role is controversial and should itself be explored through an aporematic inquiry. Sometimes resolution of the puzzle comes by rejecting the original question as ill-formed or confused; sometimes it comes in rejecting one or another of the conflicting claims as unwarranted.

Puzzles from different subject areas interact with each other, so that in theorizing about metaphysical topics, for example, attention to the broader picture is required. Any results achieved will be revisable as inquiry proceeds.

On this view metaphysics is not, at least in the traditional philosophical sense, a foundational project at all: it is not a quest for self-evident premises on which one can build the edifice of knowledge. Aporematic metaphysics might reasonably be considered immanent metaphysics: the questions, the puzzles, and the proposed answers arise within our thinking in response to current theoretical and practical demands. My sketch is rough enough to accommodate a variety of different non-foundational epistemologies; but it is certainly common for theorists working in this model to adopt an account of justification that is *holist*—a belief is justified if it coheres widely with other beliefs one has—and is, in two senses, *fallibilist*—all beliefs are revisable, and one might be epistemically justified in believing something that is nonetheless false.

Moreover, there is no suggestion that an aporematic approach to metaphysics need be foundational in the senses suggested by the feminist critique briefly mentioned. On an aporematic approach, making justified claims about the world does not require direct access to it; and metaphysics makes no claim to authority over other forms of inquiry: it is perfectly consistent with, and is in fact required by this approach that our metaphysical inquiry should be responsive to a broad range of experience as well as theoretical pressures from other domains, including normative inquiry in epistemology and moral theory.

It is in this last respect, I believe, that contemporary Anglophone metaphysics tends, in practice, to fall short of its epistemic responsibilities: the common strategy of "analytic" philosophy to break down questions to simpler ones and to focus on everyday examples masks the selectivity involved in prioritizing the phenomena the theory needs to accommodate. Feminist and anti-racist theorizing is especially attentive to phenomena that have been eclipsed both by dominant theorizing and "common sense," and is highly sensitive to unstated priorities; for these reasons metaphysical discussion would more fully approximate the aporematic ideal by attending to and engaging with the feminist and anti-racist literature.

Still, it should be recognized that feminist theorists are not merely tilting at windmills when they argue against metaphysics as a "foundational" project. Feminist theory is an interdisciplinary field, and often theorists are responding to philosophical claims or assumptions made in their field, rather than to current work in philosophy. Consider, for example, Joan Scott's characterization of history:

> History has been largely a foundationalist discourse. By this I mean that its explanations seem to be unthinkable if they do not take for granted some primary premises, categories, or presumptions. These foundations (however varied, whatever they are at a particular moment) are unquestioned and unquestionable; they are considered permanent and transcendent . . . In the minds of some foundationalists, in fact, nihilism, anarchy, and moral confusion are the sure alternatives to these givens, which have the status (if not the philosophical definition) of eternal truths.[20]

In many cases the feminist challenge to foundationalism is a request to reconsider the starting points of the author's field, to ask whether these starting points are biased, and what purposes have been served by treating these

---

[20] J. Scott, "Experience," in Butler and Scott, eds., *Feminists Theorize the Political*, p. 26.

assumptions as unquestionable. Because very often the starting points take the form of a commitment to certain kinds of entities, to certain kinds of explanation, to a certain basic conceptual framework, and because these are entities, explanations and concepts that also fall within the subject matter of metaphysics, the critique is reasonably lodged against the use of metaphysical assumptions in the field in question. But this does not make it a critique of metaphysical inquiry within academic philosophy.

If we take an aporematic approach to metaphysics, then we must acknowledge that what questions we ask, and what puzzles arise in our attempts to give answers is going to be, to some significant extent, a parochial matter: it will depend on cultural and historical context, broader theoretical needs, and so on. In a social context in which sexist and racist views are widely held and institutionalized, there is a compelling need for theories that diagnose, explain, and replace the sexist and racist beliefs. We need not suppose that these theories will be gynocentric—in the sense that they privilege a special female or feminine perspective; rather, they are feminist insofar as they engage the realities of women's oppression with the goal of ending it.[21] As these theories emerge, they may be relevant to metaphysics in two ways: feminist theories—including feminist moral and political theory and epistemology—may have repercussions that must be accommodated in our metaphysics; and feminist insights into the cultural/historical context of the metaphysical puzzles we consider may defuse and/or replace them.

Admittedly, all this remains very vague and abstract. To enrich the discussion, let us return to the issue of "direct access" and consider a topic of considerable importance in both metaphysical and feminist theorizing: natural kinds.

Feminist Metaphysics: Natural and Social Kinds

One of the major preoccupations of traditional metaphysics is the extent to which the mind is involved in constructing the world. Is there a structured world existing independent of us, whose "joints" we can sometimes capture in our theorizing? Or is the appearance of structure entirely dependent on us?

The question of the mind's involvement with the world is also of primary concern to feminists theorizing gender (and race). Traditional efforts to justify what we now view as racist and sexist institutions have portrayed women and people of color as "different," and often explicitly "inferior," by nature. In these contexts there is an unmistakable pattern of projecting onto women and people of color, as their "nature" or as "natural," features that are instead (if manifested

---

[21] See H. Longino, "In Search of Feminist Epistemology," The Monist 77 (1994), 472–85.

at all) a product of social forces. This projective error has led feminists to be ex-tremely suspicious of natural kinds and objective types: if one function of refer-ences to "nature" or "natures" is to mark the boundaries of what is socially possible, thereby "justifying" pernicious institutions, we must be wary of the suggestion that any category is "natural."[22] Yet feminists have also recognized that there are some limits on what social arrangements are possible for human agents. So we are left with a host of questions. Is there any meaningful (and politically viable) distinction between the natural and the social, and if so, where does the line fall? Is there any way to theorize about what's natural that does not depend on the projection of our political biases? If so, how?

The terminology of "natural kind" is used in several different ways, so it will be helpful to draw a couple of distinctions. The term 'kind' is sometimes used in the classification of substances, where the paradigm substances are ordinary (physical) objects. Substances are to be classified according to their essence, so kinds consist of groups of objects with a common essence. For example, tigers constitute a kind of thing because each tiger has essentially a certain cluster of properties that define the kind. On other occasions, the term 'kind' is used to refer to what I'd like to call here *types*. Types are groups of things, sometimes substances, but possibly (e.g. in the case of higher-order types) non-substances, that have a certain unity. This unity is typically not a matter of sharing essential properties. So, for instance, red things constitute a type (their unity consists in their all being red), even though redness is seldom an essential property of the things that have it. Unity seems to come in different degrees, so, for instance, the things on my desk might be thought to constitute a weak sort of type (they have in common the fact that they are on my desk), and at the limit there are highly gerrymandered sets of things that have no unity at all and so fail to con-stitute a type.

Given these different uses of the notion of "kind," the problem of "natural kinds" appears in different forms. One version concerns whether there are groups of things, in particular, substances, that share a common essence. (This debate links directly to debates over "Aristotelian" essentialism.) Another ver-sion is whether there are what I will call *objective types*. Assuming that there is a distinction between types and random gerrymandered sets, the question is what distinguishes types from the rest? A realist about objective types is someone committed to there being a kind of unity independent of us that distinguishes certain groups of individuals—the objective types—from others. Anti-realists may simply be *skeptical*, arguing that we cannot know whether there are objec-tive unities, or they may be *nominalist*, granting that there is a distinction

[22] See my "On Being Objective and Being Objectified," chapter 1 of this volume, and "Ontology and Social Construction," chapter 2 of this volume.

between types and random sets of things, but maintaining that the basis for being a type is non-objective, that is, dependent on us. In the context of feminist theory, *realism* about both kinds and types—the view that there are natural kinds/types and that we can come to know what they are (or at least what some of them are)—is generally assumed not to be an option. Forms of skepticism and nominalism are by far the preferred positions. This, I think, is a mistake. In what follows I'll look briefly at some feminist concerns about kinds, but will concentrate on the issue of types. My goal is to indicate why a modest realism about types is compatible with feminist insights into the problematic political rhetoric of "natures" and what's "natural."

The Social Construction of the Body

For some time feminists have been concerned to challenge the idea that there is such a thing as "women's nature" (or "men's nature"). Historically dominant views about men and women assume that anatomical sex, social position and sexual preference come in two distinct packages: there are those who are anatomically male, socially men and sexually desire (only) women; and there are those who are anatomically female, socially women and sexually desire (only) men. Those who don't fit into one or the other of these packages are considered deviant, and are devalued and abused. The picture driving this package deal seems to be one in which individuals have gendered natures or essences that explain the "normal" combinations of anatomy, social position, and sexuality; and various institutions (from medicine to the law) justify their treatment of individuals by taking the alleged natures as normative—the law protects individuals who are appropriately expressing their gendered/sexual nature, and it punishes those who are not; medicine is framed with the "normal" packages in mind and undertakes to rebuild those who aren't normal in this sense.

It has been a primary goal of feminist theory to challenge the givenness, naturalness and stability of this picture. Judith Butler, for example, along with many others, argues that the normalized conjunctions of body/gender/sexuality are not grounded in natures or essences (as she puts it: genders are not substances); rather, we come to think of these conjunctions as natures through participating in social institutions that are structured to take advantage of the limitations they also impose upon us.[23] Butler, in particular, suggests that we should work to break up the dominant model by proliferating alternative bodily possibilities, and specifically encourages gender crossings that parody the assumption of natural gender configurations (such as drag).

---

[23] J. Butler, *Gender Trouble* (New York: Routledge, 1990), and *Bodies That Matter* (New York: Routledge, 1993).

These arguments at the very least provide an important case study for debates about essentialism and natural kinds (in the first sense mentioned). If our investment in gendered natures is as politically grounded and as misguided as suggested, then we need to reflect carefully on our broader commitments in the area to determine whether our inquiry has been biased in favor of an ontology that serves particular political ends. What other ontologies have been ignored? Why? And at what cost?

Recent feminist discussion has gone on to question not only our commitment to natures, but also objective types. Turning again to Butler, it is clear that simply rejecting the idea of gendered natures wouldn't by itself destabilize the idea that there are two acceptable sexes (male/female) with two acceptable sexualities (male desire for female; female desire for male). One can grant that gender is constructed and still maintain that there are right and wrong ways for bodies to be, and to be sexual. Butler's somewhat unexpected next move is to reconsider the category of sex:

> And what is "sex" anyway? Is it natural, anatomical, or hormonal, and how is a feminist critic to assess the scientific discourses which purport to establish such "facts" for us? Is there a history of how the duality of sex was established, a genealogy that might expose the binary options as a variable construction? If the immutable character of sex is contested, perhaps this construct called 'sex' is as culturally constructed as gender ...[24]

The point of her rhetorical questions here is to suggest that sex, that is, the distinction between male and female, is not a natural "given," but a construction, and moreover, a construction parasitic on the social categories of gender. Roughly, the idea is that if we ask why we divide human beings into the two groups we do, along the lines of "sex," then the answer can't simply be: because bodies naturally come in these two forms; a complete answer will have to make reference to the gendered structure of our social worlds.

To illustrate this point, consider Monique Wittig's analysis of the social category of gender.[25] On Wittig's account, gender is defined in terms of the social/sexual positions made available under regimes of compulsory heterosexuality: *very roughly*, one is a woman by virtue of serving the heterosexual and reproductive needs of others; and one is a man by having one's heterosexual and reproductive needs served. Compulsory heterosexuality in this context is understood as a social institution regulating what sorts of bodies we recognize—and it does so by treating one of many anatomical distinctions between people as fundamental

---

[24] *Gender Trouble*, p. 7.
[25] M. Wittig, "The Category of Sex," in *The Straight Mind* (Boston: Beacon Press, 1992), pp. 1–8.

and, importantly, casting this choice of distinctions as determined entirely by natural facts about our bodies. Under such regimes, what matters most in thinking about human bodies is who has a penis and who has a vagina, and so these are the markers we focus on in making our basic distinction between kinds of human beings.[26]

Butler's discussion of sex suggests that the distinction between males and females is not objectively grounded even in non-essential facts, and instead is motivated by forces that are politically problematic; in particular, by the forces sustaining compulsory heterosexuality. In other words, we're not (or not simply?) mapping nature's joints in distinguishing males and females; we're enforcing a political regime.

Anti-realist Commitments?

There is no doubt that oppressive regimes justify themselves and eclipse alternative political arrangements by casting their representation of the world as revealing nature's real structure. This motivates Butler's broad argumentative strategy: when an oppressive regime purports to be grounded in objective or independent facts, show that the supposed facts are neither objective nor independent, but are "constructed" by the regime itself. Then add to this critical project positive suggestions for new sorts of distinctions that would at least provide the conceptual space for alternative social arrangements. This strategy is in many respects familiar and appealing; and the creativity and insight feminists have demonstrated in challenging the objectivity of entrenched categories is remarkable. But it is not clear that this line of thought provides reasons for accepting an anti-realist approach to objective types; if anything, it seems to presuppose such an anti-realism (otherwise, how can one be confident that an effort to challenge the supposed objectivity of the regime's grounding will be successful?). What is the basis for such an assumption?

It will help to return to the idea that our access to reality is mediated. Let's grant for the moment that there are many social and cultural factors—notably gender among them—that affect how we conceptualize the world, and that there is no way we can "step outside" all conceptualization to determine which, it any, will provide the resources to capture how the world really is. Gripped by these insights, it is tempting to locate ourselves once again behind a "veil of ideas," not necessarily a veil as opaque as Descartes supposed, but one at least that filters any information we might receive. A translucent veil, however, would

[26] Controversy in defining sex may emerge because reproductive and heterosexual needs focus on different body parts: heterosexual concerns with sexuality highlight perceptible bodily organs; concerns with reproduction highlight reproductive function, including hormonal/chromosomal factors.

seem to be little help so long as we're not in a position to compare what we experience through the veil with the reality behind it; we still have no way to distinguish in experience between what is real and what is a result of the veil's filtering effects. The best we can hope to accomplish is to describe the world-as-it-appears-through-the-veil, and to offer each other new veils that filter the world in different ways, hoping for ways that will invite us to restructure our political arrangements to be less oppressive. So, for example, a world consisting of males and females appears when we wear one veil, but if we change our veil we find a much more complex array of human bodies. On this view, the claim that the world itself (i.e., unveiled) really contains males and females should be regarded as suspect, for no one has access to unveiled reality. An insistence on the reality of males and females is instead serving a political function, normatively positioning certain bodies as preferable to others.

This picture, I think, guides a lot of feminist thinking about metaphysics and epistemology. Within this picture the suggestion that there are objective types of which we can gain knowledge makes little sense: perhaps we can have knowledge of types-as-they-appear-through-the-veil, but this is knowledge of types constituted in part by us, not objective types. Of objective types we must remain, at best, skeptical. I believe this picture is misguided in several ways.

Consider an argument that would seem to support it. In *Bodies That Matter*, Butler maintains that discourse does not "construct" things (such as the sexes) in the sense of bringing them (wholly) into existence; nonetheless we can only refer to things that have been partly constituted by discourse:

> To concede the undeniability of "sex" or its "materiality" is always to concede some version of "sex," some of "materiality". . . . To claim that discourse is formative is not to claim that it originates, causes, or exhaustively composes that which it concedes; rather, it is to claim that there is no reference to a pure body which is not at the same time a further formation of that body. In this sense, the linguistic capacity to refer to sexed bodies is not denied, but the very meaning of referentiality is altered.[27]
>
> Indeed, to "refer" naively or directly to such an extra-discursive object will always require the prior delimitation of the extra-discursive. And insofar as the extra-discursive is delimited, it is formed by the very discourse from which it seeks to free itself. This delimitation . . . marks a boundary that includes and excludes, that decides, as it were, what will and will not be the stuff of the object to which we then refer.[28]

---

[27] *Bodies That Matter*, pp. 10–11.
[28] Ibid., p. 11.

In short, our discursive practices mediate our relation to the world in such a way that any attempt we might make to refer to something independent of discourse compromises the independence of that to which we "refer." Why? Because any act of reference depends upon a boundary that we set (to refer to an object or a kind is to refer to something with the particular boundaries we determine), the boundaries of the objects and kinds we refer to are constituted by us. Therefore, the things we can know or refer to are not "pregiven," or "extra discursive," that is, their boundaries are not objective. But this argument is fallacious.

One way to capture the fallacy is to see it as ignoring a crucial scope distinction. The following claim is ambiguous:

> (i) We make it the case (through our discursive practices, etc.) that the things we refer to have the boundaries they do.

On one reading (i) makes a relatively uncontroversial point:

> (i_a) We make it the case (through our discursive practices, etc.) that *the boundaries of our reference*, that is, our referents *qua* things referred to, are what they are.

On (i)'s other reading, the point is highly controversial:

> (i_b) We make it the case (through our discursive practices, etc.) that *the boundaries of objects we refer to*, that is, our referents *qua* individuals, are what they are.

Butler's argument seems to slide from (i_a) to (i_b). But if we reject that inference, then it is possible to grant that our acts of reference depend upon often problematic background presuppositions, while also maintaining that some things and some kinds have objective boundaries. In other words, we can eagerly develop the political potential of (i_a), without relinquishing the belief that the world includes some "pregiven" and "extra-discursive" objects.

Two main questions underlie what is at issue here. First, does it follow from the fact that our epistemic relation to the world is mediated (by language, by concepts, by our sensory system, etc.) that we cannot refer to things independent of us? Certainly not. Intermediaries do not necessarily block access: when I speak to my sister on the phone, our contact is mediated by a complicated phone system, but I still manage to speak *to her*. And intermediaries sometimes improve access: there are many things in the world I cannot see without my glasses, and there are many things I cannot recognize without my concepts. Donna Haraway reminds us of the amazing prosthetic devices—telescopes, microscopes, listening devices, cyborgs—that enhance our access to the world through their mediation.[29] If we aren't in a position to compare our experience with the reality "behind it," then is it not as contentious to hold that our experience/discourse is a "further formation" of that reality as it is to say that it aptly captures it?

Second, does it follow from the fact that I cannot get outside of myself to "check" my experience against reality that I cannot know what's real or what's true? Again, no. This takes us back to the epistemological issues raised in the previous section. Admittedly, some philosophers have insisted on certainty as a condition for knowledge. But there are many other conceptions of knowledge that accept this limitation and set alternative, satisfiable conditions on justification. There is a temptation to think that if we cannot "get outside" of ourselves to test our beliefs against reality, then there's nothing further we can do epistemically to regulate belief; we're left with only political negotiation. But there are other epistemic considerations that can be brought to bear on belief, and provide grounds for claims to truth, for example coherence, evidential support, fruitfulness, and so on. Oddly, many feminists feel pressed to skepticism about an independent reality because they implicitly endorse a traditional conception that requires certainty or direct access to reality in order to have knowledge of it, while at the same time they often find the traditional conception of knowledge problematic In fact, metaphysical inquiry should be no more problematic than other forms of inquiry if certainty/direct access is not required for legitimate claims about what's real, and if an alternative epistemology—a feminist social empiricism, say—can be developed to replace the traditional one.

Is there now any further reason why someone sympathetic to a feminist political agenda need adopt either a nominalist of skeptical stance towards objective types? More specifically, if we acknowledge that our ways of classifying human bodies are motivated by problematic sexist, racist, and heterosexist concerns, must we deny that there is an objective difference (or a knowable objective difference), say, between males and females? I don't think so. Remember how the move to nominalism functions on the structure of Butler's strategy: if there is no objective basis for distinguishing one group from another, then no political regime—especially the dominant one—can claim authority by grounding itself in "the way the world is"; instead (I assume) the choice between political regimes will have to be made on the basis of normative argument. The worry seems to be that if we allow objective types, then we are politically constrained to design our social institutions to honor and sustain them.

But that worry is unfounded. One can easily maintain that the choice between political regimes requires normative debate while accepting a form of realism about types. Even if there are objective types, the question remains which of

---

[29] D. Haraway, "Situated Knowledges: the Science Question in Feminism and the Privilege of Partial Perspective", *Feminist Studies* 14: 3 (Fall 1988), 575–99.

them are morally and politically relevant. The realism I've been defending is an ontological view: the idea is that some properties are more important than others in structuring the world, and it's not up to us, so to speak, which these are.[30] More precisely, some properties, in themselves and not in relation to us, play a fundamental role in determining what the world (as a whole) is like and how it evolves. There are a number of factors that might be relevant to whether a property should count as fundamental—and it is certainly not settled—but traditionally philosophers have pointed to the need to account for non-trivial similarity relations and causal laws. So, if we compare the set of all hydrogen atoms with a gerrymandered set (e.g. that consisting of the Statue of Liberty, the cars currently parked in the lot at the San Diego Zoo, and the last sentence of each of Toni Morrison's novels), both may be the extension of some property, but the property determining the former set is more fundamental than the property determining the latter.

Realists and non-realists can agree that any grouping of things, however miscellaneous, constitutes a set; and they can also agree that some sets are more important to *us* than others. What makes a set important to *us* will depend on our purposes.[31] For example, the miscellaneous set of things in my refrigerator is important to me when I'm trying to decide what to make for dinner; the set of things on the top of my desk is important when I'm trying to pack my office to move. Depending on what I want to know and why, different properties of things are relevant, and how fundamental they are usually matters little. Some decisions, moreover—about who counts as an American citizen, or who counts as a mother—are politically and legally important, and cannot be settled simply by deciding what divisions are to be found in "nature." The realist can agree with the non-realist that our classification schemes are often motivated by interest-laden concerns, and that we need to look beyond questions of what is ontologically fundamental to determine how to structure our lives socially and politically; these issues are not ones that divide the two sides of the debate. The realist begins to diverge from the non-realist, however, when she claims that in some cases it is important to know what sets are fundamental, for example what properties are causally significant, in order to effectively interact with or understand the world.

The strategy of challenging oppressive regimes by arguing that their representation of the world is inadequate is a good one, and introducing alternative conceptual frameworks on which to construct new political arrangements is

---

[30] See M. K. McGowan, "Realism or Non-Realism: Undecidable in Theory, Decidable in Practice," PhD Thesis, Princeton University, 1996; and D. Lewis, "New Work for a Theory of Universals," *Australasian Journal of Philosophy* 61:4 (December 1983), 343–77.

[31] See Anderson, Elizabeth. "Knowledge, Human Interests, and Objectivity in Feminist Epistemology." *Philosophical Topics* 23, no. 2 (Fall 1995): 27–58.

essential to social change. But these political insights don't provide a basis for accepting an anti-realism about types. Even the most extreme realist about classification may grant that social factors play a role in determining what classification scheme we use, and that it is appropriate that they do so. In the case at hand, a realist could argue that there are lots of relatively objective unities to choose from in thinking about human bodies, and any one we mark will be marked for social reasons. Or she could argue that the categories of male and female are not objectively unified to any significant degree, but that we have been simply taught to think they are for political reasons. Or again, she could argue that the distinction between males and females is fundamental, but that it should still not be a basis for drawing moral or political distinctions. Any of these options allows for the social change Butler is concerned to promote. None of them denies the existence of objective types.

Conclusion

The previous section is an example, I hope, of feminist metaphysical debate. What makes the discussion feminist is not that it claims privilege for a woman's perspective, or that it assumes that women have different access to reality than men. It is feminist in its concern with the ways in which our views about the mind and reality either sustain or challenge oppressive patterns of thought and behavior. It is also, I hope, an example of aporematic metaphysics. The background issue is whether ontological realism is compatible with the feminist insight that oppressive regimes mistakenly justify themselves by claiming that their political arrangements are grounded in "nature" or are based in "the way the world really is." If one's metaphysical views must fit with other well-justified claims to be justified themselves, and if feminist argument suggests that there isn't "a way the world really is" or that we could never know what way that is, then one's realism must he put to the test. I've argued that feminist doubts need not lead one to an anti-realism about types, and in doing so I've also touched on the question whether feminist metaphysics itself—understood as a feminist inquiry into what there is—might be possible.

5

Family, Ancestry, and Self

What Is the Moral Significance of Biological Ties?

1. Introduction

In a series of recent papers, David Velleman has argued that it is morally wrong to bring a child into existence with the intention that the child will not have contact with one or both biological parents.[1] Put another way, "other things being equal, children should be raised by their biological parents" ("Family" 362fn 3). The primary targets of his argument are those who use anonymous donor egg or sperm to conceive a child. In his view, there is a significant value in being parented by and having ongoing contact with one's biological relatives. "What is most troubling about gamete donation is that it purposely severs a connection of the sort that normally informs a person's sense of identity, which is composed of elements that must bear emotional meaning, as only symbols and stories can" (363). Let's be clear. He is not just interested in the possibility of having information about one's biological progenitors, but actual knowledge by acquaintance. So the kind of profile that is typically made available by gamete donors or in closed adoptions is insufficient, and even information that is revealed through open records is not enough. Unless there are substantial overriding considerations, a face-to-face relationship with both biological progenitors is morally required.[2]

I'm interested in this argument as an adoptive parent. I have two children, adopted as infants, in fully open transracial adoptions. My husband and I have made substantial efforts to develop close relationships with the birth families of our children, both for their sakes and ours. Velleman is not opposed to adoption: although he maintains that all things being equal it is better to be raised by one's

---

[1] Cf. Velleman, "Narrative" and "Family."

[2] Note that Velleman's use of the term 'parent' for gamete donor is a controversial choice in a highly charged domain. I cannot follow him on this. Of course, not using the term 'parent' for gamete donors is also controversial. There is no neutral term, but I will often use the term 'biological progenitor' as an alternative to both 'donor' and 'parent.'

biological parents, he suggests that in the case of adoption (usually), "all things are not equal." "The child needs to be parented by someone, and [in the case of adoption we can assume that] it cannot or should not be parented by its biological parents, for reasons that would outweigh any value inhering in biological ties" (361).

However, Velleman's argument against anonymous gamete donation takes aim at what he calls "a new ideology of the family," an "ideology" that has implications for adoption and other family forms:

> The experiment of creating these children [by anonymous gamete donation] is supported by a new ideology of the family, developed for people who want to have children but lack the biological means to 'have' them in the usual sense. The new ideology has to do with the sense in which the resulting children will have families. It says that these children will have families in the only sense that matters, or at least in a sense that is good enough (360).

Although narrowly focused on anonymous gamete donation in the article just quoted, Velleman's concerns are broader. He explicitly mentions doubts about single parenthood, and gay and lesbian parenthood (360n2, 374n10). But in fact, any family form that fails to ensure an ongoing relationship with both male and female biological parents—and any choice that leads to such a family form—is (at least *prima facie*) morally suspect because the moral default is that a child should be raised by the two individuals from whose gametes he or she resulted.[3]

Like Velleman I find troubling the trend of reproductive technology and the assumptions behind it, especially the way it feeds a desire to have "designer babies" with the right sort of genetic background when there are many children in foster care and available for adoption in need of loving homes. I also support open adoption, where feasible.[4] However, I believe that even in non-kin adoptions where children have no contact with biological relatives, adopted children have families and adoptive parents *have* children in a sense that is "at least . . . good enough" and, actually, equal to the relations between biological parents and children. I do not agree with Velleman's suggestion that an ongoing connection with biological parents is so significant in forming one's identity that it is a moral wrong to deprive someone of this. And more broadly, I enthusiastically endorse the disruption of old ideologies of the family, and resist new ideologies that entrench and naturalize the value of biological ties.

So in this paper, I will argue against Velleman's position. I spend some effort to interpret his argument because, among other things, I take it to be more than an intellectual exercise: the moral standing of families like mine is at issue, and it would be too easy to dismiss his claims as just another manifestation of the culturally dominant biologism, or what I prefer to call *bionormativity*. Although I

---

[3] Velleman is not alone in defending this view. See e.g. Benatar, though his argument is quite different and conclusion is more cautious.

[4] Cf. Allen, "Open."

am also sympathetic with his desire to develop a moral theory that takes seriously empirical facts about human psychology and human flourishing, I argue that Velleman's evidence and the conceptual tools he uses for interpreting it are lacking. This may seem to leave the points on which I agree with him unexplained. So towards the end I will point to a different rationale for families being open to contact with biological relatives.

2. The Wrong in Denying Contact:
How Far Does It Extend?

Velleman's claim that "other things being equal, children should be raised by their biological parents" is not implausible ("Family" 362fn 3). Suppose it was your responsibility to place a newborn with one of two families: the Abbots or the Babbots. Suppose the families are alike in every significant respect—their income, values, personalities, extended family, social circumstances are equivalent. To strengthen the similarity, you could even imagine that both the prospective mothers are twins and fathers are twins and they live in similar houses in similar subdivisions in the same city. However, suppose the baby is the biological offspring of Mr. and Ms. Abbot (they are both genetic parents and Ms. Abbot is the gestational parent of the child). It does seem, barring some important further consideration, that the baby should be placed with the Abbots.

This thought does not entail, however, that the child has a right to be raised by the Abbots rather than the Babbots, or even that it would be good for the child. After all, the basis for thinking that the biological parents should be privileged in the case above may be due, not to the child's rights or interests, but to parental rights or interests; that is, it may be wrong to deny the biological parents the child unless there are compelling reasons to do so. But in the case of closed adoption and anonymous gamete donation, there *are* compelling reasons: the biological progenitors cannot or do not want to raise the child. Returning to the example above, if we suppose that the Abbots do not want to raise the child and are prepared to relinquish their rights, then it seems perfectly acceptable to place the baby with the Babbots who do want to raise the child, even if the Babbots are not biologically related to the Abbots.[5]

---

[5] Velleman claims that biological parents are not entitled to "abdicate their responsibilities at will. We do not think that parents are morally entitled to put a newborn up for adoption because of a last-minute social engagement, for example, or dismay at the size of its ears" ("Persons" 10). Although I agree with Velleman on the two examples, it is because I believe that the decision would be ill-informed and irrational. However, I believe that parents are morally entitled to relinquish their rights, if their decision to do so is informed and rational. Earlier in the paper Velleman uses the example of pushing a child into a swimming pool as an analogy with procreation, saying, "You shouldn't go pushing children into the deep end if you aren't willing to get wet" (8). Bracketing whether one should ever push a child into the deep end who can't swim, I think a more plausible claim would be: "You shouldn't go pushing children into the deep end if you haven't arranged for someone to jump in if and when necessary."

But *is it* acceptable? This is where Velleman resists. What about the interests of the child? Have the Abbots, in declining the responsibility to raise a child they have produced (assuming that they have the wherewithal to do so) done something morally wrong? In the case of gamete donation the question is even more pressing: is it wrong to undertake to create a child that one has no intention of raising?

Velleman's answer to the latter question is that yes, it is wrong. What Velleman thinks is the precise nature of the wrong, and how it extends to adoption, is not altogether clear. For example, how much does it matter that in the case of gamete donation, the conception was undertaken intentionally and in full knowledge of the consequences, where in the case of adoption, this is typically not the case? Threads in Velleman's argument suggest that closed or semi-open adoption (which could be safely opened fully) is on a par with anonymous gamete donation from a moral point of view, and that individuals who enter into an adoption arrangement that does not include ongoing contact between child and birth families are doing something morally wrong. In this line of thought, the biological and/or adoptive parents are doing something that they have good evidence to believe will harm their offspring without overriding reasons that would justify doing so. In his words, "a life estranged from its ancestry is . . . truncated" ("Persons" 13) and we have a moral obligation to avoid truncating a life.

If Velleman is correct, the moral basis for contact is not the right of the biological progenitors to parent their child (a right that one can, at least under some circumstances, choose to forfeit); the moral basis lies in the well-being of the child. The biological progenitors may be able to forfeit their right to parent, but they do not thereby forfeit their responsibility to the child. The non-biological parents may accept the child "as their own" but this does not negate the importance of the biological progenitors to the child's well-being. As mentioned before, Velleman's focus is on cases of gamete donation rather than adoption—and the cases may differ in some normally relevant ways—but the core issue of contact affects both cases equally. Because the vast majority of non-kin adoptions in the United States do not involve ongoing contact with birth families, even though contact would be safe, Velleman's argument supports the conclusion that these non-kin adoptions (certainly numbering in the millions) are morally suspect.

3. Self and Identity

Velleman argues that those who participate in donor conception are doing harm to the resulting child because:

> people who create children by donor conception already know—or already should know—that their children will be disadvantaged by the lack of a basic good on which most people rely in their pursuit of self-knowledge and identity formation. In coming to know and define

themselves, most people rely on their acquaintance with people who are like them by virtue of being their biological relatives ("Family" 364–65).

From this quotation and other passages in Velleman's essay, it seems that acquaintance with one's biological progenitors is important in two ways: (a) for forming a (healthy) self or identity, and (b) for gaining self-knowledge. There are really three interdependent tasks here.[6] One is to form a self. Another is to form an identity. A third is to gain self-knowledge. How are these related?[7]

Self-knowledge is the broadest notion: I know lots of things about myself, some of which are rather trivial and peripheral to my identity. For example, I know that I broke my left index fingernail earlier today. A capacity for such self-knowledge (reflecting a body awareness, a basic sense of myself as in *this* body) is an important achievement that only a few species are capable of; but this particular bit of knowledge is unimportant. I also know that as a child I sometimes played with my older sister's doll with shiny red hair. This bit of knowledge could be woven into a narrative about my relationship with my sister, but in fact it is just a random memory that doesn't mean much to me. If I hadn't noticed that I had broken my fingernail, or hadn't dredged up the memory of playing with the doll, it wouldn't have been any kind of threat to my selfhood. Although plausibly some self-knowledge is important to being a healthy, functioning individual, one can presumably have a fairly stable self and yet lack important, even extensive, self-knowledge. For example, an adult who suffers partial amnesia as a result of an accident may have a stable self, but have substantial gaps in his or her long-term memory. What is crucial for children is sufficient self-knowledge in order to gain a stable self, for a stable self seems to be a necessary condition for a fully human life.

But what is a self? And what is the difference between a self and an identity? In the context of adoption, the controversy over transracial adoption has provided one useful framework for thinking about the difference. In the early 1970s, critics of transracial adoption argued that because transracial adoptees would be brought up in families that could not provide the resources for developing a secure Black identity, Black children adopted into White families were profoundly harmed.[8] Since then, however, psychologists have argued that there are two relevant dimensions of mental health to consider:

---

[6] Is the wrong at issue here that individuals who lack access to their biological progenitors are at a *disadvantage* relative to others who live with biological relatives? This would mean that the harm could be ameliorated if everyone were adopted into non-kin families. But this is clearly not what Velleman has in mind, as is obvious from his rejection of Plato's plan for child rearing in *The Republic* ("Persons" 2).

[7] See also Witt.

[8] See National Association of Black Social Workers; for a helpful analysis of this document and the movement behind it, see Neal.

"personal identity" (PI) and "reference group orientation" (RGO) (Cross 41–42). Measures of the strength of personal identity are concerned with "self-esteem, self-worth, self-confidence, self-evaluation, interpersonal competence, ego-ideal, personality traits, introversion-extroversion, and level of anxiety"; measures of reference group orientation (in the context of these debates focused primarily on race) look at "racial identity, group identity, race awareness, racial ideology, race evaluation, race esteem, race image, race self-identification" (42).

William Cross used this distinction to study the transition from "Negro" to "Black" identity as a result of the civil rights movement. Whereas early studies of Negro identity represented it as pathological and burdened with self-hatred, Cross found that this research failed to appreciate the underlying psychological health of those studied:

> The Black Social Movement of the 1960s achieved a high degree of ideo-logical and cultural consensus among Black people, especially Black youth. But in changing their ideologies, the movement did not have to change the personalities of Black youth because most already *had* healthy personalities. Such mental health was a legacy of the personal psychological victories that their parents [who identified as "Negro"] were able to achieve and to pass on to the next generation (xiv).

With this distinction between PI and RGO, Cross was able to consider the al-leged harm to transracial adoptees and found, contrary to earlier empirical claims, that there is "no difference in the PI profile for Black children involved in transracial compared to inracial adoptions" (Cross 111; Shireman and Johnson). Given strong personal identities, transracial adoptees have the ability to nego-tiate the further task of developing a racial identity in the social context they find themselves.[9] Although developing a healthy racial identity is not a simple or easy task, many people now believe that the challenges transracial adoptees face are not so extreme that they provide a case against transracial adoption. In fact, there is reason to think that if the choice is between early adoption into an other-race family, or an extended time in foster care or group homes, the former is preferable primarily because it provides a better context for developing a strong personal identity which then forms the basis for negotiating race and other social identities over time.

---

[9] There is no consensus on how transracial adoption affects RGO. Some studies suggest that inra-cial adoptees have stronger RGO than transracial adoptees; however, at least one study found that at age four, transracial adoptees have an RGO profile that is "'stronger' and more 'Black oriented' than that of peers being reared in Black homes!" (Shireman and Johnson, qtd. in Cross 111–12). The study found the difference to disappear by age eight.

Drawing on this literature, I'll use the term 'self' to refer to the cluster of basic traits that allow an individual to function as an agent, some of which are measured by the notion of "personal identity" (PI) mentioned above, and plausibly includes others not mentioned, for example, a capacity for practical reason. I'll use the term 'identity' or 'social identity' to refer to an individual's reference group orientation (RGO), and the narrative tropes that are employed to navigate one's relation to the reference group. Damage or harm to self by circumstances that undermine the development of core capacities of agency is clearly something we have an obligation to avoid. But it is less obvious that we have an obligation to provide particular "identities" to children, especially identities that conform to the standard reference groups or the culturally dominant narrative tropes.[10]

It remains unclear at this point what the relationship is between self and identity. Are there particular reference group orientations—social identities and accompanying narratives concerned with biological origins and similarities—without which a healthy self cannot develop? Does the development of a healthy social identity require close contact with other members of the social group in question? And how malleable are the identities and narratives in accommodating difference?

4. Basic Goods

It might seem that the issues before us are fully empirical: how do human beings form healthy selves and identities? Velleman's argument in the passage quoted at the beginning of section 3 in this essay relies on an empirical fact about how "most" individuals form a sense of self, or an identity. Because "most" people form identities by contact with biological relations, we owe this opportunity to everyone. However, if we have a moral obligation to protect the opportunity for identity formation through contact with biological relations, it can't simply be because "most" people do it this way, but that it is a *good* way to do it. For example, at certain points in history most White people in the United States have defined themselves by reference to the White race and by acquaintance with other Whites. Being White was a fundamental element of one's identity (and for many, it still is). This identification with a race, tribe, or nation is not peculiar to the United States, but is a common and deep source of identity across time and culture. But the fact that "most" people in a certain context rely on racial categories to form their sense of self does not show that this is

[10] See Allen for an argument that a child does not have a right against their parents to be brought up with a particular racial or even gender identity.

good or right or something that should be promoted. And this for two reasons: the belief that there are biological races is false, and identities formed around assumed biological races, specifically a White/Non-White binary, can reinforce racial hierarchy. In his more recent paper on the topic, Velleman acknowledges that the argument cannot rest on the claim that "most" people form identities through contact with biological relations, or that it is "natural" (i.e., selected for), for many traits common or natural in this sense are morally problematic ("Persons" 2).

What's needed is an argument showing that people who rely on acquaintance with their biological relatives to form their identities gain *knowledge* by this acquaintance (not false beliefs about their similarity to or even superiority to others), and that this knowledge is "*a basic good.*" What is "a basic good"? Here are two possibilities:

    (i) A basic good is something *necessary* in order to lead a minimally good life.
    (ii) A basic good is something *helpful* in achieving a minimally good life.

(i) is too strong for Velleman's purposes. There are many people who lead a minimally good life without acquaintance with their biological progenitors. Velleman seems to grant this, for he says that it is just "very difficult" ("Family" 366) to form an identity without access to a relationship with one's biological parents, and that having such a relationship is "especially important to identity formation" (375).[11] But (ii) seems too weak. It would be helpful if I gave all the money in my savings account to the homeless person I walk by on the way to work, but I haven't done something morally wrong if I don't.

To take a first step in complicating this framework, let us distinguish between a minimally decent life, a good life, and a completely flourishing life. Different goods play a role in enabling each of these. Although access to biological relatives is not necessary for a minimally decent life, Velleman seems to suggest that it is

---

[11] In "Family," Velleman suggests a somewhat stronger claim, "Human life is important because it is a predicament faced by . . . a person, whose success at facing it will entail the flowering of personhood, and whose failure will entail a disfigurement of that value, in the form of damage to the self" (12). He continues with the thought that we must "avoid creating lives that will already be truncated or damaged in ways that seriously affect the prospects for flourishing within them. I claim that a life estranged from its ancestry is truncated in this way" (13). If denying access to ancestors will prevent someone from developing a secure self, or will damage such a self, then it would seem an essential rather than a basic good.

necessary for a good life.[12] This would suggest a better understanding of basic goods:

(iii) A basic good is something that, over and above the essential goods needed for a minimally decent life, is necessary in order to achieve a good life.

Denying someone access to such basic goods would have the effect that his or her life is more impoverished than it would need to be and it would be impossible for him or her to flourish fully. So it would be reasonable to think that in depriving someone of a basic good, all else being equal, you are harming him or her. And intentionally causing someone avoidable harm is morally wrong. [See Figure 5.1.]

Although this seems to be on the right track, it is important to note that what is necessary to achieve a good life is context specific, so it may be that what is necessary for a good life in one context, or at one time, is not necessary in another context or at another time. A famous example of this comes from Adam Smith:

By necessaries I understand not only the commodities which are indispensably necessary for the support of life, but whatever the custom of the country renders it indecent for creditable people, even of the lowest order, to be without. A linen shirt, for example, is, strictly speaking, not a necessary of life. The Greeks and Romans lived, I suppose, very comfortably though they had no linen. But in the present times, through the greater part of Europe, a creditable day-labourer would be ashamed to appear in public without a linen shirt, the want of which would be supposed to denote that disgraceful degree of poverty which, it is presumed, nobody can well fall into without extreme bad conduct (465).

[12] In correspondence, Velleman explained to me that he does not believe that his arguments concern basic goods that are "owed to everyone," but rather they concern what we owe to people we contemplate bringing into existence (Email). On his account, procreative decisions must be based on a standard of adequate provision that is different from what is owed to existing children. In the case of gamete donation, the alternative is non-existence, whereas in the case of adoption, the alternative is remaining with the birth family, foster care, or some other form of custodial care; the differences are significant. As a result, he holds that his arguments do not apply to the case of adoption except insofar as one is considering bringing children into existence in order to place them for adoption. Thus the reconstruction of his argument that I provide here should be understood as one he would not endorse. However, he does hold that due to the importance of biological ties, adoptees are at a disadvantage in comparison with non-adoptees, so the general import of his argument is relevant to the issue of open adoption insofar as one might plausibly think that one should not disadvantage someone without substantial reason. My arguments can be understood to question the existence and nature of the alleged disadvantage. I look forward to reinterpreting the details of Velleman's arguments in light of the feedback he has offered, and offer the interpretation I develop here as capturing a view that plays a role in our culture—so is worth analyzing—even if it is not a view Velleman would fully endorse.

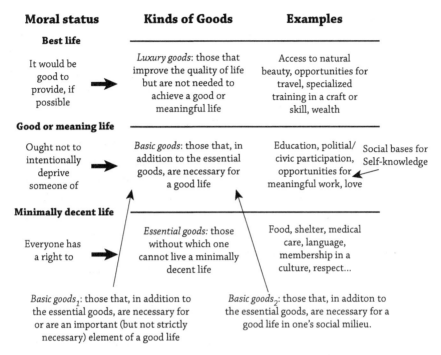

Figure 5.1 What are basic goods?

Should we think of the formation of selves and identities as sensitive to context?

One cannot provide someone a self or an identity. These are achievements that an individual must accomplish. What one can provide are the social bases for healthy selves and identities. I agree with Velleman's claim that it is morally wrong to create a child only to deprive him or her of the social basis for selfhood, of the minimal conditions that enable him or her to become a fully functioning agent. And selves are in the business of forming an identity. That's what selves do. But what counts as a healthy identity and what resources are needed for forming such an identity are culturally specific. Identities locate us within social structures and cultural narratives; they situate individuals in relation to others. Because there are indefinitely many ways of organizing ourselves, there will be variations in what is owed to individuals who are engaged in identity formation.

Difficult questions arise because not all structures and narratives are objectively sound or morally legitimate. I believe that the current racial structure (and gender structure) in the United States is morally problematic and I seek ways to undermine it, and yet I also believe that it would be wrong not to teach my children how to situate themselves as Black (and gendered) within that structure. Others believe that races are pernicious fictions and it is wrong to teach their children that they, or anyone else, are a member of a race; color-blindness is their policy. What do we owe our children here? It would be good for my children if the current racial hierarchy were weakened; if I teach them how to situate themselves within that hierarchy, their lives will be easier, but it plausibly also reinforces the structure. Justice and happiness, knowledge and security do not always coincide. How should we choose?

In spite of such complications, however, one might argue that there are some universal identity goods that we are obliged to provide children. The social bases for selfhood are, in the framework I've suggested, an essential good. And accompanying the social bases for selfhood will be social bases for *identity* formation (language, relations to others, etc.). But we should ask: what is necessary for *healthy* identity formation? Under conditions of slavery, slaves develop selves with identities, but their identities are disfigured by the cultural context. Gender and race hierarchies are harmful in part because of the limited and problematic set of identities that they make available. A minimally decent life can be achieved with an unhealthy identity. But a good life is not, or not easily, within reach.

Can we specify the social bases for a healthy identity? As I've argued, because identities situate one within a social context, it will be difficult to characterize universally necessary conditions. If Velleman's argument is sound, contact with biological relatives would be a universally necessary condition. I disagree with him about this, but would suggest that other conditions are plausible—for instance, that children should have access to basic knowledge of origins where available, opportunities to gain knowledge of themselves that can anchor a meaningful life narrative, and cultural categories and narratives that are non-oppressive. Even here, however, there are cultural differences to keep in mind, for example, in some cultures birth dates are not considered important and are not recorded, whereas in others birth dates and birthdays are central to one's legal and social identity. What counts as the relevant "knowledge of origins" will vary to some degree depending on context. However, if honesty about origins is a basic good, then lying to children about their adoptive status, or about their biological origins, would be morally wrong. But the question remains: what is the status of acquaintance with one's biological relatives? Is it a basic good?

5. The Goods of Knowing Biological Kin

Velleman points to two different epistemic goods gained by knowing one's biological relations. First, it provides a special kind of self-knowledge based on "intuitive and unanalyzable resemblances" ("Family" 368). Second, it provides a narrative within which our actions have meaning.

Note that neither knowledge of others who are similar by virtue of biological relatedness, nor biological narratives that draw specifically on such knowledge, are necessary for developing full selfhood. So in neither case is the good in question an essential good. The question is whether the knowledge gained through contact is a basic good, understood as necessary for a good life. Knowing many adoptees whose lives seem good by any ordinary standard, some of whom have, and others of whom don't have, contact with their birth families, I find it hard even to entertain the idea that contact with birth families is necessary for a good life. In fact, I think it would be insulting to adoptees I know to suggest that their lives are not good because they don't know their birth parents. Nevertheless, there may be something relevant that's easy to miss, so I will consider the issue of similarity in this section, and the issue of narrative in the next.

As Velleman points out, it is very difficult to come to know oneself simply by introspection, or by watching oneself in the mirror. The best resource, he proposes, is observation of others who are importantly similar, and the best sources for such similarity are one's biological family.

> When adoptees go in search of their biological parents and siblings, there is a literal sense in which they are searching for themselves. They are searching for the closest thing to a mirror in which to catch an external and candid view of what they are like in more than mere appearance. Not knowing any biological relatives must be like wandering in a world without reflective surfaces, permanently self-blind ("Family" 368).

As mentioned before, his argument depends on not just having information about one's relatives—this is typically available even in the case of anonymous donors—but having acquaintance with them. Why? His idea is that only by *acquaintance* can we appreciate the *intuitive* and *unanalyzable* resemblance we have to our biological relatives. We see another who is "like me." And the recognition of this resemblance is crucial to access "deeply ingrained" aspects of my self.[13]

On the face of it, however, Velleman's emphasis on biological parents and siblings is highly exaggerated. We all rely on many sources in our development of self-understanding, including friends, characters in literature and film, public figures and, in cases where biological kin are missing, custodial family members. If the crucial thing is that we have others around us who effectively mirror us to ourselves, then it isn't clear why this should be a biological relative.[14] Moreover, it is clear that self-knowledge is not *entirely* achieved by the route of mirroring Velleman describes, for if you don't have some

---

[13] Cf. Witt.

[14] Although Velleman's emphasis on narrative suggests a sympathy with a psychoanalytic notion of self, the "self psychology" of Kohut employs the notion of "mirroring" in a way that seems relevant to, but different from, Velleman's notion of mirroring (see Baker and Baker for an overview of Kohut). In Kohut's view, to develop a healthy self it is crucial that the primary caretaker "mirror" the child by providing empathetic and appropriate responses to his/her affective states. Whether the primary caretaker is capable of this has little to do with his/her similarities with the child, but depends more on the character's own narcissistic tendencies. Insofar as narcissistic projection and a failure to recognize the child as a fully separate person is more tempting with a biological child, it may even be that a non-biological parent or care-taker is better suited to this mirroring role than a biological parent.

self-knowledge prior to seeing others like yourself, then how could you tell whether they are like you or not? After all, you don't know what you are like! Given some sense of self, gained through introspection and agency, we find others to watch, to mimic, to emulate, to avoid. Although biology does sometimes provide ideal mirrors for this process, all too often it fails miserably: it is common for children to fail when they model themselves on their biological parents, and many biological parents are failures in their own lives and so are poor models even if their children could be successful.

Moreover, if the goal is to find an objective basis for self-knowledge, judgments of similarity should be viewed with caution. In the case of racial or ethnic identity, the belief in shared "blood" provides a myth of commonality. Myths of commonality run rampant in families. And such myths of commonality trace politically significant contours. For example, a female friend with two sons once commented that my son Isaac and I look alike. I was surprised since no one had ever mentioned this before. She noticed my surprise and commented: "I'm told all the time that my sons look like me. I don't think they look like me at all. They are *boys*. But that doesn't seem to matter when people are looking for parent-child similarity. People don't think Isaac looks like you because he's Black and you're White. Skin-color matters when people look for parent-child similarity. But if you actually attend to his features, he looks a lot like you." An important insight in this observation is that what similarities are salient is largely a matter of context, and some socially significant similarities are allowed to eclipse others that may be more deeply important. I don't really see our physical similarities, but Isaac and I have other emotional and temperamental similarities. This too can be easily eclipsed by our racial (and sex) difference. Social schemas tell us, among other things: Who are you allowed to look like? Who are you allowed to *be* like? (We'll return to the idea of a social schema below.)

Implicit in Velleman's discussion is a theory about why adoptees search ("they are searching for themselves") and what they find when they do ("an external and candid view of themselves"). But research on adoptees, although plagued by methodological challenges and rarely if ever reaching consensus, doesn't support this picture. Although, as Velleman notes, the number of adoptees who search has been steadily rising and may be approaching fifty percent ("Family" 259fn 1), this is not surprising, given the opening of records and changes in adoption policy and counseling. However, this increase in numbers searching does not, by itself, support his interpretation of why adoptees search or the outcome. Although I cannot provide a literature survey in this context, there are a few points worth noting.

First, it is generally recognized that adoption is a significant factor in identity development, though whether an adoptee struggles with identity is to a significant extent a matter of context, where context includes both immediate family and society. Factors that influence identity resolution in adoptive families include: type of family relationships (e.g., authoritarian or not), ways of communicating (or not) about adoption, and parental attitudes about adoption.[15] Social attitudes towards adoption influence the adoptee both indirectly by influencing parents' attitudes and directly. For example:

> Problems of identity tend to arise when we have conflicting loyalties to persons, groups or associations. Identity problems arise for adoptive children not simply because they have been told they are adopted, but because there are conflicting cultural values around them, those concerned with nurturing parenthood held by their adoptors [sic], and the values concerning biological bases of kinship that are still very much alive in the culture generally (Kirk 20; qtd. in Hoopes 155).

Interestingly, and not surprisingly, adoptees who are brought up in a family that accords significant value to being reared in biological families, a value that they are obviously missing out on, are more likely to have identity problems and search for their biological relatives. Thus it would seem that Velleman's view is locally self-affirming. But adoptees who are brought up in families where biology is treated as one source, but not the only source for identity, are normally able to form healthy identities without contact with their biological relatives.

Second, in carefully controlled studies, adoptees have been found to have "no significant differences between their behavior and characteristics and those of the matched group of biological children."[16] In studies of adult adoptees (much of the adoption research is on youth), "while adult adoptees have had unique life experiences, in many ways they are navigating their adult years no differently than their non-adopted peers" (Borders, Black, and Pasley 415). If we remember the distinction between PI and RGO in the discussion of Black identity, this research suggests that adoptees do not suffer in developing a core self measured by PI relative to non-adoptees.[17] Interestingly, however, "most of the differences found between adoptees and controls in this research could be attributed to search status. Lower self-esteem, lower family/friend support, and higher depression scores were all associated with searchers" (416). Whether this difference between searchers and non-searchers is the reason for, or a result of, searching is not clear; it is also confusing that this study apparently makes no distinction between searchers who have found family and those who have not. This research suggests, however, that contact with biological relatives is not an assured route to a healthy identity.

---

[15] See Hoopes, esp. 162f; and Kohler, Grotevant, and McRoy.

[16] Borders, Black, and Pasley; also qtd. in Carp 252.

[17] This data is not exactly what is needed to respond to Velleman's argument because the data doesn't distinguish adoptions in which there is contact with biological relations from adoptions in which there isn't. Because until recently there were very few fully open non-kin adoptions, however, the question is whether the data is primarily drawn from non-kin or kinship adoptions.

Third, adoptees search for their birth families for a variety of reasons and there are many different trajectories after reunion. Recent long-term studies suggest that in most cases, even when a good relationship is established with a birthmother, the adoptee's primary relationship remains with their adoptive mother. Moreover,

> The need to have a sense of genealogical and genetic connectedness appears strong. It is part of the drive that motivates people to search. Who do I look like? Where do I come from? Whom am I like in terms of temperament and interests, skills and outlook? But although these needs trigger people to search and seek contact, they do not necessarily imply the desire for a relationship. They are information led: they are designed to meet autobiographical and identity needs (Howe and Feast 364–65).

So even if we grant the point that it can help to gain an objective perspective on oneself through having information about or even observing biological relatives, we must ask, how much more than a glimpse is needed? How often do we need to see ourselves unexpectedly in a store window in order to form a healthy identity? Is contact needed? Apparently, an ongoing relationship is not even desired by many of those who search.

6. Identity and Culture

Where are we now? According to Velleman, the self-knowledge one gains through relationships with one's biological progenitors "is of irreplaceable value in the life-task of identity formation" ("Family" 357). So far, I've identified and criticized two claims his argument rests upon:

- Judgments of similarity with biological relations are reliable (objective?) guides to self-knowledge.
- Those who lack a relationship with biological progenitors have difficulty forming secure identities and difficulty finding meaning in life because of this lack.

However, in order to do justice to Velleman's position, we should look more closely at the role of narrative in his account of identity formation. This will help flesh out his argument, and will also enable us to explore an alternative picture of the social function of identity.

Velleman acknowledges that the construction of identity isn't primarily a matter of finding the facts about one's past. It is a process of telling a story. "I am inclined to think that a knowledge of one's origins is especially important to identity formation because it is important to the telling of one's life-story, which necessarily encodes one's appreciation of meaning in the events of one's life." He continues: "Of course, my own life provides narrative context for many of the events within it; but my family history provides an even broader context, in which large stretches of my life can take on meaning, as the trajectory of my entire education and career takes on meaning in relation to the story of my ancestors" (375–76). In describing his own family narrative—he is the grandson of Russian Jewish immigrants—he admits:

> How do I know that I have inherited these qualities [being a malcontent, a homebody] from Nathan and Golda? I don't: it's all imaginative speculation. But such speculations are how we define and redefine ourselves, weighing different possible meanings for our characters by playing them out in different imagined stories. In these speculations, family history gives us inexhaustible food for thought (377).

This is confusing, for there is a tension between the role of story-telling in identity formation, and the role of "external and candid" knowledge that is important to gain from biological progenitors.[18] Apparently Velleman's speculative imagination about his great-grandparents (Nathan and Golda) serves him adequately in constructing a story that links him to a meaningful past, so knowledge of the real events and acquaintance with actual ancestors is not required for the narrative project.

However, in the case of gamete donation or closed adoption, there is also material from which to build a story. Adoptive parents often receive not only medical information, but copies of long questionnaires filled out by one or both birthparents; the same happens in the process of gamete donation. Velleman uses the bits of evidence he gains about his ancestors—ancestors who died long

---

[18] Velleman's essay, "Narrative Explanation," argues that there is an important distinction between subjective and objective explanation. Subjective explanation works by relating events to a familiar pattern "of how things feel" in contrast to objective explanations which relate them to familiar patterns of "how things happen" ("Narrative" 19). He warns, however, that there is a common projection error in reaching a subjective explanation: "we must recognize that the audience of narrative history is subject to a projective error. Having made subjective sense of historical events, by arriving at a stable attitude towards them, the audience is liable to feel that it has made objective sense of them, by understanding how they came about. Having sorted out its feelings toward events, the audience mistakenly feels that it has sorted out the events themselves: it mistakes emotional closure for intellectual closure" (20). In some cases we are both storyteller and audience, and we are piecing together the facts of our lives. It is possible, of course, to tell a story of our own lives that gives it meaning, i.e., provides an emotionally satisfying plot, but is not a good explanation of who we are or how we got where we are. Velleman seems to suggest at some points that (a) the subjectively satisfying plots that provide for healthy identities must include details of both biological progenitors as a significant part of the story; and at other points that (b) with such a story and only with such a story can we achieve an objective explanation of who we are (because biology is an important objective determinant of who we are?), and so can only live a lie. But both (a) and (b) are mistaken. Plots are made available to people with very little information for them to fill in with what is available combined with speculation, and even those who think they have objective information about their progenitors often don't. We all live with a mix of fact and fiction pasted together with the glue that our cultural schemas provide.

before he was born—together with his knowledge of context and history, to create a story within which he can fit his life: his great-grandparents left Russia, he imagines, to find a better life, and he has benefited from their doing so. Even without contact with their biological progenitors, adoptees and the offspring of gamete donors can tell similar stories that have led up to their lives. Literature is not only filled with narratives about happy biological offspring and tragic adopted ones, but also biological offspring who feel tremendous alienation from their parents, orphans and adoptees who find loving homes and live meaningful lives with little or no knowledge of their biological relatives, and almost everything in between.[19] Velleman finds it confusing how those who do not prioritize biological ties can appreciate world literature ("Family" 369; "Persons" 14); it isn't difficult if one allows that there are a variety of narrative forms that situate one in relation to one's origins, detailed ancestral narratives being one, maybe even an important one, but not the only one. Information about "family history" may be useful "food for thought," but a relationship with biological progenitors is not necessary to creating a speculative family history—and over the long run, speculation is all any of us has anyway.

Stories we tell about ourselves, our relation to others and to our past are not unique, but follow cultural schemas. The notion of schema plays a role in both anthropology and psychology. Within the field of social psychology, schemas are understood to be representations of phenomena that organize our beliefs in a way that helps us form expectations and process new information. Groups form shared schemas that enable their members to respond similarly to circumstances they encounter. Schemas encode knowledge and also provide scripts that frame our interaction with each other and our environment; such scripts can guide group members through collective events or even organize a life. Judith Howard (a social psychologist) suggests: "Schemas, for example, are both mental and social; they both derive from and constitute cultural, semiotic, and symbolic systems" (218). Internalized schemas make the structure of our social milieu seem right and natural.

An important part of individuation and socialization involves locating oneself in relation to others, specifically one's family and society more broadly. Some kinds of similarity become salient and have weight for us because of their cultural meaning. (Recall the issue of whether Isaac and I are similar.) Cultures provide categories for individuals and scripts for those within the categories. Many of us have little choice about what category we fall into or which script we follow. However, identity crises arise when the categories are questioned or when the scripts we are following conflict or are incomplete; as we saw above, adoptees' process of identity formation involves an encounter with two conflicting schemas of the family that must somehow be negotiated and internalized.

---

[19] See Novy, *Imagining* and *Reading*.

The dominant cultural schema for the family in the recent West is articulated by Velleman in his account of how healthy families are made:

> Some truths are so homely as to embarrass the philosopher who ventures to speak them. First comes love, then comes marriage, and then the proverbial baby carriage. Well, it's not such a ridiculous way of doing things, is it? The baby in that carriage has an inborn nature that joins together the natures of two adults. If those two adults are joined by love into a stable relationship—call it marriage—then they will be naturally prepared to care for it with sympathetic understanding, and to show it how to recognize and reconcile some of the qualities within itself. A child naturally comes to feel at home with itself and at home in the world by growing up in its own family ("Family" 370–71).

This schema—let's call it the *"natural nuclear family"* schema—is so powerful as to eclipse certain facts, for example, adopted children and those produced by gamete donation *are* growing up "in their own family" and often find spending time with their biological family uncomfortable and strange. And people with certain biological predispositions are actually not well-suited to parent others with those same dispositions but actually create powerfully dysfunctional family systems.

In his more recent paper, Velleman acknowledges that not all cultures have been structured around the nuclear family ("Persons" 13). And he admits that the commonality of having children raised by their biological relatives is not an argument for the goodness of this practice. But, he suggests, the ubiquity of the practice lends credibility to the "universal common sense":

> When I say that my claim is universal common sense, I mean that people everywhere and always have based their social relationships, in the first instance, on relations of kinship, of which the basic building block is the relation between parent and child. Not every society has favored the nuclear family, of course, but virtually every society has reared children among their kin and in the knowledge of who their biological patents are (13).

Whether this is "universal common sense" is one question; whether its ubiquity lends it credibility is another. Common sense, even if "universal," is not always empirically sound, so it would be helpful if Velleman provided some empirical evidence for his own speculation about the history of the human species. I am not an anthropologist either, and hesitate to enter into debates that have persisted over a century concerning the relationship between social and biological "kinship." However, perhaps we can make progress in clarifying what's at issue. I quote at length a passage from a well-known text concerning "The History of Definitions of Kinship":

> First, there is the genetic father, the man who supplies the sperm which fertilizes the ovum. He is for all practical purposes unknown and unknowable in most societies of the world, and even in our own with the best tools of modern science it is only possible to exclude certain persons but never to positively identify any particular person. Second . . . there is the genitor. The genitor is the man who according to the particular cultural theory of the particular society we are concerned with is held to be the man by whose actions the woman was caused to be pregnant. Thus, where the genetic father is a purely scientific concept . . . the genitor is defined in terms of the folk beliefs of each culture. It is conceivable, and Barnes seems to think it is possible, that such a status may be absent from some cultures. I would take it that these would be such places as are said to deny physiological paternity or the role of coitus in conception. Finally the third concept is that of the social father, or the pater. The social father need not necessarily be a man. Thus in cases of leviratic marriage, woman-woman marriage, and so on, the culture may explicitly recognize and accord different rights, duties, and status to the (socially recognized) genitor and the pater, each different persons. It is with the genitor and the pater that anthropology is concerned and not with the genetic father. The same distinctions can be made between the genetic mother, the genetrix, and the mater, of course, and can be taken to include theories of reproduction (Schneider 110).

Summarizing these distinctions, Schneider continues:

> Thus there is genetic kinship in the sense of what the science of genetics seems to have established and there is the particular set of folk beliefs and indigenous theory of reproduction characteristic of a particular society. Finally there is the set of social conventions which consists in roles, norms, rules, rights, duties, and so forth which are attached to the culturally distinguished statuses which are embedded in the indigenous theory of reproduction (110).

Given that kinship relations might be based on genetic relations, folk reproductive theory, or social roles as sources of kinship relations, Velleman's claim about the centrality of kinship and parent/child relations is vague. There are several possible readings. Here are three:

- *Social reading*: Social kinship is the basis for all other social relations and the building block for social kinship is the relation between pater/mater and child. In every society children know who their pater and/or mater are.
- *Folk reproductive theory reading*: Presumed natural kinship is the basis for all other social relations and the building block for social kinship is the relation between genitor/genitrix and child. In every society children know who their genitor/genitrix are.
- *Biologistic reading*: Genetic kinship is the basis for all other social relations and the building block for genetic kinship is the relation between genetic parent and offspring. In every society children know who their genetic parents are.

From what I know of the anthropological literature on kinship, none of these claims would be considered uncontroversial. Given that in many societies people have had a very weak grasp of reproductive biology,[20] and given the huge variety of (social) kinship structures that anthropologists spent a good part of the twentieth century studying, the biologistic reading is the least plausible of the three.[21] However, to claim, as in the social reading, that children know their pater and/or mater is virtually tautologous, for they are defined as the social parents. (In other words, of course children know and are usually reared by their kin, because the social notion of kinship can be defined in terms of roles vis-à-vis children.) But the social reading does not support Velleman's view anyway, for it is generally agreed that the pater and mater need not be biologically related to the child.[22]

The "folk biological" reading is the most interesting, for it suggests a universal attempt at biologism, even if the beliefs about reproduction structuring kinship in a particular society are false. But there are several worries. First, in societies where the conditions for being genitor/genetrix are not conditions that pick out the genetic father and mother, the knowledge of genitor/genetrix does not provide the kind of biological resource that Velleman assumes universal. Second, even if in most societies children know *of* their genitor/genitrix

---

[20] See Beckerman and Valentine; Böck and Rao; and Merlan, for a start.

[21] It may be worth noting that "primates do not have an innate ability to identify their [genetic] relatives, even their own offspring" (Silk 73), and although it is not typical, chimps will adopt the offspring of others (Thierry and Anderson; de Waal 70–73).

[22] The further claim that social kinship is the basis for all social relations is also controversial. Although some anthropologists would probably agree, others would argue that, e.g., property, or land-holding is the basis for social relations, including the structure of family (see Pasternak, ch. 7); or, more generally, that the structure of the family is dependent on the broader social system in which it is embedded (Harrell 27).

(which, as noted in the quotation above, is controversial), it doesn't follow that they have ongoing contact with them.

> It is so self-evident to most people in Euro-American society that children should be raised by their 'natural' parents that it might come as a surprise to learn that this is not always and everywhere the case. . . . Many anthropological and sociological studies illustrate the tenuous relationship a presumed biological father or genitor may have with his children, [and] . . . In fact, to share or reassign maternal responsibilities emerges as a relatively common strategy in many societies, by no means always arising from necessity (poverty or redressing childlessness in others) (Bowie 3).

We cannot settle here whether the anthropological evidence supports Velleman's claim or not, so let us suppose he is right. What follows? Claiming that the "naturalness" or ubiquity of a practice lends it credibility is a familiar form of argument. John Stuart Mill was one of the clearest and most articulate critics of this idea. Acknowledging the universal subordination of women to men, he eloquently argued that this was no mark in its favor.

> In the first place, the opinion in favour of the present system, which entirely subordinates the weaker sex to the stronger, rests upon theory only; for there never has been a trial made of any other: so that experience, in the sense in which it is vulgarly opposed to theory, cannot be pretended to have pronounced any verdict. And in the second place, the adoption of this system of inequality never was the result of deliberation or forethought, or any social ideas, or any notion whatever of what conduced to the benefit of humanity or the good order of society. It arose simply from the fact that from the very earliest twilight of human society, every woman . . . was found in a state of bondage to some man (5).

In both the case of male domination and in biological parenting, the issue is structural. Do we have reason to think, based on the facts as we know them, that male domination is necessary, or good? Do we have reason to think, based on the facts as we know them, that a society structured around biological parenting is necessary or good? Both kinds of structures are allegedly ubiquitous (though as just noted, this is controversial). In both cases we can give explanations about how they emerged and why they survive that do not now justify them. This is the crucial point. what explains the (alleged) universality? Is the best explanation that the structures are good and, in fact, better than alternative structures that have been tried? How can we know unless we have clear evidence of the effects of other structures? Indeed, the claim of universality undermines itself: it would be easier to argue for the goodness of the structure if it weren't universal, for then we would have stronger evidence of its goodness in contrast to the alternatives under consideration.

Velleman suggests a more deliberative process: "People have tried living in vastly diverse ways, but they have almost always settled on lifeways that accord central importance to biological family ties" ("Persons" 15). Or, at least, that accord central importance to the relation between biological mother and child. To give Velleman credit, his account of the similar natures of biological parents and their offspring and the value of this for child-rearing is intended to provide a rationale for the practice. (We should note that historically, this too is a familiar form of argument: women *by nature* are in need of male supervision.) However, another explanation of the centrality of biological mother-child relations is easily available: until recently, infants needed to be breastfed. The most reliable source of breast milk for an infant would be its biological mother. It is tempting to think that just as, in Mill's words, male domination "arose simply from the fact that from the very earliest twilight of human society, every woman . . . was found in a state of bondage to some man," the centrality of biological mother-child relations arose simply from the fact that from the very earliest twilight of human society every infant was found to be in a state of needing a lactating woman, the nearest being its biological mother.

We should note, however, that Velleman doesn't need the claim that societies always and everywhere have organized themselves around the biological family to make his claim that this is a basic good. As noted above when considering the importance of linen shirts in eighteenth-century England, some goods are *contextually* basic. They are necessary in a particular culture at a particular time in order to have a good life. One could reasonably claim that because the "natural nuclear family" schema is dominant in contemporary Western societies and has been for several centuries, children are harmed who are deprived of the resources to situate themselves socially using this narrative trope. Just as lacking a linen shirt in eighteenth-century England would be shameful and suggest a history of bad conduct, likewise admission of adoptee (or birthmother or adoptive parent) status has been considered shameful and indicative of bad conduct in our recent culture, among others. Lacking knowledge of one's biological family, one is often left without answers to questions that matter culturally, and this is stigmatizing. Given the difficulty of living a good life as a member of a stigmatized group, we owe adoptees access to their biological relatives so they have answers to questions that the natural nuclear family schema assumes they will have.

Here we have come to a point on which Velleman and I agree. The natural nuclear family schema plays an important role in forming identities—including healthy identities—in our current cultural context, and many people are stigmatized by not being able to "fit" the schema; in short, early twenty-first century American culture is bionormative. Being stigmatized is harmful and it is difficult to live a good life when stigmatized in this way. However, even granting the cultural significance of the natural nuclear family schema, there are two ways to combat this stigma. One is to provide resources so that everyone can come as close as possible to fitting the schema, another is to combat the dominance of the schema. Velleman prefers the former strategy; I prefer the latter. The problem, as I see it, lies in the reification of the schema as universal, necessary, and good, and not the families that fail to match it.

I take the crucial question to be whether parents, or society more generally, is obliged to provide the social bases for healthy identity formation in terms of the dominant ideology of the culture. If the obligation is simply to provide the social bases for healthy identity formation, then if there are multiple routes to this result, the obligation is only to provide one or another of these routes. For example, if the dominant schemas for identity are implicated in structures and forms of life that are unjust, the good of fitting neatly into the culture may be compromised. The best alternative may be to find or construct alternative—counter-hegemonic—identities and narratives that complicate gender, race, ethnicity, family, and so on. In a context in which the dominant schema is biological/genetic determinism, it is useful to be acquainted with one's biological relations. But this is a conditional good and is not good by virtue of the biological relations alone. Anonymous gamete donation may make telling a life-story that fits with the dominant family schema difficult, but likewise children of interracial partnerships have (or had) more difficulty telling a life-story that fits with the dominant schema of the Black-White racial binary. This doesn't mean that interracial couples are (or were) doing something immoral by having a child. Providing our children the social bases for alternative family schemas may be not only permissible, but morally good; it may even be a moral duty to combat bionormativity. In particular, constructing and teaching narratives that normalize adoption and schemas that challenge the assumption that our biological inheritance defines who we are, may not be to spread lies (Velleman, "Family" 378), but to provide the resources to build a more just society.

In the case of the natural nuclear family schema, much more would have to be said to determine whether and to what extent its dominance is implicated in structures of injustice. Insofar as the schema underwrites traditional gender roles and heteronormative models of the family, I take it to be morally problematic. But this is a large debate that goes beyond the opportunities this chapter provides. My argument is more limited. I believe that knowing one's biological relatives can be a good thing, and that contact is valuable in the contemporary cultural context largely because this context is dominated by the natural nuclear family schema. Even in this context, the formation of a full self and the formation of a healthy identity do not require contact with, or even specific knowledge of, biological relatives. Identities are formed in relation to cultural schemas, and fortunately our culture provides a wealth of schemas that sometimes fit with and sometimes run counter to the dominant ideology. Living under the shadow of the natural nuclear family schema, it is reasonable to provide children with information about or contact with their biological relations, if and when this becomes an issue in their forming a healthy identity. However, if we are to avoid harming our children, then rather than enshrining a schema that most families fail to exemplify and which is used to stigmatize and alienate families that are (yes!) as good as their biological counterparts, we should instead make every effort to disrupt the hegemony of the schema.[23]

Works Cited

Allen, Anita. "Does a Child Have a Right to a Certain Identity?" *Rechtstheorie* 15.Sup.15 (1993): 109–19.

———. "Open Adoption is Not for Everyone." *Adoption Matters: Philosophical and Feminist Essays.* Ed. Sally Haslanger and Charlotte Witt. Ithaca, NY: Cornell UP 2005. 47–67.

Baker, Howard S., and Margaret N. Baker. "Heinz Kohut's Self Psychology: An Overview." *American Journal of Psychiatry* 141.1 (1987): 1–9.

Beckerman, S., and P. Valentine. "The Concept of Partible Paternity Among Native South Americans." *Cultures of Multiple Fathers: The Theory and Practice of Partible Paternity in Lowland South America.* Ed. S. Beckerman and P. Valentine. Gainsville: UP of Florida, 2002. 1–13.

Benatar, David. "The Unbearable Lightness of Bringing Into Being." *Journal of Applied Philosophy* 16.2 (1999) 173–80.

Böck, M., and A. Rao, *Culture, Creation, and Procreation: Concepts of Kinship in South Asian Practice.* Oxford: Berghahn, 2000.

Borders, L. DiAnne, Lynda K. Black, and B. Kay Pasley. "Are Adopted Children and Their Parents at Greater Risk of Negative Outcomes?" *Family Relations* 47.3 (1998): 237–41.

Borders, L. DiAnne, Judith M. Penny, and Francie Portnoy. "Adult Adoptees and Their Friends: Current Functioning and Psychosocial Well-Being." *Family Relations* 49.4 (2000): 407–18.

Bowie, Fiona. *Adoption and the Circulation of Children: A Comparative Perspective.* New York: Routledge, 2004.

Carp, E. Wayne. "Adoption, Blood Kinship, Stigma, and the Adoption Reform Movement: A Historical Perspective." *Nonbiological Parenting.* Spec. issue of *Law and Society Review* 36.2 (2002): 433–60.

Cross, William E., Jr. *Shades of Black: Diversity in African-American Identity.* Philadelphia: Temple UP, 1991.

de Waal, Frans. *Chimpanzee Politics: Power and Sex Among Apes.* Revised ed. Baltimore, MD: Johns Hopkins UP, 1998.

Harrell, Stevan. *Human Families.* Boulder, CO: Westview, 1997.

Hoopes, Janet L. "Adoption and Identity Formation." *The Psychology of Adoption.* Ed. David M. Brodzinsky and Marshall D. Schechter. Oxford: Oxford UP, 1990. 144–66.

Howard, Judith A. "A Social Cognitive Conception of Social Structure." *Social Psychology Quarterly* 57.3 (1994): 210–27.

[23] Thanks to Lawrence Blum, Jorge Garcia, Heather Paxson, Brad Skow, Natalie Stoljar, Charlotte Witt, and Stephen Yablo for helpful discussion of the issues in this chapter. I presented drafts of this chapter at the University of Massachusetts, Boston Philosophy Department, the Centre de Recherche en Éthique de l'Université de Montréal, McGill University Center for Research and Teaching on Women, and Encountering New Worlds of Adoption Conference at the University of Pittsburgh. Thanks to the participants at these sessions and to Marianne Novy, Emily Hipchen, and an anonymous referee for valuable feedback.

Howe, David, and Julia Feast. "The Long-Term Outcome of Reunions Between Adult Adopted People and Their Birth Mothers." *British Journal of Social Work* 31.3 (2001): 351–68.

Kirk, H.D. *Shared Fate*. New York: Free Press, 1964.

Kohler, Julie K., Harold Grotevant, and Ruth G. McRoy. "Adopted Adolescents' Preoccupation with Adoption: The Impact on Adoptive Family Relationships." *Journal of Marriage and Family* 64.1 (2002): 93–104.

Merlan, Francesca. "Australian Aboriginal Conception Beliefs Revisted." *Man* n.s. 21.3 (1986): 474–93.

Mill, John Stuart. *The Subjection of Women*. 1869. Ed. Susan M. Okin. Indianapolis, IN: Hackett, 1988.

National Association of Black Social Workers. "Transracial Adoption." Conference of the National Association of Black Social Workers. Nashville, TN. 4–9 April 1972.

Neal, Leora. "The Case Against Transracial Adoption." *Focal Point* 10.1 (1996): 18–20.

Novy, Marianne. *Imagining Adoption: Essays on Literature and Culture*. Ann Arbor: U of Michigan P, 2004.

———. *Reading Adoption: Family and Difference in Fiction and Drama*. Ann Arbor: U of Michigan P, 2007.

Pasternak, Burton. *Introduction to Kinship and Social Organization*. Englewood Cliffs, NJ: Prentice Hall, 1976.

Schneider, David M. *A Critique of the Study of Kinship*. Ann Arbor: U of Michigan P, 1984.

Shireman, J.F., and P.R. Johnson. "A Longitudinal Study of Black Adoptions: Single Parent, Transracial and Traditional." *Social Work* 31.3 (1986): 173–76.

Silk, Joan B. "Ties That Bond: The Role of Kinship in Primate Societies." *New Directions in Anthropological Kinship*. Ed. Linda Stone. Lanham, MD: Rowman and Littlefield, 2001.

Smith, Adam. *The Wealth of Nations, Books IV-V*. 1776. Ed. Andrew Skinner. London: Penguin Classics, 2000.

Thierry, Bernard, and James Anderson. "Adoption in Anthropoid Primates." *International Journal of Primatology* 7.2 (1986). 191–216.

Velleman, J. David. Email Correspondence with Author. 16 August 2008.

———. "Narrative Explanation." *The Philosophical Review* 112.1 (2003): 1–125.

———. "Family History." *Philosophical Papers* 34.3 (2005): 357–78.

———. "Persons in Prospect II: The Gift of Life." *Philosophy and Public Affairs* 36.3 (Summer 2008): 245–266.

Witt, Charlotte. "Family Resemblances: Adoption, Personal Identity and Genetic Essentialism." *Adoption Matters: Philosophical and Feminist Essays*. Ed. Sally Haslanger and Charlotte Witt. Ithaca: Cornell UP, 2005. 135–45.

6

Social Construction

Myth and Reality[1]

I have nothing against classification. I love the richness of the
different kinds of things there are in the world and of the innu-
merable ways in which they can be grouped together.
                                                    —Ian Hacking *2007, 208*

The modern idealist—the antirealist who acquiesces in minimal
realism holds that some states of affairs depend non-empirically
on *us* or *our practices*. But given the undemanding naturalism
that conditions the debate, there is nothing for this plural subject to be except a part of the natural world itself.
                                                    —Gideon Rosen *1994, 289*

Social constructionist claims are made in different contexts, different disciplines,
and with many different meanings. In many of these contexts, social construction
has come to be associated with a broad anti-realism, anti-objectivism about kinds,
and anti-naturalism.[2] My goal in this chapter is, first, to argue that although some
social constructionists are rightly described in these terms, there is a central form
of social construction—a form most often employed by feminist and race theorists when discussing the ontology of gender and race—that is compatible with
important forms of realism, an objectivism about kinds, and naturalism.

The question then arises: What is the point of defending the claim that a phenomenon is socially constructed if it is not to contrast it with a realist, objectivist,
and naturalist interpretation of it? On my view, the goal of social constructionist

[1] This chapter has been through many versions and has been presented at many colloquia. I cannot begin to thank all those who have helped me. However, a few have given me written comments
or have asked questions that have given rise to major changes, and they deserve special thanks. They
include: Penelope Deutscher, Marilyn Friedman, Lisa Guenther, Elizabeth Harman, Kate Manne,
Alexander Nehamas, Jacqueline Stevens, Kenneth Walden, Michael Weisberg, Charlotte Witt, and
Stephen Yablo.

[2] For a helpful survey of some of these differences and the complexity of the debate, see, e.g.,
Mallon 2007, 2008.

analyses is to locate the (often obscure) mechanisms of injustice and the levers for social change. It is difficult to recognize social structures, as such, and having a nuanced understanding of how social structures function is politically valuable. The constructionist metaphor remains apt, in spite of the realist ontology, because in many cases it is by understanding how complex social artifacts are put together that we can learn how to take them apart, and what we might be left with when we do.

1. Starting Points and Examples

The paradigm cases of social construction that I will be considering are: gender and race/ethnicity. Relevantly similar cases that I'm also interested in include: disability, sexuality, family, and food. In the central cases, a disadvantaged social position is marked upon and lived through the body, and the resulting condition is taken to be fixed by the natural world. This is not to say that naturalizing a category is the only way that social positions come to be fixed or assumed fixed; laws, customs, traditions, habits, and the like, function to limit not only what we can do, but also what we can imagine, at least as intractably as beliefs about what's natural. And simply calling the naturalness of a practice into question is not enough to destabilize it (since it may have plenty of social buttresses) or to critique it (since there may be good reasons to maintain it). However, the presumption that "the way things are" is due to nature, or our natures, is a serious barrier to social change. Social constructionists of the sort I have in mind (and of which I am one) attempt to unmask the processes that cause—and structures that constitute—unacknowledged parts of our social world. This is valuable both when the social is cast as natural, and when the social, considered as such, is nevertheless deeply entrenched and so exempted from critique.

Let us begin with a couple of examples. Since the 1970s, feminists have argued for the social construction of gender using the slogan: *gender is the social meaning of sex*. Although many feminists now reject this slogan, the point is to distinguish, on one hand, the anatomical features by virtue of which one counts as male or female, for example, having XX or XY chromosomes and a variety of primary and secondary sex characteristics and, on the other hand, the social position and experiences of a man or woman.[3] It is clear that the anatomical facts and the social meaning of sex can be distinguished and often are. For example, it is not incoherent for someone to say, "She is an unusual woman," or even "He's not a real man," without having any idea whatsoever of the individual's

---

[3] Throughout my discussion I will use the terms 'male' and 'female' for the currently dominant distinction between the sexes, and 'man' and 'woman' for the currently dominant distinction between genders.

biological makeup. As Beauvoir aptly noted, ". . . in speaking of certain women, connoisseurs declare that they are not women, although they are equipped with a uterus like the rest" (Beauvoir 1989 [1949], ix–x). This suggests that being a woman or a man is not just a matter of body parts. Moreover, there are many individuals for whom sex and gender do not coincide: males can live as women and females as men (in some cases without this fact being known, even to their spouses[4]).

According to the account I have proposed (Haslanger 2012 [2000]), gender, in the core sense, is defined in terms of social relations.[5] What does this mean? Consider the social categories of *landlord* and *tenant*. These are constituted by a relationship—renting to/from—that holds between the members of each category. This relationship is possible only against a larger backdrop of economic, political, and legal conditions. Members of each category vary in their identification with the category and in their experiences as members of the category; the norms associated with the categories vary from context to context; individuals can be members of neither or both categories and can move from one to the other or out of both. Although there are obvious and important differences between the categories landlord/tenant and man/woman, gender categories are likewise constituted by a set of social relations. Defining what social relations constitute gender (and race), while exploring the implications of this approach for understanding embodiment, identity, social norms and justice, is the larger project of which this chapter is a part.

Distinguishing sex and gender allows us to ask a variety of important questions, for example, what, if anything, do the social positions of women (or men) have in common across time, place, and culture? Is there some fact about sex that determines in specific ways the form gender takes? What factors other than biology determine the form of gender in a particular cultural context? Why is it that gendered social positions are generally presumed to be natural and the distinction between sex and gender is considered news?

In previous work I have argued that there are important parallels between gender and race (Haslanger 2012 [2000]). Transposing the feminist slogan yields, I argue: *race is the social meaning of "color."* "Color" in the intended sense (indicated by the use of scare quotes) includes not only skin color, but also those features in a particular context that mark the body as having presumed ancestral origins in a particular region of the world. So eye, nose, and lip shape, hair color and texture, height, and physique can all count as elements of "color" in the contemporary context. There are physical differences between members of different

---

[4] Consider, e.g., the story of Billy Tipton (Smith 1998).

[5] The term 'gender' is sometimes used as elliptical for 'gender identity,' where 'gender identity' is understood in psychological terms: one's sense of oneself as a man or woman. In my discussion I will not elide the terms in this way, for I want to hold onto a clear distinction not only between sex and gender, but also between gender and gender identity. See also chapter 9 of this volume.

races (though these differences fall along a continuum); however, races are constituted not by these physical differences, but by the implications of these differences in contexts where they are taken to be socially significant.[6] According to the details of my account (see chapter 7 of this volume), races are constituted not by just any social meaning of "color" but, in particular, meanings that situate individuals within a social hierarchy; this latter claim concerning hierarchy is not crucial for my purposes in this chapter where my focus is on the background ontology and politics of social construction quite generally, so I will elide it in this discussion.

2. Distinguishing Different Claims
The Collapse of Sex/Gender?

I maintain that gender is socially constructed. On the account of social construction that I favor, this claim is compatible with sex either being socially constructed or not. Some feminists, however, reject the sex/gender distinction. Sex, they argue, is as socially constructed as gender: we are motivated to draw sex distinctions in the ways we do to fulfill a particular social purpose; "nature" doesn't tell us where to draw the line. And if sex and gender are both socially constructed, then it doesn't make sense to introduce gender as a category distinct from sex by claiming that gender is socially constructed (Butler 1990; Wittig 1992; Fausto-Sterling 1993, 1997, 2000a, 2000b; Delphy 1993; Grosz 1994; Gatens 1996; Kessler 1998; Warnke 2001. Cf. Friedman 1996; Haslanger 2012 [2000]; Stone 2007; Mikkola 2008).[7]

The first (partial) reply to the purported collapse of sex and gender is to point out that there still may be a point to distinguishing sex and gender, even if they are not distinguishable by sex being natural and gender being social. The categories of professor and student are both social categories, each defined in relation to the other, but it is still useful to distinguish them. Moreover, even if sex and gender are both

[6] Kate Manne has helpfully suggested to me that we can see race and gender as ways of classifying people according to questions that one might initially pose a stranger: "Where are you from?," "What are you here for?." We might extend this to other categories, e.g., class ("What do you do?"), sexuality ("What can you do for *me*?"). I'm especially keen to explore the idea in later work that class is the social meaning of labor, which is also often marked on the body.

[7] In what might appear to be a parallel move, some theorists have argued that racial distinctions and "color" distinctions are, in a sense, natural, based on the claim that primitive cognitive mechanisms cause us to distinguish between individuals based on "color" differences, and to essentialize these differences (Hirschfeld 1996; see also Mallon 2007). However, it is worth noting that those exploring this line of thought are not race naturalists. Rather, they endorse a social constructionist account of the ontology of race and use research in social psychology to show how our natural belief-forming tendencies steer us wrong in this and other cases. This is significant in the context of the following discussion, for it suggests that accounts of how and why we distinguish certain groups need not have direct consequences concerning the ontological status of the categories we employ, which is my broader point.

social categories, they may be social in different ways. But these initial thoughts do not address the broader issue: What is it for something to be socially constructed (or not)? Is there a sense in which sex is socially constructed? What is that sense?

The impulse to collapse sex and gender, just sketched, also occurs when considering other purportedly socially constructed categories and relies on a particular form of inference. The premise in question asserts an explanation of why we draw certain distinctions (due, e.g., to political motivations); and this premise allegedly entails a conclusion about the ontological status of what is distinguished. Sex is socially constructed *because* the best explanation of why we draw sex distinctions as we do is that societies have an interest in managing reproduction. This form of inference is, I believe, mistaken; but exploring the mistake will illuminate the complex ontology and epistemology of social construction.

Distinctions and Differences

In what sense, if any, is *sex* (as distinct from gender) socially constructed? Human bodies come in a variety of forms, and body parts are not distributed in fixed packages. Some estimate that, depending on one's definitions, as many as 1 in 100 individuals are intersexed, that is, have a set of primary and secondary sex characteristics that do not neatly fit the classification of male or female (Intersex Society of North America; Fausto-Sterling 1993; Fausto-Sterling 2000a; Fausto-Sterling 2000b). Moreover, it is possible, even likely, that interests other than scientific taxonomy motivate the sharp divide between males and females insisted upon in most cultures. Humans have an interest in knowing with whom they are likely to reproduce and are keen to control access to reproductive resources. However, it does not follow that there is no physical basis for sex distinctions; nor does it constitute them as social differences. Some biological or anatomical distinctions may be socially *motivated* without what's distinguished thereby *being* social.

To be clearer, let us use the term 'distinction' and 'distinguish' or 'classification' and 'classify' for the linguistic/conceptual acts of noting or marking differences, and the terms 'difference' and 'differentiate' for the ontological basis for distinctions when they are apt, that is, we *distinguish* objects, properties, relations or kinds that are *different*; our *distinctions* aim to capture what *differentiates* the kinds we're interested in. For example, Granny Smith apples are different from Fuji apples in color and taste. We distinguish between these kinds of apple by using the terms 'Granny Smith' and 'Fuji.' We may distinguish these kinds of apple for agricultural or economic reasons, or because some prefer tart apples and other sweet. Some humans or communities of humans may not distinguish these two kinds of apple at all—they may be unfamiliar with apples and not realize they come in different varieties. But even if we don't have the words to distinguish them, there are color, taste, and agricultural differences between them.

On my view, the world is replete with things, and parts, fusions, sets, collections, and properties of things. Differences abound. There are more divisions than we could ever note or care about.[8] We distinguish things by classifying them, and classification is a human activity and can be done in better or worse ways. The adequacy of a classification will depend on a variety of factors, including the extent to which the classification in question serves one's goals and purposes, and the extent to which the goals and purposes are legitimate (Anderson 1995a, Anderson 1995b). Theoretical and practical norms will have different weights, depending on the task.

For example, when I am sorting my daughter's clothes to determine which should be donated to the Salvation Army, the relevant classification is "keep" and "don't keep." The "don't keep" pile may be a heterogeneous group including clothes that are too small, ones that are not attractive on her, ones she won't wear because her tastes have changed, because they evoke unpleasant memories, or because they show more (or less!) wear and tear than she will tolerate. This is a perfectly good classification and, given the purposes at hand, it captures some "joint" in the world (the joint between the clothes we have reason to keep and those we have reason to give away), even if it results in a "don't keep" set whose members are far from intrinsically unified. In this task I am appropriately guided by some epistemic goals (it would be a problem if my conditions for sorting were inconsistent, or if I applied them haphazardly), and some practical goals (I want to be efficient and generous, but also respect her preferences). Although this is not the place to argue for it in full detail, I believe that the adequacy of all classification depends on both theoretical and practical considerations.

Further examination of this example of sorting for the Salvation Army suggests that additional terminology is useful. In sorting my daughter's clothes, the distinction between "keep" and "don't keep" is motivated by a particular practical purpose—to reduce clutter while donating to a worthy cause. The *basis* for including a particular shirt in the "keep" pile consists in a set of features or conditions that the shirt manifests; these are the differentiating features that (purportedly) best serve the purpose at hand. My daughter and I might disagree about what the necessary and/or sufficient conditions for the "keep" pile should be; our disagreement may concern the overarching purpose, or how best to fulfill that purpose.

Let's suppose, for simplicity, that we agree on the condition that the "don't keep" pile should consist of all and only the clothes that are too small, that is,

---

[8] I have a kind of Lewisian picture to start with: "Any class of things, be it ever so gerrymandered and miscellaneous and indescribable in thought and language, and be it ever so superfluous in characterising the world, is nevertheless a property. So there are properties in immense abundance" (Lewis 1983, 346). I differ from Lewis, however, in not taking naturalness to be a sparse primitive. My view is closer to 'promiscuous realism' (Dupré 1993, 18).

the basis for not keeping an item is simply its fit. Additional questions arise when we come to apply this. If I'm going to make headway, I need to have a way of deciding what is too small for her without having her try everything on. Supposing that she now wears a size 12, it would make sense for me to get rid of everything that is smaller than a size 12. This the *criterion* I use for applying the distinction. Note that criteria are distinct from conditions. Criteria provide evidence that conditions are met. In this case, the criterion I've chosen is not very reliable. Clothing manufacturers are not consistent in their sizing, so some size 10 clothes may fit her and some size 12 clothes may be too small. This opens up additional space for disagreement and debate: if I sort the clothes according to marked size, she might legitimately complain that I haven't sorted correctly.

We began with a contrast between distinctions and differences, and we've added to this *purposes* for drawing the distinction or noting the differences, *conditions*—purported features of the things that differentiate them and provide a basis for applying the distinction—and (epistemic) *criteria* we use to conclude that the conditions are met. For each of these, there are relevant norms and potential for debate: We can ask whether the purposes for drawing the distinction are *legitimate*, whether the conditions are *apt* given our purposes, and whether our criteria are *reliable*.

Let us return now to the distinction between sex and gender. It may be that we are motivated to distinguish males and females by social interests and there may or may not be a legitimate social purpose for doing so.[9] It is always appropriate to ask of a classification whether and how a distinction serves our purposes (and, more specifically, whose purposes it serves) because classification is a goal-oriented activity at which we can do better or worse, both in formulating the goal and figuring out how to achieve it. But the fact that sex *distinctions* have a social function does not imply that the *difference* between the sexes—once selected as significant—is social; the conditions we settle upon for being male or female may be ones that only make reference to anatomical features. (See also chapters 3 and 4 of this volume.)

More generally, it is not uncommon to have a social purpose for drawing a physical distinction. A city official's classification of tap water as being free of coliform bacteria after the repair of a water main is apt only to the extent that the water, independently of the official's designation, meets the condition. The official's act of classification is a social act, but the quality of the water that is the basis for the classification concerns its chemical composition. In some cases, the social act of classification has its point only to the extent that it captures a difference

---

[9] I want to include both causes and reasons of our distinguishing sexes as we do, though the social constructionist metaphor has led people to think mainly in terms of causes. The focus on causes of our distinctions is sometimes a mistake and the issues should be reframed in terms of what reasons we have or what justifies us in making certain distinctions. See chapter 3 of this volume.

that is independent of that act. So, it does not follow from the fact that we are motivated to draw a distinction due to social pressures or social interests that the difference we are noting is social. (Similarly, as noted, it does not follow from the fact that there is a *nativist* explanation of my drawing a certain distinction, that the difference being noted is *natural*. It is plausible that human infants have an innate ability and predisposition to distinguish their primary caregivers from others, but being a primary caregiver is certainly a social category.)[10] In short, an inference from kind of distinction (natural/social) to kind of difference (natural/social) is not, in general, valid.

Constructing Distinctions and Constructing Differences

The observations in the previous section help us disambiguate the claim that being an F, or the category of Fs, is socially constructed.[11] First, it might mean that our drawing a distinction between Fs and non-Fs is motivated by or fulfills a *social purpose*. Most of our ideas, distinctions, and classifications have social origins (allowing for the possibility of innate ideas) and fulfill social purposes; pointing this out can be valuable, but it is not completely surprising. Second, it might mean that the differences between Fs and non-Fs are social, that is, the conditions for being F or non-F are *social features* of things. Third, it might mean that things are *caused by social forces* to satisfy the conditions that make them F or non-F.

Ian Hacking's distinction between "idea construction" and "object construction" (Hacking 1999) is useful because it calls attention to a difference between the first sort of social construction (concerning distinctions) and the other two (concerning differences); but he fails to note the further division between social features and social causes (Haslanger 2012 [2003]). To avoid ongoing ambiguity, I'll use the term 'socially distinguished' for idea construction: it is plausible that males and females are socially distinguished. We distinguish males and females and by doing so we fulfill certain social purposes. I'll use the term 'socially caused' for cases of social causation: the differences between beagles and greyhounds are socially caused (through breeding), and plausibly some differences between males and females are socially caused. I'll use the term 'socially constituted' for those cases in which the features that make for the difference in question are social: landlords and tenants are socially constituted because the conditions that must be met in order to be a landlord or tenant are social conditions. The

---

[10] This is relevant because there are some theorists who argue that there are nativist explanations of our racial classifications (see n 7). The question, then, would be whether this entails that race is a natural feature of people rather than socially constituted. See, e.g., (Hirschfeld 1996; Gil-White 2001; cf. Gelman 2003, 304f; Machery and Faucher 2005; Mallon 2007).

[11] The distinction might be between Fs and non-Fs (i.e., contradictories), or Fs and Gs (if F and G are contraries or apparent contraries). I simplify here.

category of gender (relying on the slogan that gender is the social meaning of sex) is also socially constituted, that is, one is a man or a woman (cf. male/ female) by virtue of the social relations one stands in. These three "constructionist" terms are not exclusive. The distinction between landlords and tenants is socially distinguished, and the difference is both socially caused and socially constituted.

We can now consider more carefully the claim that sex is socially constructed. It is not too hard to grant that the distinction between males and females has a social function. But what of sex differences? Is the difference between being male and being female caused by social forces? Are the conditions constituting what it is to be male or female social? In general, examples of social causation and social constitution are common. However, the suggestion that the differences between males and females are socially caused or socially constituted is unexpected: isn't being male just a matter of having XY chromosomes, a penis, and (eventually) the capacity to produce sperm? And isn't that something that just happens through a process of human biological development?

Sex Revisited

It is not my goal here to offer an argument for or against the social causation or constitution of sex. Rather, it is to illuminate how the question whether sex is socially constructed is related to the question whether gender is socially constructed. In order to determine whether the conditions sufficient for being in a category are social, or the causes of having the features in question are social, we have to look carefully at the differences in question. What distinctions we draw and what differences correspond to them depend on the purposes of sorting in that context. Human sex differentiation occurs within a framework of social meaning. An infertility specialist and an intersexed teen have different purposes and interests that will lead them, reasonably, to different conclusions about what sex is. Because there are different frameworks of social meaning, different ways of drawing sex differences will be adequate to those frameworks. It does not matter whether those who employ different frameworks in different contexts agree unless they need to communicate; and when they need to communicate, there are mechanisms available to disambiguate their terms. What matters is whether their conclusions about what sex is give good answers to their questions, where good answers involve tracking the parts of reality that do the needed descriptive, explanatory, and normative work (Anderson 1995a; Elgin 1997, Introduction, Ch. 1, Ch. 11). It is a further question which meaning is, and should be, the dominant public meaning, and what considerations are relevant to determining this (Bigelow and Schroeter 2009, e.g., also Haslanger 2012 [2008], 2012 [2010]).

For example, the question of what features *differentiate* males and females is a non-trivial matter, and is far from settled, as can be seen from the controversy over Caster Semenya, the South African runner whose female standing was challenged after she won the 800 meters in the 2009 World Championships, and only reinstated in June 2010.[12] We might start by considering physical features such as: chromosomes, reproductive organs, and such. According to standard medical dictionaries, a male just is "an individual that produces small usually motile gametes (as sperm or spermatozoa) which fertilize the eggs of a female" (MedlinePlus). If we accept this definition, then the conditions for being male appear to be physical.[13] However, sexologists have included as a basis for sex differentiation developmental features during adolescence, for example, gender identity and role, that have clear social dimensions (Money and Tucker 1976; Fausto-Sterling 1997). On this latter view, whether one is male or female is partly a function of non-biological facts, including the individual's social role. And if social role is partly constitutive of being male or female, then insofar as social context plays a role in causing one to occupy a social role, sex is (at least partly?) socially caused as well as socially constituted.

This controversy over whether sex is a physical or social category is a controversy over how we should differentiate sex, what differences count. There are certainly vested interests at stake and social pressures to select one set of conditions or the other. However, if we allow that it is possible (and in some contexts, for some purposes, even reasonable) to define sex in physical terms, then the fact that sex distinctions are socially motivated and have a social function is compatible with sex being neither socially constituted nor socially caused. The distinctions I have drawn and the argument I've offered may iterate at lower levels. What counts as a 'penis' is a decision we make in different contexts given our purposes in classifying genitalia, but we may be justified in setting conditions for being a penis that simply make reference to physical features. If not, and penises are differentiated in part by social features, for example, whether the size of the organ would result in teasing in the locker room, then penises too are socially constituted (though the distinction between conditions and criteria should be noted here: is the teasing risk a condition or a criterion?). For the purposes of this chapter, I am neutral on the question of whether and to what extent sex and sex organs are socially constructed because I do not think this question can be answered in the abstract, apart from a particular purpose for the account being offered. Instead, I defer to the extensive literature on the

---

[12] Semenya is not the only or the first to have been challenged. Others include: Stella Walsh, Dora Ratjen, Tamara Press, Irina Press, Ewa Kłobukowska ("Caster Semenya" 2010).

[13] Admittedly, the issue can iterate: do we distinguish fertile sperm from infertile sperm for social reasons? Probably so. But is being fertile a social property? No, it is a property had by a sperm with certain causal properties with respect to ova.

topic (e.g., Laquer 1990; Kessler 1998; Fausto-Sterling 2000b, 2005; Warnke 2001; Shrage 2009).

"Color" Revisited

I've devoted considerable attention to the example of sex and gender. What about the social construction of "color" and race? Recall that the contrast between "color" and race, as I've introduced it, is supposed to be analogous to the contrast between sex and gender. The slogan is: *race is the social meaning of "color."* Just as we've considered the question whether sex is socially constructed, we should ask: Is "color" socially constructed? To provide a full answer to the question, it would be important to consider what context is relevant and the purposes for distinguishing race and "color" (Haslanger 2012 [2000]).

For current purposes I think it is reasonable to assume that any plausible story about the motives and purposes for distinguishing different "colors" of people will involve some social factors (see, e.g., Omi and Winant 1994; Fields 1982), even if one holds that there are also innate tendencies leading us to form racial categories (Hirschfeld 1996; Gil-White 2001; Gelman 2003, 304f; Machery and Faucher 2005; Mallon 2007). Using the terminology of the previous sections, let us assume that both "color" and race categories are socially distinguished. The question (parallel to the discussion of sex and gender) is whether we should consider "color" to be natural and race social. More specifically, are "color" differences socially constituted or socially caused? Is it possible to define "color" in physical terms? Is "color" a natural difference?

One might argue that "color" differences are entirely physical: being "colored" white consists in having a range of lighter skin tones (under the arm pit) combined with a range of hair texture, lip shape, and such. (Think of the criteria we normally use when concluding that someone is White.[14]) Although I am willing to allow that there might be contexts in which such a physical definition of "color" could be useful, the features that form the basis for racial classification in most contexts involve the social history of the appearance in question. Consider two individuals who appear to have the same skin color, eye shape, hair texture, and so on. These similar individuals may be different "colors" because in one case their ancestry is recently African and in the other case their ancestry is recently Latin American; or in one case their ancestry is recently European, and in the other case their ancestry is recently South American. This suggests that "color" is not just a matter of the intrinsic properties of human bodies, but involves the relationships between the particular body and others over time and place (Alcoff

---

[14] Note that here and elsewhere I use the lower case 'black' or 'white' or 'brown' for the "color" markings relevant to racial designation and upper case for homonymous names of races such as 'Black,' 'White,' etc.

1998, esp. 20–21; Alcoff 2000; Alcoff 2006, Ch. 4, especially pp. 102–113; Mills 1997, esp. 53–62). To answer the question what "color" someone is, we need to have an idea about their ancestry and the (purported) migrations of their ancestors over time. For example, it is not enough to know that someone has African ancestry to interpret their "color," because we all have African ancestry. The relevant ancestral geography is not just a matter of place, but of time and culture as well. If this is the case, then "color" is not only socially distinguished, but is also socially constituted. Considering the effects of anti-miscegenation laws and immigration policy, "ethnic cleansing" through rape and the history of interracial sexual exploitation, for example, of slave women, a case could be made that "color" is socially caused as well.

The example of "color" illustrates again the conclusion I drew earlier about inferences from distinctions to differences. One cannot conclude from the fact that the best explanation of our drawing a distinction is social, that the difference the distinction aims to track is a social difference, that is, has causes or conditions that are social. And one cannot conclude from the fact that the best explanation of our drawing a distinction is non-social that the difference is non-social. What we track and why we track it are both important questions. But answering one does not give us an answer to the other.

The Social Construction of Social Kinds?

In his book *The Social Construction of What* (1999), Ian Hacking questions whether (what I've called) the social constitution of gender could be a paradigm case of social construction. This raises the question whether social constitution is really a form of social construction at all. Hacking acknowledges that feminist theorists, following Beauvoir, have been important in developing the notion of social construction; he argues, however, that it would be redundant, and so not useful, to claim that gender is socially constructed (Hacking 1999, 39). Gender is, on any definition, a social phenomenon: "no matter what definition is preferred, the word ['gender'] is used for distinctions among people that are grounded in cultural practices, not biology" (Hacking 1999, 39). He continues: "If gender is, by definition, something essentially social, and if it is constructed, how could its construction be other than social?" (Hacking 1999, 39). The point seems to be that if one means by the claim that gender is socially constructed that the conditions for being gendered are social, then one's point is no better than a tautology. And social constructionists are not simply spouting tautologies.

But social constructionists are often introducing a distinction between a familiar kind of thing (sex), and a social kind (gender) that overlaps it substantially in its extension. In doing so, they provide a characterization of the social kind and highlight it as *social* because it is typically occluded in ordinary thinking about the phenomena in question: we see the group that we assume has a set of shared physical features and miss the social dimension of the situation.[15] The social constructionist points out differences that were not noticed or understood before, and in doing so, it is useful to stipulate a new definition or clarify the type of thing being highlighted. In such cases, what might appear to be a tautology is informative, useful, and revisable.[16]

More specifically, what makes something a tautology is not that it is a definition or a necessary truth, but that it is uninformative, that it *needlessly* repeats something that has been said or restates something in a way that doesn't contribute anything. But of course, defining a word or drawing out the entailments of a concept may be highly informative and make a valuable contribution. So the claim that X is socially constructed, even if obvious to some, may be appropriate in conversation if it points to a way that X is socially constituted, caused, or distinguished that is not part of the conversational common ground.[17] This partly explains why social constructionists aren't apt to announce that washing machines or juries are socially constructed, and also why the burden falls on the social constructionist to say more about the particular X in question in order to make apparent the social dimension.

For example, take the concept of *tween*. Tweens are children of a certain age, roughly 9–12. But tweenhood is a social classification, not just a chronological one, for example, one can find several different definitions online, some of which emphasize the susceptibility of the age group to certain marketing strategies, others to their sexual interests; for example, tween girls are those "too old for toys, too young for boys" (Laurellz 2005). Some youth of the relevant age even consider it an insult to be called a "tween" (Perry C, 2006). One more extensive definition states:

> A tween is a child between the ages of 9 and 12. A tween is no longer a little child, but not quite a teenager. While a tween is not yet in the midst of adolescence, he or she will face a variety of obstacles in the next few years including transitioning from elementary school to middle school, approaching puberty, increasing responsibilities, increasing

[15] The change on forms from the regular use of a tick-box for 'sex' to one for 'gender' is not obviously due to a recognition that being a man or woman is a social rather than natural fact. Interestingly, the U.S. Census report "Gender: 2000" (Smith and Spraggins 2001) seems to assume that 'sex' and 'gender' are synonyms: "Information on gender was derived from a question which was asked of all people (see Figure 1:3. What is this person's sex? *Mark ONE box.* □Male □Female). A question on the sex of individuals was included in all censuses since the first one in 1790." However, the 2010 census report "Age and Sex Composition: 2010" (Howden and Meyer 2011) does not use the term 'gender' even once.

[16] This, I believe, is closely connected to Quine's rejection of analytic truths (Quine 1961). We are interested in sets of things that may be picked out by a variety of different properties. If our interest is in the best explanation of the things in the set and their behavior, then we must be willing to revise our understanding of them and what they have in common as our broader account of the world evolves. What we took to be a necessary truth may just be a universal generalization, and maybe not even that.

[17] Thanks to Kenneth Walden for urging me to make this explicit and helping me formulate the point.

amounts of homework, and exposure to dangerous behaviors by their peers including drugs, sex, and more. (O'Donnell)

Given this understanding of 'tween,' there were no tweens in the Middle Ages, and probably aren't tweens in many parts of the world now, though of course children did and do pass through the years 9–12. In saying that "tween" is a social construct, one is pointing out that tweenhood is more than chronological; it is a category that one falls into by virtue of occupying a certain social position that tends to overlap with the years 9–12.

Here, too, one might complain, along with Hacking, that it is "redundant," and "not useful" to say that *tween* is a social construction because it is part of the definition of 'tween' that it is a social category. But this is to miss the point. We begin to talk about tweens to call attention to the social meaning in our culture of a certain stage of life, and sometimes to highlight that this meaning is not inevitable. To do this it is useful, sometimes even necessary, to explain what tweens are.

Returning to race and gender, in both cases there are two sets of features that are relevant: sex and "color" on one hand, and social position on the other. In every known culture, males are viewed and treated differently from females; in many contemporary cultures, people with European roots are viewed and treated differently from people with non-European roots. Construed simply, genders are those social positions, within a particular culture, constituted by how sexed beings are viewed and treated. Different cultures may "sex" humans differently: the intersexed, eunuchs, and berdache may function as third sexes; but sex divisions everywhere correlate with social divisions, and the social divisions are gender. For example, mothers, daughters, wives, actresses, and Lady Spartans are social categories that organize gender in a particular culture. Analogously, races are those social positions, within a particular culture, (roughly) constituted by how we are viewed and treated in light of information and suppositions inferred from our physical appearance about our ancestral roots. Sex is to gender, and "color" is to race roughly what chronological age 9–12 is to tween (see also chapter 7 of this volume).

So, as I see it, the social constructionist is calling attention to difference along social dimensions rather than (or in addition to) physical dimensions, and considering how social difference is produced. No doubt, social difference is usually produced by social forces, but these social forces are often hard to detect because social difference is taken to be based in some way in the "natural." Why is it that women continue to be paid less than men for the same work? Why do neighborhoods remain racially segregated? Is this due to social structures that constitute races and genders? The goal is to call attention to a level of explanation that focuses on the social, rather than the individual or political, level. Once we focus our mind on social structures, the question whether the structures are social is admittedly awkward: of course they are! The point of emphasizing that they are social is to correct those who are blind to the social phenomenon.

In order to distinguish the various sorts of constructionism, and to acknowledge the awkwardness or redundancy that Hacking points to when we assert the social construction of social entities, it will be useful to introduce some terminology. I've already suggested that we should distinguish between ways in which items are *socially distinguished*, *socially constituted*, and *socially caused*, even though all three of these ways may be in involved in a particular case of construction. Of course there are additional senses I have not explored (Hacking 1986; Sismondo 1993; Hacking 1999; Taylor 2005, Ch. 4; Haslanger 2005a; Mallon 2007), for example, one might want distinguish ways that ordinary artifacts, such as buildings, are socially constructed (socially caused?); one might also want to emphasize that some things are socially maintained, even though we cannot tell what their origins were or suspect they were non-social. I don't mean to be offering an exhaustive list of ways in which the term 'social construction' is or might be used.[18]

That said, however, a *critical realist*, or *critical social realist*, as I'll be using the term, is one who aims to reveal what Ron Mallon (2008) calls *covert constructions*, that is, differences that are socially constituted but not recognized, or fully recognized, to be so. In the paradigm cases, social processes also cause the differences, and our classificatory efforts are implicated in the causal story; calling attention to this will, at least in successful cases, provide critical leverage in challenging how we think and act.[19] Critical realists eschew global claims about construction: the focus is on particular social structures, and their impact in spite of their invisibility. In my case, the term 'critical' in situates the project within a broader tradition of critical social theory.[20]

---

[18] I have no intention in this chapter to define the term 'social.' This may seem to be a cop-out; however, I believe that a rough and ready understanding of the term is sufficient for my purposes. A non-circular definition is not likely to be available, but this does not preclude an account that situates the term within a conceptual web. As in many other cases, I favor a focal analysis (see the Introduction and chapter 7 of this volume); and believe that the adequacy of any definition will depend on one's purposes. For my purposes, coordinated activity, whether or not the coordination is conscious, is central.

[19] Note that Mallon emphasizes the causal dimension: "But even local constructionist claims can be interesting to the extent that they try to show some object may be *produced by* unacknowledged social practices—when they are *covert* constructions" (Mallon 2008, italics mine). I am interested in the causal, but especially interested in the constitutive dimension.

[20] The choice of terminology here is difficult. I am not entirely comfortable with the term *critical realism* for the view I favor because that term has already been adopted by the followers of Roy Bhaskar (Bhaskar et al. 1998); some also associate it with a strand of post-Kantian German philosophy, some with Roy Wood Sellars and Wilfred Sellars (van Kooten Niekerk 2011). Critical realists have an international organization, a journal, research centers, etc.; but *their* critical realism is not mine. Hacking uses the term 'dynamic nominalism' (1986), which is appealing, but does not allow me to distinguish my view from his. The term *critical nominalism* is an option because I am a kind of nominalist about natural kinds. But because nominalism is often contrasted with realism, and I embrace a form of realism (in a different debate), this could be confusing. So although it is awkward to be a realist who embraces multiple forms of constructionism, the tension in this combination of views is also welcome because I aim to shift ordinary understandings of both realism and construcitonism. And, as I argue below, the tension is not an inconsistency.

It is important to note that although critical realism embraces the notion of social construction, it is not allied with those who argue that because our distinctions are socially motivated or fulfill a social purpose, they do not track reality. I've just argued that this form of inference is fallacious. Critical realism is committed to there being real differences in the world that we can discover through ordinary empirical and normative inquiry; in fact, as I will argue below, its ontology embraces realism, naturalism, and objectivity (of sorts).

3. Realism, Objectivism, Naturalism

As suggested above, it is often assumed that social constructionists are anti-realists, anti-objectivists, and anti-naturalists about whatever it is they are claiming is socially constructed. Although I think it is fair to say that many social constructionists adopt these views, or at least claim to, the critical realist can embrace versions of realism, objectivism, and naturalism.[21] Let me sketch briefly why they can and why they should want to.

Realism

A realist about a domain D maintains that claims purporting to describe D are truth-apt, that is, the claims are the sort of thing to be either true or false, *and* at least some of them are true. One consequence of this is that there are two ways of being an anti-realist about a domain:

1. *Non-cognitivism:* although our claims about D appear to be truth-apt, in fact they should be understood differently, for example, as imperatives or exclamations.
2. *Error Theory:* although the claims in D are truth-apt, none of them are actually true.

Plausible anti-realism in the social domain takes the form of error theories. Error theories about race are common (e.g., Appiah 1996; Zack 2002; Glasgow 2008). On this view, because there are no races, statements involving racial terms, although they purport to be true or false, are all false, since racial terms do not refer. So, because the terms 'Whites' and 'Blacks' do not refer, it is false that:

(a) Whites, on average, hold greater wealth in the United States than Blacks.

On the face of it, this is not a happy result, for if we are going to understand the effects of slavery and long standing racism in this country we need to have the resources to describe its systematic effects on racial groups. The error theorist

---

[21] For a detailed discussion of some additional forms of realism about race, see (Mills 1998, esp. Ch. 3).

will respond, however, that there are true generalizations of the sort just mentioned, but they do not depend on the existence of races; rather, the terms 'White' and 'Black' refer to racialized groups,[22] not races, and the claim in question should be reinterpreted as something like:

(b) Members of the group racialized as White, on average, hold greater wealth in the United States than members of the group racialized as Black.

Rather than:

(c) Members of the White race, on average, hold greater wealth in the United States than members of the Black race.[23]

But as I see it, this grants what the racial realist wants. According to the realist, statements involving racial terms such as 'White' and 'Black' are sometimes true. The error theorist claims that (b) is a restatement of claim (a) involving racial terms, and that (b) is true. But if (b) is a restatement of (a), and (b) is true, then (a) is also true, and the error theory is wrong. To avoid this, the error theorist has two unappealing options: on one hand she could hold that (a) is false and (b) is not a restatement of (a). But this leaves the error theorist's view disengaged with ordinary discourse and debates over the effects of racism as articulated in (a). On the other hand, the error theorist could claim that the terms 'White' and 'Black' as in (a) refer, even though they don't refer to what people have thought races are. But this is precisely the critical realist's point, and to take this route is to abandon an error theory about racial terms.[24]

The term 'realism' is used in many ways in different philosophical domains, and there is no general consensus on the requirements for realism. Even those who defend forms of non-cognitivism, which are assumed to be staunchly anti-realist views, have made a case that their position is compatible with a minimal realism (Gibbard 2003). This raises the question whether debates over realism are really worth the effort.

---

[22] How we characterize racialized groups varies from theorist to theorist. See, e.g., (Appiah 1996; Blum 2002; Glasgow 2008) among others.

[23] In the contemporary literature, realism about race is supported by (neo-) naturalists who believe that races correspond to a natural grouping, e.g., (Andreasen 2005), and by those who opt for a minimialist account of race (Hardimon 2003), in addition to the critical realist who holds that races are social kinds.

[24] The error theorist might continue by suggesting that 'White' and 'Black' are not racial terms, but are racialized group terms, and statements really involving racial terms (such as (c)) are false. The identity conditions for words or terms is complex, and worth consideration here (Epstein, 2010). My point is that we need to have claims such as (a) be truth apt and sometimes true, and for this to be the case the terms normally assumed to pick out racial groups need to refer. That is enough, as I see it, to reject an error theory of race.

Let me be clear that my aims in this section are modest. My argument is aimed at a particular form of anti-realism about race, namely, one that grants the truth-aptness of race talk, but claims that because race terms are vacuous, all such talk is false. I believe that this conclusion is a (philosophical and political) *reductio* of the account of race being offered by the racial anti-realists and, in fact, of their methodology of conceptual analysis. But the argument I've just offered doesn't pretend to establish that. Rather, I have only pointed out that there is a kind of realism whose commitments are minimal, and that because racial anti-realists are unwilling even to embrace these minimal commitments, they are invested in a substantial revision of our ordinary ways of speaking and thinking. This is noteworthy because (unlike me), anti-realists about race tend to be very concerned about revisionary proposals and defend their view based on arguments from ordinary language and common sense. Insofar as these are the terms of the debate, realism is my friend.

There are significant questions in the background, however, that are sometimes cast in the language of realism. As Gideon Rosen puts it: "We can epitomize the realist's basic commitment by saying that for the realist as against his opponents, the target discourse describes a domain of genuine, objective fact" (Rosen 1994, 278). We turn to some of these questions now.

Objectivism about Kinds

Whatever else social constructionism might stand for, it seems plausible that it must oppose a commitment to natural kinds. More specifically, the claim that Fs are socially constructed should oppose the claim that Fs constitute a natural kind. However, the term 'natural kinds' is used in a variety of ways with different implications; as Hacking suggests, "There no longer exists what Bertrand Russell called 'the doctrine of natural kinds'—one doctrine. Instead we have a slew of distinct analyses directed at unrelated projects" (Hacking 2007, 203).

This chapter cannot sort out the history of the concept of natural kinds, but it is useful to provide a glimpse of some of the different understandings of 'natural kind' in order to set up the points I want to make. Here are a few examples:

> The existence of natural kinds underlies most pre-scientific generalizations, such as "Dogs bark" or "Wood floats." The essence of a 'natural kind' is that it is a class of objects all of which possess a number of properties that are not known to be logically interconnected. (Russell 1948, 317; quoted in Hacking 1991, 112)

> We shall say that any property had essentially by some object and accidentally by none determines a natural kind, and that the set of objects having that property is a natural kind. (Brody 1980, 131)

> There are natural kinds. Each natural kind is determined by a real essence, a property or set of properties necessary and sufficient for

membership of the kind in question. The real essence, in turn, grounds the causal powers of individual members of the kind. (Wilkerson 1993, 16)

Not all sets are natural kinds, but any set whose members share a natural property are a natural kind. (Bird and Tobin 2010, describing Quine's view in (Quine 1969))

Scientific disciplines divide the particulars they study into *kinds* and theorize about those kinds. To say that a kind is *natural* is to say that it corresponds to a grouping or ordering that does not depend on humans. (Bird and Tobin 2010)

As these quotes demonstrate, several issues surface repeatedly in discussions of natural kinds: essences and essentialism, universals and nominalism, necessary and sufficient conditions, "joints in nature," causal explanation and induction, and naturalness, though there is little consensus on what a commitment to natural kinds actually entails. In fact, all but possibly the fourth characterization allow for the possibility that things of all sorts—social, psychological, political, ethical, and, in general, artifacts—fall into natural kinds.

For example, the relation between natural kinds and essences, in particular, is highly controversial.

Do natural kinds have essences? When discussing kinds and essences we need to distinguish two quite different claims. The first claim is that the kind a particular belongs to is essential to that particular: if *a* belongs to kind *K*, then it is an essential property of *a* that it belongs to *K*. [As in Brody's quote above.] The second claim is that the kinds themselves have essential properties: for each kind *K* there is some property Φ of kinds such that it is essential to *K* that $\Phi(K)$. [As in Wilkerson's quote above.] What is the logical relation between these two claims? The first claim obviously implies the second, but it is far from clear that the second implies the first. (Bird and Tobin 2010)

In my view, it is not obvious that either of the claims mentioned implies the other. Note further that neither Russell's, Quine's, nor Bird and Tobin's quotes suggest that natural kinds entail essences at all. Moreover, there is no reason to think that kinds, whether natural or not, must be definable in terms of necessary and sufficient conditions; some kinds may be primitive or unanalyzable, and others may be unified along degrees of similarity: "The notion of a kind and the notion of similarity or resemblance seem to be variants or adaptations of a single notion" (Quine 1969, 117).

For our purposes, however, the task is to consider the notion of natural kind that is purportedly opposed to that of social construction. An important candidate is that of an *objective* kind or type that carries some unspecified naturalness credentials.[25] Let's postpone the issue of naturalness to the next section and focus on the idea of an objective kind first. The claim before us, then, is that although some kinds are objective, socially constructed kinds are not.

Because the terminology of 'kind' carries connotations of essence, and this is potentially confusing since we have taken essence off the table, I suggest we switch to the terminology of 'type' (Armstrong 1989). Types are familiar and ubiquitous: paperbacks are a type of book; chickens are a type of bird. Pin oaks are a type of oak and a type of tree; oak wood is a type of hardwood used to make furniture; oak furniture is a type of furniture I especially like. Is it possible for gender or race to be socially constructed and also objective types? I believe it is.

The existence of types, as I am using the term, depends on members of a set of things having some degree of unity. Unity comes in varying degrees: some sets of things are highly unified (the members may have much in common, and what they have in common may be causally potent), and other sets of things are barely unified at all. The set of all apples is more unified than the set of things currently on my kitchen counter (including some apples, oranges, a banana, several sheets of paper, a screwdriver, a vise grip, some screws, a salt shaker, a pepper grinder, a cutting board, a knife, two forks, etc.). We are interested in some sets of things and not others: it is not particularly useful for me to know what is in the set of things exactly one mile from my dog's nose at this moment, or the precise genetic structure of a family of sparrows living in my back yard; it may be very useful to know what is in the set of things currently in the top drawer of my desk (when I am looking for my stapler), or the set of things I've inherited from my mother (when I'm considering a birthday gift for my daughter). So there may be no reason to take an interest in some substantially unified sets, and the ones that matter deeply to us may be only minimally unified. Given that some degree of unity is all that is required for a set of things to constitute a type, there are more types than we could possibly have any use for or words to name.

But what exactly, if anything, does the notion of *objective* type add to the notion of a type? This is hard to pin down because the notions of "objectivity" and "subjectivity" are notoriously ambiguous. Objectivity comes in two major forms: epistemic and metaphysical. Epistemic objectivity concerns the method by which something comes to be believed and the degree to which it counts as (scientific?) knowledge; objective methods are supposed to root out bias and

---

[25] The issue of essentialism in feminist theory is certainly an important topic. However, I don't believe it is helpful to cast the debate as one in which essentialism is opposed to social constuction- ism. Feminist anti-essentialists come in different varieties. Some oppose the idea that it is possible to define "what a woman is," or to give necessary and sufficient conditions for being a woman; some oppose the idea that anyone is essentially a woman (or a man); some oppose biological determin- ism. As I understand social constructionism, it does not entail any of these anti-essentialist claims, though it is compatible with them. See, e.g., (Witt 1995; Witt 2011).

enable us to gain knowledge of the world that does justice to the facts.[26] Metaphysical objectivity concerns the reality of things. To say that some thing or feature is metaphysically objective is to say that it is real: the objective world just is the real world. So objective types are types that can be found in the real world.

The claim that something is socially constructed is often taken to imply that it is unreal, or that its reality is somehow sketchy; it is not really real, not objectively real. Maybe it is only real-to-us, that is, an illusion we project onto the world that corresponds to nothing really real. These alleged implications of social construction concern the metaphysical objectivity of social constructs. So we should consider whether the following two claims are compatible:[27]

> *Type Objectivism about Fs:* the Fs are a (metaphysically) objective type.[28]
> *Social Constitution of Fs:* the Fs are socially constituted.[29]

If to be metaphysically objective is to be real, then we should consider what it is for a type to be real. I take this to mean that the boundaries of the type—what is and what isn't a member of the type—correspond to real differences. In other words, there is something about how things are in virtue of which the members of the type differ from non-members. Let's try to apply this to a straightforward social type: landlords are socially constituted, that is, to be a landlord is (roughly) to rent one's property to others. (I'm sure there are details to be figured out, but you have the idea.) Are landlords an objective type? Why not? They differ from non-landlords by virtue of owning property and renting it to others. There is a real difference between being such that you rent your property and being such that you don't (even if there are grey areas). It is just not plausible to claim that relations of this sort between individuals or groups of individuals do not constitute

---

[26] A fascinating discussion of the history of the epistemic concept of objectivity can be found in (Daston and Galison, 2010).

[27] Further discussion might also consider challenges to the epistemological objectivity of social construction. I am not undertaking that here, though as I see it, such a challenge would have to make a case that it is not possible to undertake social inquiry in a way that is objective. This is not plausible. But it calls for further discussion.

[28] In debates over race and gender, what I'm calling kind objectivism is sometimes simply called 'gender realism,' or 'race realism' (Mikkola 2008; Glasgow 2008). In keeping with other philosophical debates, I've used the term 'realism' for a different view (see above). The terminology of gender or race 'essentialism' is also common in this context; but 'essentialism' is an even more slippery term than 'realism' in the debates over race and gender. Admittedly, 'objectivity' is also a complex and contested notion, but I believe it is the best of the choices available.

[29] Strictly speaking, metaphysical objectivity could concern either social constitution or social causation. I've chosen to focus on social constitution because it would be so implausible to argue that X is socially caused, but X is unreal. I assume that if X has causes, then X exists and is real, even if we are the cause. We humans might cause the idea of a unicorn to exist; but even if unicorns don't exist, ideas of unicorns do. We don't cause unicorns to exist (or haven't yet!), though if someone did, there would be unicorns, they would be real.

real differences. So landlords are a metaphysically objective type. No problem. Type objectivism about Fs is compatible with the social constitution of Fs.

Although I believe this argument is sufficient to make the point, it depends on a highly deflationary conception of metaphysical objectivity. Some would suggest that this degree of deflation is tantamount to giving up the concept of metaphysical objectivity altogether. I'm happy with either way of interpreting the result. If to be metaphysically objective is just to be real, then the existence of an object, a fact, a difference (etc.) is sufficient for its objectivity. If the distinction between the metaphysically objective and the non-objective is supposed to be a division *within* reality, then it isn't clear what the relevant difference is supposed to be. Without greater clarity on the distinction and why it matters, we have no reason to think that social phenomena are not metaphysically objective.[30]

Perhaps the most relevant consideration counting against the metaphysical objectivity of social constructions is the idea that the objective world is not simply what's real, but what exists "independent of us." On this interpretation, the fictional, illusory, and mistaken are not objective because they aren't real; in addition, some *real* things are not *objectively* real. Which are these? By hypothesis, everything that depends on us. But the point cannot be that everything that causally depends on humans is not objectively real: that would include everything that humans have made, including our children. What could the point possibly be of saying that the cities we have built, the food we produce, our pets and our children are not objectively real? The notions of 'independent' and 'dependent' would appear to have a special meaning in this context.

It is an important fact that humans are prone to illusion through projection from their experience. As Hume characterized it: "[Reason] discovers objects, as

---

[30] For an excellent discussion of this issue, see (Rosen 1994). Rosen's arguments suggest that the notion of metaphysical objectivity is confused and that there is no meaningful question about the objectivity of some kinds or others. I agree with him, that there is no meaningful notion of (metaphysical) 'objectivity' that can be used to draw a line *within the totality of facts*. "The persistence of the Kantian imagery suggests, however, that for many writers there is a residual dispute—one that arises only after minimal realism has been accepted. The residual issue concerns not the existence of the objects, properties, and facts described by the disputed discourse, but rather what we have called their objectivity. The challenge, then, is to indicate a line within the world (considered as the totality of facts, or the totality of things together with their properties an relations) between the objective items and the rest. A solution need not actually say which things fall where. It will be enough to say, in relatively non-metaphorical terms, what it is for an item to fall on one side or the other" (Rosen 1994, 282). He continues, "Until the challenge is met, our sense that there is a genuine issue for realists and their rivals to debate—over and above the 'flat' ontological issues associated with the debate over minimal realism—can represent at best the pious hope that one of the most compelling problems of traditional philosophy is a real problem after all and not just a rhetorical illusion" (Rosen 1994, 283). His paper is a sustained attempt to show how attempts to meet the challenge fail. I am using the notion of 'objectivity' in a very thin sense here, equivalent to 'real' within a minimal realism, rather than purporting to divide what's real into the objective and non-objective. Another option would be to simply cast the issue as whether or not there are types, entirely dropping the notion of 'objective.' This, however, would not make a substantial difference in the arguments.

they really stand in nature, without addition or diminution: [Taste] has a pro-ductive faculty, and gilding or staining all natural objects with the colours, bor-rowed from internal sentiment, raises, in a manner, a new creation." (Hume 1983 [1751], Appendix 1, para 21/21). Taste, on this view, creates illusion by "gilding" objects with the phenomenal contents of experience. The standard ex-ample is of secondary qualities such as color or flavor. I take a bite of an apple and it tastes tart to me. I experience the tartness as "in the apple," but it only exists in relation to me. Because flavors such as tartness are not in the world independent of us, the argument goes, they are not objective. The apple is not really tart; its tartness is not objectively real. On this view, only primary qual-ities of things are metaphysically objective.

In response to such examples, it is tempting to argue that there are several items to consider: the chemical composition of the apple that causes me to expe-rience tartness; the disposition of the apple to produce tartness sensations in humans; the sensation of tartness that I experience (however you want to char-acterize it—in mental or physical terms); the causal relation between the com-position of the apple and the sensation produced. In addition, there is a false projective belief that gilds the apple: the belief that the phenomenal quality of tartness experienced is "in the apple" apart from its relation to me. This sup-posed quality of the apple is not objectively real because it isn't real at all: there is no such quality of the apple. This is not to deny that the apple is tart, which it surely is. Rather, the point is that our experience of tartness is sometimes mis-leading: it represents tartness in a way that doesn't take our relation to the apple—in particular, the temptation to gild—into account. Assuming the rest of the items involved are real, including the sensation of tartness, it isn't clear why they should be counted as anything less than metaphysically objective. Here again, the failure of objectivity is a failure to be real.

Admittedly, if one maintains a commitment to the original belief about the concept, for example, that tartness is a certain phenomenal quality, then one has the option of adopting an error theory: it is false that the apple is tart because it lacks that quality. On this approach, our experience (and/or back-ground assumptions) yields necessary truths about the concept in question.[31] However, the cost is that the concepts then have no application: our judgments

---

[31] Although here I focus on secondary qualities and phenomenal content, this is due to the hypo-thesis under consideration that some non-objective parts of the world fail to be sufficiently "inde-pendent" of us. The issue, however, is much broader: are we more reliable about the content of our concepts, or about our judgments whether the concept applies? If occasions arise when the concept we *thought* applied doesn't, we have two options: give up the judgment (accept error), or adjust the concept. The same sort of issue came up in the previous section concerning judgments about race. I argued that we should not accept an error theory about race because the cost of accepting wide-spread error was unacceptable; others hold that a commitment to what we think *race* is (or what some of us think race is) is more important, and widespread error is tolerable. I discuss some of the broader issues in chapter 16 of this volume.

employing those concepts are all false. Taken generally, this can lead to a view in which there are no colors, sounds, tastes, or values in the world. Nothing is really funny or beautiful. The alternative option is that we can adjust our understanding of what the concept requires, for example, what is involved in being tart or funny. We were misled about the concept, but happily, once we make the corrections, much of what we thought was true, is true. The apple is tart and the joke is funny. Both approaches have their place. Which approach is preferable will depend on the project, and on the broader costs of accepting widespread error in the domain in question. However, the critical realist project of revealing covert constructions depends on the possibility that sometimes we are not aware of the social factors that contribute to making our judgments true.

The problem of "gilding" and "staining" certainly happens in the social world. We experience people and things as having properties, thinking they are inherent or intrinsic to it, that aren't features of them at all, or are so only relationally. And even recognizably relational properties are misconstrued as involving fewer relata than they actually have.[32] Consider money. A $20 bill lying on the street draws our attention. There is no doubt that it has value. But its value is a complex relational matter that is not part of our experience, and often not even understood by those who experience the money as valuable. (Think of coupons that indicate their "cash value" as being, say, 1/20th of a cent. Is this to correct the tendency to gild the coupon as having an intrinsic value that it only has in relation to a particular product at a particular store?) Similarly, many experience Barack Obama as Black in a way that represents his race as an inherent feature passed down from his ancestors. This gilding (or in some minds, the staining) is an illusion. But it doesn't follow that race is an illusion, any more than the tartness of the apple or the value of money is an illusion. What's an illusion is the kind of property that race (tartness, monetary value) seems to be.

The moral here is that objective types are sometimes constituted by relational properties, for example, those things that are taller than the Empire State Building, those things that are bigger than a breadbox, those things that earned over $50K last year, those things that are someone's spouse, those things that annoy Fox Terriers (Rosen's example (1994)). And there is no reason why a relation to someone's experience should disqualify a type from being objective. Advertising companies and the film industry count on being able to determine those types of thing that

---

[32] In the adoption world, it is commonly recognized that adoptive families consist not just of parents and children, but that there are three dimensions to the adoption "triad": the adoptee, the birthfamily, and the adoptive family. In a paper presented at a recent adoption conference, the author proposed that there are really four dimensions: the adoptee, the birthfamily, the adoptive family, and the state. Others wanted to add the adoption agency and/or social worker. The point here is not to discuss the merits of these proposed additions, but to show how the experience of family as a relation between parents and children may be taken to mislead about what constitutes a family because there are additional relata that may be eclipsed.

we respond to with desire, empathy, shock, and horror; there are real differences between what produces such responses and what doesn't. Advertisers also take advantage of our tendency to "gild" and "stain" objects with phenomenal or emotional qualities of our experience, and to form false or misleading beliefs about their products because of this tendency.

Our tendencies both to project from our experience and to ignore what is not directly in our experience lead us to be mistaken about the basis for distinguishing one type of thing from another. The difference between a $20 bill and a counterfeit $20 bill is not the ink or paper (though these are reliable signs), but the process by which something made out of this ink and that paper is constituted as legal tender in the United States. Even if someone printed an exact copy of a $20 bill in her basement, it would still be a counterfeit. Social constructionists aim, on the whole, to reveal the error of gilding and staining and the relational conditions that are obscured by such projective errors; the point is to set us straight by revealing the metaphysically objective basis for our judgments.[33]

But surely, one might argue, the contrast between objective and non-objective types makes no sense in cases where there is *nothing* about the objects being sorted that warrants including *them* as opposed to another candidate in the set. Philip Pettit discusses a case of this sort:

> Take the concept of *U-ness* that used to be in vogue—courtesy of Nancy Mitford—among what we might describe as the Sloane Square set or, for short, Sloanes. To speak of lavatories is *U*, of bathrooms *non-U*; to lay cloth napkins at table is *U*, to lay paper napkins *non-U*; and so on through a myriad of equally trivial examples. I assume that there is something distinctively collusive in the way Sloanes use the *U*-concept: that as they individually decide whether something is *U* or *non-U* they look over their shoulders to make sure they stay in step—the community is the authority—rather than looking to the thing itself to see what profile it displays. In other words I think that whether something is *U* or not is a matter of the say-so of those in the appropriate set; the members of that set have an authoritative, dictating role in regard to the concept. That they have this role is borne out by the fact that as the regular bourgeoisie try to get in on the game, Sloanes are notorious—at least in the oral tradition—for shifting the extension of the *U*-concept. (Pettit 1991, 611)

Pettit argues that there is an important difference between concepts like *red* and ones like *U*, for

---

[33] For an excellent discussion of a different interpretation of the metaphysics of construction and the basis for the sex/gender distinction, see (Sveinsdóttir 2010).

> *U*-responses are determined, under my characterization of the case, by
> the efforts of Sloanes to keep in step with one another in their classification
> of things. But clearly red sensations do not generally spring from such
> collusive machinations, even if people sometimes succumb inappropri-
> ately to group pressure. When subjects see something as red, even when
> normally functioning and normally positioned subjects see something as
> red, they do so, or so we generally assume, because the thing presents
> itself—and, if there is no misrepresentation, because it is—a certain way.
> (Pettit 1991, 613)

Pettit is claiming that certain social concepts, such as *U*, are not like color or
flavor concepts: "it is not the case that something looks *U* to such subjects
because it is *U*; it is not the case that its *U*-ness is responsible in any part for
evoking the *U*-response: the *U*-response is driven by different pressures." (Pettit
1991, 615)

Although Pettit does not take his discussion of *U* to directly bear on the issue
of objectivity, many would hold, I believe, that the *Us* do not constitute an objective type. But this conclusion is, I think, mistaken. Consider, for example, Lotto
machines. Lotto machines generate random numbers, usually using balls with
numbers painted on them. Consider the set consisting of those balls that were
selected by the New York State Lottery on January 1, 2011 (= the balls marked
14, 16, 18, 23, 27, 54 in one of their sets). The members of this set were randomly
generated; there is nothing that distinguishes the balls in the set from other
balls, besides the fact that they were selected. But the set of balls is, I submit, an
objective type (with minimal unity, admittedly).

In the case of the Lotto machine, there is no suggestion that the balls are in
the set chosen because they have some mysterious intrinsic quality. Their membership in the set is explicitly based on their relational features. And there is no
reason to challenge the objective credentials of the set just because a machine
determines the members randomly. In the case of the Sloanes, we are supposing
that things are randomly selected to be *U*, much like the Lotto balls. But in the
Sloanes case, there is also a (false) attribution of a special quality *U-ness* to the
trivial accoutrements of social class, a quality that purportedly makes them desirable. Although the Sloanes themselves are not taken in by this attribution,
their followers are (and no doubt come to gild the actions and objects with
value). As I see it, however, the set of *U* things is no less unified than the Lotto
balls (though neither is significantly unified), for what differentiates the things
in the sets in question from other similar things is simply the fact that they have
been selected. However, in the case of the Sloanes there is a further erroneous
attribution of a special property to the things in the set. The Sloanes purport to
be tracking a feature that *independent of their judgment* things have; but by hypothesis, they aren't tracking any such feature, and they know they aren't. In fact,

they are deceiving others in order to reinforce the social hierarchy. When we see through the gilding that accompanies secondary quality experience and status goods, it isn't that there is nothing at all there; rather what's there is not exactly as it is purported to be. Cloth napkins do bring status, but it isn't because of any special quality they have; it is because they have been deemed a status good by the Sloanes.[34] Nevertheless, the relational properties *being selected by the Sloanes* and *being selected by the official New York Lotto machine January 1, 2011*, do unify the sets and constitute them as objective types.

The example of *being U* is directly relevant to the social kinds that critical realists are most interested in. Critical realists argue that although it might seem that *being a woman* or *being White* are intrinsic features of individuals, this is, in fact, an error. What it is to be gendered or raced is, in part, a matter of how you are viewed and treated in a social context, that is, these are relational features. However, the common error of projecting our experiences, desires, and values onto things does not undermine the objectivity of the type we are projecting onto—in the cases at hand, genders and races. However, to correct this error does require a change in our thinking, and ultimately our perception. Some things are tart, some are *U*, some are women, and some are White. These claims, however, may not have the implications we are tempted to think (Haslanger 2012 [2000]).

Recall that the goal of this section is to consider whether a social constructionist about a category C is committed to the idea that Cs do not form an objective type, for example, that women or men, Blacks or Native Americans, have no objective unity. Is a critical realist about gender committed to the claim that gender difference is not objective? Let us return to the example of *tween*. Recall that according to the critical realist, to say that tweens are socially constructed is to say that what it is to be a tween is to satisfy not just a set of chronological conditions, but also social conditions, for example, to be on the verge of entering a stage when one is socially expected to become interested in the opposite sex and facing the challenges of secondary education. Do tweens form a (metaphysically) objective type? Even those who hold a more robust account of metaphysical objectivity than I do have reason to think so, for the category plausibly fits into a systematic social theory about the social meaning of certain stages of development under patriarchal heteronormative capitalism. It may be that tweenhood is "up to us" in the sense that if we didn't organize ourselves as we do, there would be no tweens. And it may be that a theory that postulates the existence of tweens is not epistemically objective because the inquirers are biased or fail to meet other epistemic standards. But assuming epistemic standards are met, the theory is apt insofar

---

[34] We are supposing, with Pettit (1991), that the Sloanes make their selection of what's *U* and what's not randomly. But it is worth noting that such status designations come to have a "logic" of their own: Sloanes can correct past designations, and often it isn't impossible to predict what judgment they would make when asked which members of a set of things are *U*. Thus the type picked out by the predicate '*U*' usually has more unity than simply the fact that they were selected.

as it captures and explains what's going on in a part of the social world. And when the critical realist draws attention to tweens, the point is to demystify how we organize ourselves socially. If tweens have enough unity to be a type, it is an objective type. The same is true of genders and races.

A commitment to kinds is often associated with a number of further claims, for example, that there is a finite set of necessary and sufficient conditions for being a member of the objective type; that there is a universal (an abstract entity) that all members of the type share; that members of an objective type are necessarily members of that type (i.e., that it is part of their Aristotelian essence). None of these claims follows, however, from a commitment to objective types. There may be primitive unanalyzable types (Lewis, 1983); one may be a nominalist about objective types; and many types are accidental to their members, for example, my son used to weigh exactly ten pounds but has grown much larger. Type objectivism about Fs takes a stand against those who hold that Fs being a type is "due to us" in a way that makes the type less than fully real (Cf. Rosen 1994). This is compatible with the type being socially constructed.

Naturalism

The question initially raised in the previous section was whether a social constructionist about Fs can also claim that the Fs constitute a natural kind. We've just considered the issue of objective kinds—or what I have called objective types—and I argued it is possible for the Fs to be both socially constructed and an objective type. Could this type also be natural?

Who knows what it is, exactly, to be a naturalist? In Gideon Rosen's words,

> . . . a flexible and relatively undemanding naturalism functions for us as an unofficial axiom of philosophical common sense. This naturalism is so vague and inchoate that that any simple formulation will sound either empty or false. But it is a real constraint: and one of its implications is that if we believe in minds at all, they are the embodied minds of human beings and other animals. (Rosen 1994, 277)

I take a naturalism of this sort to be consistent with plausible feminist and antiracist projects. It is, in effect, a commitment to seeing ourselves as parts of a universe in which all things are interdependent. Naturalism does not entail that there are only physical things, but if there are non-physical things, they must be part of the causal order, that is, they must either have causes and effects, or must supervene on things that do.[35]

---

[35] I don't want to take a stand here on whether and to what extent a vague naturalism of the sort I'm endorsing has consequences for the metaphysics of math and logic. Nothing I say depends on that, so if we need to qualify naturalism so that it allows room for such abstracta, it won't be a problem.

In addition to the general plausibility of naturalism, there are several reasons for wanting a critical theory that embraces its commitments: (i) The framework of causal forces that link us to each other and connect us to the non-human world *just is* the natural world. This framework is clearly relevant to understanding categories such as race, gender, sexuality, and disability, for all of these exist within this causal nexus. Moreover, if we are concerned to improve social arrangements, we need to have good accounts of these forces. (ii) Attempts to draw a clear distinction between the natural and the social run into the problem that social phenomena depend on and are partly constituted by human minds, and human minds are natural by-products of—they are caused and conditioned by—human bodies. Human embodiment, both its limitations and opportunities, is a natural phenomenon and cannot reasonably be ignored by critical theory. And (iii) the best critical epistemology we have depends on viewing knowledge production as a social practice that can be affected, and distorted, by many different features of the context. A crucial resource for critique is to consider the causes and effects of belief. The idea is not that beliefs should be evaluated only in terms of their causes, but that the social and natural context of belief is relevant, for it may bias the information available and so the appearance of justification.[36]

Does social constructionism require a rejection of naturalism? Should we endorse:

> *Anti-Naturalism:* If the Fs are socially constructed, then the being an F is non-natural, or is not caused by natural processes.[37]

A plausible explanation of why social constructionists have urged that the phenomena in question are social *rather than* natural is that there is a widely held assumption that what's social, being up to us, is more malleable than the natural, being due to forces beyond our control. But even if we can draw a distinction between the social and the non-social, it is not the case that the social is more malleable—in ways that matter to justice—than the non-social. Consider, for example, the effects of the birth control pill. After millennia of efforts to control their fertility, women finally gained the resources to do so through chemical

---

[36] Virtually all of feminist epistemology is relevant here. See, especially, (Mills 1988; Longino 1990; Antony 1993; Anderson 1995b; Anderson 2010).

[37] It is interesting to note that 'The Fs are socially constructed' has both a distributive and a collective reading. On the collective reading, the point is that the Fs *as a group* are socially constructed, i.e., what makes the Fs a group is due to social factors. On the distributive reading, the F-ness of each F is socially constructed. This ambiguity may partially explain the confusion over whether social construction is a claim about differences or distinctions. The collective reading is more plausible if we are talking about distinctions: we draw a distinction between the members of this group and other things. The distributive reading is more plausible if we are talking about differences: each thing that is F is so by virtue of social factors. I intend the distributive reading here.

manipulation of their menstrual cycle. This, in turn, had a huge effect on women's social position. The ability to control the physical basis of reproduction had an impact on women's liberation far greater than generations of efforts to control social norms concerning sexuality. Another example is something as simple as curb cuts.

> Curb cut feminist analysis follows the activist model of the Americans with Disabilities movement and *begins* by privileging the knowledge of people with disabilities in designing the solution for existing infrastructure and the design for future structures . . . While designed with attention to people in wheelchairs, the curb cuts, access ramps, automatic doors, multiple access points, and clearly indicated wheelchair accessible routes enhance the mobility of others as well. People pushing strollers and delivery dollies, people carrying lots of books, and people recovering from an injury for example, are all able to move more freely. (Ackerly 2008, 134)

Materialist feminists have long emphasized the material basis for oppression, and this insight depends on an appreciation of the ways in which the social is part of the natural world.

Naturalism acknowledges that the natural world—including our biology—is not outside our control, as the example of the birth control pill shows. But it is important to see that this isn't due to some special supernatural power we have, but a wholly natural power: we are part of the natural world, and the natural world is, by definition, a causally interdependent system. Moreover, our interpretation of our biological condition is crucial in determining what effect it has on us, and what effect it should have (Antony 2000). As Beauvoir so eloquently puts it:

> [Society's] ways and customs cannot be deduced from biology, for the individuals that compose society are never abandoned to the dictates of their nature; they are subject rather to that second nature which is custom and in which are reflected the desires and the fears that express their essential nature. It is not merely as a body, but rather as a body subject to taboos, to laws, that the subject is conscious of himself and attains fulfillment—it is with reference to certain values that he evaluates himself. And once again, it is not upon physiology that values can be based; rather, the facts of biology take on the values that the existent bestows upon them. If the respect or fear inspired by woman prevents the use of violence towards her, then the muscular superiority of the male is no source of power. (Beauvoir 1989, 36)

In short, although clearly natural forces play out within the social domain, it is also the case that we—as individuals and societies—have influence within the natural domain. Understanding how and where to act in order to counteract existing unjust conditions is crucial for effective social change.

If we endorse a broad naturalism that takes the world to be a natural world that includes as part of it social and psychological events, processes, relations, and such, then it would seem that to be non-natural (at least within the empirical domain) is to be nonexistent. In the previous section I have argued that there is no reason to think that being socially constructed in any way tarnishes one's credentials as real. If the Fs are socially constructed and constitute an objective type, and if (as in the cases we are considering) the type is not one consisting only of abstract objects (as in mathematics), then there is no reason to count the Fs as non-natural. In fact, the Fs should be considered fully natural.

The basic idea I'm endorsing about objective natural types (or kinds) is quite simple: there are no things or divisions in the world that are real, but not fully real. The only kind of mind-dependence is ordinary mind-dependence in which the mind in question is an ordinary human mind that exists in the natural world, interdependent with other natural things. Some things are mind-dependent: my thoughts (on my mind), your thoughts (on your mind), agreements between us (on our minds). My mind causes things to happen, and we can put our minds together to make more happen. There is an important sense, moreover, in which the natural world is all there is. Our activities, our minds and their contents, our language and its meaning, our interactions, are all natural (or supervene on the natural). This is not to embrace biological determinism, of course, for the social and the psychological are both in the web of causation. Rather than distinguishing the natural and the social, the social should be understood as part of the natural. Critical realism, as I have characterized it, need not deny any of this, and in fact, should embrace it.

However, it is a reasonable claim that *within the natural*, it can be useful to distinguish the social from the non-social. Marriage may be part of the natural world, but it is a social part of the natural world. H_2O is part of the natural world, but it is a non-social part of the natural world. Lest this last claim be considered controversial, consider again the contrast between distinctions and differences I elaborated above. H_2O may be distinguished from other clear liquids for social reasons/motivations, but the difference between H_2O and other clear liquids, that is, the conditions that make something H_2O rather than, say, rubbing alcohol or gin, concern the chemical composition of the liquid. In embracing naturalism, I am not denying that some similarities and differences in the world concern social interactions, and some similarities and differences do not. My claim is simply that this contrast is not helpfully cast as a contrast between the social and the natural; rather, it is better viewed as a spectrum from the non-social to the social within the natural.

Thus far I have embraced a minimalist kind of realism, objectivism, and naturalism and have argued that each are compatible with the sort of critical realism

I favor. In each case, however, I have rejected some elements of what philosophers (and others) have taken to be central to the notions of objectivity, reality, and nature. A reasonable worry might be that I have succeeded in showing only that one can redefine philosophical terms to make it *seem* that there is a compatibility between the incompatible, and there is little genuine progress in this.

I want to allow that my arguments are compatible with a quite different strategy in which the point is to reject the traditional dichotomies between the objective and subjective, natural and social, real and unreal, and to develop an account of the categories of race, gender, and such, outside the conceptual frameworks that rely on such terms. This we might call *the rejectionist project*, in contrast to a *reconstructive project*.[38] I favor the reconstructionist project in this context for two reasons. First, I think there are good philosophical reasons, *apart from feminist considerations*, to jettison aspects of the traditional metaphysical notions of objectivity, nature, and reality. So I take myself to be embracing the strongest philosophical positions on these issues, not simply revising the concepts for my purposes. Second, I strongly favor feminist theory that is broadly interdisciplinary, that is engaged with social and natural science, and that builds on empirical research. Science is a complex social practice with many problems, but it is both intellectually and politically powerful. To reject the core terms of scientific inquiry, when in fact there are continuities that can be illuminated, would be a mistake.

4. Why Social Constructionism?

If the point of claiming that a phenomenon is socially constructed is *not* to take an anti-realist, anti-essentialist, and anti-naturalist stance towards it, what could the point possibly be? I suggest that the critical constructionst's goal is to show how the phenomenon in question depends, *in ordinary ways*, on us, particularly on our attitudes and our interactions. But why is this important? Two possibilities come to mind: (a) all and only phenomena that depend on us fall within the sphere of morality and justice, so to show that something depends on us is to show that we are morally responsible for it; (b) if we know both that, and how, a phenomenon depends on us, we are in a better position to intervene to change it.

I myself am wary of (a), for I am doubtful about the assumption that *only* those things "that depend on us" fall within the sphere of justice. First, as indicated above, there is a temptation to think that the class of things that "depend on us" is the class of "mind-dependent" things, that is, our attitudes and interactions.

---

[38] The contrast between rejectionist and reconstructionist I make here is familiar within feminist debates. For example, feminists have wondered whether to be rejectionist or reconstructionist about such matters as autonomy, privacy, marriage, etc.

But we are certainly morally responsible for much more than this, for we have all sorts of impact on the natural world, and we are responsible for that impact. I am responsible for the pollution my car causes, and that pollution is not mind-dependent in any metaphysically interesting sense. (And imagine if someone accepted both the claim that what's objectively real is what's "independent of us" and also that we are only morally responsible for what "depends on us." Would that leave us morally responsible for nothing that is objectively real? The notions of 'independence' and 'dependence' are clearly much in need of explication, as I hope I've demonstrated.)

Second, there are all sorts of ways we can have an impact on the natural world to make it more hospitable to justice. In particular, we can affect the natural world sometimes more easily than we can affect the social world. The development of birth control has been an intervention in the natural world towards justice, because, I believe, the biological division of labor between males and females in reproduction is unjust. (Admittedly this is highly controversial.) An improvement on the responsibility principle might be that something falls within the sphere of justice only if it is, in principle, something we can affect. However, even then we must keep in mind that we can affect much more than we normally imagine and not nearly as much as we might hope.

So I would rather not focus on the idea that social constructionists bring apparently natural phenomena into the social domain to place them in the sphere of justice. Instead, my own view is that if we are going to change the world, we need to know how the problematic parts are created and maintained. We need to find the *levers for change*. And if the goal is to find the levers for change, then it is important to understand ways in which the social and non-social are interdependent. This is what the critical realist aims to provide.

Works Cited

Ackerly, Brooke. 2008. *Universal Human Rights in a World of Difference*. Cambridge: Cambridge University Press.

Alcoff, Linda Martín. 1998. Toward a phenomenology of racial embodiment. *Radical Philosophy* 95, May/June 1998, 15–26

———. 2000. Habits of hostility: On seeing race. *Philosophy Today* 44 (Supp.): 30–40.

———. 2006. *Visible Identities: Race, Gender, and the Self*. New York: Oxford University Press, USA.

Anderson, Elizabeth. 1995a. Knowledge, human interests, and objectivity in feminist epistemology. *Philosophical Topics* 23(2): 27–58.

———. 1995b. Feminist epistemology: An interpretation and defense. *Hypatia* 10: 50–84.

———. 2001. Unstrapping the straitjacket of 'preference': A comment on Amartya Sen's contributions to philosophy and economics. *Economics and Philosophy* 17(1): 21–38.

———. 2010. Feminist epistemology and philosophy of science. *The Stanford Encyclopedia of Philosophy* (Fall 2010 Edition), Edward N. Zalta (ed.) http://plato.stanford.edu/archives/fall2010/entries/feminism-epistemology/.

Andreasen, Robin. 2005. The meaning of 'race': Folk conceptions and the new biology of race. *Journal of Philosophy* 102(2): 94–106.

Antony, Louise. 1993. Quine as feminist: The radical import of naturalized epistemology. In *A Mind of One's Own: Feminist Essays on Reason and Objectivity*. Ed. Louise Antony and Charlotte Witt. Boulder, CO: Westview Press, pp. 185–226.

———. 2000. "Natures and Norms." *Ethics* 111(1): 8–36.

Appiah, K. Anthony. 1996. Race, culture, identity: misunderstood connections. In A. Appiah and A. Gutmann, *Color Conscious: The Political Morality of Race*. Princeton: Princeton University Press, pp. 30–105.

Armstrong, David. 1989. *Universals: An Opinionated Introduction*. Boulder, CO: Westview Press.

Beauvoir, Simone de. 1989 [1949]. *The Second Sex*. Trans. H. M. Parshley New York: Vintage Books.

Bhaskar, Roy, et al. 1998. *Critical Realism: Essential Readings*. New York: Routledge.

Bigelow, John, and Laura Schroeter. 2009. Jackson's classical model of meaning. In *Minds, Ethics and Conditionals: Themes from the Philosophy of Frank Jackson*. Ed. Ian Ravenscroft. Oxford: Oxford University Press, pp. 85–110.

Bird, Alexander, and Tobin, Emma. 2010. Natural kinds. *The Stanford Encyclopedia of Philosophy* (Summer 2010 Edition), Edward N. Zalta (ed.) http://plato.stanford.edu/archives/sum2010/entries/natural-kinds/.

Blum, Lawrence. 2002. *I'm Not a Racist, But . . .* Ithaca, NY: Cornell University Press.

Brody, Baruch A. 1980. *Identity and Essence*. Princeton: Princeton University Press.

Butler, Judith. 1990. *Gender Trouble*. New York: Routledge.

"Caster Semenya." Caster Semenya. http://en.wikipedia.org/wiki/Caster_Semenya.

Daston, Lorraine, and Peter Galison. 2010. *Objectivity*. New York: Zone Books.

Delphy, Christine. 1993. Rethinking sex and gender. *Women's Studies International Forum* 16(1): 1–9.

Dupré, John. 1993. *The Disorder of Things: Metaphysical Foundations of the Disunity of Science*. Cambridge, MA: Harvard University Press.

Elgin, Catherine Z. 1997. *Between the Absolute and the Arbitrary*. Ithaca, NY: Cornell University Press.

Epstein, Brian. 2010. History and the critique of social concepts. *Philosophy of the Social Sciences* 40(1): 3–29.

Fausto-Sterling, Anne. 1993. The five sexes: Why male and female are not enough. *The Sciences* 33(2): 20–24.

———. 1997. How to build a man. In *The Gender/Sexuality Reader: Culture, History, Political Economy*. Ed. Roger N. Lancaster and Micaela di Leonardo. New York: Routledge, pp. 244–48.

———. 2000a. The five sexes, revisited: The varieties of sex will test medical values and social norms. *The Sciences* July/August: 18–23.

———. 2000b. *Sexing the Body: Gender Poltics and the Construction of Sexuality*. New York: Basic Books.

———. 2005. The bare bones of sex: Part 1, Sex and gender. *Signs: Journal of Women in Culture and Society* 30(2): 1491–527.

Fields, Barbara. 1982. Ideology and race in American history. *Region, Race, and Reconstruction: Essays in Honor of C. Vann Woodward*. Eds. J. Morgan Kousser, J. M. McPherson. Oxford: Oxford University Press.

Friedman, Marilyn. 1996. The unholy alliance of sex and gender. *Metaphilosophy* 27(1&2): 78–91.

Gatens, Moira. 1996. A critique of the sex-gender distinction. In *Imaginary Bodies: Ethics, Power and Corporeality*. New York: Routledge.

Gelman, Susan A. 2003. *The Essential Child: Origins of Essentialism in Everyday Thought*. New York: Oxford University Press.

Gibbard, Allan. *Thinking How to Live*. Cambridge MA: Harvard University Press (2003).

Gil White, Francisco J. 2001. Are ethnic groups biological 'species' to the human brain? *Current Anthropology* 42: 515–54.

Glasgow, Joshua. 2008. *A Theory of Race*. New York: Routledge.

Grosz, Elizabeth. 1994. *Volatile Bodies: Toward a Corporeal Feminism*. Bloomington: Indiana University Press.

Hacking, Ian. 1986. Making up people. In *Reconstructing Individualism: Autonomy, Individuality, and the Self in Western Thought*. Ed. Thomas C Heller, Morton Sosna, and David E. Wellbery. Stanford: Stanford University Press.

———. 1991. A tradition of natural kinds. *Philosophical Studies* 61(1): 109–26.

———. 1999. *The Social Construction of What?* Cambridge, MA: Harvard University Press.

———. 2007. Natural kinds: Rosy dawn, scholastic twilight. *Royal Institute of Philosophy Supplement* 82(61): 203–39.

Hardimon, Michael O. 2003. The ordinary concept of race. *The Journal of Philosophy* 100(9): 437–55.

Haslanger, S. 2012 [1995]. "Ontology and Social Construction." Chapter 2 of this volume.

———. 2012 [2000]. "Gender and Race: (What) Are They? (What) Do We Want Them To Be?" Chapter 7 of this volume.

———. 2012 [2003]. "Social Construction: The "Debunking" Project." Chapter 3 of this volume.

———. 2005a. Gender and Social Construction: Who? What? When? Where? How? In *Theorizing Feminisms: A Reader*. Ed. Sally Haslanger and Elizabeth Hackett. Oxford: Oxford University Press.

———. 2012 [2005b]. You Mixed? Racial Identity Without Racial Biology. Chapter 9 of this volume.

———. 2012 [2008]. A Social Constructionist Analysis of Race. Chapter 10 of this volume.

———. 2012 [2010]. Language, Politics, and "The Folk": Looking for "the Meaning" of 'Race'. Chapter 16 of this volume.

Hirschfeld, Lawrence. 1996. *Race in the Making: Cognition, Culture, and the Child's Construction of Human Kinds*. Cambridge, MA: MIT Press.

Howden, Lindsay M., and Julie A. Meyer. 2011. Age and sex composition: 2010. Washington, DC: US Census Bureau. www.census.gov/prod/cen2010/briefs/c2010br-03.pdf (accessed August 27, 2011).

Hume, David. 1983 [1751]. *An Enquiry Concerning the Principles of Morals*. Ed. Jerome Schneewind. Indianapolis, IN: Hackett Publishing Company.

Intersex Society of North America, "How Common is Intersex?" http://www.isna.org/faq/frequency/ (accessed March 8, 2010).

Kessler, Suzanne. 1998. *Lessons from the Intersexed*. New Brunswick: Rutgers University Press.

Laquer, Thomas. 1990. *Making Sex: Body and Gender from the Greeks to Freud*. Cambridge, MA: Harvard University Press.

Laurellz. 2005. "tween." http://www.urbandictionary.com/define.php?term=tween (accessed January 30, 2010).

Lewis, David K. 1983. New work for a theory of universals. *Australasian Journal of Philosophy* 61(4): 343–77.

Longino, Helen E. 1990. *Science as Social Knowledge: Values and Objectivity in Scientific Inquiry*. Princeton: Princeton University Press.

Machery, E., and L Faucher. 2005. Social construction and the concept of race. *Philosophy of Science* 72(5): 1208–19.

Mallon, Ron. 2007. A field guide to social construction. *Philosophy Compass* 2(1): 93.

———. 2008. Naturalistic approaches to social construction. *The Stanford Encyclopedia of Philosophy* (Winter 2008 Edition), Edward N. Zalta (ed.) http://plato.stanford.edu/archives/win2008/entries/social-construction-naturalistic/.

Mikkola, Mari. 2008. Feminist perspectives on sex and gender. *The Stanford Encyclopedia of Philosophy* (Fall 2008 Edition), Edward N. Zalta (ed.) http://plato.stanford.edu/archives/fall2008/entries/feminism-gender/.

Mills, Charles. 1988. Alternative epistemologies. *Social Theory and Practice* 14: 237–63.

———. 1997. *The Racial Contract*. Ithaca, NY: Cornell University Press.

———. 1998. *Blackness Visible: Essays on Philosophy and Race*. Ithaca, NY: Cornell University Press.

Money, John, and Patricia Tucker. 1976. *Sexual Signatures: On Being a Man or a Woman*. Boston, MA: Little Brown & Co.

O'Donnell, Jennifer. Definition of tween. http://tweenparenting.about.com/od/tweenculture/g/TweenDefinition.htm (accessed January 30, 2010).

Omi, Michael, and Howard Winant. 1994. *Racial Formation in the United States*. New York: Routledge.

Perry C. 2006. Tween. http://www.urbandictionary.com/define.php?term=tween (accessed January 30, 2010).

Pettit, Philip. 1991. Realism and response-dependence. *Mind* 100(4): 587–626.

Quine, W. V. O. 1961. "Two Dogmas of Empiricism." In *From a Logical Point of View*. Cambridge, MA: Harvard University Press.

———. 1969. Natural kinds. In *Essays in Honor of Carl G. Hempel*. Ed. Nicholas Rescher. Synthese Library 24. Dordrecht: Klewer.

Rosen, Gideon. 1994. Objectivity and modern idealism: What is the question? In *Philosophy in Mind: The Place of Philosophy in the Study of the Mind*. Ed. J. M. Michael. Dordrecht: Kluwer Academic Publishers, pp. 277–319.

Russell, Bertrand. 1948. *Human Knowledge, Its Scope and Limits*. London: Allen and Unwin.

Shrage, Laurie. 2009. *You've Changed: Sex Reassignment and Personal Identity*. Oxford: Oxford University Press.

Sismondo, Sergio. 1993. Some social constructions: Finding the limits of the constructivist metaphor. *Social Studies of Science* 23: 51.

Smith, Denise I., and Renee E. Spraggins. 2001. Gender: 2000. Washington DC: US Census Bureau. http://www.census.gov/prod/2001pubs/c2kbr01-9.pdf (accessed August 27, 2011)

Smith, Dinitia. 1998. Billy Tipton is remembered with love, even by those who were deceived. *New York Times*, June 2. http://www.nytimes.com/library/books/060298tipton-biography.html (accessed January 21, 2010).

Stone, A. 2007. *An Introduction to Feminist Philosophy*. Cambridge: Polity Press.

Sveinsdóttir, Ásta. 2010. The metaphysics of sex and gender. In *Feminist Metaphysics: Explorations in the Ontology of Sex, Gender and the Self*. Ed. Charlotte Witt. New York: Springer.

Taylor, Peter J. 2005. *Unruly Complexity: Ecology, Interpretation Engagement*. Chicago: University of Chicago Press.

van Kooten Niekerk, Kees. "Critical Realism." *Encyclopedia of Science and Religion*. http://www.enotes.com/science-religion-encyclopedia/critical-realism (accessed June 10, 2011).

Warnke, Georgia. 2001. Intersexuality and the categories of sex. *Hypatia* 16(3): 126–37.

Wilkerson, T. E. 1988. Natural kinds. *Philosophy* 63(243): 29–42.

Witt, Charlotte. 1995. Anti-essentialism in feminist theory. *Philosophical Topics* 23(2): 321–44.

———. 2011. *The Metaphysics of Gender*. Oxford: Oxford University Press.

Wittig, Monique. 1992. *The Straight Mind and Other Essays*. Boston, MA: Beacon Press.

Zack, Naomi. 2002. *Philosophy of Science and Race*. New York: Routledge.

PART TWO

GENDER AND RACE

7

Gender and Race

(What) Are They? (What) Do We Want Them to Be?[1]

> If her functioning as a female is not enough to define woman, if
> we decline also to explain her through "the eternal feminine,"
> and if nevertheless we admit, provisionally, that women do
> exist, then we must face the question: what is a woman?
>   —Simone de Beauvoir, *The Second Sex*

> I guess you could chuckle and say that I'm just a woman trapped
> in a woman's body.
>   —Ellen DeGeneres, *My Point . . . and I Do Have One*

> The truth is that there are no races: there is nothing in the world
> that can do all we ask race to do for us.
>   —Kwame Anthony Appiah, *In My Father's House*

It is always awkward when someone asks me informally what I'm working on
and I answer that I'm trying to figure out what gender is. For outside a rather
narrow segment of the academic world, the term 'gender' has come to function
as the polite way to talk about the sexes. And one thing people feel pretty confident about is their knowledge of the difference between males and females.
Males are those human beings with a range of familiar primary and secondary

[1] Special thanks to: Elizabeth Anderson, Larry Blum, Tracy Edwards, Marilyn Frye, Stephen
Darwall, Elizabeth Hackett, Elizabeth Harman, Donald Herzog, Will Kymlicka, Ishani Maitra, Mika
Lavaque-Manty, Joe Levine, Elisabeth Lloyd, Mary Kate McGowan, Toril Moi, Christine Overall,
Gerald Postema, Phyllis Rooney, Debra Satz, Geoff Sayre-McCord, Barry Smith, Jacqueline Stevens,
Natalie Stoljar, Martin Stone, Ásta Sveinsdóttir, Paul Taylor, Greg Velazco y Trianosky, Catherine
Wearing, Ralph Wedgwood, and Stephen Yablo for helpful comments on earlier versions of this
chapter. Extra thanks to Louise Antony for her extensive and tremendously insightful comments
and editorial advice. Thanks to audiences in the philosophy departments at the University of Ken-
tucky, University of North Carolina, Queens University, Stanford University, Tufts University, and
the University of Utah where I presented this material in talks. Research on this project was supported by the National Humanities Center where I was a fellow during 1995–6; thanks to Delta Delta
Delta Sorority whose support of the Center underwrote my fellowship there.

sex characteristics, most important being the penis; females are those with a different set, most important being the vagina or, perhaps, the uterus. Enough said. Against this background, it isn't clear what could be the point of an inquiry, especially a philosophical inquiry, into "what gender is."

But within that rather narrow segment of the academic world concerned with gender issues, not only is there no simple equation of sex and gender, but the seemingly straightforward anatomical distinction between the sexes has been challenged as well. What began as an effort to note that men and women differ socially as well as anatomically has prompted an explosion of different uses of the term 'gender.' Within these debates, not only is it unclear what gender is and how we should go about understanding it, but whether it is anything at all.

The situation is similar, if not worse, with respect to race. The self-evidence of racial distinctions in everyday American life is at striking odds with the uncertainty about the category of race in law and the academy. Work in the biological sciences has informed us that our practices of racial categorization don't map neatly onto any useful biological classification; but that doesn't settle much, if anything. For what should we make of our tendency to classify individuals according to race, apparently on the basis of physical appearance? And what are we to make of the social and economic consequences of such classifications? Is race real or is it not?

This chapter is part of a larger project, the goal of which is to offer accounts of gender and race informed by a feminist epistemology. Here my aim is to sketch some of the central ideas of those accounts. Let me emphasize at the beginning that I do not want to argue that my proposals provide the *only* acceptable ways to define race or gender; in fact, the epistemological framework I employ is explicitly designed to allow for different definitions responding to different concerns. It is sometimes valuable to consider race or gender alone or to highlight the differences between them; however, here I will begin by exploring some significant parallels. Although there are dangers in drawing close analogies between gender and race, I hope my discussion will show that theorizing them together can provide us valuable resources for thinking about a wide range of issues. Working with a model that demonstrates some of the parallels between race and gender also helps us locate important differences between them.

1. The Question(s)

It is useful to begin by reflecting on the questions: "What is gender?," "What is race?" and related questions such as: "What is it to be a man or a woman?,"[2] "What is it to be White? Latino? or Asian?" There are several different ways to

---

[2] I use the terms 'man' and 'woman' to distinguish individuals on the basis of gender, the terms 'male' and 'female' to distinguish individuals on the basis of sex.

understand, and so respond to, questions of the form, "What is X?" or "What is it to be an X?" For example, the question "What is knowledge?" might be construed in several ways. One might be asking: What is *our* concept of knowledge? (looking to a priori methods for an answer). On a more naturalistic reading, one might be asking: What (natural) kind (if any) does our epistemic vocabulary track? Or one might be undertaking a more revisionary project: What is the point of having a concept of knowledge? What concept (if any) would do that work best?[3] These different sorts of projects cannot be kept entirely distinct, but draw upon different methodological strategies. Returning to the questions, "What is race?" or "What is gender?" we can distinguish, then, three projects with importantly different priorities: *conceptual, descriptive*, and *analytical*.

A *conceptual* inquiry into race or gender would seek an articulation of our *concepts* of race or gender (Riley 1988). To answer the conceptual question, one way to proceed would be to use the method of reflective equilibrium. (Although within the context of analytic philosophy this might be seen as a call for a conceptual *analysis* of the term(s), I want to reserve the term 'analytical' for a different sort of project, described below.)

In contrast to the conceptual project, a *descriptive* project is not concerned with exploring the nuances of our concepts (or anyone else's for that matter); it focuses instead on their extension. Here, the task is to develop potentially more accurate concepts through careful consideration of the phenomena, usually relying on empirical or quasi-empirical methods. Paradigm descriptive projects occur in studying natural phenomena. I offered the example of naturalistic approaches to knowledge above: the goal is to determine the (natural) kind, if any, we are referring to (or are attempting to refer to) with our epistemic talk. However, a descriptive approach need not be confined to a search for *natural* or *physical* kinds; inquiry into what it is to be, for example, a human right, a citizen, a democracy, might begin by considering the full range of what has counted as such to determine whether there is an underlying (possibly social) kind that explains the temptation to group the cases together. Just as natural science can enrich our "folk" conceptualization of natural phenomena, social sciences (as well as the arts and humanities) can enrich our "folk" conceptualization of social phenomena. So, a descriptive inquiry into race and gender need not presuppose that race and gender are biological kinds; instead it might ask whether our uses of race and gender vocabularies are tracking social kinds, and if so which ones.

The third sort of project takes an *analytical* approach to the question, "What is gender?" or "What is race?" (Scott 1986). On this approach the task is not to explicate our ordinary concepts; nor is it to investigate the kind that we may or may not be tracking with our everyday conceptual apparatus; instead we begin

---

[3] See Stich 1998. Stich uses the term 'analytical epistemology' for what I would call a "conceptual" rather than an "analytical" project.

by considering more fully the pragmatics of our talk employing the terms in question. What is the point of having these concepts? What cognitive or practical task do they (or should they) enable us to accomplish? Are they effective tools to accomplish our (legitimate) purposes; if not, what concepts would serve these purposes better? In the limit case of an analytical approach the concept in question is introduced by stipulating the meaning of a new term, and its content is determined entirely by the role it plays in the theory. But if we allow that our everyday vocabularies serve both cognitive and practical purposes, purposes that might also be served by our theorizing, then a theory offering an improved understanding of our (legitimate) purposes and/or improved conceptual resources for the tasks at hand might reasonably represent itself as providing a (possibly revisionary) account of the everyday concepts.[4]

So, on an analytical approach, the questions "What is gender?" or "What is race?" require us to consider what work we want these concepts to do for us; why do we need them at all? The responsibility is ours to define them for our purposes. In doing so we will want to be responsive to some aspects of ordinary usage (and to aspects of both the connotation and extension of the terms). However, neither ordinary usage nor empirical investigation is overriding, for there is a stipulative element to the project: *this* is the phenomenon we need to be thinking about. Let the term in question refer to it. On this approach, the world by itself can't tell us what gender is, or what race is; it is up to us to decide what in the world, if anything, they are.

This essay pursues an analytical approach to defining race and gender. However, its analytical objectives are linked to the descriptive project of determining whether our gender and race vocabularies in fact track social kinds that are typically obscured by the manifest content of our everyday race and gender concepts.[5] Although the analyses I offer will point to existing social kinds (and this is no accident), I am not prepared to defend the claim that these social kinds are what our race and gender talk is "really" about. My priority in this inquiry is not to capture what we do mean, but how we might usefully revise what we mean for certain theoretical and political purposes.

My characterization of all three approaches remains vague, but there is one reason to be skeptical of the analytical approach that should be addressed at the outset. The different approaches I've sketched differ both in their methods and their subject matter. However, we come to inquiry with a conceptual repertoire in terms of which we frame our questions and search for answers: hence, the subject matter of any inquiry would seem to be set from the start. In asking

---

[4] Cf. Appiah and Gutmann 1996, pp. 30–105. Appiah doesn't consider an analytical approach to race except rather elliptically on p. 42.

[5] On the distinction between manifest and operative concepts, see my 1995, esp. p. 102. (this volume, p. 92).

what *race* is, or what *gender* is, our initial questions are expressed in *everyday* vocabularies of race and gender, so how can we meaningfully answer these questions without owing obedience to the everyday concepts? Or at least to our everyday usage? Revisionary projects are in danger of providing answers to questions that weren't being asked.

But ordinary concepts are notoriously vague; individual conceptions and linguistic usage varies widely. Moreover, inquiry often demonstrates that the ordinary concepts used initially to frame a project are not, as they stand, well-suited to the theoretical task at hand. (This is one reason why we may shift from a *conceptual* project to an *analytical* one.) But precisely because our ordinary concepts are vague (or it is vague which concept we are expressing by our everyday use of terms), there is room to stretch, shrink, or refigure what exactly we are talking about in new and sometimes unexpected directions.

However, in an explicitly revisionary project, it is not at all clear when we are warranted in appropriating existing terminology. Given the difficulty of determining what "our" concept is, it isn't entirely clear when a project crosses over from being explicative to revisionary, or when it is no longer even revisionary but simply changes the subject. If our goal is to offer an analysis of "our" concept of X, then the line between what's explication and what's not matters. But if our goal is to identify a concept that serves our broader purposes, then the question of terminology is primarily a pragmatic and sometimes a political one: should we employ the terms of ordinary discourse to refer to our theoretical categories, or instead make up new terms? The issue of terminological appropriation is especially important, and especially sensitive, when the terms in question designate categories of social identity such as 'race' and 'gender.'

Are there principles that determine when it is legitimate to appropriate the terms of ordinary discourse for theoretical purposes? An answer, it seems to me, should include both a semantic and a political condition (though in some cases the politics of the appropriation will be uncontroversial). The semantic condition is not surprising: the proposed shift in meaning of the term would seem semantically warranted if central functions of the term remain the same, for example, if it helps organize or explain a core set of phenomena that the ordinary terms are used to identify or describe.[6] Framing a political condition in general terms is much more difficult, however, for the politics of such appropriation will depend on the acceptability of the goals being served, the intended and unintended effects of the change, the politics of the speech context, and whether the underlying values are justified. We will return to some of these issues later in the chapter once my analyses have been presented.

---

[6] It is important to keep in mind that what's at issue is not a criterion for *sameness* of meaning, but the boundary between what could count as a revisionary project and a new project altogether.

2. Critical (Feminist, Antiracist) Theory

In an analytical project we must begin by considering what we want the concept in question for. Someone might argue, however, that the answer is simple: our concepts must do the work of enabling us to articulate truths. But of course an unconstrained search for truth would yield chaos, not theory; truths are too easy to come by, there are too many of them. Given time and inclination, I could tell you many truths—some trivial, some interesting, many boring—about my physical surroundings. But a random collection of facts does not make a theory; they are a disorganized jumble. In the context of theorizing, some truths are more significant than others because they are relevant to answering the question that guides the inquiry (Anderson 1995).

Theorizing—even when it is sincerely undertaken as a search for truth—must be guided by more than the goal of achieving justified true belief. Good theories are systematic bodies of knowledge that select from the mass of truths those that address our broader cognitive and practical demands. In many contexts the questions and purposes that frame the project are understood and progress does not require one to investigate them. But in other contexts, for example, especially when debate has seemed to break down and parties are talking at cross-purposes, an adequate evaluation of an existing theory, or success in developing a new one, is only possible when it is made clear what the broader goals are.

With this sketch of some of the theoretical options, I want to frame my own project as a *critical analytical* effort to answer the questions: "What is gender?," "What is race?" and the related questions "What is it to be a man?" ". . . a woman?," ". . . White?" ". . . Latino?" and so on. More specifically, the goal of the project is to consider what work the concepts of gender and race might do for us in a critical—specifically feminist and antiracist—social theory, and to suggest concepts that can accomplish at least important elements of that work (Guess 1981). So to start: why might feminist antiracists want or need the concepts of gender and race? What work can they do for us?

At the most general level, the task is to develop accounts of gender and race that will be effective tools in the fight against injustice. The broad project is guided by four concerns:

(i) The need to identify and explain persistent inequalities between females and males, and between people of different "colors";[7] this includes the

---

[7] We need here a term for those physical features of individuals that mark them as members of a race. One might refer to them as "racial" features, but to avoid any suggestion of racial essences I will use the term 'color' to refer to the (contextually variable) physical "markers" of race, just as I use the term 'sex' to refer to the (contextually variable) physical "markers" of gender. I mean to include in "color" more than just skin tone: common markers also include eye, nose, and lip shape, hair texture, physique, etc. Although the term 'people of color' is used to refer to non-Whites, I want to allow that the markers of "Whiteness" count as "color."

concern to identify how social forces, often under the guise of biological forces, work to perpetuate such inequalities.

(ii) The need for a framework that will be sensitive to both the similarities and differences among males and females, and the similarities and differences among individuals in groups demarcated by "color"; this includes the concern to identify the effects of interlocking oppressions, for example, the intersectionality of race, class, and gender (Crenshaw 1993).

(iii) The need for an account that will track how gender and race are implicated in a broad range of social phenomena extending beyond those that obviously concern sexual or racial difference, for example, whether art, religion, philosophy, science, or law might be "gendered" and/or "racialized."

(iv) The need for accounts of gender and race that take seriously the agency of women and people of color of both genders, and within which we can develop an understanding of agency that will aid feminist and antiracist efforts to empower critical social agents.

In this chapter I will begin to address the first two concerns, though the fourth will become relevant later in the discussion. Let me emphasize, however, that my goal in this chapter is not to provide a thoroughgoing explanation of sexism and racism, if one wants by way of explanation a causal account of why and how females have come to be systematically subordinated throughout history, or why and how "color" has come to be a basis for social stratification. My goal here is in some ways more modest, and in other ways more contentious. Prior to explanation it is valuable to provide clear conceptual categories to identify the phenomenon needing explanation, for example, categories that identify the kind of injustice at issue and the groups subject to it. In the case of racial and sexual subordination this is not as easy as it may seem. In the first place, the forms of racial and sexual subordination are tremendously heterogeneous and it would help to have accounts that enable us to distinguish *racial* subordination and *sexual* subordination from other sorts. But further, we must be cautious about treating familiar demarcations of "color" and "sex" as purely natural categories, as if the question at hand is simply why one's "color" or sex—where we take for granted our familiar understandings of these terms—has ever seemed to be socially significant. At least at this stage of the inquiry we must allow that the criteria for distinguishing "colors" or "sexes" differ across time and place, and that the boundaries are at least partly political; but in spite of this variation, we are still dealing with an overarching phenomenon of racial and sexual subordination.

3. What is Gender?

Even a quick survey of the literature reveals that a range of things have counted as "gender" within feminist theorizing. The guiding idea is sometimes expressed with the slogan: "gender is the social meaning of sex." But like any slogan, this one allows for different interpretations. Some theorists use the term 'gender' to refer to the subjective experience of sexed embodiment, or a broad psychological orientation to the world ("gender identity"[8]); others to a set of attributes or ideals that function as norms for males and females ("masculinity" and "femininity"); others to a system of sexual symbolism; and still others to the traditional social roles of men and women. My strategy is to offer a focal analysis that defines gender, in the primary sense, as a social class. A focal analysis undertakes to explain a variety of connected phenomena in terms of their relations to one that is theorized as the central or core phenomenon. As I see it, the core phenomenon to be addressed is the pattern of social relations that constitute the social classes of men as dominant and women as subordinate; norms, symbols, and identities are gendered in relation to the social relations that constitute gender.[9] As will become clearer below, I see my emphasis as falling within, though not following uncritically, the tradition of materialist feminism.[10]

Among feminist theorists there are two problems that have generated pessimism about providing any unified account of women; I'll call them the *commonality problem* and the *normativity problem*. Very briefly, the commonality problem questions whether there is anything social that females have in common that could count as their "gender." If we consider *all* females—females of different times, places, and cultures—there are reasons to doubt that there is anything beyond body type (if even that) that they all share (Spelman 1988). The normativity problem raises the concern that any definition of "what woman is" is value-laden, and will marginalize certain females, privilege others, and reinforce current gender norms (Butler 1990, Ch. 1).

It is important to note, even briefly, that these problems take on a different cast when they arise within a *critical analytical* project. The emphasis of an analytical project is not on discovering commonalities among females: although the empirical similarities and differences between females are relevant, the primary goal is an analysis of gender that will serve as a tool in the quest for sexual justice (see section 2). Moreover, a critical project can accept the result that an effort to define "what women is" carries normative implications, for critical projects explicitly embrace normative results; the hope is that the account's implications

---

[8] There are at least four different uses of the term 'identity' that are relevant in considering the issue of gender or racial "identity"; here my comments about "gender identity" are admittedly superficial.

[9] Very roughly, feminine norms are those that enable one to excel in the social position constituting the class *women;* feminine gender identity (at least in one sense of the term) is a psychological orientation to the world that includes the internalization of feminine norms; and feminine symbols are those that encode idealized feminine norms. What counts as a "feminine" norm, a "feminine" gender identity, or a "feminine" symbol is derivative (norms, symbols, and identities are not intrinsically feminine or masculine), and depends on how the social class of women is locally constituted.

[10] For a sample of materialist feminist work, see Hennessy and Ingraham 1997.

would not reinforce but would help undermine the structures of sexual oppression. However, we will return to these issues below.

Given the priority I place on concerns with justice and sexual inequality, I take the primary motivation for distinguishing sex from gender to arise in the recognition that males and females do not only differ physically, but also systematically differ in their social positions. What is of concern, to put it simply, is that societies, on the whole, privilege individuals with male bodies. Although the particular forms and mechanisms of oppression vary from culture to culture, societies have found many ways—some ingenious, some crude—to control and exploit the sexual and reproductive capacities of females.

The main strategy of materialist feminist accounts of gender has been to define gender in terms of women's subordinate position in systems of male dominance.[11] Although there are materialist feminist roots in Marxism, contemporary versions resist the thought that all social phenomena can be explained in or reduced to economic terms; and although materialist feminists emphasize the role of language and culture in women's oppression, there is a wariness of extreme forms of linguistic constructivism and a commitment to staying grounded in the material realities of women's lives. In effect, there is a concerted effort to show how gender oppression is jointly sustained by both cultural and material forces.

Critiques of universalizing feminisms have taught us to be attentive to the variety of forms gender takes and the concrete social positions females occupy. However, it is compatible with these commitments to treat the category of gender as a genus that is realized in different ways in different contexts; doing so enables us to recognize significant patterns in the ways that gender is instituted and embodied. Working at the most general level, then, the materialist strategy offers us three basic principles to guide us in understanding gender:

(i) Gender categories are defined in terms of how one is socially positioned, where this is a function of, for example, how one is viewed, how one is treated, and how one's life is structured socially, legally, and economically; gender is not defined in terms of an individual's intrinsic physical or psychological features.

(This allows that there may be other categories—such as sex—that are defined in terms of intrinsic physical features. Note, however, that once we focus our attention on gender as social position, we must allow that one can be a woman without ever (in the ordinary sense) "acting like a woman," "feeling like a woman," or even having a female body.)

---

[11] Some theorists (Delphy, Hartmann) focus on the economic exploitation of women in domestic relations of production; others (Wittig) focus on sexual and reproductive exploitation under compulsory heterosexuality; others (MacKinnon) focus on sexual objectification.

(ii) Gender categories are defined hierarchically within a broader complex of oppressive relations; one group (viz., women) is socially positioned as subordinate to the other (viz., men), typically within the context of other forms of economic and social oppression.

(iii) Sexual difference functions as the physical marker to distinguish the two groups, and is used in the justification of viewing and treating the members of each group differently.

(Tentatively) we can capture these main points in the following analyses:

S *is a woman* iff$_{df}$ S is systematically subordinated along some dimension (economic, political, legal, social, etc.), and S is "marked" as a target for this treatment by observed or imagined bodily features presumed to be evidence of a female's biological role in reproduction.[12]

S *is a man* iff$_{df}$ S is systematically privileged along some dimension (economic, political, legal, social, etc.), and S is "marked" as a target for this treatment by observed or imagined bodily features presumed to be evidence of a male's biological role in reproduction.

It is a virtue, I believe, of these accounts, that depending on context, one's sex may have a very different meaning and it may position one in very different kinds of hierarchies. The variation will clearly occur from culture to culture (and sub-culture to sub-culture); so for example, to be a Chinese woman of the 1790s, a Brazilian woman of the 1890s, or an American woman of the 1990s may involve very different social relations, and very different kinds of oppression. Yet on the analysis suggested, these groups count as women insofar as their subordinate positions are marked and justified by reference to (female) sex (also Hurtado 1994, esp. 142). Similarly, this account allows that the substantive import of gender varies even from individual to individual within a culture depending on how the meaning of sex interacts with other socially salient characteristics (e.g., race, class, sexuality, etc.). For example, a privileged White woman and a Black woman of the underclass will both be women insofar as their social positions are affected by the social meanings of being female; and yet the social implications of being female vary for each because sexism is intertwined with race and class oppression.

There are points in the proposed analysis that require clarification, however. What does it mean to say that someone is "systematically subordinated" or "privileged," and further, that the subordination occurs "on the basis of" certain

---

[12] These analyses allow that there isn't a common understanding of "sex" across time and place. On my account, gendered social positions are those marked by reference to features that are generally assumed *in the context in question* to either explain or provide evidence of reproductive role, whether or not these are features that *we* consider "sex."

features? The background idea is that women are *oppressed*, and that they are oppressed *as women*. But we still need to ask: What does it mean to say that women are oppressed, and what does the qualification "as women" add?

Marilyn Frye's account of oppression with Iris Young's elaborations provides a valuable starting point (Frye 1983; Young 1990). Although these ideas are commonplace within certain intellectual circles, it is useful to summarize them very briefly here. There are of course unresolved difficulties in working out a satisfactory theory of oppression; I'm afraid I can't take on that further task here, so I can only invoke the rough outlines of the background view with the hope that an adequate account can at some point be supplied. Nonetheless, oppression in the intended sense is a structural phenomenon that positions certain groups as disadvantaged and others as advantaged or privileged in relation to them. Oppression consists of, "an enclosing structure of forces and barriers which tends to the immobilization and reduction of a group or category of people" (Frye 1983, 11). Importantly, such structures, at least as we know them, are not designed and policed by those in power, rather,

> . . . oppression refers to the vast and deep injustices some groups suffer as a consequence of often unconscious assumptions and reactions of well-meaning people in ordinary interactions, media and cultural stereotypes, and structural features of bureaucratic hierarchies and market mechanisms—in short, the normal processes of everyday life. (Young 1990, 41)

Developing this concept of oppression, Young specifies five forms it can take: exploitation, marginalization, powerlessness, cultural imperialism, and (systematic) violence. The key point for us is that oppression comes in different forms, and even if one is privileged along some dimension (e.g., in income or respect), one might be oppressed in others.[13] In fact, one might be systematically subordinated along some social axis, and yet still be tremendously privileged in one's *overall* social position.

It is clear that women are oppressed in the sense that women are members of groups that suffer exploitation, marginalization, and so on. But how should we understand the claim that women are oppressed *as women*. Frye explains this as follows:

> One is marked for application of oppressive pressures by one's membership in some group or category. . . . In the case at hand, it is the category, *woman*. . . . If a woman has little or no economic or political power, or achieves little of what she wants to achieve, a major causal

---

[13] On the importance of disaggregating power and oppression, see Ortner 1996.

factor in this is that she is a woman. For any woman of any race or economic class, being a woman is significantly attached to whatever disadvantages and deprivations she suffers, be they great or small. . . . [In
contrast,] being male is something [a man] has going *for* him, even if
race or class or age or disability is going against him. (Frye 1983, 15–16)

But given the diffusion of power in a model of structural oppression, how are we
to make sense of one's being "marked" and the "application" of pressures? In the
context of oppression, certain properties of individuals are socially meaningful.
This is to say that the properties play a role in a broadly accepted (though usually
not fully explicit) representation of the world that functions to justify and motivate particular forms of social intercourse. The significant properties in question—in the cases at hand, assumed or actual properties of the body—mark you
"for application of oppressive pressures" insofar as the attribution of these properties is interpreted as adequate, in light of this background representation, to
explain and/or justify your position in a structure of oppressive social relations.
In the case of women, the idea is that societies are guided by representations
that link being female with other facts that have implications for how one should
be viewed and treated; insofar as we structure our social life to accommodate the
cultural meanings of the female (and male) body, females occupy an oppressed
social position.

Although I agree with Frye that in sexist societies social institutions are
structured in ways that on the whole disadvantage females and advantage males,
we must keep in mind that societies are not monolithic and that sexism is not
the only source of oppression. For example, in the contemporary US, there are
contexts in which being Black and male marks one as a target for certain forms
of systematic violence (e.g., by the police). In those contexts, contrary to Frye's
suggestion, being male is not something that a man "has going *for* him"; though
there are other contexts (also in the contemporary U.S.) in which Black males
benefit from being male. In examples of this sort, the systematic violence against
males *as males* is emasculating (and may be intended as such); but there are
important differences between an emasculated man and a woman. On the sort
of view we're considering, a woman is someone whose subordinated status is
marked by reference to (assumed) female anatomy; someone marked for subordination by reference to (assumed) *male* anatomy does not qualify as a woman,
but also, in the particular context, is not socially positioned as a man.

These considerations suggests that it may be useful to bring context explicitly into our account. Recent work on gender socialization also supports the
idea that although most of us develop a relatively fixed gender identity by the
age of three, the degree to which the marked body makes a difference varies
from context to context. In her study of elementary school children, Barrie
Thorne suggests:

> Gender boundaries are episodic and ambiguous, and *the notion of "borderwork"* [i.e., the work of contesting and policing gender boundaries] *should be coupled with a parallel term—such as "neutralization"—for processes through which girls and boys (and adults . . .) neutralize or undermine a sense of gender as division and opposition.* (Thorne 1993, 84)

Thorne's study is motivated by a recognition that gender is a well-entrenched system of oppression. However, her comments here are intended as an antidote to two problematic tendencies in speaking of girls and boys, men and women: first, the tendency to over-generalize gender differences based on paradigm or stereotyped interactions; second, the tendency to view individuals (specifically children) as passive participants in gender socialization and, more generally, gendered life.

In some respects, Frye's and Thorne's approaches appear to be in tension with one another. Frye is keen to highlight the structural facts of sexist oppression: like it or not, your body positions you within a social hierarchy. Thorne, on the other hand, examines how oppression is lived, enforced, and resisted at the micro level. There are important advantages to both: without a recognition of oppressive structures and the overall patterns of advantage and disadvantage, individual slights or conflicts can seem harmless. But without a recognition of individual variation and agency, the structures take on a life of their own and come to seem inevitable and insurmountable. But can both perspectives be accommodated in an account of gender? The idea seems simple enough: there are dominant ideologies and dominant social structures that work together to bias the micro-level interactions, however varied and complex they may be, so that for the most part males are privileged and females are disadvantaged.

Although an adequate account of gender must be highly sensitive to contextual variation, if we focus entirely on the narrowly defined contexts in which one's gender is negotiated, we could easily lose sight of the fact that for most of us there is a relatively fixed interpretation of our bodies as sexed either male or female, an interpretation that marks us within the dominant ideology as eligible for only certain positions or opportunities in a system of sexist oppression. Given our priority in theorizing systems of inequality, it is important first to locate the social classes men and women in a broad structure of subordination and privilege:[14]

---

[14] This proposal depends on the claim that at least some societies have a "dominant ideology." Others have employed the notions of "background," "hegemony," "habitus," for the same purpose. Rather than debating what is the preferred notion, I'm happy to let the term 'dominant ideology' serve as a placeholder for an account to be decided upon later. Given the strategy of my accounts, however, we must be sure to allow for multiple ideological strands in any society. See Geuss 1981, Hoy 1994.

S is a woman iff

(i) S is regularly and for the most part observed or imagined to have certain bodily features presumed to be evidence of a female's biological role in reproduction;

(ii) that S has these features marks S within the dominant ideology of S's society as someone who ought to occupy certain kinds of social position that are in fact subordinate (and so motivates and justifies S's occupying such a position); and

(iii) the fact that S satisfies (i) and (ii) plays a role in S's systematic subordination, that is, *along some dimension*, S's social position is oppressive, and S's satisfying (i) and (ii) plays a role in that dimension of subordination.

S is a man iff

(i) S is regularly and for the most part observed or imagined to have certain bodily features presumed to be evidence of a male's biological role in reproduction;

(ii) that S has these features marks S within the dominant ideology of S's society as someone who ought to occupy certain kinds of social position that are in fact privileged (and so motivates and justifies S's occupying such a position); and

(iii) the fact that S satisfies (i) and (ii) plays a role in S's systematic privilege, that is, *along some dimension*, S's social position is privileged, and S's satisfying (i) and (ii) plays a role in that dimension of privilege.

These accounts are, however, compatible with the idea that (at least for some of us) one's gender may not be entirely stable, and that other systems of oppression may disrupt gender in particular contexts: a woman may not always function socially as a woman; a man may not always function socially as a man.[15] To return to a previous example, when systems of White supremacy and male dominance collide, a Black man's male privilege may be seen as so threatening that it must be violently wrested from him. In an effort to accommodate this variation, we can add:

---

[15] We noted before that on a materialist account sex and gender don't always coincide. I'm making here a further claim: one may be gendered man or woman without functioning socially in that gender every moment of one's life.

S *functions as a woman* in context C iff$_{df}$

(i) S is observed or imagined in C to have certain bodily features presumed to be evidence of a female's biological role in reproduction;

(ii) that S has these features marks S within the background ideology of C as someone who ought to occupy certain kinds of social position that are in fact subordinate (and so motivates and justifies S's occupying such a position); and

(iii) the fact that S satisfies (i) and (ii) plays a role in S's systematic subordination in C, that is, *along some dimension*, S's social position in C is oppressive, and S's satisfying (i) and (ii) plays a role in that dimension of subordination.

And mutatis mutandis for functioning as a man in context C.

It is important to note that the definitions don't require that the background ideology in question must use (assumed) reproductive function as itself the justification for treating men or women in the way deemed "appropriate"; (assumed) reproductive features may instead simply be "markers" of supposedly "deeper" (and morally relevant?) characteristics that the ideology supposes justifies the treatment in question (Appiah 1992, 13–15).

Although ultimately I will defend these analyses of *man* and *woman*, I'll argue below that there are reasons to modify the broader materialist strategy in defining *gender*. In short, I believe that gender can be fruitfully understood as a higher order genus that includes not only the hierarchical social positions of man and woman, but potentially other non-hierarchical social positions defined in part by reference to reproductive function. I believe gender *as we know it* takes hierarchical forms as men and women; but the theoretical move of treating men and women as only two kinds of gender provides resources for thinking about other (actual) genders, and the political possibility of constructing non-hierarchical genders.

4. What is Race?

One advantage of this account of gender is the parallel it offers for race. To begin, let me review a couple of points that I take to be matters of established fact: First, there are no racial genes responsible for the complex morphologies and cultural patterns we associate with different races. Second, in different contexts racial distinctions are drawn on the basis of different characteristics, for example, the Brazilian and U.S. classification schemes for who counts as "Black" differ. For these reasons and others, it appears that race, like gender, could be fruitfully understood as a position within a broad social network.

Although suggestive, this idea is not easy to develop. It is one thing to acknowledge that race is *socially* real, even if a biological fiction; but it is another thing to capture in general terms "the social meaning of color." There seem to be too many different forms race takes. Note, however, that we encountered a similar problem with gender: is there any prospect for a unified analysis of "the social meaning of sex"? The materialist feminist approach offered a helpful strategy: don't look for an analysis that assumes that the meaning is always and everywhere the same; rather, consider how members of the group are *socially positioned*, and what *physical markers* serve as a supposed basis for such treatment.

How might we extend this strategy to race? Transposing the slogan, we might say that race is the social meaning of the geographically marked body, familiar markers being skin color, hair type, eye shape, physique. To develop this, I propose the following account.[16]

First definition:

> A group is *racialized* iff$_{df}$ its members are socially positioned as subordinate or privileged along some dimension (economic, political, legal, social, etc.), and the group is "marked" as a target for this treatment by observed or imagined bodily features presumed to be evidence of ancestral links to a certain geographical region.

Or in the more elaborate version:

> A group G is *racialized* relative to context C iff$_{df}$ members of G are (all and only) those:
>
> (i) who are observed or imagined to have certain bodily features presumed in C to be evidence of ancestral links to a certain geographical region (or regions);
>
> (ii) whose having (or being imagined to have) these features marks them within the context of the background ideology in C as appropriately occupying certain kinds of social position that are in fact either subordinate or privileged (and so motivates and justifies their occupying such a position); and
>
> (iii) whose satisfying (i) and (ii) plays (or would play) a role in their systematic subordination or privilege in C, that is, who are along some dimension systematically subordinated or privileged when in

---

[16] On this I am deeply indebted to Stevens 1999, Ch. 4, and Omi and Winant 1994, esp. pp. 53–61.

C, and satisfying (i) and (ii) plays (or would play) a role in that dimension of privilege or subordination.[17]

In other words, races are those groups demarcated by the geographical associations accompanying perceived body type, when those associations take on evaluative significance concerning how members of the group should be viewed and

---

[17] There are aspects of this definition that need further elaboration or qualification. I will mention four here.

First, on my account, those who actually have the ancestral links to the specified region
but who "pass," do not count as members of the racialized group in question. This is parallel to
the case of a female functioning socially as a man or a male functioning socially as a woman.
Because the goal is to define race and gender as social positions, I endorse this consequence of the
definitions.

Second, as it stands the definition does not accommodate contexts such as Brazil in which membership in "racial" groups is partly a function of education and class. It excludes privileged ("Whitened") members from the subordinate races they might seem—considering only "color"—to belong
to, and subordinated ("darkened") members from privileged races, because they don't satisfy the third
condition. But it cannot handle the inclusion of the "Whitened" members in the privileged group or
the "darkened" members in the subordinated group because they don't satisfy the first condition.
However, we could take the definition to capture a *strong* version of racialization, and develop another
version on which appropriate "color" is relevant but not necessary by modifying the second condition:

> (ii*) having (or being imagined to have) these features—*possibly in combination with
> others*—marks them within the context of C's cultural ideology as appropriately oc-
> cupying the kinds of social position that are in fact either subordinate or privileged
> (and so motivates and justifies their occupying such a position).

The first condition already allows that the group's members may have supposed origins in more than
one region (originally necessary to accommodate the racialization of "mixed-race" groups); modifying the second condition allows that racialized groups may include people of different "colors," and
depend on a variety of factors.

Third, need racialized groups be "marked" by actual or assumed body type? What about Jews,
Native Americans, and Romanies? (Romanies are also interesting because it isn't entirely clear that
there is a supposed place of origin, though I take "no place of origin" to be a factor in their racialization, and to serve as the limit case.) I would suggest that there are *some* (perhaps imagined) physical
features that are regarded as salient in contexts where Jews and Native Americans are racialized,
though not every member of the group need have those features if there is other evidence of ancestral links. However, ultimately it might be more useful to allow racial membership to be determined
by a cluster of features (such as physical appearance, ancestry, and class) weighted differently in
different contexts.

Finally, I want the definition to capture the idea that members of racial groups may be scattered
across social contexts and may not all actually be (immediately) affected by local structures of privilege and subordination. So, for example, Black Africans and African-Americans are together members of a group currently racialized in the U.S., even if a certain ideological interpretation of their
"color" has not played a role in the subordination of all Black Africans. So I suggest that members
of a group racialized in C are those who are *or would be* marked and correspondingly subordinated
or privileged when in C. Those who think (plausibly) that all Blacks worldwide have been affected by
the structures and ideology of White supremacy do not need this added clause; and those who want
a potentially more fine-grained basis for racial membership can drop it.

treated. As in the case of gender, the ideology need not use physical morphology or geography as the entire basis for "appropriate" treatment; these features may instead simply be "markers" of other characteristics that the ideology uses to justify the treatment in question.

Given this definition, we can say that S is of the White (Black, Asian . . .) race [in C] iff Whites (Blacks, Asians . . .) are a racialized group [in C], and S is a member.[18] On this view, whether a group is racialized, and so how and whether an individual is raced, is not an absolute fact, but will depend on context. For example, Blacks, Whites, Asians, Native Americans, are currently racialized in the U.S. insofar as these are all groups defined in terms of physical features associated with places of origin, and insofar as membership in the group functions socially as a basis for evaluation. However, some groups are not currently racialized in the US, but have been so in the past and possibly could be again (and in other contexts are), for example, the Italians, the Germans, the Irish.

It is useful to note a possible contrast between race and ethnicity. I don't have a theory of ethnicity to offer; these are some preliminary comparisons. One's ethnicity concerns one's ancestral links to a certain geographical region (perhaps together with participation in the cultural practices of that region); often ethnicity is associated with characteristic physical features. For our purposes, however, it might be useful to employ the notion of "ethnicity" for those groups that are like races as I've defined them except that they do not experience systematic subordination or privilege in the context in question.[19] Ethnic groups can be (and are) racialized, however, and when they are, one's membership in the group positions one in a social hierarchy; but (on the view I'm sketching) the occurrence of this hierarchical positioning means that the group has gone beyond simply being an ethnic group and functions in that context as a race. In short, we can distinguish between grouping individuals on the basis of their (assumed) origins, and grouping them *hierarchically* on the basis of their (assumed) origins, and the contrast between race and ethnicity might be a useful way to capture this distinction.

---

[18] As in the case of gender, I recommend that we view membership in a racial/ethnic group in terms of how one is viewed and treated regularly and for the most part in the context in question; though as before, one could distinguish *being* a member of a given race from *functioning as* one by considering the degree of one's entrenchment in the racialized social position (not on the basis of biology or ancestry).

[19] We may want to allow there to be kinds of social stratification between ethnic groups that fall short of the kind of systematic subordination constitutive of race. My account remains vague on this point. Clarification might be gained by plugging in a more sophisticated account of social hierarchies. The body is also relevant: are ethnicities distinguishable from races by the degree to which they are perceived as capable of assimilation?

5. Normativity and Commonality

So what, if anything, is achieved by adopting the above analyses? Are they the tools we need? Let's first consider the problems of commonality and normativity, and begin with gender.

Remember, the problem of commonality questions whether there is anything social that all females can plausibly be said to have in common. If we ask whether females share any intrinsic (non-anatomical) features such as psychological makeup, character traits, beliefs, values, experiences or, alternatively, whether there is a particular social role that all females have occupied across culture and history, the answer seems to be "no."

On my analysis women are those who occupy a particular *kind* of social position, namely, one of sexually marked subordinate. So women have in common that their (assumed) sex has socially disadvantaged them; but this is compatible with the kinds of cultural variation that feminist inquiry has revealed, for the substantive content of women's position and the ways of justifying it can vary enormously. Admittedly, the account accommodates such variation by being very abstract; nonetheless, it provides a schematic account that highlights the interdependence between the material forces that subordinate women, *and* the ideological frameworks that sustain them.

One might complain, however, that there must be *some* women (or rather, females) who aren't oppressed, and in particular, aren't oppressed *as women*. Perhaps there are; for example, some may "pass" as men, others may be recognizably female but not be subordinated in any way linked to that recognition. I'm not convinced that there are many cases (if any) of the latter, but I'll certainly grant that there *could be* females who did not satisfy the definition that I've offered. In fact, I believe it is part of the project of feminism to bring about a day when there are no more women (though, of course, we should not aim to do away with females!). I'm happy to admit that there could be females who aren't women in the sense I've defined, but these individuals (or possible individuals) are not counterexamples to the analysis. The analysis is intended to capture a meaningful political category for critical feminist efforts, and non-oppressed females do not fall within that category (though they may be interesting for other reasons).

But this leads us directly from the commonality problem to the normativity problem. The normativity problem raises the challenge that any effort to define *women* will problematically privilege some women and (theoretically) marginalize others, and will itself become normative. One worry is that bias inevitably occurs in deciding which experiences or social roles are definitive; a second worry is that if someone wants to be a "real" woman, she should conform to the definition of women provided, and this will reinforce rather than challenge male dominance.

On the account I've offered, it is true that certain females don't count as "real" women; and it is true that I've privileged certain facts of women's lives as definitive. But given the epistemological framework outlined above, it is both inevitable and important for us to choose what facts are significant on the basis of explicit and considered values. For the purposes of a critical feminist inquiry, oppression is a significant fact around which we should organize our theoretical categories; it may be that non-oppressed females are marginalized within my account, but that is because for the broader purposes at hand—relative to the feminist and antiracist values guiding our project—they are not the ones who matter. The important issue is not whether a particular account "marginalizes" some individuals, but whether its doing so is in conflict with the feminist values that motivate the inquiry. And as far as I can tell, *not* focusing our theoretical efforts on understanding the position of oppressed females would pose just such a conflict.

The question remains whether my definition of woman helps sustain gender hierarchy by implicitly offering a normative ideal of woman. Given that women on my definition are an oppressed group, I certainly hope not! Instead, the definition is more likely to offer a negative ideal that challenges male dominance.

I won't defend here my account of racialized groups against an extension of the normativity and commonality complaints, for I would simply repeat the strategy just employed. Although there are interesting nuances in adapting the arguments to apply to racialized groups, I don't see anything peculiar to race that would present an obstacle to developing the same sort of response.

6. Negotiating Terms

Let me now turn to summarize some of the advantages of the proposed definitions. At this point we could bracket the terminological issues and just consider whether the groups in question are ones that are important to consider given the goals of our inquiry. I hope it is clear from what I've already said how the analyses can help us identify and critique broad patterns of racial and sexual oppression (MacKinnon 1987), and how they accommodate the intersectionality of social categories. But a further and, I think, more interesting question is whether it is useful to think of these groups *in these terms*: Does it serve both the goal of understanding racial and sexual oppression, and of achieving sexual and racial equality to think of ourselves as *men* or *women*, or *raced* in the ways proposed?

By appropriating the everyday terminology of race and gender, the analyses I've offered invite us to acknowledge the force of oppressive systems in framing our personal and political identities. Each of us has some investment in our race and gender: I am a White woman. On my accounts, this claim locates me within social systems that in some respects privilege and in others subordinate me. Because gender and racial inequality are not simply a matter of public policy but implicate each of us at the heart of our self-understandings, the terminological shift calls us to reconsider who we think we are.

This point highlights why the issue of terminological appropriation is especially sensitive when the terms designate categories of social identity. Writing in response to a *NY Times* editorial supporting the terminological shift from "Black" to "African-American," Trey Ellis responded:

> When somebody tries to tell me what to call myself in all its uses just because they come to some decision at a cocktail party to which I wasn't even invited, my mama raised me to tell them to kiss my black ass. In many cases, *African-American* just won't do.[20]

The issue is not just what words we should use, and who gets to say what words to use, but who we take ourselves to be, and so, in some sense, who we are. Terms for social groups can function as descriptive terms: it may be accurate to say that someone is a woman when she satisfies certain conditions. However, terms for social groups serve other rhetorical purposes. Typically the act of classifying someone as a member of a social group invokes a set of "appropriate" (contextually specific) norms and expectations. It positions her in a social framework and makes available certain kinds of evaluation; in short, it carries prescriptive force. Accepting or identifying with the classification typically involves an endorsement of some norms and expectations, however, not always the socially sanctioned ones. The question whether I should be called a "woman" or a "wommon," "White" or "Euro-American," is not just a matter of what words to use, but what norms and expectations are taken to be appropriate; to ask what I should be called is to ask what norms I should be judged by (Haslanger 2012 [1993], esp.).

Although "identifying" someone as a member of a social group invokes a set of "appropriate" norms, what these norms are is not fixed. What it means to be a woman, or to be White, or to be Latino, in this sense, is unstable and always open to contest. The instability across time is necessary to maintain the basic structure of gender and race relations through other social changes: as social roles change—prompted by the economy, immigration, political movements, natural disasters, war, and so on—the contents of normative race and gender

---

[20] Trey Ellis, *Village Voice*, June 13, 1989; quoted in H. L. Gates 1992, "What's in a Name?," p. 139. Gates quotes the passage differently, leaving out "black" before "ass." Although he adds Ellis's conclusion, he robs the quote of its self-exemplifying power by the alteration.

identities adjust. The flexibility across contexts accommodates the complexity of social life: what norms are assumed to apply depends on the dominant social structure, the ideological context, and other dimensions of one's identity (such as class, age, ability, sexuality). But this instability and flexibility is exactly what opens the door for groups to redefine themselves in new ways. One strategy is for the group to adopt new names ('African-American', 'womyn'); another is to appropriate old names with a normative twist ('queer'); but in some cases the contest is over the meanings of the standard terms ("Ain't I a woman?"). Because individuals are so deeply invested in gender and, at least in the US, race categories, it remains of crucial importance to be and to be perceived as a 'woman' or a 'man' and as a member of one of the standard races. But even so (although this is something of an exaggeration), it is possible to view our gender and race vocabulary as, in effect, providing terminological place-holders marking space for the collective negotiation of our social identities.

Given the normative force and political potential of identifying someone (or self-identifying) in racial or gendered terms, how do we evaluate a terminological appropriation of the kind I'm proposing? For example, isn't there something disingenuous about appropriating race and gender terminology *because* it is used to frame how we think of ourselves and each other, in order to use them for new concepts that are *not* part of our self-understandings?

This latter question is especially pressing because the appropriation under consideration intentionally invokes what many find to be positive self-understandings—being Latina, being a White man—and offers analyses of them which emphasize the broader context of injustice. Thus there is an invitation not only to revise one's understanding of these categories (given their instability, this happens often enough), but to revise one's relationship to their prescriptive force. By offering these analyses of our ordinary terms, I call upon us to reject what seemed to be positive social identities. I'm suggesting that we should work to undermine those forces that make being a man, a woman, or a member of a racialized group possible; we should refuse to be gendered man or woman, refuse to be raced. This goes beyond denying essentialist claims about one's embodiment and involves an active political commitment to live one's life differently (Stoltenberg 1989). In one sense this appropriation is "just semantics": I'm asking us to use an old term in a new way. But it is also politics: I'm asking us to understand ourselves and those around us as deeply molded by injustice and to draw the appropriate prescriptive inference. This, I hope, will contribute to empowering critical social agents. However, whether the terminological shift I'm suggesting is politically useful will depend on the contexts in which it is employed and the individuals employing it. The point is not to legislate what terms to use in all contexts, but to offer resources that should be used judiciously.

7. Lingering Concerns, Promising Alternatives

There is, nonetheless, a broader concern one might have about the strategy I've employed: Why build hierarchy into the definitions? Why not define gender and race as those social positions motivated and justified by cultural responses to the body, without requiring that the social positions are hierarchical? Wouldn't that provide what we need without implying (implausibly) that women are, by definition, subordinate, men, by definition, privileged, and races, by definition, hierarchically positioned?

If we were to remove hierarchy from the definitions, then there would be two other benefits: first, by providing a place in our model for cultural representations of the body *besides* those that contribute to maintaining subordination and privilege, we could better acknowledge that there are positive aspects to having a gender and a race. And second, the accounts would provide a framework for envisioning the sorts of constructive changes needed to create a more just world. The suggestion that we must eliminate race and gender may be a powerful rallying call to those who identify with radical causes, but it is not at all clear that societies can or should avoid giving meanings to the body, or organizing themselves to take sexual and reproductive differences into account. Don't we at least need a concept of gender that will be useful in the reconstructive effort, not only the destructive one?

Consider gender. I am sympathetic to radical rethinkings of sex and gender. In particular, I believe that we should refuse to use anatomy as a primary basis for classifying individuals and that any distinctions between kinds of sexual and reproductive bodies are importantly political and open to contest. Some authors have argued that we should acknowledge the continuum of anatomical differences and recognize at least five sexes (Fausto-Sterling 1993). And if sexual distinctions become more complex, we would also need to rethink sexuality, given that sexual desire would not fit neatly within existing homosexual/heterosexual paradigms.

However, one can encourage the proliferation of sexual and reproductive options without maintaining that we can or should eliminate *all* social implications of anatomical sex and reproduction. Given that as a species there are substantial differences in what human bodies contribute to reproduction, and what sorts of bodies bear the main physical burdens of reproduction, and given further that reproduction cannot really help but be a socially significant fact (it does, after all, produce children), it can seem difficult to imagine a functioning society, more specifically, a functioning *feminist* society, that doesn't acknowledge in some way the difference between those kinds of bodies that are likely able to bear children, and those that aren't. One could argue that we should work towards a society free of gender in a materialist sense—one in which sex-oppression does not exist—while still allowing that sexual and reproductive differences should be taken into account in a just society (Frye 1996; Gatens 1996).

I will not debate here the degree to which a just society must be attentive to sexual and reproductive differences. Whether we, as feminists, ought to recommend the construction of (new) non-hierarchical genders or work to abolish gender entirely is a normative issue I leave for another occasion. Nonetheless, at the very least it would help to have terminology to debate these issues. I propose that we use the definitions of *man* and *woman* offered above: it is clear that these dominant nodes of our current gender structures are hierarchical. But borrowing strategies employed before, we can define gender in generic terms under which the previous definitions of *man* and *women* fall,[21] thus allowing the possibility of non-hierarchical genders and breaking the binary opposition between man and woman.

A group G is *a gender* relative to context C iff$_{df}$ members of G are (all and only) those:

> (i) who are regularly observed or imagined to have certain bodily features presumed in C to be evidence of their reproductive capacities;[22]
>
> (ii) whose having (or being imagined to have) these features marks them within the context of the ideology in C as motivating and justifying some aspect(s) of their social position; and
>
> (iii) whose satisfying (i) and (ii) plays (or would play) a role in C in their social position's having one or another of these designated aspects.

I offer this analysis as a way of capturing the standard slogan: gender is the social meaning of sex. Note, however, that in imagining "alternative" genders we should be careful not to take for granted that the relevant biological divisions will correspond to what *we* consider "sex."[23] (Alternative groupings could include: "pregnant persons," "lactating persons," "menstruating persons," "infertile persons," (perhaps "homosexuals," depending on the story given about physical causes)). Neither should we assume that membership in a gender will constitute one's personal or psychological identity to any significant degree. Recall that on the accounts of gender and race I am proposing, both are to be

---

[21] Thanks to Geoff Sayre-McCord for suggesting this approach.

[22] It is important here that the "observations" or "imaginings" in question not be idiosyncratic but part of a broader pattern of social perception; however, they need not occur, as in the case of *man* and *woman*, "for the most part." They may even be both regular and rare.

[23] I leave it an open question whether groups that have been identified as "third genders" count as genders on my account. Some accounts of gender that purport to include third genders pay inadequate attention to the body, so cannot distinguish, e.g., race from gender. See, e.g., Roscoe 1996.

understood first and foremost as social groups defined within a structure of social relations; whatever links there might be to identities and norms are highly contingent and would depend on the details of the picture. For example, we might imagine that "after the revolution" gender is a component of one's overall social position because, for example, there are legal protections or medical entitlements granted to individuals classified as having a certain sort of "sexed" body; but this need not have broad implications for psychological identity or everyday social interactions, for the "sex" of bodies might not even be publicly marked.

Turning briefly to race, the parallel issue arises: Do we need a concept of non-hierarchical "races" in order to frame and debate different visions of a "racially" just society? It would seem that we have the terminological resources available without a further definition: let races be, as previously defined, those hierarchically organized groups that are defined (roughly) by physical features and (assumed) geographical origins, and call those that aren't hierarchically organized (in the context in question) "ethnicities." Admittedly, ethnicity as we know it does have implications for social status and power, so my proposal is to employ the term for a somewhat idealized conception.

As in the case of gender, the question arises whether it ought to be part of an antiracist project to recommend the preservation of existing ethnic groups or the formation of "new" ethnicities. And more generally, we need to ask whether a feminist antiracism should treat genders and ethno-racial groups in the same way over the long term. Should we seek, for example, to eliminate all genders and ethno-racial groupings; to preserve and proliferate them; to eliminate gender but not ethnicity (or vice versa)? These questions deserve careful attention but I cannot address them here.

Because the structure of definitions has become quite complex, it may help at this point to provide a diagram:

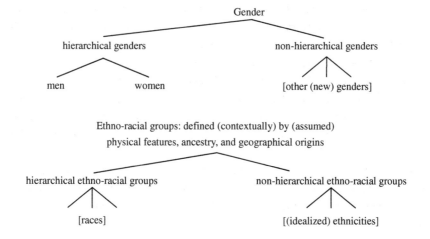

8. Conclusion

On the accounts I've offered, there are striking parallels between race and gender. Both gender and race are real, and both are social categories. Neither gender nor race is chosen, but the forms they take can be resisted or mutated. Both race and gender (as we know it) are hierarchical, but the systems that sustain the hierarchy are contingent. And although the ideologies of race and gender and the hierarchical structures they sustain are substantively very different, they are intertwined.

There are many different types of human bodies; it is not the case that there is a unique "right" way of classifying them, though certain classifications will be more useful for some purposes than others. How we classify bodies can and does matter politically, for our laws, social institutions, and personal identities are profoundly linked to understandings of the body and its possibilities. This is compatible with the idea that what possibilities a human body has is not wholly a function of our understandings of it. Our bodies often outdo us, and undo us, in spite of the meanings we give them.

Within the framework I've sketched, there is room for theoretical categories such as *man, woman,* and *race* (and particular racial groups), that take hierarchy to be a constitutive element, and those such as *gender* and *ethnicity* that do not. As I have suggested before, I am willing to grant that there are other ways to define race or gender, man or woman, that are useful to answer different questions, motivated by different concerns and priorities. I'm sure we need several concepts to do all the work needed in understanding the complex systems of racial and gender subordination.

In short (speaking of my analyses), I'm less committed to saying that *this* is what gender is and what race is, than to saying that *these* are important categories that a feminist antiracist theory needs. As I've explained above, I think there are rhetorical advantages to using the terms 'gender', 'man' and 'woman,' and 'race' for the concepts I've defined, but if someone else is determined to have those terms, I'll use different ones. To return to the point made much earlier in characterizing analytic projects: it is our responsibility to define gender and race for our theoretical purposes. The world itself can't tell us what gender is. The same is true for race. It may be as Appiah claims that "there is nothing in the world that can do all we ask race to do for us" (Appiah 1992, 45), if our project inevitably inherits the concept's complex history; but we might instead ask "race" to do different things than have been asked before. Of course, in defining our terms, we must keep clearly in mind our political aims both in analyzing the past and present, and in envisioning alternative futures. But rather than worrying, "what is gender, really?" or "what is race, really?" I think we should begin by asking (both in the theoretical and political sense) what, if anything, we want them to be.

References

Anderson, Elizabeth. (1995) "Knowledge, Human Interests, and Objectivity in Feminist Epistemology," *Philosophical Topics 23*: 2:27–58.

Appiah, K. Anthony and Amy Gutmann. (1996) *Color Conscious*. Princeton, NJ: Princeton University Press.

Appiah, K. Anthony. (1992) *In My Father's House*. New York: Oxford University Press.

Butler, Judith. (1990) *Gender Trouble*. New York: Routledge.

Crenshaw, Kimberle. (1993) "Beyond Racism and Misogyny: Black Feminism and 2 Live Crew,"
Words That Wound, ed., M. Matsuda, C. Lawrence, R. Delgado, and K. Crenshaw. Boulder, CO:
Westview, 111–32.

Fausto-Sterling, Anne. (1993) "The Five Sexes: Why Male and Female Are Not Enough," *The Sciences 33*:2: 20–24.

Frye, Marilyn. (1996) "The Necessity of Differences: Constructing a Positive Category of Women,"
Signs 21:4: 991–1010.

Frye, Marilyn. (1983) *The Politics of Reality*. Freedom, CA: Crossing Press.

Gatens, Moira. (1996) "A Critique of the Sex-Gender Distinction," *Imaginary Bodies*. New York:
Routledge, 3–20.

Gates, Jr., Henry Louis. (1992) *Loose Canons*. New York: Oxford University Press.

Geuss, Raymond. (1981) *The Idea of a Critical Theory*. Cambridge: Cambridge University Press.

Haslanger, Sally. (2012 [1993]) "On Being Objective and Being Objectified," chapter 1 of this volume.

Haslanger, Sally. (2012 [1995]) "Ontology and Social Construction," chapter 2 of this volume.

Hennessy, Rosemary, and Chrys Ingraham, eds. (1997) *Materialist Feminism*. New York: Routledge.

Hoy, David. (1994) "Deconstructing Ideology," *Philosophy and Literature* 18:1.

Hurtado, Aida. (1994) "Relating to Privilege: Seduction and Rejection in the Subordination of
White Women and Women of Color," *Theorizing Feminism*, ed. Anne Hermann and Abigail
Stewart. Boulder, CO: Westview Press, 136–54.

MacKinnon, Catharine. (1987) "Difference and Dominance: On Sex Discrimination," *Feminism
Unmodified*. Cambridge, MA: Harvard University Press, 32–45.

Omi, M. and H. Winant. (1994) *Racial Formation in the United States*. New York: Routledge.

Ortner, Sherry. (1996) "Gender Hegemonies," *Making Gender*. Boston: Beacon Press, 139–72.

Riley, Denise. (1988) *Am I That Name?* Minneapolis: University of Minnesota Press.

Roscoe, Will. (1996) "How to Become a Berdache: Toward a Unified Analysis of Gender Diversity,"
Third Sex, Third Gender, ed., Gilbert Herdt. New York: Zone Books, 329–72.

Scott, Joan. (1986) "Gender: A Useful Category of Historical Analysis," *American Historical Review
91*:5: 1053–75.

Spelman, Elizabeth. (1988) *The Inessential Woman*. Boston: Beacon Press.

Stevens, Jacqueline. (1999) *Reproducing the State*. Princeton: Princeton University Press.

Stich, Stephen. (1988) "Reflective Equilibrium, Analytic Epistemology, and the Problem of Cognitive Diversity," *Synthese* 74: 391–413.

Stoltenberg, John. (1989) *Refusing To Be a Man*. New York: Meridian Books.

Thorne, Barrie. (1993) *Gender Play*. New Brunswick, NJ: Rutgers University Press.

Young, Iris. (1990) *Justice and the Politics of Difference*. Princeton: Princeton University Press.

8

Future Genders? Future Races?

1. Background[1]

In the social world as we know it, two of the most salient dimensions of human difference are race and gender. If I mention that I met an interesting person while waiting for the subway last week, a first step to understanding the nature of our contact would be to identify whether the person was a man or a woman, and what race they were. (Also especially useful would be their relative age.) To describe someone by their race and gender is not simply to describe their appearance, but to situate them in a framework of meaning and indicate the social norms that govern our interactions.

Drawing on the insight that one's sex has quite well-defined and systematic social implications, feminists have argued that it is helpful to distinguish sex and gender. Very roughly, as the slogan goes, gender is the social meaning of sex. The idea is that gender is not a classification scheme based simply on anatomical or biological differences, but marks social differences between individuals. Sex differences are about testicles and ovaries, the penis and the uterus (and on some theories, quite a bit more (Money and Tucker 1975, Fausto-Sterling 2000));[2] gender, in contrast, is a classification of individuals in terms of their social position, as determined by interpretations of their sex.

To help understand this, consider, for example, the category of landlords. To be a landlord one must be located within a broad system of social and economic relations which includes tenants, private property, and the like. It might have

---

[1] Much of the material presented in this section can be found in a more fully developed form in (Haslanger 2012 [2000]). Thanks to Lawrence Blum, Jorge Garcia, Koffi Maglo, Ishani Maitra, Tommie Shelby, and Stephen Yablo for helpful discussion of the issues discussed here.

[2] As we saw above, the everyday distinction between males and females leaves out the intersexed population that might have been given its own sex category (or categories); so it may be appropriate to introduce terms for additional sexes, for example, 'merms', 'ferms', and 'herms' (Fausto-Sterling 1993). A study of the construction of sex—meaning the genealogy of sex categories—is itself an interesting and valuable project (Laqueur 1990; Fausto-Sterling 2000), but it is not my focus here.

been that all and only landlords had only four toes on their left foot. But even if this were the case, having this physical mark is not what it is to be a landlord. Being nine-toed is an anatomical kind; being a landlord is a social kind. Similarly, we can draw a distinction between sex and gender: sex is an anatomical distinction based on locally salient sexual/reproductive differences, and gender is a distinction between the social/political positions of those with bodies marked as of different sexes (see also Haslanger 2012 [1993]).

To be clear, I'll use the terms 'male' and 'female' to designate sexes, 'man' and 'woman' to designate genders.[3] Because one is a female by virtue of some (variable) set of anatomical features, and one is a woman by virtue of one's position within a social and economic system, we should allow, at least in principle, that some males are women and some females are men. Although it is clear enough for our purposes here what distinguishes males and females, the question of what it is to be a man or woman is not at all clear. And this has been a major site of controversy among feminists.

I'll return to how we might define gender shortly. In the meantime it is interesting to note that there is a parallel to the sex/gender distinction in the case of race. Just as one's primary and secondary sex characteristics are socially meaningful, so are the color of one's skin, shape of one's eyelids, color and texture of one's hair, and such. So we can distinguish the physical markers of race from the social implications that these markers have. To register this terminologically, let's distinguish "color" and "race" as parallel to sex and gender. I will use the term 'color' to refer to the (contextually variable) physical "markers" of race, just as I use the term 'sex' to refer to the (contextually variable) physical "markers" of gender. I mean to include in "color" more than just skin tone: common markers also include eye, nose, and lip shape, hair texture, physique, and so on. And in principle I want to allow that virtually any cluster of physical traits that are assumed to be inherited from those who occupy a specific geographical region or regions can count as "color." (Although the term 'people of color' is used to refer to non-Whites, I want to allow that the markers of "Whiteness" count as "color.") Borrowing the slogan we used before, we can say then that race is the social meaning of "color."

So far I've characterized race and gender very vaguely. It is one thing to say that race and gender are social categories that capture the social implications of

---

[3] It is by no means a simple question what criteria should be used to distinguish different sexes. Sexologists such as John Money have argued that there are ten indicators of sex including: chromosomal sex, gonadal sex, fetal hormonal sex, internal morphologic sex, external morphologic sex, brain sex, sex assignment and rearing, pubertal hormonal sex, gender identity and role, procreative sex (Fausto-Sterling 1995). Clearly, not all of these indicators are anatomical. However, as I will be using the term, sex primarily concerns anatomy. Additional sex-related characteristics, femininity, feminine identity, etc., go beyond sex towards gender.

certain bodily traits, but can we give them more content? For example, what are the specific social implications of sex in terms of which we should define gender?

Among feminist theorists there are two problems that have generated pessimism about providing any unified account of women; I'll call them the commonality problem and the normativity problem. Very briefly, the commonality problem questions whether there is anything social that females have in common that could count as their "gender." If we consider all females—females of different times, places, and cultures—there are reasons to doubt that there is anything beyond body type (if even that) that they all share (Spelman 1988). The normativity problem raises the concern that any definition of "what woman is," because it must select among the broad variation in women's traits, cannot help but be value-laden, and so will marginalize certain females, privilege others, and reinforce current gender norms (Butler 1990, Ch. 1).

A primary concern of feminist and antiracist theorizing is to give an account of the social world that will assist us in the struggle for justice. Given this goal, I take the primary motivation for distinguishing sex from gender to arise in the recognition that societies, on the whole, privilege individuals with male bodies. Although the particular forms and mechanisms of oppression vary from culture to culture, societies have found many ways—some ingenious, some crude—to control and exploit the sexual and reproductive capacities of females. So one important strategy for defining gender has been to analyze it in terms of women's subordinate position in systems of male dominance.[4] Recognizing the legitimate goals of feminist and antiracist theory, we can allow, then, that certain values guide our inquiry. Pursuing this line of thought, here is a (rough) proposal for specifying what it is to be a man or a woman:[5]

> S *is a woman* iff$_{df}$ S is systematically subordinated along some dimension (economic, political, legal, social, etc.), and S is "marked" as a target for this treatment by observed or imagined bodily features presumed to be evidence of a female's biological role in reproduction.[6]
>
> S *is a man* iff$_{df}$ S is systematically privileged along some dimension (economic, political, legal, social, etc.), and S is "marked" as a target for

---

[4] Some theorists (Delphy 1984) focus on the economic exploitation of women in domestic relations of production; others (Wittig 1981; Wittig 1982) focus on sexual and reproductive exploitation under compulsory heterosexuality; others (MacKinnon 1987) focus on sexual objectification.

[5] This is a simplified version of the account I offer in (Haslanger 2012 [2000]).

[6] These analyses allow that there isn't a common understanding of "sex" across time and place. On my account, gendered social positions are those marked by reference to features that are generally assumed in the context in question to either explain or provide evidence of reproductive role, whether or not these are features that we consider "sex."

this treatment by observed or imagined bodily features presumed to be evidence of a male's biological role in reproduction.

It is a virtue, I believe, of these accounts, that depending on context, one's sex may have a very different meaning and it may position one in very different kinds of hierarchies. The variation will clearly occur from culture to culture (and sub-culture to sub-culture); so for example, to be a Chinese woman of the 1790's, a Brazilian woman of the 1890's, or an American woman of the 1990's may involve very different social relations, and very different kinds of oppression. Yet on the analysis suggested, these groups count its women insofar as their subordinate positions are marked and justified by reference to female sex.

With this strategy of defining gender in mind, we can now consider whether it will help in giving some content to the social category of race. The feminist approach recommends: don't look for an analysis that assumes that the category's meaning is always and everywhere the same; rather, consider how members of the group are *socially positioned*, and what *physical markers* serve as a supposed basis for such treatment. Elaborating the earlier slogan, we might say that race is the social meaning of the geographically marked, that is, "colored" body. To develop this, consider the following account.[7]

> A group is *racialized* (in context C) iff$_{df}$ its members are socially positioned as subordinate or privileged along some dimension (economic, political, legal, social, etc.) (in C), and the group is "marked" as a target for this treatment by observed or imagined bodily features presumed to be evidence of ancestral links to a certain geographical region.

In other words, races are those groups demarcated by the geographical associations accompanying perceived body type, when those associations take on evaluative significance concerning how members of the group should be viewed and treated. Given this definition, we can say that S is of the White (Black, Asian . . .) race [in C] iff Whites (Blacks, Asians . . .) are a racialized group [in C], and S is a member.[8]

---

[7] On this I am deeply indebted to (Stevens 1999, Ch. 4), and (Omi and Winant 1994, esp. pp. 53–61). I develop this definition more fully in (Haslanger 2012 [2000]).

[8] As in the case of gender, I recommend that we view membership in a racial/ethnic group in terms of how one is viewed and treated regularly and for the most part in the context in question; though as before, one could distinguish being a member of a given race from functioning as one by considering the degree of one's entrenchment in the racialized social position (not on the basis of biology or ancestry). For more work that compares race and gender, see (Thomas 1980, Appiah 1990, Corlett 1997).

Note that on this view, whether a group is racialized, and so how and whether an individual is raced, is not an absolute fact, but will depend on context. For example, Blacks, Whites, Asians, Native Americans, are currently racialized in the U.S. insofar as these are all groups defined in terms of physical features associated with places of origin, and insofar as membership in the group functions socially as a basis for evaluation. However, some groups are not currently racialized in the U.S., but have been so in the past and possibly could be again (and in other contexts are), for example, the Italians, the Germans, the Irish.

Given these accounts it should be clear that a primary task in the quest for social justice is to eliminate those social structures that constitute races (or racialized groups) and eliminate men and women. Of course this is not to say that we should eliminate males and females, or impose a "khaki" appearance on everyone. Rather, it is to say that we should work for a day when sex and "color" markers do not have hierarchical implications.

2. Alternatives

At this stage one might reasonably ask, however: Why build hierarchy into the definitions? Why not define gender and race as those social positions motivated and justified by cultural responses to the body, without requiring that the social positions are hierarchical? Wouldn't that provide what we need without implying (implausibly) that women are, by definition, subordinate, men, by definition, privileged, and races, by definition, hierarchically positioned?

Recall the suggestion that gender is the social meaning of sex and race is the social meaning of "color." Consistent with this, one could allow that the social implications of sex and "color" are, *as we know them*, hierarchical, but insist that sex and "color" can nonetheless be meaningful under conditions of justice. If so, then in envisioning a just future we should include the option of preserving race and gender while working towards race and gender *equality*.

Pursuing this strategy we could use the definitions of *man* and *woman* offered above: it is clear that these dominant nodes of our current gender structures are hierarchical. Bur rather than assuming that gender is simply the genus under which the more specific categories of men and women fall, we could define gender as a broader genus allowing both hierarchical and non-hierarchical cases. For example (roughly),

A group G is a *gender* (in context C) iff$_{df}$ its members are similarly positioned as along some social dimension (economic, political, legal, social, etc.) (in C), and the members are "marked" as appropriately in this position by observed or imagined bodily features presumed to be evidence of reproductive capacities or function.

A similar approach to race would yield the following:

> A group G is *racialized* (in context C) iff$_{df}$ its members are similarly positioned as along some social dimension (economic, political, legal, social, etc.) (in C), and the members are "marked" as appropriately in this position by observed or imagined bodily features presumed to be evidence of ancestral links to a certain geographical region.

As in the case of gender, we could retain the hierarchical analysis for existing races, for example, Black, White, Latina/o, and so on, are hierarchical groups. But we might envision a new egalitarian structure of races, that is, new races, to take their place.

In what follows, I will argue that there are interesting and important differences between race and gender that count *against* treating them as parallel.

Because sex is, from a political point of view, inevitably meaningful, we need to envision new egalitarian genders; but race is different, and we should not take a parallel approach to race.

3. "Sex," "Color," and Biology

Start with gender. I am sympathetic to radical rethinkings of sex and gender. In particular, I believe that we should refuse to use anatomy as a primary basis for classifying individuals and that any distinctions between kinds of sexual and reproductive bodies are importantly political and open to contest. Some authors have argued that we should acknowledge the continuum of anatomical differences and recognize at least five sexes (Fausto-Sterling 1993). And if sexual distinctions become more complex, we would also need to rethink sexuality, given that sexual desire would not fit neatly within existing homo-sexual/heterosexual paradigms.

However, one can encourage the proliferation of sexual and reproductive options without maintaining that we can or should eliminate all social implications of anatomical sex and reproduction. Given that as a species there are substantial differences in what human bodies contribute to reproduction, and what sorts of bodies bear the main physical burdens of reproduction, and given further that reproduction cannot really help but be a socially significant fact (it does, after all, produce children), it can seem difficult to imagine a functioning society, more specifically, a functioning *feminist* society, that doesn't acknowledge in some way the difference between those kinds of bodies that are likely able to bear children, and the we that aren't. One could argue that we should work towards a society free of gender in a materialist sense—one in which sex-oppression does not exist—while still allowing that sexual and reproductive differences should be taken into account in a just society (Frye 1996; Gatens 1996).

The argument just sketched (more is certainly needed to flesh it out) asserted that sexual difference—allowing variations in what cultures consider or should consider relevant in marking sex differences—would be in some way meaningful in any society of people with bodies like ours, at least in any society in which humans are sexual beings and reproduce biologically; so doing away with gender categories altogether, that is, eliminating social categories that take sexual difference into account, would not be an effective way to create a just future. On this issue I am sympathetic to Beauvoir's argument that females, on the whole, bear a greater physical burden for the species than males, and it is the responsibility of society to address this in order to achieve justice (Beauvoir 1989/1949, Ch. 2).

So instead of attempting to eliminate gender, we should try to envision new non-oppressive ways of being gendered *without* being a man or a woman, and should eventually incorporate these new gender concepts as parts (possibly very small parts) of our self-understandings. In other words, in a just society gender (in some as yet unknown form) should constitute a thin social position, and to the extent that one's social position has an impact on one's "identity," we should allow for the development of non-hierarchically grounded gender identities.[9] Consequently, it is an important project within a feminist antiracism to construct alternative social positions and identities (hopefully many of them!) for people of different sexes.[10]

The idea here is that justice requires that we radically rethink the structure of relationships that constitute our societies. But this does not mean that "anything goes." There are some limits to what alternatives are viable, for example, there may be features that are necessary for the society to function at all, or for it to be just, or that are especially desirable in some way. Sexual reproduction, I submit, imposes some limits in forming a just society, though it is not clear what those limits are. Given that sex needs to be meaningful in order to achieve justice, a conception of gender that allows new non-hierarchical cases will be valuable in our efforts.

The question arises, however, whether there is something about race that should also constrain us. Is there something significant we are in danger of

---

[9] For more on "thin" and "thick" identities, see (Haslanger 2012 [2003]).

[10] It should also be part of that project to identify those reproductive (and potentially also erotic) differences that should be taken into account in order to achieve justice, i.e., in identifying legitimate sexual/sexuality differences.

losing track of should we pursue the elimination of race?[11] It would seem that *racial equality* should be our goal (as opposed to the *elimination* of race), only if we have reason to view "color" as a justifiable way for societies to differentiate groups of people, that is, if "color" is a legitimate basis for a thin social position. Although it appears that there are reasons for *any* functioning society to take sex and reproduction seriously, there does not seem to be any comparable reason for thinking that functional societies must acknowledge those physical differences that distinguish "color." Classifications based on "color" vary tremendously depending on the socio-historical-legal context, and are not grounded in meaningful biological categories (Appiah 1992, Ch. 2; Appiah 1996; Root 2000; Mills 1998, Ch 3; Zack 2002; Lewontin 1982; cf. Mosely 1995; Kitcher 1999; Andreason 1998; Andreason 2000).[12] The markers of "Blackness" differ when considering, for example, the contemporary United States, Brazil, and South Africa, and the rules for racial marking change over time (Davis 1991). Moreover, "color" classification is not just an informal practice, but is often legally imposed and based on biological myths of "blood" (think of the "one drop" rule, enforced under Jim Crow). It is not plausible to explain the variation and development of "color" distinctions in terms of increased understanding of biology or genetics. Rather, the best explanations point to their social and political implications (Fields 1982; Fields 1990; Stocking 1994; Mills 1997).

These facts indicate an important difference between race and gender. Although gender as we know it is a site of social injustice, just societies should be concerned with those functions of human bodies that matter for reproduction. But "color"—those clusters of features such as skin tone, hair texture, eye and lip shape, imagined "racial gene," and other imagined anatomical differences that are used to mark races—does not seem to correlate with any feature that carries sufficient biological weight that it must be socially addressed.

It is important to note that even if society should not be structured to recognize "color" distinctions, this does not entail a politics of "race blindness." Race, as I've argued, is more than just "color"; it concerns the systematic

---

[11] Note that there are several different questions at issue. Considering a just future when the effects of contemporary racialization have been remedied: (i) Must the state, in its laws and policies, be "color-blind" or is attention to "color" differences required for justice? (ii) Must we eliminate "color" categories in our social practices and our self-understandings in order to achieve justice? (iii) Is there something socially valuable in "color" classification, and would its elimination destroy something valuable? (iv) Even if not required for justice, would the elimination of "color" as a way of organizing ourselves socially be better overall? It may be helpful to rethink the discussion that follows with a greater attention to these different questions.

[12] Note that even though there is controversy over whether races are biologically meaningful categories, there is general consensus on the claim that "color" distinctions do not track biologically meaningful categories except to the extent that "color" takes on a meaning that has social implications.

subordination of groups of people marked by "color."[13] The effort to end racism must recognize racialized groups in order to understand the processes by which they are formed and sustained, and in order to remedy the ongoing injustice done to their members. Recognizing racialized groups is not only compatible with justice but essential to achieving it. But to recognize the social positions created by existing racist ideologies and institutions is not to endorse the formation of public or personal identities based on "color."

For example, in the contemporary US, there are many groups that define themselves by reference to race and racial injustice: some form on the basis of a common history of racial oppression, or in solidarity against such oppression, others on the basis of cultural practices that have evolved within racialized groups (e.g., Kwanzaa). However, note that it is neither necessary nor sufficient for group membership that one have a particular inherited body type per se; what is required is a common history, a moral stand against injustice, or the enjoyment of a celebratory practice. These groups, or at least many of them, do not define themselves by reference to "color," even if in the context of racial oppression some of them correspond in their membership roughly to groups that are marked by "color." Such group conceptions avoid false assumptions about biology and geography in constructing group solidarity, and also avoid the entrenchment of social divisions along existing racial lines: at least in principle and often in practice, the membership of such groups is "multi-racial" by the dominant standards of racialization.

The Medical Necessity of "Color" Coding

But perhaps this is too fast. What about racial patterns in susceptibility to disease? Shouldn't societies be prepared, as a matter of justice, to address disadvantages that some suffer due to genetic risk factors? And don't some of these correlate with "color"? The weight of current research suggests not (Root 2001). Although there are significant generalizations linking race/"color" with disease in the United States, the basis for these generalizations is social not biological:

> Blacks are seven times more likely to die of tuberculosis than whites, three times more likely to die of H.I.V.-A.I.D.S. and twice as likely to die of diabetes. The diseases are biological but the racial differences are not; How is this possible? . . . No mystery. Race affects income, housing, and healthcare, and these, in turn, affect health. Stress suppresses the immune system and being black in the U.S. today is stressful. (Root 2000, S629)

---

[13] For a useful discussion of related issues, see (Wasserstrom 1987; also Gotanda 1995).

Given the contextual variability of "color" classifications, it is not surprising that generalizations linking "color" with disease are only local and do not support a biological basis for race. For example,

> An individual with sickle-cell disease can be black in the U.S., but white in Brazil, for the category of black or white is defined differently here and there. As a result, rates of sickle-cell disease for blacks differ from place to place, in part because race does. (Root 2000).

Thus, it seems that although there are reasons for a society to take "color" seriously as an indicator of risk under conditions where groups are racialized (or are suffering the long-term effects of racialization), this only shows that prior injustice imposes constraints on the construction of a just society; it does not show that "color," or a biological fact correlating with "color," imposes such a constraint. As a result it may be appropriate for societies to be structured so that there are social implications of having suffered injustice—implications that attempt to redress the injustice or prevent recurring injustice—but history rather than biology is what requires our response.

One might insist, however, that although we currently think of "color" as something that is easily observable in everyday interaction, perhaps instead it should be genetically defined. If so, then in keeping with the terminology I've introduced, the genetic traits in question would count as "color." And to be more explicit, we might adjust our slogan for race: race is the social meaning of certain (to be specified) genetic traits.

In pursuing this approach, we cannot assume that such genetically defined groups will correspond with the groups we currently count as races, that is, that the external appearance of the groups will correspond to the "color" divisions we make now, or even that the external appearance of members of a single group will be similar. But that's just to say, on this view, that our current classification is misguided. Moreover, one might argue, we need to treat such genetic groups as socially relevant because they correlate with socially meaningful traits, for example, susceptibility to disease. Because medical care is something that a just society must be concerned to provide, "color," like sex, must be taken into account even under conditions of justice. As a result, we should treat *race* like gender as a category that currently has hierarchical forms, but need not.

The question whether there are genetically defined groups that are medically significant and should count as races is a large issue in contemporary genomics and biomedical ethics. I will not be in a position to address fully the literature on this topic here. However, there are three points that count against revising my account of race to include non-hierarchical groups defined by reference to generic traits.

First, according to my definition, racial divisions are marked by *observed or imagined clusters of physical traits that are assumed to be inherited from those who occupy a specific geographical region or regions*. Consequently, not just any medically relevant genetic division among humans will count as a basis for race: the genetic traits must be interpreted as geographically significant. The connection between race and geography is, I believe, a key factor in distinguishing race from other social categories that are marked on the body and assumed to be natural, for example, gender, certain forms of disability and disease, (sometimes) sexual orientation, and (sometimes) caste. The link with geography also helps explain the role of racial concepts in the context of imperialism and the process of nation-building (Mills 1997). So there are good reasons to maintain the geographical element in the definition of race.

Second, although my definition of "color" does not require that the physical traits in question be easily observable in ordinary interaction, the marking of racialized bodies involves appearance. For example, at certain times and places, Jews have been racialized. The specifics of the racialization process vary, but on one scenario Jews are imagined to have some physical feature inherited from populations originating in what is now the Middle East. In some cases, however, it is recognized that there is no reliably observable physical feature that distinguishes Jews from non-Jews, so other devices have been introduced to make sure that their race is identifiable in casual encounters, for example, yellow stars. So even if geneticists can find ways of dividing humans into groups based on genetic features that are assumed to be inherited from populations originating in a particular region, as I see it, those groups are racialized in a context only if in that context it is thought that there are observable markers, either anatomical or artificial, that—at least in paradigm cases—distinguish members of the group. Such observable marking is important to the process of racialization, for a key factor in racializing a group is the invocation of social norms that differentiate "appropriate" behavior towards the members of the group (normally) before any interaction is possible. You experience the "color," behave in accordance with the norms for individuals of that kind, and ask questions later, if ever (Alcoff 2000a, Alcoff 2000b).

Granting these two points, it would seem that it is still possible for races, in my sense, to be constituted by social responses to genetic facts. A genetic division among humans, together with assumptions concerning geography and practices of marking, can create social groups which are either privileged or subordinated. In other words, it is possible for genetics to function as an element of "color" in a process of racialization. However, the question now before us is whether there are good reasons to count non-hierarchical groups constituted in this way as races. Is "color" genuinely analogous to "sex" or not? (Recall, I've suggested there is good reason to treat differently sexed bodies differently even under conditions of justice.)

For example, consider those who have a genetic susceptibility to sickle cell anemia. Although it is often thought that sickle cell is a "Black disease," the "color" designation "black" does not correlate at all well with those who have the relevant gene (*HbS*), or with those who have the disease. (I'll use the capitalized term 'Black' for the racialized group; I'll use lower-case 'black' for the body schema designated for those with relatively recent Sub-Saharan African ancestry.) Sickle cell is found primarily among populations whose ancestors have lived where malaria is common. So it occurs among those with ancestors from central and western Africa, but not southern Africa; it is also found, for example, in Turks, Yemenis, Indians, Greeks, and Sicilians (Adelman 2003).

Should we treat carriers of the sickle cell gene as a group whose genotype-plus-geographical origins is relevant in structuring a just society? Given that presumably justice requires that we treat *HbS* carriers as a morally significant group (they should be entitled to certain medical care, perhaps to health education concerning reproductive options, accommodation for any resulting disabilities, etc.), it appears that "color" features do matter in setting constraints on how we organize ourselves. In order to guarantee needed accommodation, *HbS* carriers might also be "marked" by health alert bracelets or necklaces (note that I'm not recommending this, but raise it to make a more exact analogy with race). If so, then it would seem that the disanalogy between sex and "color" breaks down.

But this leads to my third point against treating non-hierarchical genetic-cum-geographical groups as racial groups. Insofar as justice requires that we accommodate the needs of such a group, it is by virtue of their health status. Of course, medical conditions are relevant in considering what justice requires, and it may be that medical conditions sometimes correlate with geographical origins (for obvious cases think of children born or brought up in highly polluted areas). But the basis for the differential treatment in these cases is the medical condition; any real or imagined links with geography is, from the medical point of view, accidental. For example, suppose a large percentage of individuals born in a certain area have a specific genetic defect. Presumably an individual born in or with ancestors from a very different area with the same genetic defect should be grouped with them from the medical point of view.

As I see it, the main issue is how we draw distinctions between humans for the purposes of justice. I've argued that it is important to distinguish existing races and genders because of historical and contemporary forms of oppression; I've argued that we should distinguish new forms of gender in order to accommodate the special burdens some humans carry in the process of reproduction; I have also suggested that we should distinguish groups with respect to medical conditions in order to provide adequate care and support. These different categories of concern require different strategies of response. Although there are cases where the genetics, geography, and marking relevant to medicine can trigger racialization, I submit that this is when hierarchy is imposed. In effect, there will be cases in which racism and ableism overlap and in which antiracists and antiableists are confronting structurally similar injustice. However, for the most part, the challenges facing those who have suffered racial injustice and those who have suffered medical/ableist injustice are very different; and race and disability require different responses in order to achieve justice. This provides good reason for not expanding the definition of race to include non-hierarchical genetic divisions between us as racial divisions.

Evolution, Populations, and Life-worlds

But perhaps there are other biological explanations of the persistence of race. Lucius Outlaw provides further reason to pause before we reject "color" as a legitimate, perhaps even inevitable, source of social meaning. He asks, concerning the number and persistence of differently "colored" populations,

> Might these populations not be the result of bio-cultural group attachments and practices that are conducive to human survival and well-being, and hence must be understood, appreciated, and provided for in the principles and practices of, say, a liberal democratic society? (Outlaw 1996, 13)

He seems to answer that populations defined at least in part by "color" are valuable and virtually inevitable. Communities, he argues, constitute "life-worlds" of meaning which include interpretations of the body. "[O]f particular importance," he points out, "are norms of somatic aesthetics that help to regulate the preferences and practices in terms of which partners are chosen for the intimacies that frequently (must) result in the birth of new members . . ." (Outlaw 1996, 16).

Because, he argues, humans on the whole desire "to achieve relative immortality" by having offspring "who look and carry on somewhat like ourselves" (Outlaw 1996, 17),[14] moreover, because we have reason to be fearful of "significantly different and objectionable strangers" (Outlaw 1996, 17), and finally, because the "valorization of descent" increases our chances of survival by motivating cooperation (Outlaw 1996, 18), our communities develop into "self-reproducing

---

[14] This claim puzzles me: not only is it asserted without evidence (the nuclear family is, in fact, a relatively recent and socially specific phenomenon!), but it would seem that if one reproduces biologically, one cannot avoid having a child who looks like you, to some extent. Perhaps the idea is that because "looks like" is socially defined, one is in danger of not passing on the socially salient features if one mates with an out-group member.

populations that share distinguishing physical and cultural features that set the demographic boundaries of a life-world" (Outlaw 1996, 17). On his view, when such a population is defined to a significant degree by physiological factors, it is a race; when to a lesser degree, it is an ethnicity (Outlaw 1996, 136). Races are, then, enduring, if not inevitable, facts of social life, and because they promote cooperation, security, and so survival of a community's life-world, they are valuable.

Although I am sympathetic to Outlaw's interest in the embodiment of social norms and the development of an aesthetic of "color" (see, e.g., Haslanger 2012 [2004]), there are a number of points in this narrative that strike me as worrisome. In particular, I wonder about the implicit gender assumptions and the supposed "naturalness" of mate selection among humans. For example, it appears that Outlaw is taking as given that individuals tend to choose mates of the same "color" (allowing that "color" differences depend on context), and the task is to provide an explanation of this that will show such choices to be conducive to the survival of their society. There are potentially two connections with biology here: on one hand, individual choices for "same-color" mates are being cast as, although admittedly shaped by cultural cues, nonetheless "natural"; and on the other hand, the model of natural selection is being applied to the society: the societies that are "color"-conscious in their choices are more "fit" than others, and so survive.

However, considering the broad extent of human history, the option of an individual "choosing" his or her mate has not been uniformly granted, and in particular, has more often not been granted to women; fathers or tribal elders typically control the reproductive options for women and girls. Moreover, women have been regularly used in the context of gift exchange between "foreign," even hostile, groups as a means of increasing the chance of friendly relations (Rubin 1975), not to mention a way of expanding the gene pool. So much more would need to be said to support Outlaw's suggestions that individuals naturally choose mates who are marked as being the same "color," for the alleged "choice" of mates is plausibly accounted for by a broad range of social facts rather than any biological predisposition on the part of individuals.[15] And given the potential value of out-group mating (as evidenced by the practices of gift-exchange), more is also needed to support the claim that in-group mating is the most successful strategy.

A further concern is whether, even if the choice of a same-"color" mate is common, and even if to some extent "natural," whether this is good. Outlaw suggests that it is valuable because it promotes the survival of the "life-world" of

---

[15] There is reason to believe, in any case, that for many populations geographical isolation made it difficult *not* to mate primarily with others of the same "color"; is there any evidence that when a variety of "colors" are available, and there are no social sanctions, there is a preference for in-group mates?

the community. But of course, not all "life-worlds" are ones that should be preserved, even within a "liberal democratic society." For example, Outlaw speaks of
the "valorization of descent" as a factor that contributes to the uniformity of
"color" in a population, and which also serves as a means of promoting cooperation between members of the population. Setting aside the empirical question of
whether this is an effective way to promote cooperation, it would seem that the
valorization of descent would (and does) create an unjust hierarchy of family
forms. The history of adoption provides a rather gruesome tale of the effects of
the "valorization of descent": orphaned and "illegitimate" children are systematically abandoned, women who give birth to "illegitimate" children are cast out,
even murdered, if discovered; parentless and adopted children through history
have been mistreated, denied legal protections, and severely stigmatized. Families that are formed through (either formal or informal) adoption are very often
not regarded as "real" with the implication (among many others) that individuals and couples who want children nevertheless remain childless and leave children without homes, rather than face the stigma of adoption. This suggests that
the "valorization of descent" should be rejected in a "liberal democratic society,"
not preserved.

In summary, it appears that "color" may in some hypothetical contexts and by
accident be morally significant. But this is not sufficient reason to treat race like
gender as a response to a physical fact that even a just society must address.
Although both "color" and sex as we know them are socially significant, "color"
need not, and in most cases, should not be. However, thus far I've supposed that
if "color" does impose constraints on what can be just, it would be due to the
biological basis of "color." Are there other aspects of "color" that might legitimately constrain us?

4. "Color" and Culture

It is hard to imagine any function essential to a society that could only be served
by distinguishing people along the lines of "color."[16] So it does not appear that an
argument for treating "race" as a genus of social categories that includes both
hierarchical and non-hierarchal forms, analogous to the argument offered for
gender, is available. But given the purposes of an engaged feminist antiracism, it
is important to know not only what sorts of idealized societies there might be,

---

[16] What about health policy? Are there racially specific diseases or vulnerabilities that might
make it important to have different health care options for people of different races? Are the explanations of the differences socio-economic or biological? Is there a basis for a parallel to the argument
for gender here?

but what a just society would look like that could plausibly evolve as a successor to ours. One might argue, for example, that racial groups, although originating as offshoots of racist practices and policies, develop cultural forms and self-understandings that are valuable. It might seem, more specifically, that a society without race couldn't plausibly evolve from ours without cutting itself off from its own history and doing damage to meaningful communities. Linda Alcoff argues in her paper, "Mestizo Identity":

> . . . within the context of racially based and organized systems of oppression, racial identity will continue to be a salient internal and external component of identity. Systems of oppression, segregated communities, and practices of discrimination create a collective experience and a shared history for a racialized grouping. It is that shared experience and history, more than any physiological or morphological features, that cements the community and creates connections with others along racial lines. And that history cannot be deconstructed by new scientific accounts that dispute the characterization of race as a natural kind. Accounts of race as a social and historical identity, though this brings in elements that are temporally contingent and mutable, will probably prove to have more persistence than accounts of race that tie it to biology. Ironically history will probably have more permanence than biology. (Alcoff 1995, 272)

Here Alcoff suggests that race might be best understood as "a social and historical identity," and that race is more meaningfully centered on "shared experience and history" than on body type.

The suggestion that racial unity stems more from shared experience and history is especially significant as we move away from the "Black-White binary" and think more carefully about the racialization of Latina/os and Asians. For example, Latinas/os do not fit many of the assumptions typically made about races. Latin America is highly diverse in the "color" of its populations and the cultures it includes:

> By U.S. categories, there are black, brown, white, Asian and Native American Latinas/os. There are many Latinas/os from the southern cone whose families are of recent European origin, a large number of Latinas/os from the western coastal areas whose families came from Asia, and of course a large number of Latinas/os whose lineage is entirely indigenous to the Americas or entirely African. (Alcoff 2000b, 31)

Moreover, the cultures of Cuba, Brazil, Panama, Mexico, Chile, Columbia, Costa Rica, to name a few, vary widely in their dominant (and regional) languages, cuisine, holidays, political structures, and virtually every other dimension of culture. Comparable diversity can be found in Asia. (And it should not be forgotten that there is tremendous cultural diversity in all of major groups racialized in the U.S., e.g., the cultures of Sub-Saharan Africa and the African Diaspora are by no means homogeneous.) This is, of course, compatible with Latinas/os and Asians being racialized in the United States.

Such diversity of appearance and culture raises the question whether there is anything other than being racialized that unifies Latinas/os and Asians. Although racial identity has been imposed by systems of oppression, there are and have been movements within the groups to construct positive identities (pan-Latina/o, pan-Asian) to counter stigmatized identities and fight against the injustices inherent in the process of racialization.[17] Do these count as "racial" identities? Should we reconceive the notion of racial group in their terms? Should a feminist antiracism support the formation of racial identities and racial groups in this sense?

History, Experience, and Self-interpretation

One goal of this inquiry is to provide an account of race and racial identity that will be useful in the quest for social justice. As Alcoff suggests, this will be to a significant extent a constructive project requiring us to look not only back to history but also forward towards a better future. In developing my accounts of race and gender I have focused on the task of identifying groups who have suffered from certain forms of embodied oppression; we should not ignore, however, that the members of these groups are not passive victims, but are agents engaged in the construction of their own meanings (Lugones and Spelman 1986). For members of subordinated races, their racial affiliation—as it has been constructed from within the group—is often not only a source of pride and value in their lives, but has provided resources to combat racial oppression. So if we are thinking about the possible future of race, one option is to build on these positive racial reconstructions, rather than the damaging structures of oppression.

For example, among those working on reconstructions of "Blackness," one theme emphasized is shared history as opposed to "color," and cultural *interconnections* as opposed to common culture (Gilroy 1993; Hall 1992; Gooding-Williams 1998). This option is also considered by those working on Latina/o and Asian identity (Gracia 2000a; Gracia 2000b; Alcoff 2000; Shah 1994), though as suggested above, the prospects of finding a plausible way to characterize the

---

[17] For example, Simón Bolívar, José Martí, and Che Guevara have promoted a pan-Latina/o solidarity (Alcoff 2000b, 27). There have also been moves, especially among feminists of color, to embrace mixed identity, e.g., (Anzaldúa 1987, Zack 1993, Zack 1995).

historical and cultural connections are diminished as the group becomes more diverse. Moreover, insofar as a reconstruction of race in terms of history and experience will have to provide an interpretation of that history and experience, and so select what aspects to highlight, we re-encounter the problem of normativity.

One of the arguments that has been used to challenge the usefulness of the category of gender for feminist politics raises the concern that women are so diverse that there is no way to capture *what women are* that does not privilege some women as paradigmatic and others marginal. This is a not merely an abstract concern in the context of women's studies, for there have been strands of feminist research that focus on White privileged women as if their issues and experiences are representative of all women. In developing my own account of gender I argued that theoretically privileging certain features of a group or certain members of a group over others is not always pernicious, if the basis for privileging is justified by a legitimate purpose of the theory. In the case of feminist research, one legitimate purpose is to develop a framework that enables us to identify and better understand forms of injustice. Because my theory defines women as those who suffer from sex-based oppression, it theoretically privileges oppressed females. But this is justified given the purpose of the inquiry.

I suggested that an analogous argument might also hold for race. For example, there is a danger in determining what history and experiences should count as definitive of Blackness, or of Asianness, that a narrative would be constructed that privileges men, heterosexuals, the economically advantaged, the educated, and so on. The suggestion that reconstructed races would be defined by those who are its members is, if we imagine it happening through some highly democratic process, one strategy of addressing this concern (Gooding Williams, 1988). However, even democracy doesn't guarantee equitable inclusion. Given that the effects of such efforts are not merely symbolic, but also have substantial ramifications in law and politics, there is reason to be extremely cautious. It may be possible to provide a positive reconstruction of race or of particular races; my point here is to highlight the challenge of simultaneously accommodating the broad diversity of people who count as members of a race, and the selectivity involved in constructing a basis for group membership.

I agree with Alcoff that there are a variety of groups unified by social/historical background and/or culture, and these are valuable and are likely to persist. In the case of pan-ethnicities, their formation and self-definition is still in progress. If we build on the positive reconstructions of race to envision the future of race, then we might pursue Alcoff's suggestion that the future of race lies in pan-ethnicities, or what she calls (following David Goldberg) ethnoraces, that are unified around the history of being racialized as a group and the positive cultural forms that have evolved in response.

Ethnorace

What exactly is an "ethnorace"? I've argued that there is a conception of race in terms of racialized group that is valuable for thinking about certain forms of embodied oppression. This is how I characterized it in section 1:

> A group is *racialized* (in context C) iff$_{df}$ its members are socially positioned as subordinate or privileged along some dimension (economic, political, legal, social, etc.) (in C), and the group is "marked" as a target for this treatment by observed or imagined bodily features presumed to be evidence of ancestral links to a certain geographical region.

How is an ethnonrace different from a race? Is the notion of an *ethnorace* more useful than race (as I've defined it)? In considering a more just future, should we aspire to preserve ethnoraces or eliminate them and the conditions that sustain them?

Alcoff introduces the notion of ethnorace because social and historical reality does not seem to fit the standard classifications of race or ethnicity. For example, Latina/os as a group are not racially homogenous, although Latina/o (or Hispanic) in many contexts counts as a race. Some have suggested that a better strategy is to replace racial classification with ethnic classification. Ethnicities, as Alcoff is using the term, concern "cultural practices, customs, language, sometimes religion, and so on" (Alcoff 2000, 25). Some ethnicities, in this sense, are sub-groups of existing races (all of the standard races include various ethnic groups); and some ethnicities cross racial lines.

Alcoff recommends that we think of currently racialized groups (perhaps especially groups such as "Latina/os") in terms of ethnoraces rather than ethnicities for three main reasons[18]: (i) culture, especially the cultures of racialized groups, tends to be naturalized and to entail membership in a race. For example, as soon as one reveals information about one's *culture* of origin, one is immediately racialized. If one has grown up in Mexico and is culturally Mexican, then regardless of how one physically appears, one is assumed to be Latina/o (Alcoff 2000, 37–8). (ii) The racial coding of the body trumps cultural identification:

> . . . race, unlike ethnicity, has historically worked through visible markers on the body that trump dress, speech, and cultural practices. . . .

---

[18] She also provides reasons for not thinking of Latinas/os as a race. On this see also (Mendieta 2000).

in popular consciousness—in the implicit perceptual practices we use in everyday life to discern how to relate to each other—ethnicity does not "replace" race. When ethnic identities are used instead of racial ones, the perceptual practices of visual demarcation by which we slot people into racial categories continue to operate because ethnic categories offer no substituting perceptual practice. (Alcoff 2000, 38)

Because current social perception is conditioned to interpret "color" as culturally meaningful, classifications of individuals into ethnic groups will continue to rely on the physical markers of race. And (iii) positive group solidarity among currently racialized groups in the United States is likely to provoke anxiety and resistance because the long history of their subordination is a threat to the dominant American self-image. Insofar as the United States identifies with and takes pride in its commitment to equality and freedom for all, the affirmation of Otherness is a reminder of a shameful history that many long to erase (Alcoff 2000, 39). Because racialization has been rhetorically crucial to the legitimizing narratives of white supremacy, deracialization will be resisted.

So because race and racialization is intimately bound up with culture and so ethnicity, Alcoff recommends *ethnorace*:

Unlike race, ethnorace does not imply a common descent, which is precisely what tends to embroil race in notions of biological determinism and natural and heritable characteristics. Ethnorace might have the advantage of bringing into play the elements of both human agency and subjectivity involved in ethnicity—that is, an identity that is the product of self-creation—at the same time that it acknowledges the uncontrolled racializing aspects associated with the visible body. (Alcoff 2000, 42)

Although intriguing and suggestive, I'm not sure I have a firm grasp on the notion. My best guess is that an ethnorace is a group of people who have been "marked" as of the same race (this is the uncontrolled racializing aspect), who share some common cultural elements and are collectively involved in the constitution of their shared identity. Ethnorace differs from race, as I've defined race, in including the conditions of common culture and agency in the construction of identity. Races, as I've characterized them, do not require any commonality in culture, commitment, or identity. They only require that members are similarly positioned structurally in society, whether they want to be or not, whether they even notice this or not. Races are more ascribed than embraced. However, plausibly Alcoff's ethnoraces count as a subset of races in my sense: if races are groups whose "color" affects their social position, ethnoraces are those among them that have developed a common culture and a commitment to shared identity. Some, but not all, races are ethnoraces.

Alcoff offers the notion of ethnorace not as a vision of the groups that should be part of a utopian future, but as a reconstruction of the notion of race that applies to (some of) us now and what the next step in the elimination of race might look like. I would assume that in a context where racialization is long past, ethnorace could be replaced by ethnicity. In effect, not only the condition of common descent, but also the practice of "color" marking would disappear.

Are ethnoraces a valuable interim category? This is controversial. I take it that Alcoff (and others) encourage the formation of ethnoraces because they highlight and encourage agency in group formation and acknowledge some degree of common subjectivity among those who are similarly racialized. Others, however, will urge us to resist racism by rejecting membership in "color"-defined groups, and resisting identities formed around "color." I prefer not to take a stand on this normative issue. In any case, we have reason to be theoretically attentive to the formation of such groups as we trace the workings of racializing practices and active resistance to them.

However, I believe that we also need to maintain a conception of *race* or *racialized group* that is not as concerned with culture or agency. For example, internationally adopted children of color who are brought up in the United States are ethnically American; often if they are adopted transracially they are not involved in the self-creation of an ethnic identity associated with their birthcountry, or even a pan-ethnic identity. And yet they are raced; they don't become the race or ethnorace of their adoptive parents (see also Corlett 2000, 227; Corlett 1999). At least we need some way of including such adoptees within the racialized group they are taken to belong to in order to understand some of the injustices they face in the United States.

Moreover, although it is clear that ethnicity is racialized, race is also "ethnicized" in problematic ways. Alcoff herself points out that because she is Latina, she is assumed to enjoy spicy food, even though in Panama (her ancestral home) the food is mild (Alcoff 2000, 33). Racial stereotypes that allegedly capture "cultural" differences abound (Blacks enjoy basketball, Asians value education). In the context of adoption, a link between race and culture has been a site of controversy for decades. In the 1950s, internationally adopted children were forced to assimilate and were allowed to have little, if anything, to do with the culture of their birthcountry. By the early 1970s, transracial adoption (both domestic and international) was challenged for, among other things, denying a child "her" culture. By the 1990s, when international adoption boomed and domestic transracial adoption began to significantly increase, the pressure on adoptive parents to become educated in the child's culture and to provide "cultural competence" in this culture to the child, remained very strong (in some cases being written into policies determining who could adopt). There is a way of seeing this as an enforcement of ethnorace.[19] Such practices are, I believe, at odds with Alcoff's recommendations. However, they alert us to both concerns about the normative import of the category of ethnorace and also the need for a category that allows us to keep race and ethnicity apart.

5. Conclusion

I recommend that we opt for the account of race that I've proposed as useful for doing the work of identifying those affected by racialization and remedying its harms. I further propose that we employ the notions of culture, ethnicity, pan-ethnicity, and ethnorace, for understanding the more constructive efforts to form new identities that do justice to our histories and our experiences. This proposal leaves open the possibility that currently racialized groups will either form a more encompassing identities describable in terms of shared history and experience (a pan-Latina/o identity) or will retain a variety of more local identities (Puerto-Rican, Brazilian, Cuban-American, Chicana/o).

I have argued (though the argument is far from conclusive) that in the long run, social justice does not require the formation or maintenance of groups defined by "color," though "color"-based groups may be valuable as part of an interim strategy. Race, as I've proposed we understand it, is something to be rid of. Ethnicity or ethnorace, if understood as involving both "color" and culture, may be helpful in the short term, but I believe that an ongoing social investment in "color" is harmful. In short, "after the revolution" we should anticipate that there will be no men and women, but there will be males and females (and herms, merms, ferms, etc.), and these sexual differences will have distinct but egalitarian implications. And although, we should hope, people will come in the broad variety of skin tones, shapes, and appearances they do now and will organize themselves around a rich array of cultural practices, there will be no races. Although from the point of view of justice, it would be irresponsible not to accord differences between our bodies some social meaning, it would also be irresponsible not to overturn the meanings we now assume to be natural and right.

---

[19] I agree that it is extremely important for transracially adopted children to be given the resources to develop positive self-esteem and to combat the racism they will confront. And in some cases this will involve building a connection to a community of people of the same race. However, my concern is that the argument for such involvement is often based on the idea that by virtue of having a race the child already has a culture; on this view, transracial adoption is inherently problematic because it uproots a child from her culture (cf. Allen 1993).

References

Adelman, Larry. 2003. "Race and Gene Studies: What Differences Make a Difference" (website). California Newsreel 2003 [cited July 31, 2003]. Available from http://www.newsreel.org/guides/race/whatdiff.htm.

Alcoff, Linda M. 1995. "Mestizo Identity." In *American Mixed Race: The Culture of Microdiversity*, edited by N. Zack. Lanham, MD: Rowman and Littlefield.

———. 2000a. "Habits of Hostility: On Seeing Race." *Philosophy Today* 44(Supp.): 30–40.

———. 2000b. "Is Latina/o Identity a Racial Identity?" In *Hispanics/Latinos in the United States: Ethnicity, Race, and Rights.*, edited by Jorge J. E. Gracia and Pablo De Greiff. New York: Routledge.

Allen, A. 1993. "Does a Child Have a Right to a Certain Identity?" *Rechtstheorie* 15, Supplement 15: 109–19.

Andreasen, R. O. 1998. "A New Perspective on the Race Debate." *British Journal of the Philosophy of Science* 49(2): 199–225.

———. 2000. "Race: Biological Reality or Social Construct?" *Philosophy of Social Science* 67(Proceedings): S653–S666.

Anzaldúa, Gloria. 1987. *Borderlands/La Frontera: The New Mestiza*. San Francisco: Aunt Lute Books.

Appiah, Kwame Anthony. 1990. "'But Would That Still Be Me?' Notes on Gender, 'Race,' Ethnicity, as Sources of 'Identity.'" *Journal of Philosophy* 77(10): 493–99.

———. 1992. Illusions of Race. In. *In My Father's House: Africa in the Philosophy of Culture*. New York: Oxford University Press.

———. 1996. "Race, Culture, Identity: Misunderstood Connections." *In Color Conscious: The Political Morality of Race*, edited by K. A. Appiah and A. Gutmann. Princeton: Princeton University Press.

Beauvoir, Simon de. 1989. *The Second Sex*. Translated by H. M. Parshley. New York: Vintage Books. Original edition, 1949.

Butler, Judith. 1990. *Gender Trouble*. New York: Routledge.

Corlett, J. Angelo. 1997. "Parallels of Ethnicity and Gender." In *RACE/SEX: Their Sameness, Difference and Interplay*, edited by N. Zack. New York: Routledge.

———. 1999. "Latino Identity." *Public Affairs Quarterly* 13: 273–95.

———. 2000. "Latino Identity and Affirmative Action." In *Hispanic/Latino Identity in the United States: Ethnicity, Race, and Rights*, edited by J. J. E. Grada. New York: Routledge.

Davis, F. James. 1991. *Who Is Black? One Nation's Definition*. University Park: Pennsylvania State University.

Delphy, Christine. 1984. *Close to Home: A Materialist Analysis of Women's Oppression*. Trans. Diana Leonard. Amherst, MA: University of Massachusetts.

Fausto-Sterling, Anne. 1993. "The Five Sexes: Why Male and Female Are Not Enough." *The Sciences* 33(2): 20–24.

———. 1995. "How to Build a Man." In *Constructing Masculinity*, edited by M. Berger and B. Wallis. New York: Routledge, pp. 127–34.

———. 2000. *Sexing the Body: Gender Politics and the Construction of Sexuality*. New York: Basic Books.

Fields, Barbara. 1982. "Ideology and Race in American History." In *Region, Race and Reconstruction: Essays in Honor of C. Vann Woodward*, edited by J. M. Kousser and J. M. McPherson. Oxford: Oxford University Press.

———. 1990. "Slavery, Race, and Ideology in the United States of America." *New Left Review* 181: 95–118.

Frye, Marilyn. 1996. "The Necessity of Differences: Constructing a Positive Category of Woman." *Signs* 21(4): 991–1010.

Gatens, Moira. 1996. "A Critique of the Sex-Gender Distinction." In her *Imaginary Bodies*. New York: Routledge, pp. 3–20.

Gilroy, Paul. 1993. *The Black Atlantic: Modernity and Double Consciousness*. Cambridge, MA: Harvard University Press.

Gooding-Williams, Robert. 1988. "Rate, Multiculturalismi and Democracy." *Constellations* 5(1): 18–41.

Gotanda, Neil. 1995. "A Critique of 'Our Constitution is Color-Blind.'" In *Critical Race Theory*, edited by Kimberle Crenshaw et al. New York: The New Press, pp. 257–75.

Gracia, Jorge J.E., ed. 2000a. *Hispanics/Latinos in the United States. Ethnicity, Race, and Rights.* New York: Routledge.

———. 2000b). *Hispanic/Latino Identity*. Oxford: Blackwell Publishers.

Hall, Stuart. 1992. "What Is This 'Black' in Black Popular Culture?" In *Black Popular Culture: A Project by Michelle Wallace*, edited by Gina Dent. Seattle: Bay Press.

———. 1996. "New Ethnicities." In *Black British Cultural Studies*, edited by H. A. J. Baker, M. Diawara and R. H. Lindenborg. Chicago: University of Chicago Press.

Haslanger, Sally. 2012 [1993]. "On Being Objective and Being Objectified." Chapter 1 of this volume.

———. 2012 [2000]. "Gender and Race: (What) Are They? (What) Do We Want Them To Be?" Chapter 7 of this volume.

———. 2012 [2003]. "Social Construction: The 'Debunking' Project." Chapter 3 of this volume.

———. 2012 [2004]. "You Mixed? Racial Identity Without Racial Biology." Chapter 9 of this volume.

Kitclier, Philip. 1999. "Race, Ethnicity, Biology, Culture." In *Racism*, edited by L. Harris. Amherst, NY: Humanity Books.

Laqueur, Thomas. 1990. *Making Sex: Body and Gender From the Greeks to Freud*. Cambridge, MA: Harvard University Press.

Lewontin, Richard C. 1982. *Human Diversity. New York*: Scientific American Press.

———. 1991. *Biology as Ideology: The Doctrine of DNA*. New York: Harper Collins.

Lugones, Maria, and Elizabeth Spelman. 1986. "Have We Got a Theory for You! Feminist Theory, Cultural Imperialism, and the Demand for 'The Woman's Voice.'" In *Women and Values: Readings in Recent Feminist Philosophy*, edited by M. Pearsall. Belmont, CA: Wadsworth Publishing Co.

MacKinnon, Catharine. 1987. *Feminism Unmodified*. Cambridge, MA: Harvard University Press.

Mendieta, Eduardo. 2000. "The Making of New Peoples." In *Hispanics/Latinos in the United States: Ethnicity, Race and Rights*, edited by J. J. E. Gracia. New York: Routledge.

Mills, Charles. 1997. *The Racial Contract*. Ithaca: Cornell University Press.

———. 1998. *Blackness Visible: Essays on Philosophy and Race*. Ithaca: Cornell University Press.

Money, John, and Patricia Tucker. 1975. *Sexual Signatures: On Being a Man or a Woman*. Boston: Little, Brown, and Co.

Mosely, Albert G. 1995. "Negritude, Nationalism, and Nativism: Racists or Racialists?" In *African Philosophy: Selected Readings*. Englewood Cliffs, NJ: Prentice Hall.

Omi, Michael, and Howard Winant. 1994. *Racial Formation in the United States*. New York: Routledge.

Outlaw, Lucius T., Jr. 1996. *On Race and Philosophy*. New York: Routledge.

Root, Michael. 2000. "How We Divide the World." *Philosophy of Social Science* 67(Proceedings): 628–39.

———. 2001. "The Problem of Race in Medicine." *Philosophy of the Social Sciences* 31(1): 20–39.

Rubin, Gayle. 1975. "The Traffic in Women: Notes on the 'Political Economy' of Sex." In *Toward an Anthropology of Women*, edited by R. R. Reiter. New York: Monthly Review Press.

Shah, Sonia. 1994. "Presenting the Blue Goddess: Towards a National, Pan-Asian Feminist Agenda." In Karin Aguilar-San Juan, ed., *The State of Asian America: Activism and Resistance in the 1990's*. Boston: South End Press.

Spelman, Elizabeth. 1988. *The Inessential Woman: Problems of Exclusion in Feminist Thought*. Boston: Beacon Press.

Stevens, Jacqueline. 1993. *The Politics of Identity: From Property to Empathy*. Ph.D., Political Science, University of California, Berkeley.

———. 1999. *Reproducing the Slate*. Princeton: Princeton University Press.

Stocking, George W., Jr. 1994. "The Turn-of-the-Century Concept of Race." *Modernism/Modernity* 1(1): 4–16.

Thomas, Laurence. 1980. "Sexism and Racism: Some Conceptual Differences." *Ethics* 90: 239–50.

Wasserstrom, Richard A. 1987. "Preferential Treatment, Color-Blindness, and the Evils of Racism." *Proceedings of the American Philosophical Association*, Supplement 61: 27–42.

Wittig, Monique. 1981. "One Is Not Born a Woman." *Feminist Issues* 1(2): 47–54.

———. 1982. "The Category of Sex." *Feminist Issues* 2(2): 63–68.

Zack, Naomi. 1993. *Race and Mixed Race*. Philadelphia: Temple University Press.

———, ed. 1995. *American Mixed Race*. Lanham, MD: Rowman and Littlefield.

———. 2002. *Philosophy of Science and Race*. New York: Routledge.

‖ 9 ‖

You Mixed?

Racial Identity without Racial Biology

To set the context for this chapter, it will be useful to begin with an anecdote. One recent summer I was in my neighborhood park with my then five-year-old son, Isaac. We live in a racially mixed, though predominantly Black neighborhood. The park consists mainly of a cement basketball court and a play structure set in a huge sandbox. We had been playing basketball for about 45 minutes; for the first part of it I had been helping him with his shots, but eventually a few other kids had joined us and I had stepped to the sidelines to let them negotiate their play on their own. For the time we were there, as is common, I was the only White person in the park; Isaac, my son, is Black. In order to capture the potential import of what follows, it is worth mentioning that in appearance I am quite WASPy looking—straight brown hair, gray eyes, pale skin, and Isaac is dark with nearly black eyes and black (virtually shaved) hair. The time came to leave, and we took our ball and headed down the sidewalk toward home. A boy about nine years old rode up to us on his bike—he wasn't one of the ones we'd been playing with and I didn't recognize him, but let's call him "James"—and asked me a familiar question, "Is he your son?" I replied, "Yes." He looked at me hard with a somewhat puzzled expression and continued, "You mixed?" I paused. I wasn't entirely sure what he was asking. Although I am well aware that African Americans may have straight brown hair, gray eyes, and light complexions, it seemed a huge leap of the imagination for anyone to read my appearance as mixed-race. I suspected that he might be asking whether I am (or was when Isaac was conceived) in an interracial relationship, thus explaining the disparity in Isaac's and my appearance by an absent (Black) father. Sensing that this wasn't one of those times when a long explanation was called for, I replied, somewhat misleadingly (given what I took him to be asking), "I'm not mixed, but my family is mixed." He responded, "Oh, cool," and rode off.

This sort of conversation isn't at all uncommon when you're in a family like mine, and it's the sort that tends to rattle around in the back of your mind for at least a few days, if not weeks or months. What is "a family like mine"? My family consists of me and my husband Steve (also White) and two African American children: Isaac (I've already mentioned) and our daughter Zina (at the time this essay was originally published, they were aged nine and seven, respectively). We adopted the children when they were infants. They have different birth families, and their adoptions are "fully open": we have regular contact with their birth families—including phone contact every few weeks, and visits lasting several days where typically we stay in their homes and they stay in ours. The birth families are an important part of our extended family.

Many conversations rattle around in the back of my head because I worry about what they meant, what I should have said (in contrast to what I did say), or what my kids took away from the contact and how I can usefully follow up on it with them; but most of them don't inspire philosophical reflection. However, this conversation puzzled me about a number of issues, and this chapter is an effort to sort out what I think about them.

The philosophical questions arise from a tension between certain theoretical claims about race and my own lived experience. Theoretically, I agree with many others in law and the academy that our everyday racial classifications do not track meaningful biological categories: there are no "racial genes" responsible for the different clusters of physical or cultural differences between members of racial groups, and divisions between "racial" groups are a product of social forces that vary across history and culture. But if that's the case, a certain dialectic develops that raises questions about my response to James and opens further ones.

First, if race is not biologically real, then on what basis do I so easily describe myself as White and my son as Black? On what basis can I claim so confidently to James that I'm not "mixed" (even though my family is)? This is not just a question about the facts of my ancestry—although none of my known ancestors are Black, there are many gaps in the record, and for all I know I may have some fairly recent African roots. The more pressing question for my purposes here, however, is that if race is a biological fiction, then what does it even mean to affirm or deny that I'm "White" or that I'm "mixed"?

Although I reject the idea that there are biological races in which membership is determined by "blood," and along with this reject the idea of "mixed blood," I don't agree with some theorists who conclude that "there is no such thing as race," simply because there are no racial essences or racial genes. I am a social constructionist about race: I believe that races are social categories, and no less real for being social rather than "natural." As a result, I think it is accurate to classify myself socially as White and my son as Black, and to classify others as "mixed race." But I have a rather complicated and non-standard interpretation of what that means that takes races to be social classes defined in a context of what might usefully be called "color" oppression. In the first section of the chapter I'll sketch my account of race and say a bit about how it might handle the claims that I am White and Isaac is Black.

But it will become clear that as it stands my account doesn't provide sufficient resources to understand the phenomenon of racial identity, especially in contexts where race and racial identity come apart. So in the middle of the chapter I will discuss racial identity with special attention to the phenomenon of life "on the color line" hoping that this discussion may also be of use in thinking about the phenomenon of "passing."[1] I will suggest that there is a sense in which I can claim a "mixed" identity (though certainly not in any of the senses that James probably had in mind) and in which it is probably true that my kids do and will continue to have somewhat "mixed" identities. However, the suggestion that my kids may grow up without the "correct" racial identity—that their identity may be, at least in a certain sense, "mixed" rather than "Black" or "African American"— raises issues that, of course, are one concern in debates over the legitimacy of transracial adoption. So in the final section I will consider briefly what I take to be the import of my arguments regarding the obligation of parents who adopt transracially to raise their children to have the "right" racial identity.[2]

Race as Social Class

In chapter 7 of this volume, "Gender and Race: (What) Are They? (What) Do We Want Them To Be?," I argue that for the purposes of an antiracist feminist theory, it is important to develop accounts of race and gender that enable us to identify the groups who are targets of racial and sexual oppression.[3] Although it may well be that in the long run ("after the revolution") we may hope that both race and gender will be eliminated, in the short run it would be a mistake not to recognize the ways in which race and sex oppression divide us into hierarchical classes in which membership is "marked" on the body.

In that chapter I propose that in order to accommodate the broad variety of ways in which the notions of race and gender are employed (apparently to refer to quite different things, for example, racial norms, racial symbols, racial identities, racial social roles) we should take a "focal meaning" approach to race and

---

[1] Some powerful recent accounts of "life on the color line" include Williams (1995); McBride (1996); Lazarre (1997); Derricotte (1997); Piper (1992); Dalmage (2000). Some recent accounts of living in (Black/White) transracial adoptions include Rush (2000); Thompson (2000); Simon and Roorda (2000). The issue of "passing" has received significant attention recently, and I will not be able to do justice to it here. However, some useful (non-fiction) work beyond that already mentioned includes Ginsberg (1996); Delgado and Stefancic (1997).

[2] For a glimpse of the transracial adoption controversy, see NABSW (1972); Bartholet (1991); Bartholet (1993); Perry (1993–94); Howe (1995); NABSW (1994); Simon (1994); Smith (1996); Patton (2000); Neal (1996). On the question of the "right identity" see also Allen (1993).

[3] The definitions of race below, and some of the text surrounding them, are taken directly from Haslanger 2012 [2000].

gender. A focal analysis undertakes to explain a variety of connected phenomena in terms of their relations to one that is theorized as the central or core phenomenon. As I see it, the core phenomenon to be addressed is the pattern of social relations that constitute certain social classes as racially/sexually dominant and others as racially/sexually subordinate; norms, symbols, and identities are gendered or raced derivatively, by reference to the social relations that constitute the relevant hierarchy of social classes.[4] Although my definitions of race and gender help organize and clarify some of our everyday beliefs (or so I maintain), I do not offer them as analyses of our *ordinary* concepts of race and gender (whatever they might be). Instead, I offer these accounts in a revisionary spirit as part of an explicitly political project.

My guiding idea is that systems of racial and sexual oppression are alike (in spite of their many differences) in taking certain real or imagined features of the body as markers for oppressive social divisions. Societies structured by racial and/or sexual oppression will produce culture that "helps" us read the body in the requisite ways and will provide narratives or rationalizations linking kinds of bodies to kinds of social positions; they will also be organized so that the roles and activities assigned to certain kinds of bodies systematically disadvantage them (and to other kinds of bodies systematically privilege them) in concrete material ways. Sex and race oppression are structural—institutional—but they are also internalized in our basic interpretations and understandings of our bodies, ourselves, and each other.

Feminists have often used an (albeit contested) slogan to capture the notion of gender: gender is the social meaning of sex. In keeping with the ideas above,

---

[4] To understand the notion of a 'social class' as I am using the term, it may be helpful to consider other examples. A social class is a group of individuals who are members of the class (or set) in question by virtue of having a certain social property or standing in a particular social relation. So, for example, the class of husbands is a social class. Men who are legally married are husbands, and their standing in a legal marriage relationship is the basis for their membership. Homeowners constitute a social class: they are those individuals who are legal owners of the property that serves as their domicile. I use legal relations for these examples because they arc very straightforward cases of social relations, but other relations, for example, being a neighbor of, being a pastor of, are social but aren't encoded in law. Note especially membership in the sets is not determined by and does not presuppose any common set of beliefs, psychological attitudes, behaviors, etc., among the members. (One can be a homeowner without even being aware of it, for example, if a child inherits the home she or he lives in when the parents die.) For example, consider the class of scapegoats, or the class of teacher's pets. In these cases membership is determined by the way one is both viewed and treated, though even here, we should not assume that the individuals who fall into the classes are aware that they are scapegoats or that they function as teacher's pets; and likewise, we cannot assume a common subjective experience of being in this position. Yet we may want to say of scapegoats, for example, that some *do* come to have a scapegoat identity. My point is that one might distinguish being a scapegoat from having a scapegoat identity, just as one might distinguish being a member or a race from having a racial identity. On the strategy I will be employing, explaining what it is to have a racial identity will depend on the prior notion of having a race.

materialist feminists have argued that we must understand the use of "social meaning" here along two axes—on one hand, social meaning includes the cultural readings of the body, and on the other hand, the material (economic, political, legal) divisions between the sexes. It is distinctive of materialist feminism that it refuses to prioritize either the cultural or material dimension as (causally) prior. In other words, it is a mistake to suggest that the ultimate source of the problem is "in our heads" (in our conceptual scheme, our language, or our cultural ideals), or alternatively that it is in the unjust structure of our social arrangements, as if it must be one or the other; "culture" and "social/institutional structure" are deeply intertwined, so much so, that they are sometimes inextricable.[5]

On one materialist account of gender (in particular, one I support), men and women are defined as those hierarchical classes of individuals whose membership is determined by culturally variable readings of the reproductive capacities of the human body. In contexts in which the reproductive body is not a site of subordination and privilege (presumably no contexts we know of, but ones we may hope for), there are no men or women, though there still may be other (new) genders.

Is this strategy useful for thinking about race? Perhaps, though off-hand this idea is not easy to develop. It is one thing to acknowledge that race is *socially* real, even if a biological fiction; but it is another thing to capture in racial terms the "social meaning" of the body. There seem to be too many different forms that race takes. Note, however, that the same problem arises for gender: is it possible to provide a unified (cross-cultural, trans-historical) analysis of "the social meaning of sex"? The materialist feminist approach offered a helpful strategy: don't look for an analysis that assumes that the meaning is always and everywhere the same; rather, consider how members of the group are *socially positioned*, and what *physical markers* serve in a supposed basis for such treatment. Let this provide the common framework within which we explore the contextually variable meanings.

To extend this strategy to race it will help first to introduce a technical notion of "color." What we need is a term for those physical features of individuals taken to mark them as members of a race. One might refer to them as "racial" features, but to avoid any suggestion of racial essences I will use the term 'color' to refer to the (contextually variable) physical "markers" of race, just as I use the term 'sex' to refer to the (contextually variable) physical "markers" of gender. Note that I include in 'color' more than just skin tone: common markers also include eye, nose, and lip shape, hair texture, physique, and such, and it is presumed of the physical markers of *race* that the features in question are inherited through an ancestry that can be traced back to a particular geographical region. Although

---

[5] The interdependence of the cultural and material is an explicit commitment of materialist feminism as articulated in, for example, Young (1990), 33. See also Delphy (1984), and more generally Hennessey and Ingraham (1997).

the term 'people of color' is used to refer to non-Whites, I want to allow that the markers of "Whiteness" count as "color"; however, I still use the phrases 'people of color' and 'children of color' as they are used to refer to non-Whites.

Transposing the slogan used for gender, then, we might say that race is the social meaning of "color", or more explicitly, of the geographically marked body. To develop this, I propose the following account (see also Stevens 1993; Stevens 1999).[6] First definition:

> A group is *racialized* iff$_{df}$ its members are socially positioned as subordinate or privileged along some dimension (economic, political, legal, social, etc.), and the group is "marked" as a target for this treatment by observed or imagined bodily features presumed to be evidence of ancestral links to a certain geographical region.

Or in the more elaborate version[7]:

> A group G is *racialized* relative to context C iff$_{df}$ members of G are (all and only) those:
>
> (i) who are observed or imagined to have certain bodily features presumed in G to be evidence of ancestral links to a certain geographical region (or regions);
>
> (ii) whose having (or being imagined to have) these features marks them within the context of the background ideology in C as appropriately occupying certain kinds of social position that are in fact either subordinate or privileged (and so motivates and justifies their occupying such a position); and
>
> (iii) whose satisfying (i) and (ii) plays (or would play) a role in their systematic subordination or privilege in C, that is, who are *along some dimension* systematically subordinated or privileged when in C, and satisfying (i) and (ii) plays (or would play) a role in that dimension of subordination or privilege.

In other words, races are those groups demarcated by the geographical associations accompanying perceived body type, when those associations take on (hierarchical)

---

[6] Special thanks to Jacqueline Stevens for help in formulating these definitions. My version is quite similar to the one she offers in Stevens (1999), chap. 4. See Omi and Winant (1994), 53–61.

[7] There are aspects of this definition that need further elaboration or qualification. For details see Haslanger (2012 [2000]), n. 17. Note also that there may be reasons to claim that a particular group is more racialized than another, depending, for example, on the degree of subordination or privilege, or on the role of physical marks. I would accommodate this by saying that like many concepts, there are central and peripheral cases depending on the extent to which something satisfies the conditions.

socio-political significance concerning how members of the group should be viewed and treated. It is important to note that the ideology in question need not use physical morphology or geography as the entire or explicit *basis* or *rationale* for the supposed "appropriate" treatment; these features may instead simply be "markers" of other characteristics that the ideology uses to justify the treatment in question.[8]

On this view, whether a group is racialized, and so how and whether an individual is raced, is not an absolute fact, but will depend on context. For example, Blacks, Whites, Asians, Latinos/as, Native Americans, are currently racialized in the United States insofar as these are all groups defined in terms of physical features associated with places of origin, and insofar as membership in the group functions socially as a basis for evaluation. However, some groups are not currently racialized in the United States but have been so in the past and possibly could be again (and in other contexts are), for example, the Italians, the Germans, the Irish.

The definition just provided focuses on races as groups, and this makes sense when we are thinking of group-based oppression. But the analysis as it stands does not do justice to the ways in which an individual's race is negotiated and depends on context. Racialization is definitely more pronounced in some contexts than in others, and in most cases individuals are not simply passive victims of its effects but are agents who are capable of undermining or collaborating in the process. With this in mind, we can say that S is of the White (Black, Asian . . .) race iff Whites (Blacks, Asians . . .) are a racialized group in S's society, and S is *regularly and for the most part* viewed and treated as a member.[9] Yet we may also want to allow that some people don't have a stable race at all. and that even if some are consistently racialized in the society, there are disruptions in this broad pattern when we consider narrower contexts. To accommodate the contextual racialization of individuals (and not just groups), let's say:

> S *functions as a member* of a racial group R in context C if and only if (by definition)
>
> (i) S is observed or imagined in C to have certain bodily features presumed to be evidence of ancestral links to a certain geographical region (or regions) where the group R is thought to have originated;
> (ii) that S has these features marks S, within the background ideology of C, as someone who ought to occupy certain kinds of social positions that are, in fact, subordinate or privileged (and so motivates and justifies S's occupying such a position); and

---

[8] The point here is that the racist ideology that sustains the hierarchy may be a form of either *intrinsic* or *extrinsic* racism in Appiah's sense. Appiah (1992), 13–15.

[9] As in the ease of gentler, I recommend that we view membership in a racial/ethnic group in terms of how one is viewed and treated regularly and for the most part in the context in question.

(iii) the fact that S satisfies (i) and (ii) plays a role in S's systematic subordination or privilege in C, that is, S is systematically subordinated or privileged *along some dimension* when in C, and satisfying
(i) and (ii) plays (or would play) a role in that dimension of privilege
or subordination.

Identifying Our Races

Of course, there are many controversial aspects of this account that merit further
discussion. But I hope it is clear that on an account of this sort (in some sense the
details don't even really matter for our purposes here), it is possible for individuals
to be members of a race even if there is no biological basis for racial classification.
On my view, biological ideology is just one of several possible ideologies that might
link "color" with social/political hierarchy. For example, in the contemporary United
States, even some who grant that race is not a meaningful genetic category believe
that "color" is a marker for "culture," and use such color-culture assumptions to
justify social/political hierarchy. On my view, groups that are subordinated or privileged on the basis of color-culture assumptions are no less racial groups than those
who are subordinated on the basis of color-genetics assumptions. (Hence, it makes
sense to speak of "cultural racism.") What's important and interesting about the
phenomenon of race, on my account, is not the invocation of biology to justify
hierarchy (after all, prior to the development of genetic theory, theology was invoked
to provide a basis for color oppression [Stocking 1993]), but the historically persistent ways in which the marked body—in terms of color-ancestry-geography—takes
on meaning and is used to justify and motivate social/political status.

Although on my account *there are races*—understood as social classes—this
claim is not directly incompatible with a view that might be stated as, "There are no
races." Typically in current discussions those who deny that there are races believe
that the concept of race is committed to a naturalistic form of racial essence. I can
agree with those who employ the term 'race' with such commitments that there
are no races—*in their sense*. My disagreement, instead, is with their background
philosophical assumptions about language and conceptual analysis. To clarify my
point, then, we might want to employ the terminology *'biological* races' and *'social*
races.' I maintain that there are no biological races, but there are social races, that
is, racialized groups. And I not only maintain that the concept of race is sufficiently
open-ended to include social races, but that there are philosophical and political
reasons to explicate the notion of race in a way that accounts for racialized groups.

Let's return, though, to my conversation with James. Given this account of
race, we now have some way of accounting for the idea that I am White and Isaac
is Black, even though race is not an adequate biological classification. I count as
White because I reap tremendous White privilege by virtue of the ways people

regularly interpret my "color"; Isaac, although he reaps some of the benefits of White privilege through my privilege, is already disadvantaged by the interpretation of his "color" and its social implications. Because Isaac is socially "marked" as of African descent, and this is a factor in the disadvantages he experiences, he counts as Black.

However, it is not uncommon in the adoption world to hear people describe the effects of transracial adoption (of children of color by Whites) by saying. "You will become a minority family." The purpose of such comments is not to alert prospective adoptive parents to the fact that interracial families are in the statistical minority, which of course is obvious, but to suggest that a family with children of color counts as a family of color; the strongest version of the claim would be that by virtue of the race of my children, mine is a Black family. I appreciate some of the intentions behind this comment: it is meant to alert the naïve White prospective parents that they will suffer some forms of discrimination hitherto unknown to them once they adopt children of color. This is true. But I strongly resist the idea that my family or I become Black by including Black children, mainly because my family and I retain enormous White privilege. A weaker version of the claim is just that my family becomes an interracial family and so is exposed to some kinds of and some degree of discrimination not felt by White families; to this weak version of the claim I am more sympathetic. If it makes sense to say that a family has a race (as opposed to an individual), it may be that our family is racialized as non-White (our collective "colors" are interpreted as a basis for some forms of subordination/discrimination)—but this must be unpacked in a way that acknowledges the White privilege we, the parents, bring to the family.

However, even if it is true that I am not able to exercise some of my own White privilege when in the company of my family, I maintain that this does not mean that *I* somehow become racialized as Black (or more vaguely as non-White). For me to be a member of the Black race (to any degree), it would have to be that my subordination (or in this case, my diminution of privilege) was due to interpretations of my "color" as linked to recent ancestry in Africa. In those cases in which my privilege is weakened by virtue of my being a parent of Black children, it is not on the basis of anyone viewing me as Black, though my Whiteness may be relevant to my status in their eyes.[10]

---

[10] This is complicated. It may be on the basis of my status as a *White* adoptive mother of *Black* children that my privilege is denied. In this case I would want to say that the subordination is intersectional—racial assumptions are working together with other non-racial assumptions to disadvantage me. What this highlights is that race often does not function (does it ever?) as a single variable in oppression. It may be in contexts such as we are imagining that my Whiteness is diminished, and this in turn may suggest that race, even as I have defined it, is a scalar notion, not all-or-nothing, that is, some individuals as well as some groups of individuals may be more "racialized" than others. Thanks to Larry Blum for helping me think though some of these complexities; as I understand his view, Blum would argue that this is evidence that I am giving an account of racialization (and racialized groups), but not race. See Blum (2001).

But there is also something more I want to say about the possibilities of racial "crossing" in the context of transracial adoption. To put the point bluntly, I believe that my own racial identity has been substantially altered by being a mother of Black children, and although I am White, there are ways of thinking about identity on which my racial identity is better understood as "mixed." But so far the account of race I've offered provides no resources for thinking about this, for although it offers one way of thinking about *race*, as it stands it doesn't begin to address the issue of *racial identity*. Although races as social classes are the central phenomenon to be considered on my approach, a crucial next step is to make the link between race and racial identity.

Racial Identity

In the interdisciplinary literature on race and gender there are many different senses of the term 'identity.' I do not want to argue that there is one true sense of "identity"; I am happy to allow that there are several senses that are important. My goal here is modest—to highlight a sense of identity that is often left out of philosophical discussion.[11]

On the approach I've proposed, the social construction of race depends on both a set of symbolic and narrative resources for interpreting human bodies and a set of social and political institutions structured to privilege certain of those bodies, as interpreted. One strategy for thinking about racial identity would be to focus first on the social and political institutions in which racial injustice is materially implemented, and to view racial identities as the normative subjectivities that are deemed appropriate for (and help sustain) those institutions. The relevant analogy would be to see gender identities as the modes of subjective femininity and masculinity that are regarded as suitable to females and males respectively, and whose "proper" or "appropriate" development create subjects who, more or less, function effectively in the institutions constituting gender. Black, White, Asian (etc.) identities are made available to us as part of the process of constituting racial subjects who can function effectively in the institutions constituting race.

There are some advantages to this strategy: societies/cultures have ways of constructing subjects whose lives "unfold" in the sort of ways that fit within the structure of social life. Racial identity becomes the (idealized) self-understanding

---

[11] Note that one of the uses of "racial identity" is for the notion of race (or racialized group) as I've defined it above (or for a similar notion). In the context of this chapter I use the term 'racial identity' to draw a contrast with the notion of race as social class. I don't mean to legislate that the term 'racial identity' should not be used to refer to one's racial class membership (one's race); I'm using the term as I do largely because I'm drawing on work in psychology and feminist theory where the more psychological/somatic meaning I am explicating is one of the standard uses.

of those who are members of racialized groups. Individual members may have the relevant self-understanding to a greater or lesser extent, but the strength of their racial identity is evaluated relative to the "ideal."

This strategy, however, is problematic for several reasons. First, it (at least) appears to prioritize the institutional over the cultural: subjectivity is formed in order to suit the needs of social structures. But we must acknowledge that social structures also mutate in response to cultural shifts in symbolic resources available for the construction of subjectivity. This is a corollary, I believe, of the claim that racism is the joint product of social structures and cultural meanings. On this approach, the shape and evolution of culture, and so of subjectivity, cannot be accounted for by a simple social functionalism.

Second, this strategy appears to make us victims of racial and gender identities: it is unclear to what extent we are agents in constructing our own identities, and it is unclear whether identities that are, admittedly, constructed in the context of race or sex oppression, can have emancipatory elements. If one has a racial identity only to the extent that one is a "good" racial subject, that is, a subject whose "identity" enables him or her to "fit" with and so sustain institutions of racial domination, then we have no way to accommodate the importance of racial identity, particularly in subordinated groups, in *resisting* racism.

One possible response is to think of identity, and so racial identity, as a much more self-conscious and potentially political kind of awareness. On this account to have a racial identity is not just to have a certain kind of self-understanding, but for that self-understanding to include as an explicit (and perhaps chosen or at least "owned"?) part that one is a member of a particular race. As an example of an account that leans in this direction, consider Anthony Appiah's account of racial identity in "Race, Culture, Identity: Misunderstood Connections" (Appiah and Gutmann 1996, 30–105). On Appiah's account racial identity involves a process of "identification," and "identification" according to him is defined as

> the process though which an individual intentionally shapes her projects—including her plans for her own life and her conception of the good—by reference to available labels, available identities. (Appiah and Gutinann 1996, 78)

He goes on to define racial identity (roughly) as:

> . . . a label R, associated with *ascriptions* by most people (where ascription involves descriptive criteria for applying the label); and *identifications* by those who fall under it (where identification implies a shaping role for the label in the intentional acts of the possessors, so that they sometimes act *as an R*), where there is a history of associating possessors of

the label with an inherited racial essence (even if some who use the label
no longer believe in racial essences). (Appiah and Gutmann 1996, 83–84)

As I understand this view, "White," for example, is a racial identity just in case it
is a label that has a history of being associated with a racial essence, and it is
ascribed to people on the basis of descriptive criteria, and those who are White
identify with the label in the sense that they sometimes form intentions to act
as a White person, and subsequently so act.

The part of this view that is of primary interest for our current purposes concerns what it is for an individual to have a particular racial identity. (The suggestion
that the identity is the label puzzles me somewhat.) Taking White identity as our
example, Appiah's answer seems to be that X has a White (racial) identity just in
case "White" is a racial identity (it is a label of the right sort) and the label "White"
plays a role in X's self-understanding, so at least some of X's intentional acts are
performed *as a White person*. (Is it also required that X be considered White?)

This account solves several of the problems mentioned above, while also providing a model that could be adapted to my account of race. Appiah makes explicit that he does not view racial identities as (wholly) voluntary (Appiah and
Gutmann 1996, 80), but insofar as the main role of racial identity is in the
framing of one's intentional action, and this is a primary site of agency, this account frees us from the concern that we are victims of our racial identities.
Moreover, the racial labels Appiah has in mind are linked with a history of racial
essentialism, but there seems to be no functionalist assumption that requires us
to explain the use or evolution of the labels in terms of their role in supporting
the background social structure. Admittedly, Appiah counts certain labels as
"racial" by virtue of their association with racial essences, and my account of race
makes no reference to supposed racial essences; but it would be possible to
require instead that the labels count as "racial" by virtue of their association
with a hierarchy of "colors," that is, geographically marked (and ranked) bodies.

However, I don't think this captures much of what is at stake in theorizing
racial identity. So I want to offer a different notion (perhaps just to add to the
collection) that I think is better suited to understanding how race is not just an
idea acted upon or acted with, but is deeply embodied. Part of what is motivating
me is the sense that most people whom I'd locate centrally as having a White
identity do not seem to employ the label "White" in the way Appiah's view would
require, since Whites, as the privileged group, tend to think of themselves as
"raceless," and I suspect that most would find it difficult to point to any actions
they perform "as a White person." They don't "identify" as White in the strong
sense in question, but they are White, and I would like to claim that they also
have a White identity.

What worries me most about Appiah's approach is its hyper-cognitivism, particularly its intentionalism. There are important components of racial identity, I

want to argue, that are somatic, largely habitual, regularly unconscious, often ritualized. Our racial identities deeply condition how we live our bodies and relate to other bodies. Individuals are socialized to become embodied subjects, not just rational, cognitive agents; so race and gender socialization isn't just a matter of instilling concepts and indoctrinating beliefs, but are also ways of training the body—training the body to feel, to see, to touch, to fear, to love. I do not claim that our identities are entirely non-cognitive, but to focus entirely on the cognitive, especially the intentional, is to miss the many ways that we unintentionally and unconsciously participate in racism and sexism.

A further concern that arises in philosophical discussion of identity is that there is a tendency to think of identities as something that either one has or one doesn't, and there is a canonical way of having one. Psychologists, however, tend to see identity formation as a developmental process, as something that happens in stages, that can be disrupted, that can be revisited (e.g., Tatum 1997). One also finds in the psychological literature a strong interest in disaggregating the elements of identity; for example, in one study (Cross 1991, 42), Black identity has been theorized as having two main components (personal identity and reference group orientation), the first of which (PI) is broken down into nine elements,[12] the second (RGO) into eight.[13] This disaggregation allows, among other things, that an individual's racial identity can be strong along one axis and not another, and can shift with respect to the balance of elements over time.

Although I think that the philosophical and political uses of the notion of "identity" shouldn't bow to the psychologists as experts on the sense we want or need, it is helpful, nonetheless, to bear in mind that identities may not be all or nothing (e.g., racial identities may come in degrees and have different formations), and that a conception of identity that we happen to be focused on may be only one stage of a much broader developmental process. I have a particular interest in the developmental issues, because I am keen to understand the process by which societies construct individuals with particular race and gender identities, and how those identities are lived and unlived, embodied and disembodied. To make this point more vivid, let me turn to some more personal reflections.

Let me emphasize to begin, however, that I am speaking from my own experience and a very small sample of others, and I don't mean to suggest that the phenomena I describe occur in all adoptive families or all interracial families. Moreover, I certainly want to allow that some of the experiences I describe can happen in other contexts besides transracial parenting, for example, in close interracial friendships and love relationships; further, as our communities

---

[12] Sell-esteem, self-worth, sell-confidence, self-evaluation, interpersonal competence, ego-ideal, personality traits, introversion-extroversion, level of anxiety.

[13] Racial identity, group identity, race awareness, racial ideology, race evaluation, race esteem, race image, racial self-identification.

become more antiracist, the boundaries on racial identity—should there be any—will have very different meanings than I describe here and, in fact, one may find important generational differences already. What interests me, however, are the ways that racial identity can be disrupted and transformed, and how.

Crossing the Color Line

Begin with the body. Although adoptive parents do not have a biological connection to the bodies of their children, like most (at least female) parents, adoptive parents of infants are intimately involved in the physical being of their baby. Parents learn to read the needs and desires of the baby from cries, facial expressions, body language, and in some cases it is as if the patterns of the child's hunger and fatigue are programmed into your own body. You know when to expect hunger; and when they are a little older, you know when to suggest that they use the potty or take a nap. In the case of older adoptees from other countries, the same may happen in the early phases of trying to parent across language barriers. This empathetic extension of body awareness, this attentiveness to the minute signals of another's body, does not in any metaphysically real sense make the other body part of your own. but taking on the needs and desires of another body *as if* your own, perhaps especially if the other's body is marked as different, alters your own body sense, or what some have called (following Lacan) the "imaginary body." Moira Gatens has argued, "[The] psychical image of the body is necessary in order for us to have motility in the world, without which we could not be intentional subjects. The imaginary body is developed, learnt, connected to the body image of others, and is not static" (Gatens 1990, 12). In some cases of transracial parenting I think it would be correct to say that one's "imaginary body," that is, the largely unconscious sense of one's own body, becomes racially confused.[14]

The constant attentiveness to the other's body trains one to read it: one is cued to respond to it. But importantly, as a parent, one comes to love it. The child and future adult to which one will have some person-to-person relationship is not there yet, and so parental love often takes the form of a delight in the body of the infant—its shape, movements, warmth, and so on. The playful and loving engagement of a White parent with a Black infant, however, disrupts what some theorists have called the "racial social geography" (Mills 1999, 52; Frankenberg 1993). Charles Mills develops this notion: "Conceptions of one's White

---

[14] I've heard a story recounted in which a White mother of two Korean-born adoptees returns with them to Korea when they are still children. Upon arriving, she expresses a delight in being somewhere where "everyone looks like us," only registering after receiving some curious and puzzled looks that (in the relevant sense) she doesn't look like those around her. On the "imaginary body" see Gatens (1996), viii and chap. 1: Cornell (1995), chap. 1. Both Gatens and Cornell discuss the gendered imaginary; here I am suggesting that their discussions are relevant to the racial imaginary.

self map a micro-geography of the acceptable routes through racial space . . . imprinted with domination" (Mills 1999, 52). Among other things, such maps "dictate spaces of intimacy and distance" and carry with them proscriptions and punishments for violation. A White parent's daily routine demands these violations. However, the experience of "trespassing" does not give way just to a sense of neutral ground; the experience of holding and physically cherishing one's child can bring the Black body into one's intimate home space—that space where the boundaries of intimacy expand to encompass others.

Interestingly, the effect is not just to alter one's "micro-geography" of race to accommodate one's relationship to one's children; one's entire social map is redrawn.[15] For example, I can find many changes in my physical presence among others: whose faces do I first notice in a group? With whom do I make eye contact? Next to whom do I sit? How close do I stand to others in conversation? Whom do I touch in an affectionate greeting? These questions have different answers than they used to. I am physically at home among African Americans in a way I was not before.

It is hard to lovingly parent a child without finding him or her beautiful—sometimes exceptionally beautiful. For a White parent of a Black child, this process also disrupts the dominant society's "somatic norm image" (Mills 1999, 61; Hoetink 1973). Insofar as the dominant society teaches us the aesthetics of racism—which is common, but fortunately not ubiquitous—Black bodies are regarded as less beautiful than White ones; or at least more typically under the current aesthetics of racism only those Black bodies that fulfill certain White stereotypes of Blacks (the exotic, the "natural") count as beautiful. Mills suggests:

> The norming of the individual also involves a specific norming of the *body*, an aesthetic norming. Judgements of moral worth are obviously

---

[15] It is important to think about the similarities and differences between the White parent of a Black child, and the Black nanny of a White child. I argue here that the "trespassing" involved in a White's allowing a Black child into intimate space disrupts some important aspects of White identity. But it would seem that there is an asymmetry in the case of a Black nanny of a White child: the nanny allows the White child into intimate space, but this arguably does not (in most cases?) disrupt her Black identity. How can I account for this? Although I don't have a full answer, I think attention should devoted to thinking about different modes of intimacy, the specific contours of racial geography, and what counts as racial trespassing: Black caretaking of Whites carries a very different meaning than White caretaking of Blacks. Perry (1998), sec. I. So the operative factors include not just contact and affection, but power relations and the details of the transgressive relationships. Even with this in mind, it isn't clear that the asymmetries can be accounted for in any simple way. Consider, for example, the relationship between Cora (a Black servant) and Jessie (Cora's white employer's daughter) in Langston Hughes's "Cora Unashamed" (Hughes 1962 [1933]. 3–18): "In her heart [Cora] had adopted Jessie." Although the relationship altered Jessie's racial geography to be closer to Cora's, arguably Cora's racial geography was not affected. Is this because the danger to Cora of such a shift would be so clear and present?

conceptually distinct from judgments of aesthetic worth, but there is a
psychological tendency to conflate the two . . . (Mills 1999, 61)

But a White parent's (White) somatic norm image cannot remain intact in the
face of her child's beauty. One can find lengthy conversations on adoption email
lists showing how dramatically the transracial adoptive parent's personal aesthetic does change: White babies come to appear pale, wan, even sickly . . .
there's a magnetic pull to babies of color. Although some have suggested that
such an aesthetic and emotional response to babies that look like your own is a
"conditioned reflex" that parents develop (Register 1990, 45), it isn't just an
infant or child aesthetic that changes. One's response to and "evaluation" of
adult bodies and, in my own case, even my own body—my shape, my skin, my
hair—can change.

Sometimes, through parenting a child of another race, one is drawn into cultural rituals concerning the body. In the case of White parents of Black children,
the most obvious are the rituals of caring for hair and skin. I remember vividly
our first trip to a Black barbershop for Isaac's first haircut, our anxiety at crossing
an important color line. Having moved several times since Isaac joined our
family, each time we've had to negotiate the dynamics of entering with him a
predominantly Black male space. And when Isaac met his birth grandparents for
the first time (we visited them for a long weekend), one of the most important
trips of the weekend was to the barbershop, where we were introduced as family.

The issue of girls' hair is even more laden and contested: a friend and mentor
confided in me shortly after our daughter Zina joined our family that when she
gave birth the second time and the doctor announced, "It's a girl" the very first
thing that went through her mind was, "Oh my gosh, *three* heads of hair to do
each morning!" I had only the vaguest appreciation of what she meant until I
found myself trying to comb out my sleeping (toddler) daughter's hair to find
myself two hours into it with her awake, screaming, and me in tears. But I have
been guided and coached, by friends and acquaintances, by beauty store clerks,
the crowd at the barbershop, by Zina herself. It is not just that I have learned
various techniques and the use of products I never knew existed, but the hours
and hours Zina and I spend together doing her hair have a deep effect on our
relationship, and I'm certain that this would have no correlate with a biological
daughter of mine. Moreover, this experience has affected my relationship with
Black women (both friends and strangers!)—we talk of hair, of the effects of hair
rituals on mother-daughter relationships, of aesthetic and political values represented by hair.

Steve and I master the rituals of the body not just for Isaac and Zina's sake,
but because norms of appearance vary across race, and we as parents are judged
by those norms. Although it is not the case that there is a single unified African
American "culture" or set of appearance norms—these vary by class, region of

the country, even neighborhood—norms of appearance for children, for example, how the hair should be worn, what sorts of clothes and shoes are appropriate, in most contexts are race-specific. These norms are gradually internalized: I feel anxious at not meeting the standards; I judge others by them, and so on. Although I don't uncritically accept the norms of the local Black community in deciding on the appearance or behavior of my children (isn't everyone's relationship to their local norms complex and negotiated?), those norms are ones that I daily consider and respond to.

My own sense of community has dramatically changed. I'm not entirely comfortable anymore in an all-White setting; if I go to a large event that is filled with a sea of White faces, I'm unsettled. Some of the discomfort may come from the wariness that develops when my children are with me in such contexts; I'm concerned about other people's responses to them, their own sense of belonging. This may rub off so that similar feelings arise even when they aren't with me. But it is more than this, for I think it is similar to the discomfort that arises sometimes for those with non-White ancestry who are not distinctively marked physically as a person of color. One carries a background anxiety that someone, not knowing your family, your background, is going to assume that you're White or of a White family and display their racism (Piper 1992; Derricotte 1997). And then you'll have to say something, or not, and you'll have to live with what they said or did. In my own case, it is actually easier for me to bear offensive actions actually directed at me, than to bear them, whether performed knowingly or not, directed at my kids. Racism is no longer just something I find offensive and morally objectionable; I experience it as a personal harm. There is an important sense in which a harm to my kids is a harm to me; by being open to that harm. I am more fully aware of the cost of racial injustice for all of us.[16]

But it isn't just a matter of anxiety around large groups of White strangers; in mixed settings where there is a tendency to group by race or at least by White/non-White. I am drawn to those who aren't White. Often I feel that I have more in common with them, that their life concerns are closer to mine. I am a mother of Black children, my extended family is at least one-third Black. When I want to talk about my kids, their future, our family, there's a lot that I don't think my White friends and family understand.

---

[16] Sharon Rush (2000) suggests the concept of "transformative love" for this experience:

> Transformative love . . . moves beyond racial empathy because it does not depend on Whites imaginations. A person who experiences transformative love literally *feels* some of the direct pain caused by racism. . . . importantly, I am not saying that I *know* what Blacks feel when racism hits them; I don't and never will. I am saying that I used to think empathy was as close as one could get to understanding another's pain. Loving across the color line, I am feeling something that is deeper and more personal than empathetic pain. Ironically, this new feeling, although situated in feeling the pain of racial injustice, is more empowering than empathy when it is mixed with love (169).

Racial Identity Revisited

Is there some way to organize these anecdotes toward a more theoretical account? It appears that together they highlight several different dimensions of racial "identity" we might want to capture:

- unconscious somatic (routine behaviors, skills, and "know-hows")
- unconscious imaginary (unconscious self-image/somatic image)
- tacit cognitive (tacit understandings, tacit evaluations)
- perceptual (perceptional selectivity, recognitional capacities)
- conscious cognitive (fear, apprehension, attraction, sense of community)
- normative (aesthetic judgments, judgments of suitability or appropriateness, internalized or not?)

Many of these, I believe, cannot be captured in the kind of intentionalist account Appiah offers (Rorty and Wong 1990). And plausibly we will need a quite complex model to do justice to all of them. At this point we may have to make do with metaphors that point to a model.

In his book on African American identity, William E. Cross provides a compelling account of the development of racial identity. According to him,

> In a generic sense, one's identity is a maze or map that functions in a multitude of ways to guide and direct exchanges with one's social and material realities. (Cross 1991, 214)

(Remember, the map image was also present in Mills.) Does the image of an internal map help in rethinking racial identity? In the context of feminist work on gender, the image of a map is more often replaced with the image of a script. But the map image might be preferable insofar as it need not be understood linguistically, and may involve a "map" of one's own body. Some may prefer the notion of a "program," since it seems even less cognitive than a map—but it can also invoke the specter of determinism.

There are some advantages to the metaphor of a map: map boundaries vary—what's included and what's not; their design is responsive to different concerns (contrast road maps with topographical maps) and different values (what's central, what's marginal); they vary in scale and effectiveness. Maps also function to guide the body: they are a basis for exercising "know-how," they provide information on the basis of which we can form intentions and act. And yet, the image of a map suggests that one's racial identity is something conscious (to be consulted?) and still rather cognitive (e.g., the idea that one knows how to ride a bike because one employs an internal "map" is not plausible). Moreover, we need racial identity not only to guide social interactions but also to frame in a much more basic way our perceptions and evaluations of ourselves and others. (Yet when navigating in unfamiliar locations, don't we sometimes fail to see what is not included on our map?) Perhaps the solution is to think of "maps" as sometimes tacit and unconscious, sometimes more explicit and conscious. Interestingly, it is plausible that in crossing "the color line," as in transracial adoption, the tacit racial maps are forced into consciousness and made explicit.[17]

Nonetheless, keeping in mind these limitations of the metaphor (and perhaps drawing on Cross's other suggestion of an internal "maze"—a framework or structure of (thought), is there some way to distinguish different racial maps that function as different racial identities? And is there a way to do it without assuming that all Blacks, or all Whites, or all Asians have the same substantive identity, that is, that their identities have the very same content?

Here is a proposal. The account of race I offered above gives some way of identifying the "social and material realities of race" for particular groups: the social and material realities of Whiteness, for example, concern the cultural process of marking the body as apparently descended (predominantly) from Europeans, and the structural privileging of those so marked. Given this, however, we can then focus on those aspects of our overall identity, that is, our broad map—perhaps our atlas?—that guides and directs exchanges with the racial dimension of our lives. So, someone has a White racial identity just in case their map is formed to guide someone marked as White through the social and material realities that are (in that context) characteristic of Whites as a group. More generally, one has an X racial identity just in case their map is formed to guide someone marked as X through the social and material realities that are (in that context) characteristic of Xs as a group.[18] Note that on this account a White person who resists the privileges of Whiteness—and so works from a map that navigates them *around* those privileges, rather than *toward* them—nonetheless has a White identity, for their map is formed in response to (though not necessarily accepting) the material realities of being White. Likewise, a Black person who resists the disadvantages of Blackness—navigating around those disadvantages in any number of different ways—has a Black identity.

Note that this proposal addresses the two concerns raised before: it does not entail that a White racial identity is constructed to sustain White privilege (or

---

[17] So, anticipating what is yet to come, not only is a transracial adoptee's (and transracial parent's) racial identity different from other racial "typicals," by being "mixed," but is also different in being less tacit and taken for granted, and more conscious and navigated. Thanks to Charlotte Witt for helping me think through this point.

[18] Note that this analysis depends on the prior definition of race (or racialized groups) insofar as it presupposes that we can specify the markings and social/material realities of particular races; but because I am offering a focal analysis in which racial identity is the derivative notion and race the central or focal notion, this is not problematic. It is in fact an important feature of the project that the derived notions depend in this way on the central notion.

that the identity of a person of color must be constructed to sustain their subordination); the point is rather that the identity is formed in navigating the social and material impact of one's race. In special cases, one's identity is formed or reformed in navigating the impact of one's loved one's race, or perhaps a race one wants or needs to have; it can also be formed or reformed through a conscious commitment to anti-racism. This account allows that, at least insofar as it is possible to have some critical agency with respect to the maps that guide us, we are not helpless victims of racial socialization. Moreover, it allows that racial identity comes in degrees: we vary in the extent to which our lives and self-understandings are formed in response to the social frameworks of race. Let me conclude this section, however, by saying that although I am hopeful that uses of the notion of a map by Cross and Mills will be helpful in developing further this account of racial identity, I think quite a bit more work needs to be done in explicating it.

"Mixed" Identities

Earlier I suggested that there is at least one sense of identity in which my racial identity has changed tremendously through the experience of parenting Black children. It would be wrong, I think, to say that I am Black, or that I see myself as Black, or that I intend sometimes to act "as a Black person"; I don't even think it is correct to say in a much weaker sense that I have a Black identity. But I do think that my map for navigating the social and material realities of race has adjusted so that I'm now navigating much more often as if my social and material realities are determined by being "marked" as of African descent. As I've emphasized, I am not marked as of African descent. But as a parent of children who are, my day-to-day life is filled with their physical being and social reality, and by extension, the reality of their extended families and their racial community. And their realities have in an important sense become mine.

But it is also the case that there is much of my life in which I continue to rely on old (White) maps, and in which I work to contest and challenge the realities of my Whiteness from the position of being White. As a result, I'm tempted to conclude that my racial identity, in at least the specific sense I've outlined, should count as "mixed." I have, in an important sense, been resocialized by my kids, and although I do not share their "blood," I have "inherited" some aspects of their race.[19]

It may be worth taking a moment, however, to consider different ways in which racial identity might count as "mixed." The term 'mixed' is typically used

---

[19] Thanks to Jackie Stevens for pointing out this inversion.

to refer to individuals whose recent ancestors are differently marked racially. And in contemporary racial politics, there is a movement to affirm the identities of those who count as "mixed" (note the recent change on the U.S. Census to include a biracial category). My point here is not to claim a mixed identity in this sense:

> X has a racially "mixed" identity$_1$, just in case (and to the extent that) X's internal "map" is formed to guide someone marked as of "mixed" ancestry through the social and material realities that structure (in that context) the lives of those of "mixed" ancestry as a group.

But there is an alternative notion that may also, at least in some contexts, characterize those of "mixed" ancestry:

> X has a racially "mixed" identity$_2$ just in case (and to the extent that) X's internal map is substantially fragmented, that is, is formed to guide, in some contexts and along some dimensions, someone marked as of one race, and in other contexts and other dimensions, a person marked as of a different race.

In contexts where it is important to keep our terminology clear, we might speak of racially "mixed" identity (the first sense) and racially "aggregated" (or fragmented?) identity (in the second sense).

But what of my kids? What is their racial identity? Of course the racial identity of young children is a very different matter than the racial identity of adults. But what are the prospects for their racial identities? Given that neither have any prospect for passing as White, they will grow up with the realities of racism and will develop identities that are responsive to those realities. A more pressing question, however, is whether they can, as our children, develop healthy Black identities. Living in a Black neighborhood, attending integrated schools and a Black church, having Black friends and extended family, I think it is almost certain that they will have resources for developing strong and healthy Black identities, that is, it will be possible for them to construct maps that guide them in self-affirming and racial group-affirming ways. But no doubt they will also be sheltered from certain aspects of racism by living with us, they will learn by our example some patterns of social interaction that are responsive to White privilege, and they will develop some primary somatic connections to White bodies. So it is arguable that their identities will also be, at least to some extent, "mixed" (i.e., "aggregated"). But is this a problem? Is this by itself grounds for doubting that transracial adoption is acceptable?

To begin, let me note that there are many different reasons for questioning the practice of transracial adoption, especially as it occurs under current social conditions.[20] Even if one believes that in many cases transracial adoption is permissible, one might object to the child welfare policies and broader context of economic injustice that make transracial adoption appear to be the best option for some birth families and children of color (Perry 1998; cf. Bartholet 1999). It is important to keep in mind that the debate over transracial adoption is not *just* about "identity" but also concerns questions of power (racial, sexual, cultural, and economic) and autonomy (individual, community, and national).

With this in mind, I want to maintain that the fact that transracial adoptees plausibly develop "mixed" ("aggregated") racial identities is not a basis for opposing transracial adoption. First, it is plausible that many middle-class Blacks have similarly "mixed" identities, and it is problematic, I think, to insist that there is a form of "pure" Black (or other raced) identity that should be the ideal for anyone, including adopted children. Second, although there is much of value to be found in racialized communities. I would argue that organizing ourselves (both psychically and as communities) primarily around race—rather than, for example, values, histories, cultures—should not be our long-term objective. It is politically important to recognize that race is real and has a profound effect on our lives, but it is also important to resist being racialized and participating in racial forms of life. (Recall that on my view, race is inherently hierarchical; ethnicity is its non-hierarchical counterpart [see chapter 7 of this volume]). To this end, the formation of "aggregate" or "fragmented" identities is one strategy (of many) for disrupting the embodiment of racial hierarchy and the hegemony of current racial categories. Another (not incompatible) strategy might involve working against racial hierarchy (and so, on my view, against race) in a way that maintains extensional equivalents of racial categories that function more like ethnicities: by re-valuing racialized traits, reconfiguring racialized practices to be more egalitarian, eliminating racist institutions.

But perhaps my argument does not address the real issues. The more common objections to transracial adoption are not to cases in which children of color are part of an integrated community in open adoptions. The cases of greater concern are those in which the parents' identity does not shift, because the ordinary somatic norms and racialized maps are entrenched, or in which the children are given little or no resources for forming the kinds of identity that will enable them to integrate into a Black community (or a community of individuals

---

[20] The term 'transracial adoption,' although sometimes used to refer to international adoptions in which the adoptee's race differs from that of the adoptive parents, tends to be used more often in the context of domestic Black-White adoptions, specifically where the adoptees are Black and the adoptive patents are White. ("Cross-cultural" adoption is more commonly used for international adoptions of children of color by White parents.) Throughout this chapter I have focused on the domestic Black-White "transracial adoption," mostly because I've been explicitly drawing on my personal experience in such a family. However, I intend the points I am making here to apply under the broader sense of the term. See Perry (1998).

"marked" in relevantly similar ways as the child), or to form adequate defenses against racism. This can happen, no doubt about it. And it certainly would be a horror to be brought up by parents whose racial identities cast you, their child, as a racialized Other. If it can be determined in advance that particular prospective adoptive parents would be incapable of a loving attachment to a child of a different race, this is obviously a good reason not to allow a transracial adoption in the particular case. Whether placement would be absolutely precluded would have to depend, I think, on what the other options for the child are. But I hope that the anecdotal evidence offered above shows at least that it is possible for the racial identities of White parents to shift in significant ways, for their racial "maps" to be profoundly altered.[21] This is crucial in order for parents to mirror back to the child the kind of affirmation and love that enables self-love, and that one demands of healthy parenting.[22]

It does seem possible for White parents to overcome some of those aspects of their identity that would make transracial parenting only a poor imitation of same-race parenting; and it does seem possible for White parents to provide a context in which children of color can form healthy racial identities. This is not easy; it is a challenge for any parent (biological or adoptive) of a child of color to raise a child with secure self-esteem and effective strategies to combat racism. White parents of a child of color will no doubt have to depend on the skills and knowledge of the child's racial community in order to succeed.

But a further question is whether and to what extent encouraging the development of a racial identity is a good thing. If, after all, race is a system of dominance and subordination, shouldn't we be attempting to bring up children who do not identify with one race or another, shouldn't we foster color blindness? And aren't transracial families the ideal place to do this?

On the rough account I've given of racial identities, they are responsive to the realities of race and racial subordination/privilege, but they don't necessarily sustain those realities, for the maps we use to navigate our racial positions may also guide us in resisting them. I would argue that it would be irresponsible to bring up kids who will inevitably face racism without the resources to handle it and identities that provide a defense against it. This requires attention to the social differences between White parents and children of color and, I think, over time, requires providing children the tools to construct their own political analysis of those differences. But the sense of race they develop need not be essentialist and can be pragmatic. My hope is that ultimately cultural/ethnic differences will replace racial differences. In the terms of my account, that cultural/ethnic difference will not be marked as a site of subordination and privilege. When that time

---

[21] In fact, Cross cites one study in which the RGO of transracially adopted children at age four is "stronger" and more "Black oriented" that that of then inracially adopted peers. See Cross (1991), 111.

[22] On the development of self-love in a context of injustice, see Thomas (2000).

comes, I think we will no longer have the need of racial identities; that is to say that we will no longer need maps that guide us in navigating the social and material injustices of race. I am deeply committed to bringing about that day, but clearly it is not today, nor will it be tomorrow. Until then, the best I can do is to navigate the racial spaces of my life with maps that support and guide me in resisting racial dominance and subordination, and to offer my children resources for constructing maps that will sustain them in the face of it.

Acknowledgments

For helpful comments and discussion, thanks to Linda Alcoff, Louise Antony, Margaret Burnham, Ann Cudd, Derek Darby, Jorge Garcia, Robert Gooding-Williams, Diana Henderson, Ishani Maitra, Ruth Perry, Jacqueline Stevens, Ásta Sveinsdóttir, Laurence Thomas, Jennifer Uleman, Elizabeth Wood, Stephen Yablo, and members of the audience at colloquia given at Syracuse University, Northwestern University, Smith College, University of Chicago, and the Greater Philadelphia Philosophy Consortium. Special thanks to Charlotte Win and Lawrence Blum, who each wrote extensive comments on an earlier draft.

References

Allen, Anita. (1993) "Does a Child Have a Right to a Certain Identity?" in *Law, Justice, and the State*, ed., Mikael Karlsson, Ólafur Páll Jónsson and Eyja Margrét Brynjarsdóttir. *Rechtstheorie* Supplement 15: 109–19; also in (Ladd 1996).

Appiah, Kwame Anthony. (1992) *In My Father's House*. New York: Oxford University Press.

Appiah, Kwame Anthony, and Amy Gutmann. (1996) *Color Conscious: The Political Morality of Race*. Princeton: Princeton University Press.

Bartholet, Elizabeth. (1992) "Where Do Black Children Belong? The Politics of Race Matching in Adoption." *Reconstruction* 1(4): 22–53.

———. (1993) *Family Bonds: Adoption and the Politics of Parenting*. Boston: Houghton Mifflin Company.

———. (1999) *Nobody's Children: Abuse and Neglect, Foster Drift, and the Adoption Alternative*. Boston: Beacon Press.

Blum, Lawrence. (2001) *"I'm Not a Racist, But . . .": The Moral Quandary of Race*. Ithaca: Cornell University Press.

Cornell, Drucilla. (1995) *The Imaginary Domain: Abortion, Pornography and Sexual Harassment*. New York: Routledge.

Cross, William E., Jr. (1991) *Shades of Black: Diversity in African-American Identity*. Philadelphia: Temple University Press.

Dalmage, Heather M. (2000) *Tripping on the Color Line: Black-White Multiracial Families in a Racially Divided World*. New Brunswick: Rutgers University Press.

Delgado, Richard, and Jean Stefancic. (1997) *Critical White Studies: Looking Behind the Mirror*. Philadelphia: Temple University Press.

Delphy, Christine. (1984) *Closer to Home: A Materialist Analysis of Women's Oppression*, trans. Diana Leonard. Amherst: University of Massachusetts Press.

Derricotte, Toi. (1997) *The Black Notebooks: An Interior Journey*. New York: W.W. Norton.

Frankenberg, Ruth. (1993) *White Women, Race Matters: The Social Construction of Whiteness.* Minneapolis: University of Minnesota Press.

Gatens, Moira. (1996) *Imaginary Bodies: Ethics, Power and Corporeality.* New York: Routledge.

Ginsberg, Elaine K. (1996) *Passing and the Fictions of Identity.* Durham: Duke University Press.

Haslanger, Sally. (2012 [2000]) "Gender and Race: (What) Are They? (What) Do We Want Them To Be?" Chapter 7 of this volume.

Hennessey, Rosemary, and Chrys Ingraham. (1997) *Materialist Feminism: A Reader in Class, Difference, and Women's Lives.* New York: Routledge.

Hoetink, Harry. (1973) *Slavery and Race Relations in the Americas.* New York: Harper Torchbooks.

Howe, Ruth-Arlene. (1995) "Redefining the Transracial Adoption Controversy." *Duke Journal of Gender Law and Policy* 2: 131–164.

Hughes, Langston. (1962) "Cora Unashamed." In *The Ways of White Folks.* New York: Random House.

Ladd, Rosalind Ekman. (1996) *Children's Rights Re-visioned: Philosophical Readings.* Belmont, CA: Wadsworth Publishing Co.

Lazarre, Jane. (1997) *Beyond the Whiteness of Whiteness: Memoir of a White Mother of Black Sons.* Durham: Duke University Press.

McBride, James. (1996) *The Color of Water: A Black Man's Tribute to His White Mother.* New York: Riverhead Books.

National Association of Black Social Workers. (1972) New York: Position Paper: "Transracial Adoption."

———. (1994) Detroit, MI: Position Statement: "Preserving African-American Families."

Neal, Leora. (1996) "The Case Against Transracial Adoption." *Focal Point* 10(1): 18–20.

Omi, Michael, and Howard Winant. *Racial Formation in the United States.* New York: Routledge.

Patton, Sandra Lee. (2000) *Birthmarks: Transracial Adoption in Contemporary America.* New York: New York University Press.

Perry, Twila L. (1993–4) "The Transracial Adoption Controversy: An Analysis of Discourse and Subordination." *Review of Law and Social Change* 21(1): 33–108.

———. (1998) "Transracial and International Adoption: Mothers, Hierarchy, Race, and Feminist Legal Theory." *Yale Journal of Law and Feminism* 10: 101.

Piper, Adrian. (1992) "Passing for White, Passing for Black." *Transition* 58: 4–32.

Register, Cherrie. (1990) *Are Those Kids Yours?* New York: The Free Press.

Rorty, Amelie, and David Wong. (1990) "Aspects of Identity and Agency." In *Identity, Character and Morality*, ed., Owen Flanagan and Amelie Rorty. Cambridge, MA: MIT Press.

Rush, Sharon. (2000) *Loving Across the Color Line: A White Adoptive Mother Learns About Race.* Lanham, MD: Rowman and Littlefield.

Simon, Rita, Howard Altstein, and Marygold Shire Melli. (1994) *The Case for Transracial Adoption.* Lanham, MD: American University Press.

Simon, Rita James, and Rhonda M. Roorda. (2000) *In Their Own Voices: Transracial Adoptees Tell Their Stories.* New York: Columbia University Press.

Stevens, Jacqueline. (1993) "The Politics of Identity: From Property to Empathy," Ph.D. Dissertation, UC-Berkeley.

———. (1999) *Reproducing the State.* Princeton: Princeton University Press.

Stocking, George W. (1993) "The Turn of the Century Concept of Race." *MODERNISM/modernity* 1(1): 4–16.

Tatum, Beverly. (1997) *Why Are All the Black Kids Sitting Together in the Cafeteria? and Other Conversations About Race.* New York: Basic Books.

Thomas, Laurence. (2000) "Moral Health: Living in an Unjust World." In *African-Americans and Social Justice: Essays in Honor of Bernard Boxill*, ed., Tommy L. Lott. Lanham, MD: Rowman and Littlefield.

Thompson, Becky. (2000) *Mothering Without a Compass: White Mother's Love, Black Son's Courage.* Minneapolis: University of Minnesota Press.

Williams, Gregory Howard. (1995) *Life on the Color Line: The True Story of a White Boy Who Discovered He Was Black.* New York: Penguin Books.

Young, Iris. (1990) *Justice and the Politics of Difference.* Princeton: Princeton University Press.

10

A Social Constructionist Analysis of Race

In the contemporary world the term 'race'[1] is used widely both in American popular culture and in a variety of academic disciplines, and its meanings evolve in
different ways in response to the pressures in each. This chapter brings philosophical analysis to bear on the debate among geneticists, humanists, and social
scientists over the meaning of the term 'race' in a genomic age—a debate that
extends beyond our immediate disciplines and into the public domain. What are
the genuine disagreements and what are only apparent disagreements due to
the use of different vocabularies? Why does it matter which of the positions we
accept? What sort of evidence is relevant to adjudicating the claims? How should
we go about resolving the controversy? In answering these questions, I develop
a realist, social constructionist account of race. I recommend this as an account
that does justice to the meanings of 'race' in many ordinary contexts and also as
an account that serves widely shared antiracist goals.

I argue that in debates over the meaning of 'race' in a genomic age we are
better served by shifting from the metaphysical/scientific question: Is race real?
to the political question: What concept of race should we employ in order to
achieve the antiracist goals we share? To answer this question, I contend that
we must also look at the semantics of the term 'race' in public—specifically
nonscientific—discourse, for this popular notion of race is what we use to frame
our identities and political commitments. My argument is based on a view of
language as a collective social practice rather than a set of terms stipulated by an
authority. On this view, the issue is not whether groups of people—experts in a
particular field or folk in a neighborhood—are entitled to use the term 'race' for
the divisions in which they are interested. Of course they are: there are no

---

[1] In this chapter, I follow the philosopher's convention of distinguishing between use of an expression and mention of it. When a word is mentioned, that is, when the subject matter is the word
or term and not what the word or term usually means it is enclosed in single quotes. 'Race' in single
quotes refers to the word itself; without the quotes it has the conventional meaning. Double quotes
are used for quotation of another's text or as scare quotes. Scare quotes indicate that the author is
distancing himself or herself from the choice of term and is relying on a known, potentially problematic, usage.

Ha, tell the French that [handwritten margin note]

"Language Police," and people can appropriate and transform language for their own purposes. Similarly, what 'race' means outside of the stipulated meaning operative in the biology lab is not up to the biologist.[2] Just as there is no Language Police to judge that the biologist is wrong to use the term 'race' in a particular way, likewise there is no Language Police or even Language Legislature to determine what a term will mean in public discourse. Language evolves in complicated and subtle ways. Thus, l argue that anyone using the term 'race' in public life should be aware of its ordinary meanings; and if we want to change or refine the concept of race, we should be aware of where we are starting from as well as the normative basis for where we want to go.

Race Eliminativism, Race Constructionism, and Race Naturalism

(A.306 [handwritten margin note])

(P.385 [handwritten margin note])

Questions of what the term 'race' means and whether race is *real* have become tied up with different political goals and strategies for achieving them.[3] Race *eliminativists* maintain that talk of races is no better than talk of witches or ghosts, and in order to achieve racial justice we should stop participating in a fiction that underwrites racism (Appiah, 1996; Zack, 2002). Race *constructionists* argue that races are real, but that they are social rather than natural groups; on the constructionist view, racial justice requires us to recognize the mechanisms of racial formation so that we can undo their damage (Omi and Winant, 1994; Mills, 1997; Haslanger 2012 [2000]). Present-day race *naturalists* agree with the eliminativists and constructionists that races are not what they were once thought to be—they are not groups with a common racial essence that explains a broad range of psychological and moral features of the group's members—but they disagree with both other views in maintaining that the human species can be divided on the basis of natural (biological, genetic, physical) features into a small set of groups that correspond to the ordinary racial divisions (Kitcher, 1999; Andreason, 2000; Rosenberg et al., 2002; Mountain & Risch, 2004), *and* that this natural division is socially and politically important for the purposes of achieving racial justice, for example, by enabling us to address racially divergent

Pres. day contrast [handwritten margin note]

---

[2] Note that the term 'race' did not originate as a biological term but plausibly has religious/metaphysical origins (Stocking, 1994).

[3] I sometimes frame the question as whether race is real as opposed to whether races exist because sometimes the debate is muddled by those who want to allow that *races exist* (e.g., "in the head" or "in society") but that they aren't *real*. As I see it, if races exist only in the head, then they don't exist (just as people may believe in unicorns, but this is not to say that they exist); and if races exist in society, then they do exist, since social categories are real. But to avoid potential disagreements over what it means to say that something exists, I've framed the question instead as whether races are real.

medical needs (Risch, Burchard, Ziv, & Tang., 2002; cf. Lee, Mountain, & Koenig, 2001).

Although the choice between these approaches to race may seem to some as "just semantics" (in the pejorative sense), the debate plays a role in framing and evaluating social policy. For example, consider the FDA approval of BiDil, a drug to treat heart failure, for Black[4] patients. Eliminativists, naturalists, and constructionists will have very different approaches to this decision. For example, if, as the eliminativist argues, race is not real, then the approval of BiDil for Blacks is as (un)justified as the approval of BiDil for witches. The category *Black*, on the eliminativist view, is a fiction projected onto the world, and the FDA has done social harm by reinforcing the illusion that the category is scientifically grounded. In contrast, a race naturalist could support the FDA's action—or if not in the particular case of BiDil, in a similar sort of case—arguing that racial categories map biological categories that may have significant health consequences and should not be ignored in developing new medicines. On the naturalist's view, it is as politically important for the FDA to address the biological implications of race differences as it is to address the biological implications of any other genetic differences that have medical implications; in fact, to ignore the real differences between the races would be a form of injustice. The constructionist would disagree with the naturalist that there are natural differences between the races that warrant different medical treatment, but could allow that the social differences race makes must be taken into account in deciding a course of treatment or the approval of a drug. Although disagreeing with the eliminativist's rejection of race, the constructionist would be sympathetic with the eliminativist's worry that the FDA has reinforced a pernicious belief in the natural basis for racial categories. But how should we adjudicate these different positions?

Natural and Social Kinds

Some are tempted to view the debate between eliminativists, constructionists, and naturalists as (primarily) a metaphysical/scientific debate about the reality of race. On this construal, the question is whether races are natural kinds. Eliminativists and naturalists agree that races, *if they exist*, are natural kinds. Naturalists hold that races are a natural division of human beings, that is, a division which rests entirely on natural properties of things; eliminativists deny it. Constructionists reject the claim that races are natural kinds, that is, they allow that races are kinds, but hold that the division rests at least partly on social properties (being viewed and treated in a certain way, functioning in a certain

---

[4] In this chapter, upper case is used for names of races, that is, Black and White; lower case is used for color terms.

social role, etc.) of the things in question. This requires understanding social kinds as just as fully real as natural kinds (see table 10.1). There are semantic issues: What does 'race' mean? Is it part of the *meaning* of 'race' that races are natural kinds? There are scientific/metaphysical issues: Is race real? Do races exist? And there are moral/political issues: How should we, as a nation, address the problem of racial injustice?

Following Aristotle, the term 'kind' is sometimes used to capture the classification of objects in terms of their *essence*. On this view, objects—genuine objects as opposed to heaps or weird scattered bits and parts of things—are distinctive because they have an essence. The rose bush in my garden is an object because of its rose-essence; the scattering of petals, leaves, dirt, pebbles, gum wrappers, and fertilizer under it is not an object because it has no essence. The essence of the individual is (roughly) that set of properties without which the object cannot exist and which serves in some important way in explanations of the object's characteristic behavior.

Are *races* Aristotelian *kinds*? Traditional racialists would probably think they are (Appiah, 1993, chap. 2): Whites and Blacks have different natures that explain their characteristic behaviors, and this nature is essential to who they are. However, this view is not credible at this point in time. It would be implausible to claim that an individual could not have existed as a member of a different race. In fact, people can travel from the United States to Brazil and function socially as a member of a different race; and features as superficial as skin color, hair texture, and eye shape are clearly not essential (they, too, can be changed with chemicals and surgery). If one thinks that one has one's entire genetic makeup necessarily (something with even a slight difference from your genetic makeup wouldn't be you) then there might be a case to be made for the claim that one could not have been a member of a different race. But essences are supposed to be rich explanatory resources for explaining the characteristic behavior of the individual and there is no support for the idea that there are racial essences of this sort.

Locke has a different account of kinds than Aristotle. For Locke, kinds are highly unified, but not by virtue of the essences of their members So, for example, red things constitute a kind (their unity consists in their all being red),

Table 10.1 **Sources of Agreement and Disagreement**

	Eliminativism	Constructivism	Naturalism
Is race a natural category?	Yes	No	Yes
Is race real?	No	Yes	Yes

even though redness is seldom an essential property of the things that have it. On a Lockean view, the main contrast to consider is between "real" kinds and "nominal" kinds. Real kinds are those types unified by properties that play a fundamental role in the causal structure of the world and, ideally, in our explanations. Nominal kinds are types unified by properties that happen to be useful or interesting to us. Whether there are real kinds corresponding to (and underlying) the nominal kinds we pick out is an open question. On this view *concepts* or *properties* (and, contra Aristotle, not individuals) have essences.

Are races Lockean kinds? Can we give necessary and sufficient conditions for being a member of a particular race? This question actually opens a long debate between realists and nominalists that (fortunately!) we don't need to get into about whether one can *ever* give necessary and sufficient conditions for membership in a kind. If our goal is to do justice to our pre-theoretical judgments about membership in a given race, then there are reasons to doubt whether races are definable in the sense required. However, if we stipulate a definition, either as a nominal essence to pick out a group of things we are interested in, or in postulating explanatory categories as part of a theoretical project, then the definition will give the Lockean essence of the kind.

Note that on both the Lockean and Aristotelian accounts, kinds or types may be either social or natural. Types are *natural* if the properties that constitute their unity are natural, and *social* if the properties are social. It is notoriously difficult to characterize the distinction between natural and social properties (and relations), but for our purposes we could take natural properties of things to be those studied by the natural sciences and the social properties to be those studied by the social sciences. So the set of quarks is a natural type; the set of adoptive families is a social type. Plausibly, there is *some* degree of unity in the members of a race, for example, one could list a cluster of physical, historical, and sociological properties associated with each race such that members of the race share a weighted subset of those properties. If for a category to be real is just for it to pick out a set with some loose connection among the members, then there is a sense in which, on any non-empty construal of race, races are real. It takes very little to be an objective type in this sense.

Can "Facts" Settle the Matter?

Some may find it tempting to respond that to resolve this issue, we just need to look at the facts: either there are races or there aren't; either races are social or they aren't. One significant problem with this approach is that we can determine whether there "really are" races only if the term 'race' has a specified meaning; and what it means—at least for the purposes at hand—is part of the question. Consider a different example. Suppose we ask, What percentage of the U.S. population is on welfare? Well, it depends on what you mean by 'welfare.' Do we include only those who receive TANF (Temporary Assistance for Needy Families, the successor to "welfare as we know it")? Or do we include those who receive social security benefits? What about "corporate welfare" in the form of tax breaks? We ask, Is race real? Well, it depends on what you mean by 'race.'

This is not to say that the controversy will dissipate if we only would make clear our stipulated definitions. If I maintain that 99% of the U.S. population is on welfare, then presumably I am using a non-mainstream definition of 'welfare.' For me to justify my claim it would not be sufficient to say that given *my* meanings, I've uttered a truth, if *my* meaning of 'welfare' is idiosyncratic and beside the point. But it may be that what I say is true and especially useful in the context of the debate in which I engage. In such a case the task of justification would be to show that my definition of 'welfare' better tracks what is important for the purposes at hand (Anderson, 1995).

The reason why the facts don't settle the issue is that simply establishing that there is a fact of the matter about something doesn't establish that it is a significant or relevant fact for the purposes at hand. Suppose I say that I'm going to use the term 'White' for all and only those who have blonde hair. Whites, then, are a natural kind. Turn now to the public context in which we are discussing, say, affirmative action. If I argue that non-Whites should be given preferential treatment because of historical injustice, my claim sounds familiar, but the category I am using is not the most apt for considering the justice of affirmative action. The fact that 'White,' as I defined the term, captures a real kind, even combined with the truth that (some) non-Whites have been treated unjustly, does not usefully further the debate because I have chosen categories for addressing the problem that are ill-suited to the task (see Anderson, 1995). Truth alone does not set us free; there are too many irrelevant and misleading truths. The choice of truths must—at the very least—be insightful and judicious.

Lessons from Philosophy of Language

So it would seem that the next step in our inquiry should be to adjudicate what the term 'race' means. As I mentioned before, there need not be only one meaning for the term. But for the purposes of engaging in discussion concerning matters of biological research on race, it would be useful to have a shared understanding of race. And to achieve this, we should have a sense of what the folk concept of race is. This is not because I believe that we should honor the folk concept as the *true meaning*, but because in any context where communication is fraught, it is useful to understand the competing meanings at issue. If there is a socially dominant understanding of race, then even if we want to recommend a change in the concept, we should know what it is.

This suggests that we must not simply resolve semantical disagreements in order to make headway in the debate. We must look more closely at our purposes and how we might achieve them: should we as biologists social scientists, scholars, citizens, and as people who care about social justice frame our dialogue— our narratives of explanation, justification, and justice—in terms of race? And if so, then what concept of race should we employ? These questions can be broken down further:

- Is there currently a single or dominant public meaning (or folk concept) of 'race'? If so, what is it (or what are the contenders)?
- In the quest for social justice, for example, in debating health policy, do we need the concept of race? For what purposes? If so, can we make do with the folk concept or should we modify the concept?
- If the folk concept of race is not an adequate tool to help achieve social justice (if, perhaps, it is even a barrier), then how should we proceed?

In what follows, I will suggest that an answer to the first question, in particular, is not straightforward; and yet if we are going to speak meaningfully in a public context, then we need to recognize the force and implications of our words in that context. In science it is commonplace to define or redefine terms in whatever way suits the theory at hand (e.g., 'atom', 'mass,' 'energy,' 'cell,'), without much concern with the ordinary meanings these terms have or the political import of stipulating new meanings. But semantic authority cannot be granted to the biologist in considering a term like 'race' that plays such a major role in our self-understandings and political life.

In undertaking conceptual analysis of, say, *Fness* (in our case, *Fness* might be 'Blackness,' 'Whiteness,' 'Asianness,' or the broader category, 'race'), it is typically assumed that it is enough to ask competent users of English under what conditions someone is *F*. After all, if competent speakers know the meaning of their terms, then all that is needed is linguistic competence to analyze them. However, this stance is not plausible if one takes into account arguments in philosophy of language over the past 30 years that call into question the assumption that competent users of a term have full knowledge of what the term means. This assumption in particular is challenged by the tradition of semantic externalism. Externalists maintain that the content of what we think and mean is determined not simply by what we think or intend, but at least in part by facts about our social and natural environment. For example, one can be competent in using the term 'water' without knowing that water is H_2O; one can use the term 'elm' meaningfully even if one cannot tell the difference between a beech and an elm. When I say, 'Elm trees are deciduous' I say something meaningful and true, even though I couldn't identify an elm or give any clear description of one. The externalist holds that these sorts of cases point to two features of language that the traditional picture ignored: *reference magnetism* and *the division of linguistic labor*. These ideas can be expressed *very* roughly as follows:

> *Reference magnetism* (Putnam, 1973, 1975; Kripke, 1980): type-terms (such as general nouns) pick out a type, whether or not we can state the essence of the type, by virtue of the fact that their meaning is determined by a selection of paradigms together with an implicit extension of one's reference to things of the same type as the paradigms. For example, the marketing department and the R&D department of a toy manufacturer have a meeting. R&D has produced a new "squishy, stretchy substance that can transform into almost anything," and they present a sample. The marketing director points to it and says, "Let's call the stuff 'Floam.'" Bingo. 'Floam' now refers to a whole kind of stuff, some of which has not yet been produced, and the ingredients of which are totally mysterious. Which stuff? Presumably, 'floam' refers to the most unified objective type of which the sample is a paradigm instance. This example is artificial, but the phenomenon of reference magnetism is ubiquitous.
>
> *Division of linguistic labor* (Putnam, 1975, Burge, 1979): the meaning of a term used by a speaker is determined at least in part by the linguistic usage in his or her community, including, if necessary, expert usage. For example, before the invention of chemistry, people used the term 'water' to refer to H_2O because the kind H_2O was a "reference magnet" for their term. However, in cases where one cannot even produce a paradigm, for example, when I can't tell the difference between a beech and an elm, my use of the term 'elm' gets its meaning not from *my* paradigms, but from the linguistic labor of others in my community, including botanists. The division of linguistic labor may also play an important role if I have idiosyncratic paradigms. The idea is that what I mean in using a term such as 'elm' or 'arthritis' is not just a matter of what is in my head, but is determined by a process that involves others in my language community.

Most commonly, externalist analyses have been employed to provide *naturalistic* accounts of knowledge, mind, and so on; these seek to discover the *natural* (non-social) kind within which the selected paradigms fall. But it is possible to pursue an externalist approach within a social domain as long as one allows that there are social kinds or types, such as 'democracy' and 'genocide,' or ethical terms such as 'responsibility' and 'autonomy.'

Of course, an externalist analysis of a social term cannot be done in a mechanical way and may require sophisticated social theory both to select the paradigms and analyze their commonality. It may take sophisticated social theory to determine what 'parent' or 'Black' means. In an externalist project, intuitions about the conditions for applying the concept should be considered secondary to what the cases in fact have in common: as we learn more about the paradigms, we learn more about our concepts.

Is Race a Fiction?

If we are externalists about meaning, which is the approach I am recommending, then the eliminativist about race is in a very weak position. We can all confidently identify members of different races. Martin Luther King, Nelson Mandela, Malcolm X, Toni Morrison, Oprah Winfrey, W. E. B. DuBois, Kofi Annan, Thabo Mbeki (insert here your choice of various friends and relatives) are Black. George Bush, Arnold Schwarzenegger, Margaret Thatcher, Golda Meir, Bertrand Russell, Vincent Van Gogh (insert here your choice of various friends and relatives) are White. Similar lists can be constructed for Asians, Latino/as, and other groups usually considered races. But if this is the case, then the terms 'Black' and 'White' pick out the best fitting and most unified objective type of which the members of the list are paradigms—even if I can't describe the type or my beliefs about what the paradigms have in common are false. What that type is is not yet clear. But given how weak the constraints on an objective type are, undoubtedly there is one. The term 'race' then, picks out the more generic type or category of which 'Black,' 'White,' and so on are subtypes.

I believe that these considerations about meaning show that eliminativism is the wrong approach to understand the public or folk meaning of 'race.' It is compatible with this that we should work to change the public meaning of 'race' in keeping with the eliminativist strategy so that it becomes clear that the racial terms are vacuous. In other words, eliminativism may still be a goal for which to aim. But as things stand now, race is something we *see* in the faces and bodies of others; we are surrounded by cases that function to us as paradigms and ground our meanings. The eliminativist's suggestion that "our" concept of race is vacuous is not supported by the observation that we tend to think of races as natural kinds because the meaning of 'race' isn't determined simply by what we think races are. So the eliminativist project needs to be rethought.

Race as a Social Kind

Recent work in race genetics and biology leads me to believe that there are no very unified natural types that are good candidates for the reference of race terms, where the reference of these terms is fixed by generally acceptable paradigms of each race (see Feldman and Lewontin, 2008; Bolnick, 2008). What "we" in public discourse call race is not a natural or genetic category. Rather, the ordinary term 'race' picks out a social type, that is, the objective type that attracts our reference is unified by social features rather than natural ones.[5] Let me sketch one suggestion along these lines.

Feminists define 'man' and 'woman' as *genders* rather than sexes (male and female). The slogan for understanding gender is this: gender is the social meaning of sex. It is a virtue, I believe, of this account of gender that, depending on context, one's sex may have a very different meaning and it may position one in very different kinds of hierarchies. The variation will clearly occur from culture to culture (and subculture to subculture); so, for example, to be a Chinese woman of the 1790s, a Brazilian woman of the 1890s, or an American woman of the 1990s may involve very different social relations and very different kinds of oppression. Yet on the analysis suggested, these groups count as women insofar as their subordinate positions are marked and justified by reference to (female) sex.

With this strategy of defining gender in mind, let's consider whether it will help in giving some content to the social category of race. The feminist approach recommends this: don't look for an analysis that assumes that the category's meaning is always and everywhere the same; rather, consider how members of the group are *socially positioned* and what *physical markers* serve as a supposed basis for such treatment.[6]

I use the term 'color' to refer to the (contextually variable) physical markers of race, just as the term 'sex' to refers to the (contextually variable) physical markers of gender. "Color" is more than just skin tone: racial markers may include eye, nose, and lip shape, hair texture, physique, and so on. Virtually any cluster of physical traits that are assumed to be inherited from those who occupy a specific geographical region or regions can count as "color." (Although the term 'people of color' is used to refer to non-Whites, the markers of "Whiteness" also count

---

[5] It is a controversial issue as to what counts as a "social fact" and in what sense the social is "constructed." In my discussion I assume very roughly that social facts are "interpersonal" facts or facts that supervene on such facts. So, simplifying considerably, *I am Deb's friend* is a social fact because it supervenes on a certain base set of interpersonal actions and attitudes. Others, such as John Searle (1995), have much higher demands on what counts as a social fact, including controversial "we-intentions," assignment of function, and the generation of constitutive rules. These elements are more plausibly required in creating institutional facts or conventional facts (his standard example is the social constitution of money); it is too demanding to capture much of ordinary, informal social life. E.g., we can have coordinated intentions without them being "we-intentions"; things can have a social function even if they aren't assigned it; and social kind membership isn't always governed by rules. Searle's analysis is not well-suited to the project of analyzing gender and race, which are the heart and soul (so to speak!) of ordinary, informal social life.

[6] This analysis is part of a larger project aiming to identify sites of structural subordination; other projects, such as those undertaking to define a basis for racial or ethnic identity (McPherson and Shelby, 2004) or those offering reconstructions of the notion of race (Gooding-Williams, 1998; Alcoff, 2000), are not incompatible with this.

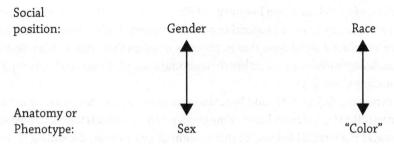

Figure 10.1 Meanings given to the body generate social positions, which, in turn, produce new interpretations of (and sometimes modifications of) the body.

as "color.") Borrowing the slogan used before, we can say then that race is the social meaning of the "colored," that is, geographically marked, body (see figure 10.1).

To develop this briefly, consider the following account.[7] A group is *racialized* (in context C) if and only if (by definition) its members are (or would be) socially positioned as subordinate or privileged along some dimension (economic, political, legal, social, etc.) (in C), and the group is "marked" as a target for this treatment by observed or imagined bodily features presumed to be evidence of ancestral links to a certain geographical region.

In other words, races are those groups demarcated by the geographical associations accompanying perceived body type when those associations take on evaluative significance concerning how members of the group should be viewed and treated. Given this definition, we can say that S is of the White (Black, Asian, etc.) race (in C) if and only if (by definition) Whites (Blacks, Asians, etc.) are a racialized group (in C) and S is a member.[8]

Note that on this view, whether a group is racialized, and so how and whether an individual is raced, will depend on context. For example, Blacks, Whites, Asians, and Native Americans are currently racialized in the United States insofar as these are all groups defined in terms of physical features associated with places of origin and membership in the group functions as a basis for evaluation. However, some groups are not currently racialized in the United States but have been so in the past and possibly could be again (and in other contexts are), for example, the Italians, the Germans, the Irish.

I offer the constructionist analysis of 'race' just sketched as one that captures our ordinary use of the term. The social constructionist analysis of race presents

[7] On this I am deeply indebted to Stevens (1999, chap. 4) and Omi and Winant (1994, esp. pp. 53–61). I develop this definition more fully in Haslanger 2012 [2000]. Note that if this definition is adequate, then races are not only objective types but are Lockean (social) kinds.

[8] As in the case of gender, I recommend that we view membership in a racial/ethnic group in terms of how one is viewed and treated *regularly and for the most part* in the context in question; one could distinguish *being* a member of a given race from *functioning* as one in terms of the degree of entrenchment in the racialized social position.

the strongest conceptual framework and consensus point for cross-disciplinary and public discussions around race and genetics research. I believe it also provides important resources in politically addressing the problem of racial injustice; specifically, it gives us a way of capturing those groups that have suffered injustice due to assumptions about "color." These are groups that matter if we are going to achieve social justice. Moreover, we already use racial terms in ways that seem to track these groups (or groups very close to them). So by adopting the constructionist account we can proceed politically without recommending a semantic revolution as well.

Conclusion

I have argued that the debate between eliminativists, constructionists, and naturalists about race should be understood as not simply about whether races are real or whether they are natural kinds, but about how we should understand race and employ racial concepts in our public discourse. I have argued that the debate cannot be settled simply by considering "the facts" of genetics, but requires close attention to the language of 'race' and 'kind' as well as contemporary racial politics. With this reframing of the question, I have argued that our ordinary concept of race is of a social kind and for a particular analysis of race that highlights social hierarchy. Given the history of racial injustice and the need to address this history, it is important for us to attend publicly to those who have suffered from what we might call *color hierarchy*. Since we have reason to track racial injustice, and since the naturalist and eliminativist accounts do not come close to matching our ordinary term for 'race,' constructionism about race is currently the best candidate of the three views considered. My conclusions are qualified, however. I do not argue that my account of race captures *the meaning of 'race'* (or what we should mean by 'race') for all time and in all contexts; it would be foolhardy for anyone to attempt that. More specifically, it would reveal a misunderstanding of how language, as a collective social practice, works.

References

Alcoff, L. M. (2000). Is latino/a identity a racial identity? In J.E. Gracia and P. De Grieff (Eds.), *Hispanics and Latinos in the United States: Ethnicity, race, and rights* (pp. 23–44). New York: Routledge.

Anderson, E.S. (1995). Knowledge, human interests, and objectivity in feminist episte mology. *Philosophical Topics*, 23, 27–58.

Andreason, R. (2000). Race: Biological reality or social construct? *Philosophy of Science*, 67(supplementary volume), S653–66.

Appiah, K. A. (1993). *In my father's house*. New York: Oxford University Press.

Appiah, K. A. (1996). Race, culture, identity: Misunderstood connections. In K. A. Appiah and A. Gutmann (Eds.), *Color conscious: The political morality of race* (pp. 30–105). Princeton: Princeton University Press.

Armstrong, D. (1989). *Universals: An opinionated introduction.* Boulder, CO: Westview Press.

Bolnick, D.A. (2008 [this volume]). Individual ancestry inference and the reification of race as a biological phenomenon. In B.A. Koenig, S.S. -J. Lee, & S.S. Richardson (Eds.), *Revisiting race in a genomic age* (pp. 70–85). New Brunswick, NJ: Rutgers University Press.

Burge, T. (1979). Individualism and the mental. *Midwest Studies in Philosophy,* 4, 73–121.

Burge, T. (1986). Intellectual norms and foundations of mind. *Journal of Philosophy,* 83, 697–720.

Delphy, C. (1984/1970). *Close to home: A materialist analysis of women's oppression* (D. Leonard, Trans.). Amherst: University of Massachusetts Press.

Feldman, M.W., & Lewontin, R.C. (2008). Race, ancestry, and medicine. In B.A. Koenig, S.S. -J. Lee, & S.S. Richardson (Eds.), *Revisiting race in a genomic age* (pp. 89–101). New Brunswick, NJ: Rutgers University Press.

Gooding-Williams, R. (1998). Race, multiculturalism, and democracy. *Constellations,* 5,18–41.

Hartmann, H. (1981). The unhappy marriage of Marxism and feminism: Towards a more progressive union. In Lydia Sargent (Ed.), *Women and revolution* (pp. 1–42). Cambridge, MA: South End Press.

Haslanger, S. (2012 [1995]). Ontology and social construction. Chapter 2 of this volume.

Haslanger, S. (2012 [2000]). Gender and race: (What) are they? (What) do we want them to be? Chapter 7 of this volume.

Haslanger, S. (2012 [2003]). Social construction: The "debunking" project. Chapter 3 of this volume.

Kitcher, P. (1999). Race, ethnicity, biology, culture. In L. Harris (Ed.), *Racism* (pp. 87–117). New York: Humanity Books.

Kripke, S. (1980). *Naming and necessity.* Cambridge, MA: Harvard University Press.

Lee, S. S.-J., Mountain, J., & Koenig, B. (2001). The meanings of "race" in the new genomics: Implications for health disparities research. *Yale Journal of Health Policy, Law and Ethics,* 1, 33–75.

MacKinnon, C. (1987). *Feminism unmodified.* Cambridge, MA: Harvard University Press.

McPherson, L., & Shelby, T. (2004). Blackness and blood: Interpreting African-American identity. *Philosophy & Public Affairs,* 32, 171–92.

Mills, C. (1997). *The racial contract.* Ithaca, NY: Cornell University Press.

Mountain, J. L., & Risch, N. (2004). Assessing genetic contributions to phenotypic differences among "racial" and "ethnic" groups. *Nature Genetics,* 36 (II Suppl) S48–53.

Omi, M., & Winant, H. (1994). *Racial formation.* In M. Omi and H. Winant, *Racial formation in the United States* (pp. 53–76). New York: Routledge.

Putnam, H. (1973). Meaning and reference. *The Journal of Philosophy,* 70, 699–711.

Putnam, H. (1975). The meaning of "meaning." In H. Putnam, *Mind, language, and reality,* Vol. 2 of *Philosophical Papers* (pp. 215–71). Cambridge, MA: Cambridge University Press.

Risch, N. Burchard, E., Ziv, E., & Tang, H. (2002). Categorization of humans in biomedical research: Genes, race, and disease. *Genome Biology,* 3, 2007. 1–2007. 12

Rosenberg, N. A., Pritchard, J. K., Weber, J. L., Cann, H. M., Kidd, K. K., Zhivotovsky, L. A., et al. (2002). Genetic structure of human populations. *Science,* 298, 2381–85.

Scott, J. (1996). Gender: A useful category of historical analysis. In J. Scott (Ed.), *Feminism and History* (pp. 152–80). Oxford: Oxford University Press.

Searle, J. (1995). *The construction of social reality.* New York: The Free Press.

Stevens, J. (1999). *Reproducing the state.* Princeton, NJ: Princeton University Press.

Stocking, G. (1994). The turn-of-the-century concept of race. *Modernism/Modernity,* 1(I), 4–16.

Wittig, M. (1992). *The straight mind and other essays.* Boston: Beacon Press.

Zack, N. (2002). *Philosophy of science and race.* New York: Routledge.

11

Oppressions

Racial and Other

The term 'racism' is used in many different ways and, at least in the contemporary United States, many things count as racist: racial hatred and racial contempt (whether overt or covert), explicit discrimination, subtle exclusion, unintentional evasion, cultural bias in favor of Eurocentric norms of behavior and beauty, negative racial stereotypes portrayed in the media, arts, and public discourse. The list could go on. My focus in this chapter will be on racial oppression. The phenomena of racial oppression in general and White supremacy in particular are ones that anyone concerned with racial justice has reason to attend to, regardless of disagreements about how to use the term 'racism.'[1] I believe that racial oppression is counted as a form of racism both in popular discourse and in some academic contexts. So an inquiry into what racism is and how we should combat it reasonably includes attention to racial oppression.

What is racial oppression? Group domination is caused and perpetuated in many different ways. Presumably, in order to understand racial oppression, we should consider oppression in general, as well as historically specific instances where racial injustice is at issue. I believe that an adequate understanding of racism cannot be achieved a priori, but depends on a close analysis of historical examples where race is a factor in the explanation of injustice. Philosophical tools are important, especially at points where the analysis becomes normative, but work done by historians, social scientists, legal theorists, and literary theorists is

---

[1] I prefer to capitalize the names of races ('White,' 'Black,' 'Latina/o,' 'Asian'). Doing so is warranted, I believe, in order to be consistent between races that are referred to using color terms and those referred to using names of continents, to highlight the difference between ordinary color words and the homonymous use of such words as names for some races, and to highlight the artificiality of race in contrast to the apparent naturalness of color (or geography). Moreover, in other work I use the lowercase terms 'black,' 'white,' 'latina/o,' and 'asian' to refer to body schemas associated with races and reserve the uppercase terms for racialized groups; making this distinction between "color" and race explicit is, I believe, theoretically important.

invaluable in revealing the sometimes subtle ways that injustice is woven through our social life.

This chapter is an attempt to explicate how racism and other forms of social injustice can be seen as structural, and as crucially concerned with power. Work on race and racism in philosophy often focuses on the individual (Piper 1990, Piper 1993, Appiah 1990; cf. Ezorsky 1991); and some argue that the primary wrong of racism is individual and structural or institutional racism is derivative (Garcia 1996,1997a, 1999). In the first part of the chapter I develop a contrast between what I will call 'structural' oppression and 'agent' oppression and discuss briefly the normative basis for the wrong of each. In the second part I consider the group component of group oppression. In particular, I ask what link between the group—the race, sex, class, and so on—and the injustice should define group oppression. I will argue that group oppression does not require that the group be explicitly targeted by the unjust institution, but more than just an accidental correlation between the members of the group and those unjustly treated is necessary. My goal is to articulate a middle ground between these two options.

1. Oppression: Agents and Structures

What is oppression? The notion of oppression has been used to point to the ways in which groups of individuals are systematically and unfairly disadvantaged within a particular social structure.[2] This said, the notion of oppression remains elusive. Let's start with a brief overview of some circumstances that might reasonably be considered oppressive in order to explore the basic grammar of oppression.

The most familiar notion of oppression is one that implies an agent or agents misusing their power to harm another.[3] Drawing on this, we might begin with the idea that x oppresses y just in case x is an agent with some power or authority and that y is suffering unjustly or wrongfully under x or as a result of x's unjust exercise of power. This leaves open what sort of power is exercised, and whether x and y are individuals or groups. Consider, first, oppression's agents and patients. There are four possible combinations: individual oppresses individual, individual oppresses group, group oppresses individual, and group oppresses group.

Are there plausible examples of each type? The fourth definition of oppression listed in the *Oxford English Dictionary* (2d ed.), although marked as obsolete,

---

[2] It would be interesting to look at the history of the term 'oppression' and its uses in the context of political debate. I have chosen this term as the subject of the chapter mainly in order to situate our discussion within a certain tradition of political interpretation central to feminist and antiracist work, and with the hope that by explicating the notion further, those suspicious of this tradition will find it more accessible and valuable.

[3] I'm leaving out cases such as "oppressive heat," or "oppressive headache," or "oppressive sadness."

appears to provide an example in which an individual oppresses another individual: "forcible violation of a woman, rape." Although the use of "oppression" as a synonym of rape is obsolete, people do classify individual relationships as oppressive—for instance, a particular parent-child or husband-wife relationship. An example of the second type (individual oppresses group) is perhaps the most common use of the term historically, as it captures a relationship gone wrong between a sovereign and his subjects: the tyrant is one who oppresses the people. The simplest examples of cases in which groups are oppressors would simply extend the previous ones: if rape is oppression, gang rape would be the oppression of an individual by a group; also lynching, and the torture of an individual by a group. Similarly, if an individual tyrant can oppress the people, presumably so can an oligarchy (or even a democracy!).

We will look shortly at senses of oppression that do not imply an oppressing agent (group or individual), but before doing so let's start by disentangling two distinct sources of power in the definitions and examples we've considered thus far. Often examples of oppression concern an unjust exercise of power where the source of power or authority is social or institutional; such examples presuppose a background social hierarchy (possibly just, possibly unjust) already in place. Consider the example of rape. In a contemporary context, where rape is often acknowledged to be about social power and not just about sex, it is easy to read cases of rape in these terms: men who rape are exercising their social power over women unjustly through coerced sex. (Plausibly in rape they are exercising their *unjust* social power unjustly!)

However, it is arguable that some rapes aren't exercises of social power: it isn't inconceivable for a rapist to have equal or even less social power than the rape victim (recall the possibility of same-sex rape). If we continue to think of rape as a paradigm of individual/individual oppression, then perhaps we should conclude that oppression's wrong lies in the use of power—not just social power but power of any kind, including physical power—to harm another unjustly. In short: *x* oppresses *y* iff *x* unjustly causes harm to *y*. On this view oppression is more than simply causing harm (allowing that causing harm is sometimes just or warranted, for example, in self-defense);[4] but oppression is not necessarily about the exercise of social power: a terrorist may oppress a hostage through brute force (capture, torture, or the like). The hostage-taking may even be motivated by the fact that the hostage has greater social power and authority than the terrorist himself.

So is this notion—causing unjust harm—the core notion of oppression? It may seem promising insofar as it defines oppression in terms of something that is clearly morally wrong;[5] and as we've seen, the term is sometimes used to capture

---

[4] If one maintains that the notion of "harm" is of *wrongful* injury, then of course the point should be restated so to allow that causing injury is sometimes warranted.

[5] This criterion for an acceptable analysis of racism is suggested by Garcia 1997a: 6.

the harm that one individual, the oppressor, inflicts on another, the oppressed. And yet, unless more can be said about *unjust* action as distinct from immoral action, oppression would just collapse into wrongful harm. This suggests that there is something missing from the account.

Undoubtedly there is more than one way of thinking about oppression and its wrongs. However, it is helpful, I believe, to begin by contrasting two sorts of cases. In one sort of case, oppression is an act of wrongdoing by an agent: if oppression of this kind occurs then a person or persons (the oppressor(s)) inflicts harm upon another (the oppressed) wrongfully or unjustly. Let's call these, unsurprisingly, cases of agent oppression. It is not clear that all cases of an agent wrongfully causing harm should count as oppression; the quote we started with suggests that the harshness of the action and the abuse of power are factors that may distinguish oppression from other sorts of wrongful harm.

In the other sort of cases, the oppression is not an individual wrong but a social/political wrong; that is, it is a problem lying in our collective arrangements, an injustice in our practices or institutions. Consider tyranny. Tyranny is wrong not because (or not just because) tyrants are immoral people intentionally causing harm to others, but because a tyrannical governmental structure is unjust. Theorists will vary on what exactly constitutes its injustice, but key considerations include such matters as the fact that tyranny is not a structure in which individuals count as moral equals. (On a broadly liberal account one could argue that such a structure could not be justified in terms that a community of reasonable equals would accept, and the distribution of power and resources under tyranny depends on invidious and morally problematic distinctions between individuals and groups.) The oppressiveness of a tyranny may be compounded by the evil designs of the tyrant, but even a benign tyrant rules in an oppressive regime. Let's call this second kind of case structural oppression.[6]

In cases of agent oppression, the focus is on individuals or groups and their actions; it is the job of our best moral theory to tell us when the action in question is wrong. In cases of structural oppression, the focus is on our collective arrangements—our institutions, policies, and practices—and a theory of justice should provide the normative evaluation of the wrong. Of course there are contexts where we need to consider both the individuals and the structures, the moral and political wrongs.[7]

---

[6] This form of oppression, sometimes more narrowly construed, has also been called "institutional oppression" ("institutional racism"). See, for example, Ture and Hamilton 1992, Ezorsky 1991, Blum 2002: 22–26.

[7] The boundaries of moral theory and political theory are by no means clear. I will tend to speak of moral theory as a theory of human conduct, so concerned primarily with individuals (and by extension, groups); the focus of political theory is our collective arrangements, i.e., our practices, institutions, policies, and so on Of course it is consistent with this that individual wrongdoing and structural injustice are both morally wrong.

The idea of an agent oppressing another is relatively familiar; it may be less familiar to think of laws, institutions, and practices as oppressive. So it will be helpful to consider some plausible cases of structural oppression:[8]

- Cases of explicit formal discrimination appear to be straightforward cases of structural oppression: for example, "Jim Crow" legislation enforcing racial segregation in the United States; the disenfranchisement and broad disempowerment of women in Taliban-ruled Afghanistan.
- Under "Jim Crow," poll taxes and (often rigged) literacy tests prevented nearly all African Americans from voting; although such practices did not explicitly target Blacks, they were oppressive. In 1971, the U.S. Supreme Court considered a case in which Blacks were systematically disqualified for certain jobs due to mandated tests that could not be shown to correlate with successful job performance. The Court found that "practices, procedures, or tests neutral on their face, and even neutral in terms of intent, cannot be maintained if they operate to freeze the status quo of prior discriminatory practices" (*Griggs v. Duke Power Co.* 401 US 424).
- U.S. civil rights legislation of the 1960s has been interpreted so that policies and practices that have an unjustified disproportionate adverse impact on minorities can be challenged. In 1985, the Supreme Court recognized that injustice toward the disabled can occur when, for example, architects construct buildings with no access ramps (*Alexander v. Choate* 469 US 287). In the opinion, the Court emphasized that unjust discrimination can occur not just as a result of animus but simply due to thoughtlessness and indifference.
- Cultural norms and informal practices that impose unfair burdens on or create disproportionate opportunities for members of one group as opposed to another are oppressive. Gender norms concerning child care, elder care, housework, appearance, dress, education, careers, and so forth oppress women.
- Cultural practices and products that foster negative stereotypes of particular groups are oppressive, not simply because they are insulting to members of those groups or foster contempt or hatred toward them, but also because they can have a distorting effect on the judgment of those who are asked to apply discretionary policies. We'll consider some cases of this below (Roberts 2002: 47–74).

I suggested above that oppression is importantly linked to the abuse of power. This fits well with a paradigm of power being abused by an individual who wields power without due regard for moral constraints. But how do we make sense of this in the structural cases? Focusing entirely on individuals and their

---

[8] Thanks to Elizabeth Anderson for suggesting some of these examples.

wrongdoings can prevent one from noticing that social power—the power typically abused in oppressive settings—is relational: it depends on the institutions and practices that structure our relationships to one another (Foucault 1978, Fraser 1989a). When the structures distribute power unjustly, the *illegitimate imbalance* of power becomes the issue rather than an individual abuse of power per se.

For example, in certain contexts (though not all) professors have greater power than their students by virtue of the rules, practices, and expectations in force in academic contexts. Individuals can gain power by developing skills in navigating the practices; they can also lose power by failing to understand or conform to them. If the professor/student relationship in question is structured justly, then we should plausibly look for individual moral failings to account for any wrongs that might occur under its auspices. For example, consider a case in which the practices and institutions constituting the role of professor are just, but an individual in that role, let's call him Stanley, gives low grades to all women of color who take his class, regardless of their performance. In such a case, the injustice arises through the abuse by the particular individual of what would otherwise be a legitimate relationship of unequal power. In cases where the practices constituting a social relationship are just, if someone is wrongly harmed, it is plausibly due to one party or the other acting immorally.

In other cases, however, the problem lies in the structure of relationships and the distribution of power. Contrast the case of the benighted professor, Stanley, who abuses the power granted him within a just social framework, with a case of institutional injustice in which, for example, only males and White women are allowed to serve as professor and to enroll as students. The women of color treated unfairly in the former case are not structurally oppressed, although they are the victims of Stanley's moral wrongdoing. In the latter case they are structurally oppressed, even if the educational resources were made available by professors attempting to undermine the unjust framework: perhaps another professor, Larry, opens his classrooms to unmatriculated women of color.

If we consider only agent oppression, then if some are oppressed we should look for the oppressor. But in cases of structural oppression, there may not be an oppressor, in the sense of an agent responsible for the oppression. Practices and institutions oppress, and some individuals or groups are privileged within those practices and institutions. But it would be wrong to count all those who are privileged as oppressors.[9] Members of the privileged group, for example, Larry in the case above, may in fact be working to undermine the unjust practices and institutions. Nevertheless, in the context of structural oppression, there may be some who are more blameworthy than others for perpetuating the injustice; they may be more responsible for creating, maintaining, expanding, and exploiting

---

[9] For a useful discussion of attributions of blame in contexts of oppression, see Calhoun 1989.

the unjust social relationships. In such cases an individual counts as an oppressor if their moral wrongdoing compounds the structural injustice, that is, if they are agents of oppression within an oppressive structure.[10] But not all those who are privileged by an oppressive structure are oppressive agents.

These considerations suggest that both agent oppression and structural oppression can sometimes be intentional and sometimes not, and sometimes there are individuals to blame for the harm and sometimes not. In the case of agent oppression, the question is whether the agent has wrongfully harmed another through an abuse of power.[11] Malicious or hostile intentions are not required: one can abuse one's power to wrongfully harm another by being insensitive and indifferent. Whether the agent is blameworthy is a further matter still; in some cases blameworthiness will depend on the agent's intentions, yet in other cases what matters is the agent's negligence with respect to determining the full impact of his or her actions.

In the case of structural oppression, the question is whether the structure (the policy, practice, institution, discursive framing, cultural norm) is unjust and creates or perpetuates illegitimate power relations. Again, the oppressive structures in question may be intentionally created or not. A structure may cause unjustified harm to a group without this having been anticipated in advance or even recognized after the fact; those responsible for the structure may even be acting benevolently and with the best information available. Whether an individual or a group is blameworthy for the injustice will depend on what role they play in causing or maintaining the unjust structure.

2. Individualist and Institutionalist Approaches

An important factor motivating the distinction between agent oppression and structural oppression is that although sometimes structural oppression is intentionally caused, say, by policy makers, it is possible for a group to be oppressed by a structure without there being an agent responsible for its existence or the form it takes. Admittedly, individuals play a role in creating and maintaining the social world, but most of the practices and institutions that structure our lives, although made up of individuals and influenced by individuals, are not designed

[10] The precise conditions for being an oppressor will depend on one's background moral theory; the question is: when does someone's moral wrongdoing compound the structural injustice? On some accounts one's actions may be morally wrong if one is simply a passive participant in an unjust structure; on other accounts not.

[11] I am suggesting here that oppression involves an abuse of power or an imbalance of power, though I have not argued specifically for this claim, nor will I resolve here whether we should ultimately endorse it. It is a promising way, however, to distinguish oppression from other forms of moral and political wrong.

and controlled by anyone individually. The government, the economy, the legal system, the educational system, the transportation system, religion, family, etiquette, the media, the arts, our language, are all collective enterprises that are maintained through complex social conventions and cooperative strategies. And they all distribute power among individuals—for example, a public transportation system that is inaccessible to the disabled disempowers them relative to the able-bodied. Rules of etiquette that preclude women from asking a man on a date, or that require a man to pay for all expenses incurred on the date, are not neutral with respect to the distribution of power.

In some cases social institutions have relatively costless exit options. But even what might seem to be the most malleable practices depend on background expectations and communicative cues that are not within the control of a single individual; so it would be wrong to think of them, except in the rare instance, as created or directed by an individual (or collective) agent.[12] If power resides in the relationships created by practices, and no individual agent is responsible for a particular practice, then there is an important sense in which the distribution of power may be unjust and yet the injustice not be properly explicated in terms of an agent's wrongdoing.

This point, that social structures are often beyond the control of individual agents, counts against what we might call an *individualistic approach* to oppression. On an individualistic approach, agent oppression is the primary form of oppression and the agent's wrongdoing is its normative core: oppression is primarily a moral wrong that occurs when an agent (the oppressor) inflicts wrongful harm upon another (the oppressed); if something other than an agent (such as a law) is oppressive, it is so in a derivative sense, and its wrong must be explicated in terms of an agent's wrongdoing. For example, one might claim that laws and such are oppressive only insofar as they are the instruments of an agent (intentionally) inflicting harm. The individualistic approach rejects the idea that structural oppression is a distinct kind of wrong.[13]

As I mentioned, a theoretical reason to reject the individualistic approach is that it cannot account for some forms of injustice for which no individual is responsible. Although I've suggested some examples to support this, a fuller

---

[12] Moreover, although it may be possible to determine in the case of an individual's action what the "meaning" of the action is, for example, by considering the intention behind it, social practices and institutions are embedded in a complex web of meanings with multiple consequences that might be relevant to evaluating their point or purpose. Although in some contexts we are offered legal opinions or transcripts of legislative debate that help sort out the intention behind a law or policy, most institutions are governed by informal norms based in conflicting traditions.

[13] Although Garcia does not frame his discussion of racism in terms of oppression, his view of racism seems to fall under what I describe here as an individualistic approach to oppression (Garcia 1996, Garcia 1997a, Garcia 1999). See also the debate between Garcia and Mills (Mills 1997, Garcia 2001a, Mills 2002).

discussion would consider specific individualist proposals that attempt to accommodate such cases.

However, there are also more pragmatic reasons for thinking that the individualistic approach is inadequate, namely, what counts as evidence for oppression and what counts as an appropriate remedy. For example, to show that a group suffers from agent oppression, we must establish that there is an agent(s) morally responsible for causing them unjust harm; but tracing the wrong back to an agent (perhaps also determining the agent's intentions) may not be possible. In contrast, to say that a group suffers from structural oppression, we must establish that power is misallocated in such a way that members of the group are unjustly disadvantaged. Likewise, the remedy in the first case will plausibly focus on the individual agent(s) responsible for the harm, whereas in the second it will plausibly focus on restructuring society to make it more just.

Of course both kinds of situation certainly obtain and are of concern: our societies are unjustly structured, and immoral people with power can and do harm others. Moreover, individual and structural issues are interdependent insofar as individuals are responsive to their social context and social structures are created, maintained, and transformed by individuals. Nonetheless, there will be situations that are clearly unjust even when it is unclear whether there is an agent responsible for the oppression; we don't need a smoking gun to tell that a system of practices and policies that result in women being denied adequate health care is unjust. I also submit that we should have more hope in the prospects of social and political change bringing about a significant improvement in people's lives than in the prospects of anything like the moral improvement of individuals. As Liam Murphy (1999: 252) suggests: "it is obviously true that, as a practical matter, it is overwhelmingly preferable that justice be promoted through institutional reform rather than through the uncoordinated efforts of individuals—a point worth emphasizing in an era characterized by the state's abandonment of its responsibility to secure even minimal economic justice and by politicians' embrace of 'volunteerism' as a supposed substitute." I will not attempt to justify this hope in structural as opposed to moral reform here. But in my experience, not only is structural reform usually more sweeping and reliable, but it also allows ordinary individuals who unwittingly contribute to injustice to recognize this and change their ways, without the kind of defensiveness that emerges when they find themselves the subject of moral reproach.

However, those who emphasize the force of social structures in our lives, and reject an individualistic approach to oppression, sometimes err in the opposite direction. A structuralist or—what may be a better term to avoid other connotations—an 'institutionalist approach' to oppression takes structural oppression as the primary form and either denies that individuals can be oppressors or maintains that acts are oppressive insofar as they contribute to maintaining an oppressive structure (Frye 1983, chaps. 1–2, esp. p. 38). Although it is important to capture the sense in which all of us perpetuate unjust structures by unthinkingly participating in them, it is also important to distinguish between those who abuse their power to harm others and those who are attempting to navigate as best they can the moral rapids of everyday life.

On the view I've sketched here, oppression is something that both agents and structures "do," but in different ways. Structures cause injustice through the *misallocation* of power; agents cause wrongful harm through the abuse of power (sometimes the abuse of misallocated power). Allowing space in our account for both kinds of oppression provides greater resources for understanding the ways in which social life is constrained by the institutional and cultural resources available, and the ways in which we have agency within, and sometimes in opposition to, these constraints.

For example, one theme in discussions of oppression is the systematic, and one is sometimes tempted to say inescapable, constraint imposed upon the oppressed (Frye 1983, chap. 1). The idea that oppression is a structural phenomenon helps capture this insight. Return once again to the contrast between the benighted professor (Stanley) in a just system and the morally responsible professor (Larry) in the unjust system. The relevant contrast between the two cases and those like them is not simply the degree to which the constraint is avoidable (Stanley may be very powerful, the institution of segregation quite weak), nor is it the systematic nature of the harm (the benighted professor can be quite systematic). Nor is it the multiplicity of the barriers (presumably just the illegality of marriage alone would be enough to oppress gays and lesbians), or the macroscopic aspects of social phenomena (it may be that one has to look at the minute details of a practice to see its injustice) (cf. Frye 1983, chap. 1). The contrast lies in the extent to which the injustice resides in the structure of the institutions and practices—for example, the ways they distribute power—and the extent to which the wrong is located in the particular acts and attitudes of individuals within them. Structural oppression occurs where the structures are unjust, not where the wrong lies simply in the moral failings—the acts and attitudes—of an agent.

At this stage I have not provided an argument for the conclusion that the notion of oppression should be "analyzed" in terms of agent and structural oppression; nor have I argued that such an analysis should be framed as the misuse or misallocation of power to cause harm. I have simply suggested that a concept of oppression developed along these lines is useful for those concerned with group domination. I believe that an individualistic approach to group domination is inadequate because sometimes structures themselves, not individuals, are the problem. Likewise, an institutionalist approach is inadequate because it fails to distinguish those who abuse their power to do wrong and those who are privileged but do not exploit their power. I recommend a "mixed" approach that does not attempt to reduce either agent or structural oppression to the other. I've opted to use the term 'oppression' to cover both kinds of case.

3. Group Oppression

So far I have suggested an outline for a theory of oppression that provides place-holders for accounts of justice and of individual moral wrongdoing. At this point it might seem that further progress in understanding oppression depends on providing substantive normative theories. As an example of a structural account of justice I have pointed toward a broadly liberal sentiment that requires of a social structure that it be one that reasonable equals could accept. To this (and related) liberal sentiments I am sympathetic, though one can endorse the kind of approach to oppression I've outlined without endorsing liberalism. Obviously I cannot develop and defend full accounts of justice and moral wrong in the context of this chapter. So what further can be accomplished?

As indicated at the outset, a crucial task for a theory of oppression is to explicate the link between groups and wrongs that make for group-based oppression. In what follows I will focus on this link in structural as opposed to agent oppression in order to understand structural racism, sexism, and the like. Of course my discussion will not be normatively "neutral" between competing conceptions of justice. In the background will lie a broadly democratic, egalitarian, and materialist sensibility, but this will not be articulated or made the focus of discussion.[14] No doubt there are particular conceptions of justice which, if plugged into my account, would yield unacceptable results by any standards. However, my goal at this stage is simply to make progress in understanding how an account of structural oppression can be sensitive to multiple group memberships without falling back on an individualist model that specifies who suffers oppression in terms of an agent's (or agents') intentions. I will be happy if I can describe a framework within which further discussion of the different factors and their interplay will be fruitful.[15]

---

[14] It may be helpful to make explicit some background assumptions that will continue to guide the discussion. First, injustice occurs not just in courts and state houses, but in churches, families, and other cultural practices. Second, although an understanding of justice and oppression must employ a meaningful notion of "group," we must avoid overgeneralizing about the attitudes, experiences, or social position of members of the groups. Third, those in subordinate positions are not passive victims of oppression, nor are those in dominant positions full agents of oppression. Society "imposes" dominant and subordinate identities on members of both groups, and groups negotiate and transform them. However, some identities are more empowering and more empowered than others. Fourth, oppression cannot be explained by reference only (or primarily) to any single factor, such as the attitudes or psychologies of social groups, economic forces, the political structure of society, culture. Fifth, injustice and so the wrongs of structural oppression consist not simply in unjust distributions of goods, opportunities, and such, but in inegalitarian social relationships, that is, in relational obligations and expectations that distribute power hierarchically (Anderson 1999: 312; Young 1990a, chap. 1).

[15] Methodologically, I see the search for counterexamples to a proposed account useful in understanding the phenomenon, even if they show that the proposal as it stands fails. Presumably, an account of justice that cannot capture the broad range of phenomena that are plausibly structurally oppressive would be, for that reason, inadequate. Some have argued that Rawls's account of justice is inadequate for this reason (e.g., Cohen 1997).

So, what makes a particular instance of structural oppression "group-based oppression," such as racist, sexist, or class oppression? As I see it, there are two parts to the question. One part is to determine whether there is oppression: whether there is a misallocation of power causing wrongful harm. This is a part where one must rely on a substantive theory of justice. Another part is to determine how or whether the wrong is linked to membership in a group. In many cases one can at least analytically distinguish between the fact that something is unjust and the fact that the injustice is specifically "racial" and/or "sexual."[16] It is this latter question to which we turn now.

On its face, the issue seems simple enough: sex oppression is injustice that targets women; racial oppression targets members of racial minorities. But how should we understand this idea of "targeting"?

Several ideas come to mind: perhaps whether something counts as a "racial injustice" depends simply on whom the injustice affects; does it affect almost all and almost only members of a particular race in a particular context? This, at least stated this simply, can't be right. There are racially homogeneous contexts in which an injustice affects virtually everyone, but we wouldn't want to say that the injustice was racial. For example, a Japanese company with all Japanese workers might exploit those workers, but this would not make the exploitation a racial injustice.[17]

Moreover, given that individuals are always members of multiple overlapping groups, even when a group is adversely affected, it is not always clear under what guise they are being subjected to injustice. For example, since the 1970s socialist feminists have argued that class exploitation and sex oppression should not be seen as two autonomous systems each with their own distinctive causal/explanatory principles and their own (overlapping) target groups (Young 1980). Instead, class exploitation and sex oppression are intertwined, not just in the sense that there are some who suffer both, or that one system affects the other, but in the sense that the relationships that distribute power along the lines of class also distribute power along the lines of sex. Broadly speaking, this is the phenomenon of *intersectionality* (Crenshaw 1995). So to analyze the situation of Mexican-American domestic workers by looking only at class, or only at nationality/ethnicity, or only at race, or only at gender, would be inadequate. An account that correctly determines whether a particular situation is just or not must include multiple categories of critical analysis; it must also attend to the different ways, in different kinds of relationships, that the demands of justice

---

[16] I leave open whether there are some inherently racial or sexual wrongs, where the wrongness of the act or the injustice of the structure is not separable from its racial or sexual meaning. Hate crimes could be an example.

[17] Although this is true in general, it isn't guaranteed, for if the company relied on particular Japanese cultural norms or practices to exploit the workers, it might count as a kind of ethnic oppression. Thanks to Roxanne Fay for pointing this out.

may be violated. The particular form injustice takes may depend on the mix of group memberships in the target population.[18]

Alternatively, one might insist that the injustice must be motivated by racial animus or intended to disadvantage members of a racial group. But as we've seen, this requirement is too strong, for not only are there cases of racial injustice where racial animus is not the cause, but there may not even be an individual or group of individuals in any clear sense perpetrating the injustice. So effects alone and motivations alone are not the key. Where should we look next?

In *Justice and the Politics of Difference*, Iris Young suggests that oppression occurs when a social group suffers any of (at least) five different forms of subordination: exploitation, marginalization, powerlessness, cultural imperialism, and systematic violence (1990a: 48–63). Although tremendously valuable for its insight into the variety of forms oppression can take, for the most part Young's discussion assumes preexisting social groups and examines the variety of structural injustices they might suffer. As a result, she avoids some of the questions that arise in understanding the relationship between the group membership and injustice.

Let's pause to reflect a bit on the idea of a group. Some groups are well-defined social entities whose members recognize themselves as such and take their membership in the group to be important to their identity (Young 1990a: 44–45). However, some social groups have little or no sense of themselves as a group, and may in fact come to understand themselves as such only as a result of policies imposed on them. Consider two cases: suppose at a particular company, call it BigCo, wage employees are required to submit to drug testing as a condition of continued employment. One might argue that the policy is unjust, and the injustice extends to all wage employees even if some have no objection to being drug tested.[19] (If you are unhappy with the suggestion that mandatory drug testing is unjust, then substitute your own example of an unjust burden placed on the employees in question.) In many work contexts, the distinction between wage employees and salaried employees is a meaningful division that organizes the individual interactions within and between the two groups. The imposition of a policy that relies on this distinction may reinforce the division and affect the groups' interactions, but the division was meaningful prior to the policy.

However, policies can also make divisions meaningful that were not before. Suppose that BigCo distinguishes types of job by numbering them from 1 to 100. The salaried positions are coded from 80 to 100 and the wage positions 1 to 79. If the company institutes the drug testing policy for employees in positions coded 25–50, this might well make salient a distinction among the wage employees that

× P. 331 "the Slogs"

---

[18] Given that there are laws against some forms of discrimination and not others, it can matter tremendously how to characterize the group basis for the injustice. See, for example, *DeGraffenreid v. General Motors* (413 F. Supp. 142 [ED Mo. 1976]).

[19] For insight into the effects of such policies on employees, see Ehrenreich 2001.

was not significant before. The employees in these categories may come to identify with each other, may organize against the policy, and may come to interact quite differently with employees in other categories. If the policy is unjust, however, it would be wrong, I think, to claim that oppression only occurs once the employees see themselves as a group and identify as members of the group. So to say that someone is oppressed as an *F* is not to imply that they *identify* as an *F*. Rather, the point can be that one is oppressed by virtue of being a member of the *F*s; that is, being an *F* is a condition that subjects them to an unjust policy or practice (regardless of whether being an *F* is meaningful to them or not).

Social groups are dynamic entities whose membership and sense of identity change in response to sociopolitical circumstances. Their origin, shape, and development is crucially bound up with the institutions within which they are embedded and the history and future of those institutions (Lieberman 1995: 438–40). So the question before us can't simply be: Is this preexisting (racial, sexual, socioeconomic) group being exploited, marginalized, or the like (cf. Young 1990a, chap. 2)? But rather: How does a particular policy or practice construct or affect the identity of the group, as well as its position within the broader sociopolitical system? To answer this question we will need to ask such questions as: Do different institutions define the group in the same way? Does the policy divide a social group into new groups, granting benefits to some members and not others?

However, there are disadvantages in focusing too much on policies and practices that name or specify the oppressed groups as such. First, as we've seen, given a history of group domination, the effects of earlier injustice position subordinate groups socially and economically so that their members have much more in common than their group membership. Policies framed to pick up on these other commonalities can reinforce the unjust social divisions (Lieberman 1998: 11). This is sometimes called "secondary discrimination" (Warren 1977: 241–43; Rosati 1994: 152–59).   p. 331 "the slogs"

Second, although for convenience we've been considering explicitly stated policies, we want the account to apply to both formal policies and informal practices.

Third, sometimes policies and practices that are articulated in a way that is "blind" with respect to a social group may nonetheless be motivated by animus toward the group and may have serious consequences for its members. In fact, as oppression is identified and condemned, it is a familiar tactic of the dominant group to reframe discriminatory structures to have the same effects without the discrimination being explicit.

Fourth, if oppression requires that the policy or practice make membership in a group an *explicit* condition for the policy's application, then there is a temptation to think that the basis for the wrong is in the intentions of the policy's framers. But this is to return to a more individualistic approach to oppression. We want to allow that a structure motivated by good intentions may be unjust in its distribution of goods and power and in the social meaning of the relationships it creates.

Thus it appears that in some cases the institution in question targets a social group explicitly; in some cases it does not explicitly target such a group but has clear ramifications for it; and in other cases its target is a group that has not previously had an established sense of itself. Is there some useful way to organize these different sorts of cases?

4. Structural Oppression of Groups: An Attempt at a Definition

Race-Ladenness

In analyzing the Social Security Act of 1935 and its legacy for contemporary race relations, Robert Lieberman offers the term "race-laden" to describe institutions that perpetuate racial injustice without doing so explicitly:[20]

> By "race-laden," I refer to the tendency of some policies to divide the population along racial lines without saying so in so many words. . . . But race-laden policies are not *simply programs whose tendency to exclude by race is merely incidental or accidental.* . . . Moreover, they can be expected *to affect Blacks and Whites differently in the normal course* of their everyday operations, whether or not their framers or administrators intended that result. (Lieberman 1998: 7, italics mine)

The notion of "race-laden" policies is suggestive. Some institutions may accidentally map onto unjust power relations without being oppressive; but some institutions that appear to map only accidentally onto unjust power relations are not only rooted in a history of such injustice but also perpetuate it.

Drawing on these insights, here's a first proposal for understanding structural oppression of groups:

(SO$_1$) *F*s are oppressed (as *F*s) by an institution *I* in context *C* iff$_{df}$ in ($\exists R$) (being an F nonaccidentally correlates with being disadvantaged by standing in an unjust relation R to others) and I creates, perpetuates, or reinforces R.)

---

[20] This characterization of 'race-laden' does not quite capture what Lieberman is after because it does not distinguish between just and unjust institutions. Although in the context it appears that he intends the term 'race-laden' to refer to unjust policies, it is possible for an institution to "reflect" racially structured power arrangements and to have differential racial effects, but also function to lessen injustice. One might argue that certain affirmative action plans designed to aid socioeconomically disadvantaged groups reflect racially structured power arrangements, and have racially differential effects, but are nonetheless just.

Consider a couple of examples:

- Nonfluent English speakers are oppressed (as such) by English-only ballots in California in 2002, iff in California in 2002 being a nonfluent English speaker nonaccidentally correlates with being disadvantaged by being disenfranchised, and English-only ballots create, perpetuate, or reinforce the disenfranchisement.
- Women are oppressed as women by cultural representations of women as sex objects in the United States in the late twentieth century iff being a woman in the United States in the late twentieth century nonaccidentally correlates with being subjected to systematic violence, and cultural representations of women as sex objects creates, perpetuates, or reinforces the systematic violence.

As mentioned before, I leave open for present purposes the large and important issue of how to understand the specific requirements of justice. However, there are several elements of this proposal that deserve further discussion:

1. How does this analysis of *group* oppression apply to individuals: under what condition is an *individual* oppressed by a structure?
2. Why am I supposing that the injustice involves being disadvantaged by a standing in an unjust *relation*?
3. What is meant by a *nonaccidental correlation* between the group membership and the injustice?
4. What sort of relation between the institution and the injustice counts as *creating, perpetuating, or reinforcing*?

I will speak to each of these in turn.

First, the proposal thus far is ambiguous in its mention of "*F*s being oppressed" for it is unclear whether the claim is that (in the context in question) *all F*s are oppressed or only some *F*s are oppressed. Is the claim in the second example that *all* women in late-twentieth-century America were oppressed by the cultural representation of women as sex objects, or that *some* women were?

My view is that the practices in question are oppressive to all members of the group, but of course to different degrees and in different ways, depending on what other social positions they occupy. For example, a wealthy woman who can afford to take a taxi whenever she is anxious about her security on the street is not oppressed by the prevalence of violence against women to the same extent as a poor woman who must use public transportation and walk several blocks home from the bus stop after her shift is over at midnight. But that women are at greater risk of rape, domestic violence, and sexual harassment than men is an injustice that affects all women, whether or not they are ever the direct victim of such acts, and whether or not they are typically in a position, by virtue of their wealth or their location, to protect themselves. As a result, I would endorse the general claim for any individual x:

x is oppressed as an F by an institution I in context C iff$_{df}$ x is an F in C and in $C(\exists R)$ ((being an F nonaccidentally correlates with being disadvantaged by standing in an unjust relation R to others) and I creates, perpetuates, or reinforces R.)

Further examples would include:

- Tyrone is oppressed as a Black man by race/gender-profiling in the United States in the early twenty-first century iff Tyrone is a Black man in the United States in the early twenty-first century and in that context being a Black man nonaccidentally correlates with being subjected to police harassment and brutality, and race/gender-profiling creates, perpetuates, or reinforces the police harassment and brutality.
- William is oppressed as a gay man by the health insurance policies at BigCo in 1990 iff William is a gay man employed at BigCo in 1990 and in that context being a gay man nonaccidentally correlates with an inequitable distribution of benefits based on sexual orientation, and the health insurance policies create, perpetuate, or reinforce the inequitable distribution.

Some may prefer to limit oppression to those who suffer directly from the specified disadvantage (the victims of violence, those denied benefits, and the like). However, plausibly the imposition of certain risks on groups is itself oppressive, so I endorse the wider account; I will not defend it here, however, and it is open to one who prefers the narrower account to qualify the proposal as indicated.

Second, on relations: I've indicated several ways that injustice is relational: it concerns relative distributions of goods and power, and relationships that define the expectations, entitlements, and obligations of the different parties. In oppressive circumstances there will be, then, a background framework of relationships that disadvantages some and privileges others. Consider Young's example of powerlessness (Young 1990a: 30–33). Although it may be possible to define, say, powerlessness in nonrelational terms (e.g., lacking autonomy in crucial areas of life), powerlessness occurs within a system of social relations that defines the spheres of freedom and control within which we are entitled to act. My proposal, as it stands, is articulated to encourage a recognition of such background relational structures.

Third, on "nonaccidental correlations" between group membership (F) and injustice (R): Let me first note two points: First, in order for there to be a correlation between *being an F* and *being a G*, it is not necessary that all *F*s are *G*, or that only *F*s are *G*. There might be a nonaccidental correlation between smoking and lung cancer even if not all smokers get lung cancer and some nonsmokers do. Similarly, women in the United States might be oppressed by wage discrimination even if a subset of women earn fair wages and some men don't. Second, in requiring that the correlations must be "nonaccidental," the point is to find a middle ground between requiring that the unjust policy or practice *explicitly target* a group, and requiring only that there be *some adverse effect* of the policy on the group. In some circumstances unjust policies will affect a group "merely accidentally" without there being any evidence that the group identity is relevant to the injustice. For example, suppose NASA implements an unjust policy applying to all astronauts; in fact, there will be a correlation between those affected by the policy and White men. But in most such scenarios it would be wrong to maintain that those White men affected by the policy are thereby being oppressed as *White men*.

What might count, then, as a nonaccidental correlation? In general, a correlation counts as nonaccidental because it supports certain kinds of counterfactuals; the idea is that the group's being a group of *F*s is causally relevant to the injustice. A full account should specify exactly what counterfactuals are necessary and sufficient for the kind of nonaccidental correlation in question. I will not be able to provide that here; instead I will offer a series of examples that suggest a set of relevant counterfactuals to consider.

Example: Racism and Child Welfare

Let's turn to a more sustained analysis of a real life case. In her work *Shattered Bonds*, Dorothy Roberts argues that current child welfare policy is racist. She uncovers ways in which state intrusion into Black families in the name of child welfare systematically (i) reinforces negative stereotypes about Black families, (ii) undermines Black family autonomy, and (iii) weakens the Black community's ability to challenge discrimination and injustice (Roberts 2002: ix). But as Roberts acknowledges, we must be careful in charging that the system is racist, for there are other variables that might explain why the Black community is disproportionately affected: "Because race and socioeconomic status are so intimately entwined, it is hard to tell how much of what happens to Black children is related to their color as opposed to their poverty" (47).

There is evidence that Black children are more likely to be separated from their parents than children of other races, that Black children spend more time in foster care and are more likely to remain in foster care until they "age out," and that Black children receive inferior services. This, of course, is disturbing, but by itself it doesn't show that the system is racially biased; it could also be that there are other features of the cases in question—level of poverty, degree of substance abuse, incarceration of parents and other family members—that better explain the rate of removal, time in foster care, quality of service, and so forth. Is there further evidence that race is the relevant variable that explains the disparity in the numbers? The evidence is mixed.

Roberts points to considerations supporting the conclusion that the system is racially biased. First, there is a huge racial imbalance in child welfare involvement between Black and non-Black families, even though studies show that children in Black families are no more likely to be mistreated than children in non-Black families (Roberts 2002: 47–52). Yet both popular opinion and expert studies are ridden with racial stereotypes and misunderstandings of cultural differences that sustain the belief that Black families are dysfunctional and dangerous. Because decisions about removal and reunification are "discretionary," the result is that removal of children from Black families often appears warranted when it isn't.

> Such a random process for identifying maltreated children could not so effectively target one group of families without some racial input. I am not charging that [caseworkers and judges] deliberately set out to break up Black families because they dislike their race. To the contrary, they may believe that they are helping Black children by extricating them from a dangerous environment. But race negatively affects their evaluation of child maltreatment and what to do about it, whether they realize it or not. (Roberts 2002: 55)

Second, looking at the history of child welfare policy, Roberts notes that there has been a major shift in its goals and policies. Whereas once the idea was to provide programs to help families in need, currently "The system is activated only after children have experienced harm and puts all the blame on parents for their children's problems. This protective function falls heaviest on African-American parents because they are the most likely to suffer from poverty and institutional discrimination and be blamed for the effects on their children" (Roberts 2002: 74). Over the past thirty years, the changes in the system have correlated with the racial makeup of the population it serves: "child protective services have become even more segregated and more destructive. As the child welfare rolls have darkened, family preserving services have dried up, and child removal has stepped up" (Roberts 2002: 99). And yet, the harsh policies do not address the deeper social problems: "At the same time that [the child welfare system] brutally intrudes upon too many Black families, it also ignores the devastating impact of poverty and racism on even more children. . . . The child welfare system reinforces the inferior status of poor Blacks in American both by destroying the families who come within its reach and by failing the families who don't" (91).

Third, Roberts considers the claim that the child welfare system is not racially biased because—*all things being equal*—Black families are no more likely to be disrupted than White families. Roberts argues that even if this were true, "all things are not equal" (Roberts 2002: 94) for there is, of course, a history of racial oppression that has systematically disadvantaged Black families. If Black families make up a disproportionate number of those in extreme poverty—due in part to a history of racial oppression—and if those in extreme poverty suffer unfair disadvantages (which research clearly shows), then the unfair treatment of the poor in fact perpetuates the injustice Black families have suffered.

This point is important for several reasons. Our focus at the moment remains on nonaccidental correlations. In the case we're considering, a history of unjust institutions has explicitly targeted African Americans, and these institutions are largely responsible for the current disproportionate number of Blacks in poverty. Recent child welfare policies, however, unjustly disadvantage those in poverty. It would be plausible to claim that Black families suffer the current injustices in child welfare because of the history of racist policies: if Blacks as a group hadn't suffered historical injustices, they wouldn't be suffering the current ones in the child welfare system. I maintain that this is sufficient to count as a nonaccidental correlation between being Black and being subject to demeaning and disempowering child welfare policies. The point is that the racial correlation occurs, not because those designing and implementing the policies have intended to harm Blacks as such, but because an adequate explanation of the current disadvantage must rely on the history of unjust policies that have targeted Blacks.

Clearly the Roberts analysis is highly controversial, and I have not attempted to summarize the research supporting her view. But for our purposes, whether her analysis is ultimately correct is not the issue. The point is to illuminate some of the ways that there *could* be a nonaccidental correlation between group membership and injustice. Drawing on the form of Roberts's arguments, we can articulate several factors that are relevant in determining whether there is a nonaccidental correlation of the type required by the proposed definition of oppression (this list is not intended to be exhaustive):

1. Does the unjust institution in question explicitly target (or was it designed to target, but not explicitly target) those who are *F*?
2. Does the unjust institution allow discretion in its application, in a context where there is widespread misperception of and bias against *F*s?
3. Does the history of the institution reveal a correlation between an increase in the harshness/injustice of its policies and practices and the *F*ness of the target population?
4. Is there a history of injustice toward the group *F*s which explains how members of that group are now affected by the injustice resulting from *I*?

The Slogs

Even with these considerations in mind, however, a problem remains.[21] Consider a fictional society in which there is a group, call them the Slogs, who are truly lazy. They don't like to work, and when they are given work they are irresponsible about getting it done and do it badly. Let's suppose too that this laziness of the Slogs is not the result of a previous injustice. Further, in this society the Slogs and only the Slogs are lazy, and the Slogs and only the Slogs are poor; although the Slogs are provided at least the minimum that justice requires, everyone else earns a more generous income and has a significantly better standard of living. Suppose now that the society imposes a harsh policy affecting the poor—for example, the denial of medical care to those who can't afford to pay for it. Note that in this society there is a nonaccidental correlation between being lazy and being denied medical treatment. Should we say then that the Slogs are oppressed as *lazy*? Is this a case of secondary discrimination against the lazy, or only primary discrimination against the poor? On the proposal as articulated, because of the nonaccidental correlation between laziness and poverty, and between poverty and denial of medical care, the case would satisfy the conditions for "laziness-oppression"—that is, if we substitute "lazy" for F in the condition, then we seem to have a case of group oppression of the Slogs (and individual Slogs) *as lazy*.

Let me be clear: the issue is not whether there is primary oppression against the poor. This can be granted. The question we are addressing is not just who is oppressed, but what groups are oppressed *as such*. In our fictional society the Slogs are oppressed because they are poor and the poor are being unjustly denied medical care. But are they oppressed *as lazy*? Could the Slogs claim that an injustice has targeted them as lazy? Or only as poor?[22]

If, as seems plausible, we don't want to allow this to be a case of "laziness oppression," then the example highlights that "secondary discrimination" does not occur in every case in which one is subject to injustice due to the effects of a prior condition, but occurs only when there is a primary injustice on which the current injustice piggybacks. In keeping with this, one might argue that it is not

[21] Thanks to Jimmy Lenman for this example. A similar one was brought to my attention by Roxanne Fay and Ishani Maitra: If it isn't an accident that astronauts are predominantly White men, then an unjust policy that targets astronauts may be sufficient for a "nonaccidental correlation" between being a White man and being subject to the injustice. But intuitively this would not be a case of "White male oppression." The revised formulation below would avoid this because the privileges granted White men don't count as a primary oppression of them.

[22] Although this question may seem to be splitting hairs (see note 18 above), it is often a matter of serious political and legal concern whether a form of injustice or a crime is group based or not, and if so, what the relevant group is.

an injustice that the Slogs are poor, given their laziness (recall that they were initially provided the minimum that justice requires). It is an injustice, however, that they are now denied medical care, given their poverty. The proposal I've offered does not capture this distinction. Drawing on the Roberts example, here is the kind of secondary discrimination we want to capture, in contrast to the Slogs case:

> Blacks are oppressed *as Blacks* by child welfare policies in Chicago in the 1990s because in that context being poor results in having one's family unjustly disrupted, and being poor nonaccidentally correlates with being Black *due to a prior injustice*, and the child welfare policies cause or perpetuate unjust disruption of families.

Hopefully, this captures what we're after in a more general way:

> (SO$_2$) Fs are oppressed (as Fs) by an institution I in context C iff$_{df}$ in C ($\exists R$) (((being an F nonaccidentally correlates with being unjustly disadvantaged either primarily, because *being F* is unjustly disadvantaging in C, or secondarily, because ($\exists G$) (*being F* nonaccidentally correlates with *being G* due to a prior injustice and *being G* is unjustly disadvantaging in C)) and I creates, perpetuates, or reinforces R.)

On this account, Blacks are oppressed both *as poor* (primarily) and *as Black* (secondarily), in the context in question. The Slogs, however, are only oppressed primarily, namely, as poor.

Fourth and finally, let us address the question: What is involved in saying that an institution *creates, perpetuates, or reinforces* injustice? In considering oppression it is important to ask three separate questions:

1. Does the institution *cause* or *create* unjust disadvantage to a group?
2. Does the institution *perpetuate* unjust disadvantage to a group?
3. Does the institution *amplify* or *exacerbate* unjust disadvantage to a group?

There is a tendency to focus on (1) when asking whether an institution is oppressive. But (2) and (3) are no less important to promote justice.

We considered above how the child welfare system perpetuates racial injustice. Consider also the situation of women in a context where women were not educated and so, for the most part, were not literate. If one then argued that women should not have the vote because they were not literate, the policy would perpetuate sexism, even if sex were not a basis for discriminating between those eligible to vote and those not. This suggests that in order for a system or a structure to be nonracist it must not remain "neutral" with respect to the

Add a "eliminativist" approach to race

impact of past racial harms. Institutions conveniently becoming "race" or "gender" blind after great harm has been done are not just; systems that remain "neutral" in such contexts actually perpetuate injustice (see MacKinnon 1989, esp. chap. 12).

In some cases institutional "blindness" to groups keeps groups in an unjust status quo; in other cases it actually exacerbates the problem. Returning to Roberts, she argues that recent child welfare policies not only perpetuate racism, but exacerbate it by, for example, disrupting the Black community. What's at issue is the effects of the policy, not just on individuals or particular families, but on the Black community more broadly. So *even if* a policy doesn't discriminate between similarly situated Black and White families, it still may be the case that it affects Black and White communities differently. If the Black community starts out in a bad position due to past racism and the policy makes things worse, then it doesn't just perpetuate the unfairness but amplifies it. Poor White communities are also unfairly disadvantaged, for the policies augment their class oppression, but there is a racial dimension to the disadvantage that affects Blacks as *a racial group*: by systematically perpetuating racist stereotypes and preventing the Black community from becoming more powerful in having its needs addressed, Blacks suffer a racial injustice.

Primary

Primary + secondary

5. Racial Oppression

Given the definition of structural oppression offered in the previous section, we can now explicitly apply it to races or ethnoracial groups. Let the *F*s be the ethnoracial group in question. Earlier examples of oppression and the Roberts case study have, I hope, given sufficient examples of what could be plausible substituends for *I* and *R*.

I have not attempted to explicate what it means to be oppressed *simpliciter*. Some may want to reserve the claim that someone is *oppressed* for only those cases in which they suffer from substantial and interconnected oppressive structures, on the grounds that to show that a single policy oppresses someone is not to show that they are oppressed. Nothing I say here counts against such a view. Of course, not all oppressive structures are equally harmful, and they should not all be regarded with the same degree of concern. My goal has not been to analyze ordinary uses of the term 'oppression' or to legislate how the term should be used, but to highlight how we might better understand structural group domination.

w/o qualification of condition absolutely

That said, it is worth considering whether the proposal for understanding structural oppression is also useful in thinking about agent oppression. We saw before that an agent may oppress another without intending to. Unconscious racism and sexism are common. So just as we needed to ask what "links" an

unjust structure with a group to constitute *structural* oppression, we should ask
what "links" an agent's action with a group to constitute *agent* oppression, that
is, a racial or sexual wrong. Here's a straightforward application of the first proposal to agent oppression (O = oppressor, V = victim):   *p. 335*

> O oppresses V as *an F* by act A in context C iff$_{df}$ in C (V is an F (or O
> believes that V is an F) and (being an F (or believed to be so) nonacci-
> dentally correlates with being morally wronged by O) and A creates,
> perpetuates, or reinforces the moral wrong.)

For example, Oscar oppresses Velma as a woman by paying her less than her
male counterpart at BigCo iff, at BigCo, Velma is a woman (or Oscar believes that
she is) and being a woman (or being believed to be so) nonaccidentally correlates
with being wrongly exploited by Oscar (i.e., Velma's being exploited is at least
partly explained by Oscar's belief that she is a woman), and Oscar's paying Velma
less than her male counterpart contributes to her exploitation. The point again
is that membership in the group (or groups) in question is a factor in the best
explanation of the wrong. As before, we'll need to complicate the proposal to
take into account the issue of secondary discrimination in the agent case. (I
leave this to the reader.)   attempt in notes

One might object, however, that the account I've offered is not helpful, for
whether group membership is relevant in explaining an injustice will always be a
matter of controversy. In short, the account does not help us resolve the very
disagreements that gave us reason to develop an account of group oppression in
the first place. see ~p. 314- 316

Admittedly, in depending on the notion of "nonaccidental correlation," I inherit many of the philosophical concerns about such connections—for example,
by what method should we distinguish between accidental and nonaccidental
correlations? Empirically, they will look the same. If the difference between
them rests on counterfactuals, don't we need a clear method for evaluating the
relevant counterfactuals? Such a method is not readily available.

Note, however, that the point of this discussion has not been to offer an *epistemic* method or criterion for distinguishing oppression (or group oppression)
from other rights and wrongs. In many cases the judgment that an action or
policy is oppressive is convincing on its face, and the question is how to understand the content of our judgment and its implications. Of course there are
controversial cases for which it would be helpful to have a clear criterion for
resolving our disagreements: Does affirmative action oppress White males?
Does pornography oppress women? Does abortion oppress fetuses? However,
in a majority of the controversial cases, the real disagreements are moral/
political—they concern one's background theory of right and wrong, good and
bad—rather than epistemic. Even if the parties to the controversy agreed on

relevant counterfactuals (e.g., if no one in the United States produced or consumed pornography, then women in the United States would not be coerced to perform sex acts on film), they would still disagree on the moral conclusion. Because I have bracketed substantive moral and political questions, my discussion cannot render verdicts in such controversies. Instead, my hope is that I have clarified the content of some claims being made and identified where the agreements and disagreements lie.

Finally, one might complain that I am helping myself to racial categories that are illegitimate. If, as many argue, there is no such thing as race, then by what rights am I invoking races as groups that suffer oppression? I have argued elsewhere that we can legitimately employ the term "race" for racialized social groups (Haslanger 2012 [2000]). If one is unhappy with this terminology, then one may speak instead of "racialized group" rather than "race"; the issue then becomes "racialized group-based oppression" rather than "race-based oppression" (Blum 2002, chap. 8). see ch.10 es p. p320

How does all this help us understand racism? Bigotry, hatred, intolerance are surely bad. Agreement on this is easy, even if it is not clear what to do about them. But if people are prevented from acting on their bigotry, hatred, and intolerance—at least prevented from harming others for these motives— then we can still live together peacefully. Living together in peace and justice does not require that we love each other, or that we even fully respect each other, but rather that we conform our actions to principles of justice. Should we be concerned if some members of the community are hypocrites in acting respectfully toward others without having the "right" attitude? Of course, this could be a problem if hypocrites can't be trusted to sustain their respectful behavior; and plausibly hatred and bigotry are emotions that involve dispositions to wrongful action. Nonetheless, for many of those who suffer injustice, "private" attitudes are not the worst problem; systematic institutional subordination is.

Moreover, love, certain kinds of respect, and tolerance are no guarantee of justice. A moment's reflection on sexism can reveal that. For women, love and respect have often been offered as a substitute for justice; and yet unjust loving relationships are the norm, not the exception.

Persistent institutional injustice is a major source of harm to people of color. Of course, moral vice—bigotry and the like—is also a problem. But if we want the term 'racism' to capture all the barriers to racial justice, I submit that it is reasonable to count as "racist" not only the attitudes and actions of individuals but the full range of practices, institutions, policies, and suchlike that, I've argued, count as racially oppressive. Cognitive and emotional racial biases do not emerge out of nothing; both are products of the complex interplay between the individual and the social that has been a theme throughout this chapter. Our attitudes are shaped by what we see, and what we see, in turn, depends on the institutional structures that shape our lives and the lives of those around us. For example,

> Is it hard to imagine that young White people who look around and see police locking up people of color at disproportionate rates, might conclude there is something wrong with these folks? Something to be feared, and if feared then perhaps despised? . . . Is it that difficult to believe that someone taught from birth that America is a place where "anyone can make it if they try hard enough," but who looks around and see that in fact, not only have some "not made it," but that these unlucky souls happen to be disproportionately people of color, might conclude that those on the bottom deserve to be there because they didn't try hard enough, or didn't have the genetic endowment for success? (Wise 2000)

Of course, individuals are not merely passive observers; attitudes are not inert. We stand in complicated relationships to the collectively formed and managed structures that shape our lives. Structures take on specific historical forms because of the individuals within them; individual action is conditioned in multiple and varying ways by social context. Theory, then, must be sensitive to this complexity; focusing simply on individuals or simply on structures will not be adequate in an analysis or a normative evaluation of how societies work.

In this chapter I have been especially keen to highlight the role of structures in oppression to offset what I find to be an undue emphasis on racist *individuals* and racist *attitudes* in recent philosophical work. Unjust societies full of well-meaning people can exist and even flourish. Working for social justice while ignoring structural injustice is, I believe, a sure recipe for failure. The battle to end racism and other forms of oppression must take place on many fronts, but without due regard for the power of structures to deform us—our attitudes, our relationships, our selves—we cannot hope to end racial oppression in particular, or group domination in general.

Acknowledgments

Thanks to Jorge Garcia, Michael Glanzberg, Elizabeth Hackett, Lionel McPherson, Ifaenyi Menkiti, Tommie Shelby, Ajume Wingo, and Stephen Yablo for helpful conversations related to this chapter. For this and for comments on earlier drafts, thanks to Elizabeth Anderson, Lawrence Blum, Tracy Edwards, Roxanne Fay, Eva Kittay, Michael Levine, Ishani Maitra, Mary Kate McGowan, Tamas Pataki, Lisa Rivera, Anna Stubblefield, Ásta Sveinsdóttir, and Charlotte Witt. An earlier version was presented at the University of Glasgow, August 2002, and to the New

York Society for Women in Philosophy, November 2002. Thanks to the participants in these discussion, especially Anna Stubblefield (my commentator at NY-SWIP) and Jimmy Lenman, for helpful questions and suggestions.

Works Cited

Anderson, Elizabeth. 1999. "What Is the Point of Equality?" *Ethics* 109:2: 287–337.

Appiah, K.A. 1990. "Racisms." In *Anatomy of Racism*, ed., David Theo Goldberg. Minneapolis: Univ. of Minnesota Press, pp. 3–17.

Blum, Lawrence. 2002. *I'm Not a Racist, But . . .* Ithaca, NY: Cornell University Press.

Calhoun, Cheshire. 1989. "Responsibility and Reproach." *Ethics* 99:2 (January): 389–406.

Cohen, G.A. 1997. "Where the Action Is: On the Site of Distributive Justice." *Philosophy and Public Affairs* 26:1: 3–30.

Ehrenreich, Barbara. 2001. *Nickel and Dimed: On Not Getting By in America*. New York: Metropolitan Books, Henry Holt and Company.

Ezorsky, Gertrude. 1991. *Racism and Justice: The Case for Affirmative Action*. Ithaca: Cornell University Press.

Foucault, Michel. 1978. *The History of Sexuality*, vol. I: *An Introduction*. Trans. Robert Hurley. New York: Random House.

Fraser, Nancy. 1989. "Foucault on Modern Power: Empirical Insights and Normative Confusions." In her *Unruly Practices: Power Discourse and Gender in Contemporary Social Theory*. Minneapolis: University of Minnesota Press, pp. 17–34.

Frye, Marilyn. 1983a. "Oppression." In *The Politics of Reality*. Trumansburg, NY: The Crossing Press.

———. 1983b. "Sexism." In *The Politics of Reality*. Trumansburg, NY: The Crossing Press.

Garcia, J. L. A. 2001. "The Racial Contract Hypothesis." *Philosophia Africana* 4: 27–42.

———. 1999. "Philosophical Analysis and the Moral Concept of Racism." *Philosophy and Social Criticism* 25:5: 1–32.

———. 1997. "Current Conceptions of Racism: A Critical Examination of Some Recent Social Philosophy." *Journal of Social Philosophy* 28:2(Fall): 5–42.

———. 1996. "The Heart of Racism." *Journal of Social Philosophy* 27:1: 5-46.

Haslanger, Sally. 2012 [2000]. "Gender and Race: (What) Are They? (What) Do We Want Them To Be?" Chapter 7 of this volume.

Lieberman, Robert C. 1998. *Shifting the Color Line: Race and the American Welfare State*. Cambridge, MA and London: Harvard University Press.

———. 1995. "Social Construction (Continued)." *The American Political Science Review* 89:2 (June): 437–41.

MacKinnon, Catharine. 1989. *Towards a Feminist Theory of the State*. Cambridge, MA: Harvard University Press.

Mills, Charles. 2002. "The "Racial Contract" as Methodology (Not Hypothesis): Reply to Jorge Garcia." *Philosophia Africana* 5:1 (March): 75-99.

———. 1997. *The Racial Contract*. Ithaca: Cornell University Press.

Murphy, Liam. 1999. "Institutions and the Demands of Justice." *Philosophy and Public Affairs*. 27:4: 251–91.

Simpson, J. A., and E. S. C. Weiner, ed. 1989. *Oxford English Dictionary*. 2nd ed. Oxford: Clarendon Press. OED Online. Oxford University Press. "oppression, n." 4 April 2002. http://dictionary.oed.com/cgi/entry/00164218.

Piper, Adrian. 1993. "Two Kinds of Discrimination." *Yale Journal of Criticism* 6:1: 25–74.

———. 1990. "Higher-Order Discrimination," in Amelie O. Rorty and Owen Flanagan, Eds. *Identity, Character and Morality*. Cambridge, MA.: MIT Press, 285–309.

Roberts, Dorothy. 2002. *Shattered Bonds: The Color of Child Welfare*. New York: Basic Books.

Rosati, Connie S. 1994. "A Study of Internal Punishment." *Wisconsin Law Review* 1994: 123–70.

Ture, Kwame (aka Stokely Carmichael), and Charles Hamilton. 1992 [1967]. *Black Power: The Politics of Liberation*. New York: Vintage Books.

Warren, Mary Anne. 1977. "Secondary Sexism and Quota Hiring." *Philosophy and Public Affairs* 6: 240–61.

Wise, Tim. 2000. "Everyday Racism, White Liberals, and the Limits of Tolerance." *LiP Magazine*: http://www.lipmagazine.org/articles/featwise_11_p.htm.

Young, Iris. 1980. "Socialist Feminism and the Limits of Dual Systems Theory." *Socialist Review* 50.51 (Summer): 169–88.

——. 1990. *Justice and the Politics of Difference* Princeton: Princeton University Press.

PART THREE

LANGUAGE AND KNOWLEDGE

12

What Knowledge Is and What It Ought to Be

Feminist Values and Normative Epistemology

1. Introduction[1]

Much of contemporary analytic epistemology has been concerned with the semantics of claims to know: What are the truth conditions of claims of the form S knows that p? With some notable exceptions, feminist epistemologists have not taken up this project—at least not in this form—so for those who are engaged in mainstream epistemology it may seem tempting to think that what feminists are doing is not relevant to their concerns, and to ignore feminist work as addressing a different set of issues.[2] Although I think it is right that a lot of feminist epistemology is addressing different issues, this response does not take into account that a significant amount of feminist writing explicitly undertakes to critique the mainstream epistemological questions; it is not simply that feminists are interested in something else, but that they have principled reasons for *not* engaging the issues as standardly framed.

My interest in this chapter, however, is not in evaluating the feminist challenges to the search for the truth conditions for knowledge claims. Although

[1] Thanks to Elizabeth Anderson, Donald Baxter, Cheshire Calhoun, Margaret Gilbert, Jim Joyce, Jeffrey Kasser, Krista Lawlor, Ruth Millikan, Peter Railton, Laura Schroeter, David Velleman, and Stephen Yablo for helpful discussion of issues taken up in this chapter. Special thanks to Karen Jones for excellent commentary on an earlier version presented at the Central Division meetings of the American Philosophical Association, May 1998. And thanks to audiences at the University of Connecticut and Colby College for their helpful discussion. An earlier version of this chapter also appears as "Defining Knowledge: Feminist Values and Normative Epistemology," in the *Proceedings of the World Congress of Philosophy*, 1998.

[2] One of the "notable exceptions" is Helen Longino, "The Fate of Knowledge in Social Theories of Science," in F. Schmitt, ed., *Socializing Epistemology: The Social Dimensions of Knowledge* (Lanham. MD: Rowman and Littlefield, 1994), pp. 135–57.

I am sympathetic with the complaint that there are many other epistemological topics that mainstream epistemology could and should consider, I am not convinced that this project itself is misconceived or irretrievably sexist or androcentric. I do think, however, that there are problems with the ways that philosophers have undertaken to provide an analysis of knowledge, and the problems suggest that an alternative approach informed by feminist concerns is desirable. My goal in this chapter is to suggest a way of approaching the task of specifying the truth conditions for knowledge, that (hopefully) will make clear how a broad range of feminist work that is often deemed irrelevant to the *philosophical* inquiry into knowledge is in fact highly relevant.

2. The Questions

Questions of the form "What is X?" (or What is it to be an X?) are often used to demand an articulation or clarification of the concept of X: What is the (ordinary?) concept of *knowledge?*[3] What is the proper analysis of the concept? I'll call this kind of project a *conceptual* investigation into X. Traditionally conceptual projects were treated as wholly a priori affairs, but contemporary efforts sometimes allow a degree of sociological or anthropological investigation in considering the variety of uses of the term or concept in question.

In contrast to the conceptual project, a *descriptive or naturalistic* project concerning X is not primarily concerned with exploring the nuances of our concepts (or anyone else's for that matter); it focuses instead on their (purported) extension, that is, the things that (purportedly) fall under the concept. Here, the task is to develop potentially more accurate concepts through careful consideration of the phenomena; this is achieved by establishing empirical or quasi-empirical generalizations about the domain in question. Paradigm descriptive projects occur in the natural sciences where the goal of understanding, for example, what water is, is not to analyze our ordinary concept of water, but to offer an account based in an empirical study of the relevant phenomena. In the case at hand, projects in naturalized epistemology seek to answer questions such as "What is knowledge?" through an a posteriori investigation of what we normally take to be paradigm instances.

In recent years there have been two different kinds of naturalistic projects in epistemology. The first and more radical form assimilates epistemology to

---

[3] Allowing for differences in conceptual resources across time and place, it might be important to specify the group whose concept is at issue: what is the dominant concept of knowledge within such and such a culture at such and such a time? However, it is notable that some traditional epistemologists seem to assume that there is one true concept of knowledge and the question is what is the proper analysis of that.

psychology (or sometimes sociology): the idea is to take our ordinary knowledge attributions to fix the reference of our epistemic terms, and then to undertake an (a posteriori) investigation of the natural (or social) kinds that are (allegedly) being referred to. The question is what, if anything, do those things that normally get called knowledge have in common? Do they deserve to be considered a kind—are they a unified collection? And if so, what is the basis for their unity? An alternative and recently more popular version makes explicit room for a normative component in knowledge by seeing the project as an investigation into the supervenience base for our ordinary epistemic evaluations.[4] Assuming that the normative supervenes on the non-normative, and that epistemology is normative, the question is: On what non-normative (physical, psychological, or social) facts does knowledge supervene? Both kinds of naturalizing approach begin the inquiry with pre-theoretic intuitions about cases that "fix the reference" of the term, and yet the resulting accounts often demonstrate the need for conceptual revision and can even serve to debunk the ordinary concept entirely (e.g., if the extension of our term 'knowledge' is not a natural kind, or if nothing is found to provide the supervenience base).

In practice, conceptual and descriptive projects can't be kept entirely separate, for each typically borrows substantially from each other. Conceptual projects depend upon a careful consideration of "normal" or paradigm cases and descriptive projects can provide the detailed accounts of them needed; in turn, descriptive projects require a rough specification of the boundaries of the phenomenon to be investigated and depend on conceptual projects to circumscribe what sorts of cases are at issue. In fact, the difference in these kinds of projects might be best taken to be a matter of emphasis. But the two sorts of project differ importantly in both their guiding questions and conditions of success: a conceptual project is concerned to specify, of all the candidate concepts, which concept of knowledge is *ours*; a descriptive project is concerned to specify, of all the candidate (natural) kinds, which we are referring to by the use of our epistemic terms. Although conceptual and descriptive projects are the most common (contemporary) approaches to questions of the form "What is X?" they are not the only ones; in fact, we'll consider a third approach later in this essay.

3. Knowledge and "Everyday Practices"

There is no doubt that much of modern and contemporary epistemology has been framed as an effort to respond to epistemological skepticism. The main anti-skeptical strategy of 20th century epistemology has been to challenge the

---

[4] See, e.g., Jaegwon Kim, "What Is "Naturalized Epistemology"?" Philosophical *Perspectives* 2 (1988): 381–405.

skeptic's conception of knowledge by taking our actual knowledge practices as providing definitive cases of knowledge. Beginning with the assumption that we do have knowledge in at least some ordinary contexts, the task is to use these contexts as a basis for articulating a conception of knowledge—possibly a naturalized conception—that might properly be called "ours." and that also rules out the skeptical hypothesis. The broad suggestion is that we should reject a "transcendental" epistemology that imposes conditions on knowledge that presume a standpoint outside of our practices, and should instead pursue what we might call an "immanent" epistemology that undertakes to elucidate the conditions on knowledge embedded in our everyday language, thought, and action.[5] Although the skeptic purports to be using the term 'know' as we do in claiming that we do not know there is an external world, attention to our use of epistemic terms shows that the skeptic is in fact employing a different concept whose conditions for use are not ours. Hence the skeptical challenge does not undermine our ordinary claims to know.

Of course even if there is broad agreement on the strategy of "immanent epistemology," controversy remains, for it is unclear what conception of knowledge is embedded in our "ordinary practices." Epistemologists, whether engaged in a conceptual or naturalistic project, have undertaken to uncover the "embedded" concept. For example, ordinary language philosophers have attempted to elucidate a nuanced analysis of our concept through a more or less a priori investigation. And radical naturalizers use our everyday attributions as the starting point for their investigation into the natural kinds that we are (allegedly) referring to. With this focus on our ordinary knowledge attributions, defenders of skepticism have, in turn, argued that in fact the conditions for knowledge embedded in our everyday practices are the skeptic's after all. But even if this is so, at this stage of the debate any theorizer—skeptical or not—who wants to maintain that the account they offer is an account of "our" concept of knowledge is committed to showing how it is to be found in our practices.

4. Feminism and the Pragmatics of Knowledge

On the face of it, then, it would seem that feminist work examining and critiquing our everyday knowledge practices would be extremely valuable to anyone undertaking an analysis of knowledge. If the goal is to offer an account of "our" concept of knowledge, then it is an important question whether the concept "embedded" in our practices is sexist, androcentric, or otherwise politically problematic.

---

[5] This is a slight revision of the slogan Stephen Stich uses to characterize "analytic epistemology." See Stephen Stich, *The Fragmentation of Reason* (Cambridge, MA: MIT Press, 1993), p. 93.

In fact, feminists have documented in impressive detail that our actual practices of knowledge attribution are both sexist and androcentric. Consider three kinds of questions about our ordinary practices (I raise them here for gender, but they can also be raised for race and class):

(i) Is an individual's gender relevant to whether he or she is likely to claim and/ or to be attributed knowledge? And is one's gender relevant to the *domain* in which one is likely to claim and/or be attributed knowledge?

(ii) Are the methods that are likely to be counted as knowledge-producing more often associated with men than women? Can the hierarchy of kinds of belief/method be justified on epistemic grounds or does the hierarchy reflect gender bias?

(iii) Are the conventions of authorizing certain individuals as knowers and the social rituals that accompany such authorization, for example, rituals involved in deferring to those authorized and in challenging authority, problematically sexist (or problematic in other ways)? Do these conventions have problematic effects on the workings of knowledge communities, for example, do they exclude women and protect ideological views from being challenged? Do they foster attitudes towards the natural world and towards other people that are androcentric and morally questionable?

In addressing these questions, feminists have accumulated substantial evidence that our actual knowledge attributions and practices of authorization privilege men and help sustain sexist and racist institutions. It is not essential to my project here to make the case that there is sexism in our everyday epistemic practices, for my concerns are more methodological. I would hope that it is obvious to anyone who has reflected for even a moment on their own behavior and the behavior of those around them that cognitive authority is not taken or granted in gender-neutral ways, and the prima facie plausibility of that claim is enough to raise the questions I want to address. But it may also be helpful to indicate briefly some of the main areas in which feminists have documented concerns [6] (again some of these points are directly parallel to ones that can be made concerning race and class):

[6] A valuable summary of the kind of research 1 have in mind can be found in Elizabeth Anderson, "Feminist Epistemology: An Interpretation and a Defense," *Hypatia* 10:3 (Summer 1995): 50–84. A full bibliography of recent work in feminist epistemology would no doubt be helpful, but not something I can provide here. I encourage the reader to consult the bibliography of Anderson's paper. In addition to other feminist work I've cited in this essay, there are three recent collections that are especially useful: L. Antony and C. Witt, ed., *A Mind of One's Own* (Boulder. CO: Westview. 1993): L. Alcoff and E. Potter, ed., *Feminist Epistemologies* (New York: Routledge. 1993); and the special issue of *Philosophical Topics* 23:2 (Fall 1995) on "Feminist Perspectives on Language, Knowledge, and Reality." These collections provide exposure to a broad range of authors and through their bibliographies to the extensive work in feminist epistemology.

- Sexism and sex-stereotyping in attributions of knowledge:
  - Refereeing: acceptance rate of papers by women increases when procedures are implemented to prevent the referee from knowing the sex of the author.
  - Classroom climate: women/girls and men/boys are asked different sorts of questions with different sorts of follow-up; men/boys are more often assumed to be capable in learning the subject and women/girls are not.
- "Masculine" and "feminine" coding of methods and fields:
  - Quantitative "hard" research is coded as masculine and is considered more important and more valuable; but these privileged methods are not uniformly successful and often what is considered "feminine" research is more effective and/or addresses different though equally valuable domains of inquiry.
- Entrenchment of sexist ideology:
  - Theories that affirm the naturalness of current sex roles (and other ideological expectations) are more quickly endorsed.
  - Use of sexist/gender metaphors in understanding non-gendered phenomena reinforce the idea that sexist social arrangements are "natural."
- Outright sexism in research communities.

Feminist discussions of these phenomena are tremendously rich and suggestive. However, the standard reply to taking these feminist studies to be philosophically illuminating is that it is "just sociology, not philosophy"—feminism tells us a lot about the sexism in our communities, but not much about our concept of knowledge. Stated as simply as this, however, the reply doesn't have much force coming from an epistemologist who favors an "immanent" strategy, for if we are trying to discern the concept embedded in our practices, "sociological" information about those practices should be relevant.

However, even though the simple reply can be dismissed, more needs to be said to link the sexism in our practices with the truth conditions for knowledge claims: How exactly should one go about reading our "embedded" concepts off our practices? Let me use a somewhat exaggerated example to demonstrate the problem. Suppose that there is substantial and systematic sexism in our attributions of knowledge. Should we conclude from this that "our" concept of knowledge is one that requires the knower to be male (or masculine)? For example, should we analyze the concept embedded in "our" practice along these lines:

S knows that p iff S is justified in believing p, p is true, and S is male (or S is in some relevant respects masculine).

Or should we provide an account with different justification conditions for men and for women, for example, requiring women to have greater justification than men in order to count as having knowledge? These suggestions are implausible (and I don't think it has been part of feminist epistemology to defend anything like this). The problem is that there are several ways to account for sexist attributions of knowledge other than claiming that the concept of knowledge being employed has the sexism built in to its truth conditions. For example, one might claim that the conditions for knowledge are gender neutral, but that background sexist beliefs lead people to believe that men are more likely to satisfy the conditions than women.[7] One way to develop this explanation would be to draw on a distinction between linguistic or conceptual competence and performance.[8] It is not unusual for ordinary and perfectly competent speakers of the language to get things repeatedly wrong due to systematic distortions present in the context; perhaps we should understand pervasive sexism as one of those systematic distortions that prevents us from making correct epistemic evaluations even by our own lights.

Alternatively, one could resist the charge that the sexism in our practices reveals a gendered concept of knowledge by arguing that in making knowledge attributions we are doing more than asserting that someone meets the conditions for knowledge, that is, the utterance conditions for knowledge attributions should be distinguished from the truth conditions.[9] If so, then our practices involving epistemic utterances may have us differentiate men and women not because the concept of knowledge employed in these utterances is somehow gendered, but because what we are doing with these utterances (besides asserting the knowledge attribution) is politically problematic.

To take this latter route is to allow that claims to know do more than assert propositions. Knowledge claims may well have propositional content, but expressing that propositional content is not the sole function of our speech act in claiming to know. As Austin so vividly puts it:

> . . . saying, 'I know' . . . is *not* saying 'I have performed an especially striking feat of cognition, superior, in the same scale as believing and being sure, even to being merely quite sure': for there *is* nothing in that

---

[7] Louise Antony has made this point in several contexts, e.g., in "Comment on Naomi Scheman." *Metaphilosophy* 26:3 (July 1995): 191–98.

[8] Note that Stich considers this move in response to the fact of "cognitive diversity" in *The Fragmentation of Reason*, pp. 80–82.

[9] See also Barry Stroud, *The Significance of Philosophical Skepticism* (Oxford: Oxford University Press, 1984), pp. 57 ff; also J. Joyce, "The Lasting Lesson of Skepticism" (1998 manuscript).

scale superior to being quite sure. Just as promising is not something superior, in the same scale as hoping and intending, even to merely fully intending; for there *is* nothing in that scale superior to fully intending. When I say, 'I know'. *I give* others my word: I *give* others *my authority for saying* that 'S is P'.[10]

He later continues:

> If you say you know something, the most immediate challenge takes the form of asking, 'Are you in a position to know?': that is, you must undertake to show not merely that you are sure of it, but that it is within your cognizance.[11]

Austin's reflections suggest that in making first person claims to know one is not (or not simply) reporting a psychological or cognitive state; one is performing a certain kind of socially meaningful act: among other things, one is claiming epistemic authority, an authority that may be "given" to others, and that may, in turn, be challenged.[12] Admittedly, one might interpret Austin as reading the truth conditions for knowledge claims directly off of our practices of knowledge attribution, but his own distinction between the locutionary and illocutionary force of an utterance provides room for a wedge between our epistemic practices and our epistemic concepts.

As I understand it, a lot of feminist work in epistemology focuses on the illocutionary force of knowledge claims—what's done, how it is done, the rituals and conventions that govern the distribution of epistemic power—rather than specifically addressing the question of truth conditions. As suggested above, the question isn't only *who* is authorized, and *what* methods are authorized, but how the rituals of authorization create and sustain self-affirming ideological communities. But acknowledging that our epistemic practices are mechanisms for the distribution of power and authority still leaves open a difficult question: what is the relationship between the (plausibly problematic) conditions of utterance for knowledge attributions and the truth conditions? Couldn't one reasonably maintain that feminist theorists should engage in a critique of our epistemic

---

[10] J. L. Austin, "Other Minds," in *Philosophical Papers*, second edition, ed., J. O. Urmson and G. J. Warnock (Oxford: Oxford University Press, 1970), p. 99.

[11] "Other Minds," p. 100.

[12] Although Austin himself focused on first person knowledge claims, his suggestions might be extended to second and third person attributions as well. I don't mean to suggest that an expressivist account of knowledge would be easy to provide, for all the reasons expressivist accounts are difficult (e.g., how to deal with embedding, connectives. etc.). Nor am I convinced that Austin's account is best understood as expressivist. Rather, I'm suggesting that in asserting that S knows that p one may also be performing another illocutionary act concerned with authorization.

practices, and even allow further that this is an important part of epistemology, but still claim that in spite of a devastating critique of our practices our basic concept of knowledge remains intact?

5. Reflective Equilibrium and the Search for "Our" Concepts

Note that both of the replies just sketched—one drawing on the distinction between performance and competence, the other between utterance conditions and truth conditions—assume that if we are careful about how we proceed, then there is some way to home in on a concept of knowledge that can rightly be considered "ours" through an examination of our ordinary epistemic practices. But what we need is some way to sort our attributions of knowledge into those that are properly indicative of our concept, and those that are not. What is the best way to do this? The standard procedure is to employ some form of reflective equilibrium: (roughly) consider the range of typical applications of the term in question and the generally agreed upon ("pre-theoretic") principles thought to govern its use, and determine the set of conditions that best accommodate both the applications and principles (allowing that cases and principles can be weighted according to centrality or importance).

This use of the method of reflective equilibrium, it might be thought, does well to set a standard for competence that allows performance errors: once examined closely the mistaken performances will be shown not to accord with the principles we endorse. And it might be possible to develop a sophisticated version of a reflective equilibrium test in order to distinguish truth conditions from utterance conditions. But there are compelling reasons, I think, not to rely on the method of reflective equilibrium (or at least "narrow" reflective equilibrium) as a basis for defining "our" concept of knowledge, reasons that should lead us to consider another way of pursuing an "immanent" approach to epistemology.

My doubts overlap substantially with those articulated by Stephen Stich in his critique of (what he calls) "analytic epistemology."[13] Stich's critique does not arise from feminist discussion of our epistemic practices, but in his case as in ours, the question is what to make philosophically of the messy reality of our epistemic and doxastic lives. As Stich points out, employing the method of reflective equilibrium in order to find the target concept in our practice presupposes (i) that there is no more than one such notion embedded in our practices, (ii) that there are general principles that govern our use of the notion or notions,

---

[13] *Fragmentation of Reason*, Ch. 4.

(iii) that there are effective ways of distinguishing principles that constitute meaning and ones that are part of our background "folk" theories (that is, analytic from synthetic principles), and (iv) that our practices and the concept in question are each coherent.[14] But most of these assumptions are highly questionable, especially for our epistemic notions.

But the second, and more important, question is why we should place so much weight on "our" concept in the first place. If we allow (which, given both the depth of our capacity for cognitive error, and the depth of our sexism, seems reasonable) that our practices might be systematically misguided; and if we take the primary task of epistemology to be a normative investigation into knowledge—one investigating how we ought to reason, on what basis we ought to form beliefs, and more generally what is epistemically *valuable*—then there is something peculiar about pursuing an "immanent" strategy in epistemology that undertakes simply to describe "our" concept, or to discover the (natural?) kind we ordinarily refer to. Normative epistemology certainly has much to learn from close attention to the ways we proceed epistemically, but to suppose that what we value epistemically is what we *ought* to value epistemically is to leave the normative part of normative epistemology undone.[15]

More specifically, the reflective equilibrium strategy of using our intuitions about principles to check our intuitions about cases and vice versa is not a plausible way to sift out sexist assumptions if we have reason to think that our everyday intuitions about cases and principles are interdependent, and both subject to pernicious background influences. For example, consider the question: can emotions count as (defeasible) evidence for a claim? Whatever pressures there are to think that they can't would seem to apply both to the specific judgments we make about cases (of course Susan is not justified in believing p, she is just in a fit of rage . . .), and the principles we affirm (to be justified in believing p one must have engaged in critical reflection upon one's beliefs . . . and so those who believe p in a moment of rage cannot be justified).

---

[14] *Fragmentation of Reason*, pp. 87–89.

[15] I take it to be a broad assumption in philosophical approaches to epistemology that the goal is to provide a normative account (e.g., see Kim, "What Is 'Naturalized Epistemology'?"). Though some see there to be two projects, one non-normative and another normative, e.g., Alvin Goldman, "Epistemic Folkways and Scientific Epistemology," in *Liaisons: Philosophy Meets the Cognitive and Social Sciences* (Cambridge, MA: MIT Press, 1992), pp. 155–75, reprinted in Paul K. Moser and Arnold vander Nat, ed., *Human Knowledge*, second edition (New York and Oxford: Oxford University Press, 1995). pp. 439–53. Note, however, that those who resist a normative inquiry are not in a good position to complain that feminist discussions are "just sociology, not philosophy," for the same question might be asked of their work: what makes it philosophy rather than sociology or psychology In short, if feminists are acknowledged to be making useful sociological/psychological observations, then the non-normative epistemological project should take those observations seriously; but (as I will argue) if the project is normative, then there too feminists have something to contribute to the discussion of value.

Note that I'm not suggesting that we should retreat from an "immanent" approach to epistemology altogether, if we understand an immanent approach to be one that undertakes to provide an analysis of knowledge *informed* by our "everyday language, thought, and action." In fact, it is through reflection on our everyday practices of knowledge attribution that I think we can confirm that our epistemic vocabulary functions normatively.[16] Nor am I suggesting that we abjure all use of the method of reflective equilibrium, for it may be that our best method for determining what is valuable is to engage in a wide reflective equilibrium—where what's involved is a broad critical reflection on one's beliefs, attitudes, and practices, to determine what combination, if any, is reflectively endorsable.[17] My concern is that because we employ our epistemic vocabulary to evaluate each other cognitively, we must undertake a normative inquiry into what is epistemically valuable, and not simply assume that "our" ordinary concept of knowledge—even when modified by recognized experts—captures what we should value. The approach I favor, then might reasonably be considered a form of immanent epistemology, but a *critical or normative* immanent epistemology.

6. Babies and Bath Water

Let's step back for a moment to consider where we stand. So far I've suggested that we—meaning to include both feminist and non-feminist epistemologists—may have good reasons for resisting a non-critical/non-normative approach to epistemology. A purely "descriptive" approach to the analysis of knowledge, I've argued, either ignores the normative question of what epistemic concepts we ought to employ, or assumes implausibly that the epistemic concepts we do employ are the ones we ought to.

---

[16] Can a very sophisticated but still narrow "reflective equilibrium" method capture the normative dimension here, and so do justice to the question of epistemic value? Stich argues not, and I would agree, since in principle what matters is not that we achieve a "reflective equilibrium" among our ordinary epistemic intuitions/judgments but that we determine what's valuable, and what's valuable may not show itself in our epistemic intuitions/judgments. Things will have to get more complicated to spell out this argument, however, since what we ought to value may be something that we can only determine via a method of wide reflective equilibrium. I will discuss this further below. My point here need only be that a narrow reflective equilibrium that takes into account only our intuitions/judgments regarding epistemic matters is insufficient.

[17] On the idea of reason as reflective self-government, see, e.g., Elizabeth Anderson. "Feminist Epistemology," pp. 52–53. Lest one be concerned that the introduction of value into epistemology render it non-objective, consider that many hold that there are standards for objective normative inquiry. Sec also Elizabeth Anderson, "Knowledge. Human Interests, and Objectivity in Feminist Epistemology," *Philosophical Topics* 23:2 (Fall 1995), esp. pp. 32–37.

But from a feminist point of view it may seem that I've thrown the baby out with the bath water: Wasn't my main point earlier that immanent epistemology cannot afford to ignore feminist research on the role of gender in our epistemic practices because it is committed to articulating the concept "embedded" in those practices? If our goal is no longer to explicate our actual concept of knowledge, how does the feminist research remain relevant? How does the discussion so far help us see how feminist research matters to epistemology at all?

My answer, I'm afraid, is going to be very programmatic. As I see it, the best way of going about a project of normative epistemology is first to consider what the point is in having a concept of knowledge: what work does it, or (better) could it, do for us? and second, to consider what concept would best accomplish this work. To frame the project this way is to employ a different approach to answering the question "What is knowledge?" (or more generally, "What is X?") than either the conceptual or the descriptive approaches outlined above. I'll refer to this third sort of project as an *analytical* approach.[18]

On an analytical approach the task is not simply to explicate our ordinary concept of X; nor is it to discover what those things we normally take to fall under the concept have in common; instead we ask what our purpose is in having the concept of X, whether this purpose is well-conceived, and what concept (or concepts) would serve our well-conceived purpose(s)—assuming there to be at least one—best.[19] Like the descriptive approach, this approach is quite comfortable with the result that we must revise—perhaps even radically—our ordinary concepts and classifications of things.

Some analytical projects are oriented towards theoretical concepts: the concept X is explicitly introduced or adopted as a theoretical tool within a larger inquiry, where the emphasis in determining the content of the concept

---

[18] I use the term 'analytical' for this approach because of its use in contemporary feminist theory lo designate such a project. In particular 1 have in mind Joan Scott's important essay, "Gender: A Useful Category of Historical Analysis," *American Historical Review* 91:5 (1986) 1053–75. Sandra Harding also employs this term, e.g., in "The Instabilities of the Analytical Categories of Feminist Theory," in Sandra Harding and Jean F. O' Barr, eds., *Sex and Scientific Inquiry* (Chicago and London: Univ. of Chicago Press, 1987), pp. 283–302, and Sandra Harding, *The Science Question in Feminism* (Ithaca and London: Cornell Univ. Press, 1986), e.g., p. 30. Note that my use of the term differs from Stich's in his phrase "analytic epistemology."

[19] My own temptation to view philosophical questions "analytically" is partly due to the influence of Paul Grice. Consider, e.g., "Reply to Richards," in R. Grandy and R. Warner, ed., *Philosophical Grounds of Rationality* (Oxford: Oxford University Press, 1986), pp. 45–106, and "Method in Philosophical Psychology (From the Banal to the Bizarre)," *Proceedings of the American Philosophical Association*, vol. 78 (November 1975): 23–53. Grice provides one of the important recent philosophical precedents for this approach.

is placed on the theoretical role it is being asked to play.[20] But an analytical approach is also possible in exploring non- (or less-) theoretical concepts if we are willing accept an answer to the question "What is X?" that does not exactly capture our intuitive concept of X, but instead offers a neighboring concept that serves our legitimate and well-conceived purposes better than the ordinary one.

So on an analytical approach, the specifically epistemic questions "What is knowledge?" or "What is objectivity?" require us to consider what work we want these concepts to do for us; why do we need them at all? The responsibility is both to investigate our purposes in having them, and then to define them in a way that best meets our legitimate purposes. In doing so we will want to be responsive to ordinary usage (and to aspects of both the connotation and extension of the terms). However, there is also a stipulative element to the project: *this* is the phenomenon we need to think about; let us use the term 'knowledge' to refer to it.[21] In short, on this approach, it is up to us to decide what to count as knowledge, and more radically, whether there is anything in our current usage of the term that compels us to carry on with any distinctions along those lines at all.[22]

It is plausible to think that there are several different purposes being served by our epistemic practices, and we need to ask what those purposes are, how

[20] In the limiting case of the analytic project, the meaning of the term is simply stipulated without reference to standard examples—this happens when a new theoretical term or notation is introduced—though in many projects there is some concern to draw on and address common (ordinary or theoretical) usage. In the latter case, it is within the scope of such a project both to challenge the idea that we need any such concept, i.e., that there is valuable work to be done in the vicinity, and to challenge the particular concept that has been employed to do it.

[21] On different sorts of definition and the possibility or impossibility of revisionary analytical projects, see W. V. O. Quine, "Two Dogmas of Empiricism," in *From a Logical Point of View* (New York: Harper and Row, 1963) section 2, and R. Rorty, "Metaphilosophical Difficulties of Linguistic Philosophy." introduction to *The Linguistic Turn* (Chicago and London: University of Chicago Press, 1992) pp. 1–39.

[22] Just as descriptive and conceptual projects cannot be kept entirely separate, analytic projects cannot be kept entirely separate from either. For example, descriptive projects unearth important and often novel similarities and differences in the items under consideration, and often provide innovative explanations aiming to do justice to the richness of the phenomena. But there comes a point when it's necessary to re-evaluate the conceptual tools the project started with, and to focus the inquiry by reassessing its aims: this invites a shift to a more analytical mode. Analytical projects reflect on, evaluate, and revise the conceptual tools we have for organizing phenomena, but in order to assess realistically what tools we need, and why we need them, they depend crucially on descriptive efforts. Stated crudely, a descriptive project begins with a rough conceptual framework in place, and looks to the world to fill in the details; an analytic project begins with a rough understanding of the salient facts, and works to construct a conceptual framework that can offer a useful way of organizing them. In both cases we do well to have a sensitive and thorough understanding of our existing concepts.

they are related, and to what extent they are legitimate.[23] Feminist work is relevant to normative epistemology because such work contributes to the exploration of what our purposes are, what they could be, and what they ought to be, in employing an epistemic framework. Feminist work also provides creative alternatives to existing conceptual frameworks for serving our legitimate purposes; given the revisionary potential of normative epistemology, the broadening of our conceptual resources offered by feminists should be welcome.

These suggestions are too general to be convincing, however, so it is probably better to describe the task less blandly and more politically. Some of our purposes in having an *epistemic* framework are likely to be very basic animal purposes—we need to have some relatively reliable information to help us get around in the world, we need to be able to adjudicate when other animals have information we can effectively use, and so on. Cognitively, we are both limited and empowered by our animal embodiment. But knowledge is not, and has never been thought to be, simply true belief, and human knowledge communities and the norms that define them do more than facilitate the gathering and exchange of information: they draw lines of authority and power, they mediate each person's relationship with herself (in defining conditions for self-knowledge), they circumscribe common ground for public debate and the basis for public policy (and much more). To decide what is epistemically valuable we need to decide what kind of knowledge community is desirable, and this can't help but involve political priorities and political choices. Feminists have much to contribute in considering such priorities and choices.

7. Constitutive Epistemic Values

One might object to the picture I've started to sketch by insisting that there are narrowly defined epistemic goals that should dictate our epistemic commitments, and consideration of political goals is not appropriate in determining what constitutes knowledge. To develop this point we can borrow a distinction drawn by Helen Longino between the *constitutive* and *contextual* values of our epistemic practices: the constitutive values of a practice are those that constitute the goal or end of that practice, or are necessary means towards those ends; in contrast, contextual values are those present in the context where knowledge is sought, discovered, attributed, denied, forgotten, and so on, but that do not

---

[23] Consider, e.g., Miranda Fricker. "Rational Authority and Social Power: Towards a Truly Social Epistemology," *Proceedings of the Aristotelian Society*, vol. XCVII, Part 2 (1998): 159–77; and Edward Craig, *Knowledge and the State of Nature: An Essay in Conceptual Synthesis* (Oxford: Oxford University Press, 1990).

define what the practice is, or what makes it an *epistemic* practice.[24] The thought then is that communities can decide what weight to give epistemic values such as truth, objectivity, coherence, and so on, compared to other values (e.g., some communities may decide that objectivity is not as important as solidarity),[25] and this is certainly a political matter, but the *epistemic* status of such values as truth and coherence is not up for political negotiation, for they are the constitutive values of anything that could be considered an epistemic practice in the first place. On this view, feminist debate about the politics of knowledge is not relevant to determining what knowledge is, or better *ought to be*, for what epistemic concepts we ought to employ should be determined by what is epistemically valuable, and not by political concerns.

There is something right about this complaint, but as it stands it is inadequate, for defining what's *epistemically* valuable in terms of the constitutive values of our epistemic practices just pushes the normative question back. Given the critique of non-normative/non-critical epistemology we've just been through, the question ought immediately to arise: what recommends our epistemic practices as opposed to some others? Why care about the epistemic values embedded in our actual practices, especially if we have reason to be critical of those practices?

It might be argued, however, that this reply misunderstands the objection: the constitutive values/goals of knowledge are not to be understood by considering the goals of our actual practices, but by reflection on the attitude of knowing (and perhaps the idealized practices that are required of those who aim for knowledge). What we're looking for are the constitutive values of knowledge itself, not our current knowledge practices. To get a handle on this it is useful to begin with belief: our epistemic evaluations involving the concept of knowledge look to be concerned with the question of what it takes to be exemplary in believing something. And beliefs are just the sorts of things that bring with them their standards of evaluation: a belief is correct if true; moreover, if a state isn't in the business of being true, then it isn't belief.

So consider the claim that truth is the constitutive goal of belief, that it is essential to anything that might count as a belief that it "aims at" the truth.[26] This is a claim about the nature of belief: for a psychological state to qualify as a belief it must represent its content as true, and in addition, the belief is correct

---

[24] Helen Longino, *Science as Social Knowledge* (Princeton: Princeton University Press. 1990), pp. 4–7.

[25] Consider, e.g., R. Rorty. "Solidarity or Objectivity?" in *Objectivity, Relativism, and Truth: Philosophical Papers*, vol. 1 (Cambridge U. Press, 1991), pp. 21–34.

[26] For a useful discussion of truth-directedness is an "internal" goal of belief, see P. Railton, "Truth, Reason, and the Regulation of Belief," *Philosophical Issues* 5 (1994): 72–75; and David Velleman, "The Possibility of Practical Reason," *Ethics* 106 (July 1996): 694–726, esp. pp. 708–14.

only if the content is true [27] (Contrast, for example, believing p from imagining p, or considering p. Many cognitive states represent their contents as true, but belief is distinctive in that the point of belief is to represent p as true only if it is.[28] Likewise a belief is correct or apt only if it is true; this is not the case of imaginings or considerings.) So if we are looking for what we ought to value in the cognitive domain, and if we frame these questions in terms of what believers ought to value, how believers ought to proceed, then it would be paradoxical to deny the value of truth. To be a successful believer is to represent the world accurately. (This is not because we must assume that all believers value the truth; some don't. The claim that belief aims at the truth does not entail that all believers value or aim at the truth; e.g., I may not endorse my own tendency to hold beliefs.[29]) Because knowledge plausibly requires true belief, we can conclude that likewise to be a successful knower is, among other things, to represent the world accurately. It thus appears that we can discover some constitutive epistemic values without reflecting on the social or political context of knowledge. Why not just continue in this fashion to provide the desired necessary and sufficient conditions for knowledge?

It may be that some constitutive epistemic values (such as truth) can be discovered without a consideration of contextual values, while others require attention to social context. But before granting that even this small part of epistemology can proceed without attention to social and political matters, I think it is valuable to reconsider the basis for regarding truth as an epistemic value. After all, truth may be a constitutive goal of belief, but is there some reason we should see ourselves as committed to forming *beliefs* (as opposed to, say, acceptings)? Is there some value in being a *believer*? Should we push the normative project back one more step?

8. Cognitive Values for Beings Like Us

In the discussion thus far I have suggested that we should approach the question "What are the truth conditions for knowledge claims?" by looking first at our epistemic practices to determine what we do with knowledge attributions, and what legitimate purpose might be served by them. At least in many contexts we use epistemic attributions and judgments in ways that are evaluative: in saying that S knows that p, I am saying that S has met certain cognitive/doxastic

---

[27] See "Truth, Reason, and the Regulation of Belief," p. 74

[28] For valuable discussion and elaboration of this point, see David Velleman, "How Belief Aims at the Truth" (manuscript, May 1998).

[29] Again, Velleman's work is very helpful in explaining this point. See "The Possibility of Practical Reason," pp. 709–10.

standards, with respect to p, where those standards capture something of cognitive value. But it isn't clear what the standards should be until we have a clear idea of the value or values at stake. So my suggestion is that we should begin our investigation of what it is to know by investigating what it is that is cognitively valuable (for creatures like us?), that is, what kinds of cognitive processes, states, and activities, we should endorse. But how do we decide what is cognitively valuable for creatures like us? And should everything that has cognitive value—even something that has only instrumental value—be properly considered relevant to an analysis of knowledge?

I'd like to be pluralistic about value in general and cognitive value more specifically. But pluralism comes in many forms, and to assert that we should be context-sensitive in judging what is valuable, or that different sorts of things might be instrumentally valuable depending on background goals or purposes, is compatible with claiming that certain things, in fact many things, are intrinsically valuable. For example. I am inclined to say that having beliefs is a good thing for human beings for many reasons, but one reason is that beliefs are an essential component of a kind of agency that is intrinsically valuable.[30]

I'm not going to offer an argument to defend my suggestion that it is a kind of (moral/autonomous) agency that is the over-arching value. I'm not sure I even have an argument for it yet. But the ideal of agency can at least function as a place-holder in my discussion, for my main goal is to sketch a broad structure for an account of epistemic value generally and knowledge more specifically. To emphasize the structural point, let me contrast my view with two others. The first is the view that epistemic/cognitive virtues constitute a realm of sui generis epistemic value, for example, that truth is good simply for its own sake. The second is the view that epistemic virtues are instrumentally valuable, for example, we should value truth and so belief (merely?) for survival purposes (the idea being that we need to know what the world is like so we can get around in it). Viewing truth as good because it is conducive to survival strikes me as insufficient, for empirical adequacy, or not too grossly false beliefs, are enough for survival. And although I don't have an argument against a realm of sui generis epistemic value, it is not a realm that I find compelling. Instead, I'd like to claim that something is epistemically valuable if it is a cognitive disposition, ability, or achievement that figures in a kind of (moral, autonomous) agency that is intrinsically good.[31] An analogy here may be helpful, for the notion of a complex

---

[30] Thanks to David Velleman for conversation on this and related points. For further discussion of links between epistemic concerns and agency, especially in the skeptical tradition, see Christopher Hookway, *Scepticism* (Routledge 1990), pp. 132–36. Thanks to Jeffrey Kasser for bringing Hookway's book to my attention.

[31] Note that to flesh out this picture I'd have to make a case that the kind of agency that is intrinsically valuable requires belief/truth rather than acceptance/empirical adequacy. This task goes well beyond the scope of this chapter.

intrinsic good that I have in mind is somewhat Aristotelian. *Eudaimonia* is intrinsically good; and yet it is a complex good. Other things are intrinsically good because they are constituent parts of a *eudaimon* life. These further goods are not merely instrumental goods, even though their goodness is conditional, that is, they are good conditional on the kind of being we are, but they are *intrinsically* good for us.

Having beliefs is intrinsically good because it is a constitutive requirement of a kind of agency that is part of a *eudaimon* life; because truth is a constitutive value of belief, then we ought also to value truth. Of the many sorts of epistemic evaluations we make, our knowledge attributions seem to be specifically oriented to evaluation of belief: in saying that S knows that p, I am saying that S has met certain cognitive/doxastic standards, with respect to the belief that p; because truth is a constitutive goal of belief, this partly explains why we take truth to be a primary condition for knowledge. But what else should we value in the cognitive domain and, more specifically, in the domain of belief? After all, it is normally thought that knowledge is not simply true belief. Is there something more? Traditionally, of course, the "something more" beyond true belief has been justification. And controversies have raged over the nature of justification. Pursuing the analytic strategy I outlined above, the prior question should be: What is at stake in seeking justification? Why are we interested in justified true belief rather than simply true belief?[32]

There is a tradition in epistemology which understands justification to be a matter of fulfilling epistemic responsibility. One is justified in believing p iff one has been epistemically responsible in forming and maintaining the belief that p. We might ask: What is the point of pursuing epistemic responsibility? We should also ask: What counts as epistemic responsibility? What one requires of epistemic responsibility may depend a lot on what view one has about the self and the self's relation to others. For example, one may think that epistemic responsibility requires that one undertake a solipsistic foundational justification for p because doing anything less (such as relying on the reports of others) is irresponsible. Or one may think that epistemic responsibility requires that one consult with others about whether they also believe that p (because one's own access to truth is presumed limited). Even the issue between internalists and externalists may arise here: an internalist will want the conditions for epistemic responsibility to be ones that we can self-monitor because we shouldn't be held

---

[32] William Alston's paper "Epistemic Desiderata," *Philosophy and Phenomenological Research*, vol. 52, no. 3 (September 1993): 527–51, is very useful in challenging the idea that there is an ordinary conception of justification that our epistemic inquiry must do justice to, and discusses several different purposes for the notion. Alston's argument is effective in showing that participants in the contemporary debate over justification may well be talking past each other. I'm sympathetic to Alston's methodological project, though my turn to a broader conception of value to resolve some of the questions is one he doesn't consider.

epistemically responsible for what we have little or no control over, and the externalist will not care about self-monitoring because (to put it crudely) value is placed more on effective agency rather than autonomous agency.

There is a lot of room here for debate over how we should think of ourselves and our cognitive situation, and what we should value cognitively. One might argue that all that matters is truth (though I think they'd have to add, and the avoidance of error), but there's still the question why truth matters. Truth matters *for beings like us* (and not for lots of other sorts of beings), because we have certain capacities (for representing the world and acting on our representations), and the exercise of these capacities is intrinsically good. And although I haven't offered here a view about why justification matters, the strategy I've been pursuing would have us look to the role of justification in informed and autonomous agency.

Note, however, that my intention is not to suggest that what we really need is a "virtue epistemology" (or that we don't); the competing ideas of epistemic responsibility and the conditions for justification they generate may be cashed out in terms that do not bring in virtues.[33] At least it is no part of my view that the primary locus of epistemic evaluation ought to be persons or dispositions rather than particular cognitive states such as beliefs; though I do think that we must consider the fact that the cognitive states are states of beings of a certain sort in order to properly evaluate them. (In other words, my reference to Aristotle is intended to highlight the notion of a conditional intrinsic good, not to invoke his entire ethical legacy.)

So what is my point? How is feminist inquiry into gender and the sexism of our epistemic practices relevant to this project? My suggestion is that questions of value are already implicit in traditional epistemological debates, and that these questions should be raised more explicitly. And feminist work on the self, on agency, and on social/political values can fruitfully inform and engage these debates. Can feminist inquiry tell us something about what conditions we should include in an "analysis" of S knows that p? If you think that the question is "what is our concept of knowledge?" you might want to do the traditional a priori investigation and spend a lot of time thinking about fake barns; if you think that the question is "what is the natural kind underlying our epistemic evaluations?" you might want to map out the core cases and then do psychology. But if you aren't convinced that what we do value epistemically is what we ought to value, and if you think (as I do) that there is no reason to favor a natural kind over a non-natural kind as the basis for our evaluations (e.g., the supervenience base for our evaluations may be highly disjunctive), then the question is: what should

---

[33] See, e.g., Linda T. Zagzebski, *Virtues of the Mind: An Inquiry into the Nature of Virtue and The Ethical Foundations of Knowledge* (Cambridge: Cambridge University Press. 1996). Thanks to Karen Jones for bringing Zagzebski's work to my attention.

our concept of knowledge be? But once this is the question, then an adequate definition of knowledge will depend on an account of what is cognitively valuable for beings like us, which raises moral and political issues on which feminists have much to contribute.

One might complain at this stage that my discussion has been too schematic to be convincing. Couldn't one easily maintain that although discussion of what's cognitively valuable has its place, the point and value of knowledge is best captured by regarding it simply as a matter of reliably formed true belief? Then my suggestion that feminist inquiry into our social and cognitive lives is essential to normative epistemology has little or no bite.

This is not the place to debate the virtues of reliabilism. My argument is intentionally schematic for my point is not to settle any debates but to open up space for further debate. Methodologically my response to the objection is that a defense of reliabilism cannot simply assume that reliably formed true belief constitutes the point and value of knowledge and would need to address the social and moral dimension of belief. For example, consider that although a reliabilist account of knowledge captures some of our concern with knowledge, it has often been observed that reliability is not all that matters in forming beliefs—if it were, then it would make epistemic sense to adopt a method of believing only tautologies. Falsehood is certainly an epistemic vice, but if avoiding falsehood were the single overriding epistemic virtue, then it could make sense to believe nothing.[34] But this makes no sense if our concern is what's cognitively valuable for beings like us, and if we also attach significant value to (informed) agency, for perfectly reliable processes of belief formation provide agents no meaningful basis for action (one cannot act on tautologies alone!).

Moreover, when asked why reliability is cognitively valuable, a plausible answer will point to the value of reliable information in enabling us to act. But this answer is weak if the connection between true belief and action is purely instrumental; as mentioned before, reliably true beliefs are not necessary for getting around effectively. Rather, there is a deeper connection between our cognitive lives and our practical lives. Reliable methods are valuable because they produce true beliefs, and true beliefs are necessary to achieve a kind of agency that is good; likewise having a coherent and fruitful system of beliefs is good because it promotes the effective exercise of a kind of agency that is good. An adequate account of knowledge must take a variety of characteristics into account, for example, truth, coherence, reliability, informativeness. fruitfulness, and so on. Again, the point here is not to suggest that reliable and fruitful methods, coherent belief sets, and such, are instrumentally good because they

---

[34] These points are eloquently put by W. James in his "The Will to Believe," in *The Will to Believe and Other Essays* (New York: Dover Publications, 1956). See also Hartry Field, "Realism and Relativism." *Journal of Philosophy* (1982), p. 565–66.

serve the political goal of furthering agency. Rather, the point is that they are intrinsically good for beings like us; their intrinsic goodness is conditional on certain facts about us as moral agents.

But once we begin to think in a more robust way about the value of agency and the cognitive life of a flourishing agent, it becomes clear that there are also more general issues at stake: how should we organize ourselves and our cognitive activities within communities so as to promote effective and informed agency? What is cognitively valuable for us *as a group*, that is, how might we best cooperate in our cognitive efforts, if we value the capacity in each individual to exercise their agency? (Or to achieve *eudaimonia*, or some other intrinsic good?) For example, there has been considerable discussion in the context of feminist moral theory of the notion of autonomy. The charge has been that traditional moral theory has not been sufficiently attentive to the social requirements for and limitations on autonomy. The charge is that not only have certain (exaggerated) ideals of independence and self-sufficiency been overrated, but valuable and sometimes unavoidable forms of interdependence have been ignored and/or scorned. A parallel discussion has emerged in the context of feminist epistemology: the lone epistemic agent is in some important sense a myth (wolf children are not plausible models for moral or epistemic life). Not only are we dependent on others for what we know, but our epistemic interdependence is a good thing; but at the same time we should be attentive to the value of epistemic autonomy.[35]

At this stage of my discussion I don't want to get involved in the details of these debates, but I think feminist theorizing has been effective in showing that different sets of norms and practices "construct" different kinds of knowers. An important task for epistemology, as I see it, is to consider the full range of norms, practices, and conventions, that together enable autonomous cognitive/epistemic agency. So, for example, even if we allow that there is a refined conception of epistemic independence that is valuable—one that recommends having a "mind of one's own," taking responsibility for one's own beliefs, and so on— and that this is a factor in achieving epistemic autonomy, epistemic autonomy is not just a matter of being independent in this sense, for it requires participation in a social network with other epistemic agents, whose own agency (and independence) provides a crucial check on our own beliefs.[36]

Here one might again object that I have managed to show how feminist work is relevant to the task of defining knowledge only by conflating that task with the project of describing the norms and practices that, in a particular context,

---

[35] Louise Antony has been good at reminding us all of this. See, e.g., Louise Antony. "Sisters Please, I'd Rather Do It Myself: A Defense of Individualism in Feminist Epistemology," *Philosophical Topics* 23, no. 2 (Fall 1995): 59–94.

[36] Thanks to Peter Railton for discussion of this issue.

enable one to be a more successful knower. For example, a reliabilist could grant that it is both difficult and important to determine what epistemic practices—considered both individually and socially—are more likely to enable individuals to gain knowledge. Because our epistemic practices are very messy affairs that vary tremendously across context, feminist inquiry may help us uncover some of the limitations of our actual practices and propose more effective ones. But none of this requires us to incorporate feminist insights regarding effective epistemic norms into our analysis of knowledge. The proper analysis of knowledge should simply focus on truth-tracking; the rest—including how we think of ourselves and our relations to each other—is just heuristics.[37]

I'm happy to grant that on a reliabilist view, much of what I am counting as relevant to determining the proper analysis of knowledge falls under the rubric of heuristics. But to consider the issue from the point of view of a reliabilist is to beg the question—for what recommends reliabilism over the various alternative epistemic positions? On what basis do we value truth, and grant it place as the dominant value in our cognitive practices? Even if in the end reliabilism turns out to be the most compelling epistemic view, some explanation must be given of its normative grip on us, of why we ought to evaluate ourselves and others in its terms.

I've suggested that one way of thinking about epistemic value is to resist the suggestion that epistemic values need be either instrumental or sui generis; there may be a more basic value of which they are constituent parts. Although in this chapter I've pointed to the value of a certain kind of agency as a basis for adjudicating what's epistemically valuable, I'm far from certain this can be spelled out, and in fact I am tempted by other alternative framings of our epistemic evaluations.

My remarks here are not sufficient to provide a very clear example of what sorts of conditions on knowledge we might consider, informed by the feminist research I've been alluding to. I'm afraid I haven't gotten quite that far in the program! My own inclination would be to resist the suggestion that we need to focus on one overall evaluative notion in this area: knowledge. This allows me to bring a pragmatist theme in my discussion back to the surface: on a critical analytical approach to the question "What is knowledge?" we begin by asking what we need the concept for, what work it is doing for us. I've argued that the theoretical work we want it to do is primarily evaluative: to say that S knows that p is to offer an evaluation of S's belief that p with respect to standards for belief formation and retention. This allows that there may be other jobs that need to be done, and some may want to retain the term 'knowledge' for those jobs; or one may prefer to reserve the term 'knowledge' for our current concept. That's fine with me; I don't want to quarrel about who gets to use the term. But even

---

[37] Thanks to Karen Jones for raising this objection.

considering the evaluative work that needs to be done, there are a variety of different purposes one might have in making epistemic evaluations. I've suggested that one way of thinking about epistemic value is to understand it in the context of a broader notion of autonomous agency (though I've only briefly sketched how this might work). But here, too. I want to allow that there are many different kinds of value and that alternative conceptions of epistemic value may depend on those. Ultimately I would hope for a proliferation of epistemic notions. Again. I'm not intending to close off inquiry, but to open it up.

However, the normative question, I think, is not in the end optional: a discussion of the truth conditions for knowledge claims that does not critically reflect on the broader purposes for our use of the concept, and that does not take up the issue of epistemic value is impoverished. But once we do engage in this critical reflection, feminist research into the sexism in our current practices and into alternative conceptions of agency and value become highly relevant and important.

References

Alcoff, Linda, and Elizabeth Potter, eds., *Feminist Epistemologies* (New York: Routledge, 1993).

Alston. William P. "Epistemic Desiderata," *Philosophy and Phenomenological Research* 52: 3 (September 1993): 527–51.

Anderson, Elizabeth. "Feminist Epistemology: An Interpretation and a Defense," *Hypatia* 10:3 (Summer 1995): 50–84.

———. "Knowledge. Human Interests, and Objectivity in Feminist Epistemology," *Philosophical Topics* 23:2 (Fall 1995): 27–58.

Antony, Louise. "Comment on Naomi Scheman" *Metaphilosophy* 26. no. 3 (July 1995): 191–98.

———. "Sisters Please, I'd Rather Do It Myself: A Defense of Individualism in Feminist Epistemology," *Philosophical Topics* 23:2 (Fall 1995): 59–94.

———, and Charlotte Witt, eds., *A Mind of One's Own* (Boulder, CO: Westview, 1993).

Austin. John L. "Other Minds." in *Philosophical Papers*, second edition, ed., J. O. Urmson and G. J. Warnock (Oxford: Oxford University Press, 1970), pp. 76–116.

Craig, Edward. *Knowledge and the State of Nature: An Essay in Conceptual Synthesis* (Oxford: Oxford University Press, 1990).

Field, Hartry. "Realism and Relativism." *Journal of Philosophy* 79 (1982): 565–66.

Fricker, Miranda. "Rational Authority and Social Power: Towards a Truly Social Epistemology," *Proceedings of the Aristotelian Society* 97, Part 2 (1998): 159–77.

Goldman, Alvin. "Epistemic Folkways and Scientific Epistemology," in *Human Knowledge*, second edition, ed., Paul K. Moser and Arnold vander Nat (New York and Oxford: Oxford University Press, 1995), pp. 439–53, reprinted from *Liaisons: Philosophy Meets the Cognitive and Social Sciences* (Cambridge, MA: MIT Press, 1992), pp. 155–75.

Grice, H. Paul. "Reply to Richards," in *Philosophical Grounds of Rationality*, ed., R. Grandy and R. Warner (Oxford: Oxford University Press, 1986), pp. 45–106.

———. "Method in Philosophical Psychology (From the Banal to the Bizarre)," *Proceedings of the American Philosophical Association* 78 (November 1975): 23–53.

Harding, Sandra. "The Instabilities of the Analytical Categories of Feminist Theory," in *Sex and Scientific Inquiry*, ed., Sandra Harding and Jean F. O'Barr (Chicago and London: Univ. of Chicago Press, 1987), pp. 283–302.

———. *The Science Question in Feminism* (Ithaca and London: Cornell Univ. Press, 1986).

Haslanger. Sally, ed., *Feminist Perspectives on Language. Knowledge, and Reality*, special issue of *Philosophical Topics* 23:2 (Fall 1995).

James, William. "The Will to Believe," in *The Will to Believe and Other Essays* (New York: Dover Publications, 1956).

Joyce, James. "The Lasting Lesson of Skepticism" (1998 manuscript).

Kim, Jaegwon. "What Is 'Naturalized Epistemology'?" *Philosophical Perspectives* 2 (1988): 381–405.

Longino, Helen. "The Fate of Knowledge in Social Theories of Science," in *Socializing Epistemology: The Social Dimensions of Knowledge*, ed., F. Schmitt (Lanham, MD: Rowman and Littlefield, 1994), pp. 135–57.

Quine. W. V. O. "Two Dogmas of Empiricism," in *From a Logical Point of View* (New York: Harper and Row, 1963), pp. 20–46.

Railton, Peter. "Truth, Reason, and the Regulation of Belief," *Philosophical Issues* 5 (1994): 72–75.

Rorty, Richard. "Metaphilosophical Difficulties of Linguistic Philosophy," in *The Linguistic Turn* (Chicago and London: University of Chicago Press, 1992), pp. 1–39.

———. "Solidarity or Objectivity?" in *Objectivity, Relativism, and Truth: Philosophical Papers*, vol. 1 (Cambridge U. Press, 1991), pp. 21–34.

Scott, Joan. "Gender: A Useful Category of Historical Analysis," *American Historical Review* 91:5 (1986): 1053–75.

Stich, Stephen. *The Fragmentation of Reason* (Cambridge, MA: MIT Press, 1993).

Stroud, Barry. *The Significance of Philosophical Skepticism* (Oxford: Oxford University Press, 1984).

Velleman, David. "The Possibility of Practical Reason," *Ethics* 106 (July 1996): 694–726.

———. "How Belief Aims at the Truth" (manuscript, May 1998).

Zagzebski, Linda T. *Virtues of the Mind: An Inquiry into the Nature of Virtue and the Ethical Foundations of Knowledge* (Cambridge: Cambridge University Press, 1996).

13

What Are We Talking About?

The Semantics and Politics of Social Kinds

When we talk of gender and race, at one level it is pretty clear what we're talking about. Although there are cases where it is hard to tell from casual observation what race or gender a person is, and although there are borderline cases in which our ordinary criteria don't give us a clear answer, we are all pretty well versed in the practice of assigning people a race and a gender. Yet, at another level, it is not so clear what we mean when we say "I'm a white woman" or "Barack Obama is a black man." For example, race eliminativists maintain that talk of races is vacuous (no one is white or black, Asian or Latino, because there are no races); others argue that race continues to be a meaningful biological kind; and still others argue that race is a social category. Feminists have questioned the legitimacy of dividing us into two sexes, males and females, and many have grown dubious of the sex/gender distinction altogether; in everyday discourse the term 'gender' now seems to be equivalent to 'sex'; and yet many feminist theorists still argue that gender is a social category. How do we make sense of all this? Are the apparent disagreements real disagreements, or are the different parties to these discussions really talking about different things?

Elsewhere I've defended social constructionist accounts of race and gender (Haslanger 2012 [2000]). I believe that races and genders are real categories to be defined in terms of social positions. I have come to this conclusion by considering what categories we should employ in the quest for social justice. Although I believe there is reason to conclude that biological essentialism about race and gender is false, to deny that people are raced and gendered within (at least) the contemporary United States would be to ignore facts about our social arrangements that those who seek justice cannot ignore. On my view, to say that I am a white woman is to situate me in complicated and interconnected systems of privilege and subordination that are triggered by interpretations of my physical capacities and appearance. Justice requires that we undermine these systems, and in order to do so, we need conceptual categories that enable us to describe them and their effects. A consequence of my view is that when justice is achieved, there will no longer be white women (there will no longer be men or women, whites or members of any other race). At that point, we—or more realistically, our descendents—won't need the concepts of race and gender to describe our current situation. However, we (they) will probably need the concepts in order to understand our past, just as, for example, to make sense of American social history, it is valuable to have the concept of 'quadroon,' 'octoroon,' 'spinster,' and the like.

Much recent debate over race, in particular, seems to have become bogged down in the question whether this or that account of race can claim to be an analysis of *our* concept of race (see, for example, Mallon 2004, Hardimon 2003). In developing constructionist accounts of race and gender, I've maintained that my goal is *not* to capture the ordinary meanings of 'race' or 'man' or 'woman', nor is it to capture our ordinary race and gender concepts. I've cast my inquiry as an analytical—or what I here call an *ameliorative*—project that seeks to identify what legitimate purposes we might have (if any) in categorizing people on the basis of race or gender, and to develop concepts that would help us achieve these ends. I believe that we should adopt a constructionist account not because it provides an analysis of our ordinary discourse, but because it offers numerous political and theoretical advantages.

However, in this chapter, I want to reconsider the strategy behind my own proposals, and social constructionist proposals more generally, and argue that they stand in a more complicated relationship to the project of analyzing ordinary discourse or explicating our concepts than I previously suggested. In doing so, I will offer a framework that clarifies the relationship between social constructionism and other philosophical projects, both naturalistic and a priori. The broad goal of this chapter is to question what's at issue in doing philosophical analysis of a concept, and to disrupt the assumptions behind the common revisionary/nonrevisionary contrast.

I begin by sketching a number of different projects that might legitimately count as providing an analysis of our concepts or speech. It is by now a familiar theme in philosophy of language that meanings (or at least some meanings) "aren't in the head"; yet it is a complicated matter to figure out the relationship between what is in our heads and the content of what we say, and think, and do. When thinking about socially and politically meaningful concepts, we must also be attentive to the possibility that what's in our heads may not only be incomplete, but may be actively masking what's semantically going on. Part of the job of ideology may be (somewhat paradoxically) to mislead us about the content of our own thoughts. How can we make sense of this? And, if this is the case, what becomes of the project of philosophical analysis?

Genealogy: Tardiness

The project of conceptual analysis in philosophy takes many forms, partly depending on the particular concept in question, and partly depending on what methodological assumptions the philosopher brings to the issue. There are at least three common ways to answer "What is X?" questions: *conceptual*, *descriptive*, and *ameliorative*.[1]

For example, consider the question: What is knowledge? Following a *conceptual* approach, one is asking: What is *our* concept of knowledge? and looks to a priori methods such as introspection for an answer. Taking into account intuitions about cases and principles, one hopes eventually to reach a reflective equilibrium. On a *descriptive* approach, one is concerned with what kinds (if any) our epistemic vocabulary tracks. The task is to develop potentially more accurate concepts through careful consideration of the phenomena, usually relying on empirical or quasi-empirical methods. Scientific essentialists and naturalizers, more generally, start by identifying paradigm cases—these may function to fix the referent of the term—and then draw on empirical (or quasiempirical) research to explicate the relevant kind to which the paradigms belong. Paradigms for knowledge could include my knowledge that there is a pencil on the desk in front of me, my daughter's knowledge that 2 + 2 = 4, the scientist's knowledge that $E = mc^2$, a sampling of further cases of memory, testimony, and the like. The question is whether these states form a natural kind, and if so, what kind? A descriptive approach in philosophy of mind and epistemology sometimes draws on cognitive science.

Ameliorative projects, in contrast, begin by asking: What is the point of having the concept in question—for example, why do we have a concept of knowledge or a concept of belief? What concept (if any) would do the work best? In the limit case, a theoretical concept is introduced by stipulating the meaning of a new term, and its content is determined entirely by the role it plays in the theory. If we allow that our everyday vocabularies serve both cognitive and practical purposes that might be well-served by our theorizing, then those pursuing an ameliorative

---

[1] Quine distinguishes different forms of definition, the third being what he calls (drawing on Carnap) "explicative." In giving explicative definitions, "an activity to which philosophers are given, and scientists also in their more philosophical moments . . . the purpose is not merely to paraphrase the definiendum into an outright synonym, but actually to improve upon the definiendum by refining or supplementing its meaning" (Quine 1963: 24–25). "Ameliorative" captures better than "explicative" the sort of project Quine is characterizing as especially philosophical; it is this sort of project that I've also called "analytical" (Haslanger 2012 [2000]). Because "analytical" is commonly used to characterize Anglo-American philosophy in general, and because I'm attempting here to introduce a more fine-grained framework, using "ameliorative" rather than "analytical" will sometimes avoid ambiguity. It should be understood, however, that on my view, whether or not an analysis is an improvement on existing meanings depends on the purposes of the inquiry.

approach might reasonably represent themselves as providing an account of our concept—or perhaps the concept we are reaching for—by enhancing our conceptual resources to serve our (critically examined) purposes. Conceptual, descriptive, and ameliorative projects cannot, of course, be kept entirely distinct, but they have different subject matters and different goals.

In this chapter, I consider an additional approach: *genealogy*. Later, I consider whether it should be considered a more specific form of the three approaches just mentioned, or in a distinct category. The idea of a genealogical approach stems from Nietzsche and Foucault, though it has been taken up by a wide range of scholars in the humanities. Very roughly, a genealogy of a concept explores its history, not in order to determine its true meaning by reference to origins, and not for sheer historicist fascination, but in order to understand how the concept is embedded in evolving social practices. Two points are crucial here: First, our concepts and our social practices are deeply intertwined. Concepts not only enable us to describe but also help structure social practices, and our evolving practices affect our concepts. Second, there is often a significant gap between the dominant or institutional understanding of a domain and its actual workings, for example, in the interplay between concept and practice, developments on one side can get ahead of or stubbornly resist the other.

For example, in some school districts, there are complex rules and consequences constructed around the notion of being *tardy*. There are forms for tracking tardiness; school officials looking out for tardiness; if you are tardy too many times in a year, you can be suspended or expelled, can't be promoted to the next grade, and so on. In school districts where this is the case, there are local understandings of how to navigate the system. For example, one morning when we were running especially late, my son Isaac reassured me by saying, "Don't worry Mom, no one is ever tardy on Wednesdays because my teacher doesn't turn in the attendance sheet on Wednesday until after the first period." This fact, together with the knowledge that his teacher would mark him present as long as he arrived before the attendance sheet was turned in, meant that *in practice* 'tardy' was defined differently in his classroom from the way it was, say, in the classroom next door.

How should we understand this? It might be tempting to insist that Isaac *really was* tardy when he arrived after the bell, even if his teacher didn't mark him as such on the attendance sheet. In other words, there is one *real* definition of tardy (the school district's: any student arriving in his or her homeroom after the 8:25 A.M. bell is tardy), and the others are only approximations and would be recognized as such by those involved.[2] However, we should note that such

---

[2] If there is a single correct definition of *tardy* it should probably generalize over all cases, for example, someone is tardy for X just in case they arrive after the official starting time for X (without an officially recognized excuse), and they are required or expected to arrive on time. But one might argue that even this sort of definition privileges the institutional structure rather than the local practice.

insistence would involve privileging the explicit institutional definition of *tardy* over the more implicit meaning established within the particular classroom practice.[3] In a slightly different context, one might imagine a teacher arguing with an overzealous school official by saying something like: "Yes, Sophia arrived two minutes after the bell rang, but students were still hanging up their coats. She wasn't *tardy*."

A genealogical approach is interested in the social and historical circumstances that give rise both to the disciplinary structures within which tardiness has its institutional meanings and to those that give rise to alternative, sometimes subversive, practices that arise in the day-to-day lives of those within the institution.[4] So in a genealogical account of 'tardiness' one would expect to find a story about how various conceptions of 'tardy' are embedded in the evolution of multiple and interacting social practices. My point is not to argue that either the classroom or the school district definition should be privileged; rather, (at the moment) it is to highlight that tardiness plays a role in different, and in some cases competing, practices.

In the literature on genealogy, the relevant contrast is often taken to be between broad institutional meanings and alternative local ones. However, this is one of several different axes of comparison that might be relevant. For example, in general, when we consider the use of terms or concepts in context there are important differences between:

- institutional uses v. "local" uses
- public uses v. more idiosyncratic individual uses
- what is explicit v. what is implicit in the minds of users
- what is thought (what we take ourselves to be doing with the concept) v. what is practiced (what we're actually doing with it)
- appropriate v. inappropriate uses.

In the case of 'tardy,' the school board's notion is public, explicit, more often recited than practiced and, one might think, an overly rigid definition of what tardiness really is (recall the teacher's complaint on Sophia's behalf); the local classroom notion is less public (though not private), implicit, more often practiced than recited, and, one might think, an overly ad hoc understanding of what tardiness really is (you're tardy unless you arrive around 8:25 on Mondays, Tuesdays, Thursdays, and Fridays, and before 9:00 A.M. on Wednesdays). Although a

---

[3] It might be worth noting that even the institutional definition given above—which would probably be the one articulated by the staff and students in the school—is not a general definition of *tardy* but only the definition for our school. Even in Cambridge, other public schools have different starting times.

[4] Though not always: where institutions are constructed to ensure social justice, the "subversive" meanings are often sites of injustice.

concern with power may recommend being especially attentive to the distinction between institutional and local meanings, for our purposes it will be important to have available the distinction between what I've elsewhere called the *manifest* concept and the *operative* concept (Haslanger 2012 [1995]). Roughly, the manifest concept is the more explicit, public, and "intuitive" one; the operative concept is the more implicit, hidden, and yet practiced one.[5]

Although I've focused on the simple example of 'tardy,' there are, of course, more philosophically rich examples available. Feminist and race theorists have been urging for some time that the proper target of analysis is not (or not simply) what we have in mind, but the social matrix where our concepts do their work. For example, Catherine MacKinnon says the verb *to be* in feminist theory "is a very empirical 'is.' Men define women as sexual beings; feminism comprehends that femininity 'is' sexual. Men see rape as intercourse; feminists say much intercourse 'is' rape" (MacKinnon 1987, 59). Charles Mills argues that the Enlightenment social contract is a racial contract (Mills 1997), and that an adequate analysis of personhood reveals that "all persons are equal, but only white males are persons" (Mills 1998, 70). Such analyses purport to show that our manifest understandings of crucial political notions are masking how the concepts in question actually operate (see also Mills 1998, 139–66).

It is important to note, however, that the axes of comparison I've listed introduce a contrast between what tardiness (femininity, personhood) "really is" and the competing understandings of tardiness used in practice that takes us beyond genealogy. Within a genealogical inquiry our subject matter is a set of historically specific social practices. To give an account of *what tardiness really is*, is to describe a broad matrix of practices, procedures, rules, rationales, punishments, institutions, equipment (bells, clipboards, forms), to demonstrate how power circulates within it, and how certain subject positions (the walkers, the bus-riders, the habitually tardy) are formed (see also Hacking 1999, 10–14). On the genealogical approach, this matrix is what tardiness *really is*.[6]

---

[5] I don't mean to suggest here that there is only one manifest concept and only one operative concept. The manifest and operative concepts may vary from context to context. Note also that although it may be tempting to map the manifest/operative distinction onto the more familiar conception/concept distinction, it is not going to do the work needed. For example, in the case of 'tardy' in Isaac's classroom, the manifest concept is the institutional or public one and the operative one is more idiosyncratic. This suggests that in some cases what we think may be more common and public than what we do with language.

[6] This matrix is not invisible to the alert. For example, in the March 28, 2004, *New York Times* you can find this headline: "Pollution and the Slippery Meaning of 'Clean.'" According to the article, families in the area of Love Canal "live in neat, new ranch houses and federal officials recently announced that they now consider this notorious symbol of industrial pollution clean. But what does clean mean when the pollutants that rendered Love Canal dangerous to humans remain exactly where they were? In fact, there is no accepted standard, and clean, in practical terms, often means still polluted—but in a different and less dangerous way." Similarly, the term 'clean' when contrasted with 'explicit' in describing rap lyrics doesn't exactly mean what it connotes and serves as a stand-in for a complex social matrix.

However, in suggesting above that both the local and institutional definitions of tardiness were in some respects inadequate, I was implying that there is a further way of thinking about what tardiness "really is" that should take us into normative questions: Should we have the category of 'tardy' in our school district? If so, how should it be defined? One might be tempted to think that the situation in our local school is ripe for an ameliorative inquiry that would have us consider what the point is of a practice of marking students tardy, and what definition (and corresponding policy) would best achieve the legitimate purposes.

The lack of attention to the normative is the basis for an important and influential criticism of genealogical inquiry. Although genealogy is attentive to and describes the use of normative discourse and the impact of social norms, it attempts to foreswear making normative claims; as a result, it cannot make crucial distinctions between good and bad forms of power and authority, legitimate or illegitimate force (Fraser 1989, chap. 1). Correlatively, one might complain that analytic inquiry that attempts to improve on our current definitions typically fails to understand how our current concepts have structured our practices, distribute power and authority, and bring with them false assumptions of legitimacy. It is tempting to think that genealogy without normative analysis shirks its responsibilities; and normative analysis without genealogy is out of touch with reality. Note again that to distinguish the variety of philosophical projects is not to say that they can or should be pursued independently; yet making clear the differences can help us locate our disagreements and misunderstandings.

Forms of Genealogy

So, what is the relationship between genealogy and the approaches mentioned earlier, namely, the conceptual, descriptive, and ameliorative? Insofar as the goal of genealogy is to understand how concepts are embedded within social matrices, it is possible to modify any of these more traditional approaches in the spirit of genealogy.

For example, the conceptual approach I've described focuses on a priori reflection and ideas that are relatively accessible to introspection; it is plausible to see this as an investigation of the manifest concept.[7] In undertaking conceptual analysis of, say, F-ness, it is typically assumed that it is enough to ask competent users of English under what conditions someone is F, without making any special effort to consult those whose daily lives are affected by the concept. However, if one is sensitive to the possibility that in any actual circumstance there

---

[7] Although I'm not endorsing the methods of ordinary-language philosophy, the complexity of our use of words in different contexts is something ordinary-language philosophers were well attuned to, and some of their methods and ideas are tremendously valuable for genealogy.

are competing meanings (often quite explicit) that structure alternative practices, then it seems worth considering a broad range of speakers, who are differently situated with respect to the phenomenon. A *conceptual genealogy* of 'tardy'
would not be content with reflection by a competent English speaker, but would
require attention to differently situated speakers over time. We would need to
ask: What are the range of meanings? Whose meanings are dominant and why?

Of course, some speakers may not be very thoughtful about their use of
terms, and others may simply be confused. Yet we should keep in mind that
"our" concept may not be univocal; in our haste to find a univocal concept, we
may obscure how the concept works in a complex social context. Such investiga-
tions into a broader range of ideas and practices will not only be relevant to a
conceptual genealogy, but also to an *ameliorative genealogy* that undertakes to
evaluate the point of having a concept or structure of concepts (along with related practices) and proposes improved resources to fulfill them.

In this chapter, however, I am especially interested in exploring how genealogy might affect a descriptive approach. Those pursuing a descriptive approach
will usually select paradigms from commonly and publicly recognized cases; as
suggested before, the task is to determine the more general type or kind to
which they belong. For example, the case in which Isaac arrives at school at 8:40
A.M. (when school starts at 8:25 A.M.) would count as a paradigm case of tardiness, regardless of what his teacher marks on the attendance sheet. Of course,
the aim of a descriptive project in this case is not to provide a *naturalistic* account
of tardiness—one that would seek to discover the *natural* (as contrasted with
social) kind within which the paradigms fall—given that the notion of being "on
time" concerns one's behavior in response to a complex set of norms and expectations. But it is possible to pursue a descriptive approach within a social domain
as long as one allows that there are social kinds or types.[8] In fact, I've chosen to

---

[8] Because the terminology of 'natural kind' is used in several different ways, it is helpful to make
a few distinctions. The term 'kind' is sometimes used to classify substances, in the ordinary case,
(physical) objects. Substances can be classified according to their essence; kinds consist of groups
of objects with a common essence. For example, tigers constitute a kind of thing because each tiger
has essentially a certain cluster of properties that define the kind. On other occasions, the term
'kind' is used to refer to what are sometimes called types. A type is a group of things, sometimes
substances, but possibly nonsubstances, that has a certain unity. This unity need not be a matter of
sharing essential properties: red things constitute a type (their unity consists in their all being red),
even though redness is seldom an essential property of the things that have it. Unity seems to come
in different degrees. The things on my desk might be thought to constitute a weak sort of type (they
have in common the fact that they are on my desk), and at the limit there are highly gerrymandered
sets of things that don't have any unity at all and so don't constitute a type.

One way to think about the unity of types is in terms of similarity between the members. We can
distinguish different sorts of types by distinguishing axes of similarity. Exactly six foot tall human
beings are a natural type because the commonality between the members is natural (species and
height); high school graduates are a social type because the commonality between the members is
social. Both of these types are (metaphysically) objective, however, in the sense that the commonality

speak of descriptive approaches rather than naturalistic ones for just this reason. Descriptive analyses of social terms such as 'democracy' and 'genocide' or ethical terms such as 'responsibility' and 'autonomy' are methodologically parallel to more familiar naturalizing projects in epistemology and philosophy of mind. However, the investigation of social kinds will need to draw on empirical social/historical inquiry, not just natural science.

If one were to undertake a *descriptive genealogy* of 'tardiness,' then it makes most sense to start with a social context in which tardiness plays a role. The first task is to collect cases that emerge in different (and perhaps competing) practices; then, as before, one should consider if the cases constitute a genuine type, and if so, what unifies the type. This, of course, cannot be done in a mechanical way and may require sophisticated social theory both to select the paradigms and to analyze their commonality; and it is easily possible that the analysis of the type is highly surprising. For example, it was not intuitively obvious that water is H_2O or that gold is an element with the atomic number 79. It took sophisticated natural science to determine what the terms 'water' and 'gold' mean. In any descriptive project, intuitions about the conditions for applying the concept should be considered secondary to what the cases in fact have in common; so as we learn more about the paradigms, we learn more about our concepts.

Semantic Externalism

I've suggested that there are different projects that might count as attempting to theorize what tardiness is. Because these projects will reasonably yield different accounts, one might wonder which strategy is entitled to claim that its results provide an analysis of the concept. The problem should look more familiar if we situate this discussion in the tradition of semantic externalism. Externalists maintain that the content of what we think and mean is determined not simply by intrinsic facts about us but at least in part by facts about our environment. Remember: Sally and Twinsally both use the term 'water,' but Sally means H_2O and Twinsally means XYZ (Putnam 1975). Sally thinks she has arthritis in her thigh, and is wrong because 'arthritis' in her environment is an ailment of the joints; Twinsally thinks she has arthritis in her thigh

between the members lies in properties of the objects (or relations between them), and not in their relationship to the speaker or cognizer. How to draw the line between social and natural types is difficult and not one I address here. I rely on background understandings and familiar cases. However, it is important to keep in mind that as I am using the terms, the distinction between objective and nonobjective kinds or types is importantly different from the distinction between natural and social kinds or types.

and is right because 'arthritis' in her environment is an ailment that is not confined to the joints (Burge 1979).

Externalism initially appeared in two forms, supported by the sorts of examples just recited:

> *Natural kind externalism* (Putnam 1975; Kripke 1980): natural kind terms or concepts pick out a natural kind, whether or not we can state the essence of the kind, by virtue of the fact that their meaning is determined by ostension of a paradigm (or other means of reference fixing) together with an implicit extension to "things of the same kind" as the paradigm.

> *Social externalism* (Putnam 1973; Burge 1979): the meaning of a term or the content of a concept used by a speaker is determined at least in part by the standard linguistic usage in his or her community.

It then became clear that externalist phenomena are not confined to natural kind terms (properly speaking) but occur quite broadly. For example, in the history of logic and math, inquiry can seem to converge on an idea or concept that we seemed to have in mind all along, even though no one, even the best minds, could have explicated it. (Leibniz's early efforts to define the limit of a series is an example.) In such cases, it is plausible to maintain that certain experts were "grasping a definite sense, whilst also failing to grasp it 'sharply'" (Peacocke 1998, 50). Although Fregeans are apt to capture this by invoking objective senses that the inquirers "grasp," an ontology of sparse objective properties will also do the work.

The upshot of this is that the basic strategy of natural kind externalism need not be confined to natural kinds (where it is assumed that things of the same natural kind share an essence). Externalism is an option whenever there are relatively objective types. The notion of objective type needed is not too mysterious: a set of objects is more an objective type by virtue of the degree of unity among its members beyond a random or gerrymandered set. We might account for unity in various ways (Lewis 1983), but a familiar way I'll assume for current purposes is in terms of degrees of similarity; the similarity in question need not be a matter of intrinsic similarity, that is, things can be similar by virtue of the relations (perhaps to us) they stand in. Roughly,

> *Objective type externalism*: terms or concepts pick out an objective type, whether or not we can state conditions for membership in the type, by virtue of the fact that their meaning is determined by ostension of paradigms (or other means of reference fixing) together with an implicit extension to things of the same type as the paradigms.

Sets of paradigms typically fall within more than one type. To handle this, one may further specify the kind of type (type of liquid, type of artwork), or may (in the default?) count the common type with the highest degree of objectivity. We should not assume that objectivity is only found in the natural world. There are objective types in every realm: social, psychological, political, mathematical, artistic, and so on.[9]

What does externalism have to do with genealogy? Genealogy explores the embeddedness of a concept within social practices and the history of those practices. Just above I suggested that a *conceptual genealogy* would explore the relatively explicit ideas and assumptions associated with a concept (over time), taking into account how these may vary depending on one's position within the practice structured by the concept. A *descriptive genealogy* explores how a term functions in our evolving practices and manages to pick things out. Descriptive projects, of the sort I've indicated, adopt an externalist approach to content: they set out to determine the objective type, if any, into which the paradigms of a particular concept fall. Descriptive projects become genealogical to the extent that they attend to the concrete historical workings of our practices and how the concept is actually used to structure our ongoing activities. In effect, a descriptive project will aim to disclose the *operative* concept(s), while the conceptual project explicates the manifest.

In some cases, the manifest concept and operative concept coincide: when we are clear what exactly we are talking about. But in many cases a speaker could have as the content of her thought or speech something about which she was ignorant or even seriously misguided. Given the externalist backdrop, this is not surprising. As the externalist slogan goes, "Meanings ain't in the head." The genealogist is especially keen to explore cases in which the manifest and operative concepts come apart, that is, when the operation of the concepts in our lives is not manifest to us. If one assumes that the task of philosophical inquiry is simply to explicate the dominant manifest meaning of a term, then any genealogical inquiry—almost any externalist inquiry—will seem revisionary. But philosophical inquiry—even philosophical inquiry that takes its goal to be the analysis of our concepts—should not define itself so narrowly, or else it is in danger of collapsing into lexicography (an interesting endeavor, to be sure, but not our only option).

---

[9] The third sort is supported by the idea that inquiry can seem to converge on an idea or concept that we seemed to have in mind all along, even though no one, even the best minds, could have explicated it. So, for example, in the history of logic, math, and science, it is plausible to maintain that certain experts were "grasping a definite sense, whilst also failing to grasp it 'sharply'" (Peacocke 1998, 50). I assume that these can fall within objective type externalism because at least there are some paradigms that fix the reference in question; they don't seem to qualify for social externalism because there isn't yet a standard linguistic usage.

Descriptive Genealogies of Race and Gender

I've suggested so far that there are several different projects that might plausibly be thought to provide an analysis of our concepts, and several different kinds of subject matter that might be analyzed.[10]

Conceptual analyses elucidate "our" (manifest) concept of F-ness by exploring what "we" take F-ness to be.

Conceptual genealogy: elucidate the variety of understandings and uses of F-ness over time and across individuals differently positioned with respect to practices that employ the notion.

Descriptive analyses elucidate the empirical kinds (the operative concept) into which "our" paradigm cases of F-ness fall.

Descriptive naturalism: elucidate, where possible, the *natural* (chemical, biological, neurological) kinds that capture "our" paradigm cases of F-ness.

Descriptive genealogy: elucidate the *social matrix* (history, practices, power relations) within which "we" discriminate between things that are F and those that aren't.

Ameliorative analyses elucidate "our" legitimate purposes and what concept of F-ness (if any) would serve them best (the target concept). Normative input is needed.

Although I have distinguished the different projects and subject matter, there will be cases in which they completely coincide. In other words, there will be cases in which we are aware of what we are talking about, and what we are talking about is what we should be talking about, namely, where the manifest, operative, and target concepts are the same. There will be cases in which an ameliorative project targets the kind that we are, and take ourselves to be, tracking. But there will also be times when these come apart, for example, where ignorance or ideology masks what we are doing or saying.

When the manifest, operative, and target concepts come apart, there will be different ways to unite them. For example, if the target concept and manifest concept coincide and it is our practice that fails, the best strategy is plausibly to correct the practice to meet the standards we ourselves affirm. In other instances, our practice is tracking something worth tracking, but we're misguided about what it is; so we need to improve our understanding of the phenomena. Sometimes we are clear what we're tracking, but something else is what we should be or need to be tracking.

---

[10] I put "our" and "we" in scare quotes to indicate that there may be significant contextual variation, or at least there will be room for contestation.

Social constructionists are interested in cases where there is a gap between manifest, operative, and target concepts, and in particular, where assumptions about what's natural are misleading us about what we're talking about. Constructionists come in many forms, of course, but at least a good number of us argue, concerning certain specific concepts, that contrary to common assumptions, we are tracking something social when we think we're tracking something natural, and pointing this out is a way of understanding what we're *really* talking about. So although the constructionist's analyses may seem revisionary, the proposed revisions in our understanding bring our ideas in better accord with what we have been doing (or should have been doing) all along. This sort of revisionary analysis is surely in keeping with the philosophical goal of talking about what we should be talking about, and being fully aware of what that is.

Given the different projects of analysis and different subject matters for analysis, it is not surprising that philosophers who may appear to be asking the same question are in fact talking past each other. For example, where one philosopher might assume that an adequate analysis must capture our ordinary intuitions, another may take for granted that a priori reflection is likely to be systematically misleading when we are trying to understand the social domain. Recent work on race provides an excellent example of the diversity of approaches. Some authors are engaged in a conceptual project, attempting to explicate our ordinary understanding of race (Appiah 1996, Zack 1997, Hardimon 2003, Mallon 2004); others are attempting to determine what, if any, natural kind we are referring to by our racial terms (Appiah 1996, Kitcher 1999, Andreason 2000, Zack 2002, Glasgow 2003); others have pursued genealogy (Omi and Winant 1994): and still others are invested in what I call ameliorative projects, raising normative questions about how we *should* understand race, not only how we currently do (Gooding-Williams 1998, Alcoff 2000).

What should we make of these different projects? Should we simply allow that different inquirers are interested in different questions, and nothing can be said to resolve the question what race *really is* or what we mean by "race"? I would not argue that there is one thing that race really *is* or one thing that "we" mean by "race." Nevertheless, in developing an account of race we should be attentive to our manifest, operative, and target concepts and, if there is a legitimate target notion, have them coincide. It is a mistake, then, for those engaged in conceptual analysis to dismiss inquiries into operative and target concepts, with the thought that only the conceptual project can discover "our" concept. For example, if we discover that we are tracking something that is worthwhile to track in using our racial vocabulary, then even if this is not what we originally "had in mind," it still may be what we have been and should continue to be talking about.[11]

---

[11] It might be useful to see this by analogy with other terminological developments in science. Although our understanding of and even our definition of 'atom' has changed over time, it is plausible that there is something worthwhile we have been and continue to be talking about.

There are cases, however, where the different strands of analysis confront each other more directly. Let's consider again how a gap between manifest and operative concepts arises. Working within an externalist paradigm, the standard case will be one in which the paradigms are projectible onto an objective type, but those whose manifest concept is at issue are typically ignorant or mistaken in some way or other about the type. So, for example, suppose that in a particular community a substantial number of the population take 'evergreens' to refer to plants that have needles instead of leaves. In this context, plausibly the manifest concept of 'evergreen' will be of plants with needles. However, given externalist considerations about the broader function of the term 'evergreen' in that community and plant types, it is reasonable to conclude that the term 'evergreens' picks out some broad-leaved plants such as hollies, rhododendrons, some ivies, and the like. Consider another case: suppose (as at MIT) there is a rule that says students may not receive an incomplete for a course unless 80 percent of the work has been submitted. Suppose further, however, that faculty often grant incompletes to students who have submitted less work, but each think that other faculty generally stick to the rule. Here too there will be a gap between what is generally understood by 'incomplete' and how the practice distinguishes those who earn incompletes and those who don't.

In the 'evergreen' case, there are compelling reasons to think that those restricting the meaning of 'evergreens' to plants with needles are making the mistake about what evergreens are, given that there are legitimate reasons to distinguish plants that stay green all winter from those that don't, and that members of the community who work with plants and are most familiar with plant types are able to track that distinction with their use of the term. But in the case of incompletes, it is less clear. Once the gap between rule and practice is pointed out, there may be controversy about what an incomplete "really is." The hard-nosed faculty may insist that the rule for incompletes defines what incompletes really are, and any other incompletes were given in error. Let's call this the strict *standards approach*. More accommodating faculty may argue that the actual practice (for example, of giving incompletes to any student who completes some but not all of the work) is what incompletes really are, and the hard-nosed faculty are living in a fantasy if they think the rule is followed. We could call this the *priority of practice approach*. An obvious next move would be to say that the important question is not what incompletes are, but what they *should be* that matters, and move the question to an ameliorative inquiry. However, this example highlights that conflict over what we're talking about may turn on how we draw the distinction between paradigms and errors, since of course the hard-nosed and the accommodating faculty don't agree on what the paradigm and mistaken incompletes are.

Defenders of intuition-based (that is, nongenealogical) conceptual analysis are likely to side with the hard-nosed in such cases. Our paradigms, it might be argued, should at the very least conform to our core ideas about how to apply the concept. If we agree on the 80 percent rule for incompletes, then our paradigms for incompletes ought to be those cases in which the rule is followed. If we project the type from the "right" paradigms, our manifest and operative concepts will coincide. The genealogist will insist that our regular practice of granting students incompletes should determine the paradigms, for what we're doing (and have done) with the distinction is what matters. And if we become clear what we're doing, the manifest and operative concepts will coincide.

In many such cases, we face two questions: what policy do we want to promote (or what objective type do we want to track), and what do we want to do with the bit of language we have been using? Do we want to change our policy and keep the same term, change it and introduce a new term, keep the policy and change the term, or keep the policy with the old term? How we proceed is primarily a pragmatic, political, and rhetorical issue. If the term has been long and strongly associated with a particular policy (or type), then it may take substantial work to change what we do with it; other terms are quite malleable in their operations. An important question is whether there ever are cases where the genealogist's (constructivist's) stand that the social category is what we're really talking about is the only reasonable option. Although I am inclined to believe that there are such cases, a full defense of this position is not possible here.

Considering the different forms of philosophical analysis, it should now be more clear that in charging that an account of a concept is revisionary, one must do more than show that it violates some ordinary intuitions; moreover, the claim that one's own account captures "our concept," must be explicated and defended by more than trotting out one's own intuitions (or a group of philosophers' intuitions) about how "we" tend to use the concept. Although social constructionist analyses are not what most people "have in mind" when they think about gender or race, it does not follow that they are inadequate even as analyses of *our* concepts, for a genealogical analysis undertakes not to explicate what is in our heads, but rather the constitutive social matrix for the paradigms.

In this discussion, I have done nothing to argue that the best way to account for gender or race in the United States is to undertake genealogy; rather, my aim has been to provide a framework for taking seriously social matrices within the context of philosophical inquiry. I believe that social constructionist accounts of race and gender (and other social categories) are attempts to identify what, among the complex forces and structures of social life, constitute a widespread and enduring source of injustice. Because our manifest concepts of race and gender still tend to be naturalized, it is news, but not conceptual revision, to provide analyses that explain the commonality among those of a race and a gender as social. My hope is that greater attention to the gap between manifest and operative concepts will lead philosophers to focus less on our intuitions and more on the role of concepts in structuring our social lives. Philosophical analysis has a potential for unmasking ideology, not simply articulating it.

Acknowledgments

Thanks to Louise Antony, Rachael Briggs, Alex Byrne, Jorge Garcia, Ishani Maitra, Mary Kate McGowan, Ned Hall, Richard Holton, Rae Langton, Marion Smiley, Sarah Song, Ásta Sveinsdóttir, and Steve Yablo for discussing with me the issues raised in this chapter. Special thanks to Lawrence Blum, Samantha Brennan, and Anita Superson for comments on an earlier draft. A version of this chapter was presented at the Society for Analytic Feminism Conference in London, Ontario, June 6, 2004, and benefited from the discussion.

References

Alcoff, Linda. 2000. Is Latina/o identity a racial identity? In *Hispanics/Latinos in the United States*, ed. J. J. E. Gracia and P. DeGrieff. New York: Routledge.

Andreasen, R. O. 2000. Race: Biological reality or social construct? *Philosophy of Social Science* 67(Proceedings): S653–S666.

Appiah, Kwame Anthony. 1996. Race, culture, identity: Misunderstood connections. In *Color conscious: The political morality of race*, ed. Kwame Anthony Appiah and Amy Gutmann. Princeton, NJ: Princeton University Press.

Burge, Tyler. 1979. Individualism and the mental. *Midwest Studies in Philosophy* 4: 73–121.

Fraser, Nancy. 1989. Foucault on modern power: Empirical insights and normative confusions. In *Unruly practices: Power discourse and gender in contemporary social theory*. Minneapolis: University of Minnesota Press.

Gooding-Williams, Robert. 1988. Race, multiculturalism and democracy. *Constellations* 5(1): 18–41.

Hacking, Ian. 1999. *The social construction of what?* Cambridge, MA: Harvard University Press.

Hardimon, Michael. 2003. The ordinary concept of race. *Journal of Philosophy* 100(9): 437–55.

Haslanger, Sally. 2012 [1995]. Ontology and social construction. Chapter 2 of this volume.

———. 2012 [2000]. Gender and race: (What) are they? (What) do we want them to be? Chapter 7 of this volume.

Kitcher, Philip. 1999. Race, ethnicity, biology, culture. In *Racism*, ed. L. Harris. Amherst, NY: Humanity Books.

Kripke, Saul. 1980. *Naming and necessity*. Cambridge, MA: Harvard University Press.

MacKinnon, Catharine. 1987. *Feminism unmodified*. Cambridge, MA: Harvard University Press.

Mallon, Ron. 2004. Passing, traveling and reality: Social construction and the metaphysics of race. *Noûs* 38(4): 644–73.

Mills, Charles. 1997. *The racial contract*. Ithaca, NY: Cornell University Press.

———. 1998. *Blackness visible: Essays on philosophy and race*. Ithaca, NY: Cornell University Press.

Omi, Michael, and Howard Winant. 1994. *Racial formation in the United States*. New York: Routledge.

Peacocke, Christopher. 1998. Implicit conceptions, understanding, and rationality. *Philosophical Issues* 9: 43–88.

Putnam, Hilary. 1973. Meaning and reference. *Journal of Philosophy* 70(19): 699–711.

———. 1975. The meaning of 'meaning.' In *Mind, language and reality. Philosophical Papers*, Vol. 2. Cambridge: Cambridge University Press.

Quine, W. V. O. 1963. Two dogmas of empiricism. In *From a logical point of view*. New York: Harper and Row.

Zack, Naomi. 1997. Race and philosophic meaning. In *Race/sex: Their sameness, difference, and interplay*, ed. Naomi Zack. New York: Routledge.

———. 2002. *Philosophy of science and race*. New York: Routledge.

14

What Good Are Our Intuitions?

Philosophical Analysis and Social Kinds

1. Introduction

Across the humanities and social sciences it has become commonplace for scholars to argue that categories once assumed to be 'natural' are in fact 'social' or, in the familiar lingo, 'socially constructed.' Two common examples of such categories are *race* and *gender*, but there are many others. One interpretation of this claim is that although it is typically thought that what unifies the instances of such categories is some set of *natural* or *physical* properties, instead their unity rests on *social* features of the items in question. Social constructionists pursuing this strategy—and it is these social constructionists I will be focusing on in this chapter—aim to "debunk" the ordinary assumption that the categories are natural, by revealing the more accurate social basis of the classification.[1] To avoid confusion, and to resist some of the associations with the term 'social construction', I will sometimes use the term 'socially founded' for the categories that this sort of constructionist reveals as social rather than natural.[2]

Let me emphasize: the idea in saying that a category is socially founded is not to say that social factors are responsible for our attending to the category in question (which may be true of wholly natural categories); nor is it to say that the things in the category are less than fully real (material things may be unified by social features and there is no reason to deny that social properties

---

[1] In Haslanger 2012 [2003] (chapter 3 of this volume) I contrast this sort of interpretation with one that is more common in the context of "the science wars" which are discussed at length in, for example, Hacking 1999.

[2] I'll continue, however, to speak of those whose project it is to argue that a category is socially founded as 'social constructionists,' both because 'social foundationalists' would be a serious misnomer, and also because it is reasonable to cluster those who make a variety of different social arguments together, even if their views are not always compatible. It may be down the road that this acceptance of the 'social constructionist' label is more trouble than it is worth.

and relations are fully real). The point, roughly, is to shift our understanding of a category so we recognize the real basis for the unity of its members. As we shall see, there are importantly different sorts of cases. But because the difference between a natural and a social category has significance both for what's possible and for what we're responsible, the constructionist's general project, when successful, has important normative implications.

Among those who aim to analyze our ordinary racial classifications, social constructionists are often at odds with *error theorists* (sometimes called *eliminativists*) and *naturalists*. Error theorists maintain, in agreement with social constructionists, that the items taken to fall within the category in question do not meet the supposed natural or physical conditions for membership; the error theorist often goes farther to claim that the conditions are vacuous: nothing satisfies them (sometimes even that nothing *could* satisfy them). They conclude, then, that such things are illusory and that talk purporting to refer to such categories is false or misguided. So, for example, an error theorist about race (Appiah 1996; Zack 1997) claims that there are no races, given what we mean by 'race.' Of course it is then open to the error theorist to propose terminology for new categories—perhaps social categories with an extension close to what we thought was the extension of our original categories, such as 'racial identities' (Appiah 1996)—whose conditions for membership are satisfied.

Present-day race *naturalists* agree with the eliminativists and constructivists that races are not what they were once thought to be—they are not, for example, groups with a common racial essence that explains a broad range of psychological and moral features of the group's members—but they disagree with both other views in maintaining that the human species can be divided on the basis of natural (biological, genetic, physical) features into a small set of groups that correspond *roughly* to the ordinary racial divisions (Rosenberg et al. 2002; Mountain and Risch 2004). This in itself would not be particularly interesting, however, if the natural basis for the grouping was biologically 'real' but of no real significance for explanation or prediction. Full-blooded race naturalists, however, maintain that there is a biologically significant classification that somehow captures our current racial divisions. Moreover, they argue, recognizing this fact is socially and politically important for the purposes of achieving racial justice, for example, by enabling us to address racially divergent medical needs (Risch et al. 2002; cf. Lee et al. 2001).[3]

In this chapter I shall focus on the debate between the constructionist and error theorist; I take up the disagreement between the constructionist and naturalist elsewhere (Haslanger 2006; also Ch 10 of this volume). One way of capturing the difference between the social constructionist and the error theorist is

---

[3] The interdisciplinary debate over race naturalism and the relevance of 'race' for medicine is substantial and complex. I have listed only a few of the most controversial articles as examples.

to see them as disagreeing about the content of the relevant concepts. According to the error theorist, there is reason to take our ordinary belief that the category has a natural basis to set a constraint on what could count as an adequate analysis of the concept: a successful analysis must be in terms of natural properties and relations (or involve them at least in the way required for the concept to count as expressing a natural property). In contrast, according to the social constructionist, we may employ the concept successfully even though we have a false belief about what sort of property it expresses or sort of set it determines. For example, a social constructionist about race (such as myself) will claim that there are races and that races are social categories, that is, that race is socially founded, even though it is commonly assumed that races are natural categories. It is an important part of the social constructionist picture that, to put it simply, our meanings are not transparent to us: often ideology interferes with an understanding of the true workings of our conceptual framework and our language. More specifically, ideology (among other things) interferes with our understanding of our classificatory practices, suggesting to us that we are finding in nature divisions that we have played an important role in creating.

The Concept of Race

To gain a vivid sense of the controversy, it may be helpful to consider briefly two different analyses of *race*, one constructionist, the other defended by the error theorist. These are just two examples of many that are discussed in the literature.

Anthony Appiah is perhaps the most well-known error theorist about race. On his view the concept of race is the core notion in the folk theory of racialism:

> [T]here are heritable characteristics, possessed by members of our species, that allow us to divide them into a small set of races, in such a way that all the members of these races share certain traits and tendencies with each other that they do not share with members of any other race. These traits and tendencies characteristic of a race constitute, on the racialist view, a sort of racial essence; and it is part of the content of racialism that the essential heritable characteristics . . . account for more than the visible morphological characteristics—skin color, hair type, facial features—on the basis of which we make our informal classifications. (Appiah 1993, p. 5)

Races, then, are groups with a common inherited racial essence. The implications of this for our purposes are straightforward: there are no such racial essences, so there are no races. Appiah argues, however, that there is a neighboring notion—that of *racial identity*—that does not presuppose racial essences and can be accurately attributed to people. Having a racial identity is a matter of identifying with a label (such as 'White' or 'Black')[4] that has been historically associated with a racial essence (Appiah 1996, pp. 81–2).

In contrast, I have argued for a constructionist account of race that parallels an account of gender (Haslanger 2012 [2000]). On my view (to simplify quite a bit) races are racialized groups, and:

> A group is *racialized* (in a context) if and only if its members are socially positioned as subordinate or privileged along some dimension—economic, political, legal, social, etc.—(in that context), and the group is "marked" as a target for this treatment by observed or imagined bodily features presumed to be evidence of ancestral links to a certain geographical region.

On this view, being White (in a context) is a matter of being seen as conforming to a meaningful bodily schema associated with European ancestry—such schemata I call 'color'—and being treated (in that context) as positioned in a social hierarchy appropriate for persons of that 'color'. In the contemporary United States, being marked as 'White' brings with it a broad range of social privileges, at least for the most part. However, because racial hierarchies interact with other social hierarchies—gender, class, sexuality, culture, religion, nationality—the concrete impact of being White varies depending on other aspects of one's social position. For example, a straight young White man and an elderly White lesbian will both reap privileges by virtue of their Whiteness, but the kinds of privileges they enjoy may differ considerably.

Three questions naturally arise at this point. First, it is clear that the analysis of race I offer does not capture what people consciously *have in mind* when they use the term 'race.' The account is surprising, and for many, highly counterintuitive. (Although I myself doubt that Appiah's account captures better what people consciously *have in mind* when they talk of races (or racial identities), it is at least familiar, and has some intuitive plausibility if we are looking for how people generally have thought of races.) Note that this counterintuitiveness will always be a feature of social constructionist analyses because (debunking) social constructionists aim to reveal that the concepts we employ are not exactly what we think they are. But if the adequacy of a philosophical analysis is a matter of the degree to which it captures and organizes our intuitions, and if constructionist analyses are always counterintuitive, then it would seem that philosophers would never have reason to consider social constructionist projects acceptable. However, this seems too fast. Surely philosophers cannot simply rule out constructionist analyses from the start.

Second, does the social constructionist approach make sense? Are there considerations developed in the context of philosophy of language (or related areas)

---

[4] I will use upper-case terms such as 'White' and 'Black' for races, lower-case terms such as 'white' and 'black' for the 'color' markings associated with the races.

that would prevent one from pursuing a constructionist *analysis* of race or gender and force us to adopt an error theory? I will argue that, in fact, there are considerations in contemporary philosophy of language that not only permit, but in some respects *favor* a constructionist account.

Third, what difference does it make? Does it really matter whether we say, for example, that there are no races but there are racial identities, rather than that there are races but they are social rather than natural? Are there cases where an error theory would be mistaken but a social constructionist account would be warranted? By what criteria do we decide, and is it worth worrying about?

The arguments that follow focus mainly on the first two questions; however, drawing on this discussion I will return to the question of why it might matter whether we adopt a constructionist or error strategy towards the end of the chapter. The issues are complex. My own view is that which approach is better will depend on the case at issue, and the betterness will depend on semantic, pragmatic and political considerations. Moreover, pragmatic and political factors will vary with context. Before we proceed, however, it is worth pointing out that one potential advantage of a constructionist account is that it does not simply deny the existence of the allegedly natural category and substitute another (possibly social category) in its place, but it also—at least in the best cases— provides a diagnosis of our role in bringing about the effects that appear to us (mistakenly) as natural, together with an explanation of the illusion. In such cases, the self-deception involved when we mean something, and yet mask that meaning to ourselves, is laid bare. Such unmasking can be an important step in motivating social change.

2. Kinds of Analysis

The project of 'conceptual analysis' in philosophy takes many forms, partly depending on the particular concept in question, and partly depending on what methodological assumptions the philosopher brings to the issue. There are at least three common ways to answer "What is *X*?" questions: conceptual, descriptive, and ameliorative.[5]

---

[5] Quine distinguishes different forms of definition, the third being what he calls (drawing on Carnap) 'explicative.' In giving explicative definitions, "an activity to which philosophers are given, and scientists also in their more philosophical moments . . . the purpose is not merely to paraphrase the definiendum into an outright synonym, but actually to improve upon the definiendum by refining or supplementing its meaning" (Quine 1953, pp. 24–5). 'Ameliorative' captures better than 'explicative' the sort of project Quine is characterizing as especially philosophical; it is this sort of project that I've also called 'analytical' (Haslanger 2012 [2000]). Because 'analytical' is commonly used to characterize Anglo-American philosophy in general, and because I'm attempting here to introduce a more fine-grained framework, using 'ameliorative' rather than 'analytical' will sometimes avoid ambiguity. It should be understood, however, that on my view, whether or not an analysis is an improvement on existing meanings will depend on the purposes of the inquiry.

For example, consider the question "What is knowledge?" Following a *conceptual approach*, or what we might more revealingly call an *internalist approach*, one is asking 'What is *our* concept of knowledge?', and looking to a priori methods such as introspection for an answer.[6] Taking into account intuitions about cases and principles, one hopes eventually to reach a reflective equilibrium. On a *descriptive* approach, one is concerned with what objective types (if any) our epistemic vocabulary tracks.[7] The task is to develop potentially more accurate concepts through careful consideration of the phenomena, usually relying on empirical or quasi-empirical methods. Scientific essentialists and naturalizers, more generally, start by identifying paradigm cases—these usually function to fix the referent of the term—and then draw on empirical (or quasi-empirical) research to explicate the relevant kind or type to which the paradigms belong. Do paradigms project an objective type, and if so, what type? Familiar descriptive approaches in philosophy of mind and epistemology draw on cognitive science.

Ameliorative projects, in contrast, begin by asking: What is the point of having the concept in question; for example, why do we have a concept of knowledge or a concept of belief? What concept (if any) would do the work best? In the limit case a theoretical concept is introduced by stipulating the meaning of a new term, and its content is determined entirely by the role it plays in the theory. If we allow that our everyday vocabularies serve both cognitive and practical purposes that might be well served by our theorizing, then those pursuing an ameliorative approach might reasonably represent themselves as providing an account of our concept—or perhaps the concept we are reaching for—by enhancing our conceptual resources to serve our (critically examined) purposes (see Anderson 1995). Conceptual, descriptive, and ameliorative projects cannot, of course, be kept entirely distinct, but they have different subject matters and different goals.

Given the different projects of analysis and different subject matters for 'analysis,' it is not surprising that philosophers who may appear to be asking the same question are in fact talking past each other. For example, where one philosopher might assume that an adequate analysis must capture our ordinary intuitions, another may take for granted that a priori reflection is likely to be systematically misleading when we are trying to understand the social domain. In fact, recent work on race provides an excellent example of the diversity of approaches. Some authors are engaged in a conceptual project, attempting to

---

[6] In previous work I've dubbed this the 'conceptualist' approach. However, I've been convinced by others, and by confusions in discussion, that it may be better described as an 'internalist' approach in order to highlight the contrast with the underlying externalism assumed by the descriptive approach (described next in the text). The change is useful; however, there are different degrees and kinds of internalism and externalism and I am only using the terms suggestively and not precisely here.

[7] On objective types, see Armstrong 1989.

explicate our ordinary understanding of race (Appiah 1996, Zack 1997, Hardimon 2003,Mallon 2004); others are attempting to determine what, if any, natural kind we are referring to by our racial terms (Appiah 1996, Kitcher 1999, Andreason 2000, Zack 2002, Glasgow 2003); others have pursued genealogy (Omi and Winant 1994); still others are invested in what I call ameliorative projects, raising normative questions about how we should understand race, not only how we currently do (Gooding-Williams 1998, Alcoff 2000).

What should we make of these different projects? Should we simply allow that different inquirers are interested in different questions, and nothing can be said to resolve the question what race *really* is or what we mean by 'race'? Although I would not argue that there is one thing that race *really* is or one thing that "we" mean by 'race,' we might hope that through reflection and discussion we could come to the point where (a) the concept we take ourselves to be employing, (b) the concept that best captures the type we are concerned with, and (c) the type we ought to be concerned with coincide. In such cases the conceptual, descriptive and ameliorative projects yield the same concept. It is a mistake, then, for those engaged in conceptual analysis to dismiss other forms of analysis, with the thought that only the conceptual project can discover "our" concept (see Mallon 2004, Hardimon 2003). For example, if we discover that we are tracking something that it is worthwhile to track in using our racial vocabulary, then even if this is not what we originally "had in mind," it still may be what we have been and should continue to be talking about.[8] But how should we proceed?

3. Manifest and Operative Concepts

One of the functions of concepts is to enable us to draw distinctions between things. Sometimes the activity of distinguishing things—separating them into groups—comes first, and we develop a concept of what we've distinguished later; sometimes the concept comes first, and we divide things according to it. For example, I might find myself asking my daughter to turn down her music on a regular basis without thinking that there is any pattern in my requests, only to find through conversation with her that I always ask her to turn it down when she is listening to a particular artist; or I might come to judge that a particular artist's lyrics are typically offensive and ask her to turn down the music once I discern that that artist is playing. Moreover, in practice, our activity of grouping things, even when we have a concept in mind, does not involve explicitly applying the concept to each case, that is, making sure that each object meets the

---

[8] It might be useful to see this by analogy with other terminological developments in science. Although our understanding of, and even our definition of, 'atom' has changed over time, it is plausible that there is something worthwhile we have been and continue to be talking about.

conditions for applying the concept. We typically rely on empirical assumptions linking easily accessible criteria with the conditions for membership. In the grocery, I pick up what look and feel like potatoes, without testing them genetically. Once I learn that the store sells genetically modified potatoes, I may want some further assurance of the genetic makeup of the ones I purchase; but even then, I will rely on a sticker or label rather than applying the genetic criteria myself.

Everyday life requires a steady activity of drawing distinctions, an activity which combines both the use of concepts as guides and a rough-and-ready responsiveness to things. In reflecting back on our activity, there are a number of options for describing this sort of give and take. Consider again my requests to Zina (my daughter) that she lower the volume of her music. Suppose I don't want to listen to music with misogynistic lyrics. I have a concept of misogynistic lyrics and I also have a rough-and-ready responsiveness to what she is listening to. When Zina complains about my interventions into her listening, I may come to find that my responses are not tracking misogynistic lyrics after all, even though that's the concept I was attempting to use to guide my interventions. Let's call the concept I thought I was guided by and saw myself as attempting to apply, the *manifest concept*. I find, in other words, that my manifest concept is not in accord with my practice of determining when she has to lower the volume of her music.

There are several ways to resolve the awkward position of having my self-representation, or my intentions, out of line with my practice.

(i) I can be more careful about my interventions so that I only make my request when the lyrics really are misogynist. This would be to change the occasions of my intervention to bring my responsiveness into accord with my manifest concept.

(ii) I might instead find that a different concept conforms to my pattern of interventions. I could find that my responses are prompted by, say, sexually explicit lyrics, not misogynistic ones. Let's call the concept that best captures the distinction that I in practice draw the *operative concept*. In such a case, I allow the operative concept to have priority over the (original) manifest concept in guiding my behavior; in doing so the operative concept becomes manifest (and, hopefully, is now consistent with my practice).

(iii) Rather than replacing the original manifest concept with a new operative concept, I modify my understanding of the manifest concept in light of the new cases that have emerged in the practice. So rather than being newly guided by the concept of sexually explicit lyrics, I change what I understand misogynistic lyrics to be. Let's call the *target concept* the concept that, all things considered (my purposes, the facts, etc.), I should be employing. In the ideal case, I adjust my practice and my self-understanding to conform to the target concept.

So far I've distinguished the manifest, the operative, and the target concept. The manifest concept is the concept I take myself to be applying or attempting to apply in the cases in question. The operative concept is the concept that best captures the distinction as I draw it in practice.[9] And the target concept is the concept I should, ideally, be employing. As illustrated above, the operative concept may not correspond with my understanding of what distinction I'm tracking. This is not to say, however, that the manifest and operative concepts always, or even typically, come apart. Typically, my practice will track the objective type that my manifest concept determines; in other words, my manifest concept and my operative concept coincide.[10] In the best cases, all three (my manifest, operative, and target concepts) will coincide.

The example of my responses to Zina's music locates the issue in the realm of individual consistency: how can I bring my practice in line with my intentions? To see that the phenomenon has broader scope, it may be helpful to consider an example that draws on more collective meanings. Consider the term 'parent.' It is common, at least in the United States, to address primary school memos to "Parents," to hold a "Parent Night" or "Parent Breakfast" at certain points during the school year, to have "Parent-Teacher Conferences" to discuss student progress, and so on. However, in practice the term 'parent' in these contexts is meant to include the primary caregivers of the student, whether they be biological parents, step-parents, legal guardians, grandparents, aunts, uncles, older siblings, informal substitute parents, and so on. However, it is also clear to everyone that those on the list just given are not the student's parents. So, for example, Tara's grandmother Denise (with whom she lives) counts as Tara's parent in all relevant school contexts, but is also known to be her grandmother and not her mother, and so not her parent. Given the distinction between manifest and operative concepts, it would seem that there are two different concepts of 'parent' here: parent as *immediate progenitor*, and parent as *primary caregiver*. Tara's grandmother satisfies the operative concept of *parent* but not the manifest one.

One might resist the idea that the manifest concept of *parent* is of biological mother or father; however, my own experience as an adoptive mother has convinced me that at least in many contexts the dominant understanding of 'parent'

---

[9] I don't mean to suggest here that there is only one manifest concept and only one operative concept. The manifest and operative concepts may vary from context to context.

[10] However, we often make mistakes in applying our manifest concepts. When we make a simple mistake, must we postulate an operative concept distinct from the manifest one? I'm not sure much hinges on this, but it seems to me that if we have a sparse theory of objective types a better approach would be to understand the practice as tracking a nearby (or the nearest?) objective type; if the nearby type is the type also determined by the manifest concept, we have coincidence. The operative concept will be, then, the concept that determines that type in terms that make the most sense in analyzing the practice.

frames it as a biological notion. For example, if I were Zina's biological parent, I don't think I would ever be asked (by people who know us), 'Do you know Zina's parents?' If one is uncomfortable with the assumption that the manifest concept of *parent* is biological, then we need only take the case to be describing a possible world in which the manifest concept of *parent* is more narrowly biological, possibly a world much like the US in an earlier era before adoption was common or legally institutionalized.

As in the earlier example of misogynist lyrics, there are three different responses to the gap between idea and practice in our use of the term 'parent':

(i) Bring our practice in line with the manifest concept: insist that one must be an immediate progenitor of a student to participate in Parent Nights, Parent-Teacher Conferences, and so on. (This option seems clearly misguided—not necessarily as a semantic matter, but as a social/political matter.)

(ii) Find a new manifest concept that better captures our practice: correct the memos so they are addressed to "Primary Caregivers."

(iii) Modify our understanding of the manifest concept, in this case, 'parent,' to accord with our practice. This would involve a transition in our understanding from parent as a biological category to parent as a social category.

This example is intended to show that the distinction between manifest and operative concepts is one that concerns public meanings as much as individual beliefs and intentions (see also Haslanger 2012 [2005]). If we ask, "What is the concept of 'parent'?" we have at least two places to look for an answer: the concept that speakers generally associate with the term, and the concept that captures how the term works in practice. Although so far I've focused on the relatively transparent example of 'parent,' of course there are many philosophically rich and more surprising examples available. Feminist and race theorists have been urging for some time that the proper target of analysis is not (or not simply) what we have in mind, but the social matrix where our concepts do their work. For example, Catharine MacKinnon says, "[The verb 'to be' in feminist theory] is a very empirical 'is.' Men define women as sexual beings; feminism comprehends that femininity 'is' sexual. Men see rape as intercourse; feminists say much intercourse 'is' rape" (MacKinnon 1987, p. 59). Charles Mills argues that the Enlightenment social contract is a racial contract (Mills 1997), and that an adequate analysis of personhood reveals that "all persons are equal, but only white males are persons" (Mills 1998, p. 70). Such analyses purport to show that our manifest understandings of crucial political notions are masking how the concepts in question actually operate (see also Mills 1998, pp. 139–66).

4. Concepts, Conceptions, and the Like

Can we understand the manifest/operative distinction in terms of a more familiar distinction between concept and conception? It is not an unusual circumstance in philosophy to find that 'the concept' we take ourselves to be analyzing
is not 'the concept' that the students seem to employ in their day-to-day practice.
Undergraduates are competent users of terms such as 'knowledge', 'justice,' and
'object', and yet are surprised and resistant when they learn philosophical theories of knowledge, justice, and objects. One might argue that the philosophical
theories are all false and the students are correct to reject them. But this is often
not plausible. More plausible is that ordinary usage of a term doesn't require that
one has thought carefully enough about the issues to develop consistent accounts
of central concepts in one's repertoire. Cases such as these (and in general,
accounts of language acquisition) support the idea that we need to distinguish
various ways that individuals might be related to the concept, say, of knowledge
or justice. For example, James Higginbotham (1998, pp. 149–50) distinguishes:

(i) possession
   - merely possessing a word, and so being able to use it with its
     meaning;
   - merely possessing a concept, so being able to deploy it, without
     having an accurate or full conception of it.
(ii) tacit conception
   - knowing the meaning of the word;
   - having a full conception of a concept.
(iii) explicit understanding
   - having an adequate conscious view of the word's meaning;
   - having a adequate conscious view of the nature of the concept.

There may be additional relevant distinctions, but these go some way to making
room for competent use without full explicit understanding. Over the course of
repeated use of a notion we develop conceptions of what we're talking about,
but we might be misguided in various ways. Philosophical inquiry helps us
develop more detailed, explicit, and adequate conceptions of our concepts.

But this doesn't seem to capture what's at issue in the cases we've been considering. How would we map the distinction between manifest and operative
concepts on some pair of the distinctions between possession, tacit conception,
explicit understanding? For example, consider Brenda, Tara's teacher. She has a
fully conscious and explicit understanding of the concept *parent*; she also enacts
a practice that is in some ways at odds with it. And she probably doesn't have a
full or explicit conception of the rule that she employs in practice. But the distinction between manifest and operative concepts is not simply a distinction

along the continuum of implicit–explicit, or uninterpreted–adequately interpreted. As we saw before, the manifest and operative concepts are at odds; they
are, in a sense, competing with each other within the space of practical reason.
For example, given the confidentiality laws in place, Brenda may find herself
uncertain how or what to communicate with someone she knows to be a primary caregiver of a student, but who is not legally recognized as such. For all
intents and purposes the adult in question is the child's parent and no other
parent is available, but legally speaking the adult is not the child's parent. In effect, fully developing and making explicit the operative concept does not necessarily yield the manifest concept. And as we saw above, this does not mean that
we should reject the operative concept as a "misguided conception" in favor of
the manifest.

5. Is *Parent* Socially Founded?

Let us return to consider further the gap between the manifest concept of *parent*
and the operative concept. A social constructionist in this case will plausibly
claim that the category of *parent* is "socially founded." This means both that our
manifest concept of *parent* (understood in biological terms) does not accord
with our practices involving the notion of *parent* (which extends beyond the biological), and also that we would do well to modify our understanding of 'parent'
to include a social dimension.

It appears that the constructionist could pursue more than one strategy for
making the modification. One would be to simply replace the manifest concept
of *parent* with the operative (e.g., *primary caregiver*), and appropriate the terminology of 'parent.' This would be to adjust, in a brute way, our understandings to
conform to our practice. I'll call this the descriptivist strategy.[11] A second strategy
would be to reflect on content of the manifest concept and the practice to come
up with a concept of *parent* that best suits our needs and legitimate purposes.
Let's call this the ameliorative strategy. A third strategy might be to argue for an
ambiguity in the term, with one meaning tracking a social kind; the question
then is whether a new term should be introduced, or whether there are other
ways of resolving the ambiguity.

Those favoring a conceptualist (or internalist) analysis, as I've described it,
typically argue that neither of these constructivist approaches—the descriptivist or the ameliorative—is acceptable because both amount to changing the subject. *Our* notion of parent (or *our* notion of race) is of a biological category, and
any modification that disrupts that assumption replaces *our* concept with a different one. In other words, 'parent' just means *immediate progenitor*, and if we

---

[11] Given what I say in Haslanger 2012 [2005], we could also consider it a genealogical strategy.

start using it to mean *primary caregiver* (or some more philosophically refined notion) then we have changed the meaning.[12] So social constructionists are wrong to say that *parent* is socially founded; what they are really saying is that a different concept, such as *primary caregiver*, is socially founded, which is obvious and not worth pointing out.[13] Moreover, the social founding of *primary caregiver* poses no challenge to our assumptions concerning the concept of *parent*. Similarly, a conceptualist concerned with race maintains that *our* concept of *race* is of a biological category, and nothing satisfies the biological conditions the concept requires. So the best we can do to capture the phenomena is to deny that there are races and invent (or appropriate) a new concept—such as *racial identity*—for the type tracked by our practices.[14]

I am willing to grant that each of these strategies could be reasonable in some context and we cannot decide on the basis of the simplified descriptions I've offered which is the best overall. However, the conceptualist sometimes maintains that his approach is the *only* reasonable approach and that the descriptive and ameliorative approaches cannot capture the meaning of our terms; the best they can do is propose new meanings.[15] Is there reason to think that a descriptivist or ameliorative approach is simply misguided and that social constructionists aren't really doing philosophical analysis of the terms in question at all?

---

[12] Of course, in the case of *parent*, it is not plausible to adopt a thoroughgoing error theory, since there are some people who do satisfy the conditions of being an immediate progenitor. But the internalist strategy would have us adopt a qualified error theory: all of our uses of the term 'parent' aside from the core biological cases are strictly in error because they pick out people who aren't really parents. In response to the charge that this would be inadequate in, for example, a school context, the conceptualist could also maintain that such an approach to the semantics does not entail that we retain the concept or terminology of *parent* in our school practices: perhaps we would do well to address our school memos using 'primary caregivers' or another term.

[13] Although Ian Hacking is a constructionist, he concludes that constructionists cannot simply be making the debunking point that the category in question is socially unified rather than naturally unified because the claim would be 'redundant.' I think the distinction between the manifest and operative concept helps show why it need not be redundant and may be important (see Hacking 1999, p. 39).

[14] Interestingly, Appiah (1996) does consider a kind of descriptivist approach, and still concludes that there are no races. He does so, however, because he takes it as a constraint on the type that can be projected from the paradigms that it be a natural type, since this is part of the concept, given his explorations of the history of the concept. So he does not consider the possibility that the objective type we designate with the term 'race' is a social type. This seems to be a 'mixed' approach that places, to my mind, too much weight on the history of the concept and does not adequately recognize objectivity of social kinds. My argument against error theories will only address those who defend their view using a conceptualist strategy. Those pursuing an ameliorative strategy who come, ultimately, to the conclusion that an error theory is the best option, I do not address here.

[15] I myself am not opposed to proposing new meanings and, more generally, undertaking revisionary metaphysics. Given the history of our language and our conceptual framework, it would be a miracle if we had landed upon the best framework to describe the world. I only care about what we do mean as a step in an inquiry into what we should mean. Nonetheless, I think the conceptualist is misguided, and it is worth pointing out why, since many are not so happy with radical revisions as I am.

In the case of *parent*, at least, I think it is fairly clear that the concept has evolved and continues to evolve in response to the changing circumstances of family life; significantly for our purposes, it has changed from functioning as a natural category to functioning—at least in some settings—as a social category. (In some contexts the manifest concept of *parent* seems to allow that step-parents and adoptive parents are fully included; and increasingly there are contexts where it is no longer surprising if a child has two parents of the same sex.) How do we take this evolution into account in doing philosophical analysis? What does this "evolution" involve? By granting that the concept has evolved, are we conceding to the error theorist that we are analyzing a new concept, not the concept of *parent*? If we adjust the manifest concept so that a biological relation to the child is no longer necessary, isn't this "changing the subject" in the very sense the conceptualist is worried about?

There are at least two ways of thinking of what might be involved when a concept evolves in response to social context: on one hand it may be that the term 'parent' expresses a different concept than it once did. The change is a change in our language. On the other hand it may be that the concept of *parent* remains the same, but what we take to be the shape and content of that concept changes. Perhaps we once took it to be an essential feature of parents that their children were biologically related to them, but we have come to regard this as just an empirical generalization based on a limited survey of cases that does not hold necessarily. This is a change in our conceptual knowledge. In the next two sections I will consider each of these interpretations of "conceptual change." I will argue, first, that the constructionist is not changing the subject, or changing our language; rather, the constructionist is revealing that our linguistic practices have changed in ways that we may not have noticed. Second, I will argue that although the constructionist suggests that we come to a new understanding of our concepts, this does not require replacing our old concept with a new one, but understanding our original concept better. I do not commit myself to one or another account of conceptual change here; I also want to leave it open that concepts change like other ordinary things, that is, by altering.

6. Semantic Externalism

According to the first explanation of conceptual change, the change is in what concepts our terms (such as 'race' or 'parent') express. This is plausibly understood as a semantic shift. It is not within the scope of this chapter to take a stand in debates over meaning, for example, whether the *meaning* of the term is a concept to whose content we have privileged access, or the term's extension, or a function from worlds to sets of objects, and so on. The point I want to make is quite simple and should be familiar: whatever it is that determines the extension of our social kind terms, it isn't something to which we have privileged access through introspection. If the extension of the term changes over time, it is legitimate to postulate a change in what determines the extension. Those who are familiar with an externalist approach to language and mind will find little new in this section beyond the claim that externalist insights should be applied to our thought and language about the social as well as the natural (so take yourself to be given permission to skip ahead). However, the implications of externalism are much less commonly recognized in social and political philosophy, so I'll provide a quick summary here.

I've suggested that the error theorist typically invests in a conceptualist approach to analysis that emphasizes a priori reflection and ideas that are relatively accessible to introspection. I've also suggested that it is plausible to see this as an investigation of the manifest concept. In undertaking conceptual analysis of, say, *F-ness*, it is typically assumed that it is enough to ask competent users of English under what conditions someone *is F*, without making any special effort to consult those whose daily lives are affected by the concept or who use the concept in practice. After all, if competent speakers know the meaning of their terms, then all that's needed is linguistic competence to analyze a term. A sophisticated internalist might want to allow that if one is sensitive to the possibility that in any actual circumstance there are competing meanings (often quite explicit) that structure alternative practices, then one could and should consider a broad range of speakers that are differently situated with respect to the phenomenon.[16]

However, this approach to understanding race, gender, and other social kinds is not plausible if one takes into account arguments in philosophy of language over the past thirty years that call into question the assumption that competent users of a term have full knowledge of what the term means, that is, that what's "in our heads" determines a term's referent. This assumption was already questioned once we considered the distinction between concept and conception (see section 4), but is further challenged by the tradition of semantic externalism. Externalists maintain that the content of what we think and mean is determined not simply by intrinsic facts about us but at least in part by facts about our environment. Remember: Sally and Twinsally both use the term 'water,' but Sally means H_2O and Twinsally means XYZ (Putnam 1975b). Sally thinks she has arthritis in her thigh, and is wrong because 'arthritis' in her community is an ailment of the joints; Twinsally thinks she has arthritis in her thigh and is right because 'arthritis' in her community is an ailment that is not confined to the joints (Burge 1979).

---

[16] Although I'm not endorsing the methods of ordinary language philosophy, the complexity of our use of words in different contexts is something ordinary language philosophers were well attuned to, and some of their methods and ideas are tremendously valuable for this project.

Most commonly, descriptive analyses—and the externalist picture guiding them—have been employed to provide *naturalistic* accounts of knowledge, mind, and so on; these seek to discover the *natural* (as contrasted with *social*) kind within which the selected paradigms fall. But it is possible to pursue a descriptive approach within a social domain as long as one allows that there are social kinds or types.[17] In fact I've chosen to speak of "descriptive" approaches rather than "naturalistic" approaches for just this reason. Descriptive analyses of social terms such as 'democracy' and 'genocide,' or ethical terms such as 'responsibility' and 'autonomy,' are methodologically parallel to more familiar naturalizing projects in epistemology and philosophy of mind.

Of course, an externalist analysis of social terms cannot be done in a mechanical way, and may require sophisticated social theory both to select the paradigms and to analyze their commonality; in short, the investigation of social kinds will need to draw on empirical social/historical inquiry, not just natural science. Moreover, it is easily possible that the resulting analysis of the type is highly surprising. For example, it was not intuitively obvious that water is H_2O or that gold is an element with atomic number 79. It took sophisticated natural science to determine what the terms 'water' and 'gold' mean. Likewise it may take sophisticated social theory to determine what 'parent' or 'Black' means. In a descriptive project, intuitions about the conditions for applying the concept should be considered secondary to what the cases in fact have in common: as we learn more about the paradigms, we learn more about our concepts.

[17] Because the terminology of 'natural kind' is used in several different ways, it will be helpful to make a few distinctions. The term 'kind' is sometimes used to classify substances, in the ordinary case, (physical) objects. Substances can be classified according to their essence; kinds consist of groups of objects with a common essence. For example, tigers constitute a kind of thing because each tiger has essentially a certain cluster of properties that define the kind. On other occasions, the term 'kind' is used to refer to what are sometimes called *types*. A type is a group of things, sometimes substances, but possibly non-substances, that has a certain unity. This unity need not be a matter of sharing essential properties: red things constitute a type (their unity consists in their all being red), even though redness is seldom an essential property of the things that have it. Unity seems to come in different degrees. The things on my desk might be thought to constitute a weak sort of type (they have in common the fact that they are on my desk), and at the limit there are highly gerrymandered sets of things that don't have any unity at all and so don't constitute a type.

One way to think about the unity of types is in terms of similarity between the members. We can distinguish different sorts of types by distinguishing axes of similarity. Exactly six-foot-tall human beings are a natural type because the commonality between the members is natural (species and height); high school graduates are a social type because the commonality between the members is social. Both of these types are (metaphysically) objective, however. How to draw the line between social and natural types is difficult (as is the distinction between objective and subjective) and not one I will address here. I'll have to rely on background understandings and familiar cases. However, it is important to keep in mind that as I am using the terms the distinction between objective and non-objective kinds/types is importantly different from the distinction between natural and social kinds/types.

Externalism initially appeared in two forms, supported by the sorts of examples ('water', 'arthritis') just recited:

- *Natural kind externalism* (Putnam 1973; Putnam 1975b; Kripke 1980): Natural kind terms/concepts pick out a natural kind, whether or not we can state the essence of the kind, by virtue of the fact that their meaning is determined by ostension of a paradigm (or other means of reference-fixing) together with an implicit extension to "things of the same kind" as the paradigm.
- *Social externalism* (Putnam 1975b; Burge 1979; Burge 1986): The meaning of a term/content of a concept used by a speaker is determined at least in part by the standard linguistic usage in his or her community.

It then became clear that externalist phenomena are not confined to natural kind terms (properly speaking), but occur quite broadly. For example, in the history of logic and mathematics, inquiry can seem to converge on an idea or concept that we seemed to have in mind all along, even though no one, even the best minds, could have explicated it. (Leibniz's early efforts to define the limit of a series is an example.) In such cases it is plausible to maintain that certain experts were "grasping a definite sense, whilst also failing to grasp it 'sharply'" (Peacocke 1998, p. 50).

Recognizing the possibility of reaching for a concept that is not quite within grasp provides us with a way to think about the ameliorative approach to analysis sketched above. In such cases we have perhaps a partial or vague understanding of the manifest concept, and the operative concept picks out a relatively heterogeneous set, but nonetheless we can say that there is something we mean, an objective type we are approaching. As before, I will use the term 'target concept' for the concept that is plausibly what we are getting at, even if we poorly understand it; the target concept is the object of ameliorative analysis. Although Fregeans are apt to capture this by invoking objective senses that the inquirers "grasp," an ontology of sparse objective properties will also do the work.

The upshot of this is that the basic strategy of natural kind externalism need not be confined to natural kinds (where it is assumed that things of the same natural kind share an essence). Externalism is an option whenever there are relatively objective types. The notion of objective type needed is not too mysterious: a set of objects is more an objective type by virtue of the degree of unity among its members beyond a random or gerrymandered set. Objectivity is not only to be found in the natural world. There are objective types in every realm: social, psychological, political, mathematical, artistic, and so on. We might account for unity in various ways (Lewis 1983), but a familiar way I'll assume for current purposes is in terms of degrees of similarity; the similarity in question need not be a matter of intrinsic similarity; that is, things can be similar by virtue of the relations (perhaps to us) they stand in. Roughly,

> *Objective type externalism*: Terms/concepts pick out an objective type, whether or not we can state conditions for membership in the type, by virtue of the fact that their meaning is determined by ostension of paradigms (or other means of reference-fixing) together with an implicit extension to things of the same type as the paradigms.

Sets of paradigms will typically fall within more than one type. To handle this, one may further specify the kind of type (type of liquid, type of artwork), or may (in the default?) count the common type with the highest degree of objectivity. For the purposes of capturing the operative concept, it is promising (as suggested before) to take the relevant type to be the one that we rely on in our best theory of the social/linguistic practice.

Descriptive projects adopt an externalist approach to content, that is, they set out to determine the (an?) objective type, if any, into which the paradigms of a particular concept fall. Social constructionists can rely on externalist accounts of meaning to argue that their disclosure of an operative or a target concept is not *changing the subject*, but better reveals what we mean. By reflecting broadly on how we use the term 'parent,' we find that the cases, either as they stand or adjusted through ameliorative analysis, project onto an objective social, not natural, type. So although we tend to assume we are expressing the concept of *immediate progenitor* by the term 'parent' in fact we are expressing the concept of *primary caregiver* (or some such); the constructionist shows us that our assumptions about what we mean are false, given our practice. This is not to propose a new meaning, but to reveal an existing one.

If one assumes with the conceptualist that the task of philosophical inquiry is simply to explicate through introspection what we think we mean in using a term, then almost any externalist inquiry will seem "revisionary." But the conceptualist approach to analysis is wedded to assumptions about mind and language that are certainly contested, if not outmoded. We should also ask ourselves why, given the systematic use of terms such as 'parent' to track a social category, do we persist in thinking that the term picks out a natural category? Might ideology be playing a role in masking how we organize our social lives? In any case, there is no reason to reject out of hand the constructivist's claim that a term whose manifest concept is of a natural kind may be better understood in terms of the operative social concept. The proposed analysis may be surprising; and it may even be that the term has come, through practice, to express a different concept than it used to; that is, the manifest may not have caught up with the operative. But the constructionist is not causing this, or even promoting such a change, but is rather revealing it.

7. Meaning Holism

We considered before two ways that we might interpret the idea that a concept "evolves" with social practices. On one interpretation, the point is that a term such as 'parent' expresses, say, the concept of *immediate progenitor* at one time, but, given changes in how the community organizes family life, comes to express a different concept, such as *primary caregiver*, at a later time. I've argued that the constructionist describes this shift by saying that the term 'parent' is socially founded. This is not to invoke or propose a new meaning, but rather, drawing on externalist insights, to reveal an existing meaning that might well be obscured.

However, the other interpretation we considered was that the concept in question "evolves," not in the sense that the term changes what concept it expresses, but rather, there is a change in our understanding of the concept. For example, empirical investigation might reveal that a generalization we took to be analytically entailed by the concept is in fact only contingent, or even false. The suggestion here is not that the concept itself changes (though it might be useful to spell it out that way), but rather that our understanding of it does.

Nothing I'm saying here is news; the claim that there is, at best, a blurry line between what's true by virtue of fact and what's true by virtue of meaning is one theme in the arguments against the analytic/synthetic distinction. As in the case of externalism, however, the focus of discussion has typically been on cases in natural science and the development of natural kind concepts. For example, in his essay "The Analytic and the Synthetic," Putnam contrasts examples in mathematics and science which, he argues, are not happily classified as either analytic or synthetic, with the standard example of "A bachelor is an unmarried man," which is one of the few claims that he thinks should count as analytic. He says:

> In the case of a law cluster term such as 'energy,' any one law, even a law that was felt to be definitional or stipulative in character, can be abandoned, and we feel that the identity of the concept has, in a certain respect, remained. Thus, the conclusions of the present section still stand: A principle involving the term 'energy,' a principle which was regarded as definitional, or as analytic, if you please, has been abandoned. And its abandonment cannot be explained always as mere 're-definition' or as change in the meaning of 'kinetic energy'. . . . (Putnam 1975a, p. 53)

He continues:

> But "All bachelors are unmarried" cannot be rejected unless we change the meaning of the word 'bachelor' and not even then unless we change it so radically as to change the *extension* of the term 'bachelor.' What

makes the resemblance [to the 'energy' case] superficial is that if we
were asked what the meaning of the term 'bachelor' is, we can *only* say
that 'bachelor' means 'unmarried man,' whereas if we are asked for the
meaning of the term 'energy,' we can do much more than give a definition. We can in fact show the way in which the use of the term 'energy'
facilitates an enormous number of scientific explanations, and how it
enters into an enormous bundle of laws. (Ibid.)[18]

But let's consider the example of 'bachelor' more closely. It is still commonly assumed and asserted in philosophy that: it is analytically true by virtue of the
meaning of 'bachelor' that:

x is a *bachelor* iff$_{df}$ x is an unmarried adult male (UAM).

But this claim only seems plausible if one assumes that heterosexuality is universal, or that there is no way other than marriage for one to enter into a formalized lifelong commitment. It seems plausible to say that an unmarried gay man
who has made a lifelong commitment to another—perhaps even formalized it as
a "civil union"—is not a bachelor. (So not: if UAM, then bachelor.) To press further: is it analytic that marriage is between a man and a woman, or is it only
"deeply embedded collateral information" (Putnam 1975a, p. 41)? Whose intuitions about 'marriage' should settle this?

One might suggest that a weaker claim is analytic by virtue of the meaning of
'bachelor':

If x is a *bachelor*, then x is unmarried.

But the truth of this claim depends on what sorts of institutions might qualify
as 'marriage,' and this is an issue that is highly contested and historically
complex. For example, marriage as we know it has traditionally combined an
economic institution with a quasi-religious institution setting constraints on
sexual behavior. This is, of course, not an accident, since sex tends to produce
offspring and offspring are, at least potentially, both an economic drain and an
economic resource. However, it is possible to imagine a case in which the economic institution of marriage and the sexual institution of marriage are separated to form two kinds of marriage, a sexual marriage and an economic
marriage. (Consider, perhaps, a variation on Margaret Atwood's *The Handmaid's*

---

[18] Putnam's paper is famous for going on to argue that there are scenarios in which we would
consider evidence that "All bachelors are unmarried" is false; but such scenarios are ones in which
'bachelor' comes to function as a natural kind term for those with a certain neurosis. So again, on
Putnam's account the phenomenon of conceptual evolution occurs in the context of developing natural science.

Tale.) Further, suppose that one can be sexually married to *A* and economically married to *B*. I'm inclined to think that bachelorhood is really about sexual availability, so the fact that a man is economically married to *A* does not compromise his bachelor status, since he is still available to be sexually married to someone else.

In any case, the reliance on a background social framework is apparent in the case of:

x is a *parent* iff$_{df}$ *x* is an immediate progenitor.

In some social/historical contexts this may seem analytically true by virtue of what 'parent' means. But laws and customs change so that one can become the legal parent of a child who is not biologically related, and with time, such parents are recognized as 'real parents.'

In the case of *parents* and of *marriage* there are competing models of social life, of what's essential and what's accidental to our existing social structures. But just as what is essential or accidental to being an atom or being energy will depend on the background physical theory in which the term 'atom' is used, so what is essential or accidental to being a parent, or being married, or being a bachelor, will depend on the background model of social life (see also Burge 1986). Putnam suggests that we should contrast cases such as "Bachelors are unmarried men" with scientific principles, because the former is as close to pure stipulation as we can get and the latter have "systematic import." Because of the systematic import of scientific principles, we can give up one or another of them without changing the meaning of the terms used to express them. (Putnam 1975a, p. 40) What Putnam (and others) seem to miss is that "Bachelors are unmarried men" also has systematic import; that is, the concepts, in particular, of *marriage, adult,* and *male,* although familiar from common parlance, can also be the subject of social and political theory and of social contestation. Although the scientific essentialists were apt to claim that the analytic/synthetic distinction stood in the way of scientific progress, they were not as apt to see that it may also stand in the way of social progress.

What these cases reveal is that often what we take to be analytic principles actually encode certain social arrangements, and the relationship between terms encode certain power structures. For example, the term 'parent' brings with it a certain normative weight, entitlement, and so on, that the term 'primary caregiver' doesn't. Putnam suggests that it would be difficult to imagine a physical theory that did not employ some notion of *the past,* or of *energy.* These are framework concepts. Similarly it is difficult to imagine a social theory that did not employ some notions of *male, female, parent,* even something like *marriage.* So there is a reason why social constructionists want to rethink the term 'parent' rather than substituting the term 'primary caregiver.' And it is not surprising that in the United States we are fighting over *what the term 'marriage' means* as part of the struggle for gay rights. The term 'marriage' is a framework concept that links the institution to a broad range of other social phenomena, and does so in a way that 'civil union' cannot approximate.

The constructionist about 'parent' maintains that in cases where the manifest concept of *parent* is of an immediate progenitor, it may nonetheless be appropriate to understand the concept of *parent* as of *primary caregiver* (or some such notion). Is the constructionist simply changing the meaning of the term? If the concept of *parent* is a (social) framework concept, which seems plausible, and if the work we need the term 'parent' to do is no longer best served by assuming that parents are immediate progenitors, then it is reasonable to consider this claim, not as giving the meaning of the term, but as stating a useful, though not universal, generalization.

This, then, suggests a reason to prefer the constructionist to the error-theoretic strategy in analyzing at least some social kinds. The conceptualist's insistence that the concept in question, say *parent,* should be analyzed only in terms of what is manifest to us, can have the effect of fossilizing our social structure: if we are not allowed to adjust the contents of our framework concepts in light of developments in social theory and social life, then social change will require a wholesale adoption of a new conceptual scheme. Given that this is unlikely, change will be difficult. Moreover, because framework concepts are embedded with normative principles, rejecting the concepts may leave us with old practices and no new principles to guide us. If we combine the conceptualist strategy with the retention of purportedly natural categories, we further entrench the existing framework by suggesting that its analytic structure is just tracking nature's joints, not ours. So, in effect, the constructionist is making two moves that potentially destabilize our social arrangements: revealing that a purportedly analytic statement is in fact a contingent generalization, and revealing that a natural category is in fact social.

8. Conclusion

I started this chapter by asking whether social constructionist analyses of familiar terms or concepts can ever be philosophically acceptable if such analyses aim to *debunk* our ordinary understandings and so inevitably violate our intuitions. Further, if social constructionist analyses can be counterintuitive, are there any limits on how counterintuitive they can be and still be acceptable; more generally, what makes for goodness in a constructionist analysis, if intuitions don't matter? And finally, are there any reasons why constructionist analyses should be preferred over error-theoretic accounts that remain committed to the manifest naturalizing concept as "what we mean" and offer a new social concept to capture how the term operates in our practice?

I have argued that constructionist analyses cannot be faulted *in general* for changing the subject, or for being counterintuitive. Semantic externalism allows us to claim that what we are talking about is, in fact, a social category, even if we think it isn't. And in the case of framework concepts, social theory and social life may lead us to reject principles that seemed definitional, while we still retain the concept. So the constructionist can claim to provide an acceptable analysis of a concept, even if it is not intuitive.

A successful constructionist debunking will be one in which the best account of what we are doing (or should be doing) in drawing the distinctions in question—taking into account what legitimate purposes are being served and what objective types there are—has us tracking a social type.[19] Such an account will not be purely a priori and will draw on social theory. I have not, in this chapter, argued that a social constructionist account of race is preferable to an error-theoretic or naturalistic account (though I have maintained that it is: see Haslanger 2012 [2000]); such an argument would have to delve into empirical matters that I haven't touched on here.

It would be a mistake to conclude from what I've argued that constructionist analyses are always preferable to error-theoretic analyses when there is a gap between manifest and operative concepts. Cases have to be examined individually. In particular, the arguments I've offered in this chapter only address error theorists who rely on a conceptualist picture, that is, those whose analysis of the controversial concept rests entirely on balancing intuitions. There may be some who adopt an error theory as the result of a broad analysis of our practices and purposes. My arguments do not weigh against such an account. Rather, I have urged that if our manifest concepts are misleading about our practices and mask what we are really doing with our concepts, we should consider whether there is a story to be told about how and why. If there is such a story, our accounts should reflect it.

Grounding philosophical analysis in linguistic competence or a priori intuition concerning our manifest concepts risks perpetuating social self-deception. Although we cannot proceed without intuition, neither can we proceed without critical social theory. My hope is that the example of gender and race will encourage philosophers to pay greater attention to the rather ubiquitous gap between manifest and operative concepts, leading to less focus on our intuitions and more on the role of concepts in structuring our social lives. Philosophical analysis has a potential for unmasking ideology, not simply articulating it.[20]

---

[19] On the issue of what counts as a "legitimate purpose" and how our theoretic purposes should be evaluated, I follow Anderson 1995 and trends in feminist empiricism more broadly.

[20] Thanks to Louise Antony, Lawrence Blum, Alex Byrne, Jorge Garcia, Richard Holton, Erin Kelly, Ishani Maitra, Mary Kate McGowan, Lionel McPherson, Laura Schroeter, Marion Smiley, Sarah Song, Ronald Sundstrom, Ásta Sveinsdóttir, Gregory Velazco y Trianosky, and Steve Yablo for discussing with me the issues raised in this chapter. Earlier versions of this chapter were given at the Society for Analytic Feminism, the Australian National University, The California Roundtable on Philosophy and Race (2005), the University of Colorado, Boulder, and Tufts University. I am grateful to the participants in the discussions for helpful feedback.

References

Alcoff, Linda. 2000. "Is Latino/a Identity a Racial Identity?" In Jorge J. E. Gracia and Pablo De Grieff (eds), *Hispanics and Latinos in the United States: Ethnicity, Race, and Rights*. New York: Routledge, pp. 23–44.

Anderson, Elizabeth. 1995. "Knowledge, Human Interests, and Objectivity in Feminist Epistemology." *Philosophical Topics*, 23(2), pp. 27–58.

Andreason, Robin. 2000. "Race: Biological Reality or Social Construct?" *Philosophy of Science*, 67, Supplementary Volume, pp. S653–66.

Appiah, K. Anthony. 1996. "Race, Culture, Identity: Misunderstood Connections." In K. A. Appiah and A. Gutmann, *Color Conscious: The Political Morality of Race*. Princeton: Princeton University Press, pp. 30–105.

——. 1993. *In My Father's House*. New York: Oxford University Press.

Armstrong, David. 1989. *Universals: An Opinionated Introduction*. Boulder, CO: Westview Press.

Burge, Tyler. 1979. "Individualism and the Mental." *Midwest Studies in Philosophy*, 4, pp. 73–121.

——. 1986. "Intellectual Norms and Foundations of Mind." *Journal of Philosophy*, 83(12), pp. 697–720.

Glasgow, Joshua. 2003. "On the New Biology of Race." *Journal of Philosophy*, 100, pp. 456–74.

Gooding-Williams, Robert. 1998. "Race, Multiculturalism and Democracy." *Constellations*, 5(1), pp. 18–41.

Hacking, Ian. 1999. *The Social Construction of What?* Cambridge, MA: Harvard University Press.

Hardimon, Michael O. 2003. "The Ordinary Concept of Race." *Journal of Philosophy*, 100(9), pp. 437–55.

Haslanger, Sally. 2012 [1995]. "Ontology and Social Construction." Chapter 2 of this volume.

——. 2012 [2000]. "Gender and Race: (What) Are They? (What) Do We Want Them To Be?" Chapter 7 of this volume.

——. 2012 [2003]. "Social Construction: The 'Debunking' Project." Chapter 3 of this volume.

——. 2012 [2005]. "What Are We Talking About? The Semantics and Politics of Social Kinds." Chapter 13 of this volume.

——. 2006. "Race and Natural Kinds." Conference presentation, January 9. *Revisiting Race in a Genomic Age*, Stanford Humanities Centre.

Higginbotham, J. 1998. "Conceptual Competence." *Philosophical Issues*, 9, pp. 149–62.

Kitcher, Philip. 1999. "Race, Ethnicity, Biology, Culture." In L. Harris (ed.), *Racism*. New York: Humanity Books, pp. 87–117.

Kripke, Saul. 1980. *Naming and Necessity*. Cambridge, MA: Harvard University Press.

Lee, Sandra Soo-Jin, Johanna Mountain, and Barbara Koenig. 2001. "The Meanings of 'Race' in the New Genomics: Implications for Health Disparities Research." *Yale Journal of Health Policy, Law and Ethics*, 1, pp. 33–75.

MacKinnon, Catharine. 1987. *Feminism Unmodified*. Cambridge, MA: Harvard University Press.

Mallon, Ron. 2004. "Passing, Traveling and Reality: Social Construction and the Metaphysics of Race." *Noûs*, 38(4), pp. 644–73.

Mills, Charles. 1998. *Blackness Visible: Essays on Philosophy and Race*. Ithaca, NY: Cornell University Press.

——. 1997. *The Racial Contract*. Ithaca, NY: Cornell University Press.

Mountain, Joanna L., and Neil Risch. 2004. "Assessing Genetic Contributions to Phenotypic Differences Among 'Racial' and 'Ethnic' Groups." *Nature Genetics*, 36(11 Supp.), pp. S48–53.

Omi, Michael, and Howard Winant. 1994. "Racial Formation." In M. Omi and H. Winant, *Racial Formation in the United States*. New York: Routledge, pp. 53–76.

Peacocke, Christopher. 1998. "Implicit Conceptions, Understanding, and Rationality." *Philosophical Issues*, 9, pp. 43–88.

Putnam, Hilary. 1973. "Meaning and Reference." *Journal of Philosophy*, 70, pp. 699–711.

——. 1975a. "'The Analytic and the Synthetic." In *Mind, Language and Reality: Philosophical Papers*, Volume 2. Cambridge: Cambridge University Press, pp. 33–69.

————. 1975b. "The Meaning of 'Meaning.'" In *Mind, Language and Reality: Philosophical Papers*, Volume 2. Cambridge: Cambridge University Press, pp. 215–71.

Quine, W. V. O. 1953. "Two Dogmas of Empiricism." In *From a Logical Point of View*. Cambridge, MA: Harvard University Press.

Risch, Neil, Esteban Burchard, Elad Ziv, and Hua Tang. 2002. "Categorization of Humans in Biomedical Research: Genes, Race and Disease." *Genome Biology*, 3(7), comment 2007.1–2007.12.

Rosenberg, Noah A., Jonathan K. Pritchard, James L. Weber, Howard M. Cann, Kenneth K. Kidd, Lev A. Zhivotovsky, and Marcus W. Feldman. 2002. "Genetic Structure of Human Populations." *Science*, 298, pp. 2381–85.

Zack, Naomi. 2002. *Philosophy of Science and Race*. New York: Routledge, pp. 29–23.

————. 1997. "Race and Philosophic Meaning." In *RACE/SEX: Their Sameness, Difference, and Interplay*. New York: Routledge, pp. 29–43.

15

"But Mom, Crop-Tops *Are* Cute!"

Social Knowledge, Social Structure, and Ideology Critique

> A study of the science of man is inseparable from an examina-
> tion of the options between which men must choose. This means
> that we can speak here not only of error, but of illusion. We
> speak of 'illusion' when we are dealing with something of greater
> substance than error, [it is] error which in a sense builds a coun-
> terfeit reality of its own . . . [Such illusions] are more than errors
> in this sense: they are sustained by certain practices of which
> they are constitutive.
>
> —Taylor *1985/1971, 54*

> Certainly a good deal of men's tyranny over women can be
> observed through data, experiments, and research. . . . Many
> things can be known in this way. . . . [But it does not] show that
> it is unnecessary or changeable, except speculatively, because
> what is not there is not considered real. Women's situation
> cannot be truly known for what it is, in the feminist sense, with-
> out knowing that it can be other than it is. By operating as legit-
> imating ideology, the scientific standard for verifying reality can
> reinforce a growing indignation, but it cannot create feminism
> that was not already there. Knowing objective facts does not do
> what consciousness does.
>
> —MacKinnon *1989, 100–101*

1. Introduction[1]

In the social realm, knowledge, or what purports to be knowledge, is entangled
with the reality it represents. Social institutions are constituted, at least in
part, by sets of shared beliefs and conventions; even false beliefs about social

[1] Thanks to Lauren Ashwell, Nancy Bauer, Alex Byrne, Gabriella Coleman, Philip Corkum, Nina
Emery, Caspar Hare, Cressida Heyes, Richard Holton, Bruce Hunter, David Kahane, Victor Kumar,
Rae Langton, Bernard Linsky, Victoria McGeer, Amy Schmitter, Paolo Santorio, Robert Stalnaker,
William Taschek, Catherine Wearing, Robert Wilson, Charlotte Witt, and especially Stephen Yablo
for helpful discussions and feedback.

phenomena can cause changes in the social world that result in the belief's be-coming true (Langton 2007). As a result, it is sometimes suggested that an epistemology of the social realm must not simply be concerned with whether a belief is justified and true. When social knowledge goes wrong, it may be because it has constituted a reality—and perhaps accurately represents that reality—that nevertheless falls short in some way. Following Taylor (see epigraph), the suggestion might be that the social reality created by the belief is an illusion. But if it is, in what sense is it an illusion? Is it an illusion about what's possible? About what's good? And is an evaluation of the product of knowledge a legitimate part of social epistemology?

Catharine MacKinnon's work repeatedly and forcefully raises the question how an epistemology of the social should proceed in oppressive social contexts. On MacKinnon's view (1989, see also epigraph),

> Consciousness raising, by contrast [to scientific inquiry] inquires into an intrinsically social situation, in the mixture of thought and materiality which comprises gender in its broadest sense. (MacKinnon 1989, 83)

She continues, "The process is transformative as well as perceptive, since thought and thing are inextricably and reciprocally constitutive of women's oppression . . ." (MacKinnon 1989, 84) Given the interdependence of social thought and reality, a change of meaning can transform the social world.[2] This calls, however, for a new branch of epistemology:

> This epistemology does not at all deny that a relation exists between thought and some reality other than thought, or between human ac-tivity (mental or otherwise) and the products of that activity. Rather, it redefines the epistemological issue from being a scientific one, the rela-tion between knowledge and objective reality, to a problem of the rela-tion of consciousness to social being. (MacKinnon 1989, 99)

Setting aside the challenge of interpreting her positive view, she is raising an epistemological problem about what "should" be thought in those domains where what is thought (at least partly) both determines and is determined by its object. This problem is especially pressing when this occurs at a site of injustice. My goal in this chapter is to provide some resources for developing a response.

---

[2] Roughly, consciousness raising considers the way in which social thought and social reality are interdependent, offers a critical perspective on the meanings implicit in this thought-imbued reality, and proposes alternative meanings gained from a perspective within the social context in question. I will not dwell on what consciousness raising is or what its epistemic credentials are.

2. Are Crop-Tops Cute?

To make this more concrete, consider the role of fashion in schools. The belief that certain girls are wearing crop-tops that expose their midriff partly constitutes the fact that it is fashionable to wear such tops and causes many other girls to do the same. Plausibly, in such situations it becomes "common knowledge" that, say, seventh grade girls are wearing crop-tops this spring.[3] But, one might argue, it would be better if seventh grade (roughly age 12) girls were wearing ordinary—midriff covering—tops instead (because the crop-tops sexualize the girls who wear them, further marginalize the chubby girls, and so on). So parents who are uncomfortable with the crop-top fashion, and yet find themselves faced with a daughter who is eager to join the crowd, might suggest to her that, for example, she shouldn't care about being fashionable, that she shouldn't let what the other girls are doing determine her choices, that she is beautiful in her track suit.

However, even if the daughter is individually able to retain her self-respect without bowing to the fashion trend, it may still be true that she will be marginalized if she doesn't conform and that the fashionable girls are sexualized (Warner 2007). Bucking conventions may be a partial solution that works for some individuals. But the problem is not individual. The situation would be better if "seventh grade girls are wearing crop-tops this spring" wasn't part of a set of beliefs that constitute common knowledge in the school (or the broader society).

With this in mind, consider the following familiar dialogue:

Daughter: "Can I have some money to buy a crop-top like Ashley's to wear to school?"

Parents: "You can have a new top, but not a crop-top. Crop-tops are too revealing."

Daughter: "But Mom[Dad], you're just wrong. Everyone knows that crop-tops are cute; and I don't want to be a dork."

Parents: "I'm sorry, sweetie, crop-tops *are not* cute, and you *won't* be a dork if you wear your track suit."

Under the circumstances it seems that there is something right about Daughter's reply to Parents, and their reply is not enough. And yet, aren't the parents right?

One might initially assume that in this conversation there is a disagreement over the truth-value of the following claims:

---

[3] Following Lewis (1969, 56), the state of affairs of certain (popular) girls wearing crop-tops is the basis for the common knowledge that seventh grade girls are wearing crop-tops this spring.

1. Seventh grade girls who wear crop-tops to school are cute.
2. Seventh grade girls who wear track suits to school are dorks.

One way to unpack the truth-value reading of the disagreement is to suggest that "cute" and "dork" are evaluative predicates and those who believe (1) and (2) are wrong about the objective (social/aesthetic/sartorial) value of crop-tops and track suits. But this is implausible. The patterns of social interaction at the school are what determine the extensions of 'cute' and 'dork': if a girl walks like a dork, sounds like a dork, dresses like a dork, she is a dork.

Where *objectivist readings* of statements such as (1) seem misguided, the alternative is often taken to be a *subjectivist reading* which renders the disagreement a matter of taste. On this reading the parents and daughter simply have different sartorial tastes, just as they might have different tastes in food or humor. In effect, the daughter is claiming that crop-tops are cute *to her* (or to her classmates), and the parents are claiming that they are not cute *to them* (or to their peers). But this fails to capture the sense in which the parents are disagreeing with the daughter and are in a position to offer a critique of the fashion trends. On a broader scale, although social norms and such are at least partly constituted by the attitudes of the social group they govern, an acceptable approach must make room for meaningful critique across groups.

Yet another reading of the disagreement would be to see the parent as rejecting, and urging the daughter to reject, the "cute/dork" dichotomy: these ways of classifying yourself and others based on a willingness to wear sexy clothing are misguided and should be avoided. Parents undertake to disrupt such classifications, as do teachers and school administrators who institute dress codes and such. Let's call this the *framework reading*.[4] On the framework reading (1) is true and one may be justified in believing it. But at the same time it captures and reinforces (and uttered by the right person at the right moment, might even create) a misguided distinction.

Without taking a stand yet on precisely what's at issue between parents and daughter, there are, nonetheless, the makings of a puzzle. If the social reality is organized around the cute/dork dichotomy, then there are cute girls and dorky girls, and it would be a mistake not to recognize this. This is important social knowledge. But at the same time it is tempting to say that the cute/dork dichotomy is an illusion. It is socially and morally problematic and because it is reified through a pattern of belief and expectation, it could be undermined by a refusing to have beliefs in its terms. More generally, in cases such as this we seem to be able to

---

[4] In fact, there are a number of different ways one might construe the speech act Parents perform other than a straightforward denial of Daughter's assertion. A rejection of the cute/dork dichotomy is a plausible one, but there are others worth considering. I am not claiming that there is only one way to interpret Parents' contribution to the conversation.

generate a contradiction: it is true that *p* so you should believe *p*; but believing *p* makes it true, and it would be better if *p* weren't true; so you shouldn't believe *p*.

3. "Should Believe"

So it appears that the daughter should believe that, say, seventh grade girls who wear track suits to school are dorks, and yet, if her parent is right, she should also not believe it. A first stab at avoiding the puzzle would be to suggest that there are two senses of 'should' involved in this line of thought. The girl should believe what is true; this is an *epistemic* 'should.' Yet for moral/political reasons, she should also not believe the statements in question. If she believes that track-suited girls are dorks, this will contribute to the patterns of beliefs and expectations that constitute the social fact that such girls are dorks, which would be bad. This second 'should,' it might be argued, is a *pragmatic* or *moral* 'should.' Thus, there is an equivocation in the argument and the puzzle dissolves.

Although there seems to be something right about this response, it isn't sufficient. First, it is controversial to suggest that pragmatic or moral norms apply to believing, for it isn't clear that believing is, in the relevant sense, a matter of choice (Williams 1973). The daughter experiences her friends as cute in crop-tops and the track suited others as dorky, and this may not be something she can change at will. For example, if the parent threatens, "If you continue to believe that crop-tops are suitable for seventh grade girls to wear to school, I'll cut your allowance in half," it seems there is little the daughter can do other than look for reasons that will change her mind (or lie about what she believes).

Second, the "framework" reading of the disagreement—the reading on which the cute/dork dichotomy is misguided—suggests that the tweenage categories are ill-conceived. A reason for rejecting (1) and (2) seems to involve a charge of inaccuracy or misrepresentation. Although there is something true about the claim that girls who wear track suits to school are dorks, there is also something false about it. For example, contrast the case with one in which the (non-athletic) daughter replies to her parents, "But Mom/Dad, the girls who wear track suits to school are all on the track team." The parent might try to resist the identification of athletes with what they wear. But it would be odd to reject the framework that distinguishes those on the track team, from those who aren't, in the same way that they rejected the cute/dorky framework: "But sweetie, you *won't be* on the track team if you wear a track suit." (Cf. "But sweetie, you *won't be* a dork if you wear a track suit.") Although the *cute/dorky* distinction and the *track team/not-track team* distinction both capture social categories, there is something illusory about the former in contrast to the latter.

So although some considerations that count against accepting (1) and (2) may not be epistemic, it is worth considering further the idea that there is some epistemic failing in the daughter's commitment to (1) and (2). In other words, there seems to be a sense in which the daughter both should and should not, *epistemically speaking*, believe that seventh grade girls who wear track suits are dorks. (Henceforth, I'll focus on (1) since there seems to be no significant difference between (1) and (2) for our purposes.)

4. Social Reality

The example of the seventh grade girl and her parents is a small instance of what's involved in navigating and negotiating the social world. The girl and her parents are members of different social groups (age-wise), have different experiences, beliefs, and frameworks for understanding what actions and events mean. Both seem to have important social knowledge, but they are also deeply at odds. In the background, I believe, are important issues concerning ideology and social structure. So in the next several sub-sections I will explore some aspects of the interdependence of thought and reality in the social world so we can better understand how thought can fail us without being false. My goal is not to define "the social" or to give a full-blown theory of social structure, but to illuminate the example we've been considering, and others like it, by exploring the idea that there are multiple social worlds or milieus. I will then return to the puzzle set out in the first two sections.

Ideology

In order to develop an account of social knowledge, it will be useful to think about the relationship between agents, their ideas, and social structures generally: what are social structures, and how do agents create, maintain, and change them? Let's begin with the concept of ideology.

There is much disagreement over the nature of ideology, yet in the most basic sense ideologies are representations of social life that serve in some way to undergird social practices.[5] We are not simply cogs in structures and practices of subordination, we enact them. And something about how we represent the world is both a *constitutive part* of that enactment and *keeps it going*.[6]

---

[5] Especially useful discussions of the notion of ideology include: Geuss 1981; Fields 1982; McCarthy 1990; Purvis and Hunt 1993; Shelby 2003.

[6] Although there is much controversy over the question whether 'ideology' or the Foucauldian notion of 'discourse' is better suited to the role described here, the controversies are not directly relevant to my purposes. Moreover, there seems to be a core notion shared by both. See Purvis and Hunt 1993.

> . . . ideology and discourse refer to pretty much the same aspect of social life—the idea that human individuals participate in forms of understanding, comprehension or consciousness of the relations and activities in which they are involved. . . . This consciousness is borne through language and other systems of signs, it is transmitted between people and institutions and, perhaps most important of all, it *makes a difference*; that is, the way in which people comprehend and make sense of the social world has consequences for the direction and character of their action and inaction. Both 'discourse' and 'ideology' refer to these aspects of social life. (Purvis and Hunt 1993, 474; see also McCarthy 1990, 440)

Ideology in this broad, sometimes referred to as the *descriptive*, sense, is pervasive and unavoidable. The term 'ideology' is also sometimes used in a narrower and *pejorative sense*, however, to refer to representations of the relevant sort that are somehow misguided, for example, by being contrary to the real interests of an agent or group of agents.[7] For current purposes, we can think of ideology as an element in a social system that contributes to its survival and yet that is susceptible to change through some form of cognitive critique.

The belief that "seventh grade girls who wear crop-tops are cute" is a good candidate for a piece of ideology. It is a constitutive part of the fashion norms of seventh grade girls in the school: the belief that girls are wearing such outfits functions to set up a pattern of understandings and expectations that reinforces the pattern of behavior. Moreover, it is plausibly ideology in the pejorative sense because the behavior it sustains subordinates girls. For example, empirical research shows that under conditions of stereotype threat, for example, in contexts where there is a background assumption that girls are worse at math than boys, anything that primes for gender identity—and highly gender coded clothing has been found to be one such thing—causes girls to do worse on math tests (Frederickson et al. 1998; Spencer et al. 1999; Cadinu et al. 2005). Yet we might hope that such beliefs are susceptible to cognitive critique, perhaps even parental challenges of the sort we've considered.

Given the discussion in the previous sections, however, we should be attentive to the possibility that an ideology is not just a set of beliefs, and ideology

---

[7] Sometimes ideologies are taken to be sets of beliefs, sometimes forms of "practical consciousness," that reside in the minds of individual agents; sometimes they are cultural phenomena presupposed somehow in collective social life; sometimes they are explicit theories articulated by politicians, philosophers and religious figures, among others. The causal or explanatory role of ideology within a broader social theory is also unclear. (Geuss 1981; Elster 1985, 468–9; Marx 1970/1846, 36–7).

critique is not just a matter of showing that the beliefs in question are false or unwarranted. The framework reading of the disagreement over crop-tops suggested, for example, that *the dichotomy* of cute/dorky itself was ideological; and the responses that have been conditioned to experience exposed midriffs as cute may be something less than full belief.

Further considerations suggesting that ideology is not simply a matter of belief include:

- In some cases, belief seems too cognitive, or too "intellectual."

  Ideology is concerned with the realm of the lived, or the experienced, rather than of "thinking". . . . It is precisely the "spontaneous" quality of common sense, its transparency, its "naturalness," its refusal to examine the premises on which it is grounded, its resistance to correction, its quality of being instantly recognizable which makes common sense, at one and the same time, "lived," "spontaneous," and unconscious. We live in common sense—we do not think it. (Purvis and Hunt 1993, 479)

- Ideology can take the form of practical knowledge, knowledge how to do certain things. Habitual gestures and body language that are ubiquitous in human interaction are ideological.
- Ideologies seem to work at the level of "slogans" that can be interpreted differently over time and by different constituencies, for example, *America is the land of the free and home of the brave* (Fields 1982, 155–9). Beliefs have a determinate content that is not compatible with this.
- Beliefs may be too individualistic. Social practices are ideological, but many who live in a culture and follow its practices don't have the beliefs that are ordinarily identified as the ideology undergirding the practices.

Social structure

Ideology plays a role in constituting and reinforcing social structures. But what *is* a social structure? There is considerable interdisciplinary work on this topic by social historians, social psychologists, and sociologists interested in subordination and critical resistance. As I am using the term here, 'social structure' is a general category of social phenomena, including, for example, social institutions, social practices and conventions, social roles, social hierarchies, social locations or geographies, and the like. Some social structures will be formal and so the schematic element will be precise and explicit (the structure of faculty governance at any university); some will involve intricate but not fully explicit coordination (informal traffic norms); others will be informal and vague and not well coordinated (the structure of holiday gift-giving).[8]

William Sewell (a social historian), drawing on Anthony Giddens, argues for an account that takes structures to be "both the medium and the outcome of the practices which constitute social systems" (Sewell 1992, 4, quoting Giddens 1981, 27; see also Giddens 1979). Sewell continues: "Structures shape people's practices, but it is also people's practices that constitute (and reproduce) structures. In this view of things, human agency and structure, far from being *opposed*, in fact *presuppose* each other" (Sewell 1992, 4).

More specifically, Giddens is known for identifying structures as "rules and resources." On Sewell's account, however, the combination becomes "schemas and resources" in order to avoid the assumption that the cognitive element must always take the form of a rule (Sewell 1992, 8). Sewell takes schemas to include:

> . . . all the variety of cultural schemas that anthropologists have uncovered in their research: not only the array of binary oppositions that make up a given society's fundamental tools of thought, but also the various conventions, recipes, scenarios, principles of action, and habits of speech and gesture built up with these fundamental tools. (Sewell 1992, 7–8)

It is crucial to Sewell that these schemas are not private and personal patterns of thought, but are intersubjective and transposable in response to new circumstances.

Responding to Sewell, Judith Howard (a social psychologist) points out that Sewell's (1992) use of the term 'schema' differs from its use in social psychology. Whereas social psychologists tend to think of schemas as concerned with the organization of an individual's thought, Sewell develops the notion in a way that highlights its cultural deployment. She suggests:

> A synthesis of these conceptions of schemas might prove remarkably useful: the stricter social cognitive models provide a sound basis for predicting how and when intra-individual schemas change, whereas the

---

[8] It is a controversial what counts as a "social fact." In my discussion I begin with the idea that social facts are "interpersonal" facts or facts that supervene on such facts. So, simplifying considerably, *I am Deb's friend* is a social fact because it supervenes on a certain base set of interpersonal actions and attitudes. Others, such as John Searle (1995), have higher demands, including controversial "we-intentions," assignment of function, and the generation of constitutive rules. These elements are more plausibly required in creating institutional facts or conventional facts; his analysis is too demanding to capture much of ordinary informal social life. For example, we can have coordinated intentions without them being "we-intentions"; things can have a social function even if they aren't assigned it; and social kind membership isn't always governed by rules.

more recent sociological conceptions say more about how group interactions shape the formation and evolution of cultural schemas. (Howard 1994, 218)

If we take Howard's idea seriously, we should explore the interdependence
between individual schemas and their cultural counterparts. "Schemas, for example, are both mental and social; they both derive from and constitute cultural,
semiotic, and symbolic systems" (Howard 1994, 218).

What are we to make of this? Let's take schemas to be intersubjective patterns of perception, thought, and behavior. They are embodied in individuals as
a shared cluster of open-ended dispositions to see things a certain way or to
respond habitually in particular circumstances. Schemas encode knowledge and
also provide scripts for interaction with each other and our environment. They
also exist at different depths. Deep schemas are pervasive and relatively unconscious. Surface schemas are more narrow and are easier to identify and change;
but their change may leave the deeper schema intact. For example, rules concerning gender differences in clothing have changed, yet the more formal the
event, the more strict the gender codes. Does this suggest that in contexts where
power, authority, and prestige are managed, the deep schema of women as submissive or hobbled property of men still functions?[9]

On this view, schemas are one component of social structures, *resources* are
the other. Social structures cannot be identified simply as schemas because
social structures have material existence and a reality that "pushes back" when
we come to it with the wrong or an incomplete schema. For example, the schema
of two sex categories is manifested in the design and labeling of toilet facilities.
If we're analyzing social structures, then in addition to the mental content or
disposition, there must be an actualization of it in the world, for example, an
enactment of it, that involves something material. Resources provide the materiality of social structures. On the Giddens/Sewell account, resources are anything that "can be used to enhance or maintain power" (Sewell 1992, 9). This
includes human resources such as "physical strength, dexterity, knowledge"
(Sewell 1992, 9), in addition to materials—animate and inanimate—in the usual
sense.

How do schemas and resources together constitute social structures? Sewell
suggests a causal interdependence (Sewell 1992, 13). He elaborates:

A factory is not an inert pile of bricks, wood, and metal. It incorporates
or actualizes schemas. . . . The factory gate, the punching-in station, the

[9] As Howard (1994) notes, the concept of a sociocognitive schema, leaves many questions un-
answered, for example, how and when are such schemas formed both in the individual and in the
culture? What explains their formation and disruption? How are they transposed? (etc.)

> design of the assembly line: all of these features of the factory teach and validate the rules of the capitalist labor contract. . . . In short, if resources are instantiations or embodiments of schemas, they therefore inculcate and justify the schemas as well . . . Sets of schemas and resources may properly be said to constitute *structures* only when they mutually imply and sustain each other over time. (Sewell 1992, 13)

So on Sewell's view a social structure exists when there is a causal, and mutually sustaining, interdependence between a shared or collective schema and an organization of resources. Sewell's claim that the two elements of structure "imply and sustain each other" suggests a constitutive relationship as well: the pile of bricks, wood, and metal *is* a punching-in station because schemas that direct employers to pay employees by the hour and employees to keep track of their hours are enacted with this tool. The schema for keeping track of hours *is* a punching-in schema because there is a punch-clock that the employer will use as a basis for calculating wages. Without the invention of the punch-clock, there could be no punching-in schema. There is a causal relationship, but not just a causal relationship. What else is it?

Consider a familiar example: a statue and the bronze of which it is composed. The bronze constitutes the statue, for example, the figure of Joan of Arc on horseback in New York City's Riverside Park. The bronze is the statue not only by virtue of its shape, but also by virtue of having a certain history, function, interpretation, and so on. Think of the bronze as resource; think of the dispositions that give rise to the statue's history, function, interpretation (roughly) as schema. The role of schema may be still more evident in the constitution of it as a memorial. The Joan of Arc statue commemorates "the 500th anniversary of Joan of Arc's birth."[10] The statue consists of the shaped bronze, and the statue in turn constitutes the memorial, understood as a further schema-structured resource: [[[bronze, shape], statue], memorial]. Thus it appears that the schema/resource distinction can be applied in ways analogous to the matter/form distinction.

Consider an example of a social event rather than a social object: the performance of a Bach minuet on the piano. The performance is an event that involves both the piano, the sheet music, fingers and such (as resources), and also a set of dispositions to respond to the sheet music by playing the piano keys in a certain way, plus the various ritualized gestures that make it a performance rather than a rehearsal (as schema). Considered in this light, most actions involve not only an agent with an intention and a bodily movement, but a set of dispositions to interact with things to realise the intention; think of cycling, cooking, typing.

---

[10] See: http://www.blueofthesky.com/publicart/works/joanofarc.htm.

These dispositions conform to publicly accessible and socially meaningful patterns and are molded by both the social and physical context. Because often such dispositions give rise to objects that trigger those very dispositions, they can be extremely resistant to change (think of the challenge of replacing the qwerty keyboard).

This sort of schematic materiality of our social worlds is ubiquitous: towns, city halls, churches, universities, philosophy departments, gyms, playgrounds, homes, are schematically structured and practice-imbued material things (cf. a "ghost town" or "a house but not a home" whose schemas are lost or attenuated). The social world includes artifacts which are what they are because of what is to be done with them; it also includes schemas for action that are what they are because they direct our interaction with some part of the world. Thus at least some parts of the social/cognitive world and material world are co-constitutive.

If a practice is the structured product of schema (a set of dispositions to perceive and respond in certain ways) and resources (a set of tools and material goods), it is not "subjective" in any of the ordinary uses of that term. Social structures are not just in our heads (just as the statue is not just in our heads); social structures are public (just as the bronze only constitutes a memorial by virtue of the collective interpretation and pattern of action in response to it); although social structures are not simply material things, they are constituted by material things. They are "constructed" by us in the ordinary way that artifacts are created by us. One can believe in them without accepting the idea, sometimes endorsed by "social constructionists" that our thought constructs, in a less ordinary way, what there is in the world (Haslanger 2012 [2003]).

This rough account of social structures helps to define the idea of a social *milieu*. As we saw above, the schemas that constitute social structures are intersubjective or cultural patterns, scripts and the like, that are internalized by individuals to form the basis of our responses to socially meaningful objects, actions, and events. In many cases, perhaps even most, the dominant cultural schema will also be the one that individuals in that context have made "their own." However, it is not always that simple. Individuals bear complex relations to the dominant schemas of their cultural context; they may be ignorant of or insensitive to a schema, may reject a schema, or may modify a schema for their own purposes. One may be deliberately out of sync with one's milieu, or just "out of it." It is also the case that different schemas vie for dominance in public space. For example, what happens when a group of people approach a closed door they want to go through? Some will employ a "gallant gentleman" schema and will hold the door for the ladies; others will employ a "whoever gets there first holds the door" schema; still others will employ a "first-come, first enters, hold your own door" schema. Which schema one brings to the doorway may be a matter of socialization and/or choice.

For the purposes of this chapter it will be useful to define an individual's (general) social milieu in terms of the social structures within which he or she operates, whether or not the public schemas in question have been internalized. Although we can choose some of the structures within which we live, it is not always a matter of choice, for example, I am governed by the laws of the United States whether I choose to be or not. Of course, individuals do not live within only one milieu; and milieus overlap. One's workplace, place of worship, civic space, and home are structured spaces; each of these structures are inflected by race, gender, class, nationality, age, and sexuality, to name a few relevant factors. So it will be important to specify an individual's milieu at a time and place and possibly in relation to specified others. In this chapter I will not be able to give precise conditions that specify what milieu is operative for an individual in a given context; we'll just have to rely on clear-enough cases for now.

Given the notion of a milieu, we can return to a claim introduced at the beginning of the chapter about which Parents and Daughter disagreed:

1. Seventh grade girls who wear crop-tops to school are cute.

Plausibly, cuteness and dorkiness are features that must be judged from social milieus because they are partly constituted by those milieus. In the seventh grade, the schemas that govern the responses to clothes constitute a structure that (1) accurately describes. Daughter, has internalized those schemas, and is correct in asserting (1); in Parents' milieu, however, (1) is incorrect. It is tempting to say, then, that both are saying something true because (1) is true relative to one milieu and not the other. But how should we make sense of this "milieu relativism"? In the following section I will suggest a promising model and then raise some questions to be addressed in order to fulfill the promise.

5. Social Truths

There is something tempting about the idea that we live in different social worlds (or milieus); that what's true in one social world is obscure from another; that some social worlds are better for its inhabitants than others; and that some social worlds are based on illusion and distortions. How might we make sense of this?

Relative Truth

Recent work in epistemology and philosophy of language has explored versions of relativism in order to give accounts of a wide variety of phenomena, including "faultless disagreement" (Kölbel 2003; MacFarlane 2006), statements of personal taste (Lasersohn 2005), the context sensitivity of knowledge attributions (MacFarlane 2005b). The basic strategy is to explore how the truth of a statement may be sensitive to context. Consider a sentence such as:

3. This oatmeal is lumpy.

Because there is an indexical term 'this' in (3), context—in particular, the *context of use*—must be consulted in order to determine what proposition, if any, is being expressed. In a particular context, (3) can be used to express a proposition concerning (a particular bowl of) Instant Quaker Oats, and in another context to express a proposition concerning (a particular bowl of) Scottish porridge. It is important to note, however, that whether the proposition expressed is true or not depends further on, for example, the world or perhaps the world/time pair under consideration. So even if we settle what particular bowl of oatmeal is in question, it still might be true in one world (or at one world/time) that the bowl of Quaker Oats in question is lumpy and in another world (or at another world/time) not. For example, if (3) is uttered in the actual world one morning referring to a particular bowl of oatmeal, it expresses a proposition that, at least on some accounts, is true at worlds (or world/times) where that oatmeal is lumpy and false where not.

So the context of use can play two roles in determining the truth-value of a statement such as (3):

> (i) it fixes the semantic value of any indexical in the utterance, and yields the propositional content, and
> (ii) it fixes the circumstances relative to which we should evaluate the proposition's truth or falsity.

Drawing on John MacFarlane's account of relative truth, we can then contrast *indexicality*, where context is necessary to complete the proposition expressed, and *context sensitivity*, where context is necessary to determine the truth value of the proposition by determining the circumstances of evaluation (MacFarlane 2005a, 327).

MacFarlane argues that in addition to contributions from the context of use, the context of assessment is also relevant to determining the propositional content and truth value of a statement:

> We perform speech acts, but we also assess them; so just as we can talk of the context in which a sentence is being used, we can talk of a context (there will be indefinitely many) in which a use of it is being assessed. (MacFarlane 2005a, 325)

To see why *context of assessment* is sometimes necessary to capture meaning, consider the statement:

4. This oatmeal is yummy.

Suppose Fred asserts (4), and suppose further that what proposition is expressed and what circumstances of evaluation are relevant to its truth-value is determined by the context of use (no context of assessment is involved). Suppose, though, that Ginger's intervenes:

5. Sorry, Fred, you're wrong . . . This oatmeal is not yummy.

If 'yummy' in (4) and (5) is understood indexically, then the proposition Fred utters is:

4_I. This oatmeal *is-yummy-to-Fred*.

And in denying his claim Ginger is saying:[11]

5_I. It is not the case that this oatmeal *is-yummy-to-Ginger*.

On this account, Ginger is denying a different proposition than the one Fred expressed and she isn't disagreeing with him. The indexical interpretation makes no sense of her claim "You're wrong!"

An advantage of context-sensitivity over indexicality is that the proposition expressed by (5) is the denial of the proposition expressed by (4); context plays a role not in changing the content of the proposition but in determining different circumstances of evaluation. Continue to suppose, however, that only the *context of use* is available to evaluate the disagreement between Fred and Ginger. We then have:

4_S. *This oatmeal is yummy*, relative to C_U.
5_S. Sorry, Fred, you're wrong . . . It is not the case that *this oatmeal is yummy*, relative to C_U.

The proposition expressed by 'This oatmeal is yummy' in (4_S) is denied by (5_S), yet it is not yet clear how both Fred and Ginger can be saying something correct

---

[11] There are complexities I won't address in how to interpret Ginger's utterance of Fred's original sentence, for example, is she denying Fred's token utterance or the proposition he is expressing? Note, however, that even if we allow the "hidden indexical" to continue to track Fred, Ginger succeeds in disagreeing, but her claim is false, not true: It is not the case that this oatmeal is-yummy-to-Fred.

if the context's contribution to truth-value is the same in both cases. For example, if C_U in (4_S) relativizes Fred's claim to his taste standards, then because Ginger denies (4_S) with (5_S), plausibly (5_S) is relativized to the same standards and would be false. So Ginger's utterance can get no purchase on Fred's claim. What we need is that there is something about Ginger's context of assessment that differs from Fred's context and allows (5_S) to be true relative to her context but not Fred's.

MacFarlane argues that we should allow both the context of use and the context of assessment to play a role in determining circumstances of evaluation (MacFarlane 2005a, 327). Then because Ginger's context of assessment is different from the context of Fred's use *and* assessment, the proposition (4) is true relative to Fred's context of assessment and false relative to Ginger's.

4_A. *This oatmeal is yummy* relative to C_{UF} and C_{AF}
5_A. Sorry, Fred, you're wrong . . . It is not the case that *this oatmeal is yummy* relative to C_{UF} and C_{AG}.

In (4_A) and (5_A), Fred's context of use determines the semantic value of the indexical 'this' and the contexts of assessment determine the different standards of yumminess. Fred and Ginger disagree because their statements cannot both be true relative to a common context of assessment (MacFarlane 2006). This gives us "faultless disagreement": both are, in a sense, right, even though they, in a sense, contradict each other.

One might wonder, however, why parties to such a debate bother to disagree if truth is context-sensitive and both sides can be right. MacFarlane suggests:

> Perhaps the point is to bring about agreement by leading our interlocutors into relevantly different contexts of assessment. If you say, "skiing is fun" and I contradict you, it is not because I think the proposition you asserted is false as assessed by you in your current situation, with the affective attitudes you now have, but because I hope to change those attitudes. Perhaps the point of using controversy-inducing assessment-sensitive vocabulary is to foster *coordination* of contexts. (MacFarlane 2006, 22)

Truth relative to Milieu, That Is, "Social Truth" Relativism

Can we use the model just sketched to make sense of the disagreement between Daughter and Parents? Recall:

1. Seventh grade girls who wear crop-tops to school are cute.

The suggestion would be that (1) is true relative to Daughter's social milieu and false relative to Parents'. So:

1_{AD}. Seventh grade girls who wear crop-tops to school are cute relative to C_{UD} and C_{AD}.

1_{AP}. It is not the case that Seventh grade girls who wear crop-tops to school are cute relative to C_{UD} and C_{AP}.

The context of assessment determines the milieu in question by reference to the assessor's social milieu, that is, the complex of schemas and resources operative for him or her in that context. (Recall that this is not a subjective matter, so in this respect there is an important difference between relativizing truth to an individual's taste, and to an individual's milieu.) How, though, does the context of assessment determine milieu? We saw above that it is a tricky question which structures are operative for an individual in a context and more needs to be said to make this precise.[12] I am assuming here, however, that Parents are governed by the practices and norms of a parental social role that discourages the sexualization of twelve year old girls. (This is not to say, however, that the parental role or the message is always clear.)

In initially considering the crop-top conversation, we considered three different strategies for analyzing the conflict: the objectivist reading, the subjectivist reading, and the framework reading. The relativist reading captures some elements of each. It has objectivist elements, for the statements in question are true by virtue of capturing a social reality. It also has subjectivist elements for the truth of the claims made by each party to the debate depends on their perspective, understood in terms of their social location. It is also possible to make progress in thinking about the framework reading on the relativist model.

Recall that on the framework reading, Parents are not objecting to Daughter's claim by denying it, but are instead rejecting the cute/dorky framework. It is worth noting that there is a spectrum of possible responses to a framework of this sort along two dimensions: first, the dimension of *understanding*, second the dimension of *critique*. For example:

- One can accept a distinction but object to a particular application of its terms;
- One can accept a distinction but find it confusing or misguided and recommend conceptual revisions to it;

---

[12] More needs to be said about the individual who offers a critique that is at odds with the operative social structure. This, after all, is the feminist critic whose intervention is the real subject of this chapter. Although the proposal I've developed characterizes the individual's social milieu as the one operative in the context for that individual—even if it is not endorsed or internalized—the possibility of being at odds with this operative structure is important for thinking about the location of social critique.

- One can object to a distinction and refuse to employ it, but still be able to "mimic" applications of it (as if with shudder quotes);
- One can find a distinction incoherent.

Similarly social structures, particularly their schemas, may be more or less *accessible* from other structures (this corresponds to the dimension of understanding), and may be more or less in *harmony* (this corresponds to the dimension of critique). For example, the structure of seventh grade East Coast urban social life is relatively accessible to me because I have lived within or near that milieu and its schemas are encoded in the material world around me: on billboards and shop windows, in pop music and film; in daily inter-generational interaction. It is also the case, however, that the meaning of crop-tops in my milieu is utterly at odds with the meaning of crop-tops for seventh grade girls. Correlatively, many of the cultural schemas of the immigrants on my street are relatively inaccessible to me, but our milieus are not at odds.

How should we understand the case in which Parents—let's call these the Radical Parents—are not just rejecting the Daughter's evaluation of crop-tops as cute, but are entirely rejecting the cute/dorky framework? Can a relativist model help with this sort of case? Schemas for 'cute' and 'dorky' are not part of Radical Parents' social milieu (or there is insufficient overlap with Daughter's schemas) and they have no intention to import meaning or enter a social milieu in which they have meaning. Daughter's milieu is sufficiently accessible to them that they have some comprehension of the dichotomy, but the disharmony between Radical Parents' schemas and Daughter's is so great that they refuse to invoke the schemas lest they be reinforced; they are refusing to collaborate in the collective definition of cuteness. Although Radical Parents don't disagree with Daughter by denying what she asserts, they do reject her claim (relative to their milieu); in their denial they use the terms 'cute' and 'dorky' with shudder quotes. This suggests that he degree of genuine disagreement over the truth-value of the claims in question will be, to a substantial extent, a function of the accessibility and harmony of the milieus.

6. Critique

Social milieu relativism provides a model of how Daughter and Parents might both be saying something true and important, and yet seem to contradict each other. However, a crucial problem remains: in what sense, if any, should the daughter believe that crop-tops are *not* cute? How can we make sense of the suggestion that Parents are right and that Daughter's social reality is in some sense illusory? The problem is that if social truth is relative to milieu, then it would seem that we have no basis for adjudicating social truths across milieus.

If crop-tops are cute in Daughter's milieu and they aren't in Parents' milieu, what can Parents do or say beyond exposing Daughter to their milieu and hoping she will be moved (as MacFarlane suggested) to coordinate with them? What we were looking for, initially, is a basis for genuine critique. And we don't have that yet.

The easy and inadequate answer draws on the epigraphs we started with. Both Taylor and MacKinnon emphasize that a key element in recognizing the illusion in one's social context is to see that how things are is not how they must be:

> A study of the science of man is inseparable from an examination of the options between which men must choose. (Taylor)

> Women's situation cannot be truly known for what it is, in the feminist sense, without knowing that it can be other than it is. (MacKinnon)

A simplistic hypothesis might be that once one is exposed to a different social reality by engaging with assessors from another milieu, one will come to see the weaknesses of one's own milieu. On this view, the very exposure to another milieu, even to a milieu that is not objectively better, can destabilize an investment in one's current (inadequate) milieu and provide opportunities for improvement. Critique, strictly speaking, is not necessary; one need only broaden the horizons of those in the grip of an unjust structure and they will gain "consciousness" and gravitate to liberation.

It is true that such destabilization can happen, but it is far from guaranteed; and there is a danger that not all such gravitation is toward liberation. Admittedly, both Taylor and MacKinnon only suggest that such exposure to alternatives is a necessary, not sufficient, condition for seeing through the illusion. There are two other options to consider for grounding critique.

First, it is compatible with relativism about social truth that one be an objectivist about moral and/or epistemic value. So there might be an objective basis for privileging some social milieus so that truth relative to those milieus is more valuable or more "sound" than truth relative to others. For example, compared to others, some milieus base their schemas on more epistemically sound practices, for example, allow greater freedom of speech and thought that promotes open inquiry, and welcome the evolution of structures in response to internal critique. The idea is that if some milieus are epistemically privileged relative to others, those in less (epistemically) privileged milieus ought to accept the critique of a practice from a more (epistemically) privileged milieu.[13] One might make a similar move for privileging morally or politically sound milieus.

---

[13] Drawing on Longino's analysis of scientific objectivity, one might, e.g., privilege milieus that meet certain standards for the diversity of and equal consideration of epistemic agents. (Longino 1990)

This is in many ways appealing. One challenge for such a view, would be to provide a basis for evaluating epistemic and moral practices that was not itself relative to milieus. Is it possible to evaluate the epistemic practices of a milieu by standards that are not themselves milieu-relative? If not, then it is possible that by the epistemic standards of Daughter's milieu, her milieu is more sound and by the epistemic standards of Parents' milieu, theirs is more sound, and we still lack an objective basis for critique. This is less of a problem in domains where there is an independence of fact against which we can evaluate different epistemic standards: is this practice truth-conducive or not? But in the social domain our epistemic practices, like other practices, can generate facts to be known, and even if a practice is truth-conducive, it may be problematic. For example, suppose in the seventh grade milieu there is a norm that everyone should agree with Hannah (e.g., about what's cute, dorky, fun, boring . . .). If this norm is followed, there will be a coordination of beliefs and responses that constitute social facts which can be effectively known by following the Hannah-agreement norm. However, the hope, on this quasi-objectivist approach, would be to establish conditions on epistemic (or moral) norms, for example, of universality, that downgrade milieus governed by norms like Hannah-agreement. But we must ask: what makes such conditions objective?

A second strategy would be to develop a notion of critique that requires more than just truth relative to the milieu of the assessor. For example, suppose the assessor's claim is a genuine critique of a speaker's only if there is some common ground (factual, epistemic, or social) between the speaker's milieu and assessor's milieus, and the assessor's claim is true relative to the common ground. To say that a critique is genuine, in this sense, is not to say that it is the final word; rather, it is to say that a response is called for.[14] This further condition could explain why the dialogue between Daughter and Parents seems at best incomplete and at worst pointless. For Parents to have a critique of Daughter's choices, they should offer more than a flat denial of her claim relative to their milieu; it is their responsibility to seek common ground from which Daughter can assess their critique. If Parents can find common ground with Daughter and their claim that crop-tops are not cute is true relative to that common ground, then because Daughter shares that ground, she must address Parents' concern; hopefully, the two sides will continue to engage until they reach a mutually acceptable common ground.

An advantage of this notion of critique is that it would help make sense of the idea that ideology critique is transformative. If critique isn't just a matter of reasoned disagreement, but is a matter of forming or finding a common milieu, then because a milieu is partly constituted by dispositions to experience and respond in keeping with the milieu, then possibilities for agency other than

---

[14] This sort of idea can also be found in MacFarlane 2006.

those scripted by the old milieu become socially available. In keeping with this, we might want to distinguish *critique* (in the transformative sense) from mere *criticism* (in the ordinary sense).

However, the notion of a "common ground" is symmetrical between parties to the debate, but we're looking for a basis for *privileging* some milieus over others. So more will need to be said to set conditions on a legitimate common ground. In the example we've been considering, I've assumed it is clear that Parents are right and Daughter is wrong about the appropriateness of crop-tops for seventh grade girls. But consider a case in which (one might argue) Daughter is right and Parents wrong, for example, Daughter wants to participate in a demonstration for a worthy cause that she and her friends believe in, and Parents object, or Daughter wants to take a girl to the school dance, and Parents object. (Such examples show that the soundness of a milieu is not, or not simply, a matter of the extent to which it is endorsed or its sensitivity to consequences.)

To begin, one might set conditions on an adequate common ground to exclude those formed through coercive measures; conditions should also be sensitive to information available to each side (it may be useful to consider Longino's (1990) discussion of scientific objectivity and collective knowledge). This strategy is promising, but it is a huge task to figure out what conditions will give the right results. And there is a danger of idealizing the conditions by which something counts as common ground to the point that genuine ideology critique is impossible to achieve.

7. Conclusion

I've argued that there are puzzles in understanding how social critique, or ideology critique, can work. If ideology partly constitutes the social world, then a description of the ideological formations will be true, and it is unclear what is, epistemically speaking, wrong with them. We may be in a position to provide a moral critique of social structures, and this remains invaluable; but moral critique can be too abstract or controversial to have an effect. The material world reinforces our tutored dispositions—qwerty keyboards reinforce our qwerty dispositions which reinforce the use of qwerty keyboards; racial classification reinforces racial segregation, which reinforces racial identity, which reinforces racial classification. Social structures, good or bad, constitute our lived reality and are common sense for us. Ideology critique requires not only a normative shift, but a critique of our schemas for interpreting and interacting with the world and a critique of the reality these schemas form.

Although I have not argued for a particular account of ideology critique, I have offered a relativist model that helps make sense of how two sides of a social issue may disagree and yet both be saying something true, and I have suggested strategies for developing an account of critique; on one such strategy, critique is not merely a matter of changing beliefs, but of creating social spaces that disrupt dominant schemas. This, I believe, is consistent with the value and the power of consciousness raising. The challenge remains, however, to explicate and justify when a change of consciousness is genuinely emancipatory, and when it is just more ideology, in the pejorative sense.

References

Cadinu, M., Anne Maass, Alessandra Rosabianca, Jeff Kiesner. 2005. Why do women underperform under stereotype threat? Evidence for the role of negative thinking. *Psychological Science* 16(7), 572–78.

Elster, J. 1985. *Making sense of Marx*. Cambridge: Cambridge University Press.

Fields, Barbara Jean. 1982. Ideology and race in American history. In *Region, Race and Reconstruction*, ed., J. M. Kousser and J. M. McPherson. Oxford: Oxford University Press, 143–77.

Fredrickson, B., Tomi-Ann Roberts, Stephanie M. Noll, Diane M. Quinn, Jean M. Twenge. 1998. That swimsuit becomes you: Sex differences in self-objectification, restrained eating, and math performance. *Journal of Personality and Social Psychology* 75(1): 269–84.

Geuss, Raymond. 1981. *The Idea of a Critical Theory: Habermas and the Frankfurt School*. Cambridge: Cambridge University Press.

Giddens, Anthony. 1979. *Central Problems in Social Theory: Action Structure and Contradiction in Social Analysis*. Berkeley: University of California Press.

———. 1984. *The Constitution of Society: An Outline of a Theory of Structuration*. Berkeley: University of California Press.

Haslanger, S. 2012 [2003]. Social construction: the "debunking" project. Chapter 3 of this volume.

Howard, Judith A. 1994. A social cognitive conception of social structure, *Social Psychology Quarterly* 57, no. 3: 210–27.

Kölbel, Max. 2003. Faultless disagreement. *Proceedings of the Aristotelian Society* 104: 53–73.

Langton, Rae. 2007. "Speaker's freedom and maker's knowledge." Manuscript.

Lasersohn, P. 2005. Context dependence, disagreement, and predicates of personal taste. *Linguistics and Philosophy* 28: 643–86.

Lewis, David. 1969. *Convention*. Cambridge, MA: Harvard University Press.

Longino, H. 1990. *Science as Social Knowledge*. Princeton: Princeton University Press.

MacFarlane, J. 2007. Relativism and disagreement. *Philosophical Studies* 132:1 (January): 17–31.

———. 2005a. Making sense of relative truth. *Proceedings of the Aristotelian Society* 105: 321–39.

———. 2005b. The assessment sensitivity of knowledge attributions. *Oxford Studies in Epistemology* 1: 197-223. URL: http://philosophy.berkeley.edu/macfarlane/relknow.pdf.

———. 2003. Future contingents and relative truth. *The Philosophical Quarterly* 53: 321–36.

MacKinnon, C. 1989. *Towards a Feminist Theory of the State*. Cambridge, MA: Harvard University Press.

Marx, Karl. 1970/1846. *The German Ideology*. Ed. C.J. Arthur. New York: International Publishers.

McCarthy, Thomas. 1990. The critique of impure reason: Foucault and the Frankfurt school. *Political Theory* 18, no. 3: 437–69.

Purvis, Trevor, and Alan Hunt. 1993. Discourse, ideology, discourse, ideology, discourse, ideology . . . *The British Journal of Sociology* 44, no 3: 473–99.

Searle, J. 1995. *The Construction of Social Reality*. New York: The Free Press.

Sewell, William H., Jr. 1992. A theory of structure: duality, agency and transformation. *The American Journal of Sociology* 98: no. 1: 1–29.

Shelby, Tommie. 2003. Ideology, racism and critical social theory. *The Philosophical Forum* 34, no. 2: 153–88.

Spencer, S. J., Steele, C. M., and Quinn, D. M. 1999. Stereotype threat and women's math perfor-
    mance. *Journal of Experimental Social Psychology*, 35, 4–28.
Taylor, C. 1985/1971. Interpretation and the sciences of man. In *Philosophy and the Human Sci-
    ences: Philosophical Papers 2*. Cambridge: Cambridge University Press.
Warner, J. 2007. "Hot tots and moms hot to trot," *New York Times*, March 17, final edition, p. 15.
Williams, B. 1973. Deciding to believe. In *Problems of the Self*, Cambridge: Cambridge University
    Press, pp. 136–51.

16

Language, Politics, and "The Folk"

Looking for "The Meaning" of 'Race'[1]

1. Introduction

Contemporary discussions of race and racism devote considerable effort to giving conceptual analyses of these notions. Much of the work is concerned to investigate a priori what we mean by the terms 'race' and 'racism' (e.g., Garcia 1996; 1997; 1999; Blum 2002; Hardimon 2003; Mallon 2004). More recent work has started to employ empirical methods to determine the content of our "folk concepts," or "folk theory" of race and racism (Glasgow 2009; Glasgow et al. 2009; Faucher and Machery 2009). In contrast to both of these projects, I have argued elsewhere that in considering what we mean by these terms we should treat them on the model of kind terms whose reference is fixed by ordinary uses, but whose content is discovered empirically using social theory; I have also argued that it is not only important to determine what we *actually* mean by these terms, but what we *should* mean, that is, what type, if any, we should be tracking (Haslanger 2012 [2000]; 2012 [2006]).

My own discussion of these issues, however, has been confused and confusing. In giving an account of race or gender, is the goal to provide a conceptual analysis? Or to investigate the kinds we are referring to? To draw attention to different kinds? To stipulate new meanings? Jennifer Saul has raised a series of powerful objections to my accounts of gender and race, suggesting that they are neither semantically nor politically useful, regardless of whether we treat them as revisionary proposals, or as elucidations of our concepts (Saul 2006). Joshua Glasgow has also offered a critique of my externalist approach to race as an

[1] I presented a version of this chapter at the Pacific APA, Spring 2009. Thanks to the audience for helpful discussion. Thanks also to Joshua Glasgow, Rae Langton, Janet Levine, Laura Schroeter, Manuel Vargas, and Stephen Yablo for valuable conversation on topics related to this chapter.

effort to capture "our concept" (Glasgow 2009, chs. 6–7). I agree with much of what they say, but I also believe that there is something I was trying to capture that remains valuable. So the challenge, as I see it, is to situate my accounts against a different theoretical background that can highlight what might be useful without entailing the problematic linguistic and conceptual claims. Whether and how this is possible, I have yet to determine.

However, rather than taking up this question directly in this chapter, I will undertake to explain more fully why I believe both the a priori and "experimental" investigation into the concepts of race and racism are misguided; as I do so, I will draw on recent work in philosophy of language (especially Bigelow and Schroeter 2009; Schroeter and Schroeter 2009) to suggest an understanding of meaning that better accommodates the shifting terrain of social life and our goal of tracking important types as our knowledge develops.[2] I believe that the emerging model illuminates better than the dominant descriptivist model the ways in which meanings are produced by and evolve through collaborative practices. In their best form, such collaborative practices are responsive to multiple participants in the linguistic community and take into account shifting concerns and the development of new knowledge. By unpacking such practices, however, we can also see how some speakers may be excluded from the production of meaning; this provides space for exploring briefly Miranda Fricker's notion of hermeneutical injustice (Fricker 2006; Fricker 2009). The goal of this chapter is not to argue for any particular account of meaning or account of race, but to bring to the discussion new tools that are not only useful for thinking about race and racism, but for engaging in critical feminist and anti-racist theory more broadly. I am also hopeful that some of my own work on race and gender can be fruitfully recast in the terms offered here; but that effort is for another occasion.

2. The Classical Theory of Meaning

Traditional descriptivism, following Frege, holds that terms have senses or meanings that determine their referents. These meanings are what a speaker knows when she or he uses the term; they are the basis for shared meanings and so make communication possible; and they are the subject matter of conceptual analysis. However, traditional descriptivism took a barrage of direct hits from Quine (1953), Kripke (1972), Putnam (1975), Burge (1979), and others. It is now generally acknowledged that speakers can be competent in the use of a term and can communicate using it without being able to specify conditions that determine the referent across possible worlds or even within the actual world.

---

[2] I'm by no means the first to suggest this. See, e.g., Mercier 2007, Andreasen 2005.

However, a set of plausible moves has seemed (to some) to salvage a version of descriptivism (see, e.g., Jackson 1998a, Jackson 1998b). According to this neo-descriptivism, reference is determined in two steps: speakers employ an implicit "folk theory" or meaning "template" that fixes the referent of the term relative to the actual world and tells us how reference depends on empirical information in the context of use; this folk theory, supplemented with further social, empirical, and modal facts, determines the referent. Competence in using a term is a matter of having tacit knowledge of the "folk theory" and this shared background makes communication possible. Experts, however, are needed to discover the essence of the referent fixed by the "folk theory." (Note that on the neo-descriptivist account, experts aren't needed to determine the referent, but only to discover the essence once the referent is determined; the resulting account provided by the experts is not analytic (cf. Glasgow 2008, 127–28)).

For example, what does the term 'apple' mean? 'Apple' means "that edible fruit that (actually) grows on trees in temperate climates, comes in various shades of red and green, has a thin skin and sweet flesh." Most competent users cannot specify exactly what biological kind apples belong to (*malus domestica*) or that apple trees are a member of the rose family (*Roseaceae*); but the "folk theory" contained in the suggested meaning is sufficient to refer. Even if a speaker considers what 'apple' means in a novel environment, she will apply her "folk theory" and seek information, as needed, about the biological kind of the fruit trees there. The "folk theory" that determines the referent of 'apple' in a context does not vary across contexts.

The neo-descriptivist's account consists of several key claims:[3]

1. For any term (or virtually any term) *t*, there is a set of topic-specific assumptions—a speaker's "folk theory" of what *t* purports to pick out—that guides the speaker's application of the term to cases; these assumptions do not vary with the speaker's assumptions about the environment she is in.
2. For most speakers, the "folk theory" associated with *t* is tacit and is revealed in their judgments about cases.
3. The "folk theory," together with information about the speaker's environment, as needed, determines what the speaker refers to using *t*.[4]
4. Most members of a linguistic community associate the very same "folk theory" with *t*. Competence in the standard use of *t* requires that one employ the (tacit) "folk theory" in one's applications of *t*.

---

[3] These are summarized very effectively in (Bigelow and Schroeter 2009, 98; Schroeter and Schroeter 2009, 6).

[4] Some find it useful to think of the "folk theory" in terms of the Kaplanian character which, in the context of utterance, determines the referent (Kaplan 1989).

5. Statements articulating the "folk theory" for *t* are analytic, that is, they are "analytic in the sense that [they are] guaranteed to be true on pain of changing the meaning" of the term (Schroeter and Schroeter 2009, 6). However, even though claims articulating our tacit knowledge of meaning are analytic, they do not, by themselves, give us knowledge of essences, for example, knowing that water is what actually flows in rivers and streams on Earth doesn't provide us with knowledge of the essence of water.

6. The fact that most people converge in their "folk theories" gives everyone a justifying and motivating reason to associate the standard "folk theory" with *t*. Thus, we know we co-refer; this makes communication possible.

This neo-descriptivism has some clear virtues. It provides an account of reference that also explains linguistic competence and communication. It grants competent speakers knowledge of meanings that guides them in applying terms to cases. Moreover, the neo-descriptivist succeeds in avoiding some of the critiques of the original descriptivism by the qualifications added in (2) and (3). The meaning of a term is not something an ordinary speaker can articulate because the knowledge is tacit; and the meaning does not, by itself, determine the reference, for the template may require supplementation by empirical information only available in the context of use.

However, neo-descriptivism has been repeatedly challenged (Block and Stalnaker 1999; Yablo 2000; Schroeter 2003; Byrne and Pryor 2004; Schroeter 2004; Stalnaker 2006; Schroeter Bigelow and Schroeter 2009). I present here a sample of criticisms. As might be expected, defenders of neo-descriptivism have developed responses to these arguments. I will not go into the details here because the point of this chapter is not to discuss the ultimate tenability of neo-descriptivism, but to illuminate some of its substantial weaknesses in order to dislodge it from its presumed status in theorizing about gender and race (and other social and normative phenomena).

To begin, although responsive to some of the complaints against descriptivism, the neo-descriptivist is not fully responsive to other, especially Quinean, parts of the critique. Two important themes of post-Quinean philosophy are skepticism about analyticity and epistemic holism. Recall (briefly), Quine's idea is that there is no adequate way to distinguish analytic truths from well-entrenched generalizations about the phenomena in question (Quine 1953). And there shouldn't be, for our semantic beliefs, like all other beliefs, should always be responsive to new circumstances and new knowledge. For example, there are approximately 7,500 known cultivars of apple; if a tree was cultivated using existing stock that produced an inedible, perhaps even toxic, fruit, it would be more sensible to modify our understanding of the term 'apple' to remove 'edible' from the "folk theory" rather than deny that the fruit is an apple. (In fact, there is reason to think that apple trees produced at least hardly edible fruit until cultivation improved them (Pollan 2002).) The same sort of thing could be said for 'water.' If we evolved so that we could not digest plain H_2O but required corn syrup and carbonation to be added, water would not be potable, and the "folk theory" associated with water would be false. Although in principle a neo-descriptivist could argue that all this is just evidence that our tacit folk theories associated with 'apple' and 'water' do not include edibility and potability, the worry is that there isn't, and again, for epistemic reasons *there should not be*, any fixed ideas about meaning that are "held true come what may" (Quine 1953, 42–13). This counts against claims (3) and (5).

Further, as Bigelow and Schroeter (2009, 99) point out, outliers who have idiosyncratic ideas and reject some of the standard folk theory associated with a term can remain competent even if their idiosyncratic ideas are false, for example, someone who denied that the oceans were filled with water, or that water is flavorless, doesn't thereby cease to be competent in the use of 'water.' As Burge (1979) famously argued, someone using the term 'arthritis' normally refers to the joint disease even if she believes that she has arthritis in her thigh (this is what makes her wrong, rather than right about a homonymous disease). But more importantly, it is not only possible, but in some cases epistemically required for competent speakers to reject some part of the "folk theory" associated with a term. The Schroeters' example is Galileo (2009, 100): his failure to believe that the earth is flat did not render him incompetent in the use of the term 'earth' for he had evidence that conflicted with the "folk theory" of the earth at the time. Again, this shows that commitment to analyticity is in tension with the rational revision of our beliefs in light of new knowledge. In general, successful rational inquiry does not destabilize meaning; we normally take it to provide us with a better understanding of what we were trying to understand all along (Schroeter and Schroeter 2009, 15).

In the Galileo case one might complain that being flat was never really part of the meaning of 'earth.' However, consider 'marriage.' Plausibly the standard "folk theory" of marriage has been that marriages can only occur between one man and one woman; those who refused to accept this belief, according to neo-descriptivism, were not competent users of the term. And those of us now who reject this "folk theory" have changed the meaning of 'marriage' and are talking about something else. For those of us committed to social change, these implications are unacceptable, for these are not plausibly semantic controversies, but are social and political ones. Just as Quine and Putnam emphasized that a commitment to analyticity stands in the way of scientific progress, the same might be said of its bearing on social progress.[5] These considerations are directly

---

[5] This influence is not merely hypothesized, but can be witnessed in the conservative arguments against gay and lesbian marriage (Mercier 2007). If 'marriage' *means* a union between one man and one woman, then same-sex marriage is not really marriage and should not be viewed and treated as such.

relevant to the discussion of 'race,' for even if the "folk" believe that race is a biological category, on the non-descriptivist account we're exploring, those who know that it is not can still use the term 'race' competently without the problematic belief or entailment. In light of these concerns, we should resist points (1), (4), and (6) of neo-descriptivism.

Moreover, it is difficult to see how neo-descriptivism can find any plausible "folk theories" that satisfy both conditions (3) and (4) (see Schroeter and Schroeter 2009, section 3). Condition (3) requires that the "folk theory" is sufficiently substantive and precise that it determines reference, and yet condition (4) requires that every competent speaker accepts the same "folk theory." The worry is that individual speakers may have very different ideas that actually guide their use of a term, and in order to satisfy condition (4) we must take as part of the "folk theory" the intersection of these ideas; but it is hard to believe that there is enough in the speakers' overlapping assumptions to achieve determinate reference to the purported entity or type of entity in the world.

Although I have only given a brief sketch of considerations against a neo-descriptivist account of meaning, it is clear that if we reject any form of descriptivism (traditional or neo-), some of the recent philosophical work on race and racism—work that purports to be exploring the "folk theory" or ordinary view of race—will look to be barking up the wrong tree. Regardless of whether one employs a priori reflection or empirical psychology to explore allegedly tacit assumptions we hold about what race is, the results will not give us an account of what 'race' means, for these tacit assumptions do not determine meaning. The kind of conceptual analysis presupposed by these projects is not viable because it rests on a mistaken view of language, concepts, and communication.

3. The Improvisational (or Jazz) Account of Meaning
(Pure) Reference Externalism

The descriptivist tradition has a powerful grip on our semantic imaginations and undergirds much of what happens in analytic philosophy. So if we are going to reject it, we need another model to take its place.[6] Since the 1970s externalists

---

[6] I have argued elsewhere that we should adopt an externalist approach to meaning that extends the insights of Putnam, Kripke, et al. beyond reliance on natural science to social theory (Haslanger 2012 [2006]), and that genealogical (Haslanger 2012 [2005]) and ameliorative (Haslanger 2012 [2000], 2012 [2006]) dimensions should be added to the project of elucidating meaning. My recommendations have been motivated not by following carefully every move in contemporary philosophy of language, but by thinking through what is needed for feminist and antiracist theorizing. As a result, the proposals I have made are firmly externalist about meaning, they have been rather vague, fragmented, and unsystematic.

have been developing this model. The work by Bigelow, Schroeter, and Schroeter I've been drawing on outlines an externalist approach that I believe is well-suited to politically engaged theorizing, and offers resources for thinking about the politics of meaning. In this section I will briefly sketch their account, and in the next I will consider how it might be fruitfully applied in critical race and gender theory.

Externalists about meaning maintain that the meaning of a term is determined, at least in part, by facts about the social and physical context of use, and not simply by the mental states of the individual using it. Thoroughgoing externalists hold the Millian or Russellian view that terms have a single meaning, namely, their referents, and a term does not get its referent by virtue of yet a further semantic item such as a Fregean sense along the lines the descriptivist would suggest. According to externalists of this sort, the meaning of a term is determined by a variety of complex pragmatic and causal factors. Typically we will have descriptions in mind that pick out the same referent as the term in question, or so we believe, but these descriptions are not part of the meaning of the term (as Stalnaker would put it, they are *metasemantic*, not *semantic* (Stalnaker 2006, 301)), nor do they provide a template or "folk theory" that determines, in the context of utterance, what we refer to.

Roughly, on the pure reference externalist view, what we are referring to takes priority in our use of language to how we think about it. Language is used primarily to refer to things in the world, and having latched onto the world we find multiple ways to describe it. Sometimes our descriptions are accurate and sometimes not. On the descriptivist model, in contrast, thought takes priority. We have a thought and it turns out that there are things in the world that match it. We communicate, according to the externalist, by talking about the same things; according to the descriptivist, by expressing the same thoughts.

There are a number of concerns that a Millian or pure reference externalist must address, for example, how to account for the epistemic value of true identity statements, how to handle vacuous terms, how to accommodate contingent necessities. Of course there is a substantial literature on these issues (Salmon 1986; Stalnaker 1999; Soames 2003), and I will not attempt to explicate how reference externalism might be developed to address them all. Rather, I want to emphasize the value of reference externalism in calling attention to a set of questions about meaning that descriptivists systematically evade (Stalnaker 1997, 535–36). I believe there are compelling reasons to favor the pure reference externalist account of meaning; however, my point in this chapter is not to present these reasons fully, but to show that such an account provides better access to the process of creating meanings that critical race and gender theorists have a special interest in than do the dominant descriptivism and neo-descriptivism. Although these considerations are not, by themselves, sufficient to defend pure reference externalism, they should motivate a reconsideration of the methodology of current debates over race and racism.

It is important to note that given a term t, there are many questions we might ask about its meaning. For example, we might want to know the meaning of t. This is a descriptive question about the semantics of the language in which t occurs. However, we might also ask a more foundational question: by virtue of what does the term t have its meaning? For the Fregean or neoFregean, the two questions are answered together: one explicates the meaning of t by invoking the sense or descriptive content of the term, and t refers to what it does because that is what satisfies the description associated with t. In effect, *what the speaker conveys is identified with what determines reference*. But this assumption, that what the speaker conveys is also what determines the reference, is optional. And if we reject it, it becomes clear that there is an important construal of the foundational question that is obscured by the Fregean approach. Stalnaker describes it this way:

> If we are implicitly looking for a semantic account of names that answers both [the descriptive and foundational] questions at once, then the Millian theory that says that the semantic value of a name is simply its referent looks like a non-answer; it seems to be denying the obvious fact that there must be something about the capacities, behavior, or mental state of the users of the name that make it the case that the name has the referent it has.

However,

> On the other hand, the conflation of the two questions masks the fact that the sense theory, interpreted as an answer to the question of descriptive semantics is also a non-answer to the foundational question. Suppose we were to accept the Fregean thesis that names have the referent that they have because they have a sense that determines a function whose value (at the actual world) is that referent. This simply raises the question: what is it about the capacities, behavior, or mental state of the users of the name that makes it the case that the name has the sense that it in fact has? (Stalnaker 1997, 543).

The descriptivist and the reference externalist both, in their own way, offer answers to the descriptive and foundational questions. However, once we reject the assumption that what gives a term its reference is what the speaker has in mind in using the term, we are led to important questions concerning the basis of meaning in the social and physical context of speech. Because the (neo-) descriptivist has a ready-made answer to what determines meaning, namely, the descriptive content or sense, these questions are occluded.

Referential Practices

So, how *do* we refer? And how do we know we are correctly applying our terms if we aren't applying a (tacit) rule? How do we know we mean the same thing and so communicate if we aren't applying the same rule? Here's a quick sketch of one externalist answer: interpretation of our own past linguistic practice with a term and the practice of those around us, together with empirical investigation, enables us to make judgments about how the term applies; the term refers to what a fully informed and rational judge in such circumstances would take herself to refer to.[7] To the extent that we are informed and rational, we can know the correct application of the term. And since we intend to use the term in a way consistent with our past practice and so that we co-refer with others in our linguistic community, we usually converge on the same thing and our words mean the same. Because we are collaborating on this, we know this about each other and communicate. For reasons that will become clearer shortly, let's call this the *rational improvisation account* of meaning.

It will be useful to flesh out this sketch a bit. There are two sets of questions to consider: (a) how does a term such as 'water' *get* the meaning it has and how do we know its meaning (and so use it correctly); (b) how do we communicate using the term 'water'? By virtue of what do we co-refer, not by accident, but *de jure*.

Let's begin with (a) and an individual speaker's meaning. As we considered above, on the neo-descriptivist account, speakers refer to things by virtue of the "folk theory" they tacitly hold about the things in question. We saw, however, that this account privileged certain beliefs associated with a term as unrevisable, and this required a denial of epistemic holism. In order to accommodate epistemic holism, we should allow that whatever we take to be part of the meaning of a term at some point, we may regard as a mere correlation at another point as we learn more about what we take ourselves to be tracking. When scientists found that the atom is, in fact, divisible, they adjusted their beliefs about atoms; it never was an analytic truth that atoms are indivisible, for if it were, we could not be talking about atoms as we do now. Rather than relying on a fixed template to adjudicate hard cases, the speaker will have to rely on "holistic hermeneutical

---

[7] This is what Schroeter and Schroeter call the "responsibilist approach to the determination of reference" (2009, 6). However, it is not clear to me whether on the rational improvisational account proposed (Schroeter and Schroeter 2009; Schroeter and Bigelow 2009) the verdict of the ideal judge constitutes the reference relation, or if the relation is otherwise constituted (by additional causal and pragmatic considerations) but is guaranteed, given the hypothesis of full knowledge, to be correct. In effect, this is the Euthyphro question. And as in the case of any account invoking an idealized judge, there are difficult questions about how to go about the idealization (Loeb 1995). Though important, it is not crucial for my purposes here to settle these questions.

reasoning starting from the entire relevant set of assumptions" (Bigelow and Schroeter 2009, 15).

> More specifically, a subject gets closer to the truth about what it takes to be [water] via holistic rationalizing interpretation of her own use of the term ['water']. The subject is looking for a theoretical interpretation of her term ['water'] which vindicates the most important aspects of her total practice with that term, including her changing substantive understanding of its reference, her implicit criteria for identifying instances, her proto-theoretical hunches about why certain principles are important, and so on. In this exercise of rational interpretation, the subject is trying to make sense of her *whole* practice with the term, by requiring each of her substantive assumptions to earn its keep in light of holistic reflective theorizing. (Schroeter and Schroeter 2009, 14; I've substituted 'water' for 'right' in order to simplify the case.)

On this account, the speaker relies on "rational improvisation" in light of what she knows about the world and her past practice in using the term.[8]

Schroeter and Schroeter extend the analogy with jazz as they move to consider the questions in group (b) concerning co-reference and communication:

> Consider a musical analogy. The members of a classical string quartet achieve a coordinated musical performance by settling in advance on a common score. This common score then serves as a fixed template, which guides each individual player's performance on the crucial night. The classical performance is coordinated and kept on track by each player following the template they've agreed upon. The members of a jazz quartet have a very different way of achieving musical coordination: instead of settling on a specific template for their performance, jazz musicians can rely on their improvisational skills. Each member is committed to building on whatever musical themes other members of the group try out, seeking a continuation that makes best musical sense of the whole performance so far. Each player in the group trusts that the others will try to take everyone's contributions on board and incorporate them into a coherent musical structure. The jazz musicians'

---

[8] I should note that (Schroeter and Schroeter 2009) focuses specifically on thin moral terms such as 'right' and 'good.' Their point, although general, has a special force for this domain: "reflective equilibrium constantly refines and restructures an individual's moral understanding through the addition, subtraction, and fine-tuning of moral assumptions." Presumably, it would be a mistake to entrench just those background assumptions that strike one as "obvious and central" and insist that deviation from them involves a change of meaning (Schroeter and Schroeter 2009, 13).

coordinating intentions, together with a rough congruence in musical sensibility, are what keep the joint musical performance on track, developing interesting themes rather than degenerating into a cacophony of divergent voices. (Schroeter and Schroeter 2009, 16)

Just as coordinating intentions and shared sensibility are what sustain the jazz performance, coordinating intentions and shared understandings sustain communication. The use of a common language requires not just that we aim to use terms in a way consistent with our own past use, corrected by our current knowledge. Rather, in competently using a term as part of a shared language we must "have a coordinating intention to use the term in a way that makes the best sense of the communal practice" and our understanding of the term, at least initially, "must not diverge so radically from that of others in the community as to undermine that coordinating intention" (Schroeter and Schroeter 2009, 18). This effort to coordinate involves "looking for the property that *all* of us have been talking about all along" (Schroeter and Schroeter 2009, 17).

On this account, we share meanings, not by having the same "folk theory" of the subject matter, but by both being part of a "historically extended representational tradition," within which we are each trying to make sense of that tradition as we engage with the world it purports to represent. Being part of such a tradition is consistent with substantial disagreement on any particular claim; what matters is that we are engaged collaboratively with others in a shared project of representing what or how things are in some corner of the world. So, for example, we can still mean the same thing by 'water' and communicate about water even if we disagree about the chemical composition of water, whether the ocean is filled with water, and whether water is good to drink, as long as we are each working to apply the term 'water' in light of our best interpretation of a shared linguistic tradition.

Competence with the meaning of a word constitutes an entry ticket into communal discussion: it demarcates whom we should treat as a legitimate interlocutor on a given topic, and who genuinely agrees or disagrees with us. In short, sameness of meaning allows for direct epistemic coordination on a single subject matter, whether by different speakers or by the very same speaker. (Schroeter and Schroeter 2009, 23).

4. Improvising the Meanings of 'Race,' 'Racism,' and Such

For over a decade, philosophers have taken up the debate over whether race is real or not, whether race is a social or a natural category, whether "race talk" should be eliminated. Much of the discussion has pivoted on questions concerning what the term 'race' means, fueled initially, perhaps, by Appiah's argument (1998) that it is part of the meaning of race that races are natural kinds, and that there are no natural kinds of the sort that race talk purports to capture. Given the concerns with descriptivism, what should we make of these debates? And how should we proceed to study race and racism?

First, should we be seeking the "folk theory" of race (whether a priori or by experimental methods) that determines, in the context of utterance, the extension of 'race'? If we reject descriptivism, as I have suggested, we shouldn't. However, we might want to know the "folk theory" of race (and other categories) in order to engage in hermeneutical deliberation about what we have meant and should mean, that is, in order to rationally improvise on the representational tradition and to give substance to our coordinating intentions. This does not commit us individually to accepting any particular claim of the folk theory in order to be competent with the term, or in order to co-refer.

Second, should we be aiming to provide an analysis of the concept of 'race'? If we reject descriptivism, as I have suggested, we shouldn't. Instead, we should take ourselves to be offering theories of the phenomena that the term 'race' refers to. The theories are not known a priori, nor are they analytically true. The theories we come up with may, in fact, violate some of the core assumptions concerning the phenomenon because they incorporate new knowledge. This does not entail that we are changing the meaning of the terms.

Third, does the term 'race' refer to anything? Well, one might suggest, it depends. Not only Appiah, but also many others have argued that a core component of the "folk theory" of race is that races are biological groups. If one is a descriptivist then, assuming that there are no biological kinds that meet the conditions for races, the term 'race' doesn't refer. But of course this conclusion does not follow for a pure reference externalist of the sort I've sketched; on the externalist account the question whether races exist cannot be settled on purely semantic grounds, either employing a priori intuitions or experiments concerning the "folk theory" of race. For example, using a rational improvisation model, I would argue that we can justify the claim that the best interpretation of our ongoing collective practice using the term 'race' is compatible with races being social kinds, and social constructionists about race are not shifting the meaning of the term. As a result, it is misleading to suggest (as I myself have sometimes done) that social constructionist accounts of race are revisionist; the issue is what counts as the important features of our past practice of using the term 'race' as we move forward, and our judgment about this may differ from what we thought before. Moreover, given that the realists (both social constructionists and racialists) and anti-realists at least appear to be engaged in a shared project of understanding our representational tradition in using the term 'race', there is reason to think that we co-refer with our uses of the term (in the limit case, I suppose, we all fail to refer). The question, then, is not who is misusing the term, but whose account is best at doing justice both to the historical collective practice and the worldly facts, or even, whose rational improvisation is the best extension of our past practice. This is not a question to be settled here; rather, my goal is to shift the terms of debate so it is not so focused on discussion of what our "folk theory" or ordinary ideas about race are. Although historical and semantic information about past use may be useful in the hermeneutical task of understanding our past practice, we are not bound by that history or (believed) semantics, so this sort of inquiry settles no philosophical or political problem.

5. Meaning and Politics

I suggested several times above that reference externalism is better situated to illuminate the social and political dimensions of meaning, and as such, should be taken seriously by feminist and race theorists. The idea was that on a descriptivist account, foundational questions about how words have meaning are answered in terms of what speakers have in mind, and this obscures questions about the collaborative process by which noises come to be part of a language and representational traditions are formed. Admittedly, the causal and pragmatic stories that reference externalists rely on to explain how terms refer are not always socially informed. So externalism, per se, is no more friendly to feminist and anti-racist insights than descriptivism. However, as the Schroeter and Bigelow and Schroeter and Schroeter discussions demonstrate, there is much room in externalist semantics for a study of the social dynamics of meaning. And this attention to the social dimension of what we mean and what we say has been a part of pragmatics since its inception (see, e.g., Grice (1975)).

To illustrate the sort of political analysis I have in mind, it is useful to reconsider a passage quoted above:

> Competence with the meanings of a word constitutes an entry ticket into communal discussion: it demarcates whom we should treat as a legitimate interlocutor on a given topic, and who genuinely agrees or disagrees with us. In short, sameness of meaning allows for direct epistemic coordination on a single subject matter, whether by different speakers or by the very same speaker. (Schroeter and Schroeter 2009, 23)

On the rational improvisation model, sameness of meaning is a matter of shared epistemic practice. We share a meaning if and only if we are collaborating in making sense of a shared representational tradition and our understandings are not so divergent as to undermine our collaborative intentions. With these conditions, questions arise about how to think of epistemic practices and the social conditions for knowledge. For example, the rational improvisation model gives us resources to explain how remarking that someone "doesn't mean the same thing we do" is an epistemic putdown and a move in a social practice of exclusion. As Schroeter and Schroeter put it:

> By commonsense standards, anyone with whom we can profitably participate in critical debate involving an evaluative term—whatever his initial substantive assumptions are—shares the same meaning. (2009, 21)

So denying shared meaning is a way of refusing entry into the shared epistemic project and critical debate. This, in turn, allows us to raise the possibility that meanings might be limited or deformed because they are not grounded in a broad community of speakers.

The rational improvisation model can also help us understand certain kinds of semantic disablement. In her recent work, Miranda Fricker has explored the idea of hermeneutic injustice: "the injustice of having some significant area of one's social experience obscured from collective understanding owing to a structural prejudice in the collective hermeneutical resource" (Fricker 2006, 100). On Fricker's account, hermeneutic injustice begins with a cognitive disablement caused by a simple hermeneutical lacuna: there are things that we cannot think or speak about because we do not have the words for them. Such a lacuna is not necessarily an injustice, but becomes an injustice when it results in an asymmetrical disadvantage, for example, if you are able to take advantage of me or harm me because I have no way to describe or identify the wrong you are inflicting, or if my efforts to do so, given the limits of the dominant vocabulary, do not achieve uptake. Fricker's example is the phenomenon of sexual harassment. Until the term 'sexual harassment' was introduced, women not only suffered from unwanted sexual attention from their employers as a condition of employment, but also suffered from the hermeneutic injustice of being unable to identify the problem. Other examples might include the phenomena of white privilege, racial profiling, and hate speech.

What is interesting about these examples, in the context of our current discussion, is that new terms and new connections between ideas are being forged as part of a process of hermeneutical interpretation and deliberation. In reflecting on a representational tradition one may find ways to improvise, but one may also find oneself or one's experience excluded, prompting new and alternative epistemic projects, as well as new and alternative representations. The rational improvisation model invites us to consider the social dynamics, collaboration, and reflective practice required for shared meanings. For those who are members of subordinated groups, this creates space within dominant philosophy of language to capture moments of libratory politics. Critical race and gender studies would be well served by exploring the jazz rather than the classical model of meaning.

6. Conclusion

This is not an essay that has undertaken to establish any conclusions. Rather, my point has been to call attention to trends in contemporary philosophy of language that have not been taken sufficiently seriously by those working in social and moral philosophy. The project of conceptual analysis, even if supplemented by empirical methods, cannot be taken for granted. More specifically, conceptual analysis is thoroughly rejected by many philosophers who specialize on language, concepts and meaning, and other models of inquiry have replaced it, and this cannot simply be ignored by normative theory if it is to be part of a broader project of rational inquiry. I have also suggested that for those working in critical race and gender theory, these alternative models should be attractive, for they take seriously a social and political dimension of meaning that opens space for considerations of justice. This is where social and political theory can contribute to philosophy of language. The moral of this story, insofar as there is one, is that engagement across subdisciplines of philosophy is tremendously valuable, for not only does normative theory have much to learn from philosophy of language and mind, but philosophy of language and mind can benefit significantly from a consideration of the moral background of our linguistic practices. Although there are important differences between normative and non-normative inquiry, one cannot do full justice to the phenomena without attending to both.

References

Andreasen, Robin. 2005. "The Meaning of 'Race': Folk Conceptions and the New Biology of Race," *Journal of Philosophy* 102(2): 94–106.

Appiah, K. Anthony. 1996. "Race, Culture, Identity: Misunderstood Connections," in K. A. Appiah and A. Gutmann, *Color Conscious: The Political Morality of Race*, Princeton: Princeton University Press, 30–105.

Bigelow, John, and Laura Schroeter. 2009. "Jackson's Classical Model of Meaning," in Ian Ravenscroft, ed., *Minds, Ethics and Conditionals: Themes from the Philosophy of Frank Jackson*, Oxford: Oxford University Press, 85–110.

Block, N., and R. Stalnaker. 1999. "Conceptual Analysis, Dualism, and the Explanatory Gap," *Philosophical Review* 108: 1–16.

Blum, Lawrence. 2002. *I'm Not a Racist, But . . . The Moral Quandary of Race*, Ithaca: Cornell University Press.

Burge, Tyler. 1979. "Individualism and the Mental," in P. French, et al., eds., *Midwest Studies in Philosophy IV*, Minneapolis: University of Minnesota Press, 73–121.

Byrne, A., and J. Pryor. 2004. "Bad Intensions," in M. García-Carpintero and J. Maciá, eds., *The Two-Dimensionalist Framework: Foundations and Applications*, Oxford: Oxford University Press.

Faucher, Luc, and Edouard Machery. 2009. "Racism: Against Jorge Garcia's Moral and Psychological Monism," *Philosophy of the Social Sciences* 39: 41–62.

Fricker, Miranda. 2006. "Powerlessness and Social Interpretation." *Episteme: A Journal of Social Epistemology*, 3(1): 96–108.

———. 2009. *Epistemic Injustice: Power and the Ethics of Knowing*. Oxford: Oxford University Press.

Garcia, J. L. A. 1996. "The Heart of Racism," *Journal of Social Philosophy* 27: 5–45.

———. 1997. "Current Conceptions of Racism: A Critical Examination of Some Recent Social Philosophy," *Journal of Social Philosophy* 28: 5–42.

———. 1999. "Philosophical Analysis and the Moral Concept of Racism," *Philosophy and Social Criticism*, 25: 1–32.

Glasgow, Joshua. 2009. *A Theory of Race*. New York: Routledge.

Glasgow, Joshua, Julie L. Shulman, and Enrique Covarrubias. 2009. "The Ordinary Conception of Race in the United States and Its Relation to Racial Attitudes: A New Approach," *Journal of Cognition and Culture*, 9: 15–38.

Grice, H. Paul. 1975. "Logic and conversation," in Cole, P. and Morgan, J., eds., *Syntax and Semantics*, vol. 3. New York: Academic Press.

Hardimon, Michael O. 2003. "The Ordinary Concept of Race," *The Journal of Philosophy*, 100: 437–55.

Haslanger, Sally. 2012 [2000]. "Gender and Race: (What) Are They? (What) Do We Want Them To Be?" Chapter 7 of this volume.

———. 2012 [2005]. "What Are We Talking About? The Semantics and Politics of Social Kinds," Chapter 13 of this volume.

———. 2012 [2006]. "What Good Are Our Intuitions? Philosophical Analysis and Social Kinds," Chapter 14 of this volume.

Jackson, F. 1998a. *From Metaphysics to Ethics: A Defense of Conceptual Analysis*. Oxford: Oxford University Press.

———. 1998b. "Reference and Description Revisited," *Philosophical Perspectives*, 12: 201–18.

Kaplan, David. 1989. "Demonstratives," in J. Almog, J. Perry and H. Wettstein, eds., *Themes from Kaplan*. Oxford: Oxford University Press.

Kripke, S. 1972. *Naming and Necessity*. Cambridge, MA: Harvard University Press.

Loeb, Don. 1995. "Full Information Theories of Individual Good," *Social Theory and Practice*, 21: 1–30.

Mallon, Ron. 2004. "Passing, Traveling and Reality: Social Constructionism and the Metaphysics of Race," *Noûs*, 38: 644–73.

Mercier, Adèle. 2007. "Meaning and Necessity: Can Semantics Stop Same-Sex Marriage?" *Essays in Philosophy*, 8(1).

Pollan, Michael. 2002. *The Botany of Desire: A Plant 's-Eye View of the World*, New York: Random House.

Putnam, H. 1975. "The Meaning of 'Meaning,'" *Minnesota Studies in the Philosophy of Science*, 7: 131–93.

Quine, W. 1953. "Two Dogmas of Empiricism," in *From a Logical Point of View*. Cambridge, MA: Harvard University Press.

Salmon, Nathan. 1986. *Frege's Puzzle*. Cambridge, MA: MIT Press.

Saul, Jennifer. 2006. "Philosophical Analysis and Social Kinds: Gender and Race," *Proceedings of the Aristotelian Society*, Supplementary Volume 80: 119–44.

Schroeter, Francois, and Laura Schroeter. 2009. "A Third Way in Metaethics," *Nous*, 43(1): 1–30.

Schroeter, Laura. 2003. "Gruesome Diagonals," *Philosopher's Imprint*, 3(3).

———. 2004. "The Limits of Conceptual Analysis," *Pacific Philosophical Quarterly*, 85: 425–53.

Soames, Scott. 2003. *Beyond Rigidity*. Oxford: Oxford University Press.

Stalnaker, R. 1978. "Assertion," in P. Cole, ed., *Syntax and Semantics*, vol. ix, New York: Academic Press, 31–532.

———. 1999. *Context and Content*. Oxford: Oxford University Press.

———. 2006. "Assertion Revisited: On the Interpretation of Two-Dimensional Modal Semantics" in M. Garcia-Caripintera and Macia, J., eds., *Two Dimensional Semantics*. Oxford: Oxford University Press.

Yablo, Stephen. 2000. "Red, Bitter, Best," *Philosophical Books*, 41: 13–29.

17

Ideology, Generics, and Common Ground

Introduction

Are sagging pants cool? Are cows food? Are women more submissive than men? Are blacks more criminal than whites? Taking the social world at face value, many people would be tempted to answer these questions in the affirmative. And if challenged, they can point to facts that support their answers. But there is something wrong about the affirmative answers. I deny that sagging pants are cool, cows are food, women are more submissive than men, and blacks are more criminal than whites. And moreover, I maintain that there is an objective basis for denying these claims even though the facts seem to support the face value affirmative response. But how can that be? We all know that male urban youth can barely walk with their pants belted around their thighs, that beef is a staple in the American diet, that blacks are incarcerated in the United States at a much higher rate than any other race, and that women defer to men in both work and family life. How could a denial of these facts be justified?

In this chapter I will sketch a way to interpret claims such as the ones listed in the previous paragraph that shows how they convey more than they seem. To do so, I will draw on recent ideas in the philosophy of language and metaphysics to show how the assertion of a generic claim of the sort in question ordinarily permits one to infer that the fact in question obtains by virtue of something specifically about the subject so described, that is, about women, or blacks, or sagging pants. In the examples I've offered, however, this implication is unwarranted. The facts in question obtain by virtue of broad system of social relations within which the subjects are situated, and are not grounded in intrinsic or dispositional features of the subjects themselves. At least this is what social constructionists undertake to establish. The background relations are obscured, however, and as a result, the assertion is at least systematically misleading; a denial functions to block the problematic implication. Revealing such implications or presuppositions and blocking them is a crucial part of ideology critique.

Ideology

What is ideology and how does it pose a philosophical problem? There is much disagreement over the nature of ideology, yet in the most basic sense ideologies are representations of social life that serve in some way to undergird social practices.[1] There is an important sense in which social structures are not imposed upon us, for they are constituted by our everyday choices and behaviors. We are not simply cogs in structures of subordination, we enact them. And something about how we represent the world is both a constitutive part of that enactment and keeps it going.[2] Comparing the Foucauldian notion of *discourse* with the more traditional concept of *ideology*, Trevor Purvis and Alan Hunt argue that

> . . . ideology and discourse refer to pretty much the same aspect of social life—the idea that human individuals participate in forms of understanding, comprehension or consciousness of the relations and activities in which they are involved. . . . This consciousness is borne through language and other systems of signs, it is transmitted between people and institutions and, perhaps most important of all, it makes a difference; that is, the way in which people comprehend and make sense of the social world has consequences for the direction and character of their action and inaction. Both 'discourse' and 'ideology' refer to these aspects of social life. (474; see also McCarthy 440)

Ideology in this broad sense—sometimes referred to as the descriptive sense—is pervasive and unavoidable. The term 'ideology' is also sometimes used in a narrower and pejorative sense to refer to representations of the relevant sort that are somehow misguided, for example, by being contrary to the real interests of an agent or group of agents.[3] As I will be using the term, however, 'ideology' is the background cognitive and affective frame that gives actions and reactions meaning within a social system and contributes to its survival.

I have argued elsewhere that it is not useful to think of ideology as a set of beliefs, understood as discrete and determinate propositional attitudes, though

---

[1] Especially useful discussions of the notion of ideology include Geuss, Fields, McCarthy, Purvis and Hunt, and Shelby.

[2] Although there is much controversy over the question whether "ideology" or the Foucauldian notion of "discourse" is better suited to the role described here, the controversies are not directly relevant to my purposes. Moreover, there seems to be a core notion shared by both. See Purvis and Hunt.

[3] Sometimes ideologies are taken to be sets of beliefs, sometimes forms of "practical consciousness," that reside in the minds of individual agents; sometimes they are cultural phenomena presupposed somehow in collective social life; sometimes they are explicit theories articulated by politicians, philosophers and religious figures, among others. The causal or explanatory role of ideology within a broader social theory is also unclear (Geuss; Elster 468–9; Marx 36–7; Althusser).

an ideology may include such attitudes ("But Mom"). In addition to beliefs, the ideology that undergirds social practices must include more primitive dispositions, habits, and a broader range of attitudes than just belief. (See also Langton, "Beyond Belief.") The less belief-like form of ideology is sometimes referred to as "hegemony":

> Ideology and hegemony are opposite ends of a continuum . . . At one end . . . 'ideology' is used to refer to struggles to establish dominant meanings and to make justice claims on the basis of alternative ideologies . . . At the other end . . . the term 'hegemony' is used to refer to situations where meanings are so embedded that representational and institutionalized power is invisible. (Silbey 276)

Although Silbey's quote is a bit unclear on this point, the idea is that ideologies can be more or less contested, more or less hegemonic. The more hegemonic, the less conscious and less articulate they are.

There are at least two sets of philosophical challenges posed by the phenomenon of ideology. The first concerns how ideology, usually without our awareness, constitutes the social background of our action. This is partly an empirical question that requires work in psychology and sociology to answer. But an adequate theory of ideology must also explicate how individuals know the collectively constituted framework for action, how actions draw on that framework to give them meaning, and how the framework can be contested and resisted. The second set of challenges concerns the normative evaluation of ideology. As mentioned, not all ideologies are pernicious, and ideology, as I'm using the term, is necessary for there to be any social coordination, both just and unjust. Because some ideologies constitute and sustain unjust social structures, there are normative questions about how to evaluate them. Some of these questions will be epistemic: How do we evaluate the adequacy of an ideology in relation to how the world actually is? Some questions will be moral and political: Are the social structures that a given ideology constitutes and sustains just?

This chapter engages the first set of challenges. It considers what the relationship is between ideology and social structures, and how an ideology can become hegemonic and so invisible to those who employ it as they collectively constitute their social milieu. There are serious epistemic problems in asking how ideology critique is even possible, for once we constitute our social world, descriptions of it not only appear true, but are true. For example, if laws concerning marriage require that the parties to the marriage be one man and one woman, then it is true that marriage cannot occur between two men or two women, and virtually anyone living within that the social milieu is justified in believing this: it constitutes important social knowledge. When heteronormative ideology is hegemonic, the "cannot" in this claim not only describes the boundaries of our legal system and the world as we know it but also most of our imaginations. Similarly, under conditions of male dominance, women are, in fact, more submissive than men. This is a true generalization and those who live under male dominance are justified in believing it. But again, if male dominance is hegemonic, this seems not only to describe how women happen to be, but more than this: how women *are*. Again, our imaginations are foreclosed. But the issue isn't just one of imagination: it concerns the adequacy of our frameworks for interpreting and constituting the social world.

When ideologies become hegemonic, their effects blend into and, in an important sense, become part of, the natural world, so we no longer see them as social. Hegemonic ideology and the structures it constitutes are extremely hard to change. Social scientists and psychologists offer important resources for revealing the workings of hegemony. But the work of philosophers and linguists is also necessary for the primary medium of social life is language: it forms the basis for intentional action, shared meaning, and collective organization. Attention to the ambiguities and slippages between different linguistic forms is useful in explaining how ideas become entrenched and social practices seem natural and inevitable. Or at least this is what I will argue in what follows.

Generics, Semantics, and Pragmatics

Let us return now to the statements with which we began. What is being claimed when someone says, "women are more submissive (nurturing, cooperative, sensitive . . .) than men"? Surely not *all* women are more submissive than *all*, or even *most*, men. Is the claim intentionally vague? Is it elliptical for a different claim? In fact, generalizations that omit quantifiers such as "some," "all," or "many" fall into the linguistic category of generics, and generics call for a quite different analysis than ordinary quantified statements. Plausibly, "generic sentences are not about some specific instances of the category mentioned in the [subject], but rather about the category in general" (Leslie, "Generics" 21).[4] We are not abbreviating an enumeration of cases, but are saying something about the group as an open-ended class.

[4] Note that this is a different claim from one saying that the generic is about the kind e.g., dodos are extinct. See Leslie, "Generics" 5, fn 3. Generics seem to be concerned with open-ended generalizations. Enumerative generalizations and open-ended generalizations differ in ways that matter for confirmation and induction: "this coin in my pocket is silver" doesn't inductively confirm "all coins in my pocket are silver" because it doesn't lend credibility to the untested cases. In addition, there are a number of issues concerning the use of bare plurals that deserve consideration (Carlson). In some cases, bare plurals seem to have existential rather than generalizing force, e.g., "he grew tomatoes in that plot," or "flour moths have invaded my kitchen." I will only be considering the generic bare plural.

In considering generics, we might ask: what is the *meaning* of a generic? Or, we might ask, what are generics typically used to say? The study of meaning is semantics. The study of what we say is pragmatics: "Pragmatics is the study of linguistic acts and the contexts in which they are performed. There are two major types of problem to be solved within pragmatics: first, to define interesting types of speech acts and speech products; second, to characterize the features of the speech context which help determine which proposition is expressed by a given sentence" (Stalnaker, "Pragmatics" 275). I propose that attention to the pragmatics of typical generics will illuminate ways in which politically salient ones can seriously mislead. This, in turn, will give us resources to think further about the role of social constructionist claims as part of ideology critique. My goal in this part of the chapter is to lay out components of one possible account of generics so that we see how they might mislead in a small range of cases; we'll then turn in the second part to consider what social consequences it might have. The tools we will need first are the notion of a generic, a generic essence, and the common ground of a conversation.

Generics

The first hypothesis I'd like us to consider is that with generics of the form Ks are F ("tigers have stripes"), or K_1s are more G than K_2s ("tigers are more dangerous than cheetahs") there is normally an implication that the connection between the Ks and F or G holds primarily by virtue of some important fact about the Ks *as such*.[5] This is a very broad claim that I will not be able to support because of the complexity of cases; for simplicity I will focus on non-comparatives such as "tigers have stripes," "women are submissive (nurturing, cooperative)," "blacks are criminal (violent, hostile)," and "sagging pants are cool," rather than statements that explicitly compare kinds or groups.

As mentioned above, generics of the form Ks are F cannot be understood as elliptical quantifications, for in contrast to quantifications,

> [Generics'] truth conditions seem to be enormously complex. Why, for example, is 'birds lay eggs' true, while 'birds are female' is false? It is, after all, only the female birds that lay eggs. And why is 'mosquitoes carry the West Nile virus' true, and 'books are paperbacks' false given that less than one percent of mosquitoes carry the virus while over eighty percent of books are paperbacks? Such puzzling examples abound. (Leslie, "Original Sin" 2)

---

[5] I'm actually not sure whether it is better to consider it an implication or a presupposition. I'm willing to adjust my account to accommodate evidence for either. My goal in this chapter is programmatic and I am aware that much more work needs to be done on the details.

Although there is no consensus on the best account of generics, Sarah-Jane Leslie suggests convincingly that generics are the expression of a very primitive "default mode of generalizing," that picks up on significant or striking properties and links them to a psychologically salient kind. Very roughly, the idea is that we have a very basic capacity to sort the world into kinds of things that seem to behave in similar ways and generics highlight striking or important features that members of these kinds typically exhibit.

In exploring this idea, we must be sensitive to different kinds of generalizations. For example, Prasada and Dillingham ("Principled" and "Representation") highlight two importantly different relations between the kinds and the properties of concern in generics:

> Principled connections involve properties that are determined by the kind of thing something is (e.g. having four legs for a dog). Statistical connections involve properties that are not determined by the kind of thing something is, but that are highly prevalent connections to the kind, e.g., being red for a barn. Principled connections are proposed to support formal explanations (Fido has four legs because he is a dog), normative expectations (Fido should have four legs and has something wrong with him if he doesn't), and the expectation that the property will generally be highly prevalent (most dogs have four legs). (Leslie et al., "Conceptual" 479)

Leslie notes that this distinction between principled and statistical connections, although important, is not sufficient, by itself, to accommodate the range of different generics, for, as noted above, there are true generics that do not ascribe (and are not presumed to ascribe) a prevalent property to the kind, for example, "Ducks lay eggs."

On Leslie's view, there are three kinds of cases ("Generics" 43):

- *Characteristic generics*: Cases such as "tigers have stripes" and "dogs have four legs" assert more than a statistical correlation between tigers and stripes. They purport to tell us what is characteristic of the kind, what a good example of the kind will exhibit.[6] But how, then, should we understand cases such as "birds lay eggs" or even "bees lay eggs" even if the majority of the kind don't lay eggs, and cases such as "police officers fight crime" even if there is no

---

[6] In ("Generics" 43), Leslie suggests that if the attributed property is true of almost all of the kind (almost all tigers have stripes), and there are no positive counterinstances (it is not the case that the tigers who don't have stripes have bold pink spots), then the characteristic generic is true. However, the role of positive counterinstances is more complex, for there may be abnormal counterinstances (albino tigers) that do not defeat the generalization (Leslie, private communication), so the better account will need to rely on some notion of what's a good example of the kind.

crime in their district? Leslie proposes that we have background knowledge that

> provides an outline of information to be gathered about a new kind; characteristic dimensions provide a learner with an informational template. When a value is found for a characteristic dimension of a kind, it is hereby generalized to the kind by the basic generalization mechanism, and so the generic that predicates that property of the kind is accepted. Ducks, being an animal kind, has reproduction as a characteristic dimension, so the inductive learner looks for a value to fill the dimension; even limited experience will deliver *laying eggs* as the appropriate value, and so the property is generalized to the kind and 'ducks lay eggs' is accepted as true. ("Generics" 32–3)

In the case of artifacts, institutions, and social kinds, the template has us look for information about the function or purpose of the kind and this explains the truth of statements such as "police officers fight crime" ("Generics" 43).

- *Striking property generics*: How can we accommodate such cases as "mosquitoes carry the West Nile virus," even though only a small fraction do, and those that do are not plausibly characteristic of their kind? In such cases, she maintains, "The sentence attributes harmful, dangerous, or appalling properties to the kind. More generally, if the property in question is the sort of property of which one would be well served to be forewarned, even if there were only a small chance of encountering it, then generic attributions of the property are intuitively true" ("Generics" 15). Leslie goes on to suggest that in order for these generics to be true, being a member of the kind must be a reasonably good predictor of the striking property, and members that don't have the property must be disposed, under the right circumstances, to have it[7] ("Generics" 41).

- *Majority generics*: Speakers are also willing to assent to weaker generics such as "cars have radios" or "barns are red" that only capture statistical or enumerative generalizations. However, speakers find these less natural than characteristic generics ("Conceptual" 480), and resist alternative syntactic

---

[7] A different hypothesis worth considering is that the striking property generics are picking out a feature that is remarkable or important in the context. This differs from Leslie's proposal in two ways: the feature may not be dangerous or harmful, and what properties are eligible vary from context to context. For example, Cohen ("Think Generic!") provides a contrastive account on which (roughly) generics are true just in case they attribute a property to a kind that is more likely to hold of members of that kind than the alternative that is salient in the context. Leslie argues against Cohen's account in ("Generics" 10–12), though others defend versions of it (Carr. "Generics").

forms for the generic, for example, "a tiger has stripes" is considered more natural than "a barn is red" ("Conceptual" 482, 484).

Leslie's account of generics is controversial (and also more complicated than I have suggested here[8]), but for my purposes, it is not necessary to accept her account in full detail, for my emphasis will be on pragmatics; rather than asking what generics *mean*, or under what conditions they are *true*, we are asking: what do we use generic statements to say? The point to take from Leslie is that generics are a distinctive kind of statement that should not be treated as ordinary quantified statements, and that they draw heavily on background knowledge and patterns of inference to highlight a significant property (either characteristic, striking, or common) of a kind.

Essences, Natures, and Coincidences

The notion of essence has a complicated and sometimes problematic history. Within the Aristotelian tradition, each member of a genuine kind has an essence or nature which consists of a set of intrinsic qualities that explains the characteristic behavior of things of that kind. An individual tiger has a nature without which that tiger could not be the individual it is. All full members of the kind have the essence though they may fail to fully exhibit it due to interfering circumstances, for example, an injured or deformed tiger or a tiger in a zoo may not exhibit all of the characteristic traits of healthy tigers in the wild, but it is still part of their nature to do so—they would have if they had been in the right circumstances.[9]

---

[8] For example, Leslie rightly points out that there is an asymmetry in how generics are responsive to counterinstances. Recall that "birds lay eggs" is true, even though there are a substantial number of counterexamples (the male and non-fertile female birds). "Birds are female," however, is false, even though there are almost as many counterexamples. Leslie proposes that in the case of "birds are female," the non-female birds manifest a positive alternative, namely, being male, whereas in the "birds lay eggs" case, it is not the case that there is another form of reproduction in place of laying eggs. If some birds gave birth to live young, then "birds lay eggs" would be false. "There is an intuitive difference between simply lacking a feature and lacking it in virtue of having another, equally memorable, feature instead" ("Generics" 35). She draws the conclusion that generics are highly sensitive to whether the counterinstances to the claim are *positive* or *negative* (33–7).

[9] In contemporary metaphysics, this notion of *objectual* essence (the essence of objects) has been reframed in terms of an object's essential or necessary properties. An object's essential properties are all and only those it could not exist without; its accidental properties are those that it has but might not have had. So, I am essentially a living being, but only accidentally a mother. I am interested in notions of essence that are *not* best understood as a set of necessary properties but are closer to the idea of natures that may be realized more or less fully (Fine, Correia).

However, the fundamental notion of essence within this tradition is of a definable type or kind.[10] When we ask what it is to be a human being, or an artichoke, we are looking for the essence of the kind *human being* or *artichoke*. This notion of essence has been called *generic essence* to distinguish it from *objectual* essence. So there are two ways of "having" an essence. Kinds "have$_g$" an essence that constitutes what it is to be of that kind; individuals are instantiations of this kind-essence and "have$_o$" the kind-essence as their individual essence.

This notion of generic essence can then be extended beyond genuine kinds, that is, kinds that constitute the being of their members, to properties and ways of being more generally. We can ask not only what it is to be a human being, but what it is to be a mother, to be a citizen of the United States, or to be just. For example, when Plato raises the issue in *The Republic* (Bk II) whether justice benefits the just person, he is careful to distinguish the claim that justice accidentally benefits the just person in cases where society rewards justice, and the claim that justice by its very nature benefits, and would do so even if being just accrued no social rewards. The suggestion is that justice has a (generic) essence, even if nothing is (objectually) essentially just.

Following Kit Fine and Fabrice Correia, it is useful to consider essentialist statements as making a claim about the ground of certain facts in natures. On this approach, if G is part of the generic essence of F, just in case:

Fs are G by virtue of the nature of F-ing.
G-ing is something Fs do by virtue of what it is to be an F.
It is true in virtue of what it is to F, that Fs are G.

It is important to emphasize that in the sense intended here, the generic essence of F is not to be understood simply in terms of what is entailed by being F, for essences are invoked as part of an explanatory project that assumes that some properties are prior (metaphysically, epistemically) to others (Fine). Moreover, if we grant that natures may not always be fully realized (remember the injured tiger), statements of generic essence may not even support true universal generalizations, much less necessary generalizations. Even if Fs are by nature G, it may not be that every case of F is a case of G, for there may be interfering conditions; Fs, however, are typically G, due to what it is to be F.

Ordinary English speakers don't often use the term "essence," and although the term "nature," as in "a dog's nature," is more common, we seem to find other

---

[10] In Aristotle's terms, the substantial form is the essence, the matter *has* the essence, and the matter together with the essence constitutes the material object. The species is the matter and form "taken generally." I'm using the term 'kind' in the first part of this paragraph as roughly equivalent to "substantial form," but I quickly revert to a more ordinary notion of 'kind.' See also Haslanger, "Myth and Reality."

ways of speaking about natures. Consider, claims such as, "fish swim" or "lilacs bloom in May." A speaker uttering the former would seem to be suggesting that there is an important connection between being a fish and being able to swim, that the ability is somehow grounded in what it is to be a fish; similarly for lilacs and their blooming season. It appears, now, that there is a close connection between the kind of generalization we find in at least some generics (F-ing is a characteristic dimension of Ks; F-ing is striking and Ks are disposed to F; being a K is a good predictor for being F) and claims concerning generic essence. We will return to consider this connection shortly.

Common Ground

In order for us to communicate, we must take certain things for granted as background to our conversation, that is, we must presuppose certain things as common ground (Stalnaker, "Common Ground" 701; see also Stalnaker, "Context," and Lewis). Stalnaker suggests that "to presuppose a proposition in the pragmatic sense is to take its truth for granted, and to assume that others involved in the context do the same.... Presuppositions are propositions implicitly *supposed* before the relevant linguistic business is transacted" ("Common Ground" 279–80). In the simplest case the common ground consists of the shared beliefs of the parties to the conversation; the belief may be wholly tacit, however, "presuppositions are probably best viewed as complex dispositions which are manifested in linguistic behavior" ("Pragmatics" 279), and in the more complex cases involve something less than full belief, for example, assumption, pretense, presumption ("Common Ground" 704).[11]

The common ground of a conversation is constantly changing, for as one party to the conversation speaks, the other(s) will at least adjust their beliefs to include the fact that the first party spoke. Typically other beliefs will change as well. For example, if I say to you "I'm sorry I can't make it to the 5:00 P.M. meeting because I need to pick up my son at the campus day care," you will probably come to believe not only that I will be absent from the meeting but also that I have a preschool aged son attending the day care (understanding "preschool" to cover ages prior to kindergarten). Conversation conveys information by means other than by what is explicitly stated.

One way inexplicit communication occurs is through *implicature*, another through *presupposition accommodation*. The idea is that in ordinary conversations in which we judge each other to be competent and cooperative, we aim to achieve and maintain equilibrium in the common ground, to share presuppositions at

---

[11] Rae Langton has argued that presupposition accommodation may also require accommodation of desire and other attitudes. See Langton, "Beyond Belief."

least for the purposes of the conversation.[12] For example, if it is clear from my utterance that I am presupposing something, then unless you have reason to suspect my sincerity or credibility, you can legitimately infer the proposition I presuppose, and I can assume that the common ground has adjusted to include my presupposition, unless you indicate otherwise. In conversation, we rely on general maxims that govern the common ground, but what constitutes the common ground is also always up for constant renegotiation. For example, if, after hearing my excuse for not being at the meeting, you reply, "I thought your children were teenagers," this indicates hesitation to accept the proposition "Sally has a preschool aged son," into the common ground. We need to backtrack and repair the common ground. In response, I might confirm that I do in fact have a preschooler, or clarify, "You're right, he is volunteering at the day care during spring break." At that point, the common ground may be further updated with new beliefs about my teenaged son. Similarly, updating and correction of common ground happens through implicature. If I write a letter of recommendation to graduate school for a student in my class and spend most of the letter expressing enthusiasm about his handwriting, you may infer that I do not think well of him as a philosopher (Grice). Often we say more by what we don't say than by what we do.

Whenever something said in conversation introduces a new element into the common ground, the interlocutor has the option of blocking the move. Lewis uses the metaphor of "scorekeeping in a language game" to capture the dynamic process of updating. Negation is one device for blocking. Even if a statement made in conversation is literally true, one can deny the statement as a way to block what the statement conveys (either the implicature, or the presupposition); this is known as metalinguistic negation (Horn).[13] A standard example is, "He's not meeting a woman, he's meeting his wife!" As I will explain more fully as we proceed, my point in saying that we should deny the generics with which we began (Are sagging pants cool? Are cows food? Are women more submissive than men? Are blacks more criminal than whites?) is that an assertion of them pragmatically implicates a falsehood, and our metalinguistic denial blocks that falsehood from entering the common ground.

It is worth emphasizing that the updating of the common ground is not a matter of what is *semantically* presupposed or implied by the proposition

---

[12] It is a difficult and contested matter how to distinguish what enters the common ground through implicature and what enters through presupposition. For my purposes, little hinges on this; what matters is that the common ground can be updated in ways that are not explicit and need not even be noticed by the audience or speaker. I will use the model of implicature to account for the examples we're looking at, but it may be that they are better handled differently.

[13] I recommend Horn (esp. §2) for a full discussion of metalinguistic negation with examples of some interest to feminists, e.g., "She's not a lady, she's a woman!" or "She's not an uppity broad, she's a strong, vibrant woman!"

expressed by the speaker. Rather, common ground is a *pragmatic* notion that concerns what is presupposed by the speaker and what is implicated, given certain conversational maxims, by her utterance. Updating of the common ground is a dynamic process that depends on the particular conversation; however, there is considerable social pressure on those who want to communicate smoothly with others to conform to the common ground of those around them.

Generics and Implication

We are now in a position to begin putting the pieces together. In uttering a generalization, one has several options. One can express the generalization using a quantified statement such as:

All [most/some] Fs are G.

One can also use a generic:

Fs are G.

In choosing a generic, it appears that one is saying *of a kind of thing*, specified in the statement, that its members are, or are disposed to be G (or to G) *by virtue of being of that kind*.[14] The speaker conveys that being G is somehow rooted in what it is to be an F: G-ing is what Fs do (or are disposed to do) by virtue of being F. This locates the source of the Gness in being (an) F.[15]

One might develop the pragmatics in a number of ways. I propose the following. It seems that in the case of at least some generics, the semantics requires that there is some non-accidental or non-coincidental connection between the Fs and being G (recall the truth conditions for both characteristic generics and striking generics). The details may plausibly be spelled out along the lines Leslie suggests.[16] However, given the usefulness and universality of the default mode of generalizing that Leslie describes, if one asserts

---

[14] This seems a quite straightforward claim for characteristic generics and striking generics; it is less clear for ordinary generics. It is more plausible if the subject of the ordinary generic is a basic-level kind (Leslie, "Generics"), and referred to by a term that makes the kind explicit. In such cases the correlation between the kind and the selected property seems to call for explanation in terms of the kind's nature.

[15] More needs to be said about what it is to be a "source" of truth. I'm drawing on Fine.

[16] The semantics of generics may be as complex as Leslie describes, or much simpler. I'm sympathetic with Leslie's view but I am not taking a stand on the semantics here. I believe that my claims about the pragmatics are compatible with several different accounts of the semantics.

that Fs are G, then it is implicated that under "normal" circumstances it is something about being an F that makes an F a G, that Fs *as such* are disposed to be G.[17] This is a pragmatic implicature and can normally be defeated or canceled. But if unchallenged, it licenses the inference from the generic Fs are G to a claim of generic essence: Fs are G by virtue of what it is to be (an) F. In conversations where we credit our interlocutor with the ability to recognize this default inference, we take their utterance of, say, "tigers are striped," to introduce into the common ground the further claim "tigers are striped by virtue of what it is to be a tiger."

To avoid confusion, let's look at some other examples. Consider the claims:

(a) Women have noses.[18]

This, it seems, is true. Most women have noses, it is not the case that those women who lack noses have trunks or antennae instead, and it is not a mere accident that a woman has a nose. However, it is also a very weird thing to say unless there is some doubt raised. It would be tempting, I think, if someone offered (a) as an insight to reply, "Yes, well, humans have noses." Such a reply is apt because an assertion of (a) implicates that there is something special about women *as such* that explains their having noses. But this presumption is false. The reply corrects the implication without denying the truth of the claim.

Consider another claim that seems to pose a challenge for my account:

(b) Dobermans have pointy ears.[19]

As I hear (b), it would depend significantly on context whether it would prompt resistance. On one hand, it seems apt to respond to (b), "They don't *really* have pointy ears. Their ears are cropped when they are puppies." But it might be clear from context that the question is how they typically appear as adult dogs, in which case there would be no reason to resist. In the latter case, (b) is assertable

---

[17] More should be said about why it is plausible that this presupposition or implicature is added to the common ground. Relevant support includes (i) further arguments for the value of the default mode of generalization and its connection to generics, (ii) further arguments concerning the relation between generics and inductive inference, (iii) the application of Gricean maxims of relevance and quantity, and (iv) the idea that the grammatically simpler a statement, the more paradigmatic the phenomenon described is implicated to be (Levinson).

[18] This example was raised and discussed in a graduate seminar devoted to this topic at MIT. My memory does not allow me to thank each individual for their particular contribution, so thanks to the group (all mentioned in the chapter's acknowledgments) for help with this case.

[19] Thanks to Mahrad Almotahari for this example.

because it is not a coincidence when one comes across an adult Doberman that it will have pointy ears; it is to be expected because that is the standard for the breed. Given, however, that these days the standard is being challenged, it would also be reasonable for someone to reply, "As a matter of fact, Dobermans have all sizes and shapes of ears," suggesting not only that it is not universal, but that in fact a dog's being a Doberman is not a good basis for predicting that it will have pointy ears because the standard is contested. As I hear it, however, in ordinary cases, (b) seems at least confusing and demands clarification because the default implication is that Dobermans, by nature, have pointy ears.

Finally, let us consider:

(c) Bachelors are unmarried.

Claim (c) is surely true. However, the assertion of (c) does not allow us to infer of John, who is a bachelor, that he is by *nature* unmarried. That would be to take the implication relevant to (c) to be a presumption of objectual essence, that is, that the individuals of the kind have as part of their essence the property expressed by the predicate. The account I have proposed takes the presumption to concern the nature of the kind or type, what I've been calling the generic essence. The relevant inference is that bachelors, as such, that is, insofar as they are bachelors, are unmarried; and this is true.

In light of this hypothesis about the pragmatic effect of generics, let's consider the statements we started with:

1. Sagging pants are cool.
2. Cows are food.
3. Women are submissive (nurturing, cooperative).
4. Blacks are violent (criminal, dangerous).

Case (1): We all know that sagging pants are only cool, insofar as they are, by virtue of being viewed as such by an in-group. But those who experience them as cool, experience *them* as cool. The coolness seems to have its source in the particular cut, hang, whatever, of the pants. Fashion examples are useful because for those even the least bit sophisticated, the temptation to regard the coolness of the fashion as having its source in the objects is unstable; although we can find ourselves drawn into the idea, we can also easily resist it by recognizing that the coolness is a relational fact derived from the social context. When we see through the essentializing of fashion, we need not deny the claim that sagging pants are cool, for we can allow the implicature to enter the common ground without actually believing it or even believing that our interlocutor believes it (Stalnaker,

"Common Ground" Section 5). It may be a presupposition we are willing to pretend is true for the purposes of the conversation.

An importantly similar, but more complicated, example[20] is:

(1b) Women wear lipstick.

There are a number of options for reading (1b) based on context. In some cases it might be clear that the assertion of (1b) is simply a majority generic indicating that a significant number of women (or of the subgroup of women the speaker has in mind) wear lipstick. However, as a woman who never wears lipstick, it is not hard for me to imagine (1b) being used to implicate a kind of reproach: *good* women, *real* women, *normal* women wear lipstick. This may reflect a pretense that fashion and other cultural forms are linked to our natures: consider the belief that there is something unnatural about a man wearing a dress. Along these lines, in response to the question, "Why is that person wearing lipstick?" one might find it tempting to respond, "It is a woman!" The suggestion (or pretense) is that this is just what a good instance of womanhood does, that being a woman is sufficient to explain why she is wearing lipstick; the more pressing question is why Sally, for example, doesn't.

Case (2), "cows are food," is complicated. One reason is that it is not the sort of thing people tend to say. They are more likely to say that beef is food. Being a vegetarian, I believe that beef isn't food although it is wrongly considered to be food by many. Beef is the flesh of a dead cow; "beef" is used to mask the reality of what is being ingested. Of course, humans can consume and digest dead cows. But being edible is not the same as being food. There are many edible things, even nutritious things, that don't count as food because they taste bad or smell bad; they are associated with disgusting things; they are too intelligent; they are our pets or our children. Food, I submit, is a cultural and normative category. However, if someone asserts that beef is food, understanding this as a generic, it is tempting to accept the implication that there is something about the nature of beef (or cows) that makes it food.

To accept this implication, I believe, is a mistake similar to the mistake made about fashion, but with a moral dimension. It is true that not just anything could count as food (an aluminum soda can is not food), but just containing certain nutrients or having a certain chemical composition is not sufficient. This, however, is obscured in saying that cows are food or beef is food. Creeping into the common ground is the suggestion (pretense) that cows are *for* eating,

---

[20] Thanks to Jennifer Carr for this example and suggestions for how to handle it.

that beef *just is* food.[21] Given that I believe this to be a pernicious and morally damaging assumption, it is reasonable for me to block the implicature by denying the claim: cows are *not* food. I would even be willing to say that beef is not food. This is compatible, however, with someone reasserting the claim that cows are food as a majority generic and canceling the implicature. People *do* eat cows; Beef *is* served as food. *But this is not what cows are for, it is the result of optional (and, I submit, immoral) human practices.* Or more simply, "cows are food, given existing social practices." This I would not deny.

Given the treatment of cases (1) and (2), it is likely predictable how the discussion of (3) and (4) will go. The general strategy of argument is to show that there is a set of problematic generics that introduce implicitly into the common ground a proposition about a generic essence, about how beef or women or blacks *are* by nature or intrinsically. These cases are problematic because the introduced proposition is false, so we have a reason to block it. But as we've seen already in the move from fashion to food, human convention picks up on the natural properties of things, and the line between the natural and the social can become blurred. So it will be useful to look more closely at the interaction between the natural and the social in constituting food, genders, races, and other social kinds. I will then return to (3) and (4) and the idea of ideology critique.

Structures, Schemas, and Resources[22]

What is a social structure? There is considerable interdisciplinary work on this topic by social historians, social psychologists, and sociologists interested in subordination and critical resistance. As I am using the term here, "social structure" is a general category of social phenomena, including, for example, social institutions, social practices and conventions, social roles, social hierarchies, social locations or geographies, and the like.

---

[21] This example is worth much more discussion than I will provide here. In particular, it is not clear how to understand the term 'beef.' Is beef just a slab of dead cow flesh? Or does it include as part of its meaning that the cow flesh is prepared (perhaps even just cut) in a way suitable for eating? Would a slab of cow flesh found on the road after a cow's collision with a truck be rightly called 'beef'? I am intending to be provocative here, though I also have a more substantive point: within the Aristotelian tradition, some natures must be understood functionally. Eyes are *for* seeing. I believe that it is characteristic of omnivores that they regard the slabs of flesh they consume *as food*, which is to say that they just are *for eating*. This is, I submit, to be mistaken about what they really are.

[22] Parts of this section also appear in Haslanger, "But Mom" (chapter 15 of this volume).

William Sewell (a social historian), drawing on Anthony Giddens, argues for an account that takes structures to be "both the medium and the outcome of the practices which constitute social systems" (4, quoting Giddens, "Critique" 27; see also Giddens' "Central Problems" and "Constitution"). Sewell continues: "Structures shape people's practices, but it is also people's practices that constitute (and reproduce) structures. In this view of things. human agency and structure, far from being opposed, in fact presuppose each other" (4). More specifically, Giddens is known for identifying structures as "rules and resources." On Sewell's account, however, the combination becomes "schemas and resources" in order to avoid the assumption that the cognitive element must always take the form of a rule (8). Sewell takes schemas to include:

> . . . all the variety of cultural schemas that anthropologists have uncovered in their research: not only the array of binary oppositions that make up a given society's fundamental tools of thought, but also the various conventions, recipes, scenarios, principles of action, and habits of speech and gesture built up with these fundamental tools. (7–8)

It is crucial to Sewell that these schemas are not private and personal patterns of thought, but are intersubjective and transposable in response to new circumstances. Responding to Sewell, Judith Howard (a social psychologist) points out that Sewell's use of the term 'schema' differs from its use in social psychology. Whereas social psychologists tend to think of schemas as concerned with the organization of an individual's thought, Sewell develops the notion in a way that highlights its cultural deployment. She suggests:

> A synthesis of these conceptions of schemas might prove remarkably useful: the stricter social cognitive models provide a sound basis for predicting how and when intra-individual schemas change, whereas the more recent sociological conceptions say more about how group interactions shape the formation and evolution of cultural schemas. (218)

If we take Howard's idea seriously, we should explore the interdependence between individual schemas and their cultural counterparts: "Schemas, for example, are both mental and social; they both derive from and constitute cultural, semiotic, and symbolic systems" (Howard 218).

What are we to make of this? Let's take schemas to be intersubjective patterns of perception, thought, and behavior. They are embodied in individuals as a shared cluster of open-ended dispositions to see things a certain way or to respond habitually in particular circumstances. Schemas encode knowledge and also provide scripts for interaction with each other and our environment. Understood in this way, schemas are plausibly part of the common ground we rely on to communicate. Although some may be rather specific to a small community, others will extend broadly, even across cultures.

On this view, schemas are one component of social structures, resources are the other. Social structures cannot be identified simply as schemas because social structures have material existence and a reality that "pushes back" when we come to it with the wrong or an incomplete schema. For example, the schema of two sex categories is manifested in the design and labeling of toilet facilities. If we're analyzing social structures, then in addition to the mental content or disposition, there must be an actualization of it in the world, for example, an enactment of it, that involves something material. Resources provide the materiality of social structures. On the Giddens/Sewell account, resources are anything that "can be used to enhance or maintain power" (Sewell 9). This includes human resources such as "physical strength, dexterity, knowledge" (Sewell 9) in addition to materials—animate and inanimate—in the usual sense.

How do schemas and resources together constitute social structures? Sewell suggests a causal interdependence:

> A factory is not an inert pile of bricks, wood, and metal. It incorporates or actualizes schemas. . . . The factory gate, the punching-in station, the design of the assembly line: all of these features of the factory teach and validate the rules of the capitalist labor contract . . . In short, if resources are instantiations or embodiments of schemas, they therefore inculcate and justify the schemas as well . . . Sets of schemas and resources may properly be said to constitute structures only when they mutually imply and sustain each other over time. (13)

So on Sewell's view a social structure exists when there is a causal, and mutually sustaining, interdependence between a shared or collective schema and an organization of resources. Sewell's claim that the two elements of structure "imply and sustain each other" suggests a constitutive relationship as well: the pile of bricks, wood, and metal is a punching-in station because schemas that direct employers to pay employees by the hour and employees to keep track of their hours are enacted with this tool. The schema for keeping track of hours is a punching-in schema because there is a punch-clock that the employer will use as a basis for calculating wages. Without the invention of the punch-clock, there could be no punching-in schema. There is a causal relationship, but not just a causal relationship. What else is it?

Consider a familiar example: a statue and the bronze of which it is composed. The bronze constitutes the statue, for example, the figure of Joan of Arc on horseback in New York City's Riverside Park. The bronze is the statue not only by virtue of its shape, but also by virtue of having a certain history, function, interpretation, and such. Think of the bronze as resource; think of the dispositions that give rise to the statue's history, function, and interpretation as (roughly) schema. The role of schema may be still more evident in the constitution of it as a memorial. The Joan of Arc statue commemorates "the 500th anniversary of Joan of Arc's birth." The statue consists of the shaped bronze, and the statue in turn constitutes the memorial, understood as a further schema-structured resource [[[bronze, shape], statue], memorial]. Thus it appears that the schema/resource distinction can be applied in ways analogous to the matter/form distinction.

More helpful for our purposes may be an example of a social event rather than a social object: the performance of a Bach minuet on the piano. The performance is an event that involves both the piano, the sheet music, fingers and such (as resources), and also a set of dispositions to respond to the sheet music by playing the piano keys in a certain way, plus the various ritualized gestures that make it a performance rather than a rehearsal (as schema). Considered in this light, most actions involve not only an agent with an intention and a bodily movement, but a set of dispositions to interact with things to realize the intention; think of cycling, cooking, typing. These dispositions conform to publicly accessible and socially meaningful patterns and are molded by both the social and physical context. Because often such dispositions give rise to objects that trigger those very dispositions, they can be extremely resistant to change (think of the challenge of replacing the qwerty keyboard).

This sort of schematic materiality of our social worlds is ubiquitous: towns, city halls, churches, universities, philosophy departments, gyms, playgrounds, homes, are schematically structured and practice-imbued material things (cf. a "ghost town" or "a house but not a home" whose schemas are lost or attenuated). The social world includes artifacts which are what they are because of what is to be done with them; it also includes schemas for action that are what they are because they direct our interaction with some part of the world. Thus at least some parts of the social/cognitive world and material world are co-constitutive.

If a practice is the structured product of schema (a set of dispositions to perceive and respond in certain ways) and resources (a set of tools and material goods), it is not "subjective" in any of the ordinary uses of that term. Social structures are not just in our heads (just as the statue is not just in our heads); social structures are public (just as the bronze only constitutes a memorial by virtue of the collective interpretation and pattern of action in response to it); although social structures are not simply material things, they are constituted by material things. They are "constructed" by us in the ordinary way that artifacts are created by us. One can believe in them without accepting the idea, sometimes endorsed by "social constructionists" that our thought constructs, in a less ordinary way, what there is in the world (Haslanger, "Social").

This rough account of social structures helps to define the idea of a social milieu. As we saw above, the schemas that constitute social structures are intersubjective or cultural patterns, scripts and the like, that are internalized by individuals to form the basis of our responses to socially meaningful objects, actions, and events. In many cases, perhaps even most, the dominant cultural schema will also be the one that individuals in that context have made "their own." However, it is not always that simple. Individuals bear complex relations to the dominant schemas of their cultural context; they may be ignorant of or insensitive to a schema, may reject a schema, or may modify a schema for their own purposes. One may be deliberately out of sync with one's milieu, or just "out of it." It is also the case that different schemas vie for dominance in public space. Plausibly the negotiation over schemas at least partly happens linguistically through the formation of common ground.

For the purposes of this chapter it will be useful to define an individual's (general) social milieu in terms of the social structures within which he or she operates, whether or not the public schemas in question have been internalized. Although we can choose some of the structures within which we live, it is not always a matter of choice; for example, I am governed by the laws of the United States whether I choose to be or not. Of course, individuals do not live within only one milieu, and milieus overlap. One's workplace, place of worship, civic space, and home are structured spaces; each of these structures are inflected by race, gender, class, nationality, age, and sexuality to name a few relevant factors. So it will be important to specify an individual's milieu at a time and place and possibly in relation to specified others. In this chapter I will not be able to give precise conditions that specify what milieu is operative for an individual in a given context; we'll just have to rely on clear-enough cases for now.

To summarize briefly, schemas and resources together constitute practices, and patterns of interdependent practices constitute structures. The schemas—dispositions, interpretations, experiences, beliefs and the like—are an important part of the common ground we rely on to communicate; they are also, I maintain, a form of ideology. On this view, ideology is not just a set of background beliefs that purport to justify social structures: ideology in the form of schemas partly constitutes the structures.

"Looping" and Social Kinds

In his discussion of social phenomena, Ian Hacking has emphasized the phenomenon of "looping."[23] On his view, the continuum between the natural and the social depends on a distinction between indifferent and interactive kinds (32, 102–5). Hacking describes the contrast this way:

---

[23] I discuss Hacking on "looping" kinds also in Haslanger, "Ontology" and Haslanger. "Social." See also Langton, "Speaker's Freedom."

The [kind/classification] "woman refugee" can be called an "interactive kind" because it interacts with things of that kind, namely people, including individual women refugees, who can become aware of how they are classified and modify their behavior accordingly. (32)

The classification "quark," in contrast, is an indifferent kind: "Quarks are not aware that they are quarks and are not altered simply by being classified as quarks" (32). As Hacking elaborates the idea of an interactive kind, it becomes clear that the interaction he has in mind happens through the awareness of the thing classified in being so-classified, though it is typically mediated by the "larger matrix of institutions and practices surrounding this classification" (103; also 31–2, 103–6).[24] For example, if a particular woman is not classified as a woman refugee,

> ... she may be deported, or go into hiding, or marry to gain citizenship ... she learns what characteristics to establish, knows how to live her life. By living that life, she evolves, becomes a certain kind of person [a woman refugee]. And so it may make sense to say that the very individuals and their experiences are constructed within the matrix surrounding the classification "women refugees." (11)

Hacking concludes that the individuals so affected are themselves socially constructed "as a certain kind of person" (11).

Hacking is especially interested in a certain kind of object construction, namely, construction that works by the social context providing concepts that frame the self- understanding and intentions of the constructed agent. In cases like this, agents incorporate (often consciously) socially available classifications into their intentional agency and sense of self, but as their self-understanding evolves, the meaning of those classifications evolves with them. This forms a "feedback loop" (hence the term: 'interactive kinds') between what we might think of as objective and subjective stances with respect to the classification. To emphasize the importance of the agent's active awareness in this process, we might call this "discursive identity construction." It is important to note, however, that relationship between schemas and resources in the constitution of social structures is, in general, loopy. Resources are formed to trigger dispositions (schemas) that are manifested in ways that, in turn, utilize and shape the

---

[24] The contrast between indifferent and interactive kinds is not a simple binary distinction, for there are several different factors that may play a role determining whether a kind is more or less indifferent or interactive. One factor is the degree to which we can have, and have had, a causal impact on members of the kind; in cases where we have had a causal impact, a further issue is whether the similarity among the members that forms the basis for the kind is due to our influence.

resources. Cuisine is a good example (Pollan). In a less-globalized world than ours, food crops were grown to support the local cuisine and the local tastes and culinary techniques evolved in ways that took advantage of the crops. In more complex and broadly social changes we can watch consumer taste develop so that certain products become "must haves" in a particular milieu. Trends in cuisine can become trends in production which, in turn, affect trends in labor, and this affects schemas of class and taste, and so on.

This loopiness can obscure the social dimension of social structures. When ideology is uncontested and hegemonic, it is insufficiently conscious to be aware of its own effects. So the causal impact of hegemonic schemas on resources is typically invisible. Because the "trigger" for a schema is external—in the world—we attend to this, and social structures come to seem inevitable, natural, "given":

> Although all ongoing social organizations incorporate contest and struggle over the constitution of their world, most aspects of social structure are taken for granted. . . . Social actors accept a good part of their social worlds as necessary, and often as natural, as perhaps they must do to function at all in those worlds. Often invisible, and certainly uncontested, these taken-for-granted structures are thus unlikely to be the subject of justice claims and critiques, although they may be a source of disadvantage and injustice . . . hegemony colonizes consciousness . . . (Silbey 289)

The reliance on, say, wheat in a particular cuisine may seem inevitable, natural, "given." Wheat is what is available; wheat just is what we eat. But the wheat is available because of the impact of schemas on resources that establish farming practices, food distribution, and such. Given the stability of such structures, culinary taste conforms. In this context quinoa, or soy, or spelt tastes bad and has a funny texture too; so who would want to plant it? Hegemony colonizes consciousness.

Critique

Refusing to Accept the Common Ground

If ideology partly constitutes the social world, then it seems that a description of the ideological formations will be true, and it is unclear what is, epistemically speaking, wrong with them. The material world reinforces our tutored dispositions—qwerty keyboards reinforce our qwerty dispositions which reinforce the use of qwerty keyboards; racial classification reinforces racial segregation, which reinforces racial identity, which reinforces racial classification. Social structures, good or bad, constitute our lived reality and they become a matter of common sense for us, that is, they become hegemonic.

Hegemony, just or unjust, appears inevitable, natural, "given." We've seen that this false appearance is easily generated due to the "loopiness" of social structures: we respond to the world that has been shaped to trigger those very responses without being conscious of the shaping, so our responses seem to be called for by the way the world is. This, I submit, is what our problematic generics (l)–(4), and others like them, articulate: they describe the world as if it is, by its nature, how we have interpreted it, and from there caused it, to be. Cows are food, women are submissive, and blacks are violent. In purporting just to capture the facts, the generics import an explanation, implicate that the source of the truth of these claims lies in what cows, women, and blacks *are*. Implicatures and presuppositions of this sort become part of the common ground, often in ways that are hard to notice and hard to combat, and they become the background for our conversations and our practices. Once the assumption of, for example, women's submissive nature has been inserted into the cultural common ground, it is extremely difficult and disruptive to dislodge it.

A first step in ideology critique, then, is to reject such claims and to make evident the interdependence of schemas and resources, of the material world and our interpretation of it. It is not the case that women are submissive, even if most women are submissive, in fact, even if *all* women are submissive, because submission is no part of women's nature. Let's consider examples (3) and (4) in a bit more detail.

Start with:

4. Blacks are violent (criminal, dangerous).

This seems to be an example of a striking generic because the attribution in question is "harmful, dangerous or appalling" (Leslie, "Generics" and "Original Sin"). Recall that striking generics, as in "mosquitoes carry the West Nile virus," require only a tiny percentage of the kind to exemplify the property in order to count as true. Nevertheless, the implicature is that all members of the kind are disposed, by nature, to have the property. So (4) is either itself false or highly misleading by virtue of inserting into the common ground a false claim about the nature of blacks,[25] and one would be right to object to it.

---

[25] I am not in a position to argue for a theory of the truth conditions for generics; in fact, I want to avoid taking a stand on the semantics of generics (though I admit that the line between semantics and pragmatics is unclear). My suggestion has been, however, that the generic essence claim is only pragmatically involved. If this is true, then whether (4) "blacks are violent" is false will

However, suppose someone, Bert, who is highly invested in (4), is challenged; he would probably deny intending the implication in the first place. The claim, he might say, was just intended as an ordinary quantified generalization and the implicature was not intentional. But what quantification makes sense of (4)? The fact that "some blacks are violent" is too weak to underwrite (4) as a majority generic (which requires that most of the kind have the property). But both "all blacks are violent" and "most blacks are violent" are false. So it is tempting to conclude that (4) is not assertable even if the implicature is canceled. Both (4) *and* its implicature are false. Not just metalinguistic negation is called for, but ordinary negation as well.

Bert, however, may still be convinced that there is a truth being expressed by (4), and given that striking generics can be compelling with very few instances, this may be a strong commitment. If he is committed to the claim that blacks are violent and recognizes that "some blacks are violent" is not sufficient to support the claim as a majority generic, he is likely to infer that "most blacks are violent." Why else, he asks, is it reasonable to assert (which he is committed to) that blacks are violent? Thus the falsehood, "most blacks are violent" comes to seem legitimately part of the common ground. So even if Bert rejects the claim of generic essence, namely, that blacks, by virtue of being black, are violent, there is still a tendency to reinterpret the claim and accept another falsehood in the common ground: "most blacks are violent." It is the responsible interlocutor's job, in such a case, to resist this as well.

Consider now:

3. Women are submissive (nurturing, cooperative).

What (3) implicates will, of course, depend on context. Moreover, it is not clear how the example fits into Leslie's categories of generics. Neither being submissive, nurturing, or cooperative fits the criteria for being a striking generic. Is it a characteristic generic? Are women, by nature, submissive (nurturing, cooperative)? There are definitely many positive counterinstances. But here again the idea could be that *good*, or *normal*, women are submissive (nurturing, cooperative), where "normal" is not understood as "statistically normal" but in terms of

depend on our semantic account and complicated facts about how we want to explain the apparent violence of (some) blacks. For example, if there is an explanation of black violence in terms of a response to racist oppression, then there may be a non-accidental correlation which would allow the generic to be true *as a striking generic* even if only a very few blacks are violent: but we will be right to resist or deny it by virtue of how it affects the common ground. The interlocutor's denial is a "meta-linguistic negation" that blocks the implicature that blacks are by nature violent. This is also relevant in the case of fashion because we may want it to be true that a fashion item is cool even if we don't grant the essentialist claim.

what individuals are good examples of the kind. Or is there a template in the background: Recall that we can say "birds (or bees) lay eggs" even if most don't because there is a template for animals that has a box for reproductive mechanism, and "lays eggs" is one of the options considered acceptable. Is there a template for animals, or for humans, that offers a pull-down psychology menu? There might be a story to tell: in interacting with other creatures we need to be able to predict whether they are going to be easy to interact with or hard to interact with, whether we are going to have an easy time being dominant or whether we are likely to be dominated. The claim that women are submissive provides a value for that box in the template and a basis for predicting behavior. Yet another option is that it is just a majority generic and is true just in case most women are submissive (etc.).

Given these options, I think there is reason to deny (3): it is neither characteristic (part of what it is to be a good example of womanhood) or generally the case that women are submissive (nurturing, cooperative). However, even if it is unclear what are the truth conditions for (3), we can still consider its pragmatic effects. The implication of (3), on the account I am proposing, is that women are, by nature, submissive; women who aren't submissive are, nevertheless, disposed to be under the right circumstances, because this is how women *are*. Perhaps the implication is that the category of woman is a functional kind: women are *for* nurturing, or women are *for* being dominated. Again, this is how women *are* (Haslanger, "On Being Objective"). If this is conveyed in conversation, it may be hardly noticeable, but once it takes hold, it becomes a schema that shapes our social world. Blocking the implication is called for.

In this case, the invested defender of (3), in the face of objections, might have an easier time defending the quantified substitute for the generic: "most women are submissive (nurturing, cooperative)" and may also regard this as an adequate basis for asserting (3) as a majority generic (not taking into account the many non-submissive women). But the tempting slide (and apparently good inference) from "most women are submissive," to "women are submissive," must keep us on our guard to block the essentializing implicature.

One might object, however, that feminists and antiracist theorists regularly employ generics that, on my account, have problematic implications. Consider, for example:

5. Women are oppressed.
6. Blacks in the United States suffer racism.

How should we handle such cases? If (5) and (6) are simply majority generics, then both are plausibly true (assuming, as I do, that the oppression and racism affect all women and all blacks in the circumstances at issue). In asserting (5) and (6) however, does one implicate that women are oppressed *by nature*? Or that blacks are naturally targets of racism?

I can think of two options for handling such cases. One is to claim that the context cancels the implicature because the point of making such a claim is to criticize the practice, not to justify oppression or racism as appropriate or natural to women or blacks. Thus there is no need to block the implicature. This strategy is also important for understanding majority generics such as "barns are red" and "cars have radios," more generally. The idea is that in cases where it is obvious that there is no non-accidental connection between the kind and the predicate, that is, where it is clear that what is being expressed is a majority generic rather than a characteristic or striking generic, there is no implicature, and so no implicature to be blocked or negated.[26]

The second option is to allow that there is a non-coincidental or non-accidental connection between being a woman and being oppressed, or being black and being the target of racism. The idea is not that women or blacks are naturally treated this way; rather, the point is that being a woman or being black are good predictors for the unjust treatment. So it is not necessary to block or negate the implicature because it is true. This may seem troublesome, but the appearance of trouble hinges, I believe, on a slide we need not make. According to some accounts of gender and race, being unjustly subordinated is part of what it is to be gendered man or woman and to be raced (Haslanger, "Gender and Race"). On this view, it is true that women are oppressed by virtue of being women, and a paradigm example of a woman is someone who is oppressed. So when someone asserts (5), both the utterance and the implicature are true. Does this entail that women are oppressed by their very natures? How could that be acceptable? It isn't acceptable, but neither is it entailed. Consider the comparison:

It is true in virtue of what it is to be a bachelor that bachelors are unmarried.

with:

It is true in virtue of what it is to be a woman that women are oppressed.

or

---

[26] There is empirical evidence that we are aware of the distinction between majority and characteristic generics. In the case of characteristic generics, speakers are more willing to count both bare plural and indefinite singular forms of the generic as natural to assert than majority generics, e.g., "tigers have stripes" and "a tiger has stripes" are both judged assertable, whereas speakers are more likely to differ in their assessment of "barns are red" and "a barn is red" (Leslie et al., "Conceptual" 482).

It is in virtue of being poor that the poor are disenfranchised.

In each of these cases the non-accidental link is being asserted between prop-erties. As long as one allows that no individual is by nature a bachelor, or by nature a woman, or by nature poor, then it doesn't follow that the individual is by necessity unmarried or oppressed or disenfranchised, or that they should be. There is a further scope error, however, that many find tempting. Consider:

> 7. Women are [non-accidentally, by virtue of what they are, by nature] oppressed.
> 8. Sally is a woman.
> 9. Therefore, Sally is [non-accidentally, by virtue of what she is, by nature] oppressed.

Of course this conclusion is unacceptable, but the inference is invalid and requires the stronger premise:

> 8*. Sally is [non-accidentally, by virtue of what she is, by nature] a woman.

If we deny (8*), which is needed in place of (8) to infer (9), then we can avoid the problematic conclusion.

Whether this second strategy is an acceptable option (and I'm not con-vinced it is!), will depend on several considerations. In particular, it will depend on the details of how we spell out the precise content of the implicature: what sort of non-accidental connection is being claimed between the kind and the property referred to by the generic, what is involved in a claim of generic es-sence, how should we interpret assumptions about nature(s). The issue here is, I believe, metaphysical, in the sense that we need good metaphysical distinc-tions to make sense of the alternatives, but more than metaphysical, it is psy-chological. The goal is to understand what people *tend to believe* when they hear someone assert a generic. There has been valuable research on the human ten-dency to essentialize (Gelman "Essential Child," "Conceptual Development") and a better account of the pragmatics of generics should take this research into account.

Critique?

The project of at least many social constructionists is to make explicit how the world we respond to, the world that triggers our schemas, is shaped by us and is not inevitable, natural, or "given." In other words, the project is to make evident the role of schemas in shaping resources that "fit" our schemas. Once the loop is laid bare, new questions can be asked about the adequacy of the schemas, the distribution of resources, and alternative structures that might be put in place. The goal is to make explicit the hegemonies that hold us in their grip so that they can be challenged and contested. My arguments thus far have attempted to connect this understanding of social construction and the formation of hegemony with practices of speech and conversation that help constitute the common ground. If what I have argued is correct, there is less mystery how confused and mistaken ideologies become hegemonic—they are absorbed as the background to successful communication. Moreover, we need not assume that the parties to the conversation are deviously insinuating the false beliefs into the cultural background. It may be that the mechanisms of presupposition accommodation and implicature that are essential to establishing shared meanings and the contours of our social world are simply not serving us well in these domains.

Is the point of ideology critique, then, to make explicit the content of hegemony, to bring it to the level of belief to be evaluated? There is much emphasis in discussion of ideology on this idea that what is gained through critique is an understanding that things could be different. Catharine MacKinnon emphasizes that in unveiling ideological illusion one comes to see that how things are is not how they must be:

> Women's situation cannot be truly known for what it is, in the feminist sense, without knowing that it can be other than it is. . . . Patterns of abuse can be made to look more convincing without the possibility of change seeming even a little more compelling. Viewed as object reality, the more inequality is pervasive, the more it is simply "there." And the more real it looks, the more it looks like the truth. As a way of knowing about social conditions, consciousness raising by contrast shows women their situation in a way that affirms they can act to change it. (101)

This fits with the idea that what is inserted into the common ground by the problematic generics is a claim of generic essence. If the presumption is that subordinated groups occupy the social positions they do because of facts about their nature or essence, then effective resistance requires that we first explore the possibilities that this move has foreclosed (see also Taylor "Interpretation"). But it is one thing to recognize the possibility of a different social structure and another to offer a critique of one. Is the revelation of alternatives sufficient to provide social critique?

A simplistic hypothesis might be that once one is exposed to the social workings of one's milieu, one will come to see the weaknesses of it. On this view, the unveiling of the illusion of inevitability can disrupt an investment in one's current (inadequate) milieu and provide opportunities for improvement. Further critique, strictly speaking, is not necessary; one need only broaden the horizons of those in the grip of an unjust structure and they will gain "consciousness" and gravitate to liberation.

It is true that this can happen, but it is far from guaranteed, and there is a danger that not all such gravitation is toward liberation. Ideology critique begins by taking aim at the particular masking of social schemas that occurs when they become hegemonic, but it takes further moral or political critique to determine whether the structures they constitute are legitimate or just. Questions of justice don't arise for the common sense world that is taken for granted. To raise normative issues we must first make visible the social dynamics that create our social worlds; once articulated ideology can (in principle) be debated. So showing how something is simply presupposed as common ground and that it needs critical examination is one goal of ideology critique. This is an important step, but alone is insufficient to capture the critical dimension. Moreover, as noted, schemas are entrenched dispositions and often don't change in response to cognitive engagement. A further, often unacknowledged, concern is that components of hegemony are polysemic, so we cannot assume that it is possible to articulate "the content" of hegemony (Ewick and Silbey, "Subversive Stories" 212; Silbey 293):

> The hegemonic is not simply a static body of ideas to which members of a culture are obliged to conform . . . [it has] a protean nature in which dominant relations are preserved while their manifestations remain highly flexible. The hegemonic must continually evolve so as to recuperate alternative hegemonies. (Silberstein 127. quoted in Ewick and Silbey, "Subversive Stories" 212)

This "protean" nature of hegemony can protect it from critique (Ewick and Silbey, "Subversive Stories" 212), but can also make room for resistance and counter-hegemony:

> Since power is exercised through the patterned distribution of resources and schemas, if there is resistance to this power it must also operate through the appropriation of these selfsame structures. Resistance, as much as power, is contingent upon the structural resources available to the relational participants. . . . "Counter-hegemony has to start from that which exists, which involves starting from 'where people are at.' Such a conception of counter-hegemony requires the 'reworking' or 'refashioning' of elements which are constitutive of the prevailing hegemony" (Hunt, 316). (Ewick and Silbey, "Narrating" 1335 (including Hunt quote)).

In studies of hegemony and counter-hegemony, many humanists, legal theorists, social scientists, have focused on narrative. Narrative is important because of its power to entrench social scripts that have plots which are transposable to different contexts; narratives frame the personal in cultural forms. Acts of resistance to social scripts can also be narrated using the "elements which are constitutive of the prevailing hegemony" and become subversive stories (Ewick and Silbey, "Narrating").

Narratives—subversive or not—are crucial components of the schemas we bring to social life. However, they are not the only component. For example, feminists have long noted that dualistic conceptual frameworks that oppose reason/emotion, mind/body, nature/culture, masculine/feminine guide and distort our thinking. It is also plausible that schemas include presumption rules that direct our reasoning in cases where evidence is slim (Ullman-Margalit). Such rules are often encoded in narratives, but we have seen that they are also ubiquitous in conversation and other forms of social interaction. And habits of body and mind—including non-intentional behavior, "body language," moods, feelings, emotions, suspicions, and the like—play an important role in social life, and their interpretation and coordination depends on socializing individuals to fit (roughly) within a pattern of collective dispositions.

So it would seem that ideology critique can and should take a variety of forms. For example, we can articulate the hegemonic in ways that open space for contestation and justice claims, for example, by criticizing conceptual frameworks and offering new ones, by noting and challenging presumption rules that occlude evidence of alternatives, by pointing to the effects of social practices on consciousness. We can give voice to the counter-hegemonic by describing and recommending resistant interventions and practices. We can analyze social conditions and organization in terms that are broadly accessible so that the looping of social structures is rendered visible and so less fixed or inevitable. We can also promote norms and standards for contesting ideology that are more democratic and alert to the muting (and deafening) effects of hegemony. We can reject generics that support false claims about generic essences: it is not the case that women are more submissive than men; that blacks are more violent than whites; that cows are food.

A further goal, of course, is social change resulting in greater justice. Ideology critique of the sort I've described can help create conceptual space for such change, but thought can never replace action. The power of consciousness raising is not just to offer new avenues of thought, but to create social spaces where new schemas can be acted out, and eventually new—less oppressive—practices can become hegemonic. Describing what those practices should look like is a task for further normative debate.

Acknowledgments

Thanks to Sean Aas, Mahad Almotahari, Lauren Ashwell, Laura Beeby, Sara Bernstein, Elizabeth Camp, Jennifer Carr. Candice Delmas, Melissa Fusco, Mark Johnston, Rae Langton, Heather Logue, Elisa Mai, Kate Manne, Sally McConnell-Ginet, Emily McWilliams, Susan Sauvé Meyer, Charles More, Wendy Salkin, Paulina Sliwa, Judith Thomson, Michael Weisberg, and Stephen Yablo for helpful conversations on the topic of the chapter. Thanks to Sarah-Jane Leslie and Charlotte Witt for excellent comments on an earlier draft and to Elizabeth Harman who served as a commentator when I presented this work as part of the Seybert Lectures at the University of Pennsylvania, March 2010. Thanks also to other members of the audience at Penn and at the "Workshop on Generics and Bias" at MIT, May 2010.

Works Cited

Althusser, Louis. "Ideology and Ideological State Apparatuses." *Lenin and Philosophy and Other Essays*. New York: Monthly Review Press, 1968–2001.

Carlson. Greg N. "A Unified Analysis of the English Bare Plural." *Linguistics and Philosophy* 1.3 (1977): 413–57.

Carr. Jennifer. "Generics and Gender." Unpublished manuscript, 2009.

Cohen, Ariel. *Think Generic' The Meaning and Use of Generic Sentences*. Dissertation, Carnegie Mellon University, 1996.

Correia, Fabrice. "Generic Essence, Objectual Essence, and Modality." *Noûs* 40.4 (2006): 753–67.

Elster, Jon. *Making Sense of Marx*. Cambridge: Cambridge University Press, 1985.

Ewick, Patricia, and Susan S. Silbey. "Subversive Stories and Hegemonic Tales: Toward a Sociology of Narrative." *Law and Society Review* 29.2 (1995): 197–226.

Ewick, Patricia, and Susan S. Silbey. "Narrating Social Structure: Stories of Resistance to Legal Authority." *American Journal of Sociology* 108.6 (2003): 1328–72.

Fields, Barbara. "Ideology and Race in American History." *Region, Race, and Reconstruction: Essays in Honor of C. Vann Woodward*. Eds. J. M. Kousser and J. M. McPherson. Oxford: Oxford University Press. 1982. 143–77.

Fine, Kit. "Essence and Modality." *Philosophical Perspectives* 8 (1994): 1–16.

Gelman, Susan A. *The Essential Child: Origins of Essentialism in Everyday Thought*. Oxford: Oxford University Press. 2003.

Gelman, Susan A., and Elizabeth Ware. "Conceptual Development: The Case of Essentialism." *Oxford Handbook of Philosophy and Cognitive Science*. Eds. E. Margolis, S. Stich, and R. Samuels. Oxford: Oxford University Press (2008).

Geuss, Raymond. *The Idea of a Critical Theory: Habermas and the Frankfurt School*. Cambridge: Cambridge University Press, 1981.

Giddens, Anthony. *Central Problems in Social Theory: Action Structure and Contradiction in Social Analysis*. Berkeley: University of California Press, 1979.

Giddens, Anthony. *A Contemporary Critique of Historical Materialism*. Vol. 1: *Power, Property and the State*. London: McMillan, 1981.

Giddens, Anthony. *The Constitution of Society: An Outline of a Theory of Structuration*. Berkeley: University of California Press, 1984.

Grice, H. Paul. "The Causal Theory of Perception." *Proceedings of the Aristotelian Society* Supplementary Volume 35 (1961): 121–68.

Hacking, Ian. *The Social Construction of What?* Cambridge, MA: Harvard University Press, 1999.

Haslanger, Sally. "On Being Objective and Being Objectified." Chapter 1 of this volume.

Haslanger, Sally. "Ontology and Social Construction." Chapter 2 of this volume.

Haslanger, Sally. "Gender and Race: (What) Are They? (What) Do We Want Them to Be?" Chapter 7 of this volume.

Haslanger, Sally. "Social Construction: The 'Debunking' Project." Chapter 4 of this volume.

Haslanger, Sally. "'But Mom, Crop-Tops *Are* Cute!' Social Knowledge, Social Structure, and Ideology Critique." Chapter 15 of this volume.

Haslanger, Sally. "Social Construction: Myth and Reality." Chapter 6 of this volume.

Horn, Lawrence. "Metalinguistic Negation and Pragmatic Ambiguity." *Language* 61.1 (1985): 121–74.

Howard, Judith A. "A Social Cognitive Conception of Social Structure." *Social Psychology Quarterly* 57.3 (1994): 210–27.

Hunt, Alan. "Rights and Social Movements: Counter-Hegemonic Strategies." *Journal of Law and Society* 17.3 (1990): 309–28.

Langton, Rae. "Speaker's Freedom and Maker's Knowledge." *Sexual Solipsism*. Oxford: Oxford University Press. 2009.

Langton, Rae. "Beyond Belief: Pragmatics in Pornography and Hate Speech." Unpublished manuscript, 2009.

Leslie, Sarah-Jane. "Generics: Cognition and Acquisition." *Philosophical Review* 117.1 (2008): 1–47.

Leslie, Sarah-Jane. "The Original Sin of Cognition." Unpublished manuscript, 2009.

Leslie, Sarah-Jane, Sangeet Khemlani, Sandeep Prasada and Sam Glucksberg. "Conceptual and Linguistic Distinctions between Singular and Plural Generics." *Proceedings of the 31st Annual Cognitive Science Society*. Amsterdam: Cognitive Science Society, 2009.

Levinson, Stephen C. *Presumptive Meanings*. Cambridge, MA: MIT Press, 2000.

Lewis, David. "Scorekeeping in a Language Game." *Journal of Philosophical Logic* 8 (1979): 339–59.

MacKinnon, Catharine. *Towards a Feminist Theory of the State*. Cambridge, MA: Harvard University Press, 1989.

Marx, Karl. *The German Ideology*. Ed C. J. Arthur. New York: International Publishers, 1970/1846.

McCarthy, Thomas. "The Critique of Impure Reason: Foucault and the Frankfurt School." *Political Theory* 18.3 (1990): 437–69.

Pollan, Michael. *The Omnivore's Dilemma: A Natural History of Four Meals*. New York, NY: Penguin Press, 2006.

Prasada, Sandeep, and Elaine Dillingham. "Principled and Statistical Connections in Common Sense Conception." *Cognition* 99.1 (2006): 73–112.

Prasada, Sandeep, and Elaine Dillingham. "Representation of Principled Connections: A Window Onto the Formal Aspect of Common Sense Conception." *Cognitive Science* 33 (2009): 401–48.

Purvis, Trevor, and Alan Hunt. "Discourse, Ideology, Discourse, Ideology, Discourse, Ideology . . ." *The British Journal of Sociology* 44.3 (1993): 473–99.

Sewell, William H., Jr. "A Theory of Structure: Duality, Agency and Transformation." *The American Journal of Sociology* 98.1 (1992): 1–29.

Shelby, Tommie. "Ideology, Racism and Critical Social Theory." *The Philosophical Forum* 34.2 (2003): 153–88.

Silberstein, Sandra. "Ideology as Process: Gender Ideology in Courtship Narratives." *Gender and Discourse: The Power of Talk*. Eds. A. Todd and S. Fisher. Norwood, NJ: Ablex Publishing, 1988.

Silbey, Susan S. "Ideology, Power and Justice." *Justice and Power in Sociolegal Studies*. Eds. B. Garth and A. Sarat. Evanston, IL: Northwestern University Press, 1998. 272–308.

Stalnaker, Robert. "Pragmatics." *Synthese* 22 (1970): 272–89.

Stalnaker, Robert. *Context and Content: Essays on Intentionality in Speech and Thought*. Oxford: Oxford University Press, 1998.

Stalnaker, Robert. "Common Ground." *Linguistics and Philosophy* 25 (2002): 701–21.

Taylor, Charles. "Interpretation and the Sciences of Man." *Philosophy and the Human Sciences: Philosophical Papers 2*. Cambridge: Cambridge University Press, 1985/1971.

Ullman-Margalit, Edna "On Presumption." *Journal of Philosophy* 80.3(1983): 143–63.

INDEX